Global Politics

for the IB Diploma Programme

Carolina Chavez Fregoso,
Michael O'Shannassy,
Stephan Anagnost

Published by Pearson Education Limited, 80 Strand, London, WC2R 0RL.
www.pearson.com/international-schools

Text © Pearson Education Limited 2024
Development edited by Alison Walters
Copy edited by Paul Martin
Proofread by Jane Read, Eric Pradel
Indexed by Georgie Bowden
Designed by Pearson Education Limited 2024
Typeset by Straive Ltd
Cover design © Pearson Education Limited 2024

The rights of Carolina Chavez Fregoso, Michael O'Shannassy and Stephan Anagnost to be identified as the authors of this work has been asserted by them in accordance with the Copyright, Designs and Patents Act 1988.

First published 2024

27 26 25 24
10 9 8 7 6 5 4 3 2

British Library Cataloguing in Publication Data
A catalogue record for this book is available from the British Library

ISBN 978 1 29246 352 0

Copyright notice

All rights reserved. No part of this publication may be reproduced in any form or by any means (including photocopying or storing it in any medium by electronic means and whether or not transiently or incidentally to some other use of this publication) without the written permission of the copyright owner, except in accordance with the provisions of the Copyright, Designs and Patents Act 1988 or under the terms of a licence issued by the Copyright Licensing Agency, 5th Floor, Shackleton House, 4 Battlebridge Lane, London, SE1 2HX (www.cla.co.uk). Applications for the copyright owner's written permission should be addressed to the publisher.

Printed in Slovakia by Neografia

The 'In cooperation with IB' logo signifies the content in this textbook has been reviewed by the IB to ensure it fully aligns with current IB curriculum and offers high-quality guidance and support for IB teaching and learning.

Acknowledgements

All Credits

The author and publisher would like to thank the following individuals and organizations for permission to reproduce photographs.

(key: b-bottom; c-centre; l-left; r-right; t-top)

Non-Prominent Image Credit(s):

123RF: Andriy Popov 241, art1980 013 L-R b2, artursz 262, batsheba 300, budastock 264, Dmitry Malov 325, evgeniyshkolenko 279, federicofoto 288, fontaineg1234 267, gary718 186, Gunnar Pippel 183, Henner Damke 121, Keith Levit 308, Paul Grecaud 013 L-R t2, radututa 286, rawpixel 257, Tinnakorn Jorruang 226, wetzkaz 99: **African Union:** Copyright © African Union, 2003. All rights reserved 13: **Alamy:** BNA Photographic 46, Bony/Pool/Abaca Press 252, D. Hurst 170, Ed Oudenaarden/Associated Press 110, Historic Collection 378, John Minchillo/Associated Press 290, Michael Kooren/Pool/Associated Press 196c, Pbecher/Panther Media GmbH 17, PJF Military Collection 210, Saudi Royal Court/Associated Press 192, Suman Acharya 281, Thunderstruck 371b, TKM 321, World History Archive 209, ZUMA Press, Inc. 320: **Cagle:** Paresh Nath 335: **Chad Davis:** Chad Davis 197b: **Getty Images:** FABRICE COFFRINI/AFP 153, Hugh Sitton 255, OLGA MALTSEVA/AFP 197t, mikroman6 21t, Nastasic 21b, TIMOTHY A. CLARY/AFP 144, ullstein bild 186, YASIN AKGUL/AFP 184b, **Library and Archives Canada:** Library and Archives Canada/PA-043181 215: **Polyp:** Paul J Fitzgerald 142: **Shutterstock:** 3D generator 303, 87914 224, Africa Studio 231, AHMAD FAIZAL YAHYA 275, akramalrasny 243, Alba_alioth 27, Alexander Ishchenko 30, Alexander Kirch 80, Alexandros Michailidis 318, Alexey Struyskiy 013 L-R b1, Anton Watman 031 R, Aphelleon 312, arindambanerjee 16, b900 319, bangoland 024t, bmszealand 107 R, Bohbeh 372, BortN66 185, cash1994 23, checy 145, corgarashu 92, dboystudio 284, dicogm 013 L-R t1, Dirk Ercken 87, Dmitry Demidovich 024b, Dragana Gordic 248, Drazen Zigic 307, Drop of Light 055b, durantelallera 33, Elenarts 134, etreeg 323, FellowNeko 039t, Feng Yu 004b, Fiora Watts 112b L, Fishman64 276, 278, fitzcrittle 305, Franck Legros 114, Gil C 013 L-R b3, Giorgio Caracciolo 106, Halfpoint 1c, 2, HelloSSTK 112b R, HollyHarry 315, Hyejin Kang 301, iman satria 379, infocus 219, ingehogenbijl 235, Ink Drop 374b, Jinning Li 245, John Wreford 244, justasc 196 b L, koya979 8, Kunal Mahto 258, kurt 195, Lickomicko 64, Lightspring 004t, maigi 85, Mark Fisher 259, McCarthy's PhotoWorks 100, Mclein 324, metamorworks 239, MichaelJayBerlin 117, MidoSemsem 37, Milan Adzic 013 L-R t4, M-SUR 1t, nEwyyy 168, NIKS ADS 236, oneinchpunch 269, Osugi 055t, PARALAXIS 44, Parradii Kaewpenssri 78, pathdoc 374t, pavalena 011b, Prachaya Roekdeethaweesab 039b, Prazis Images 177, ra2studio 265, railway fx 013 L-R t3, Rawpixel.com 242, Roman Yanushevsky 109, Ryan DeBerardinis 205, Serban Bogdan 011t, Sheila Fitzgerald 112t, Shutter_M 233, SpeedKingz 371t, Steve Allen 107 L, Tana888 228, TheaDesign 272, Todd Powell 189, VDB Photos 184t, Vitalii Stock 29, Yory Frenklakh 222, zef art 031 L, Zoltan Acs 285: **THOMSON REUTERS CORPORATION:** Siphiwe Sibeko 155: **Tuca Vieira:** Tuca Vieira 127: **United Nation Development Programme:** United Nation Development Programme 151: **United Nations:** copyright © United Nations 13, 145: **United Nations Environment Programme:** United Nations Environment Programme. 161: **United Nations Photo:** UN Photo/Isaac Billy 211

Acknowledgments are continued on page 398

Contents

Author's introduction   1

Global Politics Core: Understanding power and global politics   8

    Introducing Global Politics   9
    Framing global politics: stakeholders and actors   10
    Global politics as a system: structures and interactions   19
    Power in global politics   27
    Sovereignty in global politics   39
    Legitimacy in global politics   46
    Interdependence in global politics   52
    Theoretical perspectives in global politics   62

Introduction to the thematic studies   76

Thematic Studies: Rights and justice   78

    Introducing rights and justice   79
    Contested meanings of rights, justice, liberty and equality   80
    The evolution from individual rights to *human* rights   89
    The role of actors and stakeholders   102
    Debates on rights and justice: claims on individual and collective rights   116
    Conclusion: the future of human rights and justice   119

Thematic Studies: Development and sustainability   127

    Development   128
    Types of development: economic, political, institutional and social   130
    Contested meanings of poverty and inequality   138
    Nature, practice and study of sustainable development   139
    Stakeholders in development   147
    Sustainability   161
    The impacts of globalization on sustainability   169
    Contemporary debates on sustainability   171

Thematic Studies: Peace and conflict   177

    Contested meanings: peace   178
    Contested meanings: conflict and violence   186

Contents

Types of violence	188
Interactions of political stakeholders and actors	193
Causes of conflict	198
Conflict dynamics	201
The path toward resolution	207

HL Extension: Global political challenges — 219

Introduction	220
Poverty	221
Technology	232
Health	248
Identity	262
Borders	272
Security	283
Equality	299
Environment	312

Assessment support — 334

An overview of Paper 1	334
An overview of Paper 2	342
An overview of HL Paper 3	348
The Engagement Project	354

Global Politics and Theory of Knowledge — 370

What is Theory of Knowledge?	370
Knowledge in TOK and in Global Politics	372
The TOK areas of knowledge and optional themes	373
The 12 TOK concepts	377
The Global Politics and TOK connection: what is at stake?	379

The Extended Essay — 381

Students starting in 2025 onwards	381
Introduction	381
Formulating a research question	382
Conducting background research	383
Developing a research plan	383
Writing the Extended Essay	384
Revising your Extended Essay draft	385

Glossary — 387

Index — 393

Authors' introduction

Authors' introduction

Welcome to IB Diploma Programme (DP) Global Politics. In this course, you will explore the complexities of global political dynamics, interactions, challenges and actors, and observe how they unfold on the global stage in different contexts. This textbook is designed to serve as your gateway to understanding the multidimensional realm of global politics, which includes the interrelationships between nation-states, international organizations, non-state actors (NSAs) and individuals like yourself. By examining key concepts, political contexts, case studies and analytical approaches, we aim to equip you with the knowledge and critical thinking skills needed to navigate and understand the dynamics of our interconnected and interdependent world. In addition, you will explore different political issues and how these affect our everyday lives.

This book covers the syllabus and criteria of the IB DP Global Politics course. It can also serve as an introduction to other fields of study including international development, poverty, human rights, war and climate change. Even if you are not an IB DP Global Politics student, we hope that you find this book interesting and useful. We hope you enjoy reading it as much as we enjoyed writing it.

Global Politics is the study of political processes, issues and activities that occur within and across borders. It analyzes and evaluates the interactions, power dynamics and decision-making of a range of political actors and stakeholders. It also involves a variety of disciplines from the social sciences and humanities. As such, it is a multidisciplinary or even transdisciplinary field. Although Global Politics focuses on transnational and international forms of politics, it recognizes the influence that local and national politics have at an international level, and vice versa, and acknowledges that global affairs affect every single country and community. They can even affect individuals as they go about their everyday lives.

By studying Global Politics, you will gain insights into the complexities of global political challenges that we face individually and collectively. Understanding global politics is of critical importance in today's interconnected world. The decisions

Authors' introduction

made by governments, international organizations and non-state actors (NSAs), like multinational corporations and non-governmental organizations (NGOs), have far-reaching consequences that shape various aspects of our lives. Global politics influences economic systems and development, environmental policies, conflict resolution, the promotion and protection of human rights, and responses to a wide range of global challenges. By studying Global Politics, you will gain tools that you can use to critically analyze and engage with the forces shaping our societies, locally, nationally and globally.

In a rapidly changing world, where the number of political actors has multiplied, and many political issues and agencies transcend state borders, the study of global politics covers a wider and more dynamic set of interactions than ever before. The exploration of global politics will include various analytical approaches and theoretical frameworks, including realism, liberalism and constructivism. Realism focuses on power struggles among states, emphasizing self-interest and competition. Liberalism emphasizes cooperation, institutions and shared values as drivers of international relations. Constructivism examines how ideas, norms and identities shape political behavior and outcomes. These and other analytical lenses provide valuable ways of viewing and understanding the complex and contested nature of global politics.

There has never been a more interesting time to study global politics than today. From pandemics to conflicts around the world, the climate crisis, trade wars and new technological advances, so many issues are best understood by viewing them through a global lens. How do relations between countries affect the way countries react to a pandemic? To what extent are domestic politics influenced by global economic flows and phenomena? How is the rise of nationalism and populism related to migration? How might a localized armed conflict between two countries affect food security globally?

These questions can be answered from many different angles, with the use of different theoretical frameworks and with different levels of analysis. Global Politics will not (and cannot) provide you with clear-cut answers, but, instead, it presents you with the means to better understand global interactions, to consider and evaluate different policies and proposals, and to critically address global challenges.

Authors' introduction

The outline of this book

There are four chapters that cover the Core topic (Understanding power and global politics) and the three thematic studies (Rights and justice, Development and sustainability, and Peace and conflict).

'Understanding power and global politics' serves as an introduction to the study of Global Politics. We begin by considering some of the main actors and stakeholders of global politics before turning to the structure of global politics and how it operates as a system. Next, we explore the key concepts of power, sovereignty, legitimacy and interdependence, and the central role they play, individually and collectively, in shaping political processes and decision-making. Through contemporary real-world examples, we analyze the mechanisms through which these key concepts are acquired, exercised and challenged, providing a framework for understanding the complexities of global governance.

In 'Rights and justice' we explore the critical concepts of human rights and justice as fundamental pillars of global politics. We look at the historical conceptualizations and development of human rights, from their philosophical foundations to the establishment of an international human rights regime. Through contemporary case studies, including gender and disability rights, universal jurisdiction and climate justice, we examine the role of international organizations and institutions as well as non-state actors in promoting and protecting human rights. We analyze and evaluate the challenges and opportunities they face in enforcing these rights across diverse societies. We also analyze the evolving notions of justice, liberty and equality to shed greater light on the complexities of ensuring fairness and equity in a globalized world.

In 'Development and sustainability' we discuss the growth and evolution of our understanding of the concepts of development, sustainability, poverty and inequality. We use contemporary case studies and examples to examine the role of (and interactions between) state and non-state stakeholders and other actors toward a world of greater equality and equity and the challenges faced by stakeholders in this quest. We also examine critical political, economic, social, environmental, historical and institutional factors that contribute to successful or unsuccessful sustainable development, including some of the measurements used in the context of development and sustainability. Finally, we highlight the important role that globalization has played regarding our understanding of sustainability and development, as well as some of the key debates and critical views that drive meaningful discussions surrounding development and sustainability.

'Peace and conflict' begins by looking at peace in its positive and negative forms, and understanding that peace is more than the absence of violence. We explore different ways in which peace can be measured and the complexities of doing so. Next, we explore different paths to achieving peace. We consider different forms of conflict, both violent and non-violent. Using examples and contemporary case studies, we analyze the causes behind conflicts, the way conflicts evolve and transform, and the economic, legal, political, social and environmental effects they have. We also examine different approaches to the justification of violence as well as the methods used to resolve conflicts.

Authors' introduction

HL

The Higher Level (HL) extension chapter explores eight global political topic areas: poverty, security, borders, identity, equality, technology, health and environment. Each of these is presented in a separate section with its own concepts, diverse approaches, examples and contemporary case studies. We examine each topic area individually, but we will also find connections between them and between the concepts in the first four chapters. We also analyze the role of power, actors and stakeholders, as well as their relationships, to understand the complexity of these challenges faced at the local, national, regional and global level.

HL end

The Theory of Knowledge (TOK) chapter explores the relationship between Theory of Knowledge and Global Politics. This is where you, as an IB candidate, can make the most of the intersection between TOK as a core component of the IB DP Programme and your experiences in Global Politics. This chapter provides an overview of the expectations and assessments of the TOK course and then examines the connections you can make between Global Politics and TOK, specifically where Global Politics can strengthen your TOK experience and the TOK way of thinking that might help you in Global Politics. This chapter discusses the role that you, the *knower*, play in evaluating knowledge in both TOK and Global Politics, and includes hints that will support your work in Global Politics and contribute to the success of your TOK assessments.

The Assessment support chapter outlines the externally-assessed IB exams (Paper 1, Paper 2, and if you are an HL student, Paper 3). Each section provides an overview of what each assessment involves and what you will be expected to do. Each section also provides some guidance on how to successfully navigate these assessments. The Engagement Project section looks at the possible ways in which meaningful and successful Engagement Projects might be designed and carried out. Important in this chapter is the focus on developing strong political issues leading to relevant political challenges that form the basis of your Engagement Project. This section includes a discussion about typical challenges you might face when designing your Engagement Project and possible ways to work through these challenges. There are several helpful hints and possible strategies that can lead to successful Engagement Projects.

The Extended Essay (EE) is one of the core components of your IB Diploma. The Extended Essay chapter is designed to offer some guidance if you decide to write your EE in Global Politics (or if Global Politics is part of a World Studies EE). This chapter introduces the key objectives of the EE in Global Politics, emphasizing its role in enabling students to explore in greater depth a political issue of their choice. The chapter highlights the importance of formulating a precise research question and explains how you will use critical thinking to analyze complex political scenarios and construct coherent arguments. Furthermore, the chapter offers some tips on how to conduct research, how to effectively develop a research plan, and, finally, how to structure and write your EE.

Authors' introduction

There are several activities in each chapter that are designed to be completed in class, either individually or with your classmates. There are Exercise questions that will help you develop critical thinking skills, as well as allow you to conduct further research and explore topics of interest to you. There are also Practice questions that will help you prepare for your IB assessments.

How to use this book

This book has been designed with IB students in mind. We look at topics in detail but important concepts are also summarized. In line with the IB requirement that the course be grounded in contemporary, real-life examples and case studies, each chapter has a range of real-world examples and cases from all over the world that will provide you with a context for the content and concepts they cover. Any real-world examples you use should come from the past 20 years. If you do refer to an older, more historical, real-world example, then you must be able to make a direct link between it and a more contemporary issue or phenomenon. We hope that we have modeled this throughout the book. Key terms and vocabulary are defined, reinforced throughout the book and appear in the Glossary.

This book is not intended to be your only learning source for Global Politics. However, we do hope it will serve as your main support. The information in the book, while broad, leaves space for further research, questioning and analysis, and you are encouraged to explore other sources to strengthen your knowledge and interests. Our aim is that you understand the material quickly, but you also cover what is required by the IB Global Politics Guide so you are well prepared for your IB assessments.

The content of the book is matched to the IB DP Global Politics Guide for first examinations in 2026. This does not mean that the book must be read in a strict, linear order. We have designed the book so you can explore different topics at your own pace and according to your own interests. You do not need to read previous chapters to understand other chapters, although connections between the chapters will be signposted. If you come across a word or phrase that is unfamiliar, check the Glossary as the meaning may have been explained in another chapter.

Each chapter begins with a list of concepts that are important as a guide to exploring the chapter. These concepts will appear repeatedly throughout a chapter, providing the basis for understanding its content. You will use these concepts throughout the course. A list of learning outcomes is also included in each chapter. This list gives you an idea of what will be covered, but also of what you can expect to learn by the time you reach the end of the chapter. If you re-read the outcomes at the end of each chapter and feel that you can reflect on each one, you will have succeeded in your learning. The learning outcomes will help you keep track of what you may need to review, either independently or in collaboration with a peer and/or your teacher. They may also provide a guide for further research, perhaps in the context of your Engagement Project. Each chapter also includes conceptual questions. These are the starting points for the content that follows. These conceptual questions are general, and are often an overview of the topic.

There are images throughout the book to make the content more engaging. Maps, diagrams or graphs can be helpful in strengthening your understanding of the content, or can provide examples to help you apply and transfer knowledge to real-life situations.

Authors' introduction

Tables often provide further explanation or summaries of concepts, definitions and examples. Tables also make it easier for you to review important content. In each chapter, there is a summary of what you have learned, including references to some case studies and examples that should help to refresh your memory of each area.

There are Exercise questions that will help you develop critical thinking skills, as well as allow you to conduct further research and explore topics of interest to you. There are also Practice questions that will help you prepare for your IB assessments.

Features

This book includes lots of useful features to help your understanding. The boxes that you will find throughout this book include:

TOK (Theory of Knowledge) is a core component of the IB Diploma Programme. TOK boxes ask you to analyze and critically think about your knowledge of the world, where it comes from, and how it shapes you and your society.

Key fact boxes highlight and summarize important points for you to remember.

Hint for success boxes provide hints and tips on how to approach certain concepts, topics or theories, especially with regard to your IB assessments. They suggest things that must be considered, contexts that must be taken into account, and debates and opinions that continue to shape global political challenges.

These boxes explain new terms and concepts that you might not have come across before.

The IB DP Global Politics course includes eight global political challenges that are addressed in the HL Extension chapter. The HL topic area boxes help you make connections between the Core chapter, the three thematic studies and the HL global political challenges. These boxes have brief explanations of how the content relates to the HL topic areas of poverty, equality, identity, borders, health, technology, environment and security.

Core topics and the thematic studies topics are related. Connection boxes highlight these relationships.

Interesting fact boxes have interesting and curious facts about global politics to help make you think a little more widely and deeply.

Weblink boxes point you to websites so you can explore relevant information further, dig deeper into a topic that may interest you, or access interactive websites where you can learn more.

Conceptual question
In Conceptual question boxes, you will find broad questions relating to the main concepts of global politics.

Authors' introduction

> **Case/Example**
>
> Throughout the book, there are real-world cases and examples to aid your learning and help ground the content in the world around us. Cases and examples are contemporary and allow you to see how what you are learning in Global Politics can be applied to contemporary real-world issues or events.

> **Activity**
>
> Activities invite you to do short activities individually, in pairs or in small groups. These activities require you to engage more deeply with the material presented. They also provide you with the space and time to reflect on your learning and engage in further critical thinking.

As you embark on this journey through IB DP Global Politics, we invite you to engage critically with the concepts, theories and activities presented in each chapter. We hope that this book will encourage you to explore other sources of information on political issues and topics that are of specific interest to you. This book will provide you with a wide array of information on global politics, but it covers just some of the complexities and wonders of global affairs. By exploring power, rights, development, peace and conflict, we aim to develop your analytical and critical thinking skills, foster a global and internationally-minded perspective, provide you with multiple perspectives, encourage dialogue and debate, and empower you to navigate and contribute to the ever-changing world of global politics.

Carolina Chavez Fregoso, Michael O'Shannassy, Stephan Anagnost

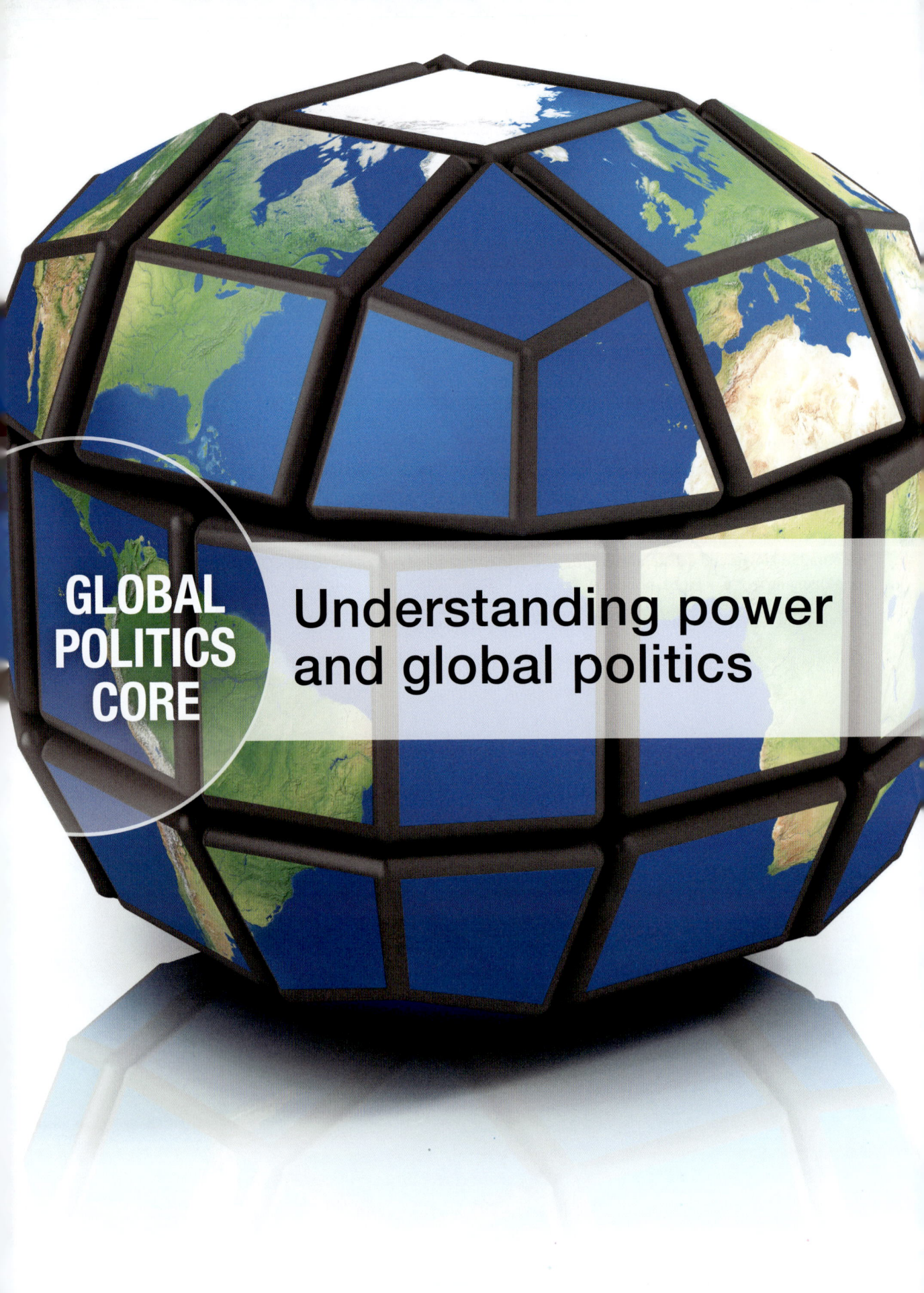

Global politics core

Concepts

Global Politics, States, Intergovernmental Organizations, Non-governmental Organizations, Non-state Actors, Norms, Institutions, Power, Sovereignty, Legitimacy, Interdependence, Theory/Theorizing

Learning outcomes

In this chapter, you will learn about:
- the nature of Global Politics as an academic discipline
- how global politics works as a field of study
- the range of prominent actors and stakeholders that help frame contemporary global politics, including states, intergovernmental organizations, non-governmental organizations and non-state actors
- ways in which global politics operates as a system within the larger construct of systems thinking
- the four key concepts of power, sovereignty, legitimacy and interdependence, and how the meaning of each is multidimensional and contested
- how each of the four key concepts is subject to challenges from within the subject as well as from the world around us
- the role that theory and theorizing plays in Global Politics.

Introducing Global Politics

Conceptual question

What is Global Politics/global politics?

The four key concepts of IB Global Politics – **power**, **sovereignty**, **legitimacy** and **interdependence** – lie at the heart of each of the thematic studies that follow. Rights and justice can be described as a conflict between the powerful and powerless. Human rights are often the basis for state legitimacy, as well as a challenge to state sovereignty. As globalization has increased, the well-being and **development** of states has come to depend more and more on the assistance of other states. This poses challenges to traditional notions of state sovereignty and the source of power in global politics.

Every discipline has its own language or jargon, a range of terms that you need to learn in order to accurately describe certain things. In this book, we have done our best to explain things in ordinary language in order to keep you engaged while, hopefully, providing you with the confidence to tackle some of the more challenging learning you may encounter during the next two years.

Global Politics is a scholarly subject that seeks to *understand* and *explain* events, processes and phenomena. However, global politics – not capitalized – is generally used to *describe* or *characterize* interrelationships between states, organizations and individuals.

You need to know certain key terms. Such understanding applies to something as basic as how to express the term Global Politics, which names both *the subject* that studies the political and economic patterns of the world, and *the field* that is being studied.

Global Politics examines how we, as humans, have organized our world. It is an interdisciplinary subject, which means that it draws on many other subjects in the social sciences and humanities for the tools it needs to examine a wide range of issues in global politics. The chapters on the thematic studies will examine many of these issues. We will first consider the Core topic *Understanding power and global politics*, which looks at some of the overarching topics and the four key concepts that lie at the heart of the subject. You will then be able to apply and expand upon these topics and the four key concepts within and between each thematic study.

While Global Politics shares much of the same DNA as International Relations, there are some crucial differences between the two subjects, not least of which is the fact that Global Politics does not share International Relations' stress on the importance of intergovernmental relations and transactions.

9

Understanding power and global politics

One way of demonstrating critical thinking in IB assessments is to consider the specific **context** within which an event occurs: actors from different places and in different circumstances may behave differently. The concept of **contingency** is another way of showing your critical thinking. To say that an event or issue is historically contingent is to say that any event or issue is dependent on a number of interrelated factors. That is, no event or issue has a *single* cause and so it is highly unlikely that any single explanation alone will work.

According to the IB Global Politics Guide, a *political issue* is any situation or matter that deals with how power is distributed and how it operates within social organization. This can be extended to the different ways that people think about, and engage with, their communities and the wider world on matters that affect their lives.

How do you *see* global politics? Think about your own (political) biases and how these shape the ways in which you approach global political challenges like conflict, climate change, human rights and immigration.

A nation-state is a territorially bounded sovereign political entity, that is, a state, that is ruled in the name of a community of citizens who identify themselves as a nation.

Exercises

1. Outline some of the similarities and differences between Global Politics and other IB Group 3 subjects such as Economics, Geography, Philosophy, ESS, etc.

2. Identify some political issues that you have been or are currently involved in as an actor or a stakeholder.

Framing global politics: stakeholders and actors

Conceptual question

Who are the prominent actors and stakeholders in global politics and how do they help frame Global Politics?

Framing Global Politics can be thought of as the process by which we determine what makes up the field of study that is Global Politics. Framing influences what we study in IB Global Politics (and, also, what we do not consider important or what issues lie beyond the scope of the subject).

One way in which we can frame Global Politics is by identifying prominent **actors** and **stakeholders** who may affect, or be affected by, a political issue. We will introduce some of the key players in global politics in order to understand some of the systems that characterize contemporary global politics.

We will start with what many consider to be the ultimate form of political power in global politics, the **nation-state**. This is a term that is usually referred to in the shorter form of *state*. It is common to hear the terms *country* or *nation* used in the media or in general conversation, but these terms are technically incorrect when used to describe one of the most significant actors in global politics.

Japan is a nation-state. It also a country and a nation. Wales is a country and a nation, but it is *not* a nation-state. Instead, it is one of four different countries within the United Kingdom of Great Britain and Northern Ireland (the UK). In this sense, the ideal of the nation-state is largely non-existent in global politics, with only a handful of possible examples – Japan, South Korea and Iceland. In fact, with 5000–8000 ethnonational groups in the world and only around 200 states,[1] most nation-states are going to be multinational and shared by more than one ethnic group. It would be more accurate to label most countries in the world as nation*s*-states.

Like Japan, the UK is a nation-state because it possesses sovereignty. If you come from or live in a federal nation-state then you might be familiar with another use of the term *state*. For example, Washington, Vorarlberg and Penang are all states that form part of the nation-states of the United States of America (USA), Austria and Malaysia, respectively. Hopefully, this brief discussion on the potential for confusion has highlighted the importance of precise language in your study of Global Politics.

Global politics core

We start with the state because it is central to the thematic studies in the following chapters. States choose to protect or violate human rights. They erect trade barriers and determine what strategies will be pursued to achieve development. They choose whether or not to establish environmental benchmarks and what they will do to meet these standards. States decide to go to war. Because states are sovereign, they possess the final authority within their territorial boundaries. As David Lake notes, states are, 'authoritative actors whose duly enacted policies are binding on their citizens and thus regulate how individuals and the collective interact with other similarly bound societies.'[2] That is, when Russia invaded Ukraine in February 2022, it did not matter whether every Russian citizen supported the war or not; Russians were at war. This applies to liberal democracies just as much as it does to **authoritarian** regimes. It is this key fact that separates the state from many of the political actors that you will be introduced to later. No matter how much a **non-state actor (NSA)** claims to speak on behalf of its members, it cannot force or bind non-members through its actions. Only the state can claim the authority and ability to act on behalf of *all* citizens. This is the foundation for those who argue that the state is the most important actor in global politics.[3]

There are some powerful critiques of this perspective. It is clear that **globalization** has weakened some of the control that states have historically had over other actors like **multinational corporations (MNCs)** and **transnational advocacy networks**. New digital technologies have also allowed transnational actors to escape state control. For example, the leaked documents that made up the Panama, Paradise and Pandora papers highlighted how wealthy individuals and corporations were able to avoid paying taxes to the relevant state.[4] **Civil society** actors can use new forms of encrypted communications technologies to increase awareness of human rights violations or the damage being done to the natural **environment** that governments would prefer to keep hidden.

It is equally clear that not all states are the same. To understand more fully the forces that are driving global politics today, we are better off thinking in terms of a continuum of state structures. At one end of the scale are **fragile or failed states**. These states are internationally recognized as **sovereign states**, but do not have authority or complete control within their own borders. Examples include Syria and the Democratic Republic of the Congo (DRC). Further along the scale are **autocratic or authoritarian states** that have some form of central government but whose authority is too weak for them to control their people effectively or completely. At the other end of the scale are **totalitarian states**, such as North Korea, where authority is highly centralized, and the state can exercise near total control over their citizens. In between are liberal strong states. Acknowledging that states exist as different kinds of political units and possess different degrees of authority over their people is critical when it comes to analyzing how states are affected by transformational forces like globalization, climate change and pandemics.

Even when we look at states that might appear similar on the surface, we should still take a critical approach. Some scholars warn against seeing any state as a single, absolute and unified actor. This means that we should recognize that most states are made up of many different components, not all of which will always move in the same direction or at the same time. We need to be careful about recognizing and clarifying

▲ The UK (top) and Japan (bottom). Only one of these can truly be described as a *nation-state*.

The term nation-state is a compound noun that joins two separate political entities. A **state** is primarily a political-legal entity characterized by a system of governance and a set of institutions with authority over those within its borders. A **nation** is primarily a psycho-cultural entity characterized as a group of people joined by a common language and a strong sense of shared identity and unity. This is commonly centered on ethnicity and/or culture. A **country** is a geographic entity, referring to physical location.

Understanding power and global politics

which parts of the state have different roles to play in different areas or issues. Figure 1.1 demonstrates this idea – when we talk about the US government, what exactly are we referring to? As political scientist Barbara Geddes puts it, 'the problem is not that there is "no there there" but that there are too many theres there.'[6] This does not mean that we need to abandon the concept of the state. We just need to be more careful when considering the role(s) that states play in global politics.

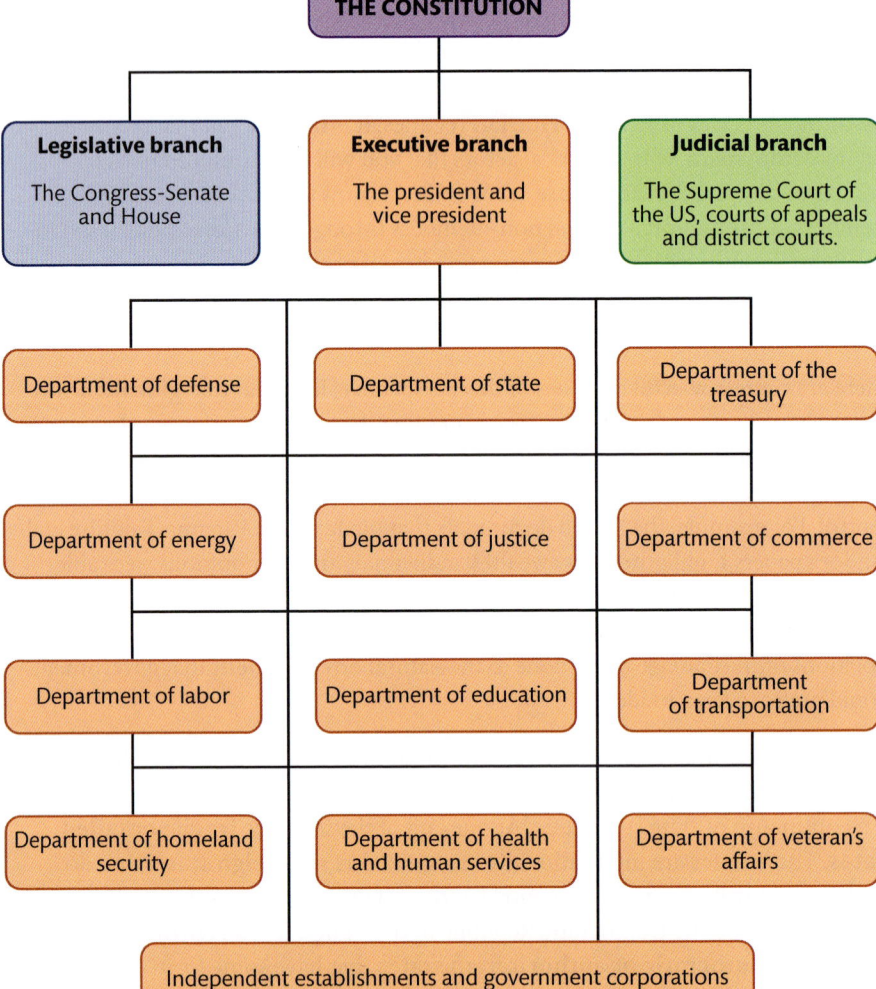

Figure 1.1 A simplified organization chart of the US Government. Adapted from: Hoffman, S. (2014, February 26). Columbia University Libraries. Journalism Library Blog.

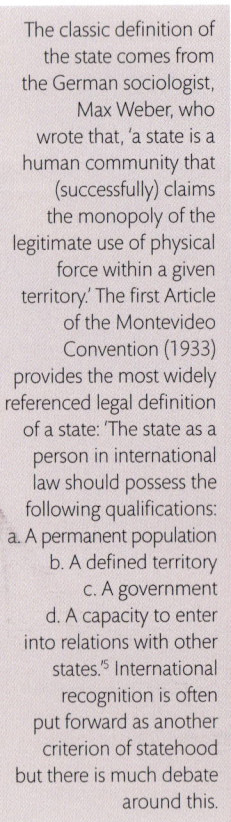

The classic definition of the state comes from the German sociologist, Max Weber, who wrote that, 'a state is a human community that (successfully) claims the monopoly of the legitimate use of physical force within a given territory.' The first Article of the Montevideo Convention (1933) provides the most widely referenced legal definition of a state: 'The state as a person in international law should possess the following qualifications:
a. A permanent population
b. A defined territory
c. A government
d. A capacity to enter into relations with other states.'[5] International recognition is often put forward as another criterion of statehood but there is much debate around this.

States remain key actors in global politics and are necessary to any explanation of international relations. However, we must be careful in specifying which states or what kind of states are most important or relevant for any issue we are considering.

Activity

Think about the structure of a government you know. Can you identify some of its component parts? (Use Figure 1.1 as a guide, if necessary). Which parts might move in the same direction as each other? Which parts might be in competition or even in conflict with one another? What might this mean for how the state engages in international relations? Share your thinking with a peer.

An **intergovernmental organization (IGO)** is a formal organization with a membership of two or more nation-states and is usually founded upon a treaty or **multilateral** agreement. IGOs like the United Nations (UN), the African Union (AU),

Global politics core

the North Atlantic Treaty Organization (NATO), the **World Trade Organization (WTO)** and the European Union (EU) are also seen as important actors in global politics. IGOs are significant for the roles they play in maintaining international order, peace and security. Among other things, IGOs help settle disputes between nation-states, deter military aggression, coordinate military or humanitarian action, regulate international trade and promote the spread of important principles like human rights and **sustainable development**.

Flags of various IGOs. From left to right: the AU, the EU, NATO and the UN.

Created in 2009, the BRICS grouping is an informal forum representing five major emerging economies: Brazil, Russia, India, People's Republic of China (PRC) and South Africa.[7] BRICS countries collectively represent around 42 percent of the world's population and 23 percent of global GDP. The group focuses on issues such as economic cooperation, trade, finance and sustainable development. It is often seen as a **Global South** version of the G7 grouping. Despite their diverse backgrounds and varying levels of development, BRICS countries collaborate on various fronts to amplify their influence in international affairs and foster a **multipolar** world order.

An **informal forum**, or **informal intergovernmental organization (IIGO)**, shares some of the characteristics of an IGO in that it is composed of sovereign states, but, unlike an IGO, an informal forum is not permanent. It is not based on a formal treaty and does not have a headquarters or a permanent secretariat (staff). Instead, informal forums often operate as an annual meeting or conference and can act as complements to and substitutes for IGOs when nation-states face high uncertainty through the state of the world and/or the preferences of other nation-states. Their informal nature offers a low-risk space where different nation-states can meet to discuss and coordinate state action, especially when there is a need for increased flexibility, speed, ambiguity or weaker enforcement. Informal forums occupy a middle ground on the spectrum of institutional forms shaping the structure of global politics between formal IGOs and norms. Prominent examples of informal forums in global politics are the Group of Seven (G7), the BRICS grouping, the Group of Twenty (G20), the World Economic Forum (WEF), the World Social Forum (WSF) and the Alliance of Small Island Nations (AOSIN).

 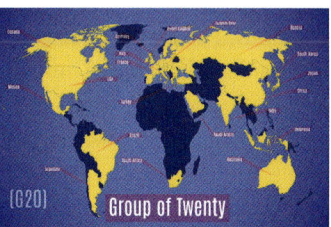 

The images (from left to right) show: the flags of the G7 members (from right to left): Japan, Italy, France, the UK, Germany, Canada, and the USA; a map showing the G20 countries (in yellow); and the flags of the BRICS members (from left to right): Brazil, Russia, India, the PRC and South Africa.

Unlike traditional International Relations analyses, Global Politics recognizes that individuals and **substate** groups, like political parties, labor unions, businesses/corporations, religious groups, social movements, the **media** and civil society organizations, may also be significant actors and/or stakeholders in global politics, largely through their effect on the interests and/or capabilities of a nation-state. The influence of any such group will depend on their capacity to engage and mobilize politically significant numbers of citizens around a common purpose. Such processes have been made easier by the phenomenon of globalization and **social media**.

Understanding power and global politics

IGOs are based on a formal treaty, have two or more member states, meet regularly and possess an independent secretariat. Informal forums (IIGOs), have shared expectations about purpose, are composed of a group of member states (although they may also include other IGOs or **non-governmental organizations (NGOs)** as observers), meet regularly, but have no independent secretariat. IIGOs, like IGOs, exist along a spectrum of formalization, with some being more formal than others. NATO is located toward the more formal end of the spectrum, for example, while the G7 is toward the more informal end.

During the Cold War, the world was divided into three ideological zones. The **First World** comprised of states that were broadly **capitalist** in their economic outlook and **liberal democratic** in their politics. The **Second World** was the Soviet Union and a range of Eastern states that were predominantly **communist/socialist**, politically and economically. Many states outside of these two international systems were **non-aligned** – giving rise to a **Third World**. In the post-Cold War world, there has been a shift to categorize states according to their economic levels of development, with Global North sometimes used to represent those states that have historically been more economically developed, and Global South to describe those states that have been historically less economically developed.

Example – The role of individuals

One example of individuals affecting global politics is a group of Pacific Island students who sought a UN resolution to make polluting countries legally accountable. This resolution calls for the International Court of Justice (ICJ) to issue an opinion clarifying nation-states' obligations to tackle the climate crisis according to two UN treaties. This opinion could then be legally binding on states that have ratified either of these two treaties.

Globalization is perceived as a challenge to the **Westphalian states system**. There are many different definitions of the term, but globalization can generally be thought of as the process of increasing interconnectedness between societies, so that events in one part of the world increasingly have effects on people and societies far away. Globalization is predominantly economic or financial in nature, but it is important to remember that it also has cultural, political and military aspects. Arguments in favor of globalization tend to focus on how the pace of economic transformation and the revolution in communications technology have fundamentally changed the way we deal with the rest of the world. Nation-states are no longer closed units. Supporters of globalization also point to the ways in which the world is becoming more similar, the emergence of a risk culture in which people realize that the main threats facing humanity are global in nature and require a global response. The world has also become more similar in terms of a related cosmopolitan culture that advocates thinking globally but acting locally. Critics of globalization point out that the spread and intensification of international exchanges, whether this is the trade of goods and services or the movement of capital/investment and people across borders, has disproportionately benefited a relatively small number of elites in the **Global North**. They argue that globalization may simply be the latest stage of **Western imperialism**. While many have widely benefited, others have suffered considerable losses under globalization. This has led some observers to argue that globalization is imperialistic and exploitative.

For example, large multinational corporations (MNCs), like Apple, Samsung, Huawei and Glencore, operate in almost every country in the world. The largest MNCs have annual revenues that exceed the Gross Domestic Product (GDP) of many nation-states, particularly those in the Global South. Their control of a sizable portion of global economic activity gives MNCs considerable political influence in global politics. There is clear evidence that MNCs have used this influence to demand changes to a government's social and economic policies, by providing tax 'holidays' or relaxing labor protection laws, for example.

Another actor whose prominence in global politics has increased with globalization is the media. Print, broadcast and social media may exert significant influence in shaping narratives in global politics. They do this by framing and controlling the dissemination of news and information in ways that can shape public perceptions, policy decisions and international relations. The media's selection of topics, framing of issues and presentation of events can influence how political events are perceived and understood by audiences. Some people have argued that the expansion of Western global news media, epitomized by CNN, played a critical role in driving the emerging doctrine of humanitarian intervention in the late 1990s. The idea that the media was driving foreign policy decision-making became known as the *CNN effect*. However, the research that followed points to a much more complex picture. The effects of media on foreign policy depends on the political costs and risks involved, and it appears that political agendas influence the media much more than the media influences politics.

Much has changed since the 1990s in the media landscape. There is now the potential for any event, real or fabricated, to be shared instantaneously across the globe. Much of the media that people consume is dictated by algorithms developed by technology companies and this means that the control of information has become increasingly problematic. Once we factor in the ways in which artificial intelligence is rewriting the media landscape, it may feel as if it is impossible to know what is fact and what is fiction. If we think of information as a form of power, then whoever controls information exerts a significant degree of control.

What impact has social media had on how we acquire and share political knowledge?

We should be careful about overstating the influence of the media on global politics. Governments devote considerable money and time to shaping public perceptions so that they fit with the government's preferred policies. Noam Chomsky has called this *manufactured consent*. Despite the presence of the Internet and the new media environment, the US and UK governments were remarkably successful at persuading most of their citizens that Iraq possessed weapons of mass destruction and that Saddam Hussein, the Iraqi president, was linked to the al-Qaeda terrorists responsible for the 9/11 attacks in 2001. This paved the way for the 2003 invasion of Iraq. Autocratic regimes also go to extraordinary lengths to control the message being received by their own populations or the wider world, whether this takes the form of state-controlled media, or by restricting media freedom. Of the 30 countries that occupy the bottom of Reporters without Borders' 2023 global ranking of press freedom, 27 were classified as authoritarian in the Economist Intelligence Unit's 2022 *Democracy Index*.[8] Governments can block access to certain websites or, in extreme cases, even turn off the Internet.

Case – European media narratives about refugees

In 2015, significant numbers of Syrians fleeing civil war attempted to make their way to Europe. In 2022, significant numbers of Ukrainians did the same after the Russian invasion of their homeland. However, there were striking differences in the way each group of refugees was covered by the European media, which both reflected and shaped national sensitivities surrounding these migrants. In each instance, civilians were escaping the widespread destruction of their country. However, differences in media portrayals of refugees, in terms of perceptions of the threat they posed, the degree to which they deserved asylum, or the economic contribution they made to the receiving countries, varied widely between 2015 and 2022. Writing in *The Irish Times*, Fintan O'Toole noted that there was only a ten-hour difference between driving from Mariupol in Ukraine to the Irish capital of Dublin and driving from Aleppo in Syria to Dublin. O'Toole then asked, 'Why does that 10-hour difference place Mariupol in our neighbourhood, while Aleppo is outside it?'[9]

Other NSAs whose membership may span the borders of nation-states include transnational activists who operate within a larger **global civil society**. The political and social activities of these activists differ from other NSAs, like corporations or businesses, in that they are driven by moral or normative concerns rather than economic self-interest. Working through NGOs, they provide humanitarian or

Understanding power and global politics

emergency aid when natural disasters strike, support refugees and internally displaced persons, pressure governments and MNCs to respect human rights, and advocate on behalf of those who lack a voice in global politics. They aim to achieve important social and developmental goals like poverty alleviation and climate change adaptation. Prominent examples of NGOs include Médecins Sans Frontières, BRAC, Greenpeace and Oxfam International.

NGOs can shape larger global narratives about the morality of government policies and actions. Amnesty International (AI) investigates and publicizes human rights violations perpetrated by governments. By encouraging other governments, international organizations and ordinary citizens within the country and overseas (for example, via their annual 'Write for Rights' campaign) to exert political pressure, AI highlights how the current era of globalization has left national borders more open than before. We now live in a world where events in one location can be immediately observed on the other side of the world, and so governments are forced to react not only to their own citizens but also, increasingly, to a global citizenry outside of their borders.

Also falling under the broad umbrella of civil society actors/NSAs that can impact global politics are **social movements**, resistance movements, interest groups and pressure groups. Social movements can be characterized as efforts by members of a society to change a situation that they view as unsatisfactory or to prevent change in a situation that they see as satisfactory. Although social movements have historically been a largely domestic phenomenon, like many other NSAs they have become more transnational in scope and influence as the world has become more globalized. Social movements can be progressive in that they seek to introduce new modes of social, political or economic behavior, for example, the LGBTQI+ movement. They can also resist change, for example, the anti-abortion movement in the USA that led to the Supreme Court overturning the legal case that granted women a constitutional right to abortion (*Roe v. Wade*) in 2022.

Resistance movements are a form of social movement that can be distinguished by their resistance or opposition to state power. While social movements are usually *for* something, resistance movements are generally *against* something, such as repression or discriminatory practices. This means that resistance movements are not limited to autocratic states but can also appear in capitalist democracies. Resistance movements will often challenge the **legitimacy** of a government or even a regime, which offers another point of potential contrast with social movements that seek to achieve their objectives within the existing political system. Resistance movements and social movements can involve collective and organized resistance through street protests, sit-ins and demonstrations. Neither are necessarily violent in nature, although violence always remains a possibility, especially if state actors respond violently to the challenge posed by social and/or resistance movements.

> The key difference between resistance movements and social movements is that resistance movements are *against* something, like social inequality or racial/gender discrimination, whereas social movements are *for* something, like free elections or greater democracy.

Protests in Toronto in solidarity with the Standing Rock protesters.

Case – Indigenous movements in the Americas

Indigenous social and resistance movements have contested mining projects throughout the Americas. In 2012, the Confederation of Indigenous Nationalities of Ecuador led thousands of people on a two-week, 650-kilometer *March for Life, Water, and the Dignity of Peoples*, demanding a new water law and the end of open-pit mining. Similar protests occurred in Guatemala and Bolivia. Indigenous movements, from

Global politics core

Canada's *Idle No More* movement to protests against damming Brazil's Xingú River Basin, have become increasingly active in demanding they be allowed to participate in decisions affecting their territories. In 2016, protesters from over 100 indigenous nations, as well as non-indigenous/settler allies, traveled to the site where the US Army Corps of Engineers was planning on placing an oil pipeline under the Mni Sose (Missouri River), and through Oceti Sakowin (The Great Sioux Nation lands). Resistance against the Dakota Access Pipeline (DAPL) took the form of a water protectors' camp at Standing Rock, which was established as a center for direct action. These camps grew to include thousands of people. Continued conflicts saw protesters treated harshly by police, including the use of dogs and water cannons on protesters in freezing weather. These police actions attracted attention on social media under hashtags such as #NoDAPL and #ReZpectOurWater, increasing national and global support for the protests. The Obama administration ordered a stop to construction of the pipeline in December 2016, but this decision was reversed by the Trump administration and the pipeline was completed in April 2017.

Like social and resistance movements, interest groups and pressure groups are interrelated NSAs, with pressure groups being a subset of interest groups. An **interest group** is any organization formed to promote a special interest. A **pressure group** is an interest group created to address a policy issue and to influence policymakers by using forceful techniques, such as money and coercive **rhetoric**. This means that pressure groups, unlike interest groups, are always political in nature. Business trade associations, like the International Chamber of Commerce (ICC) or the European Association of Business Machines and Information Technology (EUROBIT), lobby governments to ensure favorable labor codes, regulatory standards and tax structures. International networks of LGBTQI+ rights groups and indigenous peoples' groups, such as the Inuit Circumpolar Conference, lobby for the rights of their members and/or compatriots. At the global level of analysis, there are currently 5451 international public interest groups (NGOs) in active consultative status within the Economic and Social Council (ECOSOC), the UN organ responsible for promoting higher standards of living, full employment, and economic and social progress.

Not all NSAs are a positive influence on global politics. Transnational terrorist organizations and extremist groups advocate for or use terror tactics and violence, often against civilians. They do this to spread fear and undermine the capacity of governments to protect their societies and challenge their legitimacy. In extreme instances, terror organizations can shape and drive the foreign policy of a nation-state.

Global politics also includes prominent individuals. These may be the leaders of powerful states, IGOs and MNCs, whose decisions can shape the nature and practice of global politics. Global politics also recognizes the influence that ordinary individuals may have by acting as sources of inspiration that propel larger political movements.

The UN uses the term *organ* to refer to the main bodies that lie at the heart of the UN system. There are six UN organs: the General Assembly, the Security Council, ECOSOC, the Trusteeship Council, the Secretariat and the ICJ.

Interest groups and pressure groups are both political NSAs designed to lobby and influence policymakers and politicians in support of a specific objective. A pressure group is a special type of interest group that relies on more forceful techniques.

Greta Thunberg started *School Strike for Climate* in 2018.

Understanding power and global politics

Think of the impact that one person had in focusing world attention on the climate crisis when she decided in August 2018 to spend her Fridays outside the Swedish Parliament, holding up a sign reading *Skolstrejk för klimatet* (*School Strike for Climate*). By 2019, the Greta Thunberg-inspired *Fridays for Future* school strikes saw coordinated worldwide multi-city protests, each involving over a million students. In March of the same year, UN Secretary-General António Gutteres endorsed the school strikes, admitting, 'My generation has failed to respond properly to the dramatic challenge of climate change. This is deeply felt by young people. No wonder they are angry.'[10]

As a student of Global Politics, you should be aware that there is a range of actors and stakeholders who affect, and are affected by, global politics. This gives shape to how we might view global politics as a system, and it should also serve as a reminder of the contextual nature of global politics. Not every actor is equally effective in shaping the outlines of global politics and not every stakeholder is equally affected by events and issues in global politics. The model or theoretical perspective of Global Politics you adopt will also help frame how you approach different actors and stakeholders and their significance within global politics.

Table 1.1 Summary of key actors and stakeholders in global politics

Actor / Stakeholder	Summary
Nation-state	The entity formed when people sharing the same historical, cultural or linguistic roots form their own state with borders, a government and international recognition.
State	A fundamental concept within Global Politics. It is the organized political unit that has a geographic territory, a stable population, a government and is legally recognized by other states.
Intergovernmental organization (IGO)	International agencies or bodies established by states and controlled by member states that deal with areas of common interest.
Informal forum / informal intergovernmental organization (IIGO)	A type of international organization made up of states but, unlike an IGO, not permanent. Informal forums usually operate as an annual meeting or conference.
Multinational corporation (MNC)	Private enterprises or companies with production facilities, sales or activities in more than one state.
Media	The means of mass communication and the transmission of information (broadcasting, publishing and the Internet) that reach or influence people widely.
Non-governmental organization (NGO)	Private associations of individuals or groups that engage in political activity. If these activities occur across national borders, then the group is an international NGO (INGO).
Social movement	A loosely organized but sustained campaign in support of a social goal. Typically, this involves the implementation or the prevention of a change in societal structure or values.
Resistance movement	An organized group of individuals that fights for freedom or justice, usually against the government. Resistance movements can use violent or non-violent means to disrupt civil order and stability.
Interest group	A group that has some common political interest or objective.
Pressure group	An organized group of people who forcefully try to persuade a government or other authority to do something. Pressure groups are a specialized form of interest group.
Individual	One person, rather than a large group.

Global politics core

Activity

Use a Circle of Viewpoints thinking routine in a small group of 3–5 to examine a political issue, for example, the climate crisis, racial or gender discrimination, civil conflict, etc., and consider the perspectives of different actors/stakeholders with respect to the political issue you have chosen.
1. Make a list of different perspectives on your chosen political issue.
2. Each student should choose one perspective to explore, using these sentence starters:
   - I am thinking of [the political issue] from the viewpoint of [the actor/stakeholder you have chosen].
   - I think… (Describe the political issue from the viewpoint of your chosen actor/stakeholder. Take on the character of the actor/stakeholder.)
   - A question I have from this viewpoint is… (Ask a question from the viewpoint of your chosen actor stakeholder.)
3. Once everyone has had a turn, reflect as a group on how different actors/stakeholders can have different kinds of connections to the same political issue, and how these connections can influence what actors/stakeholders see and think. Be prepared to share your reflections with the whole class.

Exercises

3. Identify some of the key players in global politics. Why is it important to identify them?
4. Describe some of the differences between a nation-state, a state, a nation and a country.
5. Explain how IGOs like the UN are important in global politics.
6. In addition to the nation-state and IGOs, suggest other actors and/or stakeholders that are significant.
7. Define globalization and outline how it affects societies around the world.
8. Explain how the media has become an increasingly important actor in global politics.
9. Analyze how NGOs impact global politics.

Global politics as a system: structures and interactions

Conceptual question

What different types of structures exist in global politics and how do they shape interactions between actors?

In Global Politics, structure is a set of overarching principles, rules, roles and constraints that exist independently of political actors, but bind all actors together into a larger system. Structure can organize actors into different relative positions of power, influence and status. Structure can also help shape the interests of actors

Understanding power and global politics

and how they respond to each other in the broader system of global politics. By understanding the structures of global politics and how such structures are perceived and conceptualized, we can arrive at a deeper appreciation of how certain behaviors and outcomes are shaped by structural forces and pressures.

The system of global politics at its most basic level can be seen as a dynamic between three key actors: nation-states, IGOs and NSAs. These actors independently or together react to, are subject to and sometimes shape the political events and issues at the heart of global politics. Figure 1.2 is a crude simplification of the global system and a useful starting point.

Figure 1.2 The global system.

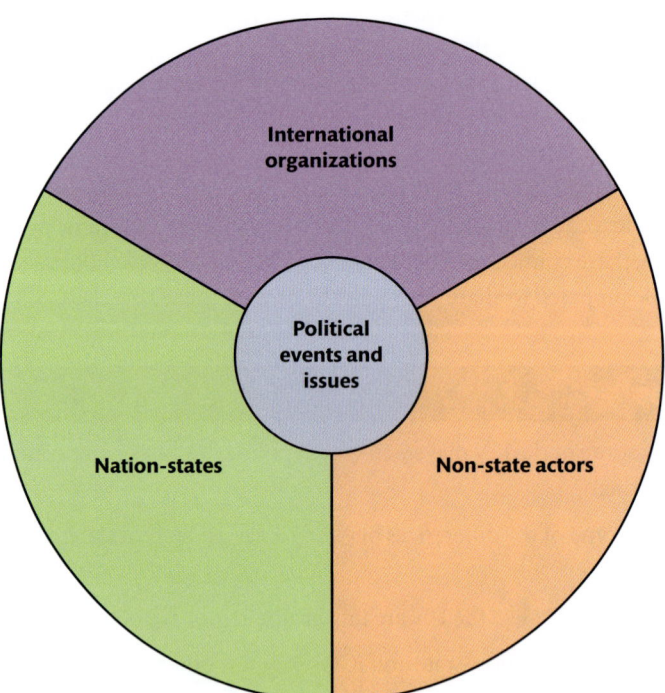

> **TOK**
> What is the purpose of a model in any academic subject? How does the use of models vary across your IB subjects and how might you explain any differences? To what extent should a model accurately reflect reality? Is there a trade-off between the accuracy of a model and its usefulness in terms of helping us better understand the world around us?

Contending views of global politics: 1648 vs 1492

Historical accounts of global politics often point to the Peace of Westphalia (1648), which ended the Thirty Years War in Europe (1618–48), as the origin of the modern system of sovereign states. Prior to this war, the European landmass was dominated by a set of city-states and small territories whose borders were unclear and whose rulers were frequently guided by the Roman Catholic Church through the Holy Roman Empire. The Peace of Westphalia produced a system in which authority would rest on the political idea of sovereignty rather than being based on religious structures. The two treaties that underpinned the Peace of Westphalia created distinct political units (states) within which a ruler could legitimately exercise political authority. States recognized one another as mutually sovereign. A key element of this new system of sovereign states was the principle of non-intervention in the domestic affairs of other states. It is worth remembering that this was still a system populated by dynastic monarchies for whom the extent of one's family tree frequently determined the extent of one's political authority. It was not until the early 18th century that the extent and limits of sovereign authority first began to be defined in terms of a state's territorial boundaries. It is not until well into the 19th century that we begin to see some of the features of the modern state system we are familiar with today.

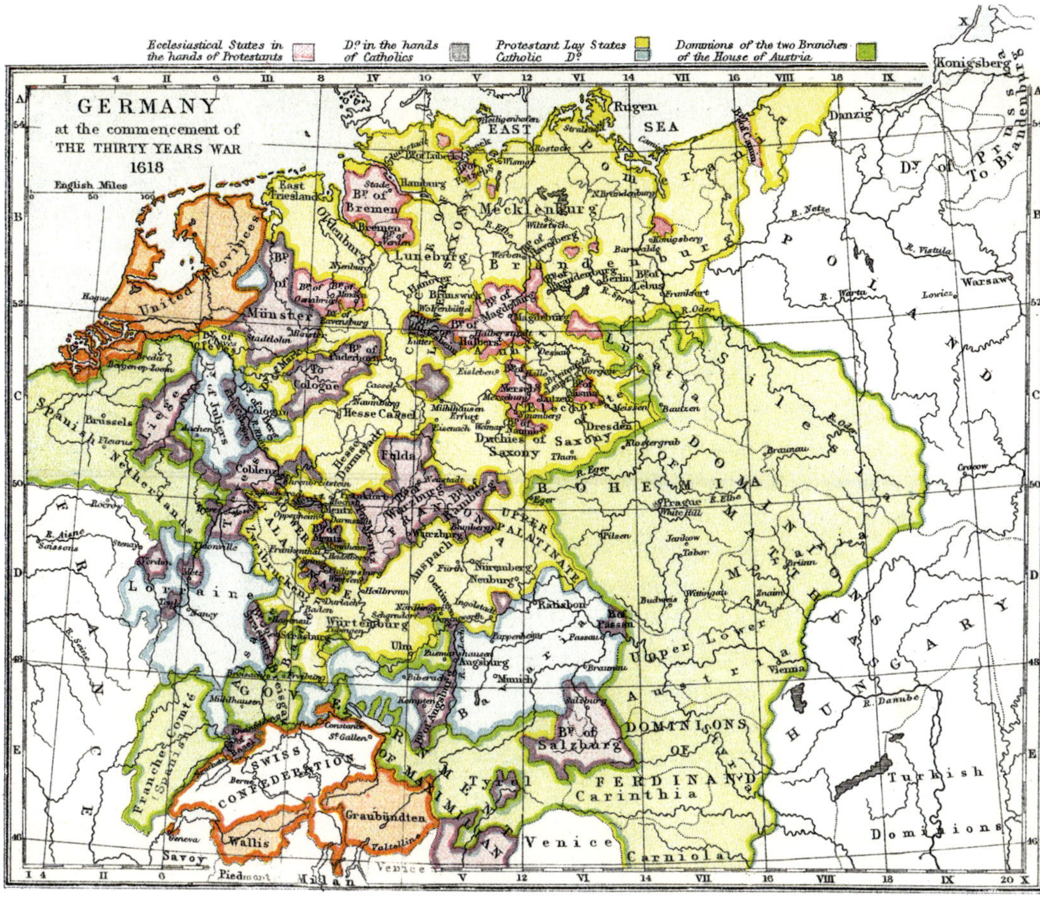

Global politics core

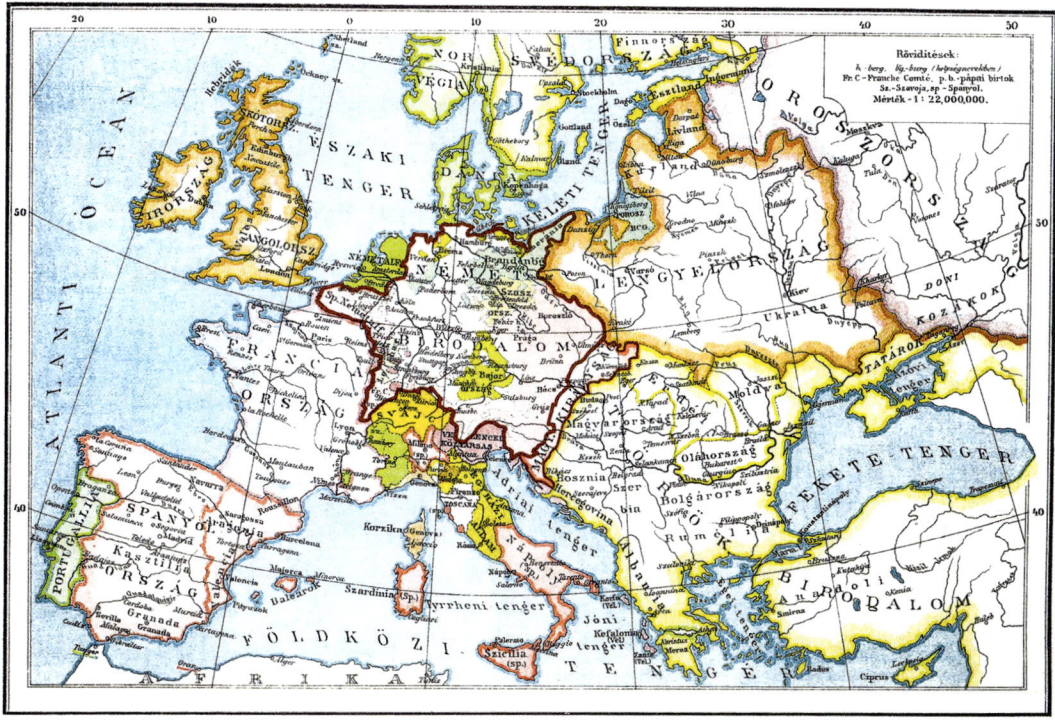

Figure 1.3 Europe in 1618 and in 1648.

Understanding power and global politics

You should be prepared to critically analyze any political narrative, particularly the historically dominant Western accounts of global politics. This means recognizing the historically contingent nature of the contemporary system of global politics and being open to non-Western histories and perspectives. There is nothing inevitable or natural about the modern global system of sovereign states.

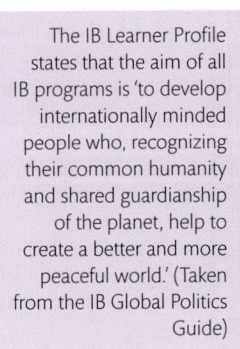

The IB Learner Profile states that the aim of all IB programs is 'to develop internationally minded people who, recognizing their common humanity and shared guardianship of the planet, help to create a better and more peaceful world.' (Taken from the IB Global Politics Guide)

How does your own position inform the way you see and approach global political challenges?

Why might it be important to explore non-dominant or **subaltern** voices and perspectives? What do we gain from doing so?

While Westphalia was a key moment in the development of our contemporary and global states system, the Westphalian settlement that identified the sovereign state as *the* legitimate actor in global politics remained a European phenomenon until the 19th and 20th centuries. It was only then that the system of sovereign states expanded first to Latin America following the Spanish-American Wars of Independence (1808–33), then to Eastern Europe after the First World War and, finally, to the rest of the world as part of the process of **decolonization** following the end of the Second World War.

The year 1492 could be seen as a more significant date for most of humanity given the international system it created. The principles of mutually recognized sovereignty and non-intervention contained within the Treaties of Westphalia only applied to a relatively small section of humanity – male, white and European Christian. Christopher Columbus' landing in the Americas in 1492 and the negative effects of conquest, including violent oppression, the theft of land and resources, slavery and genocide, impacted much of the rest of humanity. For several centuries following the Peace of Westphalia, global politics could be characterized as sovereignty at home but empire abroad for the European powers. The consequences of 1492 continue to have an impact. A 1648 perspective has little to say about the global hierarchies of humanity, often based on race and religion, that continue to justify oppression, violence and inequality. While a minority of humans living in the Global North might be living in a world where their rights to life, liberty and property are protected, most humans continue to live in the shadow of 1492.

Example – Postcolonial history

W.E.B. Du Bois, the Black American sociologist, argued for a non-linear, **postcolonial** understanding of historical time and processes. He recounted an experience of an editor asking him to 'leave out the history and come to the present', to which Du Bois wished to reply: 'Dear, dear jackass! Don't you understand that the past *is* the present; that without what *was*, nothing *is*?'[11] For Du Bois and many postcolonial theorists, to study the past was to learn about the present. In this sense time does not pass, it accumulates.[12]

Global politics before Westphalia

International relations between different peoples and political units existed before 1648. A variety of older civilizations pioneered a range of international political systems and world orders that were similar to and different from the Westphalian system of sovereign states that characterizes the world today. By considering a broader historical perspective and including non-Western examples of political orders and international relations, we can challenge and critically question some of the universal concepts that Western accounts of global politics often take for granted. In doing so, we are better able to reveal the diverse and global heritage of Global Politics as a discipline and how some of its main ideas and issues – human rights, norms, power politics, international institutions, sustainable development, conflict resolution, etc. – have multiple sources, which may give them greater legitimacy and importance. With the 'rise of the rest' in contemporary global politics, such as the PRC and India, it may be even more important to understand and apply non-Western contributions to the study and practices of contemporary global politics.[13]

Global politics core

At the heart of the modern idea of global politics as a system is the concept of **anarchy**, which is that there is no authority above the state: there is no world government. Western scholars trace this concept back to the ancient system of Greek city-states, ignoring the fact that a similar system existed in the pre-Maurya republics of India (600–400 BCE). Similarly, elements of globalization predate our contemporary period, especially the transfer of knowledge. Following his conversion to Buddhism, Indian Emperor Ashoka (268–232 BCE) of the Mauryan dynasty sent missionaries throughout Asia to spread Buddhist teachings and morals, transforming the region forever. The Islamic civilization, especially Muslim Spain (711–1492 CE), which had preserved many of the historical and scientific texts of ancient Greece, spread these ideas to Europe, eventually fueling the European Renaissance. A wider and more diverse view of global politics alerts us to some of the blind spots in the study of Global Politics that a more Eurocentric viewpoint may have.

 Anarchy refers to the absence of a central authority or overarching power governing the interactions between sovereign states. This concept emphasizes the self-help system where states operate independently and make decisions based on their own interests, often leading to a balance of power dynamics.

We should adopt a nuanced view of global politics by remembering that such systems are not static entities. History reminds us that over time such systems can move from hierarchy to anarchy and back again, as happened in ancient Sumer, India and Europe, before and after the Peace of Westphalia. What a broader historical account reveals is that it may be better to view the range of political systems and (inter)relationships in global politics as a spectrum. This is important because different types of international systems have different kinds of relationships among actors within the system. As a student of Global Politics, you should regularly challenge traditionally dominant Western perspectives because focusing only on these accounts ignores the role and contribution that other parts of the world have made and continue to make in our understanding of contemporary global politics. If the world is transitioning from a world order dominated by the Global North to something more pluralistic and decentred then it will become more important for you to appreciate such diversity.

 Although history plays an important role in understanding global politics, any examples and case studies must be contemporary. This is usually defined as within the last twenty years.

Structuring global politics: the material and the ideational

The world: upside down and reversed?

We can distinguish between the material and **ideational** foundations of structure in Global Politics. Material structures include factors associated with the physical world like wealth, natural resources, demographics, industrial capacity, military hardware and

 How do ideas have a tangible effect on the real world?

23

Understanding power and global politics

personnel, etc. Ideational approaches to structure emphasize how the physical world only becomes significant through the ideas and understandings that we have of it. The physical or material world affects human behavior once it has passed through the filter of our individual or collective knowledge and perception of it. This division is reflected in and reinforced by different theoretical or conceptual schools of thought in Global Politics.

A real-world example of this distinction between the material and ideational in Global Politics is the presence of nuclear weapons. Given their immense destructive capacity, the possession of nuclear weapons acts as a structural constraint on the behavior of *all* states in the international system. This makes the political interests, identity or regime type of the state that has such weapons irrelevant. An ideational conceptualization of how such weapons structure global politics would note how countries like the UK treat an ally with nuclear weapons, like France, very differently from a perceived foe, like Russia. At any moment, there may be several nuclear-armed French submarines off the coast of the UK without this causing alarm in London. The situation and London's reaction would likely be very different if these were Russian submarines.[14] It does seem as if calculations of the national interests and identity of states – judgments based on ideational concepts like shared values – could shape the political significance of nuclear weapons and the subsequent behavior of political actors.

We can think in terms of how the structure of the international system might shape the behavioral choices and outcomes of actors and stakeholders. The effects of structures are either direct or indirect. Direct structural effects constrain or enable the actions of political actors by rewarding or punishing certain behaviors. The presence of an economically (materially) powerful and wealthy nation-state in the global system can help enable greater international trade if this state pressures other states to lower tariffs and other restrictions. Similarly, the distribution of military power might constrain the use of military force. A more ideational example would be the presence of enduring norms in global politics. **Norms** can be thought of as unstated but widely understood standards of acceptable and legitimate behavior. They shape the actions of actors as well as their expectations about the interests and actions of other actors. One norm that underpins much of contemporary global politics is the requirement of states to respect the territorial boundaries of other states and not to seize their territory. It should be noted that the presence of widely agreed norms does not mean that states or other political actors will always act according to them.

Norms are part of the institutional framework that helps to provide structure to the contemporary system of global politics. While you may be more familiar with the use of the term **international institution** to refer to physical organizations like the UN, NATO or ASEAN, there are various types of international institutions that exist in global politics. Along with norms and organizations, the term can also be used to describe a set of rules that is meant to govern international behavior by incentivizing or disincentivizing actions and actors (states and NSAs).

Indirect structural effects are usually described in *constitutive* terms. This means that the structure of the global system helps to create actors and some of their fundamental properties. The existence of an actor and its properties, like its identity or interests, depends on, and is enabled by, the content of the larger structure. You can see real-world examples of this in the domestic constitutions and legal frameworks of many states around the world, which set out a series of rules that structure political relationships within the country. These structures define the shape of the government as well as the roles of important political actors within it. At a regional level, notions of collective identity within the EU help constitute the interests of political elites to strengthen the EU and its legal framework. Although the international level may lack the overarching structures of authority that exist at the lower levels, there are still examples of legal frameworks that shape the behavior of political actors. For instance, the United Nations Convention on the Law of the Sea (UNCLOS) articulates the normative concept of the freedom of the high seas, which permits all states the freedom to navigate the open seas beyond any country's territorial waters. States that have not signed or ratified UNCLOS

Global politics core

still follow its provisions. At a global level, we can imagine how the perceived anarchical structure of global politics creates a system in which states can only be differentiated in terms of relative power and where this external environment forces all states to maximize their relative power in order to safeguard their survival.

> **Example – Looking beyond the West**
>
> UNCLOS is an example of the need to consider non-Western impacts on contemporary understandings of global politics. The foundations of this convention can be traced back to the system of international trade that emerged in the Indian Ocean between China, India and Southeast Asia during the 15th century. It is likely that the Dutch jurist, Hugo Grotius, who wrote about the idea of *mare liberum* (freedom of the seas) in the early 17th century was influenced by this Asian trading system, which he learned about in his role as a counselor for the Dutch East India Company.

Polarity and multiplexity within global politics

The concept of **polarity** is used to describe the number of **great powers** dominating an anarchical system of global politics. **Unipolarity** describes a situation in which one state is more economically, militarily and politically powerful than any other state in the system. Some commentators believe that the USA became a unipolar state following the end of the Cold War and the dissolution of the Soviet Union in 1991 as it was the sole superpower remaining. **Bipolarity** describes a situation in which two states dominate the system. The Cold War, with the USA as one pole and the Soviet Union as the other, is the classic 20th century example of bipolarity. Some scholars suggest that bipolarity may be returning as modern rivalries increasingly shape the early decades of the 21st century. **Multipolarity** is where more than three nation-states have nearly equal amounts of power. The significance of polarity lies in its links to the stability of the international order and the likelihood of conflict (war) breaking out. It should be noted that there is disagreement among scholars as to which form of polarity offers the greatest stability and is the most peaceful.

Search online for the 2023 TED talk 'The Next Global Superpower Isn't Who You Think' by political scientist Ian Bremmer. It is an interesting source to refer to as we begin to consider the ways in which the global political order might be evolving in the 21st century.

> **Activity**
>
> How would you describe the world today in terms of polarity? Be prepared to justify your answer.

Scholars such as Amitav Acharya have advanced the idea of **multiplexity**. This describes a system where there are 'many important actors and an array of ideas, institutions and approaches to peace, security and development.'[15] Rather than being anchored by a single actor capable of shaping the international system (a **hegemon**), a multiplex world is 'a culturally and politically diverse yet economically interconnected [system].'[16] Multipolarity mainly focuses on the distribution of material capabilities and is incapable of accounting for the significance and spread of ideas, cultures and civilizations. Multiplexity recognizes that the global political challenges we face are increasingly transnational, and so it is able to capture the broad complexities of interactions that characterize the contemporary system of global politics. A multiplex system would see established powers like the USA and the EU continue to command some areas of global governance, such as the **International Monetary Fund (IMF)**,

Hegemony refers to the dominance of one state or a group of states that lead or control the international system, often through a combination of economic, military, cultural and diplomatic means. This concept implies not just the power to influence others but also the ability to shape the norms and rules of the international order to reflect the hegemon's interests and worldview.

the UN and **The World Bank**, but would also see **emerging powers** like Brazil, India, Nigeria, Indonesia and Turkey collaborate with the established powers on some issues, like climate change, while competing with them on others, such as debt and infrastructure investment. Multiplexity provides space for non-state actors, such as international NGOs (Greenpeace, Human Rights Watch), civil society activists (Greta Thunberg, Malala Yousafzai) as well as uncivil society actors (terrorist organizations, drug cartels, human traffickers) to also play a significant role.

Example – NSAs in a multiplex world

There are a growing number of NSAs taking effective action on climate change. ActionLAC, a partnership set up by the Latin American Fundación Avina, aims to strengthen climate action in Latin America by mobilizing community-based organizations, small businesses and local governments to foster inclusive climate governance in the region. ActionLAC provides support throughout the different stages of climate actions. It also aims to raise awareness and stimulate learning between local and regional actors by connecting local actors with global processes and national policy-making.

Acharya argues that multiplexity is not a futuristic fiction. The diversification of global governance and the expansion in numbers of relevant actors can be seen in the rise of regional organizations such as the PRC-led Asian Infrastructure Investment Bank (AIIB) as well as 'more complex, hybrid or multi-stakeholder interactions in areas ranging from cyberspace to climate protection.'[17] It can also be seen in how no single state or organization is able or willing to take the lead in every issue area. Different combinations of states and/or NSAs provide leadership according to the issue, with 'multiple but overlapping conversations taking place around the world on various issues of importance to world order.'[18]

Case – Multiplexity in action

In 2021, there were several instances of multiplexity in action. There were UN Security Council discussions on the conflicts in Syria and Yemen involving all the great powers. The UN Climate Change Conference in Glasgow (COP 26) saw states, civil society activists and MNCs meet to discuss the climate emergency. The Tokyo Olympic Games in 2021 functioned as a semi-diplomatic conference where a range of international leaders were able to hold informal bilateral talks. The Association of Southeast Asian Nations (ASEAN), a regional IGO, held virtual summits to reaffirm its member states' commitment to upholding and promoting multilateral cooperation and partnership across a wide range of issues of regional importance.

While a multiplex system of global politics is not guaranteed, and nation-states could continue to occupy their historically dominant position in the modern system, it seems likely that a multiplex system will emerge and expand. This is because the political events and issues at the heart of global politics may become more spread out, in terms of material and ideational capability and leadership, yet remain overlapping. Multiplexity draws upon insights from the experiences and ideas of people and institutions in the Global South as well as a greater acceptance of their role. Multiplexity, therefore, offers a more inclusive and broader approach to global politics.

Global politics core

Exercises

10. Describe structure in Global Politics, and identify how it shapes the behavior of political actors.
11. Explain the significance of the 'Westphalian settlement'.
12. Suggest some reasons why students of Global Politics should be open to non-Western histories and perspectives.
13. Define the concept of anarchy and outline its significance in global politics.
14. Define multiplexity and explain how it differs from traditional ideas of polarity in describing contemporary global politics.

Power in global politics

Conceptual question

How does the way we view power affect our analyses of global politics?

The concept of **power** is fundamental to the study of global politics. However, there is no single, universally agreed upon definition of power and its meaning has broadened over time. In general terms, power can be thought of as the ability to achieve desired goals and to influence others. This interpretation of power is not new and can be traced back to Thomas Hobbes, who defined power as '[a person's] present means to obtain some future apparent Good.'[19] Bertrand Russell thought of it as 'the ability to produce intended effects.'[20]

TOK: How do choices about what content to include and exclude shape the nature of an academic subject? How do the ways in which we think about key concepts within an academic subject, like Global Politics, shape our analytical focus?

Activity

How might the games of chess and Go (weiqi) be analogies for how power operates in global politics? Be prepared to share your answer with a peer.

Power is one of the key concepts of Global Politics, but there is very little agreement on how to define or measure it. The ideas of **power-over**, **power-to** and **power-with** can help us better understand some of the ways in which power has been conceptualized and how it might operate in global politics. Power-over refers to an uneven or asymmetrical relationship between two or more actors in which one actor is able to make another actor do what they want.[21] Power-over is usually coercive in nature. Power-to lies in the ability of the actor to reach certain specific outcomes.

Understanding power and global politics

Each of these three forms of power can be connected to the different thematic studies as well as to the HL topic areas. For example, when people are denied access to important resources and fundamental rights like land, **healthcare**, jobs, civil-political rights and a good environment, power-over sustains inequality, injustice and poverty. Power-with and power-to offer positive ways of applying power that create the possibility of forming more empowering, equitable and just relationships and outcomes.

The term *power* in English often carries a negative connotation, at least in politics and social relations, because it is usually something that is used against or held over others. But to what extent is this true in other languages? Does our perception of power depend on the language we are speaking?

Power-to does not rely on any interaction with another person or actor. Power-with exists in the ability of a group of individuals to act together to achieve collective outcomes. It is generally seen as a cooperative or co-active form of power.

Understanding power: power-to as the basis for power-over and power-with

Hanna Pitkin, the American political theorist, introduced the expressions power-over and power-to as a way of challenging the dominant narrative of power as something that existed in relations between different individuals or actors, preferring to see it in terms of ability. For Pitkin, it was important to distinguish between these two expressions of power so that we can separate situations in which an actor may have power-over others, which only occurs when that actor gets the others to do something, from those situations in which an actor has the power-to achieve something by themselves. An actor's power-to is independent of other actors. It may involve other people if what the actor has the power to do is a social or political action, but it does not have to.[22] What we see then is the relational nature of power-to and power-over / power-with. If power-to is defined in terms of one's ability to achieve a certain objective then it must exist before it can be exercised over, or with, others. Power-to is, quite literally, empowering.

Power-over: power as negative and coercive

Initially, power in global politics was understood as an entity, something that was based on tangible sources like natural resources, economic wealth, demography and military forces. Because of this, the main unit of analysis was the state as this was the political entity best able to control and command these traditional sources of power. Only great powers mattered, while smaller states were often seen to be irrelevant and NSAs were not included. The focus of analysis was on military matters and war. The early supporters of this understanding of power were **realists** like Hans Morgenthau, but similar understandings were championed later by **structural realists** like Kenneth Waltz and John Mearsheimer.

In *The Tragedy of Great Power Politics*, Mearsheimer distinguishes between *potential* and *actual* power. Potential power is based on traditional sources like the size of a country's population and its wealth because these provide a state with the opportunity to build its military strength. Actual power is expressed in the quantity and quality of a state's army, navy and air force. There are many states in the world with significant resources and large populations that would not qualify as powerful, such as the Democratic Republic of the Congo (DRC). Actual power captures the idea of causation that we often associate with power, which is that it is the ability of actor A to get actor B to do what A wants, or to get B to stop doing what A does not want them to do.[23] This is the notion of power-over. For realists, what matters most is **hard power** – the ability to command or coerce others through the use of force, the threat of force, economic sanctions or inducements of payment. At the heart of hard power is **economic power**, usually measured in terms of GDP or GDP per capita, and military power.

Because states typically are the main actors with an ability to exercise hard power, they are the central player in realist analyses. For structural realists, states compete for power because of the anarchical structure of the global system. In the absence of a governing authority, all states are ultimately responsible for their own security and survival. As Mearsheimer notes, 'anarchy forces security-seeking states to compete

Global politics core

with each other for power, because power is the best means to survival.'[24] The international system forces great powers to maximize their power *relative* to other great powers as this is the best way to maximize their security. Doing so often involves obtaining more and/or better weapons as well as the development of new military technologies, but this decreases the relative power and security of other states. If these states react by improving their own military capabilities, we see the emergence of a **security dilemma**. This is a 'a situation in which actions taken by a state to increase its own security cause reactions from other states, which in turn lead to a decrease rather than an increase in the original state's security.'[25] The tragedy that realists like Mearsheimer identify is that the pursuit of power is both necessary and self-defeating, and the accumulation of power involves a strong negative feedback effect.

> **Example – NATO and Russia's war on Ukraine**
>
> Mearsheimer has blamed NATO's expansion for the Russian invasions of Georgia in 2008 and of Ukraine in 2014 and in 2022. He has traced the origins of the war in Ukraine to the 2008 NATO summit in Bucharest, Romania, when NATO issued a statement that Ukraine and Georgia would become part of the organization. Despite the Russians making it very clear that this would be seen by them as an existential threat, NATO continued to expand eastwards. Mearsheimer argues that, faced with a decrease in Russia's relative power, which threatened the security of his regime, Russian president Vladimir Putin decided to launch a pre-emptive invasion.[26]

Understandings of power broadened in the latter decades of the 20th century as the world and global politics became more interconnected and interdependent. While conceptualizations of power still focused mainly on the ability of actors to apply pressure or influence, scholars began to recognize potential sources of power other than material resources. These included the range of relationships a state shared with other states as well as some of the norms that supported these interrelationships. While sharing realism's anarchical view of global politics, **liberal institutionalists** argued that survival was not the most significant issue for states and that the structure of anarchy did not constrain states as much as realists believed. Rather than viewing global politics as a competitive zero-sum game (where there is a winner and a loser), forcing states to always be anxious about relative power imbalances, liberals have a more optimistic view. Because they believe that states are more concerned with absolute gains rather than relative gains, liberals recognize the opportunity for states to engage in mutually beneficial cooperation (a positive-sum game, where all states can win). As long as interactions between political actors result in absolute gains for all involved, and as long as actors can reasonably expect future interactions to also be beneficial, then cooperation can emerge under anarchy. At the heart of Robert Keohane and Joseph Nye's theory of *complex interdependence* is a world in which 'security and force matter less and countries are connected by multiple social and political relationships.'[27] A core element in this liberal view are institutions, which manage international interactions and allow actors to gain **political power** without necessarily triggering a negative response from other actors. If international institutions include a wide range of actors, this reduces the likelihood of resistance from smaller powers and reduces the need for the leading power(s) to use coercion.

Another way in which liberals see evidence of this is through the concept of **soft power**. While liberals acknowledge the role that hard power can play, especially in

Understanding power and global politics

matters of national security, increased **interdependence**, particularly in terms of the different channels of contact between societies, means that security is not the main issue in global politics for them. Joseph Nye coined the term soft power in 1990, when there was a widespread belief the USA was in decline – that the Soviet Union was passing it militarily and Japan was overtaking it economically. Rejecting the narrow realist view of power as the possession of capabilities or resources that can influence outcomes, soft power expands the concept of power to include the power of persuasion, which is the ability to move people by argument. More importantly, soft power includes the power of attraction, and attraction often leads to acceptance and agreement. This is still power-over but, by stretching the concept of power, Nye hoped to explain paradoxical situations where even when actors possessed overwhelming hard power, they did not always get the outcomes they hoped for.

While hard power is easy to measure in terms of troops, weaponry and financial strength, soft power is harder to quantify. Nye put it into three categories: cultural, ideological and institutional, all of which could help to legitimize the power of a state and reduce any resistance to it from other states. That is, 'if its culture and ideology are attractive, others will more willingly follow.'[28] Unlike hard power, soft power does not rely on force or money to bring about cooperation. It uses an attraction to shared values and a common commitment to achieve those values. Soft power co-opts rather than coerces as it is based on **social power** and **cultural power**. Hip-hop is a global culture, created by artists from all around the world, but American artists dominate the genre. The US State Department has been sending musical ambassadors abroad to create connections and to improve relationships via hip-hop, just as it did previously with rock and jazz musicians.[29] This means that hip-hop is an influential soft-power tool for the USA.

Example – Eurovision

An example of soft power in action is the Eurovision Song Contest (ESC), an annual exhibition of the musical talent of European nations (and Australia). In 2023, 162 million people tuned in to watch the ESC, making it one of the largest non-sporting broadcast events in the world. Despite the efforts of organizers to limit overt political messaging, 'the performances, voting patterns, and sensibilities have become a showcase of geopolitical soft power dynamics.' Small countries within Europe embrace the vision of Eurovision as a form of cultural diplomacy, with countries like Iceland, Malta and San Marino benefiting from the contest's more level playing field. The ESC is effectively the largest election in Europe and, over the years, voting patterns in the song contest have evolved to resemble the kinds of geopolitical alliances that take place during multinational negotiations. This makes a song contest into an interesting space for exploring 'national, regional, European and even global issues.'[30] The victory of the 2022 ESC winners, Kalush Orchestra from Ukraine, only months after the Russian invasion can be seen as a reflection of European geopolitics. In the popular vote, they placed in the top three in almost every country, which was interpreted as a resounding signal of solidarity to Ukraine from the European public.[31]

Ukraine's entry into the 2022 Eurovision Song Contest, Kalush Orchestra, in Irpin (just outside of Kyiv, Ukraine).

A state's ability to use soft power is important in settings where popular opinion matters and power is dispersed rather than concentrated. Soft power recognizes the role played by substate actors like provincial or city governments. It also acknowledges the role played by NSAs like MNCs and transnational advocacy networks as globalization

Global politics core

and the spread of information technologies allows them to compete with states in terms of legitimacy and effectiveness. In many respects, '[p]olitics has become a contest of competitive credibility', and in contrast to realist power politics, where military and/or economic might matters most, the information age may 'ultimately be about whose story wins.'[32]

Up until recently, it seemed that soft power was on the rise. The number of liberal democracies and free market capitalist economies in the world increased significantly between the 1980s and 2010s. Western-led international institutions, like the WTO, The World Bank and the IMF, were enlarged and collective security alliances like NATO were expanded to include former competitors. EU expansion saw country after country giving up large parts of their sovereignty to meet shared sets of rules based on liberal values such as human rights and free markets. Technology facilitated movements toward democratization, as could be seen in the color revolutions that spread through Europe, North Africa and the Middle East in the early 21st century. In recent years, hard power is everywhere, from the Russian war on Ukraine and the Taliban's takeover of Afghanistan to North Korea's 69 ballistic missile tests in 2022. There seems little doubt that an era of soft power has given way to a new era of hard power.

However, does an increase in hard power necessarily mean a decrease in soft power? Nye never claimed that soft power could exist independently of hard power. In reality, soft power can be seen as an extension of hard power. Nye sees hard and soft power as interrelated because they are both ways in which an actor can affect the behavior of others. Hard, or command, power does so by changing what others do, whereas soft, or cooptive, power works by shaping what others want. For Nye, it is more accurate to see hard and soft power, along with their associated behaviors and resources, as existing along a spectrum (Figure 1.4). In this way, '[h]ard and soft power sometimes reinforce and sometimes interfere with each other.'[34] Soft power is not a departure from hard power, but it builds on or extends its conceptualization of power-over beyond deliberate acts of command and control to include a political actor's ability to get the outcomes it wants by shaping the preferences of others.

	Hard		Soft	
Spectrum of behaviors	Command ← Coercion	Inducement	Agenda setting	Attraction → Co-opt
Most likely resources	Force sanctions	Payment bribes	Institutions	Values, culture, policies

 In a piece for *Foreign Policy* magazine, Nye used a parenting analogy to explain soft power, saying the parents of teenagers have 'long known that if they have shaped their child's beliefs and preferences, their power will be greater and more enduring than if they rely only on active control.'[33]

 Consider these two videos – BTS Shine Spotlight on the United Nations as Envoys of the President of the Republic of Korea and BTS 'Permission to Dance' performed at the United Nations General Assembly:

To what extent did K-wave, the global popularity of South Korea's pop culture, entertainment, music, TV dramas and movies, become a key instrument of South Korea's soft power? Share your thinking with a peer.

Figure 1.4 Nye's spectrum of power.*

Understanding power and global politics

Hosting a mega-sporting event like the FIFA World Cup or the Olympics can be a way for a state to showcase and enhance its soft power ability. Germany's hosting of the 1974 FIFA World Cup could be seen as an attempt to improve its tarnished image from the Second World War. The PRC's hosting of the 2008 Olympics was designed to demonstrate its economic progress and boost its global appeal. This strategy can backfire and lead to soft disempowerment, when hosting leads to greater focus on the more controversial or problematic practices of a state, as Qatar discovered when it won the right to host the 2022 FIFA games.

Why do you think that power is a key concept in Global Politics and TOK? What role does power play in other IB subjects? How does the role/significance of power in Global Politics differ from its role/significance in other IB subjects?

Activity

In what ways might allegations that the death toll from the earthquakes that hit Türkiye in 2023 were higher than they should have been due to poor government oversight of building codes and regulations negatively impact its soft power? How might the humanitarian assistance to Türkiye by countries such as India boost India's soft power? Discuss your thinking with a classmate.

This interrelationship between hard and soft power became even clearer in 2004 when Nye argued that strategies that successfully combined both dimensions of power so that they reinforced one another could be considered **smart power**. An example is the PRC, which, since opening up and reforming its economy in 1978, has become the largest trading country in the world, with the second-largest GDP, while modernizing and expanding its military capabilities. By the first decade of the 21st century, President Hu Jintao declared that the PRC must develop its soft power, which was then expressed in the dual concepts of *a harmonious world* and *the good neighbor policy* that together emphasized multilateral diplomacy, deeper economic cooperation and cultural exchange. More recently, President Xi Jinping has called for *a community of shared destiny*. One concrete **representation** of Chinese soft power has been the Confucius Institute, whose mission is to promote Chinese language, culture and tradition. By 2018, it had over 500 branches worldwide. Even more significant has been the Belt and Road Initiative (BRI), which, since 2013, has seen Chinese firms and banks drive infrastructure-led development in many states in the Global South. Through its example of economic and developmental success, and by allowing developing states to engage in globalization without sacrificing their own culture, ideology or institutions, the PRC's smart power has gone a long way to creating an alternative world order to the one promoted by the USA and its allies.

This ability of powerful states and institutions to use hard, soft and smart power to shape the global system in ways that benefit their interests is referred to as **structural power**. Susan Strange defined structural power as the ability of a state to 'shape and determine the structures of the global political economy [or international system] within which other states, their political institutions, and their economic enterprises… have to operate.'[35] A state that has a strong military and a large economy may use its hard power to shape the rules of the international system in its favor. It could use military force to secure access to key resources or trading routes, and it could use economic coercion to influence the behavior of other states. A state with strong cultural influence or an effective diplomatic network may use its soft power to shape the norms and values of the global system in its favor, by building alliances and networks with other states or by promoting its values through cultural diplomacy. If a state uses its hard and soft power to shape the rules, institutions and norms of the global system to its own benefit, it can be said to have strong structural power. The USA has been a key player in the creation and management of IGOs like the UN, IMF and The World Bank. It has also pushed for the liberalization of trade and investment around the world, which has given US corporations and financial institutions significant influence in the global economy. The USA has historically used its soft power to shape many of the norms and values that guide international behavior, especially with respect to human rights and democracy.

States can use hard, soft and smart power within the context of their relationships with other states, using this relationship to influence other states to change their behavior.

Global politics core

Relational power is the ability of one actor to influence the behavior of another actor in a particular interaction or relationship. The conventional view of relational power involves one state knowing the strengths and weaknesses of another state so that it can determine what would be a convincing threat and what would be an attractive reward. Yaqing Qin, the Chinese political scientist, has advanced a more nuanced view of relational power, one that draws upon traditional Chinese views of the social world as ripples in a lake. Qin developed a concept of power that is not just about domination or coercion, but also involves more subtle forms of influence and control embedded in social relationships. Qin sees actors and events coexisting in 'the complex relational context, without which none of them would exist at all.'[36] Qin sees power not as a fixed or static thing that individuals or groups possess, but as a fluid and dynamic process that is shaped and reshaped by social interactions. Although he does not reject the importance of hard and soft power, Qin argues that power relations are not just about who has more resources or authority, but are also about the emotional dynamics of social relationships, such as trust, respect and solidarity. Power is 'a process of constantly manipulating and managing one's relational circles to one's advantage' and an actor becomes more powerful by increasing the size and quality of their circles, for example, the number of states and which specific states are in their relational circle.[37] This adds a different dimension to our understanding of power, which is less focused on material gains or short-term influence and more focused on reputation and reinforcing long-term ties.

> The term *ubuntu* comes from the sub-Saharan Nguni language family and refers to the idea that the individual is deeply interconnected with their community. Everyone is responsible for everyone else, which comes from a sense of being inseparably connected rather than from a sense of duty. Applied to global politics, *ubuntu* would require states to cooperate in the interests of humanity as a whole because an injustice to one would be an injustice to all. This is very different from most Western thinking, which is based on assumptions of self-interested behavior by political actors, and driven by territorially based nationalism and global capital.

The rising influence of authoritarian states in the **democratic** world throughout the 2010s led Christopher Walker and Jessica Ludwig to develop the concept of **sharp power** in 2017. They noted that Russia had spent huge amounts of money in an effort to shape public opinion and perceptions around the world through cultural activities, educational programs, media and propaganda. These efforts were not openly coercive and so did not qualify as hard power, but they also did not fit within the traditional lens of soft power as the goal was 'not principally about attraction or even persuasion; instead, it center[ed] on distraction and manipulation.'[38] Sharp power is subversive. It enables authoritarian states 'to cut, razor-like, into the fabric of a society, stoking and amplifying existing divisions' by taking advantage of the openness that exists in many democratic regimes.[39] The term helps us understand events that cannot be explained with references to hard and soft power.

A more radical and sophisticated conceptualization of power-over lies at the heart of the Italian Marxist philosopher, Antonio Gramsci's, work. Gramsci's concept

Understanding power and global politics

of **hegemony** acknowledges the active role played by subordinate or low-ranking groups in society when it comes to the operation of power-over, and presents a more subtle conception of political authority. Coercion results in a limited or domineering hegemony in which the ruling group seeks to minimize or reject the demands of the subordinate or subaltern group(s). In order to achieve an expansive or aspirational hegemony, the hegemonic group must seek the consent of subalterns, and so greater attention is paid to ideological rather than coercive domination. Gramsci's notion of hegemony is sensitive to issues of power *and* legitimacy.

According to Gramsci, consent is created and recreated by the ruling class in any system or society. Rather than dominating its junior partners, a successful hegemonic group has to recreate itself with one eye on those it rules. It does so by adopting or absorbing large parts of its subaltern's worldview to create moral, economic and political unity.[40] However, consent is inherently unstable and this notion of hegemony as a continual process emphasizes the fact that a leading group must be constantly alert to the unpredictable demands of its subalterns and to the shifting historical context within which it exercises its authority if it is to maintain power. A ruling class that asks for consent but cannot give voice to the aspirations of those in whose name it rules will not survive.

Steven Lukes, the British political and social theorist, outlined three forms that power could take in our political world. In his 1974 book *Power: A Radical View*, Lukes refers to **three faces of political power**, all of which can be seen as different ways of exercising power-over. The first face is the ability of a political actor to affect and guide the behavior of other actors within a decision-making process. In such cases, it is the person with power who gets their way.[41] The second face is the ability of a political actor to shape the agenda or parameters of a discussion. This constricts the range of possible choices that any other actor can make and denies them the opportunity to address their own interests.

Lukes' third face of power seeks to understand the fact that people sometimes voluntarily act in ways that do not appear to be in their best interests. Unlike realist and liberal analyses of power, which only see the application of power when actual cases of conflict occur, Lukes argues that, 'the crucial point [is] that the most effective and insidious use of power is to prevent such conflict from arising in the first place.'[42] There is no coercion involved in the third face of power – the dominated allow their domination in both thick and thin ways. The thick sense is where people believe the values that oppress them, perhaps due to a powerful and widespread ideological system. The thin sense is when they are simply resigned to their fate. Either way, the dominated see compliance as natural. In this case, we might say that it is the social structure of many societies that exerts power-over rather than an individual or group being responsible.

French philosopher Michel Foucault saw power as something actively performed by individuals rather than being possessed by them. Like Gramsci, Foucault argued that at its core power is based on communication and consultation rather than direct coercion. Foucault also shared some of Hannah Arendt's views, believing that power was not a thing to be held but that it emerged out of relationships. However, where Arendt saw power being created and maintained in the public sphere, Foucault saw power being distributed and dispersed throughout society. He argued that all social relations are relations of power, whether in households or in the hierarchies of government, because everyone is involved in trying to influence the actions and outcomes around them in some way or another. In his words, 'Power is everywhere and comes from everywhere.'[43]

We can see connections between Lukes' third face of power and the concept of structural violence (see 'Negative peace' (page 180) in the 'Peace and conflict' chapter.) in the sense that it is often the social structure itself that dominates or oppresses marginalized groups in society.

TOK

In what ways might the truth be subjectively determined? Are truths in Global Politics different from truths in other IB Group 3 subjects like Economics, Psychology or History? How are they different from truths in subjects like the natural sciences, mathematics or languages?

Global politics core

Foucault's historical analyses of sexuality, criminality and madness revealed how particular narratives supported dominant power structures within societies by creating accepted forms of knowledge and truth. He used the term *power/knowledge* to express how power is created through these accepted forms of knowledge. This does not mean that knowledge is power but that certain narratives are repressed while other knowledge is produced and promoted through power. Foucault wished to shift our attention away from the ways in which states historically had exercised their sovereign power by coercing their subjects to behave in certain ways. He wanted people to appreciate how a new form of **disciplinary power** had emerged so that states no longer needed to rely on force or violence to exert power-over. Disciplinary power creates a body of knowledge and behavior that defines what is acceptable behavior such that we discipline ourselves and act properly. This is a more subtle form of power-over.

Foucault also argued that power is accompanied by resistance. Because power is not domination, but is at all times a struggle, opposing forces always exist in power relationships. Like Gramsci and Lukes, Foucault saw the dominated participating in power relationships. Where Foucault differs from Gramsci and Lukes is in his assertion that power is not just a negative or oppressive thing that forces people to act in ways they would rather not, but it can also be a productive and positive force in society.[44] While power could suppress knowledge, it could also produce it and in doing so be a major source of social identities, social discipline and conformity. For Foucault, power was active in the daily activities of life (micro-practices) that create and reinforce our different identities. When you buy a coffee with money, you help maintain the power structures through which our society creates an economy. If you vote in an election, you reinforce the power structures through which your society establishes a government's authority. Society is, according to Foucault, a rich web of power relations and our daily actions serve to create and recreate these webs.[45]

Walter Mignolo, the Argentine academic, developed the concepts of **coloniality** and **decoloniality** along with other Latin American scholars. Coloniality, or the colonial matrix of power, is the system of social, economic and political relations that emerged from the historical experience of **colonialism** and that continues in many parts of the world.[46] Coloniality and decoloniality are not the same as colonization and decolonization. Colonization and decolonization are located within a specific time and are geographically defined, while coloniality and decoloniality are ongoing processes that continue to shape contemporary global politics. Coloniality is what helps justify the exploitation of the world and its resources by Western systems of domination and power-over. It acts as the basis for colonialism/imperialism, capitalism, nationalism and modernity, making them appear natural and universal even though there is nothing inevitable about such systems. The colonial matrix of power emerged from the specific historical circumstances of European colonialism and imperialism, and has been reproduced and reinforced through various forms of cultural, economic and political domination. Coloniality highlights the enduring impact of colonialism on societies, while decoloniality offers alternative ways of understanding the world and pursuing social justice/**equity** by challenging and undoing the oppressive legacies of colonialism. This includes questioning and dismantling the dominant Western-centric worldviews, power structures, and knowledge systems that have been perpetuated since the colonial era, and actively promoting and legitimizing diverse, non-Western perspectives and ways of knowing.

Edward Said's classic work *Orientalism* (1978) makes use of Foucault's thinking to demonstrate the degree to which European knowledge of and stories about the Middle East (the 'Orient') were produced as an ideological complement in support of colonial power.

TOK
Reflect on your school or your classroom. Can you identify some of the daily activities that reinforce the power structures through which knowledge is transferred? What knowledge and ways of knowing are privileged? Which are not? Share your thinking with a peer and be prepared to justify your answer.

HL
Foucault's notion of micro-practices and their role in constructing and re-constructing identities can be linked to the HL topic area *Identity*.

We earlier looked at how a 1492 view of global politics differed from a 1648 perspective. The concepts of coloniality and decoloniality would be useful analytical tools for exploring and explaining these differences.

Understanding power and global politics

Case – Decoloniality in Western global politics

Decoloniality can be observed in various contemporary examples. For instance, in countries like New Zealand/Aotearoa, there is a growing emphasis on integrating Māori knowledge and perspectives into the national curriculum, moving away from a solely Western-centric education system. Alternatively, some communities, particularly in Latin America, are exploring economic systems based on indigenous values and practices, challenging the Western capitalist model. These include concepts like Buen Vivir in Ecuador and Bolivia, which focus on communal and sustainable living. Finally, some museums around the world, such as the British Museum or the Louvre, are increasingly engaging in dialogues about repatriating artifacts to their countries of origin, acknowledging the colonial context in which many items were acquired.

The colonial matrix of power is made up of interconnected elements, including race, gender, class, language and geography. These elements work together to create racialized hierarchical systems of power relations that privilege European or Western knowledge and culture and reject indigenous, pre-colonial or non-Western systems of knowing, being and creating. Mignolo argues that the colonial matrix of power serves the interests of those who are in positions of power, particularly those in the West. It allows them to maintain their power-over other parts of the world, and to continue to extract resources and labor from those regions.

HL — The concepts of coloniality and decoloniality can be connected to the HL topic area *Borders*, both in terms of a physical border between countries and also in terms of those borders that exist between race, ethnicity and gender, for example.

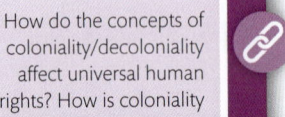

Activity

Identify examples of how coloniality operates in contemporary societies around the world, for example, specific cases of economic exploitation by Western companies in the Global South or ways in which Western powers continue to exert political influence over many formerly colonized states. How do Western values and cultural products dominate the global cultural landscape, and how are non-Western cultures often marginalized and exoticized? How do Western knowledge systems continue to be dominant in the world, while non-Western knowledge systems are often dismissed as primitive or unscientific?

How do the concepts of coloniality/decoloniality affect universal human rights? How is coloniality present in contemporary conservation strategies that often involve the creation of national parks and protected areas that dispossess and exclude indigenous and local communities from their lands?

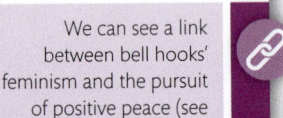

We can see a link between bell hooks' feminism and the pursuit of positive peace (see page 180 for more on positive peace). Only by eliminating all oppression and domination (structural and cultural violence) can we achieve positive peace.

By understanding the ways in which colonialism shaped and continues to shape the world, Mignolo argues that we can challenge dominant narratives and power structures, and begin to develop new ways of thinking and acting that promote greater social justice and equality. Many social movements and civil society organizations around the world have been working together (power-with) to promote international solidarity and challenge the power imbalances that are sustained by the global system. This has involved building alliances and promoting a more inclusive and equitable vision of the world. Indigenous peoples and other marginalized communities have challenged dominant Western cultural and knowledge systems by revitalizing their own languages, cultural traditions, artistic practices and knowledge systems, thereby promoting greater cultural diversity and understanding.

bell hooks[47], the feminist Black American social critic and author, wrote about how social structures of domination exerted power over individuals, especially those from marginalized and vulnerable populations. Like Mignolo, hooks' contribution to our understanding of power and how it operates lay in challenging analyses of oppression and domination that were based on only a single element – race *or* class

Global politics core

or gender. hooks argued that race, class, capitalism and gender functioned together as interdependent power structures to create the imperialist-white-supremacist-capitalist-heteropatriarchy. hooks did not coin the term **intersectionality**, but her work is viewed as having paved the way for intersectional feminism. Feminism, for hooks, was a struggle to eliminate all oppression and domination from society, and to imagine and create a counter-hegemony. What was holding so many people back was that they were under the spell of masculinist definitions of power that were negative and oppressive (power-over). hooks shared Foucault's view of power as productive, as something that could be positive and even emancipatory (liberating). hooks' most interesting definition of power is what she referred to as *the power of disbelief*. This is the power of the weak and oppressed to refuse 'to accept the definition of oneself that is put forward by the powerful… [and] to reject the powerful's definition of their reality.'[48] By drawing attention to the historically contingent ways in which oppressive social structures are created and maintained, she also highlighted the collective responsibility of individuals to work together (power-with) to challenge these local instances of repression. Doing so reminds us that we must be aware of power being exercised from above by the state, while still being cognizant of power that comes from below.

Power-with: power as positive and cooperative

German historian and political philosopher Hannah Arendt's conception of power is similarly consensual. For Arendt, power is linked with action and it is the ability for individuals to 'act in concert for a public-political purpose.'[49] Power is not a natural phenomenon but is a human creation. Power is grounded in collective engagement, in the actions and speech of individuals who come together as citizens or political equals to take on a common project of public importance. Power is never something that individuals have or exercise, but it belongs to a group and exists only so long as the group stays together.[50] Because power is based on the consent of those involved, it is not violent or coercive. Rather than being power-over, this is power-with.[51] Examples include workers' councils, demonstrations and social movements in support of struggles for justice and human rights.

Because power exists and is created *between*, rather than *in*, individuals acting together it is largely independent of material factors like economic wealth or military resources.[52] Its only limitation is people's willingness to come together as a group in public for political action. The realist view of power has a fixation on actual power and its capacity for violence. Arendt argues that power exists only as a potential, and it is not something that can be saved or stored up. Instead, it must be continually renewed. Arendt builds on James Madison's comment that 'all government rests on opinion' when she claims that power is the source of legitimacy for all political institutions: 'It is the people's support that lends power to the institutions of a country, all political institutions… petrify and decay as soon as the living power of the people ceases to uphold them.'[53] Power lies in the people and only exists with their *active* consent.

Eric Liu, the co-founder and CEO of Citizen University, a non-profit NGO promoting civics education in the USA, shares Arendt's view. For Liu, the legitimacy of political institutions and policies rests on collective action, particularly when large numbers of people are involved. He echoes Foucault's view that power is all around us, that we move through *systems of power* every day. Building upon a conventional analysis of forms of power-over (physical force, wealth, bureaucracy and social norms), Liu identifies two additional interrelated sources of power: ideas and numbers of people. An idea, such as political and civil liberty, can motivate real change in thinking and actions if

Protesters in Cairo during the Arab Spring.

Understanding power and global politics

a vocal mass of people creates the power to do so. The Arab Spring uprisings in 2011 demonstrated that large crowds of people matter. This is very much power-with.

Liu's Three Laws of Power helps us understand how power operates or is exercised in societies. The first law states that power is never static but expands or shrinks. This echoes Gramsci and Foucault thinking because this law means that if you are not taking action to increase your power then you are being acted upon. The second law also contains traces of Foucault's thinking and states that power is like water – it flows through everyday life. Liu argues that politics is the work of harnessing that flow in a preferred direction and that the act of policy-making is an attempt to freeze and sustain a particular flow of power. The third law is that power compounds, as does powerlessness. As the rich get richer, the powerful become more powerful. The sole factor that keeps us from ending up in a world where one person has all of the power is how we apply the first and second laws to ensure that the rich and powerful cannot enshrine their privilege in policy.[54] For Liu, this means organizing and mobilizing, that power-with can be developed 'out of thin air' as long as people work together to achieve a common goal. As he notes, '[w]hen one of us decides to invite two or three or five or seven other people to begin to organize, we're performing an act of magic. We're generating brand new power where it did not previously exist.'[55] Because of his focus on citizenship education and his recognition of the potential for every person to shape their life and world, we can also see some elements of power-to in Liu's conception of power, even though his action strategy remains centered on joint action and power-with.

Example – Alliance for Gun Responsibility

Following the 2012 Sandy Hook mass shooting at a school in Connecticut, USA, Eric Liu was part of a group of citizens that created the Alliance for Gun Responsibility. Based in Seattle, Washington, the Alliance wanted Washington's gun laws to be reformed. Washington State had a Democrat-controlled House and a Democratic governor, who should have been open to supporting gun control legislation. However, the gun lobby had become very effective at courting and frightening politicians, so the Alliance settled on a new strategy. Washington State has direct democracy in the form of ballot initiatives and referenda. Liu and the Alliance decided to bypass the politicians and appeal directly to the voters, who were strongly in favor of universal background checks for guns. In a show of citizenship power, hundreds of thousands of signatures were collected and the initiative won with close to 60 percent of the votes cast.[56]

Activity

Choose one perspective/theory on power and create a visual representation in the form of a diagram, mind-map, comic strip, artwork, etc. Be prepared to share and discuss your visual representation with your peers.

Exercises

15. Identify some of the main ways in which power is understood and classified in Global Politics.
16. Outline how the way in which power is conceptualized shapes our analyses of real-world political issues and phenomena.

Global politics core

17. Outline the differences between power-to, power-over and power-with.

18. To what extent is power generally coercive or cooperative in nature?

19. Explain the differences between hard, soft, smart and sharp power.

Sovereignty in global politics

Conceptual question

What is the concept of sovereignty and what is its significance in global politics?

Sovereignty is the key ordering principle of the global political system due to its central role in defining the authority, autonomy and territorial boundaries of nation-states. Sovereign states are the fundamental building blocks of the international system and the principle of sovereign statehood (the right of each state to supreme, comprehensive and exclusive rule over its territorial jurisdiction) forms the basis of governance in the world system. Sovereign states have no higher authority, they govern all areas of social life, and they do not share their authority with other states or any other actor. By separating the domestic sphere from the international (at least, in theory), and identifying and authorizing states as its key agents, sovereignty makes global politics possible. By excluding all other rivals to its domestic authority, sovereignty creates the possibility of state accountability to its own people, through **self-determination** and **democracy**.

State and sovereignty are *mutually constitutive concepts,* which means that they are interconnected and shape each other's meaning and existence. The concept of the state is closely tied to the concept of sovereignty, and vice versa. The state, as a political entity, depends on sovereignty to legitimize its authority and existence. Sovereignty is what grants the state the power and authority to govern its territory, make decisions, enforce laws and represent its population. Without sovereignty, the state lacks the essential foundation for its governance and autonomy. Sovereignty also plays a central role in defining statehood. When a state is recognized as sovereign by other states, it gains international legitimacy and enters into the community of states. Sovereignty is a criterion for statehood and provides the legal basis for a state to participate in international relations, establish diplomatic relations, and assert its rights and responsibilities as a political entity.

The concept of and practices associated with sovereignty have evolved over time. This evolution has not been uniform or even, and state experiences and state practices with respect to sovereignty have varied over time and space. While the great powers of Europe have given up many elements of sovereignty, other great powers like the USA, Russia, India and Japan have not. In various parts of the world, national borders are still things to fight over and defend, whether it is Azerbaijan reestablishing control over the historically Armenian Republic of Artsakh causing hundreds of thousands of ethnic Armenians to flee their homes, or the militarization of the US southern border with Mexico, sovereignty can be a matter of life and death.

Sources of sovereignty

The traditional notion of state sovereignty, often referred to as **Westphalian sovereignty**, is rooted in the 1648 Peace of Westphalia treaties, which marked the end

39

Understanding power and global politics

of the Thirty Year's War in Europe. There are three core elements that make up the traditional notion of state sovereignty:

- Sovereign states have exclusive authority and control over their territory, government and domestic affairs. They have the right to make and enforce laws within their boundaries without external interference.
- Sovereign states are recognized as autonomous entities with clearly defined borders, and the international community respects these borders, which are not to be violated. Traditional sovereignty emphasizes the principle of territorial integrity.
- Sovereign states have the right to govern themselves without external interference, subject to their willingness to respect international law. This is the principle of non-interference, which implies that states should not interfere in the internal affairs of other states.

We can detect some of the sources of state sovereignty in these three elements. International recognition is an important source of state sovereignty and states may choose to recognize other states as legal entities in international law for economic, moral and balance of power considerations. International law, and a state's willingness to behave according to international law and widely held norms, can also be a source of sovereignty. As far back as Thomas Hobbes, a key source of sovereignty has been the ability of a state to exercise a monopoly over legitimate use of violence within its territory and be a provider of security to its citizens.[57]

Most scholars recognize that it took several centuries for the modern sovereign state to evolve and that the notion of sovereignty as final authority has probably never existed. The writers of the US constitution created a set of checks and balances that introduced multiple sovereignties across national and local levels that were inconsistent with the notion of supreme authority. Not all states have been able to maintain exclusive authority and control within their borders, given the number of intrastate conflicts the world has experienced and continues to experience.[58] This is not something that only affects countries in the Global South, as separatist demands by Scotland in the UK, Quebec in Canada, and Catalonia in Spain demonstrate. States can be a source of insecurity and oppression to their own people, especially minorities and marginalized groups. R.J. Rummel, a political scientist at the University of Hawaii, has estimated that more than 262 million people have been killed by their own governments, which is almost seven times the number killed in international and civil wars in the 20th century alone.[59]

The idea of territorial integrity does not match the historical record. Many European states maintained colonies overseas, exercising sovereignty over territories that were distant from the borders of the parent state. The increase in the number of states in the latter half of the 20th century (Table 1.2) shows how the requirement for sovereign states to have fixed territorial boundaries is not essential in the modern period. The principle of sovereign equality and non-interference is not historically accurate either, with post-Westphalia European states regularly intervening in each other's affairs. Constant interference in the affairs of other states has continued in the modern era. Between 1990 and 2005, there were 425 interventions by major powers, non-major powers and international organizations. The Military Intervention Project at Tufts University estimates that the USA has intervened militarily overseas approximately 170 times since the end of the Cold War.[60] Even the UN, despite the provision in its Charter forbidding any intervention 'in matters which are essentially within the domestic jurisdiction of any state,' has intruded in the intrastate politics of member states when it has determined such politics to be a threat to international peace and order. Not

---

Jean Bodin and Thomas Hobbes developed the idea of sovereignty in the 16th and 17th centuries. They both realized that giving the sovereign overwhelming power could result in tyranny. However, both were writing at a time when Europe was plagued with conflict – Bodin was nearly killed in religious riots in 1572 and Hobbes lived through the English Civil War (1642–52) – and so it makes sense that they were more concerned with maintaining domestic order rather than justice.

all intervention is visible. Russia's documented hacking of the 2016 US presidential election and subsequent congressional elections shows how subtle and subversive interfering in the domestic affairs and political processes of other countries can be.

Table 1.2 Growth in the number of states in the international system

Year	Number of UN Member States
1945	51
1950	60
1955	76
1960	99
1965	117
1970	127
1975	144
1980	154
1990	159
2000	189
2010	192
2020	193

Table 1.3 The creation and disappearance of states, 1816–2011

Time Period	States Created	States Disappearing
1816–1876	24	15
1876–1916	12	1
1916–1945	16	7
1945–1973	81	1
1974–2011	52	2

As we can see from Table 1.3, many new states have come into existence since Westphalia, and a few have disappeared. This, along with the fact that state sovereignty has long coexisted alongside interventionist practice, led Stephen Krasner to argue that sovereignty was organized hypocrisy, maintained by states when it benefited them but violated whenever it suited them. Krasner's is a realist view of sovereignty (for more on realism see pages 64 and 65), and most contemporary scholars would agree that sovereignty has always been a fluid and variable concept rather than something that was absolute and unchallengeable. Modern notions of state sovereignty have evolved in response to these realities and include:

- An acknowledgment that states are interdependent. Interdependence among states has increased in scale and scope due to globalization, economic integration and transnational issues. States recognize that challenges, such as the climate crisis, terrorism and global pandemics, require cooperative efforts and collective action that may qualify a state's sovereignty. Technological change has made borders more porous, which means that it has become very difficult, if not impossible, for states to control movements across their borders of things like coffee, illegal drugs, people, capital flows, movies and social media.
- Sovereignty as responsibility rather than as an absolute right. States are expected to act responsibly and be accountable to their people and the international community. This is usually framed in terms of respect for human rights,

Understanding power and global politics

democratic governance and sustainable development, although these views are strongly contested by some states.

- Human rights and international law. The modern notion of sovereignty acknowledges the importance of human rights, and states are expected to respect and protect the rights of individuals within their borders, although the definition and content of human rights are contested. States are also expected to follow international legal frameworks that provide guidelines for and limitations on acceptable state actions.

Unlike traditional notions of sovereignty, modern notions see sovereignty as contingent. Contingent sovereignty recognizes that, while states maintain a degree of independence and decision-making authority, their actions and choices can be influenced or limited by international agreements, obligations and norms. Cooperation and shared responsibility are necessary in addressing global political challenges and maintaining order in the international system.

Activity

In his first speech to the UN General Assembly in September 2017, then US President Trump invoked the word *sovereignty* 21 times. Search online for a full transcript of his speech. Imagine you are the leader of another state speaking after Trump. Respond to his vision of sovereignty. Your speech can be critical, supportive or mixed in its assessment of Trump's speech, but it should relate your understanding of sovereignty to global politics as seen from your country, as well as your perceptions of the ideas Trump advanced.

The internal and external dimensions of sovereignty

Sovereignty has external and internal dimensions.[61] **Internal sovereignty** can be defined as 'supremacy over all other authorities within that territory and population.'[62] Internal sovereignty means that the state's institutions have final authority within the territorial borders of the state, and there is no higher authority to which people within those borders can appeal. It also implies that the state has the capacity to provide political goods like security, national defense and well-being for those it claims to represent. **External sovereignty** refers to the state's relationship with external actors and can be defined as 'not supremacy, but independence of outside authorities.'[63] It is best expressed in the state's right to territorial integrity based on mutual recognition by other states and the principle of non-interference from other states or IGOs.

Activity

Can you think of any countries that possess external sovereignty but not internal sovereignty? Can you think of any that enjoy internal sovereignty but do not have external sovereignty? Share your answers with a peer.

Robert Jackson has argued that following the creation of the UN there has been a change in the norms surrounding statehood and sovereignty. Before the early 1960s, only those countries that had internal sovereignty and could provide political goods for their populations were seen as sovereign states. Following the UN General Assembly Declaration on the Granting of Independence to Colonial Countries and Peoples in 1960, which stated that 'all peoples have the right to self-determination' and that 'inadequacy of political, economic, social or educational preparedness should never serve as a pretext for delaying independence,' there was an increase in the number of nation-states in the world. Many of these newly independent states were former European colonies that had been granted external sovereignty but had been left by the colonizers without the ability to effectively exercise internal sovereignty.[64]

Rather than seeing internal and external sovereignty as two separate qualities of the state, modern notions of sovereignty understand how these two dimensions of sovereignty influence one another. Internal sovereignty is not just about using coercive means to maintain domestic authority but it is also based on some degree of consent and legitimacy from domestic society. Internal sovereignty legitimated in this way provides the foundation for a state to exercise power internationally. Foreign policy decisions, which relate to the international political order, are made on the basis of domestic politics and the internal characteristics of a state. With many of the world's global political challenges being transnational in scope and scale, what countries do inside their borders has become an international governance issue. State sovereignty is contingent on the internal *and* external dimensions. It also depends on how state practices associated with internal sovereignty affect their external sovereignty, and vice versa (Figure 1.5).

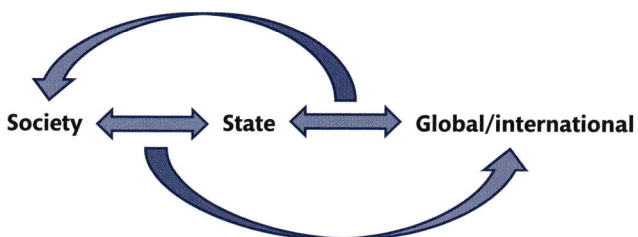

Figure 1.5 Internal and external state sovereignty.

Case – UNCLOS and the USA

The USA has not ratified the United Nations Convention on the Law of the Sea (UNCLOS), which establishes rules governing all uses of the oceans and their resources, because US politicians have seen it as an unnecessary restriction on US sovereignty. By not being a party to the treaty, the US cannot participate in the Commission on the Limits of the Continental Shelf, which examines submissions from states seeking to expand their sovereign rights beyond the 200 miles from shore boundary that marks a coastal state's Exclusive Economic Zone. This means that the USA, because of concerns over its sovereignty, cannot participate in one of the last divisions of sovereignty on the planet and cannot help set the rules that could see it exercise sovereign rights over approximately 1 million square kilometers of seafloor and sub-seafloor resources.

Challenges to state sovereignty

State sovereignty is being challenged from multiple directions. While countries still largely get to decide what happens within their borders, the world is changing. Biological or computer viruses from one state can cause massive disruptions in other states, and people migrating from one country can cause political crises in an entire region. In an interdependent world, the decisions made in one country are more likely to affect other countries. When these decisions cause harm, the affected country may try to protect its sovereignty by interfering with the decisions of the first country. These violations of external sovereignty can take many forms, such as direct military

Understanding power and global politics

intervention, cyber-attacks, election interference and economic coercion in the form of sanctions. Many states in the Global South have criticized the ways in which the global financial system violates their economic sovereignty, when IGOs like the IMF, leading bilateral state lenders, and private lenders impose strict conditions on their borrowing.

State sovereignty also faces challenges from separatist movements that challenge the state's internal sovereignty. Such movements typically fight for one of three outcomes: to become an independent state, to merge with a neighboring state or to gain more autonomy within the existing state. Real-world examples of each are Ambazonia (Cameroon), Rojava (Syria) and Wales (UK), respectively. Despite declarations and treaties in support of *all* peoples to the right of self-determination, the UN has hesitated to endorse the break-up of modern states, and only three new countries have joined the organization this century – Timor Leste, Montenegro and South Sudan. The concept of *indigenous sovereignty* has challenged the political and moral authority of sovereign states that have indigenous populations within their borders. Indigenous sovereignty challenges the uniformity of rules that characterizes internal sovereignty by advocating respect and recognition for difference and diversity across different levels of governance.

State sovereignty may be challenged in two other ways. First, economic and financial globalization is often perceived as restricting a state's ability to exercise effective control over its national economy, particularly in the key areas of public spending for income redistribution, macro-economic policy (fiscal and monetary policy) and taxation, especially when it comes to MNCs. Second, many of the environmental effects of domestic economic policies do not respect sovereign borders – the climate crisis does not recognize state sovereignty.

▲ Fires in the Amazon rainforest can be considered a global problem.

Case – Amazon wildfires

In 2019, when there was international outrage over the fires in the Amazon, the Brazilian government denied responsibility, instead blaming loggers, ranchers and farmers for starting the fires. The G7 members tried to convince Brazil to put out the fires and offered to give Brazil $22 million to help fight the fires, but Brazilian President Jair Bolsonaro refused, with a government spokesperson saying that Brazil's sovereignty was non-negotiable. Ireland and France threatened to block a trade deal between the EU and a group of South American countries unless Brazil did more to put out the fires. Eventually, Bolsonaro accepted some foreign aid money and sent the Brazilian army in to control the fires. In the following months, there were far fewer fires. Climate change remains a global challenge and Brazil is not the only state with harmful domestic policies. In the future, other countries may be targeted with incentives or possibly more direct interventions. If some modern problems ignore borders, does this mean that their solutions should also do the same?

Increased interdependence is forcing many states to consider how their desire for independence may be balanced by their need for effective international cooperation. Global challenges such as the climate crisis, migration or **public health** crises may require states to collaborate and *pool* their sovereignty to tackle these issues. **Pooled sovereignty** is a cooperative arrangement between sovereign states, in which they share and delegate certain powers, responsibilities and decision-making authority to a common international entity, often for addressing mutual challenges or pursuing common objectives. States may voluntarily coordinate their efforts and establish

Global politics core

international norms and standards to address these challenges, and so accept certain limitations on their sovereignty. This brings us back to the notion of contingent sovereignty and, many states may have to consider *sovereignty bargains*, where a state trades off some of its sovereignty to cooperate with other states on global challenges. In *Sovereignty: Organized Hypocrisy*, Stephen Krasner identified four different dimensions of sovereignty:

- International legal sovereignty, which is international recognition from states.
- Westphalian sovereignty, which is the principle of non-interference, or the ability of a state to determine its own affairs.
- Domestic sovereignty, which can be seen in terms of state autonomy and the ability of a state to maintain the monopoly of the use of legitimate violence within its territory.
- Interdependence sovereignty, which is the capacity of a government to control cross-border movements of any kind (people, goods, etc.). Interdependence sovereignty can also be thought of as the ability of a government to control the outcomes of issues it cares about.[65]

To advance its interests in a complex world may require a state to make difficult trade-offs and sacrifice some autonomy, or even authority, to gain influence over issues such as nuclear proliferation, trade, border security, migration, terrorism, the climate crisis and global pandemics.

Even though states may enter into sovereignty bargains, it is still their sovereign right to do so or not. The need for a state to bargain some of its sovereignty is not the same as saying that sovereignty is an outdated concept or the sovereign state is nearly dead. Despite sovereign equality being a foundational UN concept, the reality of global politics means that some states may be more sovereign than others. The extent to which a state can engage in sovereignty bargains, and the terms of any such bargain, can vary depending on its capabilities or on the circumstances. Different states may have different levels of participation and obligations within international frameworks. The notion of sovereignty bargains reflects the evolving nature of sovereignty in an increasingly interconnected and interdependent world.

Case – Pooling sovereignty

All states give up some sovereignty when they sign a treaty or join an IGO, and Europe has taken the process the furthest. The EU, a **supranational** organization, which as of now includes 27 member states, works to ensure that labor, goods, capital and services can move freely within its borders. By pooling (ceding) sovereignty, countries in the EU enjoy economic, political and security benefits. Goods and services are cheaper, and, as the second-largest economy in the world, the EU can negotiate better trade deals than any individual European state could alone. Although many EU member states are also members of NATO, an EU defense agreement is also part of membership. There are some downsides to pooling sovereignty as the high degree of economic interdependence means that, if one economy collapses, as Greece's did in 2010, it can threaten the economic stability of the entire bloc. As with Brexit, national identity and loyalties remain a powerful force in many parts of Europe and threaten the degree of interconnectedness that exists at the heart of the EU project.

The Treaty on Open Skies, which came into force in 2002, allows parties to conduct unarmed aerial surveillance flights over the entire sovereign territory of any of the other parties to the treaty. It is designed as a confidence building measure by allowing parties to gather information about military forces and activities that are of concern to them. Both the USA and Russia were parties to the treaty until the USA withdrew in 2020, and Russia followed them out in 2021.

Pooled sovereignty involves multiple states voluntarily combining certain aspects of their sovereign powers, typically in areas like defense, economy or governance, to achieve collective benefits or address shared challenges. This concept is often seen in supranational organizations where member states relinquish some degree of autonomy in exchange for greater collective strength, decision-making efficiency or resource sharing.

Understanding power and global politics

Exercises

20. Outline the concept of sovereignty and explain its significance in global politics.
21. Describe how the concept of sovereignty has changed over time, and outline what have been the implications of these shifts for state behavior and global politics.
22. Outline some of the challenges state sovereignty faces in the 21st century.
23. Suggest some of the ways in which sovereignty might be contingent.
24. To what extent is the principle of sovereignty an obstacle to addressing global challenges like the climate crisis?

Legitimacy in global politics

Conceptual question

What does it mean to say that a political actor or action is legitimate?

Legitimacy refers to actors or actions that are considered to be acceptable, usually by conforming to agreed norms or legal principles. In the political sense, legitimacy is the same as the right to rule. Rodney Barker has defined political legitimacy as, 'the belief in the rightfulness of a state, in its authority to issue commands, so that the commands are obeyed not simply out of fear or self-interest, but because they are believed to have moral authority, because subjects believe that they ought to obey.'[66] Unless the governed believe that their government is morally right, regardless of whether it is democratic, monarchic, communist, theocratic or authoritarian, they will not feel obliged to obey it. In such cases, we can only speak in terms of power, not authority, and political legitimacy will be challenged.

Political actors, particularly state actors, care about legitimacy as it shapes the effectiveness of domestic governance and the ways a state interacts internationally. If a government needs to rely on hard power to get its citizens to obey and follow its commands, then the right to rule will be challenged and may even lead to resistance, rebellion and revolution. Governments that are concerned about their survival will have to expend scarce resources to prop up their rule, reducing their effectiveness. If a government is perceived as legitimate, the 'social, political, and economic cost of governance will be low and the government's capacity to promote its political and socioeconomic goals will be enhanced.'[67] Without legitimacy, power can only be applied through coercion. With legitimacy, power can be exercised through voluntary or quasi-voluntary acceptance. There is often a moral aspect to legitimacy for leaders – they want or need to be seen to be serving the national interest. Legitimacy transforms raw power into authority. If there is the perception that power is being exercised for the benefit of the governed then this may soften the sharp edges of political, social and economic inequalities, and explain why people choose to obey their rulers.

▲ Patrice Lumumba was a Congolese politician and independence leader, who was the first PM of the Democratic Republic of Congo and played a significant role in the transformation of the Congo from a colony of Belgium into an independent republic. He was assassinated in 1961 by Joseph-Désiré Mobutu with the help of Belgian partisans.

Global politics core

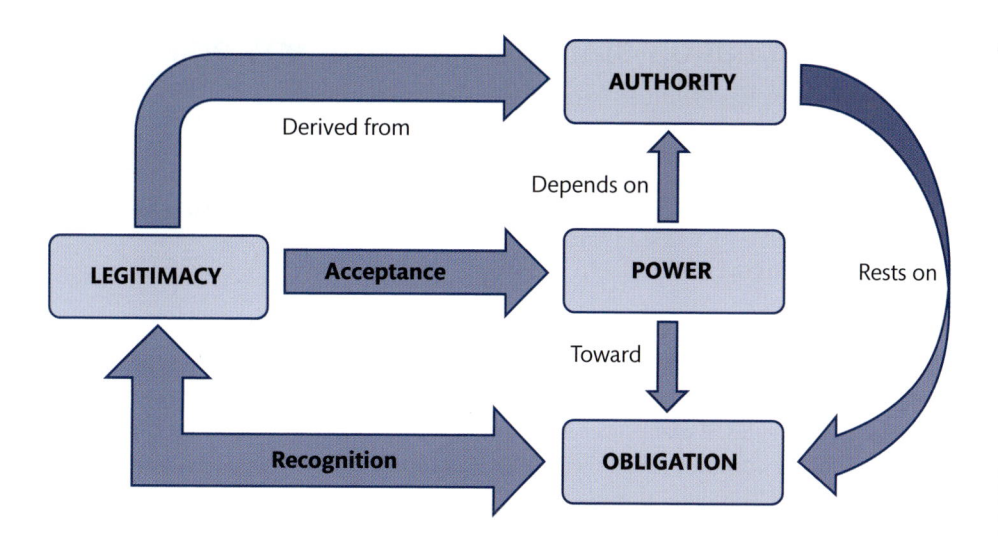

Figure 1.6 Legitimacy, power, authority and obligation.

We can see how the concepts of legitimacy, authority, power and obligation (obedience) are interdependent in Figure 1.6. While a political actor may have the authority to act, they will not be able to achieve anything if they do not also have the power to do so. If we recognize an actor as having legitimate authority (and power) then we will feel obliged to obey their commands. Legitimacy is the acceptance of the use of power and, if power is not used to benefit the ruled, we may be forced to oblige, but we may challenges to the legitimacy of such actions.

Let us reconsider the different political institutions that are the focus of legitimation efforts. A nation-state is a political community whose territorial and legal borders coincide with the boundaries of a nation. A **regime**, or political system, refers to the *type* of government a country has – democratic, theocratic, monarchical, authoritarian, totalitarian. Different regimes have different principles, institutions and procedures that make up the political system. A government refers to the organizations and people whose responsibility it is to govern and who are in control of state power – politicians, political parties, the civil/public service, military, etc. These distinctions are important because the relationship between each of the three political institutions (nation-state, regime and government) is not the same for every country. In many countries with durable political orders, governments can come and go without threatening with the legitimacy of the regime, or the nation-state. In other countries, regime and government may be fused so that a change in government brings about a change in regime. If the legitimacy of the nation-state is challenged then we may see resistance, rebellion and even wars of succession erupt. This means that you need to be precise when identifying what it is that political actors are trying to legitimize.

> Legitimacy is something that political institutions, like nation-state, regime and government, possess or seek to possess. Legitimation is what these political institutions *do* to get or to increase their legitimacy.

Activity

Research contemporary real-world examples of countries whose regime and government may be fused. Identify any nation-states whose legitimacy is under challenge. Share your ideas with a peer.

Sources of nation-state and government legitimacy

Muthiah Alagappa has identified four key elements of legitimacy:

- shared norms and values
- conformity with established rules for acquiring power
- proper and effective use of power
- consent of the governed.

Alagappa argues that the relationship between a government and its people may be defined as legitimate if, 'the political order in which it is rooted is based on shared norms and values, if the government in concern acquired power in conformity with established rules, if that power is exercised within prescribed limits for the promotion of the community's collective interest, and if the governed have given their consent…'[68] This definition captures the normative sense of legitimacy – that the government asserts it has the right to rule – and the sociological or political sense of legitimacy – that it is widely believed that the government has the right to rule.

Shared norms and values can define and shape the interactions between the state and its people and create ideological unity in support of specific goals. These goals can span a wide range, from the building of a democratic or socialist state to sustainable development, ethnic protection or survival. Ideological unity can be forcibly imposed or it can be achieved in a more consensual way if the dominant group within society appears to represent the general interest. History and culture can both act as a basis for ideological unity and legitimacy because they communicate a sense of antiquity and continuity. If all this can be packaged into a sense of national identity, this will further solidify the legitimacy of any government seen to be representing and reflecting this shared identity. Having a clear national identity is often a basis for international recognition. The presence of shared norms and values helps create a clear sense of the socially acceptable ways in which political power can be gained. A government that comes to power by following commonly accepted rules will be viewed as legitimate, what the Organization for Economic Cooperation and Development (OECD) refers to as *input legitimacy*.

The proper use of power as a source of legitimacy can be viewed in two ways, both of which speak to the quality of a state's governance. The first is a continuation of the two elements we have already seen, and it occurs when a government operates within the law or other commonly accepted rules and procedures. The second is when it uses its power effectively to advance the collective interest of the community. For instance, its economic performance or in terms of working toward sustainable development. This is what the OECD calls *output legitimacy*.

The final element of state legitimacy is the consent of the governed and the notion of popular sovereignty, which means that citizens recognize the government's right to give commands and they have *a duty* to obey these commands. Popular sovereignty can be seen as an expression of the collective will of the people, so focused on outcomes, or as a power relationship between different actors, so focused on processes. The nature, significance and role of consent will vary from state to state depending on the type of regime. In a democratic or participatory regime, consent is active and works to sustain shared norms and values. Free and fair elections are an important element in such regimes but there is more to consent than just voting. There should also be active participation in the institutions and processes that make up the political system. In traditional regimes, such political processes may be incompatible with local understandings of how legitimacy is generated. Competitive liberal-democratic elections could be alien to local custom in many places. In authoritarian and totalitarian regimes, consent 'relates more to the legitimation and execution of goals and policies… [and]… is secured through mobilization.'[69] An example is the massive civilian parades in North Korea with thousands marching in choreographed displays of loyalty to the Kim family. In theocratic and monarchical regimes, consent is more passive as the will of a deity and divine right are the basis of a government's legitimacy. Unless a ruler fails to meet appropriate religious or royal standards, a follower or subject is obliged to obey and consent is simply presumed to exist.

There are other sources of legitimacy. Max Weber identified a leader's charisma as a possible source of legitimacy. Weber used the term to refer to those individuals who possessed exceptional qualities or power, which then became the basis of authority. Lee Kuan Yew, the first prime minister of Singapore, commanded substantial power and authority, which he used to legitimate his government and the Singaporean regime over a long period of time. Vladimir Putin has built upon Russian ideas of the strong man to boost his legitimacy as a leader. Despite the importance personal authority may have, it is generally not enough by itself. We typically see such leaders relying on other sources of legitimacy to reinforce their right to rule and to ensure that the legitimacy of their government and/or regime continues after they are gone. A politically defining moment may also be a source of legitimacy in that it can create deep emotion and inspire support for a cause or government. Revolutions, national liberation and independence, and international warfare all carry significant moral authority that can be used to legitimate certain causes while delegitimating others. Much of the legitimacy of the current Iranian government rests on the legacy of the 1979 Islamic revolution. Although legitimacy is mainly a domestic issue, international support can enhance the domestic legitimacy of governments. Acceptance by the international community, as well as access to the resources of IGOs like the IMF, The World Bank and WTO, can provide status to governments. This can also potentially increase state capacity and performance, which then can be used by leaders to solidify their domestic base. However, this will depend on local perceptions of the international system and whether it is seen as a positive or negative force.

Most states rely on a range of sources of legitimacy, which are based on people's beliefs about the rightness of authority. We should be sensitive to how understandings of legitimacy may vary from context to context. The weight given to different sources of legitimacy often depends on who is making the judgment, and expectations of political actors differ between and within societies. These expectations may change and can be influenced by the media, ideology and events.

Activity

Choose a government. This could be the government of the country you are living in or the government of a country you identify with. Using a Think-Pair-Share thinking routine answer the following questions:

- What are the sources of legitimacy for the government you have chosen?
- Are some sources of legitimacy more important than others for the government?

Take a few minutes to *think* about your answers. Once the time is up, *pair* with a classmate and *share* your thoughts.

Understanding power and global politics

Challenges to nation-state or government legitimacy

Challenges to state legitimacy should be seen in light of the sources of legitimacy. Several factors might indicate a lack of shared norms and values, pointing to how legitimacy may be contested within a country. If there is significant public support for groups that promote an alternative set of values or ideologies, this may pose a challenge to the legitimacy of a government. Demands for autonomy or secession by communities that do not identify with the nation-state may also lead to ideological conflict. Such conflicts are often accompanied by political violence and extensive use of force by state actors. While some use of force by a government is acceptable and is a key component of authority, if it is not used in support of the will of the people then it will be perceived as illegitimate. Poor performance in terms of the economic, security, welfare and justice functions of government can also be the basis of challenges to a government's legitimacy. If a government or its leaders use state power to advance their own interests rather than the well-being of its citizens, this will erode its legitimacy, as will corruption. Where such abuses of power are permitted by the political system, the legitimacy of a regime can also be eroded, as in Iran in 2022.

In terms of economic performance, the increased interconnectedness and interdependence of global politics means that legitimacy is often dependent on external factors like the state of the global economy. If the costs and benefits of globalization are not shared equally or fairly then this may generate challenges to a government's legitimacy. External delegitimization of a government or regime can also occur if massive human rights violations are present. Modern notions of sovereignty depend upon respect for human rights. If a government is violating the human rights of its citizens – as, for example, is currently the case in Myanmar and Syria – it will be perceived as illegitimate by the international community.

Legitimacy and non-state actors

Non-state actors gain legitimacy through a range of strategies, although it is important to distinguish between different levels of analysis (local, national, regional, international, global) when analyzing the legitimacy of non-state actors, especially when considering their relationship with states.

One of the central domestic roles of a government is to provide public and social services for its citizens: healthcare, education, drinking water and basic infrastructure. If states are unwilling or unable to provide these services then NSAs may gain legitimacy by filling real or perceived gaps in state performance. In Somalia, Al Shabaab, the armed NSA, has provided social services, with an emphasis on justice and security. In the Philippines, another armed NSA, the Moro Islamic Liberation Front, has adopted a similar strategy. During the COVID-19 pandemic, the Mafia in Sicily and drug cartels in Mexico distributed food and aid packages to those who struggled to meet their basic needs due to loss of income. These actions may potentially weaken the legitimacy of the state in a direct sense, and there may be further indirect negative feedback effects. In Zambia, citizens who thought the state had little to do with service provision were less likely to pay tax, which further reduces the state's ability to provide services.

Non-state groups can gain legitimacy by using ideology or religion to promote social transformation, which may delegitimize existing state structures and systems of inequality. The Tamil Tigers (LTTE) in Sri Lanka used Marxism to increase their legitimacy among lower castes and other marginalized groups. Al Shabaab has used Islam to cut across Somalia's clan-based political structure and create a more pluralistic identity that appeals to younger generations and those who are members of less powerful clans. Part of the Pakistani Taliban's appeal for legitimacy rests on their support for dismantling the feudal system that exists in the province of Khyber Paktunwa to create equality between the classes (although not between genders). The Irish Republican Army (IRA) frequently referred to human rights ideology to legitimate their claims for better treatment in British prisons.

At the international or global level, the sources of legitimacy for NSAs, as well as their potential relationship with states, are different. The participation of NSAs in multilateral institutions can be seen as one way of decreasing the perceived legitimacy deficit in global governance. As the distance between citizens and decisions made at the international or global level has widened, the democratic legitimacy of global institutions and global governance has been challenged. The inclusion of NSAs is one way of bridging this distance. While states are often seen as the main sources of authority and legitimacy in global politics, globalization has created a sense that NSA participation can increase the legitimacy of global governance arrangements. This does vary according to issue area – environmental politics is a more open and inclusive policy field for NSA inclusion compared to international trade, security and finance.

The legitimacy of NSAs at the global level rests on their ability to increase the input and output legitimacy of IGOs and intergovernmental policy-making processes. NSAs can provide expertise and deliver apolitical or impartial information. This strengthens evidence-based decision-making and helps states to make better decisions. NSAs can represent interests that have an important stake in the decisions being made at the global or international level. By giving a voice to marginalized and vulnerable groups not represented at the state level, the outcomes of international policy-making processes can be improved. Popular mobilization can also help to make sure that decisions are implemented. NSAs and the participation of civil society actors can increase the transparency, representation, inclusion and accountability of IGOs and intergovernmental policy-making processes by creating a space for dialogue between those making the decisions and those likely to be affected by these decisions.

Example – CSOs

Civil Society Organizations (CSOs), along with other NSAs like businesses and city officials, are a key feature of the Conference of Parties (COP) meetings that are convened under the United Nations Framework Convention on Climate Change (UNFCCC), an environmental multilateral treaty adopted in 1992. While CSOs only have observer status and cannot take part in the negotiations, their participation is important because they are best placed to articulate the concerns of diverse local communities and to propose policies that will improve the lives of citizens.

Legitimation: multidimensional and symbiotic

The existence of interrelated elements and sources of legitimacy points to legitimacy being a complex, dynamic and multidimensional concept. David Beetham has argued that legitimacy should not be seen in terms of its different sources. He argues that legitimacy should be seen as a symbiotic relationship between two different sets of actors – those seeking legitimacy and those who can provide legitimacy. These two sets of actors influence and shape each other. Beetham notes that people's perceptions of

Understanding power and global politics

legitimacy are influenced by the justifications provided by a political actor (nation-state or government) and that the political actor's justification for its legitimacy is influenced by the shifting beliefs of the people.

Because of this, it is better to speak of states and governments existing along a spectrum rather than in terms of legitimacy/illegitimacy. The sources of legitimacy are open to change and the legitimacy of a government or state may be higher or lower depending on the time period. The reasons for obedience may vary across different groups within a state. Legitimacy is not a permanent feature, although the legitimacy of some nation-states or governments may be more solid than others. All governments and states have to work at maintaining or increasing their legitimacy so as to convert power into authority.

Activity

Identify a state or non-state actor you are familiar with and use a Claim, Support, Question thinking routine to reflect on its source(s) of legitimacy.

- Make a claim about (or give a explanation for, or offer an interpretation of) the source(s) of legitimacy for your chosen state or NSA.
- Identify supporting evidence for your claim.
- Ask a question related to your claim or the supporting evidence. What is not explained?

Be prepared to share your thinking with a peer or the whole class.

Exercises

25. Define the concept of legitimacy and outline its significance in global politics.

26. Explain the difference between legitimacy and legitimation.

27. Distinguish between legitimacy, authority, power and obligation (obedience).

28. Identify some of the sources of legitimacy for a nation-state or government.

29. Identify some of the strategies that NSAs use to gain legitimacy, and outline how these differ from the strategies employed by nation-states or governments.

30. Explain why it is better to speak of nation-state/government legitimacy existing along a spectrum rather than in terms of legitimacy/illegitimacy.

Interdependence in global politics

Conceptual question

Why do sovereign states cooperate?

In global politics, the concept of interdependence refers to the mutual reliance between different actors for access to the resources and means that sustain living arrangements. All social groups or societies are faced with the problem of how to

Global politics core

coordinate their collective actions – how to resolve conflicts, how to meet external challenges, how to manage resources and how to agree on shared goals as well as the best means to achieve them. But how is order – justice, peace, progress, prosperity, growth – possible in an anarchic global political system or in a capitalist world economy? In *Governance without Government: Order and Change in World Politics*, James Rosenau and Ernst-Otto Czempiel first outlined the concept of **global governance** in order to better describe and understand changes in the global system that had started in the 1970s. The use of the term *global* means something different than international, interstate, intergovernmental or transnational. In addition, *governance* is not the same as government. While both refer to systems of rule or deliberate behavior toward a goal, government refers to activities backed by formal authority. Governance refers to activities that may be more informal and do not necessarily rely on police powers to compel actors to obey. A single site of authority, such as the sovereign state at the national level, is missing from the global system. There is no world government or world police to enforce rules and laws. This does not prevent the possibility for cooperation between states and other actors in dealing with global issues. Global governance then is any purposeful activity designed to control or influence other actors that occurs in the space occupied by nation-states or, if it occurs at lower levels of analysis, that has an effect on that space.

Activity

Working in a group of three or four, come up with definitions and key characteristics of each of the following terms: *global governance*, *international* and *government*. Identify and discuss the differences between each term. Consider the following real-world examples that illustrate each term:

- Global governance: Discuss how international organizations like the United Nations, World Trade Organization or **World Health Organization (WHO)** work together to address global challenges.
- International: Explain how countries collaborate on trade agreements, climate accords or cultural exchanges.
- Government: Describe the structures and functions of national governments and how they operate within their borders.

Reflect on your discussions and write down one key takeaway from the activity and what you understand to be the differences between global governance, international and government.

International law

International law is a body of rules and norms that regulate interactions between states, and between states and IGOs. It may also apply to relations between IGOs, states and individuals. International law serves functional and ethical purposes by providing order while aiming to be fair and equitable. What complicates the operation of international law is the tension that exists between it and the principle of sovereignty. In practice, states do cooperate in many areas and act according to international law. Why do sovereign states do this?

Almost all law comes from customs. In the case of international law, it is the actual practice of states and their conduct that forms the basis for international law. Wherever

Understanding power and global politics

Hugo Grotius (1583–1645), a Dutch scholar and jurist, is often identified as the founder of Western international law. As an idealist, he believed that states, like people, were rational and capable of working together on mutually beneficial goals like law and order.

there exists a general practice, together with the general acceptance of this practice, we refer to this as **customary international law**. This is the principle of *opinio juris*, which means that states must act in compliance with an internationally recognized norm or practice not merely out of convenience, habit, coincidence or political benefit, but rather out of a sense of legal obligation. Presidents or prime ministers often shake hands when they first meet, but it is highly unlikely that they do so because they believe that a rule of international law requires it. However, a state would expect some form of legal repercussions if it were to prosecute a foreign ambassador without the consent of their home state. In this sense, *opinio juris* does exist for the international law rule of diplomatic immunity. While it can be difficult to identify and prove, a variety of sources tend to be used to demonstrate the existence of *opinio juris* including: diplomatic correspondence, press releases and other government statements of policy, legislation, national and international judicial decisions, treaties ratified by the state that include the same obligation(s), resolutions and declarations by the UN, and other sources.

International law also comes from treaties, the dominant source of law today. Treaties come in two forms:

- law-making, which are multilateral and aim to be universally accepted
- treaty contracts, which are bilateral.

The creation and enforcement of treaties is governed by the Vienna Convention on the law of treaties, which was adopted in 1969 and codifies a fundamental concept in international law that covenants must be kept. If a state signs onto a charter or treaty, it is bound to keep its word. While some treaties only require a signature for a state to become legally bound by its provisions, most treaties require the domestic process of **ratification** (the formal approval or confirmation of a decision, agreement or document by the relevant authorities or stakeholders). Many states have signed treaties that they did not ratify, and so they are not legally bound to the treaty's obligations. Even after ratification, a state is not legally bound until the treaty enters into force, which usually happens at a time specified by the treaty and sometimes only after specific requirements have been met. States can also join a treaty after it has entered into force, a process referred to as *acceding to the treaty*, which results in the state being legally bound to its provisions.

As sovereign actors, states can decide whether or not to comply with international law. There are examples of states that have violated international law in the 21st century. The Syrian government violated the treaty prohibiting the use of chemical weapons by employing them during the Syrian Civil War in Ghouta (2013), Khan Shaykhun (2017) and Douma (2018). However, most of the time, states do follow international law so when and why do they do so?

There are several reasons why a sovereign state complies with international law. **Vertical enforcement** occurs when an international institution has authority over a state and can force it to obey. An example of this is the EU, whose component institutions are all above the level of individual member states and can sanction any member state who is found to have violated EU law. Another example of vertical enforcement is the ICJ, which is part of the UN system and settles legal disputes between states, as well as providing advisory opinions on legal matters. However, the ICJ is seen to be a relatively weak institution because it can only deal with disputes between states and both parties must agree to the court's jurisdiction before a case is taken. National courts can also be enforcers of international law through a process known as **universal jurisdiction**, which allows a domestic court to claim jurisdiction

Global politics core

if an individual is accused of egregious (shocking and horrible) human rights abuses that violate the laws of all states. Due to the anarchical nature of global politics, courts lack the tools of enforcement required to compel sovereign states to follow international law and so other methods may be more effective.

Horizontal enforcement is a process in which the nature of the interrelationship between states determines whether a state will comply with international law. A state might conform to international law because more powerful states make them. In 2015, Iran halted its nuclear program, in part because of the economic sanctions placed on it by more powerful states working through the UN Security Council. This shows that horizontal enforcement is often most effective when many states coordinate their actions against the violator of international law. Horizontal enforcement can also rest on the idea of reciprocity; cooperation becomes habitual when the states engage in like-for-like interactions. International law can be seen as the codification of these cooperative interactions (I will cooperate with you if you cooperate with me).

Self-interest can also be a reason why states comply with international law. By committing themselves to following international law, states benefit from knowing that other states will do the same. If this was not the case then domestic and international peace and order might be threatened. There are also normative and ethical explanations for why states comply with international law. In most cases, international law reflects the most commonly held norms of the global system, and treaties are the codification of these norms. By complying with international law, states are just doing what is right. Because of the multilateral nature of many international laws, they are often viewed as legitimate, and states will behave in line with such laws so that they appear legitimate.

Example – North Korea and the NPT

In 1985, North Korea became a party to the Treaty on the Non-Proliferation of Nuclear Weapons (NPT), an international treaty whose objective is to prevent the spread of nuclear weapons and weapons technology. However, the North Korean government continued to develop a nuclear weapons program and, by the early 2000s, was prepared to test a nuclear bomb. Rather than violate the provisions of the NPT, the North Korean government withdrew from the NPT in 2003 so that it would no longer be bound to it. In 2006, North Korea tested its first nuclear weapon.

The UN

While sovereign states may be the key legal actors, today's global politics is a crowded space with different voices and interests trying to be heard. IGOs are increasingly important in helping us govern the world. They help to create habits and routines of cooperation as states become socialized to regular interactions. The most prominent IGO today is the UN, created in 1945 in the aftermath of the Second World War. There are three fundamental principles upon which the UN was founded, which are spelled out in the first two Articles of the UN Charter:

- the sovereign equality of member states
- a focus on international issues
- the maintenance of peace and security.

The UN building in New York.
A UN meeting.

Each state, regardless of its size, is legally the same as every other UN member state – each state has a single vote in the General Assembly. This sovereign equality does not extend to the UN **Security Council** where the five permanent members (P5) – the USA, Russia, the PRC, France and the UK – each have veto power over Security Council resolutions. The UN Charter is sensitive to the Westphalian notion of sovereignty as it forbids 'the United Nations to intervene in matters which are essentially within the domestic jurisdiction of any state.'[70] Peace and security feature several times in the Preamble and first two Articles of the Charter, committing member states to avoid the use of force and to settle disputes peacefully so that international order may be guaranteed.

Much has changed since 1945. The make-up of the P5 no longer reflects the distribution of power on the global stage and there have been calls to reform the Security Council. Almost everyone agrees that membership should be increased but there is little agreement on which countries should be admitted or what powers they should have. Since 1945, the distinction between domestic and international issues has become blurred as globalization, international human rights and the climate crisis have eroded traditional Westphalian notions of sovereignty. The concept of security has also broadened from its original post-Second World War focus on the protection of national territory and sovereignty to include humanitarian assistance and meeting the basic needs of people at risk of famine or in the aftermath of natural disasters. This focus on *human security* also presents a challenge to traditional notions of state sovereignty because it potentially undermines the domestic authority of a state.

Table 1.4 Principal organs of the UN

Organ	Membership and Voting	Responsibilities
Security Council	15 members: 5 permanent members each with veto power, 10 rotating members elected by region	To maintain international peace and security; decides on enforcement measures and authorizes action.
General Assembly	193 members; each state has one vote	Debates any topic within the UN Charter's scope; elects members to special bodies.
Secretariat, headed by the Secretary-General	37,000 employees; Secretary-General elected for 5-year renewable term by the General Assembly and the Security Council	In charge of the day-to-day running of the UN; gathers information. The Secretary-General is the chief administrative officer and spokesperson for the UN.
Economic and Social Council (ECOSOC)	54 members elected for 3-year terms	Coordinates economic and social welfare programs along with the action of specialized agencies like the World Health Organization (WHO), Food and Agriculture Organization (FAO) and United Nations Educational, Social and Cultural Organization (UNESCO).
International Court of Justice (ICJ)	15 judges	Rules on matters of international law between states; has non-compulsory jurisdiction.

Global politics core

The principal organs of the UN are shown in Table 1.4. The role of the Security Council is to maintain international peace and security. It has fifteen members – the five permanent members (P5) and an additional ten members that are elected on a rotating basis and represent the different regions of the world. Under Chapter VII of the UN Charter, the Security Council has the power to authorize the use of hard power, in the form of economic sanctions or military force, against any state that threatens international peace and security. All Security Council resolutions that are passed become legally binding on all UN member states. To pass, a resolution requires nine positive votes with no vetoes. The Security Council became a more powerful body following the end of the Cold War, when it was no longer deadlocked by the Soviet Union's and the USA's frequent use of the veto. Greater cooperation among the P5 saw the Security Council authorize actions to deal with armed conflicts and the rising threat of terrorism. In recent years, divisions within the council have deepened. The result of these divisions has been relative inaction on issues like the Syrian Civil War and the Russian invasion of Ukraine. Despite the Security Council's formal power, it is still reliant on states for its funding, personnel, the enforcement of sanctions and military action.

The General Assembly is the main forum of the UN where debate on any topic within the scope of the UN Charter can take place. All 193 member states of the UN are represented in the General Assembly and, while each state has one vote, debates on resolutions are typically organized around regionally-based voting blocs. General Assembly resolutions are not legally binding. Many are voted on for political purposes, but some are meaningful and provide the foundation for the development of norms and new international law. Global politics is not merely a struggle for power, it is also a contest over legitimacy, and General Assembly resolutions can provide (or deny) legitimacy to a state's actions.

Example – The role of the UN General Assembly

Between March 2, 2022 and February 23, 2023, the United Nations General Assembly passed six resolutions that condemned the Russian invasion of Ukraine. Given the paralysis of the Security Council due to Russia's veto power, the General Assembly has become the most important UN body dealing with the conflict. Each resolution passed with an overwhelming majority, serving as a useful indicator of world opinion.

The Secretariat conducts the day-to-day business and operations of the UN, with one-third of its 37,000 employees located at the UN headquarters in New York. The Secretariat operates under the leadership of the Secretary-General, who is elected by the General Assembly after being recommended by the Security Council. The Secretary-General has few formal powers, which means that their authority often depends on the force of their personality. The ECOSOC was originally created to coordinate the economic and social activities and programs within the UN system through specialized agencies. As UN membership expanded with decolonization, and the number of these activities increased, ECOSOC's tasks have become complex

Understanding power and global politics

and unwieldy. ECOSOC works with a range of non-state actors – nearly 5500 NGOs have consultative status in the Council. It also holds an annual meeting of finance ministers that includes representatives from the IMF and The World Bank. The ICJ is in The Hague and has 15 judges, elected by majority vote in the General Assembly and Security Council. The ICJ rules on disputes between states under international law. It has non-compulsory jurisdiction and so relies on both parties to agree to its jurisdiction before it can rule on any dispute.

Calls for Security Council reform have been around for a long time. They have increased in recent years because of the world becoming more multipolar/multiplex and because of the USA's indifference and, at times, rejection of multilateralism and international organizations like the UN. This can be seen in the context of broader debates over the nature of international order and the global political system (the West vs the Rest).

Global governance: IGOs and NSAs

IGOs can help states deal with major issues in the global system. IGOs seek to establish and promote procedures and processes that encourage and facilitate cooperation between states. By bringing states together, IGOs hope to increase transparency and reduce misunderstandings between states so that common issues, like the climate crisis, can be dealt with more effectively. Membership of an IGO can constrain a state's activities. By adopting international agendas, IGOs force member states to align their domestic policies with these agendas if they wish to benefit from their membership.

The UN is a very large and very broad IGO. Most IGOs are more specific in nature and often deal with a particular issue or focus on a specific geographical region/area. **Strategic alliances** are formal or informal agreements between two or more states or organizations to cooperate in pursuit of a common goal. By sharing resources and expertise, they can collaborate more efficiently, and by sharing risks, they can spread the economic and political costs of any action and reduce the likelihood of failure. By working together, states can increase their bargaining power and influence in international negotiations. In a political alliance, members can work together to promote their shared interests and values. Strategic alliances can take many forms, such as military alliances, **economic partnerships**, political agreements or cultural exchanges.

Military alliances are a type of strategic alliance, where countries that are part of a **collective security** arrangement agree to provide mutual defense and support in the event of an attack on one of the members. The goal of joining such an alliance and acting together to repel any potential aggressor is to prevent wars and preserve peace and security. These alliances can be bilateral or multilateral. Examples of bilateral military alliances include the US-Japan Security Treaty, which commits the USA to defend Japan in the event of an attack, and the UK-France Defense and Security Cooperation Treaty, which commits the two countries to work together on defense and security issues. The most prominent multilateral alliances are the Organization of American States (OAS), the Shanghai Cooperation Organization (SCO) and NATO. Originally designed to deter the Soviet Union, NATO adopted an increasingly

Global politics core

humanitarian role, with military interventions to protect Bosnian Muslims in 1994, monitoring of elections in Afghanistan, and providing humanitarian aid to Pakistan. There were concerns that with the end of the Cold War, NATO had exhausted its usefulness, but with the Russian invasions of Georgia (2008) and Ukraine (2014 Crimea, 2022), NATO found new purpose, and in 2023, neutral Finland became its 31st member state.[71] Collective security arrangements can also have a normative dimension. Both NATO and the OAS state that they support the spread of liberal-democratic values as the best way of ensuring peace, security and development. Collective security helps to ensure stability, which further reinforces peace and development.

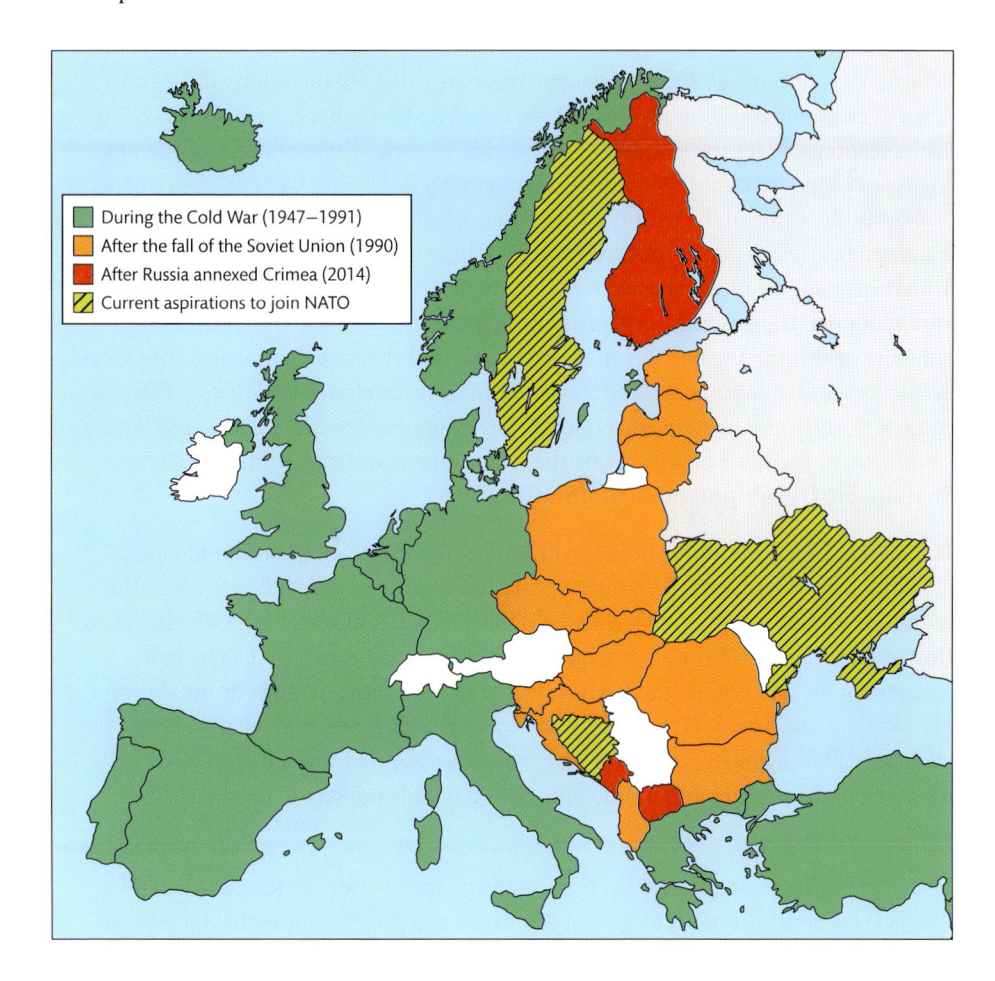

NATO member states (as of June 2023).

Legend:
- During the Cold War (1947–1991)
- After the fall of the Soviet Union (1990)
- After Russia annexed Crimea (2014)
- Current aspirations to join NATO

Economic partnerships are another form of strategic alliance, where countries agree to cooperate in areas such as trade, investment and economic development. These can be bilateral or multilateral. An example of a bilateral alliance the Australia-United States Free Trade Agreement (AUSFTA), which eliminates tariffs on trade across a range of goods and services between the two countries. Examples of multilateral alliances include the EU, Mercosur, the Common Market for Eastern and Southern Africa (COMESA) and the US-Canada-Mexico Agreement (USMCA). Political agreements can also be considered strategic alliances, where countries agree to cooperate on issues of importance to them. A bilateral political agreement is the US-India Civil

Understanding power and global politics

Nuclear Agreement, which allows for nuclear cooperation between the two states, while a multilateral political alliance is the Council of Europe, which promotes human rights, democracy and rule of law within its 46 member states. Cultural exchanges can also be considered a form of strategic alliance, where countries agree to share their cultural heritage and promote mutual understanding. Examples include artistic collaborations, sports events and academic exchanges, such as the EU's Erasmus+ program, the Chinese government's Belt and Road scholarship program or the USA's Fulbright program – all of which can also help boost a state's soft power. Strategic alliances are an important tool in international relations to promote cooperation and achieve common goals, and they can take different forms depending on the needs and priorities of the countries or organizations involved.

In terms of economic global governance, there are three organizations at the heart of the Western liberal economic order: the IMF, The World Bank and the WTO. The IMF is responsible for the stability of the world's monetary system, and it provides emergency loans to countries that are experiencing significant balance of payments problems (the value of the country's exports does not pay for all its imports). IMF loans can be used to pay for needed imports. These loans are conditional upon the borrowing country meeting a set of requirements that involve reducing government intervention in the economy and promoting trade liberalization (the process of reducing or eliminating barriers to international trade between countries). The World Bank provides loans and grants to less economically developed countries (LEDCs) to combat poverty and to support economic development. Recently, The World Bank's lending focus has been on protecting the environment and promoting the UN's **Sustainable Development Goals (SDGs)**.

The market-based economic policies promoted by the IMF and The World Bank, including tax reform, trade liberalization, reduced government intervention in the economy, and greater openness to foreign investment, is known as the **Washington Consensus**. The WTO was established in 1995 as the successor to the General Agreement on Tariffs and Trade, which was created at the same time as the IMF and The World Bank. The WTO currently has 164 member states, and its main functions include facilitating negotiations on trade agreements, providing a forum for resolving trade disputes and monitoring national trade policies to ensure they meet WTO rules.

The World Bank and the IMF are sometimes referred to as the Bretton Woods Institutions after the town in New Hampshire where they were created in 1944.

The term **Beijing Consensus** was first coined by Joshua Cooper Ramo in a 2004 *Foreign Policy* article. It refers to a set of economic and political ideas that have been associated with the PRC's rise as a global economic and political power. The Beijing Consensus is characterized by a focus on state-led development and a rejection of western-style democracy and neoliberal economic policies. The consensus emphasizes the importance of a strong central government that can guide economic development and achieve social stability. It also places a strong emphasis on long term planning and investment in infrastructure, education and technology. The Beijing Consensus has been associated with the PRC's success in achieving rapid economic growth and its success in reducing poverty over the past few decades. Other states have adopted elements of the Beijing Consensus. Vietnam has adopted a similar model of state-led development, with a focus on export-oriented manufacturing and investment in infrastructure and education, while Ethiopia's state-led development has seen infrastructure investment and a focus on agriculture and manufacturing. Supporters of the Beijing Consensus argue that it offers a viable alternative to the Western model of liberal democracy and free market capitalism, which they see as being in crisis. Critics of the Beijing Consensus argue that it has been associated with authoritarianism, and that it may not be sustainable in the long run.

The **Group of Twenty (G20)** is also a key organization in global governance. It is an informal forum that includes 19 countries and the EU.[72] By representing 60 percent of the world's population and 80 percent of its GDP, it is a more inclusive and representative organization than the G7, which is made up of seven democracies with advanced economies, and a more manageable grouping than the UN General Assembly. The G20 was created in 1999 as a response to the mishandling of financial crises in the late 1990s. It has become a key platform for global economic governance by promoting international economic cooperation and policy coordination between its members. The G20 has no formal legal authority, but it provides a platform for its members to discuss and coordinate their policies on a wide range of economic and financial issues, including trade, finance, development and climate change. Recently, the G20 has taken on a more prominent role in addressing global challenges such as climate change and sustainable development. It has committed to working toward the implementation of the Paris Agreement on climate change and the SDGs adopted by the UN in 2015.

However, there are tensions within the G20. The G20 includes countries that are major producers and consumers of fossil fuels, as well as countries that are heavily impacted by climate change. This can lead to disagreements over the pace of transitioning to clean energy and the level of commitment to international climate agreements. At a July 2021 G20 meeting of environment ministers, some countries including India, Russia and Saudi Arabia blocked an agreement on phasing out coal and fossil fuel subsidies. Other countries pushed for coal-friendly language to feature at the 2023 G20 summit meeting in India. Geopolitical tensions can spill over into G20 meetings and threaten cooperation. The G20 includes developed and developing states, and there can be significant economic imbalances between them. These imbalances can lead to disagreements over a range of economic issues, especially as many economic shocks disproportionately affect emerging economies. The massive increases in the price of energy and food imports following the war in Ukraine has seen many developing economies in the Global South that were struggling in the aftermath of the COVID-19 crisis go into debt distress. To date, the G20 has been unable to come up with a solution acceptable to all stakeholders.

NSAs, such as NGOs, MNCs and transnational advocacy networks, play a crucial role in shaping and influencing global governance. In today's interconnected world, these actors have become powerful agents of change, often filling gaps left by traditional IGOs and state-centric informal forums like the G20. One significant contribution of NSAs is their ability to address global issues that transcend state borders, such as climate change, human rights and public health crises. NGOs engage in advocacy and activism, mobilizing public support and pressuring governments to take action. Their expertise and grassroots networks allow them to raise awareness, propose policy alternatives and monitor implementation, effectively influencing global governance processes. MNCs also wield influence in global governance. Their economic power, and extensive global reach, enables them to shape policies and regulations. Through corporate social

Understanding power and global politics

responsibility initiatives that involve integrating ethical, social and environmental concerns into their business practices, companies can influence sustainable development practices, labor standards and environmental protection measures. MNCs often engage in public-private partnerships with governments and international organizations to address complex challenges. These collaborations bring together expertise, resources and innovation, resulting in more comprehensive and effective solutions. However, the influence of non-state actors in global governance raises concerns about democratic accountability and representation. The role they play highlights the evolving nature of global governance, emphasizing the need for inclusive and participatory decision-making processes that bring together the perspectives and interests of diverse actors.

Case – MNCs and global governance

An example of how MNCs engage in public-private partnerships is the Global Fund to Fight AIDS, Tuberculosis and Malaria. The Global Fund is an international financing institution that aims to combat these diseases by mobilizing resources and coordinating efforts globally. It operates through a unique model that involves collaboration between governments, civil society organizations and the private sector, including MNCs. In this partnership, MNCs contribute financial resources, expertise and technology to support the global funds programs. Pharmaceutical companies may provide discounted or free medications, diagnostics and treatments for these diseases. They also engage in research and development to develop new drugs and therapies. Civil society organizations play a vital role in educating the public, policymakers and key stakeholders about the importance of addressing these diseases. They are also directly involved in providing prevention, treatment, care and support services to communities while also monitoring the implementation of global fund supported programs to provide transparency and accountability.

Exercises

31. Define the concept of interdependence.
32. Identify the ways in which greater interdependence might undermine state sovereignty.
33. Suggest some reasons why sovereign states comply with international law.
34. Explain why strategic alliances are important in global politics, and outline what factors determine the form they take.

Theoretical perspectives in global politics

Conceptual question

What is the purpose of theory and theorizing in Global Politics?

TOK: How are theory and theorizing different in Global Politics than in other IB DP subjects?

IB Global Politics is not supposed to be a theoretical subject, but it is hard to avoid theory and theoretical perspectives. Theories offer an account of why things happened and why certain actors behaved in the ways they did. Depending on the theory you choose, you will get different answers to political issues and global challenges. The fact that there are

Global politics core

different theories in Global Politics can worry students, because they may expect a 'right' answer. Global Politics is a social science, and there is always more than one story to tell. This section covers some of the more prominent theoretical perspectives in Global Politics. If you find this topic interesting, we encourage you to explore further on your own.

One of the most common types of theory is **explanatory theory**. Explanatory theories can provide an account of why things happened the way they did. They can also act as a simplifying device by taking a more abstract view of reality and predicting behavior and outcomes based on a few key factors. Neorealism or structural realism is an example of this kind of explanatory theory.

Robert Cox, the Canadian political scientist, referred to explanatory theories as *problem-solving theories* in that they are only concerned with looking at the world as it is and attempting to understand how it operates so that they can make it work better. Cox also identified a different kind of theory, which he called **critical theory**. This type of theory begins from a point that is critical of particular social arrangements or outcomes. It sets out to identify and criticize how these came about. If theorizing builds on the identification of an unjust state of affairs and what caused it to arise, then a theory can be both explanatory and critical. Many feminist theories fit this model.

Many approaches take the additional step of demonstrating how the world would be a better place if the factors that cause unjust situations were eliminated. Once we begin to consider ways in which our world could be different and better, we have entered the realm of **normative theory**, which examines the ways in which the world *ought* to be. Marxist theory is an example of normative theory as it lays out what a communist society should look like.

Constitutive theory is another type of theory. Rather than trying to explain underlying causal factors or patterns, it asks, 'How is this thing made/created?' Constitutive theories come in two forms. The first attempts to understand how actors or concepts came to be. For example, rather than asking how sovereignty operates or how the modern nation-state behaves, constitutive theories focus on questions such as 'What is sovereignty?' or 'What makes up the modern nation-state?' The other form refers to scholars who examine the ways in which rules, norms and ideas constitute social objects and actors. For these theorists, the social world, and even the natural world, is constructed through the ideas or views that we hold. Constructivism is an example of such a theory.

Another type of theory is **theory as a lens** through which we view the world. Political and social actors move through the world and make sense of events and processes based on pre-existing patterns of thought or mental structures. These patterns or structures provide a framework for them to see the world and to organize new information about it. All actors see the world in particular ways and these do not always conform to one of the theories covered above. If we are to appreciate how social and political actors behave in global politics, we have to be aware of the lenses through which they see and understand the world.

You should be aware that all of these theoretical schools of thought are trying to get you to buy in to them. No theoretical perspective is neutral. Each of them is trying to sell their particular analytical framework to you by delegitimating alternative models or by proving their superiority over other approaches. It is your responsibility to critically reflect on the limitations of each framework and to remember that each theoretical perspective is open to criticism and challenge.

Understanding power and global politics

Activity

The map shows Vienna's metro network, with the lines, stations and some basic information to help commuters. It does not show information that is not essential to traveling on the system, like roads and shopping centers. A theory does something similar by putting different things on its map based on what theorists within that school of thought think are important. Based on what you know, what kinds of things do you think should appear on a theoretical map of global politics? Draw your map and justify your selections with a peer.

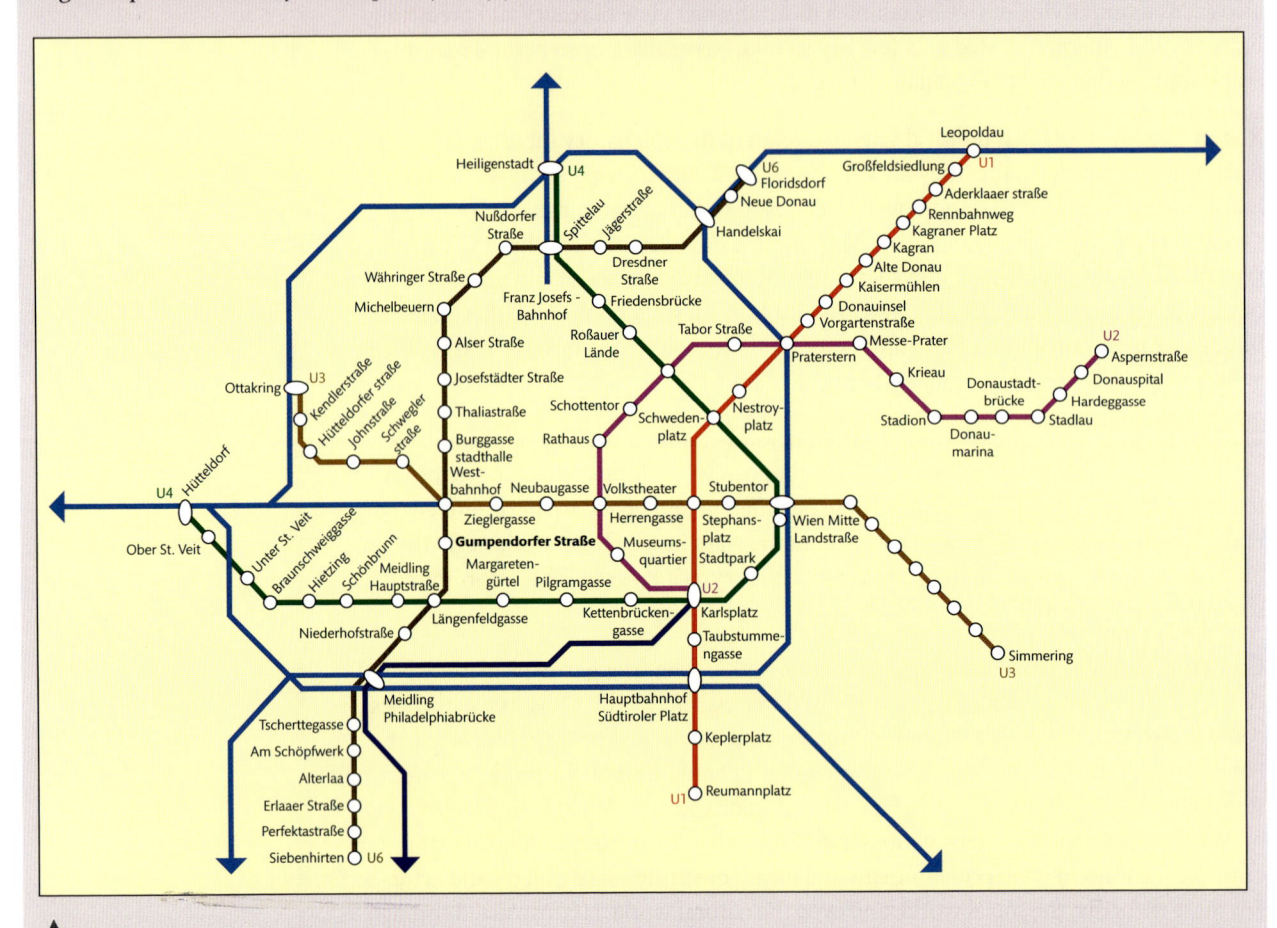

▲ A map of Vienna's metro system.

Traditional and middle ground theories

Realism aims to reflect the world as it actually is rather than what some hope it should or could be. The focus of realism lies with the state and the nature of the international system. For most realists, states are unitary actors that rationally pursue their own national interests. This means that states are focused on increasing their hard power – economic and military power – so that they can protect their security and territorial integrity. Realism comes in different forms: **classical realism** and **neorealism/ structural realism**. Realism tends to see global politics though a pessimistic lens, with competition for power and conflict dominating.

Classical realism was developed in the aftermath of the Second World War. It saw global politics as a struggle for power, especially economic and military power, that could be used by states to protect themselves from the threats posed by other states.

Global politics core

For realists, international relations is about *states* pursuing *interests* defined in terms of *power*. Classical realists such as Hans Morgenthau see this struggle for power as arising out of human nature, that human beings have a will to power hardwired into them at birth, and that states are governed by the same objective laws of human nature. The fact that the global system is anarchical and lacks a governing authority is a general condition, which means that states are always worried about their survival and are ultimately responsible for their own well-being (self-help). The primary concern for states is to maximize their power, with hegemony as their ultimate goal.

Neorealism, also known as structural realism, abandoned classical realism's assumptions about human nature and the characteristics of states and looked to the anarchical structure of global politics to provide realist analyses with a firmer foundation. For neorealists, states are made functionally similar by the constraints of this anarchical structure, with the principal differences among them determined by their capabilities. This is why neorealists tend to focus on great powers. Unlike classical realists, neorealists see security as the ultimate concern of states, with power not as an end in itself but as a means to achieving (territorial) security. This means that neorealists see states focusing on increasing their hard power *relative* to other states to protect their security. This concern for relative gains can lead to what realists call a security dilemma in which state security is seen in zero-sum terms. The result is constant tensions and power conflicts between states. For Kenneth Waltz, what determines the amount of peace and conflict in global politics is not the characteristics of individual states but the distribution of power in the system. Waltz argued that a bipolar system increased the potential for peace, as a balance of power would stabilize around the two most powerful states in the system.[73] Other neorealists have argued that the closer the distribution of power approaches unipolarity, the greater the likelihood of peace becomes.

Structural realism can be divided further into **defensive realism** and **offensive realism**. Defensive realists argue that the anarchical system encourages states to behave defensively and to maintain whatever balance of power exists between states. Defensive realists recognize that states have incentives to focus on their relative power, but they do not recommend that great powers behave aggressively. They note that few, if any, major wars have ended up benefiting the state(s) that started the war. This is because threatened states tend to balance against aggressors, eventually reversing many or all of the gains initially made by the aggressor state(s). Preserving power, rather than increasing it, is the main goal of states. Offensive realism believes that 'the international system creates powerful incentives for states to gain power at the expense of rivals, and to take advantage of those situations when the benefits outweigh the costs.'[74] Maximizing relative power is the optimal way to maximizing security in an anarchical system. Great powers 'behave aggressively not because they want to or because they possess some inner drive to dominate, but because they have to seek more power if they want to maximize their odds of survival.'[75] If a state has a reputation for being willing to use force, this can help that state get others to do what it wants because they will fear being attacked as well.

Classical realism and neorealism have biases and limitations. Classical realism tends to have a state-centric bias, focusing primarily on the interests and actions of states while overlooking NSAs and other factors that shape global politics. It also tends to emphasize power struggles and security concerns, often neglecting non-military aspects of international relations. Neorealism can be criticized for oversimplifying state behavior by focusing on power balancing and systemic constraints, and disregarding

> A zero-sum game refers to a situation where one actor's gain is inherently another actor's loss, implying that resources or power are finite and the success of one actor directly corresponds to the failure of another. In contrast, a positive-sum game describes scenarios where cooperative approaches and interactions lead to outcomes where all participants can benefit, suggesting that the total 'pie' of resources or advantages can be expanded for mutual gain.

other motivations and complexities of state actions. Both theories can be accused of overlooking the role of norms, ideas and non-material factors in shaping global politics.

Liberalism as a theoretical framework includes a range of different perspectives. What they all have in common is a belief that humans are rational and social creatures who can cooperate and create institutions capable of ensuring and advancing human welfare. Classical liberalism grew out of principles based on idealism, which has human liberty at its core and believed that a better world was possible. It did not see human rationality happening as a result of morality, but it was due to political actors acting out of self-interest. Economic interests were seen as the impetus for greater state interaction and interdependence, raising the costs of war and reducing its likelihood. Repeated interactions between states would eventually create shared norms that could be codified in international law to reduce the uncertainty caused by the global structure of anarchy.

Neoliberal institutionalism emerged in the 1970s to explain why states in the anarchical international system, contrary to realist predictions, cooperated most of the time. Robert Keohane and Joseph Nye advanced their idea of **complex interdependence** to explain this phenomenon. In their book *Power and Interdependence*, Keohane and Nye identify three components of complex interdependence. First, there are multiple channels for state interaction. While formal meetings between government leaders remain important, informal interactions, like those that occur on the sidelines of G20 meetings, can be extremely influential. Other actors like INGOs and MNCs can also connect states in significant ways. Second, while states remain concerned about their security, there are other issues, such as the environment, where they share common interests and which drive cooperation. Third, the result of this cooperation is a reduction in the use of military force as a tool of statecraft.

Neoliberal institutionalism shares many of the assumptions of realism – states are the main international actors and they behave rationally by pursuing their own self-interest in an anarchical global system. Where it differs from realism is that neoliberal institutionalism argues that states cooperate as a result of constant interaction and a focus on absolute rather than relative gains. There are many incentives for states to cooperate, particularly with respect to non-security-related, positive-sum issues such as trade. Over time, reciprocity sees the gains from cooperation grow and enjoyed by all. Economic and social power matters alongside military power. International institutions, both organizations and international law, play a key role for neoliberal institutionalists by facilitating cooperative interactions between states. Organizations like the WTO and the EU provide a framework within which mutually beneficial and reciprocal interaction is possible and expected from member states. International law or treaties in the form of the USMCA or the Paris Agreement create a context within which states are expected to engage in long-term relationships.[76]

Classical liberalism and neoliberal institutionalism have biases and limitations. Classical liberalism can be criticized for its focus on individual rights and freedoms, which may lead to an underemphasis on collective responsibilities and societal inequalities. It tends to assume that cooperation and mutual benefit will naturally arise from market forces and overlooks power imbalances and unequal distribution of resources. Neoliberal institutionalism can be accused of placing excessive faith in international institutions and their ability to promote cooperation and resolve conflicts. It may overlook power dynamics and the potential for institutions to perpetuate existing inequalities. Both theories can be criticized for their emphasis on the state as the primary actor, often neglecting the influence of NSAs.

Global politics core

Realism and liberalism have been the two main theories of global politics. However, a range of middle ground theories emerged in the last two decades of the 20th century. These theories rejected the traditional theories' obsession with the state and their focus on explaining the status quo. They did not entirely reject the theoretical frameworks of realism and liberalism and so can be seen as lying between the traditional theories and more critical theories. **Constructivism** explains phenomena in global politics through a focus on norms and identities. While many types of constructivist arguments exist, all constructivists agree that **intersubjective** rules and norms are fundamentally important in world politics as these create its structure. The concept of intersubjectivity refers to the shared understandings, beliefs, norms and meanings that exist among actors in the global system. It recognizes that states and other political actors do not exist in isolation but interact with one another, and their behavior is shaped by common understandings and interpretations of the world. Think about how much you know about yourself and what makes you distinctive because you can compare yourself to others. Intersubjectivity is a major point of difference between constructivism and the traditional theories of realism and liberalism. It allows constructivist analyses to go beyond the objective material interests of states (security, power, well-being, etc.) to look at the social and ideational factors that influence their actions. Unlike realist and liberal accounts of global politics, which treat identity and interests as given and only ask how the environment influences behavior, constructivists go a step further and ask where identity and interests come from.

Alexander Wendt, a prominent constructivist, has identified two fundamental assumptions at the heart of constructivism.[77] The first is that the structure of global politics is determined by shared ideas and not material forces. As with the example of French nuclear missile submarines off the UK coast, material forces are significant only to the extent that they are given or possess particular meanings. The second is that the relationship between individual actors and structures (such as the state) is one where structures not only constrain or limit the agency and behavior of individual actors, but also construct their interests and identities. Wendt's phrase 'anarchy is what states make of it' captures this idea. In contemporary global politics, state leaders who interact with one another have accepted that the structure of international relations is anarchical. However, if anarchy is what states make of it then anarchy can be perceived differently by states and their representatives. The characteristics and shape of anarchy as a defining principle of global politics may change over time. Anarchy could even be replaced by a different system if enough influential states/leaders agreed to this. At the core of constructivism is the argument that certain ideas or norms have real power. Constructivists pay close attention to how new ideas and norms emerge and become adopted (or not). They acknowledge the key role that NSAs like NGOs, social movements, transnational advocacy networks and individual norm entrepreneurs can play. They examine how norms are tested, challenged and changed. By recognizing how everything in global politics is socially constructed (how people make, and remake, our global system), constructivism offers a more holistic theoretical perspective by allowing us to put more variables on our maps than either realism or liberalism does. Constructivism argues that there is nothing natural or inevitable about any political or social system.

Constructivism as a theory has biases and limitations. One key bias is its emphasis on ideational factors and the social construction of reality, which may overshadow material power dynamics and economic factors. Constructivism tends to focus on norms, identities and ideas, often downplaying the significance of material interests and power struggles. It may struggle to provide concrete policy prescriptions or offer clear predictions due to its emphasis on context-specific social construction.

> Intersubjectivity refers to the shared understanding, meanings, and expectations between actors (such as states, organizations, or individuals) that shape their interactions and perceptions of the international system. This concept emphasizes how collective beliefs, norms, and social constructions influence the behavior of actors and the formation of international policies, rather than just objective material factors.

Understanding power and global politics

> **Activity**
>
> Sovereignty is the key ordering principle of the global political system. How do you think a realist, a liberal and a constructivist might see sovereignty differently?

Critical theories

The end of the Cold War in 1991 saw the emergence of a range of theories that were critical of traditional theories for minimizing or ignoring factors that caused injustice and for being unable to address the flaws that exist in the global system. What these theories have in common is that they are critical of how traditional theories seek to explain the world as it is, rather than imagining the world as it ought to be. In general, critical theories have a strong normative element. Many critical theories overlap each other and often incorporate insights from constructivism as they attempt to understand, and question, the increasingly complex world we find ourselves in. They go further than constructivism and other middle ground theories do by giving a voice to vulnerable and marginalized individuals and groups, particularly women and those from the Global South.

Critical Theory[78] is a theoretical perspective that seeks to uncover and challenge the underlying power dynamics, social inequalities and oppressive structures with the global system. It emphasizes the intersection of power, ideology and social structures in shaping global politics and challenges existing power relations. Critical Theory provides a framework for analyzing the dominant capitalist system, global governance structures and the impacts of neoliberal economic policies. It sheds light on the uneven distribution of power and resources, class struggles and the perpetuation of inequalities in the international arena. By focusing on issues of race, gender, class and other forms of oppression, Critical Theory provides a lens through which to understand how these factors intersect and shape global politics. It challenges traditional theories like realism and liberalism by highlighting the agency of marginalized actors and advocating for more inclusive and emancipatory forms of global governance and social justice.

Critical Theory has biases and limitations. Its abstract nature and lack of a unified framework can make it challenging to apply in a concrete manner. The theory's focus on power and social inequality can overshadow other important factors, like economic considerations or state behavior. Critics also argue that Critical Theory lacks clear policy prescriptions and prioritizes critique over practical solutions.

In *Eleven Theses on Feuerbach*, German philosopher Karl Marx stated that philosophers 'have only *interpreted* the world… the point, however, is to *change* it.' Modern Marxists look at the current global system and see it as inherently unequal, as something that needs to be changed. Marxists seek to change the way that global politics operates in favor of elites rather than ordinary people. At the heart of **Marxism** is a critique of the nation-state and its legitimacy. Where traditional theories take the nation-state as a given, Marxists see the nation-state as the fundamental problem in global politics. For them, the nation-state is a largely oppressive actor in people's lives, whether this is due to its monopoly on the legitimate use of force or in terms of supporting economic globalization and globalized capitalist trade systems that have led to increasing inequalities across the globe. For Marxists, only the dissolution of states and the powerful IGOs that represent them will allow humans to free themselves from such domination and inequality. At its core, Marxism is an emancipatory theory.

Global politics core

Marxism as a theory has biases and limitations. One key bias is its focus on economic factors, particularly class struggle, which can overshadow other dimensions of power, such as identity, culture and non-economic forms of oppression. Marxism's emphasis on economic determinism can also downplay the agency of individuals and the complexity of political processes. Marxism tends to view power through the lens of exploitation and inequality, often overlooking other forms of power dynamics and diverse interests that shape global politics.

Marxism focuses its critique on the inequality that exists between different classes. **Postcolonialism** centers its critique on inequalities that exist between different states or regions, which often have racial overtones. At the core of postcolonial theory is a recognition that, although decolonization may have occurred, many of the ideas, prejudices, biases and understandings that made colonialism possible did not disappear when former colonies gained their independence. A key goal of postcolonial theory is to show how the legacies of colonialism created the current inequalities that exist globally and how neocolonial power structures continue to reproduce these inequalities. Colonial economies were often structured around resource extraction for the benefit of the colonial power. Many poorer states in the Global South are still subject to indirect control and influence in the form of unequal trading practices and the political power that MNCs (often from the Global North) can exert on postcolonial governments. Postcolonial theory focuses on how the Global South is represented and how these representations reinforce impressions of Western political dominance and the appropriate exercise of Western power in the Global South. If states in the Global South are seen to be incapable of governing themselves and protecting their own citizens then this permits Western intervention in such states and also portrays it as benevolent and even beneficial. Postcolonialism alerts us to a significant blind spot in global politics – the fact that most theory has been written by white Western scholars (often men) and published in English. By highlighting the ways in which the historical legacies of colonialism produced, and continue to reproduce, current global inequalities, postcolonialism widens our focus and challenges us to reflect on the role played by diverse perspectives in our understandings of global politics.

Postcolonialism has biases and limitations. One key bias is its focus on colonial experiences and its tendency to center the experiences of the formerly colonized, often overlooking other aspects of global politics. Postcolonialism can be criticized for neglecting non-colonial forms of power relations and their impacts on the international system. The theory's emphasis on cultural and identity-based analysis can downplay economic factors and material power dynamics. The diverse range of postcolonial experiences and contexts make it challenging to develop a unified framework and generalize findings.

Example – Orientalism

Edward Said's *Orientalism* (1978) outlines how representations of North Africa, the Middle East and Asia in European literature and political theory constructed it as a place waiting for Western exploration and domination. In the Western imagination, the Orient became a barbaric place in need of Western/European civilization and these representations became so dominant that it was almost impossible to think or speak differently. Modern versions of Orientalism could be seen during the War on Terror and in the US invasion and occupation of Afghanistan.

Understanding power and global politics

> Carol Cohn analyzed how the use of sexist and sexualized language when discussing nuclear weapons disguised their ultimate purpose – the mass incineration of millions of human beings – and made it possible for officials and military leaders to 'think about the unthinkable' by making 'it possible to be radically removed from the reality of what one is talking about and from the realities one is creating...'[79]

Feminism critiques the inequalities that are inherent in the global system by focusing on the role and framing of gender in global politics. Feminists define gender as a set of socially constructed characteristics that define what the ideal man or woman ought to be. In general, we assign more positive value to masculine characteristics, like strength, rationality, independence, protector and public, than we do to feminine characteristics, like weakness, emotionality, relational, protected and private. Feminism challenges us to reflect on the historical dominance of men and the ideal masculine type. In the West, this is typically associated with whiteness and heterosexuality. It also challenges us to reflect on the widespread exclusion, until relatively recently, of the perspectives and experiences of women and femininity. There are several different forms of feminism. Liberal feminists prioritize issues of political and economic equality, arguing that if more women were represented in government and in boardrooms, and if wage equality were to occur, this would lead to wider societal changes. Marxist feminists examine how contemporary economic and political structures are built on and maintained by the exploitation of female labor, in workplaces and in households. Postcolonial feminists explore how neocolonial structures and processes impact women in the Global South. Feminist theories remind us is that gender relationships are everywhere in global politics. Feminist approaches help question the extent to which theories are created by men based on their experiences and those of other men. We should also consider how policy-making impacts women and how a lack of women's voices can influence such processes.

Feminism as a theory has biases and limitations. One key bias is its primary focus on gender and the experiences of women, which may overshadow other dimensions of power and identity in global politics. Feminism can be criticized for not accounting for the intersectionality of identities and power relations, as it tends to prioritize gender analysis over other factors such as race, class and sexuality. There can be diverse interpretations and approaches within feminist theory, leading to different perspectives and potential biases. Some critics argue that feminist theory may overlook economic considerations and fail to provide concrete policy prescriptions.

> Global Politics is not an overly theoretical course, but a reference to a theory or a particular scholar in an IB assessment can help demonstrate critical thinking. Any reference should be relevant, and it should add to the effectiveness of any argument or point you are making. If you include a theoretical reference because you think you need to, it will feel forced and will likely detract from the quality of your response.

Green theory, also known as ecological or environmental theory, helps to expose the ecological blindness that exists in many traditional theories. It emphasizes the interconnectedness of environmental issues and global politics. Green theory argues that environmental issues, such as the climate crisis, deforestation, biodiversity loss and resource depletion, are not isolated from political and social dynamics, but rather shape and are shaped by them. Green theorists assert that the focus of traditional theories on state-centric security concerns should be expanded to include the broader concept of **human security**, which includes ecological security, environmental sustainability and the well-being of present and future generations. They advocate for the integration of ecological concerns into the decision-making processes of governments, IGOs and NSAs. This is necessary to promote sustainable development, the preservation of Earth's ecosystems, and environmental justice so that ecological risks are evenly distributed among different social classes, states and regions.

> What role do models play in the acquisition of knowledge in the human sciences?

Green theory has biases and limitations. One key bias is its strong focus on ecological sustainability and environmental concerns, which may overshadow other important aspects of global politics, such as economic considerations or power dynamics. Green theory's emphasis on ecological interdependence may downplay other factors shaping international relations. The theory's application and policy prescriptions can vary, leading to diverse interpretations and potential biases. The limitations of scientific knowledge and uncertainties in predicting environmental impacts can pose challenges in formulating concrete policy recommendations.

Global politics core

Exercises

35. Explain the purpose of theory in Global Politics.

36. Describe to what extent we should be more focused on normative theories about how global politics 'ought to be' as opposed to focusing more on explaining the world 'as it is'?

Practice questions

1. Some describe the principle of sovereignty as resilient and fundamental to the world order. Others consider it obsolete. Discuss which of these perspectives is more accurate.
2. To what extent are powerful states able to manipulate global politics to their own benefit?
3. To what extent should NSAs have equal standing with sovereign states in structures of global governance?
4. Evaluate the reasons why the legitimacy of a political actor might need to be questioned.
5. 'Global politics is characterized more by conflict than cooperation.' Discuss this view.
6. Examine the place that the key actors/stakeholders and the key concepts have in each of the theoretical frameworks considered above.

Summary

In this chapter, you have learned:

- The difference between Global Politics, the scholarly subject, and global politics, the field of study.

- The role played by different stakeholders and actors in global politics, including: states, non-state actors, multinational corporations, transnational advocacy networks, intergovernmental organizations, informal forums, nongovernmental organizations, individuals, the media, social movements, resistance movements, interest groups and pressure groups.

- How the structure of global politics enables and constrains actors within the system. For example, the behavior of political actors under anarchy is very different than that under hierarchy or hegemony.

- The significance of the Peace of Westphalia (1648) in modern conceptualizations of global politics and some of the reasons why we should be critical of its prominent position.

- How material structures (resources and personnel) and ideational structures (norms and ways of seeing) help shape the behavior and outcomes of actors and stakeholders. For example, British politicians feel differently about French nuclear-armed submarines than they do about Russian submarines.

- How the concepts of polarity and multiplexity can be used to describe the structure of contemporary global politics.

- The distinction between power-to, power-over and power-with, as well as different conceptualizations and explanations of power and how it operates in global politics.
- The central role of sovereignty as one of the defining operating principles of global politics, particularly in terms of its close association with the state as a key political actor in global politics.
- The different forms of sovereignty for example, internal and external sovereignty, as well as some of the challenges to sovereignty that exist in global politics.
- The role of legitimacy and legitimation in global politics and the interrelationship between legitimacy, power, obligation and authority.
- The different sources of legitimacy for state and non-state actors, as well as some of the challenges to legitimacy, such as a poor performance by a government or state in terms of protecting the welfare of its citizens.
- The concept of interdependence and how global governance has become a more important issue as the world has become more globalized and many of the challenges states face (development, pandemics, climate change, etc.) require cooperation across national borders.
- The role of international law and why states in an anarchical system cooperate, due to vertical or horizontal enforcement.
- The central role played by the United Nations and some of its primary components such as the Security Council and the General Assembly.
- The role played by other intergovernmental organizations and non-state actors in global governance, for example, NATO, The World Bank and the G20.
- The role of theory in global politics and some of the different forms of theorizing, for example, the distinction between explanatory theory, critical theory, normative theory, constitutive theory and theory as a lens.
- Some of the main theories in global politics, including traditional theories, such as realism and liberalism, middle ground theories, such as constructivism, and critical theories, such as Marxism, postcolonialism and feminism.

Notes

1. The United Nations (UN) recognizes 206 sovereign states: 193 UN member states, 2 UN General Assembly non-member observer states and 11 other states.
2. Lake, D.A. (2008). 'The State and International Relations'. *The Oxford Handbook of International Relations* (Ser. The Oxford Handbook of Political Science). Oxford University Press, p.43.
3. States are also a common unit of analysis in many conceptual perspectives or theories of Global Politics.
4. The Panama (2016), Paradise (2017) and Pandora (2021) papers saw millions of confidential documents leaked to investigative journalists, which shed light on the secretive world of offshore companies and trusts used by many of the world's wealthiest and most powerful people and corporations to shift and store money internationally to avoid taxes and state scrutiny.
5. United Nations Office of Legal Affairs. (1999, December 31). *No. 3802. Convention on rights and duties of states adopted by the Seventh International Conference of American States. signed at Montevideo, December 26th, 1933*. UN iLibrary, https://doi.org/10.18356/57z42223-en-fr
6. Geddes, B. (1994). *Politician's Dilemma: Building State Capacity in Latin America*. University of California Press, p.7.

Global politics core

7. In August 2023, the BRICS group agreed to admit Saudi Arabia, Iran, Ethiopia, Egypt, Argentina and the UAE.
8. The Reporters without Borders ranking of press freedom can be found at: https://rsf.org/en/index. The Economist Intelligence Unit's most recent Democracy Index can be accessed via: https://www.eiu.com/n/
9. O'Toole, F. (2022). 'Would Ukrainians still feel welcome if they were not white and Christian?' *The Irish Times*, 18 June. Retrieved on June 15, 2023 from: www.irishtimes.com/opinion/2022/06/18/fintan-otoole-would-ukrainians-still-feel-welcome-if-they-were-not-white-and-christian/
10. Guterres, A. (2019, March 15). 'The climate strikers should inspire us all to act at the next UN summit'. *The Guardian*. Retrieved on 18 June, 2023 from https://www.theguardian.com/commentisfree/2019/mar/15/climate-strikers-urgency-un-summit-world-leaders
11. Du Bois, W.E.B. (1996, 1946). *The World and Africa: An Inquiry into the Part Which Africa has Played in World History*. International Publishers, p.80 (Italics in the original).
12. Irish author James Joyce expresses a similar sentiment in *The Portrait of the Artist as a Young Man* when he has Stephen Dedalus utter 'History is a nightmare from which I am trying to awake' in reference to the history of violence that Ireland seemed unable to escape, where the past was very much still a part of the present.
13. This section covers only some of the discussions challenging traditional Eurocentric or Western-centred views of Global Politics. If you are interested in learning more, see: Acharya, A. (2020). 'What "Introduction to International Relations" Misses Out: Civilizations, World Orders, and the Rise of the West', *Social Science Research Network (SSRN)*. Available online: https://papers.ssrn.com/sol3/papers.cfm?abstract_id=3750112
14. An alternative example could be US and Israeli concerns over Iran's attempts to acquire nuclear weapons, which has led both countries to allegedly consider preventive military strikes to ensure that this does not occur.
15. Mathur, S. and Acharya, A. (2022). 'Towards Global International Relations'. McGlinchey, S. (ed.) (2022). *Foundations of International Relations*. Bloomsbury Academic, p.49.
16. Ibid.
17. Mathur & Achaya, p.50.
18. Ibid.
19. Hobbes, T. (1985 [1641]). *Leviathan*. Penguin Books, p.150.
20. Russell, B. (1938). *Power: A New Social Analysis*. George Allen & Unwin, p.35.
21. The social structure itself can be seen to exert power-over individuals who exist and operate within it.
22. See: Pitkin, H. (1973). *Wittgenstein and Justice: On the Significance of Ludwig Wittgenstein for Social and Political Thought*. University of California Press.
23. This distinction is sometimes referred to as 'positive' power and 'negative' power, respectively.
24. Mearsheimer, J.J. (2014, 1001). *The Tragedy of Great Power Politics*. W.W. Norton & Co., p.19.
25. Wivel, A. (n.d.). 'Security dilemma'. *Encyclopedia Britannica*. Retrieved on May 3, 2023 from www.britannica.com/topic/security-dilemma
26. See: Chotiner, I. (2022, March 1). 'Why John Mearsheimer blames the U.S. for the crisis in Ukraine'. *The New Yorker*. Retrieved on May 3, 2023 from www.newyorker.com/news/q-and-a/why-john-mearsheimer-blames-the-us-for-the-crisis-in-ukraine
27. Keohane, R. and Nye, J. (1998). 'Power and Interdependence in the Information Age'. *Foreign Affairs*, vol. 77, p.83.
28. Nye, J. (1990). 'Soft Power'. *Foreign Policy*, p.167.
29. Sierra, G. (Host). (2022, May 27). 'Hip-Hop Diplomacy'. [Audio podcast]. Retrieved from: https://cfrwhyitmatters.podbean.com/e/hip-hop-diplomacy/
30. English, E. (2023, May 22). 'High camp and soft power: How Eurovision explains modern Europe-and more'. Bulletin of the Atomic Scientists. Retrieved from: https://thebulletin.org/2023/05/high-camp-and-soft-power-eurovision-explains-europe/

31. Aspinall, E. (2023, May 13). 'Eurovision: Glitz, glamour and geopolitics'. British Foreign Policy Group. Retrieved from: https://bfpg.co.uk/2023/05/goepolitics-eurovision/
32. Nye, J. (2004, February 8). 'The benefits of soft power'. HBS Working Knowledge. Retrieved on May 5, 2023 from https://hbswk.hbs.edu/archive/the-benefits-of-soft-power
33. Nye (1990), p.166.
34. Nye (2004).
35. Strange, S. (1988). *States and Markets*. Pinter Publishers, p.24.
36. Qin, Y. (2016). 'A Relational Theory of World Politics'. *International Studies Review*, 18(1), p.36.
37. *Ibid.*, p.42.
38. Walker, C. and Ludwig, J. (2017). 'From "Soft Power" to "Sharp Power": Rising Authoritarian Influence in the Democratic World'. *Sharp Power: Rising Authoritarian Influence*. National Endowment for Democracy, p.6.
39. *Ibid*, p.13.
40. Gramsci, A. (1971). *Selections from the Prison Notebooks*. Lawrence & Wishart, p.182.
41. Lukes, S. (2005). *Power: A Radical View* (2nd ed.). Palgrave MacMillan, p.18.
42. *Ibid*, p.27.
43. Foucault, M. (1998). *The History of Sexuality: The Will to Knowledge*. Penguin, p.63.
44. In the original French, power/knowledge is written as *savoir/pouvior*. *Savoir* is a particular kind of unspoken knowledge (the common sense) that characterizes a specific time and place, and which then shapes the explicit knowledge (*connaissance*) that becomes the dominant perspective in the human or natural sciences. While *pouvoir* is typically translated as power, it is also the infinitive form of the verb meaning to be able to. It is the most common way of saying 'can' in Romance languages.
45. See: Foucault, M. (1977). *Discipline and Punish: The Birth of the Prison*. Random House.
46. In doing so, Mignolo resolves the racial and colonial blind spot that exists in Foucault's very European/Western understanding of power. See: Alcoff, L.M. (2007). 'Mignolo's Epistemology of Coloniality'. *CR: The New Centennial Review*, 7(3), pp.80–81.
47. bell hooks was born Gloria Jean Watkins, but adopted the name bell hooks from her maternal great-grandmother and styled it in lower case in an effort to focus attention on her ideas rather than on her identity as an isolated individual.
48. hooks, b. (2015 [1984]). *Feminist Theory: From Margin to Center*. Routledge, pp.90–91.
49. d'Entreves, M.P. and Tömmel, T. 'Hannah Arendt'. Zalta, E.N and Nodelman, U. (eds.) (Fall 2022 Edition). *The Stanford Encyclopedia of Philosophy*. Retrieved on May 3, 2023 from https://plato.standford.edu/archives/fall2022/entries/arendt/
50. Arendt, H. (1958). *The Human Condition*. The University of Chicago Press, p.199, and Arendt, H. (1972). *Crises of the Republic*. Harcourt, pp.143–155.
51. Arendt used the terms 'power' and 'violence' to describe power-with and power-over, respectively. According to Arendt, every use of power-over consists of a form of violence and did not deserve the label power. Power deserved this name only when it was legitimate, when it involved the ability of the group to act together. See: Arendt, H. (1970). *On Violence*. Harcourt Brace, p.44.
52. Arendt (1958), p.200.
53. Arendt (1972), p.140.
54. Liu, E. (2014, November 4). 'How to understand power – Eric Liu'. YouTube. Retrieved on May 6, 2023 from www.youtube.com/watch?v=c_Eutci7ack
55. CBC/Radio Canada. (2017, October 10). 'The gun lobby doesn't always win: The Democratic Workaround that best the NRA'. CBC Radio. CBCnews. Retrieved on May 6, 2023 from www.cbc.ca/radio/day6/episode-358-outsmarting-the-nra-canada-s-magnitsky-act-ham-radios-for-puerto-rico-music-in-dna-and-more-1.4329733/the-gun-lobby-doesn-t-always-win-the-democratic-workaround-that-beat-the-nra-1.4329884
56. *Ibid.*
57. In *Leviathan*, Hobbes wrote: 'The obligation of subjects to the sovereign is understood to last as long, and no longer, than the power lasteth by which he is able to protect them.' See:

Hobbes, T. (2002, July 2). *The Project Gutenberg eBook of Leviathan, by Thomas Hobbes*. Project Gutenberg. Retrieved on July 22, 2023 from https://www.gutenberg.org/files/3207/3207-h/3207-h.htm. This also links to Max Weber's definition of the state.

58. The Correlates of War data set estimated that there were 41 intrastate conflicts between 2000 and 2014. Source: https://correlatesofwar.org/data-sets/cow-war/
59. Rummel, Rudolph J. (n.d.). '20th Century Democide'. Retrieved from: https://www.hawaii.edu/powerkills/20TH.HTM
60. Tufts University. (n.d.) 'MIP Research'. Center for Strategic Studies. https://sites.tufts.edu/css/mip- research/#_edn2
61. External sovereignty is sometimes referred to as juridical or negative sovereignty, while internal sovereignty is sometimes called empirical, domestic or positive sovereignty.
62. Bull, H. (1995). *The Anarchical Society: A Study of Order in World Politics*. Macmillan, p.8.
63. *Ibid*.
64. In practice, the right to self-determination only applied to former colonies and was not available to *all* peoples.
65. See: Krasner, S.D. (1999). *Sovereignty: Organized Hypocrisy*. Princeton University Press, pp.3-4.
66. Barker, R. (1990). *Political Legitimacy and the State*. Oxford University Press, p.11.
67. Alagappa, M. (1995). 'Introduction'. Alagappa, M. (ed.). *Political Legitimacy in Southeast Asia: The Quest for Moral Authority*. Stanford University Press, p.15.
68. Alagappa, M. (1995). 'The Anatomy of Legitimacy'. Alagappa, M. (ed.). *Political Legitimacy in Southeast Asia: The Quest for Moral Authority*. Stanford University Press, p.15.
69. *Ibid*, p.24.
70. United Nations. (n.d.) 'United Nations Charter (full text)'. Retrieved on June 23, 2023 from https://www.un.org/en/about-us/un-charter/full-text. This appears in Chapter I, Article 2.
71. As of September 2023, another long-neutral state, Sweden, is also in line to join NATO.
72. In September 2023, the AU was made a permanent member of the G20.
73. See: Waltz, K. (1979). *Theory of International Politics*. Waveland Press.
74. Mearsheimer, p.21.
75. *Ibid*.
76. Other forms of liberalism relax neoliberal institutionalism's assumption of the state as a unitary actor. These branches of liberal theory adopt a *bottom-up* view of global politics and argue that the domestic characteristics of a state influence the behavior of the state at the international level. They see individuals and NSAs (trade unions, interest groups, NGOs and businesses) as key actors in global politics.
77. See: Wendt, A. (2012). *Social Theory of International Politics*. Cambridge University Press.
78. Critical Theory is one form of critical theory. When the term is uncapitalized, it refers to the general field of critical theories. When it is capitalized, it refers to a specific theory within this broader field.
79. Cohn, C. (1987). 'Sex and Death in the Rational World of Defense Intellectuals'. *Signs* 12(4), p.715.
* Source: Nye, J. (2004). *Soft Power: The Means to Success in World Politics*. Public Affairs, p.8.

Introduction to the thematic studies

We now move on to the three thematic studies: Rights and justice, Development and sustainability, and Peace and conflict.

When working through these chapters, keep the content in the Core chapter 'Understanding power and global politics' in mind. None of the thematic studies can be fully understood without understanding the key concepts of power, sovereignty, legitimacy and interdependence. These concepts should not be understood as independent but as recurring concepts found in different contexts. As you engage with additional concepts and theories, you will realize how the Core chapter's key concepts are related to the three thematic studies. You will also come to understand that the three thematic studies are interrelated. The feature boxes will help you establish and strengthen these connections.

The following three chapters will provide you with contemporary real-world examples, as well as cases and case studies. These will help you to better understand how the concepts and content in Global Politics can be applied in real-life contexts. These are only a few of the examples and cases that can be studied, so do not limit yourself to just knowing these ones. Try to apply what you are learning to your own context or to topics that are of particular interest to you.

The first thematic study chapter is 'Rights and justice'. Rights and justice are crucial concepts in Global Politics as they provide insights into fairness and equality in our world. Political narratives and practices are influenced by people's perceptions of what is fair or unfair. These concepts help establish legal and standardized frameworks that determine the privileges and protections individuals and groups are entitled to. However, the meanings of rights and justice, as well as related concepts like liberty and equality, are subject to debate due to diverse historical and cultural perspectives. This chapter explores the contested meanings of rights and justice in global politics and examines their understanding and implementation. It also considers the involvement of various stakeholders in the codification, protection and monitoring of human rights. The nature and practice of rights and justice vary across socio-political contexts and regions, with different priorities given to civil and political rights or economic, social and cultural rights. Finally, it delves into debates surrounding individual rights versus collective rights, the effectiveness and legitimacy of the international human rights regime, and the influence of different actors in shaping human rights narratives and practices. Each of these debates highlights how power dynamics and interests among and between states and other actors often influence how rights and justice are organized and protected. This raises questions about the inclusivity and effectiveness of international human rights regimes in promoting universal rights and justice.

The second thematic study chapter is 'Development and sustainability'. You should keep in mind the practical and real-world nature of the concepts in this thematic study to help you see the human face behind the concepts of development, sustainability, poverty and equality. In our examination of development and sustainability, we will see how the consequences of policies intended to bring about greater equality and equity often have the opposite effect on individuals and groups in real life. The second thematic study also shows that there are specific interests behind development and sustainability policies. These interests come from the various state and non-state actors (NSAs) and stakeholders involved. Due to power imbalances between these

---

In the context of Global Politics, *real-world example* refers to a specific event or phenomenon that has taken place in the real world, which is used to make concepts and content more relatable by demonstrating how they are applied in actual political situations (for example, NATO's 2011 intervention in Libya is a real-world example of Responsibility to Protect). A *case* refers to a more specific and focused instance within a broader topic or theme. Cases are used to delve deeper into the details of a particular political event or scenario, allowing you to analyze the complexities, causes, consequences, and relevant actors involved (for example, the Syrian Civil War could be used as a case to study the dynamics of conflict in the Middle East). A *case study* is a comprehensive analysis of a particular case, typically involving an in-depth investigation of a specific global political issue or event. Case studies are used to encourage you to apply critical thinking and analytical skills to understand the nuances of a complex global political problem (for example, a case study on the EU's response to the refugee crisis could involve a thorough examination of the impact on member states).

Introduction to the thematic studies

stakeholders, some of which have developed over centuries, the outcomes of these policies do not always benefit as intended. The discussions on development and sustainability deal with these power relations and the potential marginalization and vulnerabilities that are created due to these power imbalances. We focus on what is being done to help bring greater symmetry to these relationships by the various stakeholders and actors. The development of these relationships is important, especially with regards to the impact that globalization, climate change and greater interdependence have had on development and sustainability.

The third thematic study chapter is 'Peace and conflict'. Our world is always facing armed conflict, wars and non-violent conflict. At the same time, we always wish to live in peace. There are two crucial issues that need to be understood. First, human history and the present is plagued by conflict. Second, peace is possible and, despite the presence of conflict, it does exist. In this chapter, we will look at concepts related to the peace and conflict field of studies. We will look at theories, contexts, dynamics and the role of different international actors and stakeholders involved. Perhaps most importantly, we will look at how peace and conflict are not binary opposites, but exist within a wider spectrum that needs to be understood in order to have a broader understanding of how power, sovereignty, legitimacy and interdependence play a role in global politics.

THEMATIC STUDIES

Rights and justice

RIGHTS OF WOMEN

RIGHTS OF OLDER PERSONS

SELF-DETERMINATION

INDIGENOUS PEOPLES AND MINORITIES

RIGHTS OF PERSONS WITH DISABILITIES

RIGHTS TO WORK IN FAIR CONDITIONS

PREVENTION OF DISCRIMINATION

RIGHTS OF THE CHILD

RIGHTS OF JUSTICE

Thematic studies

Concepts

Rights, Justice, Liberty, Equality, Human Rights, International Law, Responsibility to Protect, Humanitarian Intervention, Universal Jurisdiction

Learning outcomes

In this chapter, you will learn about:
- how rights, justice, liberty and equality are contested and interconnected concepts
- the evolution of individual rights to human rights
- how the modern international human rights regime developed following the end of the Second World War
- the role that the Universal Declaration of Human Rights and subsequent human rights laws and treaties have played in internationalizing human rights
- how international law has been humanized due to concerns over rights and justice, with specific reference to the norms of responsibility to protect, humanitarian intervention and universal jurisdiction
- the role played by different actors and stakeholders in codifying, protecting and monitoring human rights
- how the politicization of rights drives debates on rights and justice in Global Politics.

Activity

How is the thematic study of rights and justice connected to something you already know about? What new ideas or impressions do you have that extend your thinking about rights and justice in new directions? What do you wonder about? What might be challenging or confusing about the topic of rights and justice? Be prepared to share your thinking with your peers.

Introducing rights and justice

Conceptual question

What are rights and justice?

Rights and **justice** are fundamental concepts in Global Politics because they help us to understand how fairness and equality work (or do not work) in the world around us. Many of the narratives and practices of international relations are shaped by what people think is fair or unfair. The concepts of rights and justice help create legal and standardized frameworks that determine what privileges and protections people are entitled to. The meanings of rights and justice, along with the related concepts of **liberty** and **equality**, are often contested because there are many different historical, ideological and cultural perspectives in the world. In this chapter, we will explore the contested meanings of rights and justice in global politics and examine how these concepts are understood and practiced. We will also examine the nature and practice of rights and justice in global politics, and the involvement of various stakeholders in the **codification**, protection and monitoring of **human rights**. Additionally, we

---

Human rights concerns are often seen as a threat to state sovereignty. Conflict over human rights, and which rights and whose rights matter, has long been a feature of global politics. Human rights violations are also often a feature of armed conflict. The protection of human rights is generally seen as a requirement for successful development, and development can be seen as a human right.

Codification is the process of organizing and consolidating laws, regulations or principles into a comprehensive legal system. Protection refers to the collective efforts and mechanisms put in place to safeguard and uphold fundamental rights and freedoms. Monitoring involves gathering information, conducting investigations, and analyzing data to identify potential violations of human rights.

Rights and justice

will consider some of the debates about rights and justice, ranging from the tensions between **individual rights** and **collective rights** to questions about the effectiveness and legitimacy of the international human rights regime and its tools.

Rights and justice are complex and multidimensional, with different political actors and perspectives contributing to the discussion. State actors, international organizations, civil society groups and individuals all play a role in shaping the meaning and practice of rights and justice. These actors often have different understandings of what rights and justice look like, leading to contested meanings and interpretations. While some may emphasize individual rights or human rights as the cornerstone of global justice, others may stress collective rights, cultural rights or even the right to development.

The involvement of various actors and stakeholders in the codification, protection and monitoring of human rights is a critical part of studying rights and justice. Many of the actors and stakeholders you met in the Core chapter play a role in shaping the norms, standards and institutions that govern human rights. The roles and influence of these actors and stakeholders are often contested, reflecting power dynamics and differing interests. Some argue that states and multinational corporations (MNCs) should have the main responsibility for protecting and promoting human rights, while others emphasize the role of individuals and non-state actors (NSAs), like charities. Debates about the appropriate roles and responsibilities of different actors in this context continue to shape the narratives and practices of human rights in today's world.

The nature and practice of rights and justice also varies across different socio-political contexts and geographical or cultural regions. Some states or regions may prioritize civil and political rights, such as freedom of speech and political participation, while others may prioritize economic, social and cultural rights, such as the right to education and healthcare. The ways in which rights and justice are codified, protected and monitored also reflect power dynamics and interests among states and other actors. The involvement of powerful states in shaping and enforcing international human rights regimes may raise questions about the legitimacy and effectiveness of these regimes in promoting rights and justice for all.

Contested meanings of rights, justice, liberty and equality

The contested meanings of rights, justice, liberty and equality have been central to political narratives throughout history. These concepts are often seen as fundamental principles, yet their interpretations and applications have fueled intense debate and disagreement. As societies evolve and cultures converge or diverge because of globalization, different perspectives shape how these concepts are understood, leading to conflicts over their definitions, scope and implications.

Activity

When trying to understand rights, justice, liberty and equality, it is important to consider that these are multidimensional concepts whose meanings are contested and depend on context. Write down your own definition for each of these terms and compare them to that of a classmate or of an organization that works to promote the concepts. What are the differences between your definitions? What might the reasons for these differences be?

Thematic studies

The concept of rights

The meaning of rights in Global Politics has long been a topic of contention among various stakeholders, including governments, intergovernmental organizations (IGOs), civil society groups, such as non-governmental organizations (NGOs) and informal intergovernmental organizations (INGOs), and individuals, such as activists, politicians and academics. The contested nature of rights arises from differing perspectives on the origin, scope and universality of rights, as well as conflicting interests and cultural norms (the shared beliefs, values and behaviors that are considered typical and acceptable within a particular society or group).

One key debate revolves around the source of rights. In Western Europe, early concepts of rights first appeared as part of the theory of **natural law**. This is the system of law that was thought to exist in the *state of nature*. Natural law theory states that all people have inherent rights, conferred by 'God, nature, or reason', rather than through the laws of a state. Such natural rights exist independently from governments and were initially thought of as duties – you were expected to act according to your natural tendencies as a human.

In Western Europe, it was not until certain societal changes occurred between the 13th century and the Peace of Westphalia in 1648 (see page 20 of the Core chapter) that we start to see the shift from natural law as duties to natural law as rights, based on more liberal ideas of freedom and equality. It was not until the 17th and 18th centuries, during the European Enlightenment, that we see an elaboration of this in the writings of social contract philosophers like John Locke and Jean-Jacques Rousseau. These writings were influential in laying the foundation for what would, in the 20th century, become human rights.[1] According to these thinkers, certain rights belonged to individuals as moral beings. These were general rights, not special rights, and so did not depend on particular transactions or relationships. These natural rights were equal and everyone who was a moral being held them without distinction, particularly the rights to life, liberty (freedom from arbitrary or unjustified rule) and property. Upon entering a social contract with the sovereign state, individuals did not surrender these natural rights, but they gave the state the right to protect and enforce them. The real-world extent of these ideas can be seen in some of the key political documents of the period, such as the US Declaration of Independence (1776), the French Declaration of the Rights of Man and of the Citizen (1789), and the Constitution of the USA (1787).

The idea of natural rights and the notion that individuals were the primary rights holders came under attack in the late 18th and early 20th centuries, from utilitarian philosophers such as Jeremy Bentham, who made fun of natural rights as 'nonsense upon stilts' and for whom legal rights were the only real rights; and John Stuart Mill, who declared that all rights were founded on utility ('the greatest happiness for the greatest number'). Others, like Karl von Savigny and Sir Henry Maine, emphasized that rights were the result of unique cultural contexts. Given rising European nationalism and the spread of Marxist ideology, by the onset of the First World War not many Western rights theorists were prepared to defend natural/individual rights. Instead, rights were created and restricted by law makers or were seen to belong to communities or whole societies and nations, and subject to change only as these developed.

Despite the idea of individual rights emerging first within Western philosophy, some Western philosophers were critical of what we would call human rights. These critiques foreshadowed later, largely non-Western arguments, about the ways in which human rights may be socially constructed and shaped by specific and unique historical, political and cultural factors.

This perspective of rights being linked to duties can also be seen in non-Western sources such as the ancient neo-Sumerian and Sumerian codes of Ur-Nammu and Hammurabi, the ancient India vedas, the Buddhist kalama sutta and the Islamic notion of haqooq-al-Ebad.

While both nationalism and Marxism challenged notions of individual rights, they have also been instrumental in shaping and advancing human rights agendas. Nationalist movements have played a role in the struggle for self-determination and the recognition of cultural and linguistic rights. Marxist-inspired movements have championed social and economic rights, advocating for improved working conditions and access to basic necessities.

Rights and justice

> It is important to critically evaluate **dominant narratives** – those stories or ways of seeing the world that appear natural or have a taken-for-granted quality to them. Doing so allows for a more meaningful evaluation of key debates in Global Politics.

Natural rights as thought of during the European Enlightenment were *not* human rights as most people understand them today. We generally think of individual rights and human rights as being the same thing, but this has only been true since the end of the Second World War. Before that, individuals, especially those in the Christian West, regularly claimed and asserted rights because they were fully developed moral and political agents, while at the same time denying the same social standing and rights to other humans because of their race, religion, sex, creed, class or gender. Human rights are a special, narrow category of rights. Although some scholars trace the origins of contemporary human rights back to the natural and constitutional narratives that unfolded in the European Enlightenment, we must try to free modern human rights from broader talk of rights.

> While contemporary notions of human rights may have historical roots, it is important to remember that human rights are a modern concept that only emerged after the end of the Second World War.

Another area of contention is what our rights should be. While many agree on fundamental human rights, such as the right to life, liberty and security, there are different views on the significance, extent and specificity of rights. This sometimes occurs *within* the different generations of human rights with respect to their interpretation and enforceability.[2] Civil and political human rights, such as the right to life, equality before the law, and freedom of speech and thought, are first generation rights. Economic, social and cultural human rights, such as the right to work and to specific conditions of employment, as well as the right to food, housing, healthcare and education, are second generation rights. Third generation rights include collective or solidarity human rights, for example, rights to **self-determination** (the principle that individuals and communities have the right to determine their own political, economic and social destiny without external interference), development, a clean environment, as well as rights that protect minority groups. Since the late 1980s, there have been discussions about a fourth generation of human rights to reflect more recent technological and social developments, but no consensus has yet been reached on this.

> First generation human rights are civil-political rights. Second generation human rights are economic, social and cultural rights. Third generation human rights are collective or solidarity rights.

Table 2.1 Generations of human rights

Generation of Human Rights	Definition	Real-world Examples
First generation (civil and political rights)	These are individual rights that protect civil liberties, political freedoms and due process. They focus on individual liberty and protection from government interference.	Examples include the right to life, freedom of speech, freedom of religion, the right to a fair trial and the prohibition of torture.
Second generation (economic, social and cultural rights)	These are rights that pertain to social and economic well-being, addressing issues such as healthcare, education, employment and social security. They emphasize the importance of ensuring social and economic equality.	Examples include the right to education, the right to adequate housing, the right to healthcare, the right to work and the right to social security.
Third generation (solidarity rights)	These are collective rights that focus on broader social, environmental and developmental concerns. These often require international cooperation and solidarity. They emphasize the rights of communities and future generations.	Examples include the right to a clean environment, the right to development, the right to peace, the right to self-determination, and the right to a healthy and sustainable environment for future generations.

Thematic studies

Debates also arise *between* the different generations of rights over whether a certain set of rights should be prioritized over another. Some governments, often in developing countries, assert that economic and social rights should be prioritized over civil and political rights. Some governments argue that civil-political rights may need to be sacrificed so that the economic and social rights can be (more fully) achieved. This becomes an issue because many United Nations (UN) documents assume human rights to be *indivisible*. The notion of **indivisible rights** refers to the idea that human rights are interconnected and interdependent. They cannot be fully achieved or protected in isolation from one another. These rights are considered *universal*, *inherent* and *inalienable*, and apply to all individuals regardless of their race, gender, religion, nationality or other characteristics. The concept of indivisible rights recognizes that these rights are interconnected and mutually reinforcing (where multiple factors support and strengthen one another), and that the full achievement of one right often depends on the protection and promotion of other rights.

The view that rights are universal is contentious. Some argue that rights are universal and apply to all individuals regardless of nationality, sex, ethnicity, gender or religion. They advocate for a global standard of rights that transcends cultural differences. Others assert that rights are culturally relative, shaped by local traditions and values, and that attempts to impose a universal standard may be culturally insensitive or even hegemonic.

> **TOK**: Why might it be useful to categorize different generations of human rights? What is gained from doing this? What might be lost or sacrificed when we categorize knowledge in ways like this?

> Human rights are thought to be universal, inherent and inalienable. They are interconnected and interdependent.

> In global politics, the term *hegemonic* refers to the dominance or leadership of one state or a group of states over others, exerting significant influence and power in shaping international relations and setting the agenda.

Case – Cultural relativism and LGBTQI+ rights

A real-world example of cultural relativism and human rights is the issue of LGBTQI+ rights. In many cultures and societies, diverse sexual orientations and gender identities are met with varying degrees of acceptance or discrimination. From a cultural relativist perspective, LGBTQI+ rights can be seen as conflicting with traditional norms, religious beliefs and societal values, leading to resistance or even persecution of LGBTQI+ individuals in some parts of the world. Cultural relativists argue that these attitudes should be respected and that imposing Western concepts of LGBTQI+ rights may undermine local cultural autonomy.

From a human rights viewpoint, LGBTQI+ rights are considered fundamental and universal. International human rights frameworks, such as the **Universal Declaration of Human Rights (UDHR)**, assert the rights to non-discrimination, equality and freedom of expression, which encompass LGBTQI+ rights. The clash between cultural relativism and LGBTQI+ rights can be seen in the varying legal frameworks, social acceptance and protection of LGBTQI+ individuals across different countries and cultures. This shows the challenges of balancing cultural diversity and the protection of human rights, particularly regarding marginalized groups. It also raises crucial questions about the universality of human rights and the role of cultural relativism in shaping social norms and policies.

The concept of justice

The meaning of justice is a highly contested and complex issue that involves differing perspectives, ideologies and interests among various actors, including states, IGOs and a range of NSAs. The concept of justice focuses on the idea of fairness and accountability. Its application in the context of global politics includes addressing issues such as inequality, human rights abuses, conflict resolution and **peacebuilding**, environmental sustainability and resource distribution at different levels of analysis.

Rights and justice

The contested nature of justice arises from differing views, the application of justice in global contexts and the challenges of achieving justice in an unfair global system.

Justice is a multidimensional concept. One area of contention is the application of justice in global contexts.

- *Retributive justice* focuses on punishment for wrongdoing and is often associated with legal systems. It involves holding individuals, businesses or states accountable for their actions through penalties or punishment.
- *Distributive justice* concerns the equal distribution of resources and involves making sure that goods and opportunities are shared fairly to reduce or eliminate inequalities and promote social welfare. Distributive justice seeks to achieve a more balanced and fair distribution of wealth, power and resources among actors in global politics. Gavi, the Vaccine Alliance, aims to distribute resources and healthcare interventions to low-income countries, addressing health inequalities and promoting distributive justice in global health.
- *Corrective justice* seeks to repair harm caused by wrongful actions and focuses on restoring the victim or affected parties to a state of justice via some form of compensation. Germany's reparations and apologies for the Holocaust can be seen as an attempt at corrective justice.
- *Procedural justice* emphasizes fair and transparent decision-making processes and dispute resolution. It involves making sure that the procedures used to determine outcomes are impartial and inclusive, and that actors in global politics have equal access to justice regardless of their status or power.
- *Restorative justice* involves repairing relationships and addressing the needs of victims, offenders and communities affected by wrongdoing. It is similar to corrective justice, but it differs in its focus on processes such as **mediation**, dialogue and **reconciliation** to promote healing, forgiveness and reintegration, and to prevent further harm or conflict. Tunisia's Truth and Dignity Commission (Instance Verité et Dignité, IVD) was established in 2014 to investigate and document human rights violations that occurred during 1955 to 2013 as part of the country's transitional justice process following the Arab Spring revolution in 2011.
- *Transitional justice* addresses past injustices and human rights abuses, especially in the aftermath of conflicts or authoritarian regimes. It is also related to corrective and restorative justice. Its focus is on peacebuilding mechanisms such as truth commissions, reparations and accountability measures to promote healing, reconciliation and the rule of law in societies transitioning from conflict or oppression to peace and democracy. Numerous countries have established **Truth and Reconciliation Commissions (TRCs)**, such as South Africa's post-apartheid commission, to address past human rights abuses and foster national healing during transitions to democracy.
- *Environmental justice* addresses environmental inequalities, especially the impacts of environmental degradation, pollution and climate change on vulnerable communities, often marginalized due to race, class or geography. It involves promoting equal access to environmental resources, protecting human rights and addressing environmental inequalities to ensure a fair and sustainable environment for all. The 2015 Paris Agreement, an international treaty adopted by nearly all states to combat climate change, was designed to promote greater environmental justice.

Reconciliation is the process of building or restoring amicable relations between nations, groups, or communities that have previously been in conflict or strife. This process often involves acknowledging past grievances, seeking justice and truth, fostering mutual understanding and respect, and creating a shared vision for a peaceful and cooperative future.

Thematic studies

States and IGOs often struggle with questions of justice. These struggles are practical in terms of how resources, benefits and burdens are allocated, but they are also philosophical in the sense of who gets to define what justice is. This results in opposing viewpoints on what creates a fair outcome. Disagreements may arise over responsibilities and costs related to global challenges like climate change, weapons of mass destruction, transnational crime, migration, cybersecurity and pandemics. Challenges related to achieving justice in a diverse and unbalanced global system add to the contested meanings of justice. Issues can be complex and controversial, with different political actors advocating for different approaches to achieve justice. States and other actors may prioritize their own interests, including national sovereignty, economic gains, moral image or geopolitical influence. This can clash with principles of justice.

> **HL**: Many of these forms of justice can be linked to different HL topic areas such as *Environment* and *Equality*.

Case – Climate justice

The climate crisis disproportionately affects vulnerable communities and countries, raising issues of climate justice. The more economically developed countries of the Global North, which have historically been the major contributors to greenhouse gas emissions, have been urged to take greater responsibility in assisting developing countries in the Global South to adapt to the impacts of climate change and transition to low-carbon economies. The debate revolves around how to fairly allocate responsibilities and resources to address the global consequences of the climate crisis. The Loss and Damage fund, agreed upon at COP27 and further discussed at COP28, represents a significant step towards climate justice as it seeks to address some of these inequities in climate impacts and responsibilities. The fund aims to provide financial assistance to developing countries most affected by the climate emergency, acknowledging that those who have contributed least to global warming are often the most impacted by global heating.

> **TOK**: How is *justice* defined in different societies and who gets to decide what is *just* in any particular situation or context? How do we decide when to trust such people?

The concept of liberty

Liberty is a multidimensional and contested concept.

Negative liberty is the absence of external constraints or interference with respect to people's enjoyment of their (human) rights. Negative freedom is often conceptualized as freedom *from* something – freedom from arbitrary/unjustified detention, from torture, from expropriation of private property (when the government takes away someone's personal belongings, land or assets without their consent or fair compensation). It is associated with first generation civil and political rights.

Positive liberty is the ability to follow one's own goals and aspirations. Positive freedom is the freedom *to* something, for example, the freedom to enjoy a certain standard of living (education, healthcare, infrastructure). It is often linked to second generation economic, social and cultural rights.

The distinction between these two forms of liberty is important in Global Politics because each promotes a different idea of what the proper role of the state is. Negative liberty's focus on the individual encourages a limited political, economic and social role for the state, one in which the state's only role is to ensure that discrimination does not occur, and that legal contracts are respected so that the marketplace runs smoothly. Positive liberty demands an active and interventionist state (where the government actively involves itself in economic and social affairs) if

> You will come across many examples where the term *freedom* rather than *liberty* is used. The two terms are normally used interchangeably (as they are in this book). If English is not your first language, this may not be surprising, as many other languages have only one word or term for freedom and liberty.

85

Rights and justice

> Despite the political implications that separating positive and negative liberty might have in many states around the world, freedom may consist of *freedom from something* and *freedom to do or become something.*

the rights of the most vulnerable within society are to be protected. Such intervention often takes the form of policies and actions aimed at regulating and influencing the functioning of the market and public welfare. One key area of debate in Global Politics is the scope of liberty. While many agree that liberty involves the freedom of individuals and/or groups to act and make choices without unjustified interference, there are differing views on the extent to which this freedom should be protected or limited. Debates may arise around issues such as individual rights, freedom of speech, freedom of association and privacy, with different actors advocating for varying levels of liberty depending on their ideological, cultural or political perspectives.

Activity

Think of some human rights that may require the state to ensure that both negative and positive freedoms are met. Write these down then share your thoughts with a peer.

There is also debate over the limits of liberty. Questions may arise about the boundaries of liberty in relation to other values or interests, such as security, public order or social cohesion. In many parts of the world, issues such as surveillance, censorship, counterterrorism measures and limits on migration are the focus of debate. Opinions differ on how far freedom should be restricted to pave the way for other objectives.

On a global level, the implications of liberty are also contested, with debates arising around issues such as human rights, the nature of the rules-based global order, democracy, governance models and the legitimate basis for international interventions. Political actors may have different perspectives on how liberty should be promoted, protected or balanced with other considerations in global governance, as well as what the role of liberty in shaping global norms, policies and institutions should be. Conflicting interests and power dynamics influence the contested meaning of liberty in global politics. We may think of liberty in the following ways:

- In a *geographical* sense as the freedom of states and/or peoples to make decisions within their borders without interference from external forces or actors. This form of liberty depends upon respect for the concept of Westphalian state sovereignty and the principle of non-interference in the internal affairs of other countries.
- *Political* liberty can be conceptualized as the freedom of states and other actors to participate in international decision-making processes and engage in diplomatic and political activities without coercion. It covers issues such as global governance, international law and the right to participate in international organizations and institutions.
- The principles of free trade, open markets and fair economic competition underpin the idea of *economic* liberty, which is also expressed in the context of the rights of states to access global resources and markets on equal terms.

States and NSAs often have different priorities and interests, such as national sovereignty, economic interests or cultural norms, which shape their perspectives on the meaning and application of liberty in the broader context of human rights. Ideological and cultural differences may also impact perceptions of liberty, with differing perspectives on the relationship between individual freedom and collective interests. This is another example of the contextual and contingent nature of global politics.

Thematic studies

Example – Surveillance and privacy rights

The balance between liberty and security is often challenged in the context of surveillance measures. Some argue that increased surveillance is necessary to ensure public safety and protect against potential threats, while others view such measures as an infringement on an individual's right to privacy and personal freedom. During the COVID-19 pandemic, some countries implemented cell phone tracking and contact tracing measures to curb the spread of the virus. These initiatives aimed to identify and notify individuals who came into contact with infected persons. Such measures also raised privacy concerns over the collection and use of personal data for public health purposes.

The concept of equality

Equality is another contentious and multifaceted issue that involves differing perspectives, ideologies and interests among various actors, including states and NSAs. The contested nature of equality also arises from differing views on the definition, scope and implementation of equality in the context of global governance and relations within and between states.

One key area of debate is the definition of equality. While there is broad agreement that equality includes the principle of treating all individuals and groups with fairness and impartiality, there are differing interpretations of what equality is in practice. Discussions of equality often highlight how it is an **intersectional** concept. When we use the term negatively, it is more accurate to speak of the *inequalities* that frequently feature in global politics. These debates usually center on the different forms of equality that exist, such as economic equality, legal equality, social equality, gender equality, racial equality and equality of opportunity, and also on how each form of equality may assist or hinder another as different political actors emphasize their own interpretations based on their ideological, cultural or political views.

The scope of equality is another area of contention. Questions may arise about:

- the *fields* in which equality should be pursued, such as political, economic, social or cultural
- the best *means* for promoting equality.

Debates may occur around issues such as income distribution, access to material and technological resources, education, healthcare and political representation, with differing opinions on how far equality should be extended in different spheres. Depending on the level of analysis, discussions centered on how best to implement and promote greater equality in global norms, policies and institutions may consider approaches such as affirmative action, preferential trading agreements, social policies geared toward marginalized groups and individuals, development assistance, and diversity and inclusion measures.

Conflicting interests and power dynamics also influence the degree to which the concept of equality is contested. States and other actors may have different priorities and interests that are shaped by state sovereignty, economic and political interests, or religious and cultural norms. These shape their outlook, particularly when they address the question of which forms of equality should be prioritized or whose equality matters most. Power imbalances and historical injustices may also impact

> Intersectionality is a framework for understanding how multiple aspects of an actor's social and political identities overlap and intersect, contributing to unique experiences of advantage and discrimination. This concept highlights that power structures and social inequalities are complex and interwoven, influencing how individuals and groups engage with and are affected by global political dynamics.

Rights and justice

perceptions of equality, with differing perspectives on how to address disparities and inequalities among different groups.

> ### Example – Disability rights and accessibility
> The rights of persons with disabilities to access services, infrastructure and opportunities can be a contentious issue. Some countries have implemented accessibility measures, while others lag behind in providing equal opportunities for people with disabilities. The Americans with Disabilities Act (ADA) is a civil rights law that prohibits discrimination against individuals with disabilities in all areas of public life. Brazil's National Policy for the Integral Health of Persons with Disabilities aims to improve access to healthcare services and assistive devices. However, challenges remain in remote or less populated areas, especially for those from disadvantaged backgrounds.

Rights, justice, liberty and equality: contested but interconnected and interdependent

Rights are inherent entitlements or claims that individuals possess, and they provide the foundation for justice, liberty and equality. Rights, at least in the Western interpretation, are based on the principle that all individuals are moral agents and so have inherent dignity and worth. Individual rights impose duties and obligations on others to respect and protect these rights. Without the recognition and protection of rights, individuals may be subjected to arbitrary/unjustified treatment, discrimination or oppression, which can damage justice, liberty and equality.

Justice involves the establishment of rules, laws and institutions that ensure that individuals are treated equally and their rights are protected. Justice requires that individuals be treated according to their merits, without discrimination or favoritism. In a fair society, individuals are held accountable for their actions, and their rights are balanced against the rights of others and the collective welfare of society. Without justice, there can be no true liberty or equality, as some individuals may be denied their rights or marginalized based on random criteria, such as race, ethnicity, gender, religion, class or social status.

Liberty is the principle of individual freedom and autonomy, which allows individuals to exercise their rights and make choices about their lives without undue interference from others or the state. Liberty involves the protection of individual rights, such as freedom of speech, religion, association and privacy, as well as the freedom to participate in public life and engage in social, economic and cultural activities. Liberty likely involves the recognition of diversity and pluralism with respect to beliefs, opinions and lifestyles. Without liberty, individuals may be coerced, oppressed or marginalized, and their rights may be restricted, which can undermine justice and equality.

At its heart, equality is centered on the principle of fairness. It recognizes that all humans are entitled to the same rights and opportunities, and that they should be treated with equal dignity, respect and consideration. Promoting greater equality means addressing **systemic inequalities** or **structural inequalities**, such as poverty, discrimination and marginalization, which hinder individuals from fully achieving their rights and potential. Without equality, some individuals may be excluded, disadvantaged or oppressed, and their rights may be violated, which can weaken justice, liberty and social cohesion.

The four concepts of rights, justice, liberty and equality can separately and together help inform any global political challenge you might wish to explore in the HL topic area Equality. Equality is central to rights and social justice.

Thematic studies

The concepts of rights, justice, liberty and equality are contested, and they are interconnected and mutually reinforcing. Together, they shape many of the norms, principles and institutions that help govern the relations between states and NSAs in the global system. Rights provide the foundation for justice, liberty and equality, as they establish the entitlements and claims that individuals possess. Justice ensures that rights are protected, and individuals are treated fairly and impartially. Liberty allows individuals to exercise their rights and make choices about their lives without undue interference. Equality promotes fairness and inclusivity and ensures that individuals are treated with equal dignity and respect. Understanding and navigating these interrelationships is crucial for addressing contemporary global political challenges and promoting a more just, equitable and inclusive global order.

TOK: If rights, justice, liberty, and equality are contested concepts, what methods do individuals and communities use to determine their meaning and application in different contexts?

Rights, justice, liberty and equality are interconnected and interdependent concepts. They are mutually reinforcing concepts.

Exercises

1. Define *rights* and *justice* and explain how concerns over rights and justice help shape global politics.
2. Explain why the meanings of rights, justice, liberty and equality are often contested in global politics. Your answer should identify factors that contribute to conflicts over the definitions, scope and implications of these concepts and outline how different perspectives shape the understanding of these concepts across time and across different regions of the world.
3. Identify the different generations of human rights and outline how they differ.
4. Explain how the concepts of rights, justice, liberty and equality are interconnected and mutually reinforcing.

The evolution from individual rights to *human* rights

Conceptual question

What are *human* rights and how did the international human rights regime take shape?

In the 21st century, we often think of individual rights and human rights as the same thing – all individuals by virtue of their humanity possess certain rights that need protecting or satisfying. This equating of individual rights with human rights has only existed since the end of the Second World War, with the creation of the Charter of the UN. Before that, certain individuals or groups asserted their own rights as fully developed moral and political agents but denied such rights to other humans. It was only with decolonization after the Second World War that the zone of application of individual rights came to include all of humanity, regardless of race, religion, gender, sexuality or creed. The habit of some texts to identify pre-1945 examples of global human rights should be critically analyzed. The anti-slavery movement, which began in the late 18th century, and which is often identified as one of the first global human rights movements, did not frame its arguments in the language of human rights. The Atlantic slave trade

The UN Charter was signed at the conclusion of the UN Conference on International Organization held in San Francisco. The signing took place on June 26, 1945, with representatives from each participating country signing the document. The UN Charter's Preamble begins with: 'We the Peoples of the United Nations.' This inclusive language reflects the commitment to the equal participation and representation of all nations and peoples within the UN.

89

Rights and justice

> **TOK**
> Why might there be a tendency for us to project present-day phenomena backward in time? How does recognizing the present in the past help support an argument or position now? How is the use of history in Global Politics similar or different to its use in other subjects you are studying?

was banned in some parts of the world in 1807, but slavery was not declared illegal at the same time and was only abolished in the Caribbean and the Americas in the latter half of the 19th century.[3] Even after slavery was abolished, previously enslaved individuals and their descendants struggled to gain full socio-economic (second generation) rights due to racism and other forms of discrimination, which is a battle that continues today.

We should be careful about finding human rights in places where their applicability and significance are not so clear cut. Many of the world's major religions, for example, Hinduism, Judaism, Buddhism, Christianity, Islam and Confucianism, affirm the dignity of individuals and outline people's responsibilities to other humans, but it is unclear whether any religion asserts the inalienable rights of humans to some universal standard of treatment or if these are just duties that the faithful must fulfill. There is also little clarity on who is responsible for protecting and enforcing these duties.

The concept of rights is contested and the same is true for human rights.

Human rights are a form of general, rather than special, rights. Special rights are conditional and emerge when people enter a special relationship, typically based on a contract or custom. Special rights are limited to those involved in a special transaction or relationship – the individuals who have the right as well as those who have the associated obligation to fulfill or protect that right.[4] An example of special rights would be those that arise out of a promise one makes to another person.

> Special rights are rights that arise within specific relationships, such as contracts or customs, and are contingent upon certain conditions, granting individuals or groups specific entitlements or privileges within that context.

General rights are held by individuals 'not because of some contract or custom but because they are said to constitute a particular kind of moral being.'[5] In the case of human rights, all humans qualify, at least theoretically, as moral beings and so are entitled to such rights. General individual rights are institutionally dependent, and their recognition and protection requires some institutional authority or entity.[6] With the collapse of empires as a legitimate form of international order in the period following the Second World War, peoples in former colonies turned to newly independent sovereign states as the institutional alternative to support human rights claims. As observers have pointed out, sovereign states have shown themselves to be suboptimal protectors of human rights, responsible for entrenched forms of sexual and/or racist discrimination, the suspension of political and civil liberties in the name of national security, and human rights violations. As International Relations scholar Barry Buzan has observed, 'the sovereign state stands as both the principal guarantor of individual security and the principal threat.'[7] This fact has driven the historical development of institutional norms and practices at the international level, which have sought to qualify the limits of legitimate sovereign authority.[8]

> The idea of human rights as the rights that we have simply by being human is the most common definition of human rights, but there are other schools of thought:
> - The deliberative perspective sees human rights as the set of political values that liberal societies choose to adopt. Human rights are the product of societal agreement. The adoption of the Universal Declaration of Human Rights by the United Nations in 1948 reflects a deliberative process where representatives from various nations came together to agree upon a set of fundamental rights and freedoms.
> - Another perspective sees human rights as the product of protest. They only exist because of social struggles on behalf of the vulnerable and marginalized in society. The civil rights movement in the USA, led by activists like Martin Luther King Jr, fought against racial segregation and discrimination, contributing to the recognition and advancement of civil and political rights for African Americans.

Thematic studies

- Another school of thought sees human rights as the product of narratives, where human rights only exist because people talk about them. The #MeToo movement, which gained momentum in recent years, highlighted the prevalence of sexual harassment and assault, sparking conversations and challenging societal norms regarding gender equality and women's rights.

Activity

Why might it matter whether we conceive of human rights as given, agreed upon, fought for or talked about? Discuss your thoughts with a classmate.

We are going to adopt John Vincent's definition of human rights as, 'the rights that everyone has, and everyone equally, by virtue of their very humanity.'[9] Possessing such rights entitles all humans to make claims against 'other individuals, national communities, and humanity as a whole for the respect and satisfaction of certain civil and political freedoms and social and economic needs.'[10] To this definition, we can add the language of the 1993 Vienna Declaration and Programme of Action, which declared all human rights as *universal, indivisible* and *interdependent and interrelated*. Sometimes, the term *inalienable* is added to this vision as some argue that human rights are fundamental to every individual and so essential that they cannot be taken away.

> Human rights are the rights that everyone possesses because they are human.

Activity

Translate the terms *human rights, universal, indivisible, interdependent* and *inalienable* into another language. Are any of these terms more difficult to translate? If so, why do you think this is the case? What might this tell us about the nature or position of human rights in different places/cultures? Discuss with a classmate.

The creation of the UN: human rights as an emerging international responsibility

Human rights, when properly codified and protected, are an essential part of an effective and fair justice system. It was only with the end of the Second World War that human rights as a political, rather than philosophical, project began to take shape with the creation of the UN. The world was a different place in 1945. For many of the leading states gathered in San Francisco to create the UN, human rights were not their top priority. Prior to the end of the Second World War, there had been some discussion between the USA, the UK, the Soviet Union and the PRC about including human rights in the Charter of what would become the UN. Of the four powers, only the USA and the PRC were initially in favour of doing so.[11]

The postwar position of the USA, the UK and the Soviet Union is not surprising, as most of them had significant human rights issues within their territories. In many of the southern states of the USA, racial discrimination and segregation were widespread, human rights violations also occurred in many of the British and French colonies, and repression took place in the Soviet Union.[12] The Cold War had begun, and the great powers were primarily concerned with this approaching struggle for global

Rights and justice

supremacy. This was not an environment favorable to prioritizing human rights over **realpolitik** (a political approach that prioritizes national interests over moral principles in making decisions and conducting foreign policy).

Before the Charter meeting was convened in San Francisco in 1945, Latin American states held a separate meeting to discuss the proposals that the leading powers had distributed. Through their efforts, together with those of Australia, New Zealand and France, and supported by a range of civil society actors, seven references to human rights were added to the UN Charter. Most notable are the second clause of the Preamble, which reaffirms the organization's 'faith in fundamental human rights [and] in the dignity and worth of the human person', and Articles 55 and 56, which committed member states to provide 'higher standards of living, full employment, and conditions of economic and social progress and development', and to promote 'universal respect for … human rights and fundamental freedoms for all without distinction as to race, sex, language, or religion.'[13] The Charter also commits UN member states to the principle of non-discrimination among nations and people, and so recognizes the close association between human rights and the concept of equality that has characterized the UN since it was created.[14] Popular forces, like civil society organizations and NGOs, along with small or middle powers have, right from the start, played a central role in helping to shape the modern human rights regime that we have today.[15] We should be alert to the dangers of uncritically adopting hegemonic accounts of how human rights emerged in the modern era. We should also be aware of how such dominant narratives may unfairly impact the ways in which we evaluate the nature and effectiveness of human rights today.

Despite the inclusion of human rights in the UN's founding document, civil society actors and smaller states did not entirely get their way. There were proposals at San Francisco to insert references to the promotion and protection of human rights in the Charter, but the leading powers opposed any inclusion of the second part of that phrase. This was likely because a written commitment of their part in protecting human rights around the world would have backfired as it could have been used to support those discriminated against or oppressed in the USA, the European colonies or the Soviet gulags (prison camps).[16]

So the Charter spoke only of the promotion of human rights, a fact that would frame the evolution of global human rights norms and their related machinery in the decades following 1945.[17]

The Universal Declaration of Human Rights

The Universal Declaration of Human Rights (UDHR) was adopted by the UN General Assembly on December 10, 1948 as an elaboration and codification of the principles of human rights outlined in the UN Charter.

The horrors of the Nazi Holocaust are usually cited as the driving force behind international action to create an international declaration of human rights, but momentum for such a declaration had been building since the early 20th century. In the West and elsewhere, intellectual interest in the notion of rights, but particularly women's rights and minority rights, was clear.[18] The International Federation of Human Rights was founded in Paris in 1922 and, by the end of the decade, it was calling for an international declaration of rights. In 1941, US President Franklin D. Roosevelt gave his 'Four Freedoms' speech to Congress in which he proclaimed four essential human freedoms, references

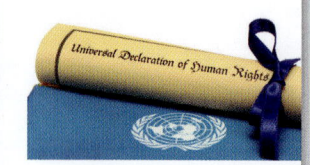

Thematic studies

to which were embedded in the Atlantic Charter that he and British Prime Minister Winston Churchill signed later the same year.[19] Roosevelt directed the US State Department to begin exploring the possibility of an international bill of human rights as part of its postwar planning. The Holocaust served as a reminder of the need to protect human rights in the postwar world, but other terrible experiences also shaped the minds of those who participated in the drafting of the UDHR. The bombing of Guernica during the Spanish Civil War (1936–39) was deeply felt by many Latin Americans, while the Nanjing massacre had seen approximately 200,000 Chinese murdered by the invading Japanese Imperial Army in 1937. Pakistan and India were waging war over Jammu and Kashmir, while tensions were widespread in Palestine between Zionist groups and Palestinian Arabs. Lynchings of African Americans and Native Americans in the USA were common, repression in the Soviet Union was extensive, and large parts of the world continued to suffer under colonial rule. There were a wide range of terrible experiences that the drafters of the UDHR could draw upon.[20]

The standard account of the drafting of the UDHR is that it was a Western political project. One of the most common arguments against the universality of international human rights norms is the lack of postcolonial involvement in negotiating the principal instruments (declarations, treaties, covenants, conventions, etc.) of the modern international human rights regime, beginning with the UDHR. As Christian Reus-Smit notes, 'the conventional narrative highlights … the critical role of Western liberal powers, constrained and cajoled by the Soviet bloc with its emphasis on social and economic rights. Yet although this narrative has assumed the status of common wisdom, it is strikingly at odds with the historical record.'[21]

Over the course of the two years during which it was negotiated (1946–48), the drafting of the UDHR was a complicated public process, involving the input and efforts of many people. During the initial 18-month phase of negotiation, a drafting committee of eight states, and then the 18-member UN Human Rights Commission, along with additional input from NGOs and states not represented in the Commission, discussed, debated and amended the text. Smaller powers and developing countries were active participants in the drafting process and frequently rejected the efforts of the great powers to limit debate and move quickly.[22]

By May 1948, when the final draft was referred to the UN General Assembly's Third Committee, which deals with human rights, humanitarian affairs and social matters, 85 sessions had been devoted to its discussion. In daily sessions over a two-month period, committee delegates looked over each Article one by one, proposing and debating amendments. The text was referred to the General Assembly for another round of speeches, debates and amendments, before the final vote on December 10, 1948.[23] Although it is not a legally binding document under international law, the influence of the UDHR has been considerable. Liberal analyses would point out that the language and provisions of the UDHR have found their way into the national constitutions of several states and it has been referenced as the basis for judgments made in national and international courts. Furthermore, UN member states have come to, 'acknowledge that the Declaration … does contain actual human rights obligations.'[24]

Without the input of smaller, developing states, the final form and content of the UDHR would likely have been very different. Leading powers, such as the USA, wanted a more inspirational and limited document, with fewer Articles. However, smaller states were instrumental in making sure that socio-economic rights were included

---

The Holocaust and other experiences of gross human rights violations were important factors in the creation of the UDHR.

Eleanor Roosevelt is often singled out as the driving force behind the creation of the UDHR, but her role is both overstated and underappreciated. With quiet yet forceful diplomacy, she steered the debate and moved it along during the critical early phase of the project. It is possible that without her efforts to create the diplomatic momentum that led to its creation the UDHR would not exist, especially given the Cold War tensions that were beginning to surface. However, she did not contribute to writing any part of the document.

Rights and justice

> The creation of the UDHR was a long and deliberate process that involved significant contributions from a range of states, including many smaller, non-Western powers.

in the UDHR.[25] It is also likely that it would have been a more gendered document. It is largely due to the persistence of Hansa Mehta, the Indian delegate, that initial references to 'all men' being created equal were replaced in the final text of the UDHR with the phrase 'All human beings are born free and equal.' Given the leading position of Western colonial powers at the time, it is highly unlikely that the UDHR would have contained condemnation of all forms of discrimination or its commitment to universality.[26] Many of the small states and developing countries attending the early sessions of the UN saw in the concept of human rights the opportunity to delegitimize colonial possessions by attaching, 'the right to self-determination on to emergent international human rights norms, casting it as a necessary precondition for the satisfaction of individuals' civil and political rights.'[27] These states would also play a crucial role in the next phase of the emerging international human rights regime.

The internationalization of human rights and the humanization of international law

The UN's next step following the adoption of the UDHR was to create a single, legally binding treaty to cover all categories of human rights and measures for implementation. Ideological conflict between the Western and Communist blocs meant that the UN Human Rights Commission was asked to draft two separate legally binding documents, each of which would codify different broad categories of rights. On December 16, 1966, the UN General Assembly adopted the International Covenant on Civil and Political Rights (ICCPR) and the International Covenant on Economic, Social and Cultural Rights (ICESCR). States could choose which, if either, of these treaties to sign and ratify.

> The UDHR is *not* an international human rights law or treaty. While UN member states may have signed the UDHR, it was not subject to processes of ratification by relevant national (domestic) authorities and so it is not a legally binding human rights document or instrument.

The ICCPR covers many first generation human rights, including rights to life, liberty and a fair trial, and freedoms of conscience, movement and peaceful assembly. It also prohibits torture, discrimination, arbitrary arrest and a range of cruel or inhuman treatment. The ICESCR safeguards many second generation human rights in areas including education, food, housing and healthcare. It also includes the right to work and labor protections. Parties to this treaty agreed to 'take steps for the progressive realization of Covenant rights to the full extent of that state's available resources.'[28] Both Covenants came into force in 1976 and, together with the UDHR, form what is known as the **International Bill of Rights**.

> First and second generation human rights can be linked to the HL topic areas *Health* and *Poverty*. The latter is supposed to guarantee access to adequate healthcare as a basic human right, while civil or political liberties may be restricted in the event of an epidemic or pandemic. Both generations of rights aim to tackle some of the inequalities that create various forms of poverty around the world.

Just as they did in the drafting of the UDHR, leading developing states from Asia and Latin America, such as Chile, India, Mexico and Peru, played an important role in the development of both Covenants and often led the way in promoting the universal application of international human rights norms.[29] They also worked to strengthen the enforcement measures contained within the Covenants, arguing that 'the protection of human rights was an international concern which limited the domestic jurisdiction [sovereignty] of states.'[30] There was even an attempt by postcolonial states to broaden the scope of the Covenants by having them recognize the right of individuals and NSAs to have direct access to the UN when their state engaged in human rights violations. In 1953, a **coalition** of small Western and postcolonial states pushed to have this right included in the ICCPR, arguing in the UN Third Committee that 'without the inclusion of provisions extending the right of petition to individuals, groups, and non-governmental organizations, the whole value of the covenants would be in question.'[31] Ultimately, they were unsuccessful in overcoming the opposition of the Soviet bloc countries, who opposed all implementation measures because they

Thematic studies

violated the sovereign right of a state to non-interference in its domestic matters, and the USA and the UK, who argued that only states should have the right to access the UN. A compromise was reached, with a separate Optional Protocol to the ICCPR, proposed by Lebanon and drafted by Nigeria, allowing individuals experiencing human rights violations in states that have signed it to petition the UN Human Rights Committee. Regardless of their subsequent human rights records, it is unlikely that this option would exist without the efforts of these smaller powers.

Christian Reus-Smit argues that the strong support for universal human rights demonstrated by many postcolonial states (as well as colonial elites fighting for independence) during 1948 to 1960 should be viewed as part of efforts to broaden the principle that 'all peoples have the right to self-determination.'[32] Rather than basing this right on the presence of racially pure or ethnically homogenous groups, the pursuit of which had been morally and politically shattered by Nazism, the era of decolonization saw self-determination being described by postcolonial elites as 'a necessary prerequisite for the satisfaction of individuals' basic political and economic rights.'[33] This connection between human rights and the right to self-determination stretches back to the initial negotiations on the two Covenants, when some postcolonial states called for the UN General Assembly to insert an article guaranteeing the right to self-determination into the draft Covenants, arguing that, 'No basic human rights could be ensured unless this right were ensured …'.[34] These moves were opposed by the colonial powers with the support of other Western states, including the USA, but the right to self-determination was eventually included in the opening Articles of both International Covenants. This signaled its status as a necessity for the realization of fundamental human rights.[35] Attaching the right of self-determination to emerging human rights norms helped shape ideals of what made a state legitimate with 'human rights increasingly provid[ing] the justificatory foundations for sovereignty.'[36] It is true that many postcolonial states later rejected international efforts to inspect their human rights practices, but it is equally true that many of these states played a central role in expanding the rights contained within the UDHR and the Covenants.

In addition to the Covenants, the UN identifies another seven instruments or treaties that it considers core to the international human rights regime (Table 2.2). For each of these core treaties, the UN has created a panel of independent experts (known as a treaty body) that is responsible for monitoring the implementation of the treaty by those nation-states that have endorsed it.

> Self-determination refers to the right of a people or nation to decide their own political status and govern themselves, often in the context of seeking independence, autonomy, or the establishment of a new state. This concept is integral to issues of sovereignty, national identity, and the rights of ethnic, cultural, or regional groups within the international system.

HL Look at the human rights treaties in Table 2.2 and notice how many of them are identity-based, reflecting how different forms of identity have often been the basis for widespread discrimination and human rights violations. There are strong links between the HL topic area *Identity* and this chapter on rights and justice.

Freedom House is an NGO that conducts research and advocacy to promote democracy, human rights and political freedom around the world, producing reports and indices that assess the state of civil liberties and political rights in different countries.

Case – Have human rights laws and treaties failed?

Even though there are many regional and international human rights treaties and institutions, human rights violations continue. Between 2009 and 2013, Amnesty International (AI) received reports of torture in 141 states, even though 173 states have agreed to the Convention against Torture.[37] At the moment, 173 states are party to the ICCPR, which has been in force for nearly 50 years and yet, according to Freedom House, only 84 states are currently classified as 'free'.[38] However, accusations that human rights treaties have failed may be inaccurate. In a conceptual sense, the goals of international human rights institutions are transformative and aspirational. Perhaps their success should not be determined by the persistence of human rights violations.

Rights and justice

Table 2.2 Additional core UN human rights instruments*

Human Rights Treaty[39]	Opened for Ratification	Entered into Force	Ratifications (as of 2023)	Focus of the Treaty
International Convention on the Elimination of All Forms of Racial Discrimination (ICERD)	1966	1969	182	Prohibits any distinction, preference or exclusion based on race, color, descent or national or ethnic origin that impairs the equal enjoyment of human rights and freedoms in any field of public life.
Convention on the Elimination of All Forms of Discrimination Against Women (CEDAW)	1971	1981	189	Designed to ensure that women have equal access in all fields of public life by eliminating all practices that are based on the idea of the inferiority of women.
Convention against Torture and Other Cruel, Inhuman or Degrading Treatment or Punishment (CAT)	1984	1987	173	States must take measures to prevent torture from occurring within their jurisdiction. Includes the duty to protect all humans (not just a state's own citizens) from torture.
Convention on the Rights of the Child (CRD)	1989	1990	196	Seeks to protect children from practices that threaten their welfare, including economic exploitation, trafficking and all forms of sexual abuse.
Convention on the Protection of the Rights of All Migrant Workers and their Families (CRMW)	1990	2003	58	Recognizes the close connection between migration and human rights and seeks to foster respect for migrant workers by requiring states to guarantee the same working conditions for migrants as those enjoyed by citizens.
International Convention on the Rights of Persons with Disabilities (CRPD)	2007	2008	186	Protects the rights of individuals with disabilities to make their own decisions in a range of areas. States are also obliged to eliminate any discrimination based on disability by any person, business or organization.
International Convention for the Protection of All Persons from Enforced Disappearance (ICPPED)	2006	2010	71	Prohibits the detention or any other denial of liberty by state actors or others acting under state authorization or acquiescence. Prohibits the concealment of disappeared persons (their fate and/or whereabouts).

There is evidence that some human rights treaties have made a difference at the national level. Examples include Chile and Argentina citing human rights treaties to overturn military self-amnesties for mass atrocities. Kenya referenced the Convention on the Elimination of All Forms of Discrimination Against Women (CEDAW) to grant women equal access to inheritances, and the EU Convention on Human Rights led Ireland to decriminalize homosexual acts. Human rights laws and treaties are a tool for individuals

Thematic studies

and domestic NGOs to hold their own governments to account, as well as a base from which they can partner with INGOs, like Human Rights Watch, to generate pressure on their government to respect any treaties that they have signed and ratified.

Human rights norms have been codified and institutionalized in a series of parallel developments at the regional and national levels. Sovereign states can ignore international human rights laws if they wish, but several states around the world have sought to incorporate (parts of) international human rights conventions into their domestic legislation, giving it the force of law within the sovereign territory of that state. Liberal analyses would point to how such norms have become 'deeply embedded in constitutional and other forms of domestic and regional law in almost every nation around the world.'[40] Canada's Youth Criminal Justice Act (2003) references parts of the UN Convention on the Rights of the Child, which Canada is a party to. Similar steps are being taken in New Zealand and Australia to write parts of the legally non-binding United Nations Declaration on the Rights of Indigenous Peoples (2007) into domestic law. Some states have even incorporated human rights provisions into their constitutions. The best examples are the South African constitution and Argentina's 1994 constitution, which provides nine international human rights treaties with constitutional standing.

There has also been codification of human rights at the regional level, although there is variation in terms of the content and scope of regional human rights systems. The European Convention on Human Rights (ECHR) was drafted in 1950 and came into force in 1953. The ECHR, whose parties include all 46 member states in the Council of Europe, prioritizes civil-political rights. Economic, social and cultural rights are not recognized as rights in this treaty but exist only as aspirations for parties to achieve. The American Convention on Human Rights followed in 1969, coming into force in 1978. Twenty-four Latin American and Caribbean states are party (signatories) to the Convention. Its initial focus was on first generation civil and political rights. However, to elevate the Inter-American human rights system by protecting second generation economic, social and cultural rights, an Additional Protocol (the Protocol of San Salvador) was drafted in 1988 and came into force in 1999. The Protocol includes provisions that cover rights to work, to health, to food and to education.[41]

The Organization of African Unity, which has since become the African Union (AU), sought to create a regional human rights system for Africa. The result was the African Charter on Human and People's Rights (also known as the Banjul Charter), which opened for signature in 1981 and came into force in 1986. The Banjul Charter acknowledged economic, social and cultural rights alongside civil-political rights, and it also recognized third generation collective or group rights in ways not seen in the European or Inter-American regional human rights institutions (this is the reference to 'Peoples'). Article 22 acknowledges the right to development, while Article 24 recognizes the right to 'a generally satisfactory environment.' In addition to outlining the rights of individuals and peoples, the Charter references in Article 29 the duties that people have, which include 'Not to compromise the security of the State', 'To preserve and strengthen social and national solidarity' and 'To preserve and strengthen positive African cultural values …'

Meanwhile, the Cairo Declaration on Human Rights in Islam was adopted in 1990 and revised in 2020 by the Organization of Islamic Cooperation (OIC), an IGO

You can look at the Office of the High Commissioner for Human Rights (OHCHR) page for an interactive Status of Ratification map.

The OHCHR has identified 18 human rights treaties, and this map shows how many and which of the 18 each state has ratified. What do you notice when you look at the map?

Rights and justice

that claims to be the collective voice of the Muslim world.[42] The Cairo Declaration is seen as an Islamic response to the UDHR and provides an overview of the Islamic perspective on human rights. The Cairo Declaration guarantees some of the rights contained within the UDHR, but it acknowledges the superiority of Sharia law.[43] Because of this, the Cairo Declaration has been criticized for failing to guarantee fundamental rights and freedoms, particularly with respect to women and non-Muslims. In 2004, the Council of the League of Arab States adopted the Arab Charter on Human Rights (ACHR), which affirmed the principles contained within the UN Charter, the UDHR, the ICCPR, ICESCR and the Cairo Declaration. Although the ACHR includes provisions covering several traditional and broadly accepted human rights (the right to liberty and personal security, the right to due process and freedom from torture), it has been criticized for establishing human rights standards that fall short of those recognized internationally. In 2008, the UN High Commissioner for Human Rights, Louise Arbour, asserted that several of its provisions were incompatible with the UN's interpretation of universal human rights, particularly those covering women's and children's rights.

The most recent regional articulation of human rights is the Association of Southeast Asian Nations (ASEAN) Human Rights Declaration (2012). The Declaration reaffirms the UDHR's civil and political rights as well as its economic, social and cultural rights. Where it differs is in the degree of detail it offers when defining who holds these rights, specifically emphasizing that human rights belong to 'women, children, the elderly, persons with disabilities, migrant workers, and vulnerable and marginalized groups.' Like the Banjul Charter, the ASEAN Human Rights Declaration goes beyond the UDHR by making explicit the right to an adequate standard of living, which includes 'the right to safe drinking water and sanitation' (Art. 28), protection from discrimination in treatment for 'people suffering from communicable diseases, including HIV/AIDS' (Art. 29), the right to development aimed at poverty alleviation and 'the creation of conditions including the protection and sustainability of the environment …' (Art. 35 and Art. 36), and the right to peace (Art. 38). While the UN High Commissioner for Human Rights welcomed the Declaration and ASEAN's renewed commitment to universal human rights norms, there was also criticism that references to the concept of **cultural relativism** in the Declaration could potentially see human rights undermined in Southeast Asia. Article 7 notes that 'the realization of human rights must be considered in the regional and national context' and Article 8 states that human rights might be restricted if 'national security' or 'public morality' are perceived to be under threat.

> Declarations are not binding in international law, but charters, conventions, statutes and treaties are legally binding.

> Links can be made to the HL topic areas *Identity* and *Environment*. More recent regional articulations of human rights emphasize specific identity-based groups of individuals whose rights need to be protected. There are also references to protecting the environment as a fundamental human right to be enjoyed by all.

Activity

Think about the following statement: *The evolution of human rights since 1948 has undermined the effectiveness of the Universal Declaration of Human Rights.* Come up with as many arguments for and against this statement as you can. Each argument should be supported by a contemporary real-world example. Be prepared to share your arguments with your peers.

Thematic studies

Universal jurisdiction and the responsibility to protect doctrine

Sovereignty should not be seen as an absolute principle. Two relatively recent developments in the way rights and justice are thought about show how the sovereignty of a state may be qualified: universal jurisdiction and the **responsibility to protect (R2P)**.

Universal jurisdiction is the principle that allows national courts in any country to exercise jurisdiction over individuals accused of serious international crimes, such as torture, slavery, crimes against humanity, genocide and piracy, regardless of where the crimes were committed or the nationality of the perpetrator. The origins of universal jurisdiction can be traced back to the ancient Romans, but it was only with the Nuremberg and Tokyo trials after the Second World War that the concept gained recognition in international law. These tribunals established that individuals could be held accountable for egregious human rights violations no matter where they were committed.

Universal jurisdiction gained further momentum after the Cold War with the creation of international criminal tribunals, such as the International Criminal Tribunal for the former Yugoslavia (ICTY) and the International Criminal Tribunal for Rwanda (ICTR) in the early 1990s. These tribunals were established to prosecute individuals responsible for atrocities committed during the conflicts in Rwanda and the former Yugoslavia. Since then, a number of countries have adopted laws allowing for the prosecution of individuals for serious international crimes committed abroad, regardless of the nationality of the perpetrator or the victim.[44] These laws have been used to bring to justice individuals accused of crimes such as torture, genocide and war crimes.

Case – Universal jurisdiction in practice

Examples of universal jurisdiction include the 2003 arrest of former Liberian president Charles Taylor in Sierra Leone for war crimes and crimes against humanity, and the conviction in 2007 of the former Argentine naval officer, Adolfo Scilingo, for crimes against humanity. More recent cases include the 2016 conviction of the former dictator of Chad, Hissène Habré, in Senegal for crimes against humanity, the 2021 conviction in a German court of an Iraqi former Islamic State in Iraq and Syria (ISIS) member for his enslavement and abuse of a Yazidi woman and the death of her five-year old daughter, and the declaration in July 2022 that 11 European countries intended starting investigations of alleged war crimes committed during the Russian invasion of Ukraine.

The use of universal jurisdiction has been controversial, with some countries expressing concerns over the potential for politically motivated prosecutions. Former US Secretary of State Henry Kissinger argued that universal sovereignty was an unjustifiable breach of state sovereignty and in conflict with the UN Charter's declaration of 'all states being equal in sovereignty.' Kissinger, who was called to provide testimony in a Spanish court about the US government's role in a covert

---

Many regions of the world have created their own human rights documents. Most take the UDHR and other UN instruments as their starting point, although there is variation between the documents each region has produced.

The Nuremberg and Tokyo war trials were post-Second World War international tribunals held to prosecute individuals responsible for war crimes, crimes against humanity and other atrocities committed during the war. The Nuremberg Trials, held in Nuremberg, Germany, from 1945 to 1946, focused on prosecuting high-ranking Nazi officials. The Tokyo Trials, held in Tokyo, Japan, from 1946 to 1948, sought to bring Japanese war criminals to justice. Both trials set precedents in international law, establishing the principle of individual accountability for gross violations of human rights, and serving as milestones in the development of modern international criminal justice.

HL Given the ways in which universal jurisdiction and responsibility to protect both challenge absolute notions of state sovereignty, there are strong links that can be made between these concepts and the HL topic area *Borders*.

Rights and justice

campaign of political repression and state terror implemented by right-wing South American governments in the late 20th century, equated universal jurisdiction with universal judicial tyranny. According to him, since any state could establish a universal jurisdiction tribunal, there was the risk that human rights would be politicized and that the process would descend into politically driven show trials. The evolution of universal jurisdiction in global politics reflects a growing recognition of the need to hold individuals accountable for serious human rights abuses and violations, but it is unsurprising that, in recent years, there have been calls for greater clarity and consistency in its application.

A different but related concept is the responsibility to protect (R2P). The practice of **humanitarian intervention** predates the 20th century, but it is only since the end of the Second World War and the development of the modern international human rights regime that we see a more formal recognition that all humans deserve protection. Ideally, it is the sovereign state that bears central responsibility for the protection of its people. Many postcolonial states connected the right to self-determination to the international human rights norms that emerged in the immediate postwar world. However, a series of humanitarian crises in the 1990s in Somalia, Rwanda, Darfur (Sudan) and Kosovo (Yugoslavia) led the International Commission on Intervention and State Sovereignty (an *ad hoc* grouping composed of scholars, senior international officials and Canadian government personnel) to change the narrative around humanitarian intervention in global politics.[45]

> The fact that states have justified military interventions on humanitarian grounds for centuries shows that the Westphalian view of state sovereignty is problematic.

The report the Commission produced in 2001 built upon pre-existing narratives that asserted that the protection of human rights was the basis for legitimate statehood. If a state's sovereignty depends upon its responsibility to protect its citizens, then it follows that, if a state cannot or is unwilling to fulfill this responsibility, the social contract between the ruler and the ruled is void and the state's claim to sovereignty is illegitimate. In such cases, and when there are violations of human rights, it becomes the responsibility of the international community to intervene, and to use military force as a last resort. This is R2P's foundation argument, which was reaffirmed in 2006 by a UN Security Council Resolution and committed the Security Council to take action to protect civilian populations from genocide, war crimes, ethnic cleansing and crimes against humanity.

The responsibility to protect continues to be questioned and challenged. The application of R2P has been problematic and it is subject to reasonable criticism for not being effectively supported. As Roberto Belloni states, 'moral decisions with weak sanctions are the worst policy.'[46] Instead of being something that protects human rights, R2P has been reduced to a morally powerful, yet ineffectual, doctrine. The international community (the UN, NATO and the Arab League) endorsed military action against the Libyan dictator, Colonel Muammar Qaddafi in 2011 when he threatened 'rivers of blood' in opposition strongholds, but stood by when the Syrian regime of Bashar al-Assad committed mass atrocities against its own people in the same year. Such inconsistencies gave rise to perceptions that R2P was invoked selectively, based on the strategic or national interests of other states. In the pursuit of geopolitical goals, states may politicize or weaponize human rights by using them as a pretext for military intervention or sanctions. This weaponization of rights can have far-reaching consequences, leading to human suffering and regional instability, and exacerbating existing conflict. The USA in 2003, and Russia in 2014 and 2022, utilized versions of R2P to justify their respective invasions of Iraq and Ukraine.

Protest by Libyan nationals against their rulers.

Thematic studies

> **Activity**
>
> R2P raises questions of scale and authorization. How bad do human rights violations have to be before R2P is triggered? Who decides when to respond to such violations? Why are some violations ignored while others are not? Share your answers with a classmate.

The politicization of human rights occurs when states or other actors use the rhetoric of rights to advance their political agenda. Powerful states may denounce rights violations in some countries while overlooking abuses committed by their allies. This inconsistency erodes the credibility of human rights as universal norms and undermines the legitimacy of interventions aimed at protecting rights. Given the historical experiences of many postcolonial and Global South states, they often distrust countries in the Global North whenever they justify their interventions on humanitarian grounds. Russia has consistently demanded that only humanitarian interventions authorized by the UN Security Council are legitimate, giving Russia the final say over any such action thanks to their veto power. However, not all interventions under R2P are sanctioned by the Security Council. In 1999, when Western countries sought UN authorization for a military intervention in Kosovo to protect ethnic Albanians from ethnic cleansing by Yugoslav forces, Russia opposed this step. Western powers sidestepped Russia and approached NATO instead. Since then, national interests have repeatedly shaped the issue. The most recent example of this is in Syria, where despite international outrage after the massacre of civilians by Syrian security forces in 2012, opposition in the Security Council meant that no UN-authorized military intervention could be sent to protect the human rights of ordinary Syrians from violations committed by their own government.

There is still support for R2P as a developing norm, although it remains stuck in controversy, especially given its selective use by great powers and the tendency for human rights to be politicized by actors and stakeholders in global politics. While some argue that external intervention is necessary to protect populations from gross violations of rights and crimes against humanity, others emphasize the principle of non-interference in internal affairs. The search continues for an acceptable balance between the principle of respecting a country's sovereignty and when intervention and the use of force might be justified to protect human rights.

HL — Human rights violations can be viewed as attacks on individuals' and groups' fundamental sense of security. There are clear links between the topics discussed here and the HL topic area *Security*.

The politicization of human rights refers to the process by which human rights issues are used as tools for political agendas, often leading to selective enforcement or double standards based on strategic interests rather than universal principles.

> **Exercises**
>
> 5. Suggest some reasons why pre-1945 examples of global human rights should be critically evaluated.
> 6. Explain why the UDHR is considered a key human rights document of the modern era.
> 7. Outline the ICCPR and the ICESCR, and explain what categories of rights they codify.
> 8. Identify some examples of regional human rights systems and outline how they differ in terms of content and scope.

Rights and justice

9. Define universal jurisdiction and identify some potential drawbacks or controversies associated with its use.

10. Define R2P and explain how it relates to humanitarian intervention.

11. Explain some of the ways in which human rights might be politicized in global politics.

The role of actors and stakeholders

Conceptual question

Which actors and stakeholders are best positioned to protect human rights and how can they do so?

We have looked at the role of the UN in setting human rights standards and spreading human rights norms. The UN Charter affirmed the importance of human rights, and subsequent covenants and conventions defined specific obligations for parties to meet. However, the principle of state sovereignty still framed what was possible, as acknowledged by the Charter itself.[47] This tension between promoting and protecting human rights, especially those of the most vulnerable and marginalized, and the need to uphold the twin principles of state sovereignty and non-interference has meant that the UN has often been constrained in its attempts to respond effectively to violations of human rights and perceived injustices. So which actors and stakeholders might be better at protecting human rights and how can they do so?

States

The principle of sovereignty and, in particular, the Westphalian conceptualization of sovereignty asserts that states are responsible for protecting and enforcing human rights standards within their territorial boundaries. Some states have referenced international human rights norms in domestic legislation and their constitution. Many liberal democratic states in the Global North have based their human rights practices on political and civil liberties, with the constitutions of many North American and European democracies emphasizing freedom of speech, freedom of conscience and due process of law. These states have also attempted to internationalize these principles by including references to human rights in their foreign policy. A key part of the process of joining the EU is that a candidate country must demonstrate significant progress toward improving political and civil liberties before they will be admitted. Many of the world's most important trading states, including Canada, the EU and Brazil, insert human rights language in their Preferential Trade Agreements (PTAs). Some European social welfare states like Germany and Sweden seek to protect economic and social rights in addition to civil and political rights because societies in these states believe that their governments have a responsibility to ensure access to necessities such as free education and affordable healthcare.

There are several tools that states can use to promote and protect human rights around the world. They can use economic incentives to try to improve human rights, often by making other benefits dependent on improvements in a state's human rights policies and practices. The USA and European states frequently tie aid and foreign assistance to better human rights policies and practices. Since 1976, the US State Department has produced annual Country Reports on Human Rights Practices for every country receiving US assistance and all UN member states (except for the USA), which cover civil, political and worker rights recognized by the UDHR. Together with reports from leading INGOs such as Amnesty International (AI) and Human Rights Watch, these are used by the US government to determine whether a country should receive foreign aid and how close a relationship it should have with them. However, strategic or political interests may override any human rights concerns that donor countries may have. An example of where strategic or political interests may override human rights concerns is the relationship between several Western countries and Saudi Arabia. Despite concerns over Saudi Arabia's human rights record, many Western nations maintain close diplomatic, economic and military ties with the country due to its significant oil reserves, geopolitical influence in the Middle East, and cooperation in regional security matters.

The use of **sanctions** is another hard power tool that states can use to punish other states' violations of human rights and modify behavior. In 2022, the US government sanctioned 17 Iranian law enforcement, prison and government officials for their role in the crackdown against protests sparked by the death of Mahsa Amini. In 2023, it targeted several entities in Myanmar, Nicaragua and Russia for enabling or engaging in human rights abuses. The EU has signaled its determination to support human rights and to punish those responsible for abuses by imposing restrictive measures on individuals and entities responsible for serious human rights violations around the world under its Global Human Rights Sanctions Regime established in 2020. In 2021, the EU sanctioned several individuals and entities responsible for serious human rights abuses and violations. Restrictive measures included an asset freeze in the EU, an EU travel ban, and prohibiting individuals or entities in the EU from financial dealings with any of the listed actors.

Case – Sanctions and counter-sanctions

The effectiveness of sanctions as a means of improving human rights in another country is contested. Imposing economic sanctions on a country frequently harms ordinary people more than the government or political elites accused of human rights abuses and violations. This means that sanctions often make the human rights situation in a country worse. Sanctioned states generally see such actions as interference in their domestic affairs and a breach of sovereignty. Depending on the state, they may retaliate with sanctions of their own, as Russia did in April 2022 with a set of counter-sanctions against 'unfriendly states', including every state that had imposed sanctions on Russia.

States can also intervene more directly in the case of extreme human rights violations, like genocide or ethnic cleansing, under the R2P doctrine. These interventions are even more controversial than the use of economic incentives and sanctions as a means to protect human rights. The main reason is that it is difficult to separate a state's strategic interests in intervening from a genuine desire to protect human rights. States may use the rhetoric of protecting human rights or responding to human rights violations when their true motivation for using force may be self-serving or otherwise not about protecting human rights.

Rights and justice

The sovereign state may be the principal protector of human rights, but it is also often the main violator of these rights. Regime type, level of development and real or perceived threats to the security of the state can be reasons for states being unwilling or unable to combat human rights abuses and violations. Authoritarian or autocratic regimes are more likely to violate civil and political rights such as freedom of expression, freedom of assembly and the right to a fair trial. Less developed states may be unable to fulfill social and economic rights due to a lack of resources.

> ### Activity
>
> Work in a group of three or four. Discuss the following questions:
> - How do you define *development* in the context of a country's progress and growth?
> - What are some key human rights that countries should protect and enforce for the well-being of their citizens?
> - How might development and the protection of human rights be interconnected?
> - Can economic progress positively impact a state's ability to protect and enforce human rights? How?
> - What are some potential challenges that a developing country might face in upholding human rights?
>
> Choose a country and do some research on it. This could be the country that you are living in, you identify with or you are interested in. The research should include information about the country's level of development, social indicators and human rights issues. Analyze the data to identify possible links between development and human rights, as well as any other factors influencing the state's capacity to protect and enforce human rights. Be prepared to share your findings and thinking with the rest of the class.

When threatened with civil unrest or terrorist attacks, states may take measures that prioritize the security of the state over individual or human rights. Article 4 of the ICCPR recognizes that state leaders may revoke some civil-political rights when a public emergency 'threatens the life of the nation.'[48] This tension between human rights and national security was evident following the September 11, 2001 terrorist attacks on the USA and subsequent debates over the use of torture. Despite a UN convention prohibiting the use of torture, former US vice president Dick Cheney argued that protecting national security outweighed individual human rights. Other military and political leaders in the USA disagreed. Senator John McCain, a victim of torture after being shot down during the Vietnam War, argued that torture was 'un-American.' Freedom from torture is one of the political-civil rights that Article 4 of the ICCPR recognizes as *non-derogable*, which means that under *no* circumstances can a government legitimately use torture. Controversy over what exactly qualifies as torture continues to be an issue in global politics.[49]

> ### Example – Human rights and the USA
>
> US government rhetoric frequently asserts that freedom, human rights and democracy are universal norms and values. However, US behavior does not always reflect this commitment. The USA never ratified the **Rome Statute**, despite having played a key role in its drafting. This was the document that created the International Criminal Court (ICC). In 2020, when the ICC called for a formal

investigation of potential war crimes by US military personnel in Afghanistan between 2003 and 2004, the Trump administration reacted with visa restrictions and sanctions on leading ICC employees. Realists would claim that the Trump administration's actions were valid as many of the provisions in international human rights treaties infringe on US sovereignty and may undermine national security. Liberals would argue that US commitments to human rights depend on the nature of the presidential administration, with Democratic administrations being more dedicated to the global promotion and protection of human rights. Constructivists would suggest that international human rights norms have become embedded in the framework of global politics.

Economic conditions may shape a state's adherence to their human rights obligations in two ways. First, a state may lack the ability to fulfill these obligations, especially those that are related to social and economic rights, because it does not have the resources to do so. Second, governments in states that are experiencing worsening economic conditions may repress political-civil rights to curb any opposition that may emerge as a result and to maintain their authority. However, even developed states that have the resources to meet the demands of economic and social rights, like free education and affordable access to healthcare, may neglect to do so on ideological grounds.

States are often the main protector of human rights for many people and the chief violator of their own citizens' human rights at the same time.

IGOs

The primary role of IGOs, like the UN and regional bodies, has been to establish the legal and ethical framework for the international human rights regime by codifying human rights standards in multilateral treaties and laws. The UN body of international human rights instruments includes 16 laws and treaties, covering everything from crimes against humanity and torture, to women's rights, children's rights and the rights of those with disabilities. Realists might criticize human rights norms for being aspirational, but they do provide objectives that can be implemented, as well as a set of benchmarks from which the actions of political actors can be evaluated.

One of the most significant roles that IGOs, such as the UN Human Rights Council, the European Court of Human Rights and the Inter-American Court of Human Rights, play in the modern international human rights regime is to monitor state behavior. This can be procedural – establishing ways for those whose human rights have been violated by state practices to voice their complaints. Or it can be investigative – gathering reports on state behavior and investigating alleged abuses and violations of human rights. Each of the international human rights treaties in Table 2.2 has a treaty body, which is a committee of independent experts that monitors the degree to which each state party is meeting its treaty obligations as well as ensuring that everyone in the state can enjoy the rights set out in the treaty. Monitoring state actions can be a sensitive operation and many states regard such in-depth inspection of a government or regime's conduct as a violation of a state's sovereignty.

Comprised of 47 states, the UN Human Rights Council (UNHRC), which replaced the UN Commission on Human Rights in 2006, is the key independent UN intergovernmental body responsible for promoting and protecting human rights internationally.[50] For many individuals around the world, the UNHRC is the only place where they can seek accountability and remedies for human rights violations. The UNHRC promotes and protects human rights in several ways. The council's Advisory

Rights and justice

Committee provides expertise on human rights issues, while a Complaints Procedure allows individuals and organizations to bring complaints of human rights abuses and violations to the attention of the Council. The most significant innovation over the Commission on Human Rights is the UNHRC's Universal Periodic Review (UPR) that has been commissioned since 2006. The UPR, which was a response to criticism of the selectivity and politicization that existed in the UNHRC's predecessor, sees all 193 UN member states assessing and reporting on the shape of their own human rights record every four years. Using these reports, other states make recommendations and suggest actions that a state could take to improve its human rights situation. NGOs use these reports as a means of applying public pressure and holding states accountable for their actions. The UPR process is thought to be more effective in promoting state compliance with human rights norms because, rather than being judged by international experts, states are appraised by their peers. Critics suggest that the UPR process has become political theater and another place where power politics is displayed.

The Office of the High Commissioner for Human Rights (OHCHR) has the lead responsibility in the UN system for the promotion and protection of human rights and has the authority to investigate and report on situations relating to human rights issues around the world. One of its most prominent roles is to ensure fair elections in line with Article 21(3) of the UDHR, which states: 'The will of the people shall be the basis of authority of government; this will shall be expressed in periodic and genuine elections.' This can take different forms, from certifying an electoral process as fair (Côte D'Ivoire, 2010) to providing expert monitoring or supervising vote counts (Afghanistan, 2014). Notions of legitimate statehood often rest on a foundation of human rights and, although cheating and electoral fraud still exists, states and governments gain legitimacy by having UN oversight of their elections.

The Headquarters of the United Nations in Geneva.

Activity

Look at a contemporary case study. Research one of the ways in which the UNHRC and the OHCHR have promoted and protected human rights. These can include:

- UPR, which examines the human rights records of UN member states and makes recommendations for improvement.
- Special Rapporteurs who monitor and report on human rights issues in specific countries or thematic areas.
- The functions and activities of the Human Rights Council, including its resolutions and reports.
- Treaty Monitoring Bodies associated with various human rights conventions and how they review state compliance and issue recommendations.
- Election monitoring to ensure that elections are free and fair.

You should be prepared to share your findings with a peer or the whole class.

Other ways in which IGOs can encourage state compliance with international human rights norms include the use of sanctions to encourage changes in state behavior. In the UN system, this is the responsibility of the Security Council. There is evidence that sanctions or the prospect of sanctions have helped protect the human rights of marginalized and vulnerable groups around the world. A 2022 Security Council meeting noted that the threat of sanctions were, 'a factor in the release of abducted women and children from military bases in South Sudan in early 2020 and in child

Thematic studies

protection workers negotiating the release of children by armed groups in the Democratic Republic of Congo.'[51] Despite the Security Council's use of more targeted sanctions since the 1990s, such actions are still criticized for some of their unintended humanitarian impacts, restricting the enjoyment of economic, social and cultural rights including the rights to food, water, shelter and health. We have seen how the EU's Global Human Rights Sanctions Regime functions in a similar way by sanctioning individuals and entities that the EU believes to be involved in serious human rights abuses (see page 103).

> **Example – EU sanctions and the Democratic People's Republic of Korea (DPRK)**
>
> In the first round of its sanctions in 2022, the EU's Global Human Rights Sanctions Regime targeted North Korea's Minister of State Security, Jong Kyong-thaek, and Minister of Social Security, Ri Yong-gil, for 'implementing the repressive security policies of the DPRK' that involve widespread human rights abuses. The effect of these sanctions appears to have been minimal because of North Korea's self-reliant economic model and closed-off economy. The effectiveness of IGO sanctions appears to vary, depending on the state being sanctioned.

Other regional IGOs also play a role in promoting and protecting human rights. The European Convention on Human Rights is enforced by the European Court of Human Rights. Any individual or organization may seek help from the court if their rights have been violated by a member state of the Council of Europe. The Organization for Security and Co-operation in Europe (OSCE) is also able to hear complaints about human rights violations occurring in any of its 56 member states, although only human rights organizations are allowed to petition it. The American Convention on Human Rights established the Inter-American Commission on Human Rights and the Inter-American Court of Human Rights. The Commission's function is similar to that of the UN bodies, including to monitor and report on the standard of human rights in member states, to recommend measures for improving human rights in the region, and to receive complaints from legally recognized NGOs or individuals who believe their human rights have been violated by a member state. The Court's main functions are to hear and rule on specific cases of human rights violations that have been referred to it by the Commission, and to provide legal interpretation and opinion of the provisions contained in the American Convention on Human Rights.

(*left*) European Court of Human Rights, (*right*) American Court of Human Rights.

In Africa, the African Commission and the African Court on Human and Peoples' Rights were created following the adoption of the Banjul Charter. The African Commission is responsible for promoting and protecting human and peoples' rights, as well as interpretation of any provision contained within the Charter if requested

Rights and justice

to do so by an AU member state, AU organ, individual or organization. The African Court was established through a separate Protocol to the Banjul Charter with a mission to reinforce the human rights system on the continent. Its jurisdiction extends to all cases and disputes related to the interpretation and application of the Banjul Charter and any other relevant human rights law or treaty approved by the states concerned, including the Covenants and subsequent human rights treaties. To date, the only region that has not established an intergovernmental human rights organization or a human rights court is Asia.[52]

There are limitations to each of the regional human rights systems. For an individual or organization to bring a case before the European, Inter-American or African human rights systems, all domestic legal avenues must first have been exhausted. In the American and African systems, each case must be reviewed by a commission whose members are appointed by the Organization of American States and the African Union, respectively, to determine if cases are admissible and of sufficient merit. Commissioners may dismiss any petition that does not involve a member state's violation of their obligations under the relevant American or African human rights instruments. The appointed commissioners act as gatekeepers of each member state's sovereignty, which can be seen to overrule human rights concerns.[53] All the courts above are limited in what they can achieve. Legal decisions and documents exist, but the protection and enforcement of human rights lies with sovereign states.

There are two other judicial institutions that play a key part in protecting human rights: the International Court of Justice (ICJ) and the **International Criminal Court (ICC)**. Established in 1945, the International Court of Justice is one of the six principal organs of the United Nations. It is the principal judicial body of the UN, responsible for settling legal disputes between states and providing advisory opinions on legal questions. The ICJ plays a key role in promoting the peaceful settlement of disputes, which is an essential element in the protection and promotion of human rights. Its most crucial role in protecting human rights is to interpret and apply international law, including human rights treaties and conventions. Over time, ICJ's judgments and opinions have contributed to the development and implementation of international human rights law, such as the right to self-determination and the prohibition of torture and genocide.

Example – Gambia's case against Myanmar

In 2019, the ICJ began hearing *Gambia v. Myanmar*, a case in which Gambia, a majority-Muslim state in West Africa, requested that the ICJ issue provisional measures for Myanmar, a majority-Buddhist state in Southeast Asia, to stop the killing of the Rohingya, a Muslim minority. Gambia's application alleges that Myanmar security forces are guilty of genocide by destroying Rohingya villages in Rakhine province. In 2020, the ICJ issued provisional measures calling on Myanmar to cease actions. In 2022, it decided that it had jurisdiction under the Genocide Convention to hear this application.[54]

The ICC is a permanent international tribunal established to investigate, prosecute and bring to trial individuals accused of the most serious crimes of international concern. Although the origins of the ICC lie in the Nuremberg and Tokyo trials following the end of the Second World War, the Court's more immediate predecessors were two

Thematic studies

temporary criminal tribunals established in the 1990s to investigate, prosecute and punish those found guilty of committing atrocities in Yugoslavia and Rwanda. From these experiences, the UN negotiated the creation of a permanent institution. In 1998, the UN General Assembly adopted the Rome Statute for the International Criminal Court, which entered into force in July 2002. This binding treaty established the ICC, giving it compulsory jurisdiction, and jurisdiction over all individuals accused of one or more of the following crimes: genocide, crimes against humanity, war crimes and crimes of aggression. By 2022, 123 states had agreed to the Rome Statute.

The ICC aims to hold accountable those responsible for these crimes and provide justice for the victims. The Court can apply jurisdiction in one of three ways:

- If a state party to the Rome Statute refers a situation committed by one of its citizens or within its own territory.
- If the UN Security Council refers a situation.
- If the Chief Prosecutor launches an investigation after determining that the alleged crimes are serious enough for a case to proceed.

The ICC functions as a court of last resort and only hears cases when domestic courts are unable or unwilling to prosecute those accused of committing human rights abuses. The ICC cooperates with national jurisdictions to ensure that those responsible for these crimes are held accountable, and that victims' rights to justice and compensation are respected.

Since 2002, the ICC has issued arrest warrants for 45 individuals. Thanks to the cooperation of several states, 21 people have appeared before the Court. Sixteen people are still fugitives. There have been ten convictions and four acquittals. By issuing arrest warrants for sitting and former heads of government and/or state, as well as military leaders, the ICC sends a clear message that no individual is immune from prosecution and serious violations of human rights will not go unpunished. The hope is that this will deter individuals and groups from committing atrocities in the future.

> **Example – The ICC and the Russian war on Ukraine**
>
> On March 17, 2023, ICC judges issued the first arrest warrants for crimes committed in the Ukraine conflict. Russian President Vladimir Putin and his children's rights commissioner, Maria Lvova-Belova, were accused of overseeing the unlawful deportation of Ukrainian children from their homes and families. Russian citizenship laws had been changed so that these abducted children could be adopted by Russians. This makes Putin only the third sitting head of state to be indicted by the ICC. Putin is likely to evade punishment for now, as Russia does not recognize the ICC's jurisdiction, but he does face limits on his freedom to travel to the ICC's 123 member states.

Criticism of the ICC takes one of two forms: it has too much prosecutorial power and threatens states' sovereignty, or it has too little authority and is inefficient at prosecuting and punishing those responsible for atrocities.

There is the perception that human rights have become politicized in the Court's proceedings. Although it had never become a party to the Rome Statute, Russia withdrew all support for the ICC in 2016 after the Court decided to open a preliminary

---

The ICJ and the ICC are both in The Hague and the courts play a significant role in protecting human rights in the world. However, there is a key difference between them: the ICJ settles disputes between *states* while the ICC prosecutes *individuals*.

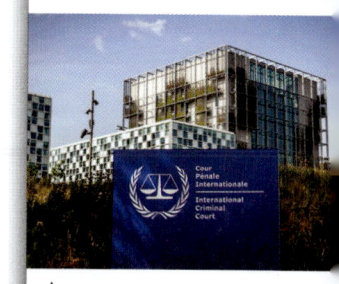

International Criminal Court, The Hague.

Rights and justice

investigation into possible war crimes perpetrated by Russian forces during Russia's 2008 invasion of Georgia. More damaging were accusations from many African countries, once strong supporters of the ICC, that the Court was disproportionately targeting African leaders, like Jean-Pierre Bemba Gombo, a former vice president of the Democratic Republic of Congo (DRC).[55] South Africa, Gambia, Burundi and the Philippines all threatened to withdraw from the Rome Statute, with Burundi and the Philippines doing so.

▲ Former vice president of the DRC, Jean-Pierre Bemba Gombo.

US policymakers originally supported the concept of an international criminal court and US officials were involved in the initial negotiations, but the USA has not backed the Rome Statute. The US position on, and relations with, the Court have varied since its inception. The administration of George W. Bush allowed the UN Security Council to refer the Darfur case to the ICC and later offered to assist the investigation. The Obama administration voted in favor of the Security Council referral for a Libya investigation and helped deliver several indicted individuals to The Hague. However, when the Chief Prosecutor pushed to investigate potential war crimes committed by US armed forces and CIA personnel in Afghanistan, while also opening a preliminary investigation into alleged Israeli war crimes in the Palestinian occupied territories, the Trump administration blocked any attempts by the Court to pursue US or Israeli citizens. The Biden administration continues to express concern over the ICC's investigations in the occupied territories, but it has been more cooperative, and it claims to be working on a reset with the Court.[56]

Criticism also questions the degree to which the ICC has been able to *deter* potential human rights violators. There is evidence to suggest that those actors who are concerned with 'their legitimacy in the eyes of domestic publics and/or the international community are much more likely to be deterred by the possibility of ICC prosecution than those who are not.'[57] However, there is empirical data showing that leaders under investigation by the ICC were more likely to allow a conflict to drag on in the hope of evading punishment. Critics point to the ICC's failure to investigate all human rights abuses around the world as a massive moral failure, and the two billion US dollars spent to secure just ten convictions as a waste of money.

It is worth acknowledging the role that IGOs play when states decide to respond to human rights violations with force. If a humanitarian emergency is so serious as to threaten 'international peace and security', then the UN Security Council can invoke Chapter VII of the UN Charter to authorize military and non-military actions that do not require the consent of the states involved. Although Chapter VII actions date back to the Korean War (1950–53), they really took off in the early 1990s and 2000s. By early 1992, a brutal civil war in Somalia, followed by intense fighting between warlords, left millions on the brink of famine. The Security Council linked gross human rights violations to security threats and authorized a UN intervention under Chapter VII. In 2011, the Security Council adopted Resolution 1973, which authorized NATO's military intervention to protect civilians under threat during the Libyan Civil War. IGOs themselves rarely intervene, either because they lack the ability to project hard power of their own or because sovereign states guard their sovereign right to non-interference. The power of the UN Security Council lies in its ability to authorize or legitimize the use of force by states or other multilateral organizations.

Thematic studies

> ### Activity
>
> Choose an IGO that focuses on human rights issues, for example, the UN, EU, AU or OAS. Research your chosen IGO. You should explore the following aspects:
>
> - What specific human rights issues does your IGO address?
> - Identify and analyze the human rights programs or campaigns your IGO has undertaken.
> - Investigate your IGO's involvement in the ratification and implementation of international human rights treaties and conventions.
> - Discuss examples of your IGO's successes in promoting human rights, as well as any challenges it has encountered in fulfilling its mandate.
>
> Critically assess the extent to which your chosen IGO can be viewed as a powerful and legitimate instrument for the protection and enforcement of human rights. You should consider the following:
>
> - Impact: Has your IGO made an impact in advancing human rights, and if so, in what areas?
> - Cooperation and support: How well does your IGO collaborate with member states and other stakeholders to address human rights issues?
> - Challenges and limitations: What challenges and limitations does your IGO face in its human rights endeavors?
> - Accountability and transparency: Does your IGO demonstrate transparency in its actions, and is it held accountable for its decisions related to human rights?
> - Public perception: How is your IGO perceived by human rights advocates, governments and civil society groups?
>
> You should be prepared to share your findings with your peers. You will be expected to reflect on the overall role of IGOs in promoting human rights globally.

NSAs

Despite their lack of hard power, NGOs and INGOs play an important and often effective role helping promote and protect human rights, particularly via their monitoring activities. Amnesty International (AI) has been tracking human rights violations since its creation in 1961 and has been involved in efforts to end such abuses. Initially, its attentions were directed toward individual cases of political prisoners around the world, but it has since broadened its agenda to include a range of more structural issues, such as abuses of economic and social rights, LGBTQI+ rights and women's rights. NGOs like AI also contribute to and complement the UN's monitoring of human rights as well as those of some nation-states.

> ### Example – Write for Rights
>
> For over 20 years, Amnesty International has run an annual *Write for Rights* campaign, which sees people all around the world writing in support of individuals whose human rights have been abused or violated, as a way of putting pressure on governments and leaders to redress the harm being done and to protect citizen's human rights. For more information, go to: /www.amnesty.org/en/get-involved/write-for-rights/. Write a letter to one of the individuals you find on this web page.

🔗 Lukes' Three Faces of Power can be applied to how transnational advocacy networks operate. The first face of power is reflected in the way these networks can shape discourse and influence what ideas and narratives gain prominence. Lukes' second face of power can be seen in the ways these advocacy networks wield power over what global issues are considered important and warrant attention. Finally, by shaping public opinion, these networks influence and shape the very beliefs and perspectives of people without their explicit awareness, demonstrating the third face of power.

Rights and justice

NGOs publicize issues and highlight human rights abuses and violations. As the world has become more interconnected, they have also formed coalitions, leading to the creation of transnational advocacy networks and social movements to promote and protect rights. As Margret Keck and Kathryn Sikkink have argued, such networks function by spreading information and framing the politics around rights issues, but they also use leverage politics. This involves calling on stronger actors like states to act on behalf of vulnerable and marginalized groups and also to hold political leaders accountable for what they have said. Transnational advocacy networks can influence dominant narratives and agenda setting,[58] which can influence state behavior and change national or foreign policy.[59]

Case – Women's rights are human rights

Transnational women's networks grew in strength once they framed violence against women as a human rights issue. Earlier attempts to highlight the discrimination and inequalities suffered by women failed to gain much attention and traction. Once activists reframed the issue in terms of human rights, they were able to take advantage of what some scholars have called an adjacency principle. If activists could persuade state actors that women's rights were human rights, it might be possible to get them to protect women, because states had already acknowledged the normative significance of human rights. Framing violence against women as a human rights violation allowed activists to overcome criticism that women's rights were just another form of Western cultural imperialism. Keck and Sikkink argue that framing the practice of female genital mutilation together with rape and domestic abuse defused culturally relative arguments and legitimized opposition to the practice.

Transnational advocacy networks and social movements have taken advantage of the spread and use of social media to shape narratives and mobilize people to act. Civil rights activists in the USA have linked the racism experienced by Black Americans to discrimination against people of color elsewhere in the world since the turn of the 20th century. During the Cold War, civil society activists in the USA leveraged their transnational alliances and global audience to expose how the mistreatment of people of color undermined the rhetoric (persuasive language and arguments) of those American leaders who wanted the USA to be seen as a champion of equal rights and democracy.[60] By taking advantage of this tension between reality and rhetoric, activists were able to advance the struggle for civil and human rights. In May 2020, a video captured George Floyd, a Black man, pleading for his life as a White police officer kneeled on his neck. The video was shared globally via social media and Floyd's final words – 'I can't breathe' – amplified the Black Lives Matter (BLM) movement, with rallies in solidarity occurring around the world from France to Costa Rica, the UK and New Zealand. Social media and technology have facilitated transnational connections between social movements, such as BLM, and other human rights and social justice organizations around the globe, albeit with the risk of persecution.

Transnational advocacy networks and social movements play a vital role in promoting and protecting rights across borders. These networks consist of diverse organizations and individuals working together to advocate for various causes, leveraging their collective power to influence governments, shape policies and raise awareness about human rights abuses. Through collaboration and the use of digital platforms, these networks amplify voices, facilitate global solidarity and exert pressure for positive change, making significant contributions to the advancement of rights and social justice on an international scale.

HL This can be linked to the HL topic area *Technology*. The Internet and social media have changed the ways in which people can communicate, making it easier for them to organize and mobilize across national borders in support of rights and justice issues around the world. However, this technology allows authoritarian governments around the world to monitor their opponents and prevent resistance.

(left) Protesting against the police treatment of George Floyd, *(right)* The words 'I can't breathe', the last words of George Floyd, became important to the BLM campaign.

Thematic studies

Social movements and NGOs can move more quickly than IGOs. NGOs can also fill gaps that exist in institutional frameworks. Asia is the only region that lacks intergovernmental human rights institutions like a commission or a court. Instead, there is the independent, non-governmental body, the Asian Human Rights Commission (AHRC). While the AHRC works to promote greater awareness of human rights in the region, and seeks to mobilize regional and international public opinion to secure justice for those whose human rights have been violated, it lacks the authority and legal standing of the commissions and courts that exist in Europe, the Americas and Africa. Research suggests that the presence of a strong civil society represented by NGOs and national human rights institutions (NHRIs), like national courts and police, ombudsmen[61] and National Human Rights Commissions, can strengthen respect for human rights and encourage national and regional court decisions that protect the human rights of the most vulnerable and marginalized in society. This is because NGOs and NHRIs can focus on national-level issues, increasing the effectiveness of monitoring and protecting human rights. The Commission on Human Rights and Administrative Justice (CHRAJ) has played a crucial role in investigating and addressing human rights violations in Ghana, as well as promoting good governance by educating public officials and citizens of their rights and responsibilities. Even though some governments may overlook the recommendations or initiatives proposed by civil society actors, the UN has acknowledged NHRIs to be one of the most important ways by which states can bridge the gap between their international human rights obligations and the enjoyment of human rights by their citizens.

Multinational corporations (MNCs) have historically argued that they do not have any role in the promotion or protection of human rights as this would constitute direct interference in the domestic affairs of a sovereign state. However, globalization has seen MNCs become an important, even essential, source of revenue and investment for many states around the world, including dictatorial regimes that abuse or violate the rights of their own people. Inspired by a growing appreciation of the essential role MNCs play in influencing domestic policies in countries where they invest, the UN launched its Global Compact in 2000, a non-binding pact requiring companies to adopt ten principles (two of which focused on human rights) and to align their practices with the UN's Sustainable Development Goals (SDGs). Thousands of MNCs have agreed to the Compact, but they are not legally required to do so and, even when they do, human rights violations still occur together with their business activities, particularly in extractive industries like mining or forestry in conflict or post-conflict areas. In June 2011, the UN Human Rights Council endorsed the UN Guiding Principles on Business and Human Rights (UNGPs), a corporate human rights responsibility initiative outlining how states and businesses should respect and protect human rights. Despite widespread support from states, civil society organizations and the private sector, some stakeholders have criticized the lack of any accountability mechanism that could make the UNGPs legally enforceable.

In 2013, Ecuador, supported by 84 states, proposed a legally binding agreement that would require MNCs to provide 'appropriate protection, justice and remedy to the victims of human rights abuses directly resulting from or related to [their] activities.'[62] While this proposition was backed by numerous civil society actors, as well as the majority of the UN Human Rights Council, the following year, the UNGPs currently remain non-binding on states and MNCs.

Trade unions/labor unions have played a crucial role in promoting and protecting human rights throughout history, especially second generation rights. Labor unions

> The SDGs are a set of 17 global goals established by the United Nations in 2015, aiming to address global challenges such as poverty, inequality, climate change and sustainable development by 2030. They provide a framework for international cooperation and action, guiding efforts to achieve a more sustainable and equitable world for all.

Rights and justice

are active in many countries in the Global North and Global South, and through their collective efforts have helped to improve the lives of workers, promote social justice and challenge discriminatory practices. The American Federation of Labor and Congress of Industrial Organizations (AFL-CIO) actively supported the fight for racial equality in the USA. Through **strikes**, **boycotts** and **collective bargaining**, trade unions fought against racial discrimination in employment, contributing to the progress of first generation civil rights, and helped to reduce many discriminatory practices. More recently, the AFL-CIO has fought for essential workers' rights during the COVID-19 pandemic and continues to be involved in addressing the challenges faced by workers in precarious employment and the gig economy. The General Confederation of Labor (Confédération Générale du Travail, CGT) is one of the largest and oldest trade unions in France, representing workers from sectors such as transportation, energy and manufacturing. Together with other unions, it opposed the proposed pension reforms of the French government between 2019 and 2023. The CGT organized strikes and protests, including major transportation strikes, to express their concerns and demand changes to the proposed reforms.

2023 protest by the CGT trade union in France against proposed pension reform.

The gig economy refers to a labor market characterized by temporary and flexible work arrangements, where individuals work on a project-by-project basis or as independent contractors, often facilitated through online platforms or apps. It represents a shift away from traditional employment structures, offering opportunities and challenges in terms of income stability, job security and worker rights.

Trade unions have also been instrumental in promoting human rights on an international or global scale. The International Trade Union Confederation (ITUC) works toward protecting labor rights and advancing social justice worldwide. The ITUC has been involved in combating modern forms of slavery and forced labor around the world, particularly within mining, agriculture and fisheries industries, to ensure that workers are treated with dignity and respect. They have also advocated for the right to freedom of association and the right to form and join trade unions. The ITUC campaigns against anti-union practices and legislation that restricts workers' right to organize and collectively bargain, while raising awareness of cases where trade unionists face persecution, violence or intimidation for their activities.

Example – Combating modern slavery

Through its Global Rights Index, the ITUC assesses the state of workers' rights in countries around the world and identifies cases of modern slavery and forced labor. The ITUC has raised awareness about these issues, advocating for stronger legislation and regulations to prevent and address such human rights abuses, and supporting initiatives to hold companies and businesses accountable for their supply chains. The ITUC's efforts have contributed to dialogue on improving the working conditions of vulnerable workers and working toward ending modern slavery.

Thematic studies

> **Activity**
>
> Work in a group of three or four. Investigate one of the following real-world examples of the ITUC's work in addressing modern-day slavery in the Global North and Global South:
>
> - Global North:
>   - Supply chain monitoring and advocacy: The ITUC campaigns for greater transparency and accountability in MNCs to ensure that labor rights violations do not occur in their operations abroad.
>   - Legal and policy initiatives: The ITUC has worked to advance legislation and policies that combat modern-day slavery and protect the rights of vulnerable workers.
> - Global South:
>   - Support for grassroots movements: The ITUC provides resources, training and capacity-building programs to empower local communities to combat labor exploitation.
>   - Forced labor and child labor eradication: The ITUC campaigns against forced and child labor in industries such as agriculture, textiles and mining.
>   - Migrant workers' rights: The ITUC advocates for improved labor protections, fair recruitment practices, and an end to debt bondage and other forms of labor exploitation faced by migrant workers.
>
> You should consider the following inquiry questions:
>
> - How has the ITUC engaged with other actors/stakeholders to address the issue?
> - What are some notable outcomes or achievements of the ITUC's work in relation to modern-day slavery?
> - What are some of the challenges the ITUC faces in its work against modern-day slavery?
>
> You should be prepared to share your findings with the rest of the class. Hold an open discussion where you can exchange perspectives, insights and questions related to the ITUC's efforts in combatting modern-day slavery. This will be a chance for you to demonstrate your critical thinking and reflect on the complexities addressing this global issue.

The evidence for whether NSAs make a difference to the promotion and protection of human rights is mixed. Research has shown that the naming and shaming activities of human rights INGOs do see states improving their human rights practices. However, reporting on a state's poor human rights situation is not enough in itself and improvements rely on the efforts of domestic NGOs, as well as pressure from third-party states and organizations.[63] Other research points to cases where accusations of human rights abuses from the UN, NGOs and the media has had no apparent effect on the countries identified, and in some instances, the number and intensity of human rights violations increased. Naming and shaming could be ineffective because NGOs and the media lack authority over sovereign states, while some IGOs may lack the legitimacy necessary for their voice to carry weight. The UN Council for Human Rights includes several states whose human rights records are questionable.[64] The principle of sovereignty casts a shadow over many human rights discussions. Even if a state has agreed to a human rights treaty, there is no guarantee it will be able or willing to meet its treaty obligations. The actions of IGOs and NGOs may help to improve human

Rights and justice

rights around the world, but these are not necessarily enough to change practices that lead to human rights abuses and violations.

> ## Exercises
>
> 12. Identify some methods that states can use to promote and protect human rights and outline what their limitations might be.
> 13. Suggest some reasons why states may be unwilling or unable to combat human rights abuses and violations.
> 14. Outline the main role of IGOs like the UN and regional bodies in the international human rights regime. Your answer should include specific reference to the UN Human Rights Council.
> 15. Explain how sanctions have been used to protect human rights around the world.
> 16. Analyze the role played by regional IGOs in promoting and protecting human rights.
> 17. Explain the role of the ICJ and ICC in protecting human rights.
> 18. Describe the ways in which the ICC has been criticized. Identify some real-world examples in your answer.
> 19. Explain how the presence of a strong civil society represented by trade unions, NGOs and NHRIs can strengthen respect for human rights and encourage court decisions that protect vulnerable and marginalized groups.

Debates on rights and justice: claims on individual and collective rights

> **Conceptual question**
>
> Who do rights belong to and why does this matter?

To whom exactly do rights ultimately belong? To individuals or to groups? What happens if individual and collective rights clash with one other? Justify your thinking to a classmate.

This is an opportunity to make connections to the HL topic area Identity. What are the effects and consequences of prioritizing one form of identity over another when it comes to rights and justice?

Rights and general individual rights are political and give rise to heated debate. They are wrapped up with issues of power and powerlessness. Rights are 'a weapon of the weak against the strong.'[65] This is because they imply a conflict between a rights holder and a rights *with*holder, which is some authority (usually the state) against which a justified claim can be made.

The key debate between individual and collective conceptualizations of human rights centers around whether these should be viewed as individual entitlements or as collective goods. Critics of individualistic approaches argue that individual rights may conflict with collective interests, and that a focus on individual rights can neglect the needs or interests of vulnerable or marginalized groups. Supporters of the individualistic approach argue that collective rights can be used to justify human rights abuses by authoritarian regimes, and that individual rights are essential for protecting the freedom and autonomy of individuals.

Thematic studies

An individualist approach stresses the importance of individual autonomy, arguing that individuals have the right to live their lives free from interference from others, including the state. This approach prioritizes the negative liberties associated with first generation civil and political rights, such as freedom of speech and freedom of religion. The collective rights approach emphasizes the positive liberties associated with second generation economic, social and cultural rights, such as the right to education, healthcare and a decent standard of living. Collective rights are seen as essential for the protection and promotion of the rights of marginalized groups, such as cultural or linguistic minorities, so they are sometimes associated with third generation solidarity rights.

Which rights should take precedence in cases where they conflict? Some argue that individual rights should always take precedence, as they are fundamental to a free and democratic society. Others argue that collective rights should sometimes take precedence, as they can help to protect the rights of vulnerable groups and promote social cohesion. There is debate over the scope of individual and collective rights. Some assert that individual rights should be seen as absolute and universal, and that any infringement of these rights is unacceptable, while others argue that there may be circumstances in which individual rights can be legitimately restricted for the greater good of society.

Example – The COVID-19 pandemic

On January 30, 2020, the WHO declared the novel coronavirus that was first detected at the end of 2019 to be a Public Health Emergency of International Concern and then, on March 11, declared the outbreak a pandemic.[66] As a pandemic, COVID-19 was a direct challenge to notions of individualistic rights, since individual responsibility and collective action were vital in combating the spread of infections and implementing social distancing measures. Countries around the world saw their social compact tested as the unwritten understanding between individuals within society, as well as between the government and society, came under enormous strain.[67] The responses of different countries to the pandemic fueled the debate over the best ways to govern a state, and mask mandates, vaccination programs and lockdowns demonstrated where many countries lay on the individualist-collective rights spectrum.

Activity

Share with a peer your observations and experiences of where you were living during the pandemic. What do you think the pandemic showed you about the social compact? In small groups, reflect on the following questions:

- What changes did you observe in the social dynamics and behavior of people during the pandemic?
- Did you notice any shifts in the relationship between individuals and the government or other authorities?
- How did the pandemic affect people's sense of community and solidarity?
- Were there any examples of people coming together to support each other during challenging times?
- Were there any instances where the social compact appeared to be strained or challenged?

Rights and justice

> Share the key points and insights from your discussion with the rest of the class. Discuss the similarities and differences between different places or communities, and place different countries or communities on a spectrum, from more individualistic to more collectivist. Be prepared to justify your choices.
>
> Reflect in writing on the following questions:
>
> - How did the social compact influence people's compliance with pandemic-related measures?
> - Did the social compact change or evolve over time as the pandemic progressed? Why or why not?
> - Were there any instances where the social compact was violated?
> - How did the government respond to challenges posed by the pandemic? Was it effective?

There is also a debate between universal and culturally relative ideas of human rights. The notion of universal human rights is best captured by the key UN human rights laws and treaties. Culturally relative perspectives criticize these human rights instruments as reflecting a Western bias. Critics of the international human rights regime argue that UN human rights instruments are broadly incompatible with the cultural foundations of many Asian and African societies. Supporters of cultural relativism see a more sinister motive behind Western attempts to universalize human rights, and say that claims based on universal human rights can be viewed as a weapon of cultural hegemony.[68]

Case – The Asian values debate

In the 1990s, several Asian leaders and intellectuals challenged the notion that human rights were universal, instead attacking them for privileging Western values unsuited for Asia. Singapore's Senior Minister, Lee Kuan Yew, said that Asians have 'little doubt that a society with **communitarian** values where the interests of society take precedence over that of the individual suits them better than the individualism of America.'[69] This view was echoed in other countries in the region, where leaders claimed that they might have to sacrifice some political and civil freedoms in order to safeguard the stability of their societies and protect the economic security of their citizens. This culturally relative view was not universally held in the region. A former president of Singapore, Devan Nair, stated that 'Human rights and values are universal by any standard, and their violation anywhere is a grievous offence to men and women everywhere.'[70]

Michael Ignatieff has presented a different interpretation of the debates between individual/universal rights and collective/culturally relative rights. He argues that the distinction between group rights and individual rights might be a false dichotomy (binary choice). Some group rights, like the right to speak your own language, are essential for individual rights to be exercised and for individuals to be able to live a meaningful life. He also rejects any necessary connection between individual rights and Western ways of life: '[b]elieving in your right not to be tortured or abused does not mean adopting Western dress, speaking Western languages, or approving the Western lifestyle.' In his view, just because someone values their individual human rights does not mean that they must abandon other cultural attachments.

Instead, it means that they wish to enjoy negative liberties: to be free from oppression and harm. What those countries that have embraced communitarian value systems are often missing, according to Ignatieff, is the degree to which demand for human rights comes from the bottom up, from the powerless, and that this is what gives them their legitimacy.[71] It may be more accurate to imagine that countries exist along a spectrum and that their position is not static, but may shift further toward one end or another (and back) over time. The sociologist Amatai Etzioni has put forward a version of communitarianism characterized by a shared culture or set of values, and also by a high level of responsiveness. In his responsive communitarian model, neither individual rights nor collective rights are better, but both are values to be negotiated and balanced. For Etzioni, this involves greater participation, deliberation and responsiveness on the part of government and society to ensure that basic human needs and rights are met.[72]

Modern ideas about human rights may have emerged first in the West, but their globalization, especially after 1945, involved contributions and efforts from many different places and cultures, so we cannot easily identify the specific contribution of any one culture. Between 1945 and 1960, newly independent postcolonial states of diverse cultural backgrounds linked the fulfillment of human rights to the right to self-determination, that '[t]he whole question of human rights … was quickly and inextricably blended with the question of national emancipation; only the emancipated sovereignty of the people, of one's own people, seem to be able to ensure them.'[73] In doing so, these states helped universalize general individual or human rights. Many states in the Global South have become some of the strongest defenders of the Westphalian concept of sovereignty, seeing appeals to human rights as an unwarranted interference in their domestic affairs and/or a form of Western cultural imperialism, However, many of these same states championed such rights in their struggles against colonialism. The broadening and deepening of the international regime of human rights can be seen as a global process.

> **TOK**: How can we decide whether individual or collective rights should be prioritized in a certain context?

> **TOK**: How do the TOK concepts of values and culture impact knowers' perspectives on individual vs collective rights?

Exercises

20. Outline the basis of the debate between individual and collective notions of human rights.

21. Describe the debate between universal and culturally relative ideas of human rights and outline how supporters of cultural relativism view attempts to universalize human rights.

Conclusion: the future of human rights and justice

Conceptual question

How might human rights and the international human rights regime change in the future?

Rights and justice

The expansion of human rights and justice in the 21st century

Human rights are often seen as a weapon of the weak against the strong. Human rights are normative principles that relatively powerless actors can use to challenge dominant or powerful actors and institutions, especially the state. While the liberal international order, and the international human rights regime that is associated with it, have been challenged by a range of authoritarian and populist leaders, human rights still have a potentially positive role to play in an emerging multiplex world order.

Constructivists would argue that developments in human rights illustrate the central notion that ideas matter and that ideas can change over time. The development and practice of human rights has expanded in focus and scope since 1945 by addressing new issues and there is no reason to think that this cannot continue in the future. One such area is the environment, and there have been several climate change lawsuits around the world based on the principle that a sovereign state has a duty to protect citizens' human rights from the effects of climate change by reducing carbon emissions. Over 100 constitutions have, to date, adopted the human right to a healthy environment. This points to a growing focus on intergenerational climate justice and calls to bridge the gap between environmental law and human rights. It also highlights a more constructivist notion of sovereignty, one that changes based on new issues that come up and how they develop.

Case – Human rights and the environment

Between 2015 and 2020, approximately 40 human rights-based climate change cases were brought before national courts and international bodies. In the 2020 *Urgenda* and 2021 *Royal Dutch Shell* cases, the Dutch Supreme Court referenced articles in the ECHR to rule that individual countries have direct obligations to protect their citizens' rights to a healthy environment. David Boyd, the UN special rapporteur on human rights and the environment at the time, noted that these cases confirmed 'that human rights are jeopardized by the climate emergency and that wealthy nations are legally obligated to achieve rapid and substantial emission reductions.'[74]

Activity

Research the *Urgenda* or the *Royal Dutch Shell* case. Identify the main arguments made – for and against – in the court case and outline the final ruling or decision made. Analyze and evaluate the significance of your case in the context of the ways in which our understanding of human rights might be evolving. Present your analysis and evaluation verbally or in writing.

Human rights have become more significant for indigenous peoples' rights. While there have been declarations in support of the collective or group rights of indigenous peoples, like the 2007 UN Declaration on the Rights of Indigenous Peoples, individual human rights have also been able to protect the rights of marginalized groups. A 2021 decision by the Inter-American Court of Human Rights declared that Guatemala was responsible for protecting the rights to freedom of expression of all its citizens, which meant that the indigenous Maya Kaqchikel people could operate radio stations and broadcast in their indigenous languages, a right that they had not been given earlier despite being the original inhabitants of the land.

This is an opportunity to make a link to the HL topic area *Environment*.

Thematic studies

There is the expansion of human rights beyond humans. Some legal bodies around the world have recognized the human rights of mountains, volcanos and rivers. Usually, this is connected to their sacred status for indigenous peoples. In Aotearoa/New Zealand and Canada, rivers have been granted the same legal rights as a person. Advances in science and technology have driven human rights discussions around artificial intelligence and robots.

TOK: To what extent can we speak of nature as a *person* and therefore entitled to *human* rights? What are the consequences if we do?

Mount Taranaki in New Zealand. Some rivers and mountains have had their human rights recognized, often for their sacred status.

Activity

If algorithms create discriminatory situations, or autonomous weapon systems select targets and engage without human control, who can be held responsible for human rights violations? Discuss your thinking with a classmate.

Practice questions

1. Evaluate the different ways in which human rights can be protected and enforced in countries that fall short of internationally agreed upon standards.
2. Discuss how the evolution of human rights since 1948 reflects contested meanings of rights and justice.
3. Discuss the claim that human rights are the foundation of legitimate state sovereignty.
4. 'The right to development is the most important human right.' Evaluate this statement.
5. To what extent is the protection and enforcement of human rights best pursued at the international level?
6. To what extent is the sovereign state the most significant protector of human rights?
7. To what extent have international human rights treaties and institutions been effective in promoting and protecting human rights?
8. To what extent are the principles of rights and justice universal?

Summary

In this chapter, you have learned:

- The meaning of rights and justice are contested due to different historical, ideological and cultural perspectives. Some of the debates have centered on individual vs group rights and some have focused on different generations of human rights.

Rights and justice

- The nature and practice of rights and justice vary across different socio-political contexts and geographical regions. Practices that might be considered socially acceptable in one part of the world might not be accepted in another.
- Debates persist about the appropriate roles and responsibilities of different actors (states, international organizations, civil society groups, individuals) in protecting and promoting human rights.
- The international human rights regime has evolved since the end of the Second World War, especially with the development and expansion of organizations intended to maintain rights for all, such as the United Nations.
- Sovereignty is not an absolute principle, as demonstrated by the concepts of universal jurisdiction and the doctrine of Responsibility to Protect (R2P).
- How states are the main protector of human rights but can also be the main violator of human rights. State authorities are often responsible for the protection and enforcement of civil-political and social-economic rights, but in many countries, the state frequently violates rights and freedoms, like the right to life or the freedom from arbitrary arrest.
- Non-state actors, such as NGOs, MNCs and individuals, despite lacking hard power, play a vital role in promoting and protecting human rights.
- How the debate between individual and collective ideas of human rights highlights the conflict between prioritizing individual autonomy and protecting the collective interests of a group. Should individual freedoms (free speech or assembly, for example) be allowed if they threaten the stability of a society?
- The expansion of human rights in the 21st century increasingly includes addressing contemporary issues such as climate change, indigenous peoples' rights, the rights of nature and advances in technology.

Notes

1. Although Rousseau argued that individual rights were subordinate to the general will.
2. This distinction was first proposed by jurist Karel Vasak in 1977. References to different generations of human rights are more about different categories of rights than chronology. There is no real sense here of certain rights emerging before others, 'first generation' rights preceding 'second generation' rights, even though technological and societal changes have seen certain rights emerge that were not formerly clear to see. The different generations of human rights are meant to mirror the three themes of the French Revolution: liberté, egalité, fraternité (liberty, equality, fraternity). Note that fraternité is brotherhood, which linguistically discounts 50% of the human population.
3. The International Convention on the Abolition of Slavery was not ratified until 1926.
4. Nelson, W.N. (1974). 'Special Rights, General Rights, and Social Justice'. *Philosophy & Public Affairs*, 3(2), p.412.
5. Reus-Smit, C. (2013). *Individual Rights and the Making of the International System*. Cambridge University Press, p.170.
6. *Ibid*.
7. Reus-Smit (2013), p.211.
8. *Ibid*, pp.170–71.

Thematic studies

9. Vincent, J. (1986). *Human Rights and International Relations.* Cambridge University Press, p.13.
10. Reus-Smit, C. (2001). 'Human rights and the social construction of sovereignty'. *Review of International Studies,* 27(4), p.521.
11. Waltz, S. (2002). 'Reclaiming and Rebuilding the History of the Universal Declaration of Human Rights'. *Third World Quarterly,* p.440.
12. *Ibid.*
13. United Nations. (1945). Article 55 and Article 56 in 'United Nations Charter (full text)'. Retrieved on April 25, 2023 from www.un.org/en/about-us/un-charter/full-text
14. As a multilateral treaty, the UN Charter is legally binding for all parties under international law.
15. It was largely thanks to the lobbying efforts of around 42 US and international NGOs that a UN Human Rights Commission was established. It was this commission that would be responsible for drafting the Universal Declaration of Human Rights and many of the subsequent treaties considered core to the global human rights system.
16. Buergenthal, T. (1997). 'The Normative and Institutional Evolution of International Human Rights'. *Human Rights Quarterly,* 19(4), pp.706–707.
17. The word *protection* was hardly ever used in UN documents or discussion until 1993, after the end of the Cold War. It was then that the newly established office for the United Nations High Commissioner for Human Rights was given the responsibility for promoting *and* protecting human rights.
18. The *Izahat dar Khusus-i Azadi* (Explanations Concerning Freedom) and *Datong shu* (The Book of Great Harmony) published in Iran and the PRC, respectively, promoted individual liberty, freedom, equality and the natural rights of all humanity.
19. The four freedoms Roosevelt identified were: freedom of speech; freedom of worship; freedom from want; freedom from fear. His speech explained that 'Freedom means the supremacy of human rights everywhere.' See: 'The Four Freedoms'. Voices of Democracy. (2016, July 5). Retrieved on 25 June, 2023 from https://voicesofdemocracy.umd.edu/fdr-the-four-freedoms-speech-text/
20. There was also the example of the Armenian genocide, which refers to the systematic extermination and persecution of the Armenian population by the Ottoman Empire during the First World War. Between 1915 and 1923, an estimated 1.5 million Armenians were massacred, forced on death marches or deprived of food, water and other necessities. Nazi Germany used the model of the Armenian genocide as a blueprint for the Holocaust.
21. Reus-Smit (2001), p.182.
22. Developing countries that were formally represented in the drafting committee included: Chile, Lebanon, Egypt, India, Panama, Philippines and Uruguay.
23. The resolution adopting the UDHR (217 A (III)) was passed in a vote of 48-0-8, the abstaining states being a range of Eastern European communist countries along with Saudi Arabia and apartheid South Africa.
24. Clapham, A. (2015). *Human Rights: A Very Short Introduction.* Oxford University Press, p.42.
25. Articles 22–27 address various social and economic rights. Article 25, which established the right to food, clothing, shelter and medical care, as well as social security, education and decent working conditions, was an extension of the provisions present in several Latin American constitutions.
26. This commitment is most clear in Article 2, which stated that 'Everyone is entitled to all the rights and freedoms set forth in this Declaration' and 'no distinction shall be made on the basis of political, jurisdictional or international status of the country or territory to which a person belongs, whether it be independent, *trust, non-self-governing or under any other limitation of sovereignty.*' (Emphasis added.)
27. Reus-Smit (2001), p.188.
28. Clapham, p.48.

Rights and justice

29. By 1953, the USA had abandoned the international human rights project it helped to create, and it was completely removed from the processes that institutionalized the work of the ICCPR's Human Rights Committee. It took nearly 30 years for the USA to ratify the ICCPR and, to date, it has not yet ratified the ICECSR.
30. Reus-Smit (2001), p.186.
31. United Nations. (1953). *Yearbook of the United Nations: 1953*. United Nations Department of Information, p.386. The coalition included Denmark, India, Iraq, Israel, Mexico and Syria.
32. 'Declaration on the Granting of Independence to Colonial Countries and Peoples'. General Assembly Resolution 1514 (XV), December 14, 1960.
33. Reus-Smit (2002), p.535.
34. United Nations. (1951). *Yearbook of the United Nations: 1951*. United Nations Department of Information, p.485.
35. Article 1 of the ICCPR and the ICESCR declares: 'All peoples have the right to self-determination. By virtue of that right they freely determine their political status and freely pursue their economic, social and cultural development.'
36. Reus-Smit (2002), p.537.
37. Amnesty International. 'Torture'. Retrieved on April 27, 2023 from www.amnesty.org/en/what-we-do/torture/
38. The map can be found here: https://freedomhouse.org/sites/default/files/2023-03/FH_World_map_2023_poster_24x16_v2.pdf
39. A number of these treaties include Optional Protocols that were subject to a separate process of signing and ratification. Many of these Optional Protocols were created to allow for individuals to directly petition or address the relevant treaty body. Typically, only states are allowed to do so.
40. Wuerth, I. (2019, March 22). 'A Post-Human Rights Era? A Reappraisal and Response to Critics'. Lawfare. Retrieved on April 27, 2023 from www.lawfareblog.com/post-human-rights-era-appraisal-and-response-critics
41. Sixteen of the 24 states that are party to the American Convention on Human Rights have also signed the Protocol of San Salvador.
42. The most significant difference between the 1990 and 2020 versions is that the former affirms Islamic sharia law as its sole source, whereas the 2020 iteration does not specifically invoke sharia law.
43. Sharia law is a system of Islamic principles and guidelines derived from the Quran, Hadith (sayings of Prophet Muhammad) and scholarly interpretations, governing various aspects of life, including personal conduct, family matters and societal norms, followed by many Muslims around the world.
44. An Amnesty International report in 2012 stated that 163 of the 193 UN member states 'can exercise universal jurisdiction over one or more crimes under international law, either as such crimes or as ordinary crimes under national law.' See: 'Universal jurisdiction: A preliminary survey of legislation around the world – 2012 update'. (2012, October 9). Amnesty International. Retrieved on April 27, 2023 from www.amnesty.org/en/documents/ior53/019/2012/en/
45. The Commission was guided by a question that then UN Secretary-General Kofi Annan had posed: 'If humanitarian intervention is, indeed, an unacceptable assault on sovereignty, how should we respond to a Rwanda, to a Srebrenica – to gross and systematic violations of human rights that affect every precept of our common humanity?' Annan's question captured the debate between those who valued the norm of humanitarian intervention above state sovereignty, and vice versa.
46. Belloni, R. (2006). 'The Tragedy of Darfur and the Limits of the "Responsibility to Protect"'. *Ethnopolitics*, 5(4), p.331.
47. Article 2[7] of the UN Charter states: 'Nothing contained in the present Charter shall authorize the United Nations to intervene in matters which are essentially within the domestic jurisdiction of any state.'

Thematic studies

48. Article 4 does not permit parties to the Convention to derogate from their obligations to protect the following rights: right to life, freedom from torture, freedom from slavery, freedom from arbitrary imprisonment, equality before the law, and freedom of conscience and thought.
49. For a discussion of the various US government committees on the use of torture, see: Jervis, R. (2015). 'The Torture Blame Game'. *Foreign Affairs*, 94(3), pp.120–27.
50. The 60-year-old UN Commission on Human Rights came under increasing criticism in the early 2000s for failing to uphold human rights norms globally, in part because its membership had expanded to include many nation-states perceived to be major human rights abusers and violators. The UNHRC still includes many of the world's worst rights-violating states.
51. United Nations. (2022, February). 'Concerned by Unintended Negative Impact of Sanctions, Speakers in Security Council Urge Action to Better Protect Civilians, Ensure Humanitarian Needs Are Met'. Retrieved on April 28, 2023 from https://press.un.org/en/2022/sc14788.doc.htm
52. There is an Asian Human Rights Commission, but this is an independent NGO.
53. Commissioners can dismiss a case if the facts have been presented to any other international body of adjudication or if the case is filed too long after the final domestic decision has been handed down.
54. The Convention on the Prevention and Punishment of the Crime of Genocide (Genocide Convention) codified for the first time the crime of genocide in international law. It was signed on December 9, 1948 (the day before the UDHR) and came into force in 1951. As of April 2022, there are 153 parties to this convention.
55. Jean-Pierre Bemba Gombo was charged with two counts of crimes against humanity and three counts of war crimes. These charges were confirmed in 2009, but he appealed and the ICC Appeals Chamber acquitted him of all counts in 2018.
56. For example, in late July 2023, the Biden administration announced that it was sharing information about Russian war crimes in Ukraine with the ICC prosecutor, Karim Khan.
57. See: Jo, H. and Simmons, B.A. (2016). 'Can the International Criminal Court Deter Atrocity?'. *International Organization*, 70(3), pp. 443–75.
58. Transnational advocacy networks can impact the beliefs, ideas and perspectives (dominant narratives) surrounding certain global issues. These networks can also influence the process of determining which issues are prioritized and addressed on an international scale (agenda setting). They can shape public opinion and policy discussions on a global level.
59. See: Keck, M.E. and Sikkink, K. (1998). *Activists beyond Borders: Advocacy Networks in International Networks.* Cornell University Press.
60. See, for instance: Blain, K.N. (2020). 'Civil Rights International: The Fight Against Racism Has Always Been Global'. *Foreign Affairs*, 99(5), pp.176–81.
61. An ombudsman is an independent and impartial official appointed to represent and advocate for the rights and interests of individuals or groups when dealing with complaints, disputes or grievances related to a specific government agency or institution.
62. 'Statement on behalf of a Group of Countries at the 24rd [sic] Session of the Human Rights Council'. (2013, September). Retrieved on April 29, 2023 from https://media.business-humanrights.org/media/documents/files/media/documents/statement-unhrc-legally-binding.pdf
63. See: Murdie, A.M. and Davis, D.R. (2012). 'Shaming and Blaming: Using Events Data to Assess the Impact of Human Rights INGOs'. *International Studies Quarterly*, 56(1), pp.1–16.
64. See: Burton, E. (2008). 'Sticks and Stones: Naming and Shaming the Human Rights Enforcement Problem'. *International Organization*, 62(4), pp.689–716.
65. Vincent, p.3.
66. Coronaviruses cause diseases in mammals and birds. In humans, they cause respiratory tract infections that can range from mild to lethal. The descriptor 'novel' is added to coronaviruses of medical significance before a permanent name is decided upon. The COVID-19 disease was caused by SARS-CoV-2.
67. The term *social compact* refers to the unwritten understanding between different stakeholders in a society and is based on the idea that there is an implicit agreement between the state and its citizens that acknowledges the interdependence and shared interests of these stakeholders in maintaining social stability, economic development and the well-being of society as a whole.

68. Article 29 of the UDHR is communitarian, however: 'everyone has duties to the community in which alone the free and full development of his [sic] personality is possible.'
69. Ignatieff, M. (2001, November 1). 'The Attack on Human Rights'. Foreign Affairs. Retrieved on April 29, 2023 from www.foreignaffairs.com/articles/2001-11-01/attack-human-rights
70. BBC World Service. 'Repression in the name of rights is unacceptable'. Retrieved on April 30, 2023 from www.bbc.co.uk/worldservice/people/features/ihavearightto/four_b/casestudy_art30.shtml
71. Ignatieff (2001).
72. Etzioni, A. (1996). 'The Responsive Community: A Communitarian Perspective'. *American Sociological Review*, 61(1), pp.1–11.
73. Arendt, H. (1979). *The Origins of Totalitarianism*. Harcourt, Brace and Co., p.291.
74. Kaminski, I. (2019, December 20). 'Dutch Supreme Court upholds landmark ruling demanding climate action'. *The Guardian*. Retrieved on April 30, 2023 from www.theguardian.com/world/2019/dec/20/dutch-supreme-court-upholds-landmark-ruling-demanding-climate-action

* Sources: United Nations. (n.d.). *UN, United Nations, UN treaties, treaties*. Retrieved on April 22, 2023 from https://treaties.un.org/pages/Treaties.aspx?id=4&subid=A&clang=_en, and Clapham, pp.49–51.

Development and sustainability

THEMATIC STUDIES

Development and sustainability

Development and sustainability are contested concepts with important links to our understanding of power as the ability to determine outcomes for others. The effective implementation of human rights and positive peace are closely associated with the different levels of development in different societies. Lower levels of development increase the possibility of internal and external conflict. Adequate sustainable development may have a reversing effect, leading to higher levels of peace and an enjoyment of rights.

Your inquiry into development and sustainability will provide you with a number of opportunities to explore all the HL topic areas. Each topic area can be used as a lens to explore the causes and impacts of sustainable and successful development. In addition, you can use your case studies to explore each of the topic areas.

Exam questions frequently ask you to consider the different circumstances, factors or conditions that contribute to successful development. You can boost your success by considering these factors and use relevant case studies to show these factors in practice.

Concepts

Development, Sustainability, Poverty, Inequality, Models of development, Stakeholders

Learning outcomes

In this chapter, you will learn about:

- four different types of development: political, institutional, social and economic
- the contested meanings and understandings of development, sustainability, poverty and inequality, and why they are important for a deeper understanding of global politics
- the power interactions of political stakeholders, policymakers, actors and others impacted by policies designed to address the political issues surrounding these concepts
- the links and relationship between sustainability, inequality and development
- the evolution and development of sustainability as an economic, social and environmental concept
- the role, interests and interactions of state and non-state stakeholders and actors impacting sustainability
- how the global legal and institutional sustainability framework continues to develop
- the interdependence of sustainability, poverty and equality
- the impacts of globalization on sustainability and inequality
- the politicization of the environment that drives many of the contemporary debates on sustainability.
- the persistent problem of poverty and how it is affected by development
- how inequality and poverty are a problem for everyone.

Activity

Look at the chapter opening image which shows Tuca Vieira's 2004 photograph of the Paraisópolis favela (informal/temporary settlement) on the left next to its wealthy neighbor, Morumbi, on the right. What does this image say to you about development and sustainability? Share your thoughts with your classmates. What similarities and differences do you notice in your interpretations of Viera's image?

Development

Conceptual question

What is development and is all development successful?

If you ask five social scientists the question 'What is development and what constitutes successful development?', each might begin with 'Development is a shift or change in circumstances, conditions or factors…', but after that you will likely get five different answers.

Why might this be the case?

Thematic studies

> **Activity**
>
> Write down your own definition or understanding of the terms 'development' and 'successful development'. Compare your definitions and understandings with your classmates. What ideas do you share about development and successful development? In what ways are your definitions and understandings different? What factors might contribute to these differences?

Economists will often emphasize the importance of economic factors such as high levels of investment and low levels of unemployment. Psychologists may see development as efforts to reduce individual and societal stress factors. Cultural anthropologists might consider the impact that development has on the ability of indigenous groups to be able to use their language and celebrate their traditions as part of the larger society they belong to. Political scientists might value the development of laws that protect the human rights of all citizens in a society equally and without discrimination.

Now consider development and successful development from the perspective of a government official responsible for trade policy, the small grocery store on the corner of your street being faced with a new tax on fizzy drinks, or an executive of a large oil company interested in exploring the possibilities of an oil field in a post-conflict environment.

There are also billions of people directly or indirectly impacted by development policies who might see development very differently.

The interpretations of development and successful development from these different perspectives might be very different, and may even be in conflict with one another.

Because there are many interpretations of development and what successful development might look like, development is a significant, high-stakes issue for all of us.

> **Activity**
>
> When trying to understand development, sustainability, poverty, and inequality, it is important to consider that these are multidimensional concepts whose meanings are highly contested and depend on context. Write down your own definition for each of these terms and compare them to that of a classmate or to that of an organization that works to promote (development and sustainability) or eliminate (poverty and inequality) the concepts. What are the differences between your definitions? What might the reasons for these differences be?

Different approaches to development are important because they contribute to the policies and practices of states, multilateral organizations like the United Nations (UN), private corporations like Nestlé and NGOs like Oxfam.

Development policies and practices have an impact on all living things on our planet and require our specific attention in Global Politics.

In Global Politics, we often speak of ideas or concepts being *contested*. Contested means that there are various different perspectives or approaches to consider. You can boost your success by researching and examining the different perspectives behind contested concepts like successful development.

Stakeholders are actors on the global, regional or national stage, such as states, organizations or groups, that have an interest in determining the outcomes and are impacted by those outcomes. In development, we look at the policies and practices of stakeholders such as states, intergovernmental organizations (IGOs), international and regional financial institutions, private companies, non-governmental organizations (NGOs) and trade unions, as well as social movements, and marginalized or vulnerable groups.

Development refers to a general improvement in standards of living, although this may come at a cost in terms of the environment, or include improvements in living standards that are not shared by everyone. Successful development refers to development that aims to be environmentally friendly and equally distributed in society.

TOK — How do we know if we have effectively measured success in development?

129

Development and sustainability

Figure 3.1 This map represents the size of each country if their sizes were determined by their proportion of worldwide wealth measured as GDP. We will consider other ways of viewing our world as we explore development and sustainability in Global Politics.

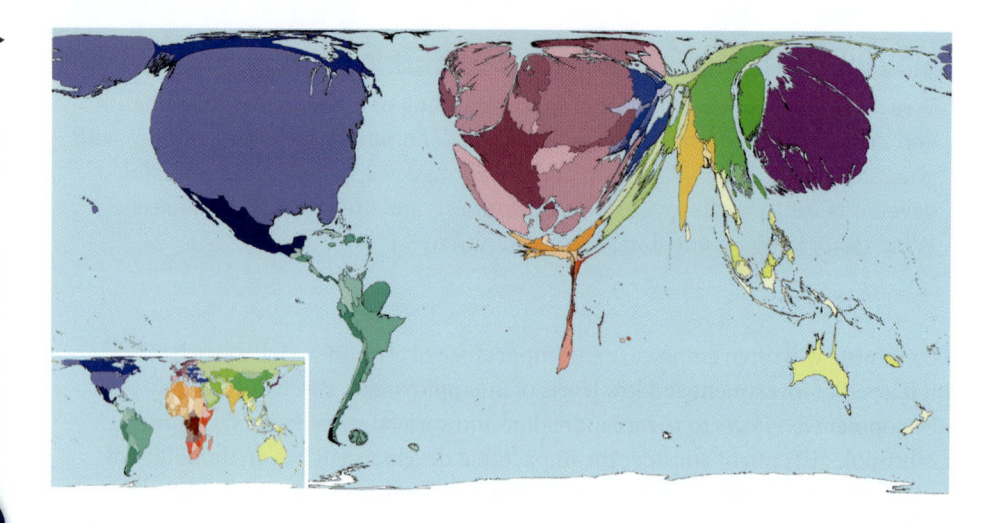

HL

When exploring what successful development looks like, you can use this opportunity to explore some of the HL topic areas. For example, consider what the *Health* outcomes look like in a high-middle- or high-income country and compare these to the health outcomes in low- and middle-income countries. You could investigate how high-middle- or high-income countries are meeting certain challenges related to the *Environment* and climate change. Consider the advantages created when a country has access to renewable energy technology and can mitigate the effects of climate change.

Types of development: economic, political, institutional and social

There are many different interpretations of development. In this section, we will begin with a straightforward definition of development: development means a sustained increase in the standard of living in a society.

Activity

Working with your classmates, interpret Figure 3.1. This map represents the size of each country if the size were determined by its proportion of worldwide wealth measured as GDP. Which countries are largest according to the map? Which ones are smallest? How did these countries get that way? Search online for the Visual Capitalist distribution of global GDP by region map to help you with this activity.

Economic development

Successful development defined in terms of a sustained increase in the standard of living usually brings to mind economic development. Economic development is an important part of our overall understanding of development.

Successful economic development is often measured by specific types of economic growth, measured in specific ways such as gross domestic product (GDP), gross national product (GNP) or gross national income (GNI) for an entire country or broken down per capita (per person). A well-managed economy is necessary for an increased standard of living. However, many would argue that development involves more than just GDP-, GNP- or GNI-measured economic growth.

Thematic studies

Figure 3.2 Top 12 countries measured in GDP per capita 2022, based on The World Bank and IMF data.

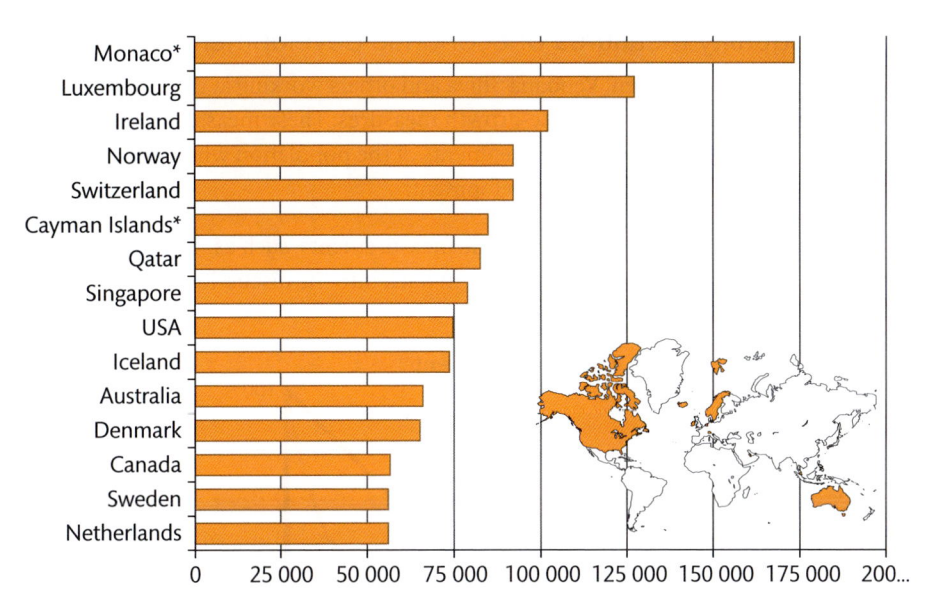

Source: World Bank, Helgi Library, IMF estimates (Oct 2020), * Data from 2020

GDP and GDP per capita help us to start understanding the levels of development in a country. It is also useful to compare countries' GDP and GDP per capita. Figure 3.2 looks at GDP per capita, and you can see a regional trend, with only a few exceptions. Our task in Global Politics is to understand and interpret what this might mean. Figure 3.2 shows the top 12 countries ranked by GDP per capita in 2022, but these countries may be very different in other areas of their development.

> GDP is the total value of all the finished goods and services produced within a country's borders in a specific time period, usually one year. It is also measured per person or per capita. To calculate GDP per capita, the overall income of a country is divided by its number of inhabitants. This gives the average income per person. When GDP per capita is increasing, the economy is growing, which is an indicator of successful economic development. If there is no growth, or a downward trend, there is negative development. Because GDP per capita is calculated as an average, however, it does not give a clear picture of how a country's wealth is distributed.
>
> GNP is an estimate of the total value of all the final products and services produced in a given period by a country's citizens.
>
> GNI is the total amount of money earned by a country's people and businesses in a specific time period, usually one year. The amount includes the country's GDP, plus the income it receives from overseas sources.

GDP, GNP and GNI do not consider how the income in a country is distributed, as they look only at the average. In very unequal societies, GDP, GNP and GNI per capita and Balance of Trade (BOT) can be misleading measures. If the rich are getting richer, this may show as an increase in GDP, GNP and GNI per capita, and an increase in exports, even if the situation of the poor does not change.

One way to bring balance to your assessment responses in Global Politics related to development is to discuss the different types of development beyond economic development. You can boost your success by including case studies that show the relationship between economic and other types of development.

HL Using economic growth measures of development like GDP, GNP and GNI might lead you to explore case studies linked to *Poverty* and strategies that promote poverty reduction. It might be helpful to look at how these strategies have been implemented over time and to consider the extent to which these policies might be considered successful or not. You could consider the connection between levels or rates of poverty and *Health* outcomes. You may also find it useful to explore poverty through *Identity* and the extent to which poverty impacts men and women, young and old, differently at different levels of income.

131

Development and sustainability

Income-equality measures of economic development

Mahbub ul Haq, Amartya Sen, Vendana Shiva and others working at the UN brought about a re-evaluation of these income-growth measures. These measures were useful to some extent, but they missed entire segments of the population who might not feel the benefits of successful economic development.

To help bring some balance, older economic measurements, such as the **Lorenz curve** and the **Gini coefficient**, were brought back into the discussion of successful economic development.

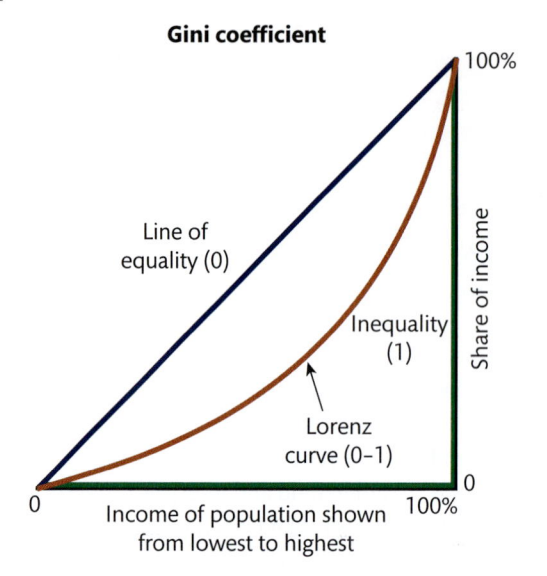

Figure 3.3 The Gini coefficient and Lorenz curve help us to understand the nature of income distribution within a country.

The Gini coefficient and Lorenz curve came about through a need to understand how the economic success of a country and the level of *Equality* were related. You can use both, for example, when exploring a country with a relatively high GDP, GNP and GNI to see the extent to which wealth is equally or unequally distributed. You might discover higher rates of *Poverty* and poorer *Health* outcomes for some *Identity* groups in high-income countries. What might this tell you about the importance of income and wealth distribution toward successful development outcomes?

When you discuss successful economic development, you can boost your success if you look at income-growth measures and income-equality measures of development before reaching a conclusion about successful development.

How might we decide when it is better to value an income-growth measure of development over an income-equality measure?

The Gini coefficient is used to measure how equal or unequal societies are. It considers the distribution of income, rather than assuming that it is distributed evenly. It measures the difference between the incomes of the richest and the poorest, and how many people earn across this spectrum. The Gini coefficient is given as a number between 0 and 1. The more equal a society is, the closer to 0 its Gini coefficient. A high Gini coefficient indicates that there is a lot of inequality and a large difference between the incomes of the wealthiest and the poorest.

The Lorenz curve is derived from calculating the Gini coefficient. The curve represents unequal distribution of wealth, or inequality, within a society.

An analysis of the data from calculating the Gini coefficient and the Lorenz curve might be used as an indicator for successful development, assuming that high inequality and unequal distribution of wealth is considered bad for development. If used with the more income-growth based measurements like GDP, GNP and GNI, an overall determination of successful economic development may be possible.

Political and institutional development

Critics of the purely economic view argue that other factors, such as human rights and democracy, are equally important in development, and an important part of the development discussion relates to the role that political development plays in successful development.

Political development might be seen as the ability of a state's national and local institutions to carry out the tasks of governance efficiently, fairly and without discrimination. In other

Thematic studies

words, political development may be seen as the extent to which a country practices good governance and implements the rule of law. The presence of high or low levels of public and private sector corruption is usually part of this discussion.

Institutional development relates to the strength of justice systems and civil rights processes, as well as the role of non-state actors (NSAs) like IGOs and NGOs working within a society to improve conditions for all. This could involve health, rights or charities, and NGOs supporting marginalized groups in society.

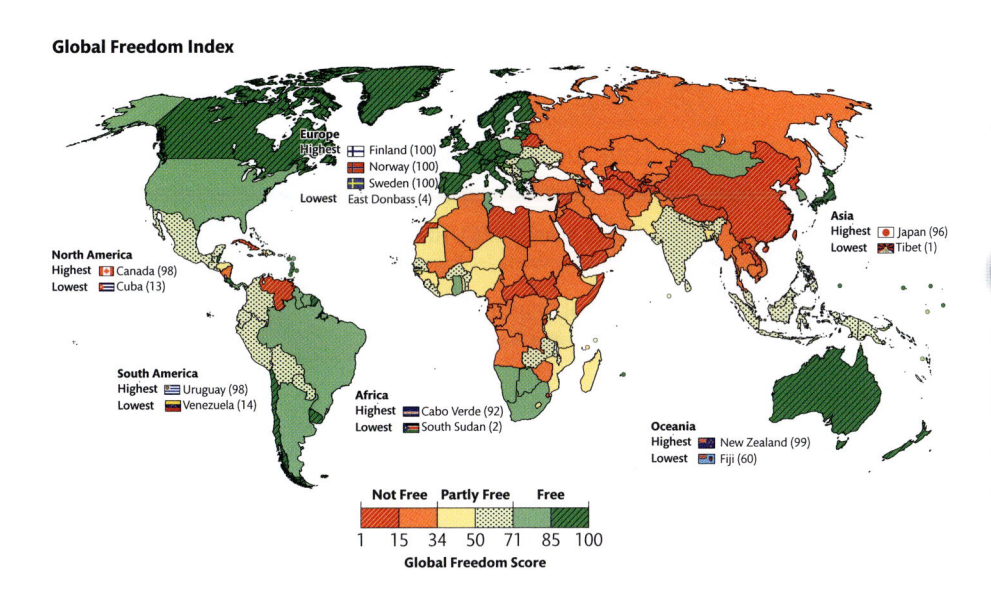

Global Freedom Index

Europe
Highest: Finland (100), Norway (100), Sweden (100)
Lowest: East Donbass (4)

North America
Highest: Canada (98)
Lowest: Cuba (13)

South America
Highest: Uruguay (98)
Lowest: Venezuela (14)

Africa
Highest: Cabo Verde (92)
Lowest: South Sudan (2)

Asia
Highest: Japan (96)
Lowest: Tibet (1)

Oceania
Highest: New Zealand (99)
Lowest: Fiji (60)

Global Freedom Score
Not Free: 1–15, 15–34
Partly Free: 34–50, 50–71
Free: 71–85, 85–100

Political development can also be understood by looking at how the citizens of a society have their voices heard and their needs met in their society. This might be through the development of political parties, trade unions, civil society organizations or social movements. Figure 3.4 shows the Global Freedom Index, which is a way of representing the level of freedom experienced in different countries. Freedom House analyzes and evaluates political development in 210 countries and regions using a number of categories including: rule of law, access to the judicial system, right to vote, freedom of expression, press freedom, etc. Each year, they publish their *Freedom in the World* report, which is used by many as a way to evaluate the extent to which a country has successful political development. Freedom House also tries to make the connection between successful political development and successful economic development.

People often refer to Abraham Maslow's hierarchy of needs (Figure 3.5) in the context of political development. It shows a progression from basic human needs, such as food and shelter, at the bottom of the hierarchy, to security and then to higher needs, such as relationships and self-esteem. The goal is self-actualization, or the fulfillment of a person's potential and wishes in life.

The assumption is that successful political development will help societies reach this higher level of the pyramid structure by making possible the physiological and safety needs at the bottom of the pyramid. The argument is that, if these are not secure, it will be difficult to achieve the upper levels. Maslow helps us to understand that successful development needs to be more than just narrowly measured GDP and GNI.

One way to strengthen your assessment responses in Global Politics related to political development is to use data related to different ways of measuring political development, like press freedom and perceptions of corruption. You can boost your success by including this data as you explore different case studies related to political development.

Figure 3.4 Global Freedom Index from Freedom House.

HL Freedom House looks at political development in regions, subregions and countries. You might consider using their methodology as you approach political development through your exploration of *Borders*. Consider the relative levels of political development by region and the role that national and regional borders have played, especially with regards to the expectations of political development found in regional IGOs like the European Union (EU), African Union (AU) and Association of South East Asian Nations (ASEAN).

HL Exploring political development, especially using such measures and rankings from Freedom House, is an opportunity to consider the relationship between political development and *Security*. You could investigate traditional forms of national security and compare how much a country spends on military and defense and where they rank according to Freedom House. You could also look into human security by investigating levels of *Equality* and *Poverty*, and *Health* outcomes.

133

Development and sustainability

Figure 3.5 Maslow's hierarchy of needs.

SELF-ACTUALIZATION
morality, creativity, spontaneity, acceptance, experience purpose, meaning and inner potential — Self-fulfillment needs

SELF-ESTEEM
confidence, achievement, respect of others, the need to be a unique individual

LOVE AND BELONGING
friendship, family, intimacy, sense of connection — Psychological needs

SAFETY AND SECURITY
health, employment, property, family and social abilty

PHYSIOLOGICAL NEEDS
breathing, food, water, shelter, clothing, sleep — Basic needs

TOK: How can we be certain that the way toward successful political development in one country is applicable in another?

HL: Consider using Maslow's hierarchy of needs as a tool to explore the HL topic areas. Fundamental needs include positive *Health* outcomes, access to a sustainable *Environment* for current and future generations, as well as low levels of *Poverty*. Basic needs also include *Security* and the support of a system including access to technologies to help guarantee these basic needs. Levels of *Equality*, including equal access to the benefits of society, can be found further up Maslow's hierarchy. You can include the right to express one's *Identity* as part of what Maslow refers to as 'psychological' and 'self-actualization'. Different countries and regions will likely have different priorities and ways in which to achieve these needs (more government intervention and support, greater reliance on private-sector firms or individuals, etc.), so *Borders* is also a topic area you can explore using Maslow.

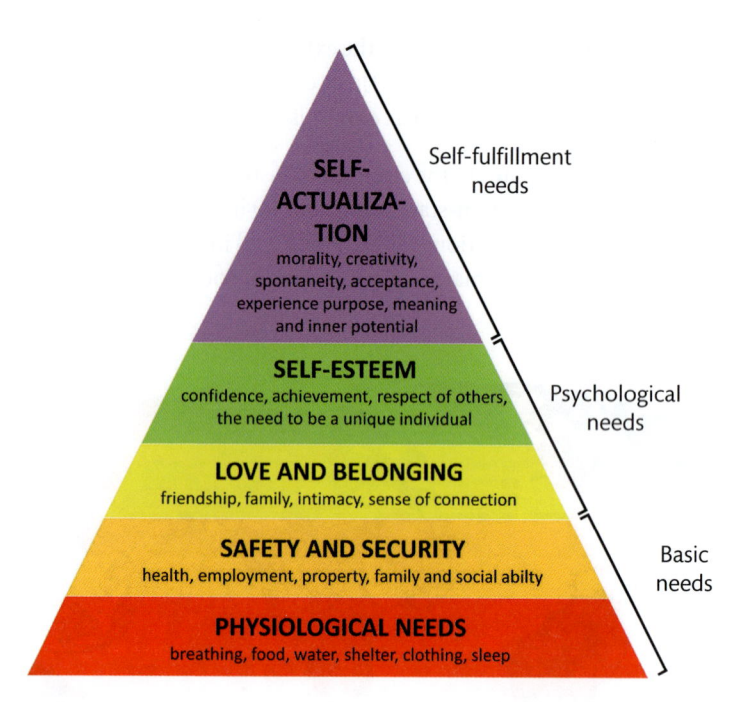

Political development is difficult to measure, in part due to how different societies prioritize different rights and freedoms. For example, does successful political development require multiple political parties, trade unions and civil society organizations for these needs to be met?

Activity

Working with a classmate, each of you pick a country that has very different rankings for press freedom or perception of corruption using the latest Transparency International Corruption Perceptions Index.

Come up with a set of reasons why these differences might exist. What circumstances, factors and conditions have you come up with? What do you think best explains why these differences exist? What might be done to reduce these differences?

Social development

Successful development also includes **social development**, which is the idea of improving the well-being of each individual member of society, as well as the different groups that make up society. When we speak of social development, we often discuss the importance of individual and group rights, and the access of all to equal opportunities and equal treatment.

One (very large) group whose rights are often restricted is women. Figure 3.6 shows women's freedom of movement in public spaces. The areas where women have free movement are shown in green. In other areas, the movement of women in public spaces is restricted.

Thematic studies

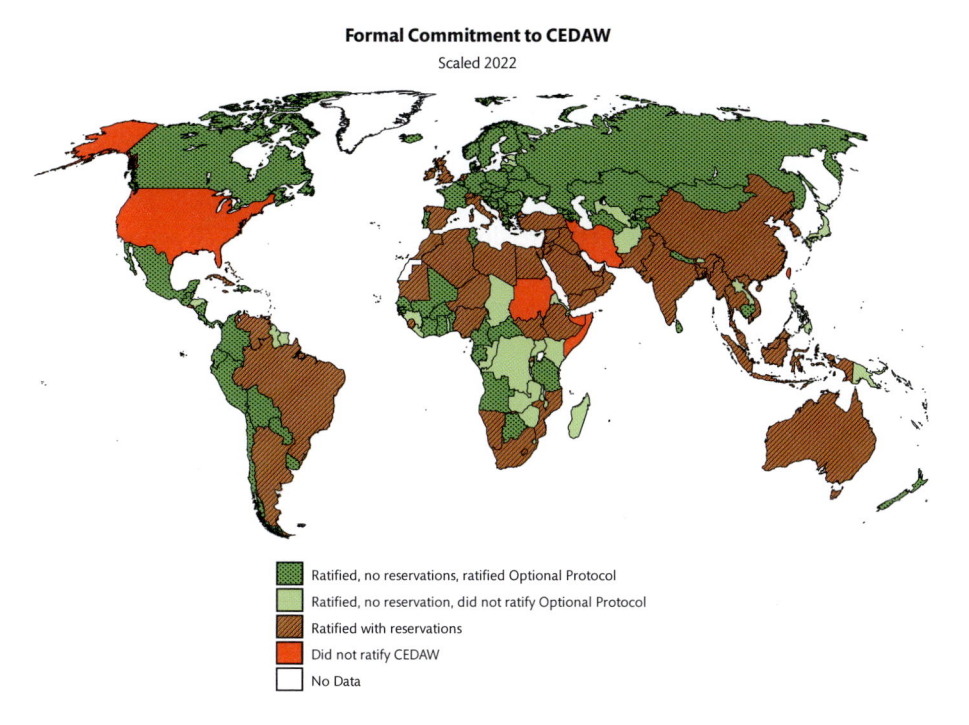

Formal Commitment to CEDAW
Scaled 2022

- Ratified, no reservations, ratified Optional Protocol
- Ratified, no reservation, did not ratify Optional Protocol
- Ratified with reservations
- Did not ratify CEDAW
- No Data

◀ **Figure 3.6** A global snapshot of women's mobility.

i — WomanStats provides visualizations and analyses of data related to the situation and security of women, and the dynamics between security, stability and the behavior of state actors toward women using various indicators and measurements. They are an excellent source of information regarding social development.

Social development is about equality as well as equity. Equality is where things are made the same for people and people are treated in exactly the same way. Equity is where the barriers faced by individuals are acknowledged and supported, for example, by providing access ramps for wheelchairs or accessible childcare provision for women who want to work.

Social development may involve healthcare and nutrition programs for children and families, or the impact of laws relating to gender equality, freedom of association, women's rights and worker's rights.

Example – The African Union's Agenda 2063

The African Union's Agenda 2063 represents a holistic vision encompassing economic, political, institutional and social development goals aimed at transforming Africa. Economically, it emphasizes infrastructure development, economic integration and industrialization to foster intra-African trade and technological advancement. Politically, the agenda prioritizes good governance, peace and pan-Africanism, focusing on fostering accountable leadership, conflict resolution, and a sense of collective identity among African nations. Institutionally, Agenda 2063 emphasizes building strong governance structures, capacity building, and fostering partnerships for development. Socially, it underscores human development, gender equality, and youth empowerment through investments in education, healthcare, social welfare and inclusion initiatives. This comprehensive approach acknowledges that sustainable development requires a multifaceted strategy addressing various dimensions to achieve a prosperous, united and thriving Africa by 2063.

HL — Your investigation of social development may bring you into contact with data and case studies linked to the HL topic areas of *Health*, *Environment*, *Poverty*, *Equality* and *Security*. Using *Identity* as your primary topic area, you could explore how each of these topic areas impact and are impacted by different identity groups. You could also explore through case studies, for example, gender equality and the impact that gender equality has on health outcomes, or the security of women.

Development and sustainability

> The HDI of the UN Development Programme (UNDP) considers life expectancy, years of education and income. The HDI adds another dimension to our understanding of development and how successful development might be measured or understood.

Human development

Human development refers to the process of enlarging people's freedoms and opportunities, and improving their well-being.[1] Human development emphasizes personal, family and community well-being, and the importance of certain types of political and economic development to support the individual in their community.

Human development focuses on the freedom and opportunities for all people and how this impacts who they want to be and how they want to live their lives. Amartya Sen's influential book on human development was titled *Development as Freedom* (1999).[2]

There is a focus on capabilities, which refers to the necessary equipment for pursuing a life of value. Examples of basic capabilities include good health, access to knowledge, the level of control over the living environment and freedom from violence.

Human development is now measured by the UN using the **Human Development Index (HDI)** (Figure 3.7), which is a collection of social measurements taken at the national and local levels.[3] You can see a strong connection between the ideas of human development and Maslow's hierarchy of needs.

The HDI, pioneered by Mahbub ul Haq, an eminent economist and development theorist from Pakistan, combines data on life expectancy, education and income.

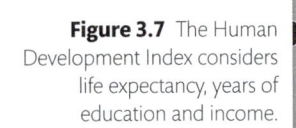

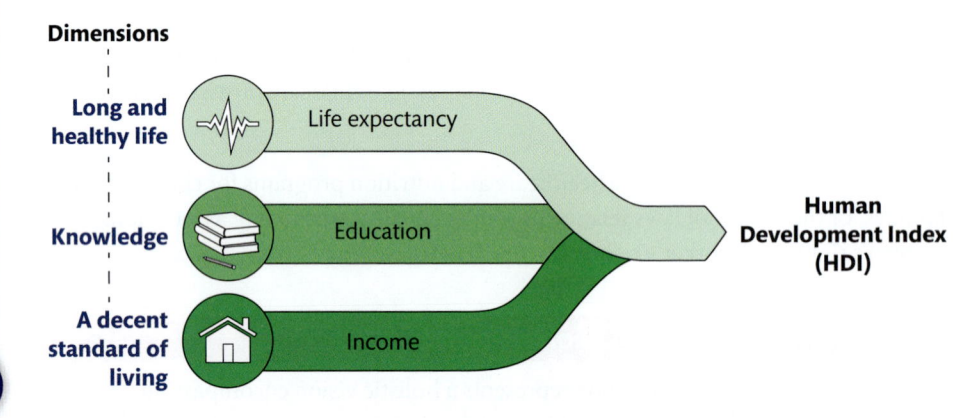

Figure 3.7 The Human Development Index considers life expectancy, years of education and income.

Dimensions
- Long and healthy life → Life expectancy
- Knowledge → Education
- A decent standard of living → Income

→ Human Development Index (HDI)

> When you find a good case study in development, you can boost your success if you find specific evidence of the different types of development at stake, such as political, economic, social and institutional.

> **TOK**
> What are the advantages and disadvantages of different ways to categorize development? Is it useful to view development in different ways?

People-centered development (PCD)

Another approach to social development can be found in the idea of **people-centered development (PCD)**.

Around the same time ul Haq and Sen were developing their approach to human development, David Korten and Vandana Shiva were working on PCD. This focuses on improving local communities' self-reliance through social justice, participatory decision-making and local empowerment.

PCD recognizes that economic growth does not contribute to human development on its own and that fair growth requires changes in social, political and environmental values and practices.

Thematic studies

> **Activity**
>
> Working with a classmate, look up the Gender Development Index (GDI) and each pick a country that has very different rankings for gender equality.
>
> Come up with a set of reasons why these differences might exist. What circumstances, factors and conditions have you come up with? What do you think best explains why these differences exist? What might be done to reduce these differences?

Another development theorist, Inge Kaul, looked at comparative data for men and women across a wide range of countries. The result was the **Gender Development Index (GDI)**, which analyzes countries and regions in the following three categories:[4]

- Health: measured by female and male life expectancy at birth.
- Education: measured by female and male expected years of schooling for children and female and male mean years of schooling for adults aged 25 years and older.
- Command over economic resources: measured by female and male estimated earned income.

Another more holistic measure of successful economic development is The Happy Planet Index (HPI) of the New Economics Foundation, launched in 2006. HPI considers income as part of the larger discussion about human well-being and also measures the impact of human behavior on the environment.[5]

Top 10 Countries		
1	Costa Rica	62.1
2	Vanuatu	60.4
3	Colombia	60.2
4	Switzerland	60.1
5	Ecuador	58.8
6	Panama	57.9
7	Jamaica	57.9
8	Guatemala	57.9
9	Honduras	57.7
10	Uruguay	57.5

There is an interrelationship between political, institutional, economic and social development that needs to be considered and applied when reaching an evaluation as to what constitutes successful development.

HL Comparing and contrasting HDI and GDI for countries with different levels of income is an excellent way to begin a discussion about the HL topic areas of *Equality, Poverty* and *Identity*. As you investigate and compare HDI and GDI for different countries, consider the extent to which different regions of countries might have similar rankings and why that might be. This should lead you to an interesting discussion about the contemporary role that *Borders* play regarding levels of development.

Figure 3.8 The HPI measures human well-being and impacts on the environment.

When you discuss successful development, you can boost your success if you add to your analysis hybrid and holistic measures of successful economic development such as GDI, HDI and HPI before reaching a conclusion about successful development.

TOK How might we decide if holistic and hybrid measures are more useful than income-growth and income-equality measures of development?

137

Development and sustainability

Contested meanings of poverty and inequality

Like development and sustainability, the concepts of poverty and inequality have contested meanings that reflect different perspectives and which generate heated debate within Global Politics. This section touches upon the dynamic and often contentious nature of how poverty and inequality are conceptualized, defined and understood in Global Politics. Examining the contested meanings of poverty and inequality reveals to us a patchwork of contrasting viewpoints, and helps to illuminate some of the different layers that underpin global policymaking, socio-economic interventions in the name of development and sustainability, as well as the pursuit of a more equitable world order.

The concept of poverty

In Global Politics, poverty is conceptualized as both a social injustice and a complex global challenge with multifaceted dimensions. One prevailing interpretation revolves around poverty as an economic condition, focusing on insufficient income or resources to meet basic human needs like food, shelter, healthcare and education. This viewpoint often employs quantitative measures such as income thresholds to assess and address poverty.

Another significant perspective looks beyond the purely economic aspects, emphasizing poverty as a multidimensional phenomenon. This approach recognizes that poverty extends beyond income scarcity, encompassing social exclusion, limited access to opportunities, health disparities, and inadequate political representation. Poverty is seen as a product of unequal power dynamics, structural inequalities, and historical injustices embedded in global systems of trade, governance and resource distribution. This view emphasizes that poverty is not merely a lack of resources but a consequence of political and economic decisions that maintain disparities. This structural perspective emphasizes inequalities, discrimination, power imbalances and policy frameworks that make poverty worse. It underscores the need for policy interventions, reforms and international cooperation to address not just the symptoms but the root causes of poverty within the global political landscape.

A more multidimensional view, popularized by the HDI and Multidimensional Poverty Index, highlights the importance of considering various aspects of well-being and capabilities when addressing poverty in global politics. Furthermore, poverty is seen as interconnected with various global issues such as conflict, human rights, migration, climate change and health crises. By acknowledging the complexity of poverty as a phenomenon, many perspectives emphasize the need for comprehensive, multifaceted approaches to effectively combat poverty and its far-reaching impacts.

The concept of inequality

Much like other concepts in Global Politics, inequality is understood through various lenses, reflecting the multifaceted nature of disparities within and between countries. As we have already seen above, one predominant interpretation of inequality focuses on economic disparities, highlighting the uneven distribution of wealth, income and resources among individuals and states. This perspective often emphasizes metrics like the Gini coefficient to measure income inequality and assess the gap between the rich and the poor. This economic lens reveals stark differences in standards of living, access to necessities, and the concentration of wealth within certain segments of societies and across countries.

Other critical viewpoints on inequality extend beyond the economic realm, however. Social inequality encompasses disparities in access to education, healthcare, social

Thematic studies

services, and access to rights or opportunities based on factors such as gender, ethnicity, race and social class. Political inequality delves into unequal power structures, limited political participation, and disparities in representation, where certain groups might hold disproportionate influence in decision-making processes. Cultural interpretations of inequality explore discrimination, exclusion and marginalization within societies based on cultural identities and norms.

Moreover, there's a global perspective on inequality, acknowledging disparities between different regions and countries, for example between developed and developing countries. This lens emphasizes the uneven distribution of resources, access to technology, trade imbalances and development levels among nations. It also considers the impact of historical factors, colonial legacies, geopolitical power dynamics and international policies on perpetuating global inequalities. Addressing these diverse forms of inequality in global politics often involves policies and initiatives aimed at promoting equity, social justice, human rights and sustainable development, while tackling root causes across economic, social, political and cultural domains. Conceptualizing inequality in global politics necessitates addressing systemic issues, advocating for policy reforms, promoting inclusive governance structures, and fostering international cooperation to mitigate disparities and create more equitable societies on a global scale.

Exercises

1. Define *poverty*. How do we compare the poverty in one country with the poverty in other countries?
2. Should we always aim for equality? Can inequality ever be fair?
3. How developed is the country that you live in? Which methods of measuring development are most important to you?

Nature, practice and study of sustainable development

The Second World War brought about big changes in global organization, structure and priorities. The second half of the 20th century was the origin of many organizations aimed at maintaining and improving security. There were also many ideas for recovery and development in countries that had suffered as a result of the war. The horror of war made people seek better lives that would prevent the bad times from coming again. This resulted in a range of economic and development theories still used today.

Models of economic development

Modernization theory

The first major model of economic development to emerge, in the middle of the 20th century, was **modernization theory**. In 1961, Walt Whitman Rostow published his influential book *The Stages of Economic Growth*, in which his market-based modernization theory model of development promoted the idea that industrialization and investments in technology and infrastructure would allow a country's economy to take off, leading to increased consumer consumption.[6]

W.W. Rostow is known for his modernization theory, a contested idea that suggests that, through increased investment, increased exposure to modernized and Western society, and changes in traditional culture and values, societies will become more highly developed.

Development and sustainability

HL — Development often involves technological advancements and this connects to the HL topic area of *Technology*. Sustainable development policies consider cybersecurity concerns, as technology can play a significant role in economic development but also poses risks if not managed securely.

Rostow identified five stages of development:

1. Traditional societies: Societies that are based on subsistence agriculture (where a family grows enough food to meet their own needs), with low levels of technology and pre-scientific values.
2. Pre-conditions for take-off: Societies that have started to introduce money and banking into their economy, and have a new class of entrepreneurs with scientific values.
3. Take-off: Societies in which values that encourage economic growth are widespread and growth of certain economic sectors, including industrial, commercial, services and government, have become common (such as Sweden and the USA in 1961).
4. Drive to maturity: Societies with an economy that is diversifying and producing an increasingly large variety of goods. Standards are rising and poverty is decreasing.
5. High mass consumption: Societies in which wealth and the production and consumption of modern consumer goods are widespread.

Example – Economic transformation

South Korea's rapid economic growth from the mid-20th century onwards often aligns with Rostow's theory. The country shifted from an agrarian economy to industrialization, experiencing significant economic development and technological advancement, eventually becoming one of the world's major economies. Another example would be Brazil's journey toward industrialization and urbanization, which also reflects some elements of Rostow's theory. The country experienced periods of economic growth and modernization, especially in its industrial sectors, contributing to its status as one of the leading economies in Latin America.

TOK — How are our current understandings of global politics shaped by historical development?

This approach became a driving force in what was understood as development. In other words, that poorer countries should follow the example of richer countries and develop just like the richer ones had done. This may, to some extent, have been partly used as a justification for colonialism (the occupation of one country by another). Colonial occupiers were often rich countries who increased their wealth by taking and trading the produce of poorer countries. Colonizing countries often said that they were helping the country that they colonized, by organizing their trade and employing workers (stages 2 and 3 above). In reality, the opposite was often true, as colonizers stood in the way of the colony's own development. In the second half of the 20th century, most colonies freed themselves from their colonial oppressors, although the legacy of colonialism can still be seen.

Modernization theory was very much a product of its time. Some questions that this theory has raised are:

! — When you include modernization theory in your assessment responses, make sure that you identify both its strengths and weaknesses. You can boost your success by providing some context about when it developed and why.

- What were the actual reasons why these newly independent countries were poorer than their former colonizers?
- Did these countries want to develop in the way Rostow suggested?
- Would increased production and consumption be equally beneficial to all who took part?
- What about the pollution and waste created by the increased production and consumption?

Thematic studies

- Who would be responsible for this pollution and waste?
- Who will ultimately benefit from Rostow's kind of development?

Modernization theory had three core ideas that proved influential in development:

- Trade between countries will increase development.
- Limited government intervention in the economy will increase development.
- Market-oriented policies will increase development.

These core ideas were also found in a branch of economic policy-making called **neoliberalism**, which relied heavily on the assumption that a country that has limited government intervention in its economy will experience growth.

Economic neoliberalism

Economic neoliberal policymakers believe that the free market is the most fair and efficient way to foster economic growth and development. Neoliberals believe that government interference in economics almost always has negative long-term consequences as it distorts the market. They believe a better solution is to encourage free enterprise by intervening in the economy as little as possible. The belief is that this leads to healthy competition, meaning that only the strongest companies survive and grow, which in turn leads to long-term economic growth.

Neoliberals argue that development in developing countries should grow from foreign direct investment (FDI), rather than government investment. The idea is that FDI should bypass the government of a developing country and go directly to an entrepreneur or company in that country.

Neoliberals also argue for a reduced role of the government and lower government spending on public services such as healthcare, education and pensions or retirement funds. This, according to neoliberal policymakers, will encourage people to work and contribute more to the economy in terms of spending and taxes. They believe that newly created economic wealth will eventually trickle down through all classes of society. As the rich get richer, they spend more money, which in turn helps various industries that employ more people who, in turn, become richer.

The Washington Consensus

In the 1970s and 1980s, neoliberal economic policymakers had a great deal of influence in the investment policies of the USA, UK and international financial institutions (IFIs) like The World Bank and the International Monetary Fund (IMF). These neoliberal policies were called the Washington Consensus because of the influence that the USA in particular had over these market-oriented, privatization policies in developing countries.

In order to achieve these neoliberal policies in developing countries, IFIs like The World Bank and the IMF created Structural Adjustment Programmes (SAPs) as a condition of giving out Structural Adjustment Loans (SALs) to developing countries. SAPs might include changes to government economic policy such as reducing government spending in

---

Nobel Prize winner for economics Milton Friedman is most closely associated with the ideas and policies of economic neoliberalism.

Economic neoliberalism is the idea that the free market is the most fair and efficient way to foster economic growth and development. Economic neoliberals believe that government interference in economics almost always has negative long-term consequences and should be avoided.

FDI is investment made in a country by an investor, company or government from another country.

Privatization is when the government transfers a business, industry or service from public (run by the government) to private ownership and control (run by a for-profit company).

141

Development and sustainability

some areas, or changing international trade policy. Governments of developing countries were encouraged to sign up to and implement a SAP to get the SALs they needed.

A SAP typically involved the lowering and eventual removal of trade barriers such as import tariffs, the devaluation of currencies, the cutting of public spending (such as subsidies) and the partial privatization of many public services (such as healthcare, education, waste management and sanitation).

▲ An interpretation of Washington Consensus neoliberal policies.

Activity

Working with a classmate, analyze the political cartoon above. Who are the characters on the left and right? What are they holding? What are they saying? What might each represent? What do you think this political cartoon is saying about neoliberal economic policies? Is it in favor of them or critical of them? What evidence do you have to support your analysis, from the cartoon and your own knowledge?

The results of Washington Consensus policies led to their reevaluation and the rise of a different set of policies to guide development. In the final analysis, most countries found that the Washington Consensus policies were designed to strengthen the national interests of the donors, not the recipients.

The conditions of the SAPs and SALs were difficult to manage, especially after reducing the ability of recipient governments to intervene or provide effective services. Many countries found themselves in a cycle of stagnation and inflation that crippled their national development. In many cases, this led to the need for more loans from IFIs.

Eventually, neoliberalism and the Washington Consensus in general, and SAPs in particular, were widely criticized for their harsh policies and the resultant dependency and the pressure that was put on governments to sign up to them, as a refusal to participate would often result in a cutting-off of further aid or credit.

HL
Development aims to provide long-term solutions for livelihoods and so can be linked to the HL topic area of *Poverty*. This involves initiatives that empower communities economically, such as promoting sustainable agriculture, microfinance and entrepreneurship, which can help break the cycle of poverty.

Import tariffs are placed on goods that are purchased from another country as trade. When a tariff is placed on imported goods, it makes these goods more expensive than goods that are grown or produced in the importing country, and so protects the trade in homegrown products. It is a way for countries to control trade with other countries and manage prices.

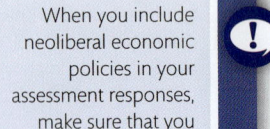

When you include neoliberal economic policies in your assessment responses, make sure that you identify and discuss specific policies. You can boost your success by providing some context about when these policies developed and why they developed.

Thematic studies

> **Example – The Washington Consensus**
>
> During the European debt crisis, Greece implemented austerity measures in line with the principles of the Washington Consensus. These measures included budget cuts, privatization of state assets, and structural reforms aimed at reducing public debt and enhancing economic competitiveness, as advised by international financial institutions. Similarly, Chile has implemented market-oriented economic policies, including trade liberalization, privatization and fiscal discipline, reflecting some aspects of the Washington Consensus. Over the years, Chile has embraced open-market policies, although the approach has evolved and incorporated social welfare initiatives.

> **Activity**
>
> With a classmate, role play stakeholders discussing the best way forward for a developing country. Discuss the strengths and weaknesses of modernization theory and the Washington Consensus' neoliberal economic policies from your point of view as a stakeholder in the country. Decide whether you would support these approaches as a stakeholder.

TOK: What would we consider adequate evidence to justify the claim that neoliberalism made positive contributions to development?

Official development assistance (ODA)

In the late 1960s and early 1970s, a shift emerged in the approach to development, stemming from critiques of modernization theory and neoliberal economics. **Official development assistance (ODA)** took shape as a response, initially focusing on short-term emergency aid termed 'bilateral aid' or 'bilateral assistance.' Countries like the US established agencies such as the US Agency for International Development to manage these policies. At the same time, a new model of development, based on the thinking of scholars like Kaul, ul Haq, Sen, and Shiva, and emphasizing environmental sustainability, systematic poverty reduction and economic equality, began to take shape.

The UN began incorporating these perspectives, integrating gender and human development ideas into its policymaking. The Brundtland Commission in 1987 acknowledged the persistence of extreme poverty despite industrialization efforts, fueling a growing consensus that economic progress at the expense of ecology and equity was unsustainable. Reports from bodies like the OECD's Development Assistance Committee echoed similar sentiments, emphasizing sustainable economic growth, broader participation and environmental sustainability. Despite Cold War tensions slowing immediate response, a consensus formed that linked prosperity with ecological balance and equitable development.

The 1970 UN General Assembly resolution urged economically advanced countries to increase ODA to less economically developed states, aiming for a minimum net amount of 0.7 percent of Gross National Product (GNP) by the mid-1970s. However, most countries fell short of this target, and international consensus on ODA coordination remained elusive until the easing of Cold War divisions in the early 1990s.

ODA between two states is called bilateral assistance. ODA from a UN agency or an IFI is called multilateral assistance.

The Brundtland Commission, formerly the World Commission on Environment and Development, was a sub-organization of the UN that aimed to unite countries in pursuit of sustainable development. The commission took its name from Gro Harlem Brundtland, a former Prime Minister of Norway, who was its chairperson.

Development and sustainability

International aid and cooperation are key aspects of global politics concerning the HL topic area of *Poverty*. Sustainable development goals often rely on partnerships between states, IGOs and NGOs to support poverty alleviation efforts through aid, technical assistance and capacity building.

Sustainable development emphasizes creating a better future for generations to come. This is linked to the HL topic area of *Poverty* as policies that address poverty through sustainable means not only alleviate current hardships but also aim to prevent future poverty.

▲ Meeting at the UN's Millennium Summit in 2000.

Development initiatives often aim to reduce poverty and inequality, which links to the HL topic areas of *Equality* and *Poverty*. Sustainable development goals prioritize lifting people out of poverty and narrowing income gaps between different socio-economic groups through policies, especially those that involve creating inclusive decision-making processes, that promote fair wages, social protection programs, and equitable distribution of resources.

Overall, this period marked a transition in developmental approaches, highlighting the need to align prosperity with environmental health and social equity, shaping contemporary understandings of ODA, and paving the way for coordinated global efforts toward human development.

Global initiatives: the Millennium Development Goals (MDGs)

Following the end of the Cold War, in the 1990s, the UN and OECD member states developed what they considered a consolidated strategic plan to address the underlying causes of poverty and low levels of well-being. Keeping in mind the 0.7 percent GNP targets set in the 1970s, in 2000, at the UN's Millennium Summit, the then 189 UN member states made a commitment to a specific set of international development goals that become known as the eight Millennium Development Goals (MDGs). These were:

1. Eradicate extreme poverty and hunger.
2. Achieve universal primary education.
3. Promote gender equality and empower women.
4. Reduce child mortality.
5. Improve maternal health.
6. Combat HIV/AIDS, malaria and other diseases.
7. Ensure environmental sustainability.
8. Develop a global partnership for development.

The MDGs marked a pivotal moment in global development by introducing a coordinated and comprehensive set of goals, notably lifting individuals out of extreme poverty (defined then as living on less than $1.25 per day), with a primary focus on Africa, Asia and Latin America. Primarily aimed at low- and middle-income countries, the MDGs necessitated the cooperation of more economically developed nations, expected to fund and implement these objectives either bilaterally or through multilateral institutions like the UN and IFIs, in conjunction with the governments of low-income countries. Over the following fifteen years, the world witnessed substantial progress on paper: a billion people emerged from extreme poverty, and global GDP more than doubled.

Yet, this progress did not imply a conclusion toward development nor an equitable impact globally. The bulk of advancements toward the MDGs occurred predominantly in the PRC and India. The PRC's rapid growth saw around 300 million people escape extreme poverty between 2000 and 2015.

Activity

Working with a classmate, pick a country that was low–middle-income in 2000 and research how the MDG process impacted this country. Using different measurements of development like poverty rates, literacy rates, HDI and others, evaluate the changes that this country went through from 2000 to 2015. Prepare a short presentation about your findings and present it to the class. Was there improvement? Consider the circumstances, factors and conditions that might have contributed to your findings. Compare your results with classmates evaluating another country. What do you notice?

Thematic studies

An evaluation of the MDGs by the US-based think tank Brookings Institution determined that the MDGs contributed to reduced 'child mortality, maternal mortality, HIV/Aids, and tuberculosis.' They concluded that, while much of the progress was likely to have happened without the MDGs and took place in the PRC and India, 'somewhere between 21–29 million more people are alive today than would have been the case if countries had continued their pre-MDG rates of progress.'[7]

While these criticisms and successes of the MDGs have been echoed elsewhere, the MDGs did represent the first concerted and global effort to 'do development' and they form the basis of 'doing development differently'.

The Sustainable Development Goals (SDGs)

> When evaluating the strengths and weaknesses of the achievements of the MDGs process, bring balance to your responses by including perspectives critical of the MDGs. You can boost your success by evaluating reports from the UN as well as other reports of the MDGs.

> **TOK** What role do experts play in influencing our understanding of the strengths and weaknesses of MDGs? What does it mean to be an expert in global politics? How do you know if you can trust someone's expertise?

Figure 3.9 The UN's 2015–30 SDGs.

Recognizing the limitations of the MDGs, the United Nations convened in 2015 to address these shortcomings and prioritize sustainable development. Recipient countries sought more involvement and influence in goal setting, emphasizing partnership over beneficiary status. Donor nations aimed for increased transparency and efficiency, while emerging economies like the PRC and India desired greater participation. UN agencies, IFIs and NGOs pressed for broader access and emphasized environmental and sustainability concerns. Overall, there was recognition of the crucial role the private sector, including both small and large enterprises, needed to play in achieving future development targets.

This led to the formulation of the seventeen Sustainable Development Goals (SDGs), which distinguished themselves from the MDGs by emphasizing sustainability, interconnectedness and a global focus. With the SDGs officially coming into effect on January 1, 2016, they represent a renewed and comprehensive approach to global development, aiming

Proportion of People Living on Less than US$1.25 a Day (Percentage)

	1990	2011	2015
World	36	15	12
Developing regions	47	18	14
Developing regions (excluding the PRC)	41	22	18

Source: Data from UN (2015) *The Millennium Development Goals Report* 2015, p. 14 (2015 data predicted)

> **HL** Many of the Sustainable Development Goals (SDGs), such as ensuring clean water and sanitation, combating climate change, and promoting sustainable cities and communities, directly impact health outcomes and so can be linked to the HL topic area of *Health*. Policies aimed at achieving these goals often have positive implications for public health. Furthermore, sustainable development aims to reduce inequalities among and within countries and so can be linked to the HL topic area of *Equality*.

Figure 3.10 Poverty reduction, 1990–2015.

145

Development and sustainability

> The UN's MDG process, as well as earlier approaches to development, is an opportunity for you to explore the impact of *Borders* and national *Identity* as part of your investigation into the HL topic areas. For background, you might consider researching how these various approaches have impacted development in the country you are focusing on. This might lead you to explore the development of *Health* outcomes, *Poverty* reduction and expanded *Equality* for different groups within that country. Consider what impact, if any, these earlier approaches have had.

> You can look at the targets on the UN site for the SDGs.

> When evaluating an ongoing process like the SDGs, find a case study that focuses on a specific SDG target in a low–middle-income country. Consider how you might measure the success of this target in practice. Consider the different stakeholders involved. You can boost your success by including different perspectives and you can find these perspectives by looking at articles written by experts coming from these low–middle-income countries.

> To what extent does our knowledge of the impacts of processes like the SDGs depend on our interactions with those impacted by them?

to address the deficiencies of the previous framework and promote a more sustainable and equitable path forward.

Activity

Look at the data presented in Figure 3.10. What factors or conditions might have contributed to this reduction in poverty?

The SDGs represent a departure from previous development models, prioritizing sustainability by encouraging environmentally friendly practices, inclusive economic growth and interconnected strategies. SDGs advocate for environmentally sound development methods, like renewable energy for factories, aiming to mitigate climate change's impact. They stress inclusive growth by questioning who benefits from economic progress and advocate for marginalized groups' advancement, eliminating discriminatory practices in development projects.

Moreover, the SDGs emphasize interconnectedness, illustrating how advancements in one area can positively impact others. For instance, initiatives supporting women's safety with solar-powered streetlights in Lebanon extend opportunities for education and employment, contributing to broader economic growth. Numerous examples highlight how sustainable methods, such as Peru's grassroots recycling initiatives led by marginalized women, align with multiple SDGs, addressing issues like gender equality and responsible consumption.

The SDGs adopt a global perspective, recognizing that developed nations also face challenges like gender inequality and environmental issues. Countries like Germany have banned fracking due to its environmental risks, demonstrating that economic growth need not compromise sustainability. Meanwhile, efforts in the United States, such as raising the minimum wage, illustrate how addressing income inequality positively impacts public health and social issues, aligning with the SDGs' inclusive growth mandate.

Adaptive development

One of the outcomes of the MDG process in particular, and an evaluation of ODA more generally, was to question how success in development is measured and evaluated. Critics highlighted the UN's tendency to attribute all development success to the MDGs when the situation was more complex than this. The fact that progress was often as much due to the domestic policies of low- to middle-income countries themselves underscored the need for collaborative efforts from various stakeholders in evaluating poverty reduction or hunger decrease.

The SDG process has learned from this and, as a result, there is a growing conversation among different stakeholders about doing development differently under the idea of **adaptive development**.

Known also as Thinking and Working Politically (TWP) or Problem-Driven Iterative Adaptation (PDIA), adaptive development challenges the idea that successful development happens only when high-income countries, the UN and IFIs provide enough money and technical capacity to recipient countries to support development.

Adaptive development recognizes that development is a deeply political and complex process, and that all stakeholders, including donor and recipient governments, play a

Thematic studies

critical role in shaping the success of development. Good governance is an important aspect of development decision-making.

At its core, adaptive development thinking encourages a multistakeholder approach and a dialogue between stakeholders, most importantly those who will be most impacted by the development projects at the local level. Entrepreneurs, small and medium-sized enterprises and other private sector stakeholders are highly valued as part of this thinking.

In the 1970s, Muhammed Yunus and his Grameen Bank pioneered **microcredit** as a form of microfinance that involves a small loan given to an individual or group to help them become self-employed and grow their business. Microcredit usually operates on a low or no interest basis, very favorable to the person or group taking out the loan. Women in developing countries, as well as other marginalized or vulnerable groups, are often the beneficiaries of microcredit.

Adaptive development might be viewed as thinking about ODA outside the box or as expanding the development box to include more stakeholders, innovations and ideas. The SDGs reflect aspects of adaptive development, as do the development strategies of bilateral donors and multilateral IFIs.

Will the SDGs meet their goals and targets by 2030? Perhaps. What we have seen is that development is now being done differently. It is more coordinated and focused, and there is more transparency and partnership than development based on Rostow's modernization theory.

There is an emphasis on increased sustainability, a reduction of inequalities and an emphasis on understanding and addressing the root causes of poverty.

Example – Bangladesh's Community Climate Change Project (CCCP)

The CCCP stands as a prime example of adaptive development in tackling climate change. The initiative focuses on empowering local communities to identify climate risks, devise adaptive strategies, and implement measures to bolster resilience. Emphasizing participatory approaches, the CCCP engages community members in decision-making, fostering ownership of adaptive measures. It integrates traditional knowledge with innovative solutions, tailoring responses to local needs. Moreover, the project employs ongoing monitoring and evaluation, allowing for dynamic adjustments and refinement of strategies based on real-time feedback and evolving climate conditions. By placing communities at the forefront and employing flexible, context-specific approaches, Bangladesh's CCCP exemplifies adaptive development in its responsiveness to changing environmental challenges.

Stakeholders in development

The baseline understanding of development in global politics is that development means a sustained increase in the standard of living in a society. This means that development is something that is done or undertaken. It is a set of policies and ideas that must be realized in practice. For this to happen, there needs to be institutions ready to contribute to and be a part of development.

Adaptive development challenges the idea that successful development happens when high-income countries, the UN and IFIs provide enough money and technical capacity.

HL Sustainable development goals can be linked to the HL topic area of *Security* in several ways. Many development goals encompass human security, focusing on addressing the root causes of insecurity, such as poverty, inequality, and lack of access to basic needs like food, water and healthcare. Similarly, policies focusing on sustainable practices help mitigate environmental risks that can lead to conflicts over resources or exacerbate security concerns.

TOK To what extent can we determine that the SDGs are an improvement over earlier development ideas like modernization theory or the Washington Consensus?

HL Sustainable development emphasizes social equity and justice and so can be linked to the HL topic area of *Equality*. Development policies that focus on addressing historical and systemic inequalities, including racial, ethnic and socio-economic disparities aim to ensure fair and equitable treatment for all individuals and communities.

Development and sustainability

> A policy is a plan of action on a particular issue, developed and implemented by certain stakeholders.

> IGOs are created by a treaty between two or more countries. The countries that sign the treaty agree to take decisions through the organization that they have created. The UN and EU are IGOs.

Not everyone agrees on the way in which a sustained increase in the standard of living is best achieved. Different groups or actors involved with development have different interests in what should be developed and how it should be developed.

Remember that stakeholders are actors on the global, regional or national stage (states, organizations or groups) that have an interest in determining the outcomes and are impacted by those outcomes. In development, we look at the policies and practices of stakeholders such as states, IGOs, international and regional financial institutions, private companies, multinational corporations, local governments, NGOs, trade unions and political parties, as well as social movements and marginalized or vulnerable groups and individuals.

Development policy and the role of stakeholders

When thinking about stakeholders in development, it is important to identify their role. In simple terms, stakeholders might:

- create development policy
- implement development policy
- be impacted by development policy
- evaluate development policy.

For example, a policy might be to reduce waterborne diseases through increased access to clean drinking water. The idea for this policy had to come from somewhere, such as a community that has a high rate of illness from unclean drinking water. Someone had to take this idea and come up with a possible solution, fund the solution and then implement it.

You might have noticed that countries that neighbor each other or are within the same region have certain political, economic, social, cultural or historical similarities, for example, the countries of Central America, West Africa or Scandinavia. You may also have noticed that some countries have similar levels of development throughout the country, with perhaps some slight difference between urban and rural populations (Norway, Sweden and Germany, for example), whereas other countries have more extreme inequalities throughout the country, with greater concentrations of wealth and more widespread poverty (such as the USA, Russia and India). All this is done by different stakeholders operating at different levels.

> **HL**
> Sustainable development can be linked to the HL topic area of *Borders* as it often involves the responsible management of shared resources, such as water bodies, forests and biodiversity that span across borders. Similarly, environmental challenges like air and water pollution, climate change and wildlife conservation often transcend national borders. Global politics often addresses agreements and collaborations between states to manage these resources sustainably and recognizes that environmental sustainability requires collective action beyond borders.

Stakeholders at the international level

Political, economic, social, cultural and environmental development at the **international level** is governed by a series of laws and agreements reached through the UN, World Trade Organization (WTO) and some of the more informal gatherings of nation-states, like the G7, G20 and OECD.

Unlike human rights law, which usually appears in the form of legally binding conventions, treaties or covenants, development does not have a set of international laws to provide a guiding framework. Instead, agreements exist between nation-states working within the UN in the form of goals such as the MDGs or SDGs, or a process such as the Conference of Parties (COP), which meets regularly to discuss the details of the Framework Convention on Climate Change.

At the international level, nation-states are extremely protective of their sovereignty and are hesitant to commit to any set of laws that might impact their ability to manage

Thematic studies

their own approach to development. As a result, development stakeholders at the international level see a great deal of activity from nation-states cooperating within these organizations or directly/bilaterally with each other. Other institutions at this level include the UN and its agencies, and IFIs like The World Bank, IMF and WTO.

The role that private companies, seeking profit, play at this level is often overlooked. The political goods of trade, access to markets and access to investment are some of the most significant factors impacting development, and for-profit companies are the primary stakeholders when it comes to trade, markets and investment.

Countries

Much of the analysis in Global Politics focuses on the actions of countries. In development, we are interested in how countries interact with each other and how countries manage their own development. We look at local corruption, GDP per capita or carbon dioxide emissions per capita, but we do most of our measuring, calculating and analyzing at the level of the country and within the country.

Countries are generally divided into or classified as different stakeholder groups or categories, sometimes based on income and sometimes based on region and subregion. There is a significant relationship between country income and region. High-income and upper middle-income countries tend to be the largest donors of bilateral and multilateral ODA, while the lower middle-income and low-income countries are generally ODA recipients. We consider these groups of countries stakeholders based on their role as ODA donors or recipients.

The World Bank Atlas Method, for example, identifies four types of countries:

- High-Income Economies (GNI per capita over $13,205 USD)
- Upper Middle-Income Economies (GNI per capita between $4256 and $13,205 USD)
- Lower Middle-Income Economies (GNI per capita between $1085 and $4256 USD)
- Low-Income Economies (GNI per capita under $1085 USD).[8]

Along with the IMF, The World Bank also refers to **heavily indebted poor countries (HIPCs)**.[9]

The World Bank classifications are updated each year on July 1 and are based on the GNI per capita of the previous year. Classifications can change if GNI increases or decreases.

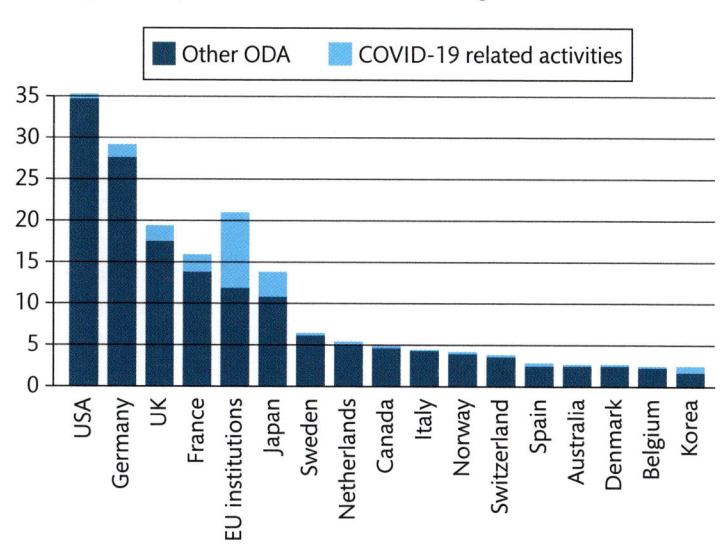

Figure 3.11 The world's top donors of ODA, and their COVID-19 related expenditures in 2020.

Development and sustainability

When discussing development, those high-income and upper middle-income countries are often considered donor countries of ODA. Low-income and lower middle-income countries are considered recipient countries or beneficiaries of ODA.

ODA donors, for example, also contribute ODA funds and work together in IFIs like The World Bank and the IMF. However, the largest share of ODA happens bilaterally, from one country to another.

These two types of countries, ODA recipients and ODA donors, make up the two main country stakeholder groups in development.

To manage these bilateral relations, donor countries have established **national development agencies (NDAs)** to manage all forms of development cooperation between themselves and the recipients of their ODA. These NDAs are usually part of a country's Ministry for Foreign Affairs, so they speak for and act on behalf of the country they represent. Their funding comes from the budget of their country.

Figure 3.12 An example of bilateral ODA from five Nordic countries carried out through their respective national development agencies.

Government aid to developing countries as percentage of Gross National Income

	1980	1990	2000	2010	2020
Denmark	0.74%	0.94%	1.06%	0.91%	0.72%
Finland	0.22%	0.65%	0.31%	0.55%	0.47%
Iceland	-	-	0.10%	0.26%	0.27%
Norway	0.87%	1.17%	0.76%	1.05%	1.11%
Sweden	0.78%	0.91%	0.80%	0.97%	1.14%

National development agencies like the US Agency for International Development (USAID) are funded by their government, coordinate and implement the development policy of their country and work directly with recipient country governments.

International development policy for Japan, for example, is carried out by its Japan International Cooperation Agency (JICA). International development assistance from Canada is carried out by its Canadian International Development Agency (CIDA).

These national development agencies coordinate directly with the governments of the recipient countries they work with. In addition, these agencies also coordinate with multilateral institutions like the UN and IFIs.

All countries (donors and recipients) have their own interests and these interests are sometimes advanced through ODA. You can strengthen your analysis and evaluation by looking at a certain country's ODA policy, as well as other policies they might have regarding security, trade and human rights, to get a more balanced assessment of where ODA fits into a country's overall priorities.

Example – JICA

The Japan International Cooperation Agency (JICA) stands as a prominent national development agency actively engaged in fostering global development partnerships and initiatives. In the 21st century, JICA has spearheaded numerous impactful projects across various regions. For instance, in Africa, JICA has collaborated with countries like Kenya and Ethiopia to bolster infrastructure development, constructing roads, railways and energy facilities to stimulate economic growth and regional connectivity. Additionally, JICA's emphasis on sustainable development is evident through projects focusing on renewable energy, water resource management and climate change adaptation in countries like Bangladesh and Indonesia.

Thematic studies

This relationship is transitioning from one of donor and recipient to one of partnership. True balanced partnership takes time to develop. There still exists a power imbalance between donor countries and recipient countries, with the donor countries in the position of being able to set certain terms and expectations. This has long been resented and resisted by recipient countries to differing degrees.

> **TOK**
> How do we know if countries have an ethical obligation to each other and, if so, what is that obligation?

Activity

Working with a classmate, identify a donor country and the largest recipient of ODA from that country. Explore the recent historical relationship between these two countries. Are there any notable events the two countries share? Consider the trade and security relationship between these two countries. What conclusions might you draw about ODA based on your investigation?

International multilateral stakeholders and IGOs

Countries also work together within international multilateral stakeholders like the UN and through IFIs like The World Bank and IMF.

The UNDP was created by the UN General Assembly in 1966 to work on issues related to poverty reduction and political, economic and social development. That same year, the UN General Assembly created the UN's Industrial Development Organization (UNIDO) to work on industrial competitiveness in some of the world's least developed countries. These two UN agencies both work on development issues.

UNDP was established by the UN General Assembly in 1966. Its mandate is to end poverty, build democratic governance, rule of law and inclusive institutions. It is one of a number of UN agencies with a development mandate.

Other UN agencies are also active in development. UNICEF has been working on development issues such as the impacts of poverty, poor health, nutrition and low education on children since 1946. The UN's High Commissioner for Refugees works on long-term sustainable solutions for conditions in predominantly developing countries that might lead to population movement, as does the International Organization of Migration, which joined the UN in 2016 after over 60 years as its own IGO.

Development and sustainability

> The UN is a single stakeholder, acting through its Security Council and General Assembly, but it is also home to a collection of agencies and operations that are part of the larger development landscape. Look up the UN online or use the link to see how it works:

> A **mandate** is the term used to describe the specific task and function of a stakeholder like an international organization or agency.

> Duplication in development is when multiple stakeholders are doing the same thing, but not cooperating and coordinating their efforts.

> **TOK** What impact might the language we use when discussing development have on our understanding of development?

> IFIs can be global in scope or more regional. They loan money to countries in need.

The UN's World Health Organization (WHO) works with all populations on issues specific to health. WHO worked closely with UN member states and their institutes of health to provide information about COVID-19 in its early stages. WHO was instrumental in working with UN member states to collect and distribute vaccines to countries that were unable to afford to vaccinate their entire population.[10]

To illustrate how vast the UN's engagement is on the issues of development, consider the UN's role within the important development area of reducing malnutrition and hunger. The **Food and Agriculture Organization (FAO)** directs international efforts to combat hunger and provides UN member states with a forum to meet on these issues multilaterally. The **World Food Programme's (WFP)** mandate is to eradicate hunger and malnutrition. It is the largest humanitarian organization in the world. The **International Fund for Agricultural Development (IFAD)** aims to fight rural poverty, hunger and malnutrition among farmers and the rural poor in developing countries.

All three of these UN agencies provide significant support for populations in need and their mandates are similar, but not quite the same. This can create some confusion if you are wondering who to contact at the UN if you have a question or need some support regarding efforts to reduce malnutrition and hunger. It also can lead to **duplication** or multiple agencies doing the same thing, and even competition between agencies as their funding comes from donations from UN member states.

The UN and its various agencies have worked hard to reduce duplication and competition for resources through the 2000–15 MDGs and 2015–30 SDG processes.

International financial institutions (IFIs)

IFIs are significant stakeholders in development. Some IFIs operate globally, while others are more regional in their focus. They are significant because they loan money to governments in need (recipient countries) and raise money from high-income countries (donor countries), who have a significant say in how this money is loaned out.

Two of the most significant IFIs are The World Bank and the IMF. Both are intergovernmental (treaty-based) and part of the UN system, but they are more independent of the UN.

The World Bank

The World Bank was founded in 1944 and loans money to low-income and middle-income countries from the funds it raises from high-income countries. The World Bank is led by a Board of Governors made up of the Ministers of Finance or Ministers of Development from the country members of the bank. The Board of Governors chooses the President of The World Bank Group. The largest donors have more decision-making powers within the bank, and the five largest donors (the USA, Japan, the UK, Germany and France) are each able to choose one of The World Bank's 24 Executive Directors. The Board of Governors meet each year to determine the development agenda for the bank.

Thematic studies

The World Bank has five branches that work on various aspects of development:

- International Bank for Reconstruction and Development: lends to low- and middle-income countries
- International Development Association (IDA): lends to low-income countries
- International Finance Corporation (IFC): lends to the private sector
- Multilateral Investment Guarantee Agency (MIGA): encourages private companies to invest in foreign countries
- International Centre for Settlement of Investment Disputes (ICSID): acts as a troubleshooter to resolve conflicts between private investors and foreign countries.

The input of the donor countries to The World Bank in these branches is significant. Donor countries guide policy development and implementation.

The International Monetary Fund (IMF)

Also founded in 1944 as an IGO, the IMF provides loans to member countries so that they can maintain their financial stability, to help them pay for things like imports, pay back loans, and stabilize their currency and support economic growth.

The IMF has a structure similar to The World Bank, with decisions taken by a Board of Governors made up of representatives chosen from the 190 IMF member countries. Voting on policy in the IMF is weighted, meaning that it is based upon the amount a country donates to the IMF. Countries like the USA, Japan and the PRC have more influence over IMF policy-making than countries who contribute less.

Ngozi Okonjo-Iweala served as a chief development economist and managing director of The World Bank, served two terms as Nigeria's finance minister and is General-Director of the World Trade Organization (WTO).

Member	Quota (millions, SDR)	Quota Share (%)	Votes	Votes Share (%)
United States	82994.2	17.46	831407	16.52
Japan	30820.5	6.48	309670	6.15
PRC	30482.9	6.41	306294	6.09
Germany	26634.4	5.6	267809	5.32
France	20155.1	4.24	203016	4.03
United Kingdom	20155.1	4.24	203016	4.03
Italy	15070	3.17	152165	3.02
India	13114.4	2.76	132609	2.64
Russian Federation	12903.7	2.71	130502	2.59
Brazil	11042	2.32	111885	2.22

Figure 3.13 Contributions to the IMF in USD. The largest donors have more voting power in the IMF.

Both The World Bank and the IMF are significant stakeholders and, because their decisions in terms of development policy are largely driven by their major donors, it is important to remember that the development interests of these donors are important.

The World Trade Organization (WTO)

The World Trade Organization (WTO) is a treaty-based IGO that helps to set and promote the rules of free trade, fair competition and non-discriminatory trade practices between nations, although it is not invested in development in the same way as The World Bank and the IMF.

The World Bank, the IMF and the WTO are excellent sources for case studies to analyze and evaluate fair development. You can strengthen your analysis and evaluation by investigating the impacts of a specific project or loan. Consider what it was designed to achieve and evaluate the extent to which it was achieved.

Development and sustainability

Ministers of Finance and Ministers of Trade for the member countries of the WTO set WTO policy. Contributions to and influence on WTO policy-making is based on the strength of a member's economy, meaning that higher-income countries are likely to contribute more and have more influence over decision-making.

> **TOK**
> Do IFIs have an ethical obligation toward developing countries when considering their policies and loans?

Activity

Choose an IGO that focuses on development and/or sustainability issues, for example, the UNDP, IMF, The World Bank, New Development Bank, Asian Infrastructure Investment Bank, or any other relevant IGO. Alternatively, you could propose another IGO with a development and/or sustainability focus. Conduct some preliminary research on your chosen IGO. You should explore the following aspects:

- What specific development or sustainability issues does your IGO address?
- Identify and analyse the various development or sustainability programs or campaigns your IGO has undertaken.
- Discuss specific examples of your IGO's successes in promoting development and sustainability or, conversely, in reducing poverty and inequality, as well as any challenges it has encountered in fulfilling its mandate.

Based on the information you've gathered, critically assess the extent to which your chosen IGO can be viewed as a powerful and legitimate instrument for the promotion of development and sustainability. You should consider the following:

- Impact: Has your IGO made a tangible impact in advancing sustainable development, and if so, in what areas?
- Cooperation and Support: How well does your IGO collaborate with member states and other stakeholders to address sustainable development issues?
- Challenges and Limitations: What challenges and limitations does your IGO face?
- Accountability and Transparency: Does your IGO demonstrate transparency in its actions, and is it held accountable for its decisions related to sustainable development?
- Public Perception: How is your IGO perceived by sustainable development advocates, governments and civil society groups?

You should be prepared to share your findings with your peers. You will be expected to reflect on the overall role of IGOs in promoting sustainable development globally.

Stakeholders at the regional level

Development at the regional level is characterized in some regions by much closer political, economic, social, cultural and environmental interdependence, such as within Europe and in Africa with the AU.

Similarities between nation-states, especially cultural and historical ties, have an impact on how nation-states view sovereignty. The EU is a good example of close political, economic, social, cultural and environmental development between a group of nation-states, and the EU frequently makes joint decisions on how to react to an international or national situation. An example of how the EU acts together

Thematic studies

on development and climate is the European Regional Development Fund (ERDF), available to EU member states. ERDF is part of the larger EU-wide goal-setting for environmental, social and economic sustainability, including standards for EU-wide carbon emissions.[11]

The EU is also active outside its own region through EuropeAid as the world's largest donor of ODA.[12] Together with all EU member states, the EU contributes over $75 billion USD in ODA each year.[13] One example of EU ODA is their Global Gateway Africa-Europe Investment Package that includes partnership projects with 20 Sub-Saharan African countries toward the **Great Green Wall** throughout the Sahel region, intended to restore and reclaim degraded land across the region while creating jobs and building greater resilience to climate change.[14]

One important relationship at the regional level is the one between political development and economic development.

Stakeholders at the regional level are similar to those at the international level, with roles being played by regional IGOs.

Stakeholders at the national level

Stakeholders at the national level in practice: South Africa's National Union of Metalworkers trade union go on strike in 2021 demanding higher wages to keep up with the increasing cost of living.

You can look at the 2030 climate and energy framework by visiting the European Commission website, or using the QR code below:

The national level is perhaps the most interesting with regards to development.

The overwhelming majority of measurements, metrics and data regarding political, economic, social, cultural and environmental development are national level measures. While policies have local implications, the policy-making itself is generally at the national level. This does not mean that these policies might not have an impact outside of the country where they are developed and implemented, but, when we analyze political issues at the national level, we generally mean that we are focusing on one country.

In terms of nation-states operating on the global stage through trade policy, as donors or recipients of ODA, this too is a result of national-level policy-making.

155

Development and sustainability

The stakeholders at this level are made up of different ministries, departments, offices and institutions of a given nation-state, including the legislature and judiciary.

In 2022, Japanese Prime Minister Kishida Fumio wanted to change the direction of Japanese ODA. Recognizing that the role of Japan in the Indo-Pacific region was growing, Fumio wanted to move from being focused primarily on promoting economic good governance to including the ability to address common challenges in the Indo-Pacific region. These political challenges include climate change, energy, food security and global health. To do this, Fumio worked with the main political parties in the Japanese parliament to create and fund a new ODA policy called the New Plan for a Free and Open Indo-Pacific.[15]

In Greece, the national governmental stakeholders and institutions have influence over national development policy, but they might not be the only government stakeholders to consider. The Greek government wants to encourage its citizens to follow EU laws on sustainable development and best environmental practices and international standards that the Greek parliament has made into national law. The Ministry of Environment and Energy is the government ministry responsible for developing these policies, but it cannot implement them alone. It must work with a number of other government ministries, including the Ministry of Development and Investment and the Ministry of Rural Development and Food, as well as several regional and local authorities within Greece. No single government stakeholder can force the others to agree and comply, which means that sustainable development and environmental policy-making and policy implementation take a great deal of time in Greece.[16]

Recipients of ODA also develop policies at the national level through national stakeholders in order to manage ODA. Nigeria, for example, received over $3 billion USD in bilateral and multilateral ODA in 2021 according to The World Bank.[17] To help manage the distribution and investment of this ODA, the office of the Nigerian President introduced Nigeria 2050, a nation-wide program involving national and local state and non-state stakeholders. Nigeria 2050 needed approval from the Nigerian parliament and is being implemented through several Nigerian government ministries.[18]

Large private, for-profit companies generally have a great deal of influence at the national level in that they will want to ensure policies are beneficial to them, for example, lower tax rates, protectionist tariffs or favorable regulations.

In most countries, trade unions are a significant stakeholder at the national level, seeking favorable policies such as better working conditions, better pay and more influence over employment-related policies.

South Africa is an example of how private, for-profit companies and trade unions have an impact on national policies. In 2021, South Africa's largest trade union, the National Union of Metalworkers (NUMSA), was negotiating for a pay increase of 8 percent to keep up with increases in the cost of living with the Steel and Engineering Industries Federation of Southern Africa (SEIFA), a group that represents the interests of private sector companies that rely on steel, like the automotive industry. The private sector companies wanted to keep wages where they were in order to ensure greater profitability for their companies. They offered a wage increase of 4 percent. This offer was rejected by NUMSA, which represents 155,000 South Africans, and workers went on strike in October 2021. The strike lasted nearly a month and had a significant

Thematic studies

impact on South Africa's automobile manufacturing sector before NUMSA and SEIFA agreed to a compromise of a 6 percent wage increase.[19]

Political parties operate at the national level, in terms of policy creation through laws coming from the legislature and articulating a specific vision and path for development.

The media also plays a significant role at the national level, bringing attention to successful and unsuccessful policies, and serving as an informal watchdog over state government practices.

In Malaysia in 2020, 110 containers of toxic waste (including dangerous heavy metals like zinc, chromium, cadmium and lead) were found at a port. The containers had been labeled as 'non-toxic'. Local media were given information about the containers and their reports helped to expose a much larger political issue of shipping companies using Malaysian and other ports in emerging economies to illegally dump dangerous toxic waste materials. This led to greater government oversight and public awareness of the issue.[20]

> Trade unions are organizations that represent workers in a particular industry, such as teachers or doctors. They ensure that workers are satisfied with their levels of pay, safety and working conditions. Trade unions have played an important role in the development of workers' rights, including education, equality and respect for all.

Stakeholders at the local level

Perhaps the most important level from a development analysis perspective is the local level because it is at this level where the impacts of policies (or the absence of policies) are felt the most. Therefore, it is the local level where you find the richest and most valuable case studies and examples to consider how stakeholders are involved in and contribute to sustainable development.

Local-level stakeholders include local government officials and employees such as police officers, teachers and tax collectors, as well as trade union organizers, youth and community organizers and owners of small businesses.

Example – the Kazakh police force

When citizens do not feel safe in their own communities, they usually look to their local police for protection. To improve law enforcement's ability to provide greater protection for its citizens, since 2000, the government of Kazakhstan has been working with several international and regional multilateral partners (such as the UN's Office of Drugs and Crime, the EU and the Council of Europe) to improve the human rights training that all Kazakh police officers receive at their police academies. The aim of these programs is to increase local police officer knowledge and practice of human rights and to reduce instances of human rights violations by law enforcement officers.[21]

It is at the local level where failed policies lead to social movements that, if left unaddressed or ignored, grow into political movements or protracted social conflicts. Consider the widely unpopular privatization of Bolivian water resources by the Bolivian government in 1999. This policy forced Bolivians to pay higher prices for water, something many people could not afford. Citizens organized and complained. This was largely ignored by the Bolivian government. Citizens protested and blocked roads. The government's response was violent. Protesters were attacked, hit with tear gas, beaten and imprisoned. Despite the government response, the protests grew in size. Finally, a year later, the Bolivian government changed the privatization law.[22]

> Each political level of analysis has its own unique characteristics, and the cause and impact of policies that make up a case study should be viewed through each of these levels if possible.

Development and sustainability

Other key stakeholders in development

Other stakeholders play an important role in development. Private sector, for-profit companies make up a significant stakeholder group. They can be large multinational or transnational companies, large companies that operate only in one country, small or medium-sized enterprises, or small family businesses.[23]

Most economic development takes place through and between these private sector, for-profit stakeholders, and all of these stakeholders have headquarters in a nation-state.

Local, smaller businesses, though significant, do not have the same power over policy as the larger MNCs do. For example, with over 135,000 employees in over 190 countries and a revenue of over $75 billion USD, consumer goods company Unilever is an example of the impact and influence that large, for-profit companies have on development.[24] In Indonesia, Unilever has developed Sustainable Living Brands products including toothpaste, laundry detergent, soaps and salad dressings, using methods to reduce the negative environmental impact of production and reducing carbon emissions in production and transportation.[25] In addition, Unilever has sought to raise the standard of living in low- and middle-income countries where they operate, such as Indonesia, Vietnam and Côte d'Ivoire.[26] The scale and size of large for-profit companies like Unilever means that they have the power to influence policy.

The NewClimate Institute warns that greater oversight of large MNCs is necessary to avoid **greenwashing** and to be sure that such companies use their size and scale to support sustainable development.[27]

NGOs, non-profits, civil society organizations and charities form another significant stakeholder group. Some of these NGOs operate internationally, such as Oxfam or Amnesty International. Others operate only in one country, and most operate only locally. All NGOs, those that operate internationally and those that work exclusively in one country, are based in a nation-state.

Groups with state-like aspirations are often overlooked but, given their reach and impact, they deserve our consideration. There are stateless nations like the Kurds and Catalans, who began as social and political movements and aspire for a nation-state of their own. There are other groups like the Fuerzas Armadas Revolucionarias de Colombia (FARC), the Liberal Democratic Party of Russia and the Citizens Coalition for Change (CCC) that wish to play a political role in the development of their nation-state.

Some fragile states, like Somalia, have numerous factions or groups wishing to undermine their existing state, secede and establish their own, like the Somali National Movement (SNM) and Rahaweyn Resistance Army (RRA). There are also organizations like Al Shabaab, Al-Qaeda and Islamic State that would like to undermine existing state structures in order to establish their own state.

For-profit organizations that operate illegally are also significant stakeholders. Narcotics, contraband and human traffickers operate across borders. Along with domestic organized crime organizations, these stakeholders have a significant impact on development. In many parts of Mexico, the Sinloa Cartel has replaced the Mexican government as the provider of services and security. Businesses in these areas generally have to pay a protection fee in addition to the taxes they pay to the federal government.[28]

Glocalization is the practice of conducting business according to local and global considerations and is generally used to describe a product or service that is developed and distributed globally with changes that allow it appeal to different consumers in different national or local markets.

Greenwashing is when a company claims that it is doing something to promote sustainability in its business practices, but there is limited evidence to suggest that this is the case.

Sustainable development initiatives can also be connected to the HL topic area of Security when they address resource scarcity concerns. In global politics, policies focused on sustainable resource management aim to reduce tensions and conflicts arising from competition over limited resources like water, arable land or energy sources.

Thematic studies

Political parties and trade unions play a significant role in policy development at the national and local levels. In some countries, these stakeholders hold a great deal of policy influence.

The media, including print, broadcast, electronic/internet and social media, have considerable influence in development policy. The CNN Effect, which is the raising of awareness and focusing on specific topics, events and issues, gives the media a large role in our understanding of some of the more important impacts of development. When the media is not reporting on certain issues of development, many of us remain unaware. Therefore, the media in all its forms is a very significant stakeholder.

University-based research and policy-making think tanks play a significant role in developing and influencing development policy in all areas. This stakeholder group provides much of the research and data that is used by states and multilateral organizations. This group is also an excellent source of critiques of existing development policies.

The most important stakeholder group in development are the people impacted by development policy themselves: local community groups, social movements, and individuals in a community. In particular, marginalized, vulnerable, and deeply affected groups and individuals are crucial stakeholders when it comes to development and sustainability. Their centrality stems from their lived experiences of socio-economic disparities, environmental degradation and systemic injustices. Recognizing them as stakeholders is not merely a moral imperative but an essential step toward holistic progress. Their involvement ensures a more comprehensive understanding of diverse needs, challenges, and aspirations within development. Embracing their perspectives and agency not only fosters inclusivity but also enhances the effectiveness and sustainability of development initiatives. Empowering these groups creates resilient and equitable systems, Their active participation not only amplifies their voices but also redefines sustainable development, making it more responsive, adaptive and genuinely transformative.

> **HL** Sustainable development aims for inclusive growth, ensuring that development benefits all segments of society and can be linked to the HL topic area of *Identity*. Global politics often addresses issues related to social identities—ethnic, religious, linguistic, or gender-related—and aims to ensure that development policies are inclusive and do not marginalize any specific identity group.

Example – Indigenous communities and sustainable resource management

In the Amazon rainforest, indigenous tribes like the Waorani in Ecuador have been instrumental in challenging oil companies' incursions into their territories. Their involvement does not merely revolve around safeguarding their lands, but embodies a profound understanding of sustainable practices deeply rooted in their traditions. By recognizing their rights and engaging them as stakeholders, not just bystanders in policy discussions, these communities offer valuable insights into balancing economic development with environmental preservation, ensuring a more equitable and sustainable future for their regions and the planet at large. Their intricate knowledge of ecosystems and holistic approaches to resource usage stand as powerful examples of how marginalized groups significantly contribute to and shape sustainable development narratives.

To have their needs met, people often form local community groups or social movements to put pressure on local and national authorities. Such groups usually ask for the reform of laws, institutions or policies that do not seem to benefit their communities and the families that live in these communities. What has kept these groups, especially marginalized and vulnerable communities, largely at the periphery of the very policies that impact them is the power imbalance that exists between local community groups and the other stakeholders.

Real-world examples of positive and negative MNC-stakeholder interactions concerning development, sustainability, poverty and inequality

Positive interactions:

- Corporate Social Responsibility (CSR) Initiatives: Many MNCs engage in CSR activities, partnering with NGOs and local communities to address social issues. For instance, Unilever's Sustainable Living Plan focuses on sustainable sourcing, reducing environmental impact and improving livelihoods, demonstrating a commitment to both sustainability and poverty alleviation.
- Supply chain transparency and fair trade: Companies like Starbucks or Nestlé engage in fair trade practices, ensuring fair wages and better working conditions for farmers in developing countries. These initiatives aim to reduce inequality and improve the livelihoods of those in the supply chain.
- Collaboration with governments on policy development: MNCs often collaborate with governments in policy-making to address societal issues. For instance, in renewable energy, companies like Tesla have partnered with governments (for example, the South Australian state government) to promote sustainable energy policies, aiming to combat both environmental degradation and energy poverty.
- Technology transfer and capacity building: Technology giants like Microsoft or Google engage in programs that transfer technology and provide skills-building opportunities in underprivileged communities, contributing to reducing the digital divide and empowering marginalized groups.
- Community engagement and development programs: Companies such as Coca-Cola or Procter & Gamble engage in community development projects, providing access to clean water, education and healthcare in impoverished areas, aiming to tackle both poverty and inequality.
- Partnerships for sustainable development goals: MNCs often align their strategies with the UN's Sustainable Development Goals (SDGs). For instance, pharmaceutical companies like Novartis collaborate on initiatives to improve healthcare access in developing nations, targeting health-related inequalities.
- Advocacy and lobbying for social causes: Some corporations engage in advocacy efforts and lobbying for policies that promote social justice and sustainability. For instance, Patagonia is known for its advocacy for environmental protection and sustainability, influencing policy debates and consumer awareness.

Negative interactions:

- Environmental exploitation and pollution: Multinational corporations often face criticism for environmental degradation due to their extraction or production processes. For instance, oil companies have faced allegations of contributing to climate change through their extensive carbon emissions.
- Labor exploitation and poor working conditions: Some clothing retailers, like fast-fashion brands, have faced accusations of exploiting cheap labor in developing countries, perpetuating poverty and income inequality by providing low wages and unsafe working conditions.

Thematic studies

- Land grabbing and displacement: Agribusiness companies that make food and drink products have been criticized for land grabbing and displacing indigenous communities to expand their agricultural operations, worsening inequalities and disrupting local livelihoods.
- Tax avoidance and revenue loss: Multinational corporations engaging in aggressive tax avoidance strategies often relocate their profits to low-tax locations, leading to revenue loss for developing countries, and hindering their ability to invest in poverty-alleviating programs.
- Water privatization and access issues: Some beverage companies have faced scrutiny for privatizing water sources in certain regions, leading to issues of unequal access to clean water and exacerbating poverty in communities reliant on those resources.
- Human rights violations: Companies involved in extractive industries, such as mining companies, have been accused of human rights violations, including displacement of communities, environmental destruction, and disregard for indigenous rights.
- Political interference and lobbying: Certain multinational corporations engage in lobbying practices that can undermine policies aimed at reducing poverty and inequality. For example, pharmaceutical companies lobbying against affordable access to medicines can perpetuate health inequalities in developing nations.

Exercises

4. Should all stakeholders in development be considered equally?
5. Can models for development used in the past still be effective now?
6. What evidence is there that stakeholders in development have learned lessons from the past about how development works?

Sustainability

The internal border between Haiti on the left and the Dominican Republic on the right suggests practices that contribute to threats to sustainability.

What is sustainability?

Conceptual question

What does sustainability mean? Does it mean the same to everybody?

161

Development and sustainability

Sustainability is directly connected to development and our current patterns of consumption and production.

> **Activity**
>
> Create a mind map with the term 'sustainability' in the middle. Add words and ideas related to sustainability. Compare your mind map with a classmate. What similarities do you notice? Where do you think your understanding of sustainability comes from?

Development is defined as a sustained increase in the standard of living in a society. It might seem that the overall increases in global and national GDP, GNP and GNI over the past decades, measured in absolute and per capita terms, would indicate successful development. Poverty has been reduced, wealth is more globally distributed, and life expectancy has increased globally. Overall, higher incomes and the possibility for further growth are positive outcomes.

However, evidence suggests that our patterns of production, consumption and economic growth have come at a cost. We cannot fully understand this cost by looking only at our patterns of consumption and production through development. This cost is best understood when viewed through the lens of sustainability.

> **Activity**
>
> Reflect on the photo of the border between Haiti and the Dominican Republic on page 161. What does the right-hand side of the image look like? Compare this to the left-hand side of the image. What do you think might have caused this stark difference?

Sustainability: a brief background

Our understanding of sustainability, like development, has evolved, due in part to the analysis of the consequences of economic growth driven development. In 1969, the USA passed a law called the National Environmental Policy Act, which established a government office called the Environmental Protection Agency. This defined sustainability as 'economic development that may have benefits for current and future generations without harming the planet's resources or biological organisms.' In 1972, the UN hosted the first Conference on the Human Environment, which was an effort to bring together developed and developing countries to discuss solutions to the connection between economic growth and pollution. Sustainability was not explicitly defined at this UN conference, but its final report, the *Stockholm Declaration and Action Plan*, called on UN member states to create international and domestic laws that would address the impacts of economic growth. This Declaration also led to the creation of the UN's Environmental Programme (UNEP) in 1973.

> **Activity**
>
> Create a key events timeline related to sustainability, with a brief description of each event. What did you choose as your start date? Where on your timeline does a definition of sustainability appear? Why is this significant? What events did you include, and why?

Sidebar: Power relationships are at the heart of the sustainability discussion. It takes significant power to change patterns of production and consumption to make them more sustainable. This means that any discussion about sustainability must also address who is responsible for making sure that these changes are made, which raises questions about who has the sovereign power and ability to make these changes. This raises questions of legitimacy and who has the legitimate right to determine what patterns are changed and how they are changed.

Sidebar: The UN's *Our Common Future* report did more than just define sustainability. Its definitions linked sustainability with sustainable development.

Thematic studies

By 1987, we had the first workable definition of sustainability at the UN level, which was 'meeting the needs of the present without compromising the ability of future generations to meet their own needs.' This will be the definition that we will use to better understand the nature, practice and study of sustainability.

Contested understandings of sustainability

If you study Economics, one question you might be familiar with is: 'Who determines what is produced and how it is produced?'

This problem of defining sustainability raises additional questions related to the environment, such as: 'If what we produce and consume is having significant detrimental impacts on the sustainability of life on our planet, whose responsibility is it to make sure that we change these patterns?'

There are two fundamental understandings of sustainability, which do not seem compatible in the short term: **weak sustainability** and **strong sustainability**. Weak sustainability assumes that sustainable development challenges will be best met through economic growth, technological innovation and natural resource substitution. In other words, we can continue our current patterns of production and consumption because we have the funds and technology to substitute or replace any of our natural environment that has been damaged by these patterns.

Strong sustainability advocates for the preservation of natural resources, and that any current economic activity that has a negative and potentially irreversible impact on future generations should be limited or halted in the short term or the near future.

Weak sustainability finds support in extractive businesses and industries with significant levels of carbon pollution, such as coal mining and oil refining. Developing countries often prefer a weak sustainability approach as it allows them to concentrate on industrial production while also attracting polluting industries from countries that have opted for the strong sustainability approach.

The UN's SDGs (see page 145), for example, represent an effort to blend these two approaches so that current production and consumption practices do not negatively impact the ability of future generations to live sustainably.

The perspective taken by stakeholders regarding sustainability, weak or strong, depends on the interests of the stakeholder.

Activity

SDG 12 is 'Responsible production and consumption'. Working with a classmate, list changes that you would need to make in order for your patterns of consumption to be more sustainable. Think about what you eat, the clothing you wear, the technology and transportation you use. Do you know where these items come from? If you made changes to your current patterns of consumption, how different would your life be?

You can explore global CO_2 emissions since 1750 by searching online for Our World in Data CO_2 emisisons.
You can see increased emissions over time from coal, oil, gas, flaring, cement, steel and other industrial processes.[29]

Weak sustainability relies on economic growth, technological innovation and natural resource substitution to achieve sustainable development. Strong sustainability prioritizes natural resources and the reduction of economic activity that has irreversible impacts on the environment and human development.

The intergenerational rights discussed in the 'Rights and justice' chapter are based on an understanding that sustainable practices today will allow future generations to live well without undue sacrifice. Unfortunately, the opposite might also be true.

TOK
To what extent can we be certain of the needs and wants of future generations?

163

Development and sustainability

Sustainability raises important questions related to peace and conflict. It has been argued by Paul Farmer and others that the lack of sustainable development over time will lead to a gradual depletion of resources necessary to maintain adequate standards of living. For developing countries that rely on the export of raw materials or commodities, this might lead to conditions of what Johan Galtung refers to as negative peace and is evidence of what Galtung and Farmer describe as structural violence.

The definitions of sustainability and sustainable development are central to discussions about *Poverty*, *Equality*, *Health* and *Environment*, and they can be a helpful part of your efforts to find effective case studies to explore political challenges raised in these four HL topic areas.

Look at this video to see Kate Raworth explain doughnut economics:

Sustainability as an economic, social and environmental concept

Sustainability refers to the capacity of countries and other stakeholders to maintain themselves by reducing factors that threaten well-being. Sustainability can be seen in terms of what John Elkington described in the 1980s as the Triple Bottom Line, which describes the impacts that the interrelationship between economic, social and environmental factors have on our planet's ability to sustain life. These are:

- economic sustainability
- social sustainability
- environmental sustainability.[30]

Economic sustainability aims to reduce factors that threaten economic well-being. Social sustainability aims to reduce factors that threaten human social well-being. Environmental sustainability aims to reduce factors that threaten environmental well-being. These **Three Pillars of Sustainability** were adopted by the 2005 UN World Summit on Social Development.

In an effort to create practical policies to help implement these pillars, in 2012, economist Kate Raworth published *A Safe and Just Space for Humanity: Can we live within the doughnut*.[31] Raworth argues that humanity exists within a delicate 'social foundation' and an 'ecological ceiling'. To continue to survive within this space, our practices of consumption and production need to be sustainable, regenerative and careful. If we overproduce or overconsume, or if these practices are unsustainable, we can expect greater biodiversity loss, more pollution and the depletion of the environment within which humanity exists. Raworth presents a workable framework of the three pillars that takes into consideration the cost of achieving sustainability.

Example – Costa Rica's Biodiversity and Climate Change Strategy

Costa Rica's Biodiversity and Climate Change Strategy reflects elements of Kate Raworth's thinking by balancing environmental preservation with social well-being. The country's commitment to environmental sustainability and social equity is evident through several initiatives. Costa Rica has focused on reforestation efforts, aiming to restore degraded ecosystems and enhance biodiversity. Additionally, the country has heavily invested in renewable energy sources, with a goal to achieve carbon neutrality by 2050, aligning with Raworth's model's emphasis on ecological balance. Moreover, Costa Rica's strategy integrates social considerations by emphasizing sustainable agriculture practices, community engagement, and policies promoting social well-being, such as investments in education and healthcare. This holistic approach addresses both environmental concerns and societal needs, by striving to meet the needs of its citizens while respecting planetary boundaries.

Economic sustainability can be measured through more holistic measurements, such as the HDI, HPI, the Gini coefficient and the Lorenz curve. Another important measure is the Social Sustainability Index (SSI). The SSI is updated each year and uses indicators to measures social, environmental and economic sustainability by country as well as globally on a scale of 1 (weak) to 10 (strong).

Thematic studies

The SSI is holistic, combining economic, social and environmental factors to provide a comprehensive overview of sustainability. Table 3.1 shows the SSI ratings for Albania for 2019, compared to the world SSI average.

Table 3.1 2019 SSI ratings for Albania compared to world average[32]

Indicator	Albania	World Average
Sufficient food	9.8	9.2
Sufficient drinking water	9.4	8.9
Safe sanitation	9.9	7.9
Education	10.0	9.8
Healthy life	9.9	8.9
Gender equality	7.9	7.1
Income distribution	6.6	6.4
Population growth	8.5	5.2
Good governance	5.4	5.1
Biodiversity	6.7	4.3
Renewable water resources	9.6	7.7
Consumption	3.0	3.7
Energy use	8.2	6.9
Energy savings	6.0	3.8
Greenhouse gases	8.6	6.2
Renewable energy	4.6	3.6
Organic farming	1.1	2.7
Genuine savings	4.0	8.2
GDP	6.2	5.6
Employment	3.2	5.9

HL — Sustainable development emphasizes responsible resource management and can be linked to the HL topic area of *Environment*. In global politics, this involves negotiations and agreements on the use and conservation of natural resources like water, forests, minerals and energy sources. Balancing development needs with the preservation of these resources becomes a key point of discussion and policy-making

Activity

Look at the Sustainable Development Report online or with this QR code.

Choose a country with a high overall ranking (close to 10) and one with a relatively low ranking (close to 1). Compare the ranking across several of the SSI indicators. What similarities or differences do you find? Investigate these countries further using some of the other measurements and rankings used to determine development. Identify and explain three reasons why these differences exist. To what extent do these differences rely on historical factors?

HL — Development initiatives that aim to bridge the digital divide by ensuring equitable access to technology and information can be linked to the HL topic areas of *Technology* and *Equality*. Global politics concerning development focuses on policies that promote universal access to digital infrastructure, internet connectivity, and technology tools to empower underserved communities and nations.

Using environmental data since 1978, the Environmental Sustainability Index (ESI) from Yale and Columbia Universities, in cooperation with the US National Aeronautics and Space Administration (NASA), The World Bank and the EU, is another measure of overall environmental sustainability. The practices of countries in areas such as land use, conservation, infrastructure and water use are evaluated on a scale of 1 (bad) to 100 (good).

Development and sustainability

Another holistic sustainability measure is the Sustainable Governance Indicators (SGI), which evaluate how governments consider and target sustainable development and are updated each year. The SGI also uses a three pillar approach and evaluates a country's specific policies in the following areas:

- Economic policy: this includes the management of the economy, overall labor market, taxation rates and integration into the global financial system
- Social policy: such as access to education, social inclusion, family support, pension and retirement support
- Environmental policy: conservation, recycling and clean energy usage.[33]

The SGI considers quality of governance as an important part of measuring a country's ability to grow and develop sustainably. The SGI interpretation of good governance includes the type of election process available, access to information, respect for human rights and the rule of law, good governance and citizen participation in governance.

The SGI also looks at a country's contributions globally in the form of ODA (see page 143) and the role a country plays in multilateral environmental agreements.

For private sector, for-profit companies, the **Sustainability Accounting Standards Board (SASB)** and the **Global Reporting Initiative (GRI)** provide guidelines for sustainable environmental, social and governance (ESG) sustainability practices. SASB and GRI provide a set of guidelines for industries such as coal, steel, oil, natural gas, and financial companies, food and beverage companies, healthcare providers and infrastructure developers to help shape their ESG sustainability practices.

You can find the SGI's key findings for Ireland's environmental policies here:

Activity

Choose a country and explore the SGI findings for the economic, social and environmental policies for that country. Consider how balanced the findings are in each policy category. Are some policy categories stronger than others? Look at the good governance measures and findings. Discuss with a classmate what the connection might be between good governance and sustainability policies. What connections, if any, have you found? Do you think the connection between good governance and sustainable policies might be valid for each country regardless of their level of development?

SASB and GRI are not UN or government initiatives, but come from the industries themselves.

What role does the bias of experts play in the creation and measurement of sustainability in different countries?

Activity

Consider the strengths and challenges of using measurement tools like SASB and GRI to measure ESG sustainability. What is the value of having an industry or group of companies evaluate and regulate themselves? What challenges might this create? Working with a classmate, identify a significant strength and a significant weakness of this approach. Which is more convincing? Can you think of other ways sustainability might be measured to complement SASB and GRI?

Thematic studies

> **Example – Alcoa and environmental and social concerns in Australia**
>
> Alcoa is a Fortune-500 mining company with over 100 years of experience. Since 2015, Alcoa publishes an annual *Sustainability Report* highlighting its ESG sustainability practices, including grants to local communities, commitments to human rights, diversity in hiring and use of renewable energy. Alcoa's revenue for 2022 was estimated at $12.5 billion USD. Alcoa employs over 4000 people in Australia.
>
> Mining is a polluting, CO_2 producing activity. In addition, mining requires the regular use and transportation of toxic chemicals and materials. Recently, Alcoa's construction of a pipeline near the Samson drinking water dam, which provides water to nearby Waroona, led to environmental and social concerns in Australia.

> **Activity**
>
> You have been given the opportunity to provide sustainability policy guidance to Alcoa and the Australian government on this recent incident. They are both looking for a workable and sustainable solution. Research the case by looking up the incident online. What is your policy advice?

Interactions of stakeholders and actors around sustainable development issues

We have looked at the main state and non-state stakeholders and actors and their role in development. It is a mix of countries, IGOs, companies, non-governmental civil society actors and local state and non-state actors.

We are going to look at the roles that these stakeholders play regarding the three pillars of sustainable development. The interests and priorities of these stakeholders determine the policies and forms of sustainable development they support. Remember the ideas of weak and strong sustainability – why would a stakeholder not support strong sustainability policies?

Look at the photo on page 168. Why would a country willingly and intentionally subject its citizens and environment to such unhealthy, life-threatening conditions? What is the root cause of these conditions? Pollution is a sign of development and weak sustainability.

Higher-income countries have cleaner air, while lower-income countries, especially those that have higher rates of economic development, have more polluted air. In fact, pollution is very high and concentrated in rapidly developing countries. The oil rich countries of the Persian Gulf and Africa experience some of the worst air quality on a regular basis.

Developing and developed countries are important stakeholders, but it is stakeholders such as larger multinational and state companies that appear to benefit from all this unsustainable development and pollution.

Sustainability measurements like SSI and SGI are connected to the concepts of human development and human security. Human security is of particular interest here as it prioritizes the existence of fundamental Maslow needs such as security and access to nutrition as necessary components of good governance and rule of law.

HL Sustainability, especially measurements used to evaluate a country's level of sustainability or sustainability policies, provides a good basis for exploring real-world examples and case studies in *Security*. You should be able to make the case using these measurements that insecurity is increased when poor or limited sustainability policies are in place. You could use of SSI and SGI to compare and contrast two or more countries.

HL The connections between sustainability and sustainable development and *Health* are an excellent source of case studies that could be used as part of the HL topic area. While pollution and air quality are one approach you might take, it might also be valuable to explore the links between rates of cancer, diabetes and infant mortality in countries that have in place effective sustainable development policies compared to those who do not.

Development and sustainability

Why would a government allow pollution like this to continue? ▶

You can see the list of NGOs working on sustainability issues by navigating to the UC Berkeley Library website, then searching for Library Guides, finding Government and Public Policy, then finding the NGO dropdown. Or follow the QR code below:

Factories are producing goods. Tankers, trucks and motorbikes are delivering and shipping the goods. Consumers are buying them and jobs are being created. This is the type of development that reflects weak sustainability at its worst. So, the answer to the question why a stakeholder would not support strong sustainability is that weak sustainability is not only easier to implement, it is also more profitable.

The UN and non-governmental/non-profit stakeholders are not without influence, but their influence is limited. According to the website of the University of Berkeley in California, there are 14 NGOs working on sustainability issues, so you might think that their influence would be greater.

Most of these NGOs are based in or have their headquarters in high-income countries, and they are very active in low- and middle-income countries.

Despite the activity of NGOs and efforts by the UN, large and small private sector companies, with their headquarters in high-income countries and with large profit margins in low-income countries, continue to influence international, regional and national debates, and laws and institutions related to sustainable development.

Example – Shell and oil spills in the Niger delta

In 2016, Nigerians from the Ogale community and the Bille community brought lawsuits against the oil company Shell in courts in the UK for harm to their health and environmental damage to their lands as the result of oil spills in the Niger Delta. They argued that the UK parent company, Royal Dutch Shell, was responsible for the systematic pollution caused by its Nigerian subsidiary, the Shell Petroleum Development Company of Nigeria Ltd (SPDC). The claimants argued that Royal Dutch Shell exercised significant direction and control over its Nigerian subsidiary and was, therefore, liable for its systematic pollution of Ogale and Bille. Shell argued it could not, in law or in fact, be held responsible for the actions of its subsidiary.

Activity

What do you think about the claim made against Shell by the Nigerians? Do you think their case might be valid? Do you think Shell might be right? Write down what you think and compare with a classmate.

Thematic studies

The impacts of globalization on sustainability

Connected to the discussion of the role of stakeholders are the impacts that globalization has on sustainability. The impacts will have a number of different interpretations; some will be positive and others will be negative.

Globalization has increased the possibility that best practices will be shared and implemented globally. Economic sustainability seems to benefit from globalization. For example, a successful ESG sustainability strategy in South Africa can be brought to Mexico and Japan. New ideas can improve the quality and sustainability of business practices. Local government can take advantage of initiatives that have been tried elsewhere. Workers can access new opportunities in markets in countries that were not available before. As industries and jobs move, more opportunities are created. Greater economic interdependence can lead to higher rates of investment, job creation, higher purchasing power, higher incomes and standards of living, while increased competition can also lead to lower prices.

This can have a positive impact on social sustainability, as more funds are available for social services, healthcare and education, and movements of populations can lead to great diversity, cultural exchange and increased opportunities.

Cleaner, greener and more efficient technologies developed in one country can find their way to other countries, making transportation, construction and farming more efficient, while helping to support greater environmental sustainability.

Globalization could be seen as successful sustainable development. However, the benefits need to be put into perspective.

There is significant evidence to suggest a growing global wealth gap, which has detrimental impacts for sustainability, especially in developing countries. The globalized marketplace has created a concentration of wealth that benefits a small global elite.

Not all companies benefit equally either. Larger MNCs have the opportunity through globalization to access markets and purchase or push out micro and small and medium-sized enterprises, greatly impacting the sustainability of local communities in developed as well as developing countries.

HL Economic development and environmental sustainability are linked to improved health outcomes and therefore feature in the HL topic area of *Health*. Sustainable economic growth enables countries to invest in healthcare infrastructure, disease prevention programs, and access to essential medicines and treatments. Practices that harm the environment, such as pollution or deforestation, can have direct repercussions on public health, leading to increased respiratory problems, infectious diseases, and other health issues.

Global Wealth Distribution in 2021

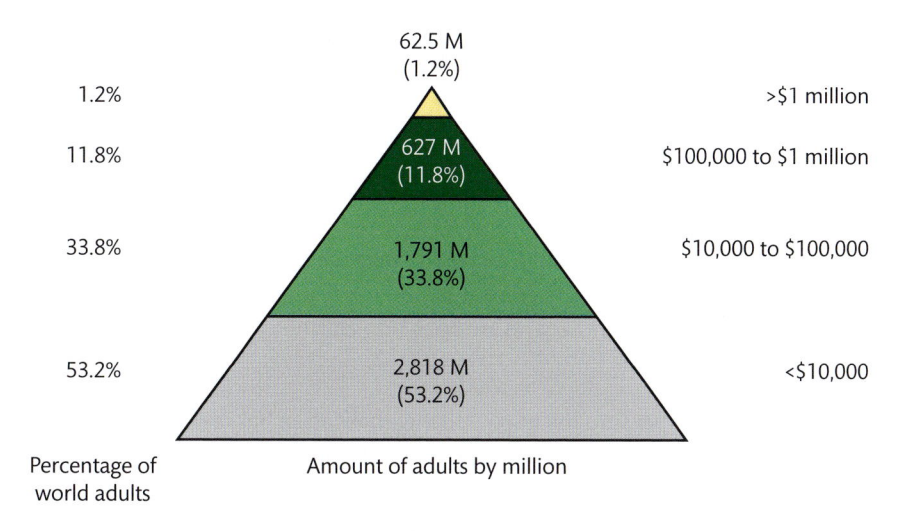

Percentage of world adults	Amount of adults by million	Wealth range
1.2%	62.5 M (1.2%)	>$1 million
11.8%	627 M (11.8%)	$100,000 to $1 million
33.8%	1,791 M (33.8%)	$10,000 to $100,000
53.2%	2,818 M (53.2%)	<$10,000

Figure 3.14 The global wealth gap as illustrated by Credit Suisse's Global Wealth Pyramid, with a significant portion of the world's wealth concentrated in a small number of hands.

169

Development and sustainability

Example – Ikea in India

Ikea is a furniture and houseware company, which has a globally recognized commitment to sustainable production. It recently opened a store in India, in Bengaluru. Ikea brings employment, cheaper priced products and slightly higher wages to an area. However, Ikea has faced criticism regarding the sustainability of the sourcing of its furniture, and the impact that its stores have on local businesses, practices and local furniture traditions. There is concern that Ikea's stores will negatively impact sustainability.

Activity

You have been given the opportunity to provide sustainability policy guidance to both Ikea and the local government in India as they tackle the realities of globalization in Bengaluru. Both are looking for a workable and sustainable solution. You can see the article about Ikea's sustainability here:

Research the case. What are the advantages and disadvantages of globalization? What is your policy advice?

There are benefits for workers, but wage competition forces workers to compete with workers in other countries and, where wages are lower, this places pressure on existing wages, potentially driving them down. Unionization efforts are made more difficult, as are government regulations to maintain sustainability practices as MNCs can threaten to relocate their factories to other places to take advantage of lower worker wages and a more relaxed regulatory environment.

Figure 3.15 The double-edged nature of economic globalization.

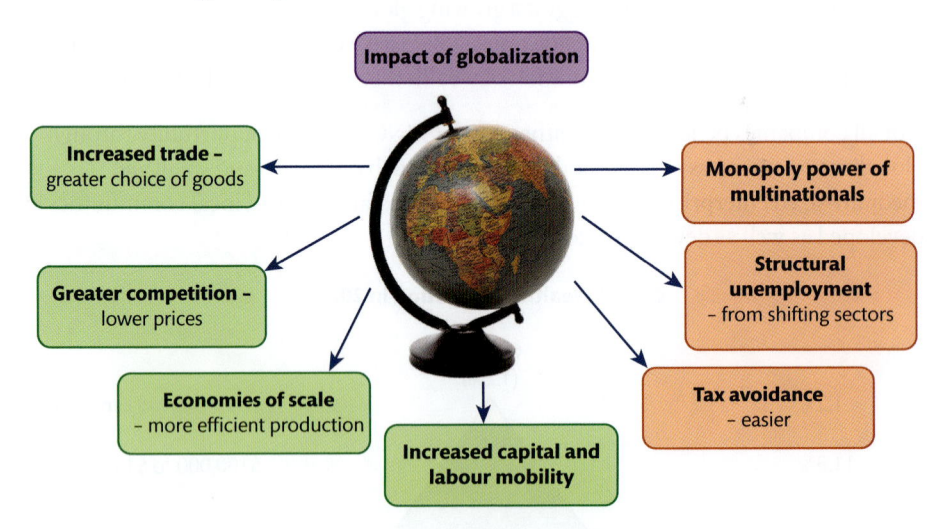

Impact of globalization:
- Increased trade – greater choice of goods
- Greater competition – lower prices
- Economies of scale – more efficient production
- Increased capital and labour mobility
- Monopoly power of multinationals
- Structural unemployment – from shifting sectors
- Tax avoidance – easier

Globalization does not always lead to an equal exchange of ideas, products and services. For example, English is becoming a dominant language, displacing other languages and advantaging those who are born into cultures where English is the most common language.

It is worth looking deeper into the impact that globalization has on sustainability in local communities in developing countries, especially given the role that micro and small and medium-sized enterprises have on sustainability.

Thematic studies

Activity

Does globalization have a negative impact on local communities being able to develop sustainably? Compare some of the advantages and disadvantages facing local communities when it comes to the businesses that operate within those communities. Use Table 3.2 as well as your own knowledge about sustainability. Consider what might be the best way forward for a local community in a developing country when it comes to their immediate and long-term sustainability. What would you recommend?

Table 3.2 Some advantages and disadvantages facing businesses in local communities

Micro and Small and Medium-sized Businesses	Larger Businesses and MNCs
• Serve a local market with less reliance on polluting transportation, though they may rely on motorbikes • Employ locally • May use older or outdated equipment that has negative environmental impacts like fuel leakage or non-filtered pollution • Less access to credit and capital for investments, expansion and improvements like refrigeration or fertilizers • May not be able to afford premises in easily accessible locations so are harder to reach • Less leverage when it comes to negotiating contracts and influencing policy • Business is more vulnerable to price changes and wage demands	• Serve a much larger market, local and further away • Can afford land near key infrastructure points such as paved roads, rail lines, canals and airports, making transport easier and cheaper; can also contribute to improvement of local infrastructure • Greater access to funds to access and upgrade technology for mechanization or land productivity, leading to decline in natural habitats and fewer skilled jobs • Use machinery and hire fewer workers • Access to lawyers to settle disputes with other businesses and individuals • Can access good quality credit, and then invest the money in their business • Use information and communication technology (ICT) to predict market changes and communicate with suppliers and buyers • Can absorb price changes more easily so less likely that business will fail

Contemporary debates on sustainability

Local vs global

The essence of the local versus global debate is the extent to which efforts to increase sustainability should come from local communities (bottom-up) or from the international community (top-down).

Supporters of the local side of the argument make the case that international efforts like the SDGs, and bilateral or multilateral ODA, are not as efficient as local initiatives. They believe that corruption creates additional levels of inefficiencies where the support does not reach the intended recipients.

Supporters of the global argument make the case that sustainable development is now done differently and with the involvement of a broader range of stakeholders,

---

HL Integrating interpretations of globalization and the connection between globalization and sustainability into your HL topic areas will have a significant impact on your exploration of case studies related to *Borders*. You could explore the changing nature of borders in free trade or economic development zones such as the EU or Economic Community of West African States (ECOWAS), or the cause and impact of population movements, migration and asylum to the countries of origin, transit and destination.

Globalization has a number of interpretations that bring us back to the discussions about sovereignty. Neoliberals argue that globalization brings about greater political, economic, social and cultural interdependence, and that greater interdependence leads to higher levels of peace and stability. They believe that countries trade some of their sovereignty for a greater share of global security. Postcolonialists argue that globalization is a modern form of neocolonialism and that the loss of sovereignty by countries in the Global South demonstrates inequality, and that those affected do not have the same share of global security as a result of globalization.

including local non-governmental actors and large and small for-profit businesses. They believe that efforts like the SDGs and other forms of multilateral and bilateral development are far more effective.

Government vs market

At the heart of the government versus market debate, also known as the public sector vs private sector or non-profit vs for-profit debate, is how much a society should rely on its government or for-profit businesses to work toward sustainable development.

The 'more government' approach makes the case that a combination of government policy, regulation and civil society participation is the best way forward in terms of strong sustainable development solutions. Supporters of this approach believe that only the government and non-governmental groups have the public interest in mind.

They argue that for-profit businesses are just interested in profit and that sustainability concerns, especially environmental ones, are secondary to increasing revenue and income. They see corruption as a product of for-profit businesses attempting to increase their influence. They also feel that for-profit businesses will settle for weak sustainability policies.

Market supporters argue that sustainability is at the core of any for-profit business. Without a market to sell their products in or provide their services to, businesses would not survive. Market supporters make the case that government corruption is evidence for greater involvement of large and small for-profit companies, for lower taxes and more favorable regulations toward businesses.

Market supporters point to efforts by companies to regulate their own sustainable practices through ESG and other initiatives. They also claim that for-profit companies are more efficient, less prone to waste and better suited to promote and carry out sustainable practices.

Trade vs aid

A debate that draws on the perspectives from the local/global and government/market debates involves which approach to sustainable development is best: trade or development aid and assistance.

The aid supporters argue that levels of development are still unequal and that more needs to be done by governments and stakeholders in developing countries to improve their sustainability. They point to levels of private sector and government corruption that impede sustainable development efforts when left unregulated and unmonitored.

Bilateral and multilateral aid supporters make the case that doing development differently has created a system that gets ODA to those who will be more productive and sustainably so.

Trade suppporters argue that ODA is unsustainable and ultimately tied to the national or institutional interest of those providing it. It might be available this year, but what happens when priorities change?

Trade and direct foreign investment, they argue, not only enhances the benefits of globalization for all involved but helps to promote sustainable development practices. Governments, bilateral and multilateral institutions have a role to play, but that role should be to make sure everyone has access to markets and loans.

Thematic studies

Global North vs Global South

At the core of the Global South side of this debate is the consensus by low- and middle-income countries that globalization continues to favor high-income countries and that real sustainable development will come only when more economically developed countries (MEDCs) open their markets to much cheaper commodities, goods, services and labor from less economically developed countries (LEDCs). They point out that many MEDCs maintain active policies that keep goods out of their markets, but expect LEDCs to open up their markets.

Supporters of the Global South make the case that most forms of ODA, including loans and funds through the multilateral IFIs, are under conditions that are unfavorable to countries of the Global South, considering it a form of neocolonialism. They point out that India and the PRC, members of the Global South, developed without ODA.

They also point out that the Global North is a symbolic name (they consider Australia and New Zealand, for example, to be a part of the Global North), meant to underscore in some cases hundreds of years of historical control of the resources, identity and people of the Global South by the Global North.

They also criticize the Global North for failing to recognize that the industrialization that began 200 years ago continues to pollute the planet that we all occupy. Now that greater wealth and living standards have come to the Global South, the Global North is attempting to limit industrialization and greater development in the Global South in the name of combating climate change.

The Global North counters that the period of colonization ended decades ago and that there is far more equity and symmetry between countries today. They point out that markets are more open than they have ever been. Open markets, they argue, are helping sustainable development efforts in all countries involved. That they have some protections still in place is a way to ease the impact of globalization on their own populations, but that these barriers to entry will be relaxed over time, just not immediately.

In addition, the MEDCs make the case that bilateral and multilateral ODA is just one part of the larger interdependent picture intended to drive sustainability and that all countries, especially those with high populations, need to do more to reduce, rather than increase, their carbon footprints, and that this can happen with a greater reliance on technology and innovation.

Deep ecology vs sustainable development

Deep ecologists and others are calling for a radical change in human patterns of production and consumption. Deep ecologists want a complete halt to polluting and extractive industries and human practices.

Supporters of sustainable development make the case that a radical transformation of our patterns of production and consumption would be too disruptive and would require countries to apply a level of force on all stakeholders that would be resisted and prove unsuccessful. They also argue that some aspects of the deep ecology philosophy and proposals have already been adopted, but that these ideas require a longer time to be implemented successfully.

Deep ecologists are of the view that the planet and life on it does not have that much time.

> Deep ecology developed in the 1960s. Deep ecologists believe that our planet is an equal stakeholder and that humans are just one component of the global ecosystem.

Development and sustainability

These key debate snap-shots are designed to stimulate a discussion between you and your classmates. The merits and weaknesses of each have been oversimplified here in order to get that conversation started. You should find ample evidence in this section, as well as your study in the other areas of Global Politics, to help guide you through the complexities of each.

Activity

Hold a class debate for one of the sustainability debates above, such as trade vs aid or Global South vs Global North. Divide the class into two teams. Each team researches one side of the argument and comes up with three points, supported by case studies or real-world examples. Each team has three minutes to make their case. Allow 5–10 minutes for questions and responses and give each team two minutes to summarize their main points. Which arguments were most persuasive? Which position did you choose and why?

Exercises

7. Is sustainability possible for all countries?
8. How should we hold people accountable if they do not follow sustainability guidance? Is it possible?
9. Does your view of sovereignty change if sovereignty is a barrier to sustainability?

Practice questions

1. Discuss different models for development. Can one model be described as entirely successful?
2. Identify indicators you believe could contribute to more accurate measurements of inequality inside a country.
3. Discuss the impact of poor governance and corruption on addressing poverty and inequality.
4. Identify reasons why sustainability, environmental and social factors should be considered for development alongside economic and political factors.
5. Evaluate the success of the Sustainable Development Goals process. What evidence would you use to argue it has been successful?
6. Discuss the view that globalization, in particular trade, has benefits for the poorest and most vulnerable in society.

Summary

In this chapter, you have learned:
- Inequality and marginalization are products of power asymmetries between state and non-state stakeholders.
- Sustained inequality is structural and a product of cultural factors and attitudes, some of which are difficult to change.

Thematic studies

- Inequality impacts different groups in different ways. Factors such as income, location, country of origin, gender, age, and other identity characteristics need to be analyzed and understood in your investigation of inequality.
- Different models of development have had mixed results, with some positive and negative outcomes. Recent development models have focused on the connection between sustainable living and inequality.
- Some efforts by richer countries to support development in poorer countries are conditional and dependent on some loss of sovereignty.
- Sustainability is a contested concept, even though it has a generally agreed upon definition. The contested nature comes in the creation and application of policies designed to achieve sustainability. Sustainability can be defined as weak or strong.
- Sustainability and development are different, but linked, concepts, especially when seen together as sustainable development.
- The understanding of sustainability has evolved to include specific terms and concepts linked to economic, social and environmental sustainability. Each of these pillars of sustainability can be measured, but these measurements are imperfect and need to be complemented.
- Interests and priorities determine the role and interactions of state and non-state stakeholders and actors impacting sustainability. The global, legal and institutional sustainability framework is impacted by the extent to which stakeholders believe in and seek to practice weak or strong sustainability.
- Approaches to sustainability and sustainable development can have positive or negative impacts on poverty and equality. Measurements exist, but they are imperfect. This very much depends on the intentions and actions of stakeholders.
- Globalization has an impact on sustainability efforts. Lower-income developing countries and lower-income populations in general tend to experience the negative impacts of globalization and wealthier populations experience the benefits.
- There are different debates regarding sustainability, such as local vs global, government vs market, trade vs aid, Global North vs Global South, and deep ecology vs sustainable development.

Notes

1. Baru, S. (1998). 'Mahbub Ul Haq and Human Development: A Tribute'. *Economic and Political Weekly*, 33(35), pp.2275–79. Retrieved on August 2, 2023 from JSTOR, www.jstor.org/stable/4407121
2. Selwyn, B. (2011). 'Liberty Limited? A Sympathetic Re-Engagement with Amartya Sen's "Development as Freedom"'. *Economic and Political Weekly*, 46(37), pp.68–76. Retrieved on August 2, 2023 from JSTOR, www.jstor.org/stable/23047282
3. UNDP. 'Human Development Index'. Retrieved from https://hdr.undp.org/data-center/human-development-index#/indicies/HDI
4. UNDP. 'Gender Development Index'. Retrieved from: www.undp.org/sites/g/files/zskgke326/files/migration/tr/UNDP-TR-EN-HDR-2019-FAQS-GDI.pdf
5. Wellbeing Economy Alliance. Retrieved from: https://weall.org/happy-planet-index-2021-launch-event-recap
6. Tsiang, S.C. (1964). 'A Model of Economic Growth in Rostovian Stages'. *Econometrica*, 32(4), pp.619–48. Retrieved on August 2, 2023 from: JSTOR, https://doi.org/10.2307/1910181

Development and sustainability

7. The Brookings Institute. Retrieved from: www.brookings.edu/articles/15-million-success-stories-under-the-millennium-development-goals/
8. The World Bank Atlas Method. Retrieved from: https://datahelpdesk.worldbank.org/knowledgebase/articles/378832-the-world-bank-atlas-method-detailed-methodology
9. IMF. Fact Sheet in HIPCs. Retrieved from: https://www.imf.org/en/About/Factsheets/Sheets/2016/08/01/16/11/Debt-Relief-Under-the-Heavily-Indebted-Poor-Countries-Initiative
10. UN News. Retrieved from: https://news.un.org/en/story/2023/05/1136367
11. European Commission. Retrieved from: https://ec.europa.eu/regional_policy/funding/erdf_en
12. EURADA. Retrieved from: https://www.eurada.org/projects/europeaid
13. European Commission. Retrieved from: https://ec.europa.eu/commission/presscorner/detail/en/IP_22_4532
14. European Commission. Retrieved from: https://international-partnerships.ec.europa.eu/countries/sub-saharan-africa_en#examples-of-regionalcontinental-initiatives-under-the-global-gateway-africa-europe-investment-package
15. Center for Strategic International Studies. Retrieved from: https://www.csis.org/analysis/kishidas-realism-diplomacy-japans-official-development-assistance-strategy
16. SGI. Retrieved from: www.sgi-network.org/2019/Greece/Environmental_Policies
17. The World Bank. Retrieved from: https://data.worldbank.org/indicator/DT.ODA.ALLD.CD?locations=NG
18. *The Guardian*. Retrieved from: https://guardian.ng/news/nigeria-abandons-vision-202020-dreams-agenda-2050/
19. *Al Jazeera*. Retrieved from: www.aljazeera.com/news/2021/10/5/south-africa-metalworkers-union-strike-car-industry
20. *New Strait Times*. Retrieved from: https://www.nst.com.my/news/nation/2020/07/609838/110-containers-toxic-waste-discovered-tg-pelepas-port
21. Human Rights Watch. Retrieved from: https://www.hrw.org/world-report/2022/country-chapters/kazakhstan
22. University of California Press. Retrieved from: https://www.ucpress.edu/blog/58831/how-bolivians-fought-for-and-won-water-access-for-all/
23. PEDIAA. Retrieved from: https://pediaa.com/difference-between-multinational-and-transnational/
24. NewClimate Institute. Retrieved from: www.foodnavigator.com/Article/2022/02/08/we-re-fooled-into-believing-that-these-companies-are-taking-sufficient-action-nestle-and-unilever-rebuff-greenwashing-accusation
25. World Economic Forum. Retrieved from: https://www.weforum.org
26. World Business Council for Sustainable Development. Retrieved from www.wbcsd.org/Overview/News-Insights/Member-spotlight/Unilever-launches-wide-ranging-set-of-commitments-and-actions-to-raise-living-standards-create-opportunities-through-inclusivity-and-prepare-people-for-the-future-of-work
27. Academy of International Business. Retrieved from: https://insights.aib.world/article/31077-the-role-of-multinational-enterprises-in-achieving-sustainable-development-goals
28. Brookings Institute. Retrieved from: www.brookings.edu/articles/how-the-sinaloa-cartel-rules/
29. Our World in Data. Retrieved from: https://ourworldindata.org/co2-and-greenhouse-gas-emissions
30. Elkington, J. 'Enter the Triple Bottom Line'. Retrieved from: https://www.johnelkington.com/archive/TBL-elkington-chapter.pdf
31. Raworth, K. (2012). 'A Safe and Just Space for Humanity'. Oxfam International. Retrieved from: https://www-cdn.oxfam.org/s3fs-public/file_attachments/dp-a-safe-and-just-space-for-humanity-130212-en_5.pdf
32. SSI Cologne. Retrieved from: https://ssi.wi.th-koeln.de/
33. SGI. Retrieved from: https://www.sgi-network.org/2022

Peace and conflict

THEMATIC STUDIES

Peace and conflict

Concepts

Peace, Negative Peace, Positive Peace, Violence, Conflict, War, Genocide, Terrorism, Resolution, Non-violence

Learning outcomes

In this chapter, you will learn about:

- peace and conflict as contested and interrelated concepts essential for a full understanding of global politics
- the idea of peace as more than the absence of violence, and the close connection between peace and other global challenges (such as development, poverty, equality, respect for human rights, the environment, etc.)
- the difference between negative and positive peace, and how this relates to the existence of conflict
- the nature and transformation of conflicts as part of human nature, emphasizing that armed conflict can be avoided
- armed conflict may seem to be necessary or even desirable in certain cases
- the complexity of conflicts, by analyzing the sources of violence, the range of possible actors within a conflict, and the possible causes that can trigger, escalate and intensify a conflict
- the existence of conflicts aside from armed conflict
- important concepts in peace and conflict studies such as war, genocide and terrorism
- why global politics always seem to be plagued by conflict
- why conflicts are so hard to address, by examining the complex dynamics through which conflicts and actors relate to one another across time
- different paths toward resolution and their strengths and limitations, allowing critical evaluation of why some conflicts have been solved successfully while others have not
- why peace is so frail and hard to achieve, yet important to work on in order to cease conflict and violence, and achieve global development.

Power is at the core of all conflicts and peace efforts. In every armed conflict, humanitarian damage is widespread, and human rights are often violated. Conflict also affects development. Positive peace seeks to halt the violence and to provide adequate conditions in which global development can exist.

Contested meanings: peace

Conceptual question

What is peace and how can it be achieved?

Peace means different things to different people. In some societies, peace refers to the absence of an armed conflict or war, while for those in which armed conflict has been absent for long periods of time, peace refers to the absence of other forms of non-violent conflict and the existence of lasting security (human and national security). Measuring a state of peace depends on the context, and on a deeper

Thematic studies

assessment on the absence of **violence**, and the levels of harmony, equity and justice that exist within a society.

Despite this lack of agreement on defining peace, it is clear that peace is underfunded, and often undervalued. Even though a state of peace is what most humans desire, it is **conflict** and war that demand enormous amounts of money, resources, energy and attention. People have different ideas about how peace can be achieved. For some, the path is through non-violent means, but for others, it is through violence.

> **Activity**
>
> Peace is often defined as the absence of violence, or the absence of the threat of violence. It is seen as a state of harmony in which the actors involved enjoy relative equity, and where justice rules. Yet, peace means different things to different people. When we talk about peace, do we mean world peace, peace between and among communities, an 'outer peace'? Or do we mean individual or 'inner peace'? When trying to understand peace, it is important to consider that its meaning is contested and depends on context. Write down your own definition of peace and compare it to that of a classmate or an organization that works for peace. Analyze how the definitions are different or similar, and evaluate what the reasons behind any differences could be.

If peace is something we all desire as humans, why do we keep engaging in armed conflicts and going to war?

In 2001, American author and journalist Chris Hedges wrote *War is a Force That Gives Us Meaning*.[1] He declares that war gives states and individuals adrenaline, a significance, a *raison d'etre* that cannot be found elsewhere. But, in 2022, he said that 'The Greatest Evil is War.'[2] Throughout history, people and states have recognized the horrors of war, and at times even its absurdity, but we keep engaging in armed conflicts.

Proposals on how to solve war are abundant and many have been implemented (at times with success). Perhaps, as David Barash and Charles Webel[3] state, some less successful solutions have not been creative, forward thinking or feasible, or they have not been attempted in the right combinations, or are not strong enough. This may be because war is a business, and a very lucrative one, while peace is not. Whatever the reasons, peace, at least in some form, is possible and we must keep thinking that way in order for life to persist.

Presenting peace and war as opposite points may not be helpful in achieving peace. Instead, we can look at peace and war as a continuum, in which peace is not just the absence of war, but a range of states and possible scenarios.

Norwegian sociologist, mathematician and peace theorist Johan Galtung, founder of the Stockholm International Peace Research Institute, referred to peace in a binary way. According to Galtung, peace could be either negative or positive. These labels did not make reference to whether peace could be seen as something positive or negative, but to how deep, stable and sustainable the state of peace actually is.

The difference between a war and an armed conflict is debatable. An armed conflict often refers to a fight between armed troops, existing with or without an official declaration by governments or states, as fights can also occur between non-state actors (NSAs). War is an intentional, disclosed, widespread and long duration armed conflict between countries. War is governed by the law of armed conflict, also called International Humanitarian Law. International law, which uses the term 'armed conflict' instead of 'war', applies whether states are fighting each other or against NSAs. Wars have evolved in many ways.

TOK

Why is it that, in spite of the increasing information and knowledge we have about the evils of war, we can become less and less emotionally impacted by it?

Understanding that peace is more than the absence of war, but a range of different scenarios, can help us engage in critical analysis when trying to achieve peace in different contexts.

Peace and conflict

How can we be certain that today's peace will be still enjoyed tomorrow? Can we make sure peace will be long-lasting?

Violence can be categorized into direct, cultural and structural violence (see the 'Types of violence' section later in this chapter). Direct violence refers to the immediate action of hurting someone physically, emotionally or psychologically. Cultural violence refers to emotional sources of violence, attitudes, feelings and values. Structural violence is an indirect form of violence inflicted through institutions, systems or established structures.

A ceasefire refers to a temporary stop in direct fighting between the parties to a conflict. It is a temporary period of truce that can serve as a preliminary step toward more permanent peace.

Resolution is the solution to a problem or conflict. In the context of conflict, resolution usually refers to the way in which two or more parties find a peaceful solution to their disagreements.

Peace is the absence of physical, cultural and structural violence that leads to a state of harmony, equity and justice.

Negative peace

Negative peace refers to the absence of direct, physical or immediate violence between people, clans, tribes, ethnic groups, states or other NSAs. This is the most common understanding of peace in the context of international relations. It is a realist view that considers that peace exists when there is no war or other direct form of violence. This type of peace is labelled as 'negative' due to the fact that the absence of physical violence does not necessarily mean the absence of an underlying, or even a structural, conflict. For example, a **ceasefire** or a declared cease of hostilities does not mean the conflict is over, but it can be a temporary pause in direct violence in order to attend to the wounded, evacuate civilians or deliver humanitarian assistance. A ceasefire can be used to regroup and reorganize the fighting forces.

Negative peace does not look deeper into the causes of conflict, or how to resolve it, nor does it address the consequences that previous violence may have had (on infrastructure, the economy, the population or diplomatic relations). Negative peace provides a first step toward possible future conflict resolution, but it can only provide a weak and artificial state of peace that can lead to further escalation. The India-Pakistan conflict frequently sees phases of an escalation of violence followed by periods, sometimes as long as several years, of relative calm. However, there is no real reconciliation. These peaceful periods are only characterized by an absence of overt violence and military activity, while the cultural and structural violence persists.

Positive peace

Positive peace refers to the absence of physical direct violence (see page 188 for a further explanation of types of violence), and it also considers the absence of cultural and structural violence (for example, xenophobia among the population and institutional discrimination in the educational system). It looks beyond reducing or stopping immediate physical violence. It identifies a deeper level of harmony by addressing the cultural and structural violence that may play a role in conflict. With positive peace, the causes of potential conflict are addressed and, ideally, solved. This type of peace refers to a social condition in the presence of social harmony that is equitable and just. It focuses on peacebuilding, political and social structures.

Positive peace exists when enemies agree to a cease of physical hostilities, but also to formally *make* peace, while addressing the social, political, cultural, economic and institutional causes of those hostilities. It takes into account the grievances that led to the conflict in the first place, and it makes the effort to disarm, demobilize and reintegrate the former combatants in order to contribute to a stable and sustainable peace. All societies should and must aim for positive peace.

Culturally, positive peace has long been something wished for by humans. Barash and Webel present examples of this.

> The ancient Greek concept of *eireinei*... denotes harmony and justice as well as peace. Similarly, the Arabic *salaam* and the Hebrew *shalom* connote not only the absence of violence but also the presence of well-being, wholeness, and harmony within oneself,

Thematic studies

a community, and among all nations and people. The Sanskrit word *shanti* refers not only to peace but also to spiritual tranquility, an integration of outward and inward modes of being, just as the Chinese noun *ping* denotes harmony and the achievement of unity from diversity.[4]

Activity

Work in a group of three. Look for other examples where negative peace exists, without positive peace being in place. Argue why you think positive peace has not been achieved.

Measuring peace

Internationally speaking, there are few efforts to measure peace because of the difficulties encountered when defining and approaching peace. The Institute for Economics and Peace in Australia created the Global Peace Index (GPI) in order to try to measure the absence of violence in connection to other factors (23 qualitative and quantitative indicators) that can correlate to a state of peace. The GPI measures peace in three broad aspects:

- a country's level of societal safety and security
- the extent of ongoing domestic or international conflict
- the degree of militarization.

The results are presented annually with countries located on a scale of 1–5, where the lower the number, the higher the level of peace.

The GPI 2023 results showed the average level of global peace deteriorating by 0.42 percent compared to the previous year (84 countries improved and 79 deteriorated). Factors that contributed to the deterioration were the war between Russia and Ukraine, the increasing costs of food and other goods, a growth in political instability in Africa, South Asia and the Middle East, and the increasing number of **refugees** and **internally displaced people (IDPs)**. The 2023 report also reported a decreasing trend in militarization, terrorism impact, nuclear and heavy weapons, incarceration rates and perceptions of criminality.

TOK: To what extent can peace be measured? How can we be sure peace measurements reflect reality?

To further analyze the results presented by the GPI, you can access the Vision of Humanity website or the QR code below:

Activity

Access the latest GPI results on the Internet. Based on the level of global peace presented and the main figures, assess what these tell you about global peace and what they do not say. Find the results of the GPI concerning your own country. Would you consider the GPI accurate, or do you have a different perception of peace as a citizen?

As of 2023, Iceland has held the position of the most peaceful country since 2008, with Afghanistan being the least peaceful country for eight consecutive years. Out of the top ten countries in the peace index, seven are in Europe.

Peace and conflict

Table 4.1 Top ten peaceful countries, GPI 2023

Rank	Region (Country)	Score
1	Iceland	1.124
2	Denmark	1.31
3	Ireland	1.312
4	New Zealand	1.313
5	Austria	1.316
6	Singapore	1.332
7	Portugal	1.333
8	Slovenia	1.334
9	Japan	1.336
10	Switzerland	1.339

The largest deteriorations recorded in 2023 were in external conflicts fought, deaths from internal conflict, political instability indicators, violent demonstrations, and the number of refugees and IDPs. This was attributed mainly to:

- the war between Ukraine and Russia (which resulted in millions of Ukrainians having to flee the country or being forced to move internally)
- the war in Yemen
- the continuous conflict in Syria
- the withdrawal of US and other NATO forces from Afghanistan, which allowed the Taliban back into power
- the increasing number of environmentally-induced migrants
- the ongoing conflicts in the Democratic Republic of Congo, Mali, Nigeria and Sudan, among others.

Within the GPI, there is a Positive Peace Index (PPI) that measures a society's resilience associated with socio-economic factors such as higher incomes and greater economic stability, and more efficient, transparent and inclusive governance.

Within the PPI, eight factors are considered pillars:

- a well-functioning government
- sound business environment
- acceptance of the rights of others
- good relations with neighbors
- free flow of information
- high levels of **human capital** (the knowledge, skills and health that people invest in and accumulate throughout their lives, enabling them to realize their potential as productive members of society)
- low levels of corruption
- equal distribution of resources.

The International Organization for Migration (IOM) defines environmental migrants as 'persons or groups of persons who, predominantly for reasons of sudden or progressive change in the environment that adversely affects their lives or living conditions, are obliged to leave their habitual homes, or choose to do so, either temporarily or permanently, and who move either within their country or abroad.' The United Nations (UN) and the UN High Commissioner for Human Rights (UNHCR) have recorded an average of 21.5 million people forcibly displaced by weather-related events since 2008. The Institute for Economics and Peace estimates that by 2050 there will be a total of 1.2 billion people displaced due to climate change and natural disasters.

Thematic studies

This means that positive peace is closely linked to opportunities, health, education and people's satisfaction with their access to basic services.

There is a direct correlation between PPI and Gross Domestic Product (GDP), the monetary value of final goods and services produced in a country in a given period of time. Countries that improved their PPI also saw an increase of 3.1 percent on average in their GDP. Inflation is also less volatile in these countries, which results in less drastic increases in prices. Where PPI improves, there is an improvement in household consumption (an increase in the amount of expenditure made by households to meet their everyday needs, such as food, clothing or housing). Countries with a decrease in their PPI also declined in the Global Peace Index (GPI).

The Institute for Economics and Peace defines positive peace 'as the attitudes, institutions and structures that create and sustain peaceful societies. Positive Peace is a gauge for societal resilience, or the ability to shield its citizens from shocks and to promote the recovery of the socio socio-economic in their aftermath.'[5] This means that the same factors that contribute to positive peace also contribute to socio-economic outcomes, such as greater income growth, better environmental conditions, higher levels of well-being, superior developmental outcomes and stronger resilience.

Positive peace, compared to negative peace, seeks a stable environment that allows all humans to be safe from physical harm, and to develop and fulfill a dignified life, with access to opportunities, equality and justice.

> Positive peace is closely related to human rights in that whenever positive peace exists, people enjoy a stable environment that provides the means for the fulfillment of their human rights. It is related to development as well. Positive peace increases people's capability to achieve the lives they want.

The road to peace

There are disagreements on how to avoid war, and people also disagree on how to achieve peace. Notable people in history have approached the road to peace through non-violent means, while others have approached it through violence. Agreeing upon which means is the best is an almost impossible task. Peace studies do not aim to eliminate conflict in its entirety. We cannot expect to eliminate competition and rivalry considering the imperfections of humans and a world with finite resources. If possible, peace studies try to develop new roads of cooperation that can lead to a reduction of violence.

One way in which peace enthusiasts oppose war and militarism, while also aiming for the creation of structures and cultures oriented toward peace, is through **peace movements**. Peace movements are a type of social movement in which people organize and sustain a campaign in support of a social goal, which looks for the implementation of, or the prevention of, a change in the society's structure or values.

Peace movements are becoming more popular due to:

- the increasing potential of global destruction through war (with the development of increasingly destructive weapons)
- the social, economic and environmental effect of armed conflicts
- the interconnectedness brought by communications and transportation (demonstrating that we are all affected by the experiences of others)
- a general increase in political involvement (warfare is no longer seen as exclusive to governments but as an issue in which every organization and individual can play a role).

Peace and conflict

Peace movements are inspired and supported by a belief in **universalism**, which sees a common interest in peace and shared humanity.

Peace movements can be grouped into three different types:

- movements that aim to eliminate war in general (for example, the War Resisters League)
- movements that aim to stop particular aspects of war (such as the use of landmines or the use of torture, for example, the International Campaign to Abolish Nuclear Weapons (ICAN))
- movements that aim to stop specific wars (such as the war in Iraq or the war in Ukraine, for example, the Peace in Ukraine Coalition).

Protesters with banners opposing racism.

Many peace movements have come under criticism for seeming to recede once the war is over. While this does happen, it is also true that opposition to war does continue, but that it is not covered by the media as much as it initially was, giving the false impression that the opposition is over.

Another anti-war response is through **civil disobedience**. American writer Henry David Thoreau argued that citizens have a higher obligation toward each other than to their own governments. Therefore, conscientious citizens are obliged to do what is right even when their defiance of governments results in retribution on them by those governments. This has been observed in many countries in which citizens protest against their government's decision to conduct war even at the risk of being physically attacked, arrested or imprisoned. The anti-war protests in Russia after the invasion of Ukraine resulted in over 1300 arrested on September 22, 2022 alone, according to the independent OVD-Info protest monitoring group. Another example is the 22,000 Iranians arrested, but later pardoned by the supreme leader in Iran, after anti-government protests following the death of Mahsa Amini (the 22-year-old Kurdish Iranian woman arrested by the morality police who later died in hospital under suspicious circumstances) in September 2022.

Anti-government protests following the death of Mahsa Amini in September 2022.

Thematic studies

Peace movements and civil disobedience have faced backlashes from opponents who are concerned about the consequences of breaking the law, or about the possibility of actions alienating the general population, resulting in counterproductive consequences.

Throughout history, war has been seen by many as a necessary evil. Prussian general and military theorist Carl von Clausewitz (b.1780) referred to war as the continuation of politics by other means. But many societies have condemned the evils of war. In global politics, efforts have been made by pacifists (those who believe war and violence are unjustifiable) to search for an alternative to the 'natural state' of anarchy in the world. For instance, the concept of sovereignty was thought to have the ability to limit power ambitions and the pursuit of these through violent means. Throughout the 19th century, pacifist organizations spread throughout Europe, leading to the creation in the 20th century of institutions such as the International Court of Justice (ICJ) and the UN, as well as the signing of international treaties. Worldwide pacifist movements appeared, such as the anti-nuclear movement, the student movements in the USA and Europe in the 1960s and 1970s, and the Indian independence movement led by Gandhi.

Pacifism has been presented as pragmatic and with a moral principle. The former sees peace as a useful and ideal policy through which conflicts can and should be resolved. The latter sees violence as morally wrong. Yet, pacifism is not exempt from criticism. Anti-pacifist views see the refusal to participate in war as a failure to carry out what can sometimes be a moral obligation (for example, carrying out a humanitarian intervention in a country at war in order to prevent worse outcomes). Critics of absolute pacifism are often referred to as 'pragmatic pacifists'[6] or relative pacifists, because they understand peace as a continuum in which, even though peace is the desired means and outcome, there is a range of options that do allow for a limited use of force under specific conditions.

Nowadays, most countries, following neorealist thinking, point to military strength as the most important way of maintaining peace. The argument is that weakness invites aggression. Therefore, the power of one (country or party) must be balanced. As Barash and Webel put it, 'peace through strength relies fundamentally on deterrence, the expectation that a would-be aggressor would refrain from attacking opponents who are more powerful than it or who are capable of inflicting unacceptable damage if attacked.' This leaves the **balance of power**, implying a continuous arms race to keep a symmetry in the international system.

According to some theorists, such as Kenneth Waltz and John Mearsheimer, the existence of a balance of power deters wars, while a slight power imbalance can result in war because the status quo feels threatened. Defensive realists (Waltz) argue that the best way to safeguard the status quo and secure a state is by maintaining the power balance. Offensive realists (Mearsheimer) believe that great powers can only secure themselves by maximizing their own power. An example of this is Russia, feeling threatened by NATO's increasing influence in Ukraine, choosing to carry out an invasion instead of waiting for the opponent to become stronger. This does not mean that a shift in the power balance leads to war. Sometimes, actors prefer to lean toward the creation of **alliances**. The problem with a focus on the balance of power is when the pursuit of one's own security creates a security dilemma. The build-up in one country makes other countries seek to do the same, resulting in all actors being less secure than in the beginning.

As seen in the Core chapter of this book, sovereignty refers to the state's ability to rule itself. A state is sovereign when it has full control over what happens inside its territory, without foreign interference.

TOK How can we be certain whether pacifism or force is the most adequate response?

Balance of power is the idea that states strive toward an equal distribution of power to avoid dominance by one, either consciously or unconsciously.

Peace and conflict

The road to peace is neither easy nor simple. Proposals on how to achieve peace are many, yet it is much easier to express one's commitment to them than to carry them out. Perhaps one of the main reasons for this is not only the complexity of peace as a concept, as a means and as an end in itself, but it also has to do with the complexities of conflict.

Exercises

1. Design a peace education program for your country. Include step-by-step suggestions.
2. Discuss with a partner whether the world would be safer with no nuclear weapons.
3. Analyze peace movements in Israel and Palestine. Compare them. Do they share any traits? Can any of them learn from the other?
4. Why do you think 'peace through strength' is still the most followed path to achieve peace? Write a paragraph to explain your opinion.

Contested meanings: conflict and violence

Conceptual question

What is conflict and what does it mean to be ever-present?

Knotted gun sculpture by Carl Fredrik Reuterswärd in front of the UN Headquarters in New York.

The concept of conflict has generally negative associations. It is frequently assumed that conflict is always violent. But conflict and violence are not the same thing, and conflict can exist without violence. Conflict is part of our everyday lives. It exists whenever people have different values, ideas, needs, interests, goals, perceptions or beliefs. This is referred to as **latent conflict**. Sometimes, conflict can exist without the actors being aware of the conflict itself.

Thematic studies

Conflict is the existence, or perceived existence, of incompatibilities, disagreements or inconsistencies that can occur among people, nations, states and any other type of actors. We could even say that conflict exists within ourselves. Think of your morning routine, when your alarm goes off and you find yourself in a conflict between getting out of bed and snoozing for 20 more minutes. Think of your dinner plans with a friend and the disagreement you might have when it comes to choosing a restaurant. In each scenario, you are not facing a war, or a violent dispute, it is simply a conflict. Conflict can be much more complicated. Incompatibilities and disagreements can involve sensitive and complex issues such as religious beliefs, language, nationalism, ethnic or racial supremacy, and control over territory. Conflicts can involve only a couple of actors, but they can also involve numerous actors at different levels.

Conflict can exist within peaceful disagreements (a peaceful demonstration, for example). It can also involve violent incompatibilities that can result in armed conflicts, war or even genocide. When people openly disagree and choose to confront, this is known as **overt conflict**. But what makes a conflict turn violent? There is no single and concrete answer because every armed conflict is different and involves a variety of actors. Although causes may be similar, they will never be the same, and they will also depend on particular contexts. All violent conflicts do involve the existence of negative emotions and tension (anger, sadness, frustration, oppression, vengeance, hatred, etc.).

Table 4.2 Examples of violent and non-violent conflicts

Violent Conflicts	Non-violent Conflicts
• Genocide • Civil war • Terrorism • Interstate war • Insurgency	• Strike • Diplomatic dispute • Civil disobedience • Peaceful demonstrations • Economic sanctions

It can be stated that conflict cannot be avoided, but violence and war can. Conflict can exist without tension and, even when tension is present, violence can still be avoided. If violence does occur, this does not necessarily lead to a war. And if war happens, it can be resolved without the further use of violence. Conflicts can involve different means of coercion without resorting to direct violence. Examples include diplomatic and economic sanctions, sabotage, trade sanctions and espionage. The use of violence is just one means of coercion out of many.

What differentiates war and conflict is the existence of, or threat of, violence. To be able to differentiate conflict from war allows policymakers to address a dispute accordingly. War has been a constant throughout human history.

Conceptual question

What is the role of violence in conflict?

Violence refers to actions, words, attitudes, structures or systems that cause physical, psychological, social or environmental damage. It is a means of coercion that can be found in different scenarios, not exclusively war. A commonly used categorization of violence comes from Johan Galtung, who divides violence into direct, cultural and structural types.

Conflict is a real or perceived state of incompatibility or disagreement that can be non-violent or violent.

Violence is one of the many tools through which power can be exercised.

TOK

Language is crucial, and it can define the actions and responses of stakeholders. Even in international law, language matters. Russia's military operations in Ukraine have been referred to as a military intervention, an invasion, a war, or by Russia as a 'special military operation'. Reflect on the implications different wordings can have.

187

Peace and conflict

Types of violence

Figure 4.1 Johan Galtung's triangle of violence.[7]

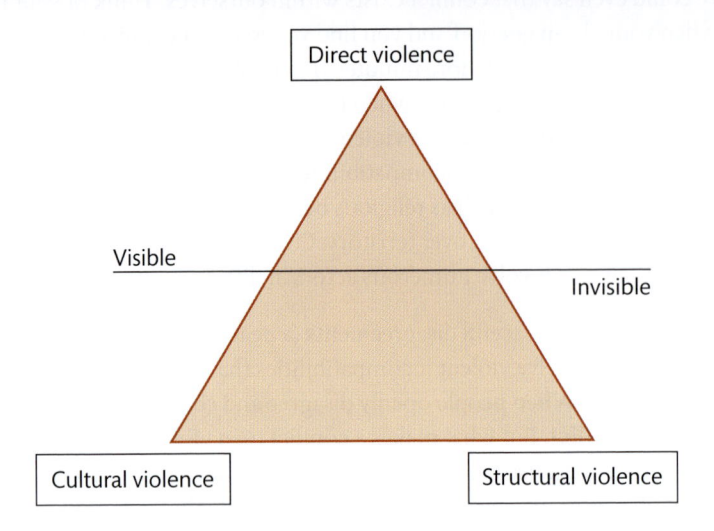

```
                    Direct violence
                         /\
                        /  \
                       /    \
              Visible /      \
              -------/--------\-------
                    /          \  Invisible
                   /            \
                  /              \
                 /_____\
          Cultural violence    Structural violence
```

In Galtung's triangle, you can see that violence has a similar structure to that of an iceberg. There is a small visible part, but underneath there are much bigger violence issues.

Direct violence

Direct violence is the immediate physical or mental harm faced by an individual or a group of people through the use of direct action, such as the torture of a prisoner, the beating of a person, the use of pepper spray against protesters or the explosion of a bomb in a market. All of these actions cause immediate direct harm to the victims.

Direct violence tends to be visible, making it straightforward to identify. The level of damage can be measured, investigated and addressed accordingly (such as treating the wounds from a gun). In the best-case scenario, the aggressor or aggressors can be identified and held accountable.

Cultural violence

Cultural violence can be found in the mindset, beliefs or values of individuals or whole societies. It involves the emotional sources of violence, attitudes, feelings and values, that are learned in private spaces such as in homes and families, as well as in public spaces such as schools and the media. Every level of society is responsible for cultural violence.

For example, boys are not born believing they are superior to girls. However, family and society can teach boys the belief of superiority based on their sex. This can create a society in which it is believed girls are inferior to boys and do not deserve the same human rights. This can lead to the creation of cultural norms and traditions from which girls are excluded or where they are given a secondary role, possibly limiting them to domestic activities, or leaving them out of the political and economically productive spheres.

Thematic studies

Cultural violence can also be government-driven, where the authority abuses its position of power to influence the society's culture and values. This type of violence can result in culturally based justifications that can lead to direct or structural violence.

Structural violence

Structural violence or **institutional violence** is the indirect form of violence inflicted by governments or any other authority through institutions, systems or established structures. It is when the actions taken by an authority or another power result in physical, mental or any other type of violence on individuals or groups of people. This violence is institutionalized. It is official and is part of the system or structure.

Apartheid in South Africa (1948–94) consisted of a policy of segregation and political, social and economic discrimination against the non-white population. During this period, the South African authorities provided differing access to and quality of services (ranging from education to public transport) to people based on the color of their skin. This was one of many discriminatory policies that existed as part of the institutional structure of the country.

As of 2023, there were 64 countries[8] with laws that criminalize homosexuality, with nearly half of these being in Africa. While some countries have moved to decriminalize same-sex unions and improve rights for LGBTQI+ people, others have tightened their laws, such as Nigeria and Uganda. A law passed in March 2023 condemned people who identify as gay in Uganda to risk life in prison or the death penalty in certain cases. Even though homosexuality in Uganda was illegal before, this law strengthened structural violence and introduced many new criminal offenses.

Realized by Roderick Sauls, the bench Non-White Only in Queen Victoria Street, Cape Town, South Africa, recreates the public benches used in the Apartheid era.

All violence contains some form of intent. *Direct* violence seeks an immediate harm. Cultural and structural violence are referred to as *indirect* types of violence because they seek an indirect harm through the denial of the equality and fundamental rights of a group of people, by reinforcing negative emotions and beliefs.

Activity

Discuss with your classmates which type of violence (direct, cultural or structural) you believe most commonly leads to other types of violence.

Peace and conflict

> **HL** Structural violence is closely related to the HL topic area *Equality*. Authorities or governments, through the use of institutions and whole systems, create an environment of discrimination that leaves certain communities, groups or individuals without the same access to opportunities and benefits as the rest of the population.

It is important to note that all three types of violence are connected. Cultural violence can provide justifications for structural and direct violence. Direct violence can be understood as a manifestation of structural and cultural violence. However, it is not necessary for all three types to exist for there to be violence. It is, for example, possible to encounter physical confrontations between different ethnic groups without violence existing in the system. A government can discriminate against a minority as a result of religious ideologies without any physical confrontation taking place. However, the presence of one type of violence is more likely to strengthen other types of violence, or even lead to other types of violence.

Non-violent conflict

Conflict can exist without violence. In global politics, it is common to find disagreements among nations, groups or states that are solved through peaceful and diplomatic means. In the international system, an active policy of **non-violence** is not only desired but expected. The opposition to war and the opposition to violence are the principles found in pacifism, which entails using peace as a means to solve disputes, opposes war and violence under any circumstance, and sees no justification for it in any context except by pragmatic pacifists.

An alternative to pacifism is what is known as strategic non-violence. Peter Ackerman and Chris Kruegler argued that non-violence could be used strategically as an advantage over the use of violence, not simply for moral reasons.[9] At the state level, countries often apply non-violent measures against violent regimes such as embargoes or sanctions, diplomatic or economic, seeking to exert pressure without using military force (maintaining a peaceful image). It is important to note that these measures tend to harm the populations greatly. In other cases, countries may choose to stay unaligned during an international armed conflict to preserve a peaceful posture. States that refrain from the use of violence, compared to others that do not, attract support for their causes. At the population level, if the opposition uses violence against an authority, the state finds legitimacy in using force against this opposition in return. Instead, people can use strategic non-violence as a powerful way to fight for justice, freedom, and their rights and liberties. Mass protests, strikes and boycotts are examples of non-violent actions where large numbers of people can unify, organize and peacefully disrupt their opponents by exerting pressure and attracting more individuals to join their movement. Non-violence is a strategy that can increase the power and influence of the people while reducing any legitimacy the state has in using force as a response.

If the state uses violence against those acting non-violently, whether another country or a population, this can create a negative image for those behind the violence, increasing sympathy for those affected by the violence. For example, social unrest in Iran has been characterized by the Western media as an unjust and violent regime acting against a peaceful society that only demands the respect of its basic freedoms and liberties.

The following case study on the 2017 diplomatic crisis in Qatar is an example of a non-violent conflict, in which the absence of violence was not only the result of moral principles, but also of strategic politics.

Thematic studies

Case – The Qatar crisis

The Middle East is a region that has known a number of armed conflicts. It is a region of constant tensions, coming from outside and within, which is rich in natural resources. The region experiences poverty, social and gender inequality, the negative economic impacts of war, insecurity and acts of terrorism. Contributory factors to the tension and violence include:

- the Iran-Iraq war (1980–88)
- the Gulf Crisis (1990–91)
- the invasion of Kuwait by Iraq (1990)
- the violent revolutions of the Arab Spring (2010)
- the war, and one of the worst humanitarian crises, in Yemen (2014–present)
- the existing tensions and hostilities between Israel and its neighbors (1948–present)
- the Syrian Civil War (2011–ongoing)
- the US invasion of Iraq (2003).

However, peaceful outcomes can sometimes occur in the Middle East.

The Qatar crisis of 2017 refers to a diplomatic dispute between Qatar and the Arab Quartet (Saudi Arabia, the United Arab Emirates (UAE), Bahrain and Egypt) that resulted in the temporary break-up of relations between these actors. It began when the Arab Quartet accused Qatar of the following:

- Having a controversial foreign policy: Qatar has always had strong relations with Iran, a regional competitor to Saudi Arabia.
- Supporting terrorist organizations: Qatar has supported groups such as Hamas in Palestine, the Muslim Brotherhood in Egypt and Hezbollah in Lebanon.
- Supporting the Arab Spring: This was a wave of social revolutions that overthrew the government of Egypt, but also posed a threat to other autocratic Arab governments.
- Using Al-Jazeera to criticize Arab governments and meddle in domestic affairs of other countries.

The accusations resulted in the Arab Quartet sending Qatar a list of 13 demands to which the government of Qatar had to respond within a period of 10 days. Among the demands were:

- Scale down diplomatic ties with Iran and close Iranian diplomatic missions. This included trade and commerce with Iran, complying with US and international sanctions.
- Shut down the Turkish military base in Qatar and halt military cooperation with Türkiye.
- Break relations with terrorist, sectarian and ideological organizations such as the Muslim Brotherhood, ISIS, al-Qaeda, Hezbollah and the al-Nusra Front (or Fateh al-Sham). At the same time, fugitives or wanted individuals by the Arab Quartet – who had previously found refuge in Qatar – to be handed over.
- Close down Al-Jazeera and affiliates.
- End interference in other countries' internal affairs, including ceasing all contact with those countries' political opposition.

Peace and conflict

> **HL**
>
> Violent and non-violent conflicts can have important negative implications in economic terms. Unfortunately, effects often hit civilians the most. From trade sanctions, economic embargoes, inflation and other economic sanctions, conflict can increase the number of people living in *Poverty* and can worsen the situation of those living in poverty already.

- Align militarily, politically, socially and economically to the rest of the countries in the region.
- Pay reparations and compensation for loss of life and financial losses caused by Qatar's policies, and consent to frequent audits.

Qatar refused to fulfill the demands, based on its view that these were baseless accusations, and also on the fact that the demands violated the country's sovereignty. On June 5, 2017, the accusing countries broke relations with Qatar, demanded their citizens to leave Qatari territory and gave 14 days to Qatari nationals to leave their countries. The diplomatic break-up also included an **embargo** on land, sea and air. This affected trade and the economy of Qatar (Qatar is a small peninsula with only one land border shared with Saudi Arabia). The air embargo prohibited the use of the air space of the Arab Quartet countries by Qatari planes, and the same applied to territorial waters.

Qatar was expelled from the Gulf Cooperation Council (GCC) and only Oman and Kuwait maintained relations with the country. Qatari families were separated, and there were negative impacts on jobs, education and other social sectors. Nationalism grew, and Qataris were banned from performing the Islamic pilgrimage (hajj) to Mecca. Foreigners, both tourists and foreign nationals living in Qatar, were also affected by the embargoes.

The sanctions imposed on Qatar had the opposite effect to what was expected. At first, the Qatari economy suffered a hard blow, as well as the Qatari food supply (the country depends highly on imports), but they eventually pushed the country to turn toward other allies to survive, strengthening relations with Iran and Türkiye.

The Saudi crown prince welcomes the Qatari Emir before signing a deal to end the blockade on Qatar.

Qatar's image was not damaged by the crisis. In fact, the only countries affected were the Arab Quartet. There was evidence of the United Arab Emirates having even stronger economic ties (much stronger than Qatar) with Iran, and of Saudi Arabia supporting and financing so-called terrorist organizations. Qatar was able to keep its image as a neutral player. It sought to play the role of mediator in other conflicts, supported the West and Saudi Arabia in wars in Syria and Yemen, expanded its soft power globally through Al-Jazeera and kept going with its plans of hosting the 2022 FIFA World Cup.

Without a single bullet being fired in almost four years, and after several negotiation efforts brokered by Kuwait, on January 5, 2021, Saudi Arabia's Crown Prince Mohammed bin Salman and Qatar's Emir Sheikh Tamim bin Hamad al-Thani met, and with the rest of the GCC members restored full relations under the Al-Ula Declaration.

Thematic studies

The reasons why relations were restored so easily without Qatar agreeing to any of the 13 demands, and without the need for armed conflict or the threat of violence to happen, are still unknown. There are several factors to consider that could have contributed to this outcome: the US change in administration from Donald Trump to Joe Biden, the economic impact on all countries involved, the strengthened relations between Qatar and Iran, the social and diplomatic damages caused to the accusers, and even the 2022 FIFA World Cup. The Qatar crisis is an example of a non-violent conflict and the possibility of non-violent solutions.

While violence and the threat of violence are coercive measures, the behavior of other actors can be influenced through non-violent means such as sanctions (as seen in the case study on Qatar). Sanctions involve economic restrictions, diplomatic break-ups, boycotts, trade sanctions, travel sanctions and punishments against specific political and influential figures. Sanctions tend to exert the most painful effects on the general population. They affect mainly the marginalized and poorest inhabitants, having little to no real impact on the wealthy and powerful elites and rulers.

> Intensification refers to a conflict becoming more visible. Escalation refers to a conflict becoming more violent.

Exercises

5. Out of the three types of violence presented by Galtung, identify which you consider to be easiest to address. Which do you consider to be the hardest?

6. Explain under what circumstances violence is unavoidable and perhaps even desirable.

7. Identify a case in which non-violent protests led to a significant political change. Discuss the (possible) reasons for their success. Identify a case in which non-violent protests did not lead to a political change. Compare the cases and examine the factors that could have led to different results.

Interactions of political stakeholders and actors

The study of conflicts has evolved throughout the years, with different theoretical approaches resulting from the changing dynamics of global politics. The role of actors within conflicts has changed with the appearance of NSAs. These have important influence in the creation of conflicts, how these conflicts transform and how they are resolved.

Nowadays, states are not the only actors involved in armed and non-armed conflicts, nor are they the sole actors that perform violent acts in order to achieve political goals. The role of intergovernmental organizations (IGOs) has been recognized for a long time. Non-governmental organizations (NGOs), the media, individuals and society, multinational corporations (MNCs), other armed groups (such as guerrilla groups) and illegal organizations are all becoming more important to the study of conflicts.

> **HL** Conflicts nowadays involve many more actors. Because of globalization and a growing global interdependence, conflicts and war have implications that cross *Borders*. Even intrastate conflicts can have international repercussions in economic, political and social areas. They can cause displacement and migration, have repercussions for global trade and affect global security.

Peace and conflict

Table 4.3 Types of conflict, meaning and examples

Type of Conflict	Meaning	Example
Interstate conflict	Conflict occurring between two or more states	The armed conflict between Armenia and Azerbaijan
Intrastate conflict	Conflict that takes place between opposing actors within a single state	The fight between Sudan's army and the paramilitary group RSF
Extra-systemic or extra-state conflict	Conflict between a state and a non-state group outside its own territory	Western NATO states fighting against the Taliban in Afghanistan

Armed conflicts are not carried out exclusively by states and their armies. They can also occur between a state and its society (such as the armed conflict in Ethiopia since 2016 between the Oromo and Somali ethnic groups), or between the state and illegal organizations (such as the fight between the Mexican and US governments and the Mexican drug cartels). The existence of these NSAs has increased the complexity of conflicts. As a result, different types of armed conflict exist. These can depend on:

- the nature of the groups involved
- the cause or nature of the conflict
- the scope of violence and the intention with which it is used.

Categorizing conflicts is not simple, because conflicts tend to involve several causes. Even if a factor is not a root cause of a conflict, it can become important over time. Until a few years ago, digital or cyber conflict would not have been considered a possibility, let alone a category in itself.

Globalization, and advances in technology and communications, have allowed for a number of non-state and smaller actors to acquire the tools and the knowledge to carry out armed actions against their enemies. British academic Mary Kaldor (b.1946) spoke about 'new wars' to characterize warfare in a post-Cold War era.[10] According to her, this new form of warfare included:

- violence occurring between state and NSAs in different combinations
- an increasing fight for identity politics, which are political agendas based upon identities created from race, nationality, religion, gender, social class, etc.
- political objectives over physical ones, and an increasing use of terror and fear to achieve these
- conflicts financed increasingly through illegal means and not the state itself.

The new wars thesis is part of a wider debate among academics on how to properly define and categorize the changing dynamics of warfare. These new wars are not necessarily new, and examples can be found throughout history. Analyzing conflicts outside of the traditional scope, recognizing that traditional battlefield tactics have changed, allows the creation of new policies and strategies to address them.

When analyzing conflicts, it is essential to consider the number and type of actors that are involved. There is always direct and indirect influence from foreign states, individuals, illegal organizations, MNCs and the media. Try mapping all actors involved in a conflict of your choice – you will be surprised by how complex it is.

Conflicts always involve *Identity* issues, whether this appears in the form of nationalism, racial issues, religion, ethnicity, gender or something different. Identity can strengthen labels that create a distinction between *us* and *them*, can serve as a factor for cohesion, and can also be a cause for conflicts when identities are a reason for discrimination, oppression or marginalization.

Thematic studies

> **Activity**
>
> Using the case study on the Qatar crisis, identify, with your classmates, the actors that played a primary role, those who had a secondary role and NSAs that influenced, or may have influenced, the outcome of the diplomatic dispute.

In order to better understand armed conflicts and war, we need to start seeing them in the context of globalization. War can no longer be understood as the actual, intentional and widespread use of violence – this is too simplistic to convey the complexity of these phenomenon. Instead, war, like peace, can be seen on a spectrum, where armed conflict and world peace are located at opposing ends.[11] This idea helps us understand that from peace to war there is a range of possible conflicts and hostilities that can occur. These in-between possibilities depend on an array of factors, from the desire to engage in violence, to strength, capabilities, diplomacy and other non-violent means of addressing hostilities (including where external actors can play a role).

It is important to introduce other common concepts in the study of armed conflicts: genocide and terrorism.

Genocide

> Kaldor's 'new wars,' though much more present after the Cold War era, have been present throughout history. Colombia began its fight against the FARC in the late 1940s, the ethno-nationalist conflict in Northern Ireland began in the 1960s, the Basque Euskadi Ta Askatasuna (ETA) Basque separatist organization in Spain appeared in 1950 and committed its first act of terrorism in 1968, and the Munich massacre (a terrorist attack carried out during the Summer Olympics in Munich, West Germany) took place in 1972.

> When studying conflicts and war, the role of globalization has to be considered at all times. We must consider the increasing interconnectedness of societies, the increasing interdependence of societies, the immediacy of communications between societies and the global interests of actors.

The concept of **genocide** was coined by Polish lawyer Raphael Lemkin in 1944 and was defined by the United Nations Genocide Convention of 1948 as 'acts committed with intent to destroy, in whole or in part, a national, ethnical, racial, or religious group.' Genocide can occur through:

- the killing of a group's members
- causing serious bodily or mental harm
- deliberately inflicting conditions that seek to bring about a group's physical destruction
- imposing measures to prevent births
- forcibly transferring children.

Genocide is not a random act. Victims are directly targeted due to their belonging, or perceived belonging, to a specific group.

Peace and conflict

After the two World Wars, it became a priority to prosecute individuals responsible for crimes referred to as 'crimes against humanity.' The Nuremberg Trials were a crucial moment for legal history, but also set the example for what would later become the ICC. On July 1, 2002, the Rome Statue established the ICC, and four core international crimes: genocide, crimes against humanity, war crimes and the crime of aggression. The ICC can only investigate and prosecute these crimes where states are unable or unwilling to do so themselves. The court has jurisdiction over crimes only if they are committed in the territory of a state party or if they are committed by a national of a state party. If Saddam Hussein had been accused of crimes against humanity or genocide for the mass killings of Yazidis in Iraq, the ICC would not have had jurisdiction over this, since Iraq is not a state party of the Rome Statute.

Radovan Karadžić, former President of Republika Srpska[12], convicted of genocide at The Hague, ICTFY, March 2016.

Burundi left the ICC in 2017 after the court decided to investigate the government's crackdown on opposition forces within the country. The Philippines also left in 2019 after the court launched an investigation of President Rodrigo Duterte's war on drugs.

After the Holocaust that took place during the Second World War, Lemkin successfully led the international community to recognize the role of international law in preventing and sanctioning genocides. Under international law, genocide is recognized based on acts being committed with full intent and knowledge, instead of recklessness or negligence.

What differentiates genocide from other crimes is intent. According to the definition above, we can identify recent examples of genocide such as the Armenian genocide, the Holocaust, the Rwandan genocide, the Guatemalan genocide and the genocide in Cambodia. Even as a legally defined concept, the label 'genocide' has been highly contested. Some crimes that have been given labels such as mass murder, crimes against humanity or war crimes, such as in Bosnia during the 1990s, the Rohingya conflict or the Yazidi conflict, could be categorized as genocides. This is despite the fact that all these fall under the jurisdiction of the International Criminal Court (ICC), established under the treaty of the Rome Statute in 1998.

The difficulty of defining genocide, added to the fact that belonging to political and social groups are excluded from the definition of genocide, has led the definition of genocide to be criticized by many who argue that the definition is too restricted. This is why it is common to find disagreement on whether the Armenian genocide was a genocide (Türkiye claims it was not), or if the genocide in Bosnia was a mass killing (which Serbia claims it was, and not a genocide).

In theory, all signatories to the Convention on the Prevention and Punishment of the Crime of Genocide (CPPCG) are required to prevent and punish this crime. In practice, things are more complicated. Often, states are incapable of prosecuting these crimes. This is why the UN created *ad hoc* tribunals. Examples of these were the International Criminal Tribunal for the Former Yugoslavia (ICTFY) in 1993, the International Criminal Tribunal for Rwanda (ICTR) in 1994 (these two contributed to the creation of the ICC) and the Extraordinary Chambers in the Courts of Cambodia (ECCC) in 2007. Sometimes states are unwilling to prosecute the perpetrators in international tribunals because they consider this goes against the perpetrator's sovereignty.

There are 123 signatory countries to the Rome Statute, 40 countries never signed it (including North Korea, Türkiye, Saudi Arabia and India), while several others signed but never ratified it (including the USA, Russia, Iran and Israel).

Terrorism

The use of **terrorism** as a means of coercion is not new or recent. Terrorism has been used for centuries. Since the beginning of the 21st century, the word has become more frequently used. This is perhaps due to the increasing role of the media, increasing illegal access to weapons, and the frequency with which terrorism is used. Defining terrorism is not simple. There is no international legal definition of what terrorism is. Despite considerable discussion worldwide, there has been a lack of consensus on a definition. Distinguishing terrorism from other forms of violence is complicated, and the lines between such forms of violence and what constitutes terrorism are often blurred. Certain characteristics are recognized by a majority in labeling an act as terrorism.

Thematic studies

Armed conflicts tend to be categorized based on the actors involved, the methods used and the purposes sought. Different definitions of terrorism can also focus on these factors, but they emphasize different characteristics, depending on the authority that is using the label.

The Global Terrorism Database defines terrorism as acts of violence conducted by NSAs. But what about state terrorism, such as that conducted in Syria under president Bashar al-Assad's regime or in North Korea with decades of the Kim family? The US Federal Bureau of Investigation (FBI) defines terrorism as violent acts or crimes committed by individuals or groups inspired by or associated with designated terrorist organizations. But what about those who act individually? In its definition, the FBI defines national terrorism as the acts committed by individuals or groups that seek to further ideological goals. In that case, how do we distinguish between terrorism and hate crimes?

Terrorism is an act or series of acts that spread terror and fear. When compared to other violent acts, the distinguishing feature is to spread terror among the civilian population. So, what differentiates terrorism from armed conflict, in which civilians are also targeted and terrorized? Terrorism seeks a political goal by deliberately targeting civilians through an unlawful use of violence or the threat of violence. Terrorism is a means of exerting pressure on the civilian population. The fear faced by the people being targeted by terrorism pushes the population to demand their government does or stops doing something to reduce their vulnerability as targets.

Terrorism needs violence, or the threat to use violence. This means that activism, political dissent or non-violent resistance are not terrorism. Human rights groups have reported numerous cases around the world of censorship, detention and arrest of individuals under the pretext of counterterrorism measures. For example:

- the Sri Lankan government's Prevention on Terrorism Act (PTA), which allows detention of political dissenters without charge (February 2022)
- arrests in Russia since the military intervention in Ukraine began (March 2022)
- arrests and charges of domestic terrorism in the USA, particularly in Georgia, of protesters seeking to stop 'Cop City' from being built (June 2023).

An act of terrorism must:

- be carried out for a political purpose (for example, the Islamic State of Iraq and the Levant (ISIL or ISIS) has openly stated its political goal of establishing a caliphate)
- seek a long-lasting psychological effect beyond immediate harm and damage
- not aim exclusively at killing or maiming, but at creating and spreading long-lasting terror.

Terrorism is the spread of fear and terror through the use or the threat of use of violence, especially against civilians or non-combatants, to achieve political goals.

Yelena Osipova, the 77-year-old protest artist and activist, opens her exhibition of pacifist paintings in Saint Petersburg on January 31, 2023.

Protesters marching in Minneapolis near Hennepin Lake remembering Manuel Teran (Tort), who was shot and killed by officers at a prolonged protest in an Atlanta forest after they say he fired upon them.

With technological advancements and the increasing reliance on computers and communication networks, a new form of terrorism has appeared: cyberterrorism. This is a form of cyberattack that uses computers or communication networks to cause disruption or destruction of data, information and systems, to generate fear or intimidate a society or state.

It is said that there is no international agreement on what a terrorist is because it is an emotionally and politically charged concept. It is politically charged because it is used to delegitimize actors, and emotionally charged because someone's terrorist can be seen as someone else's freedom fighter. What do you think about this?

Peace and conflict

This explains why violence is used without discrimination against civilians and non-combatants, disregarding the rules of warfare, and tends to be executed brutally and dramatically.

Every year, the Institute for Economics and Peace produces the Global Terrorism Index (GTI) report. This contains data on terrorist incidents, civilian damage, regional and state contexts, and armed groups, among other information (although it does not cover state repression and violence). The GTI 2023 results reported the Sahel region (a 5000 km belt of land south of the Sahara Desert including Cameroon, Chad, Niger, Nigeria, Burkina Faso, The Gambia, Guinea, Mali, Mauritania and Senegal) becoming the epicenter of terrorism, with more deaths in 2022 than the Middle East and North Africa (MENA) and South Asia regions combined. Of particular concern were Burkina Faso and Mali. The results were influenced by increased political instability, social, economic and security challenges, geopolitical tensions and counterterrorism measures against Salafi-jihadi groups (these groups are based on the political-religious ideology that seeks to establish a global caliphate and advocates for physical attacks against non-Muslims and apostate Muslim targets) that have exploited political vacuums and years-old grievances.

Table 4.4 Deadliest terror groups of 2022[13]

Rank	Organization	Attacks	Deaths
1	Islamic State (IS)	410	1045
2	Al-Shabaab	315	784
3	Islamic State – Khorasan Province (ISKP)	141	498
4	Jamaat Nusrat Al-Islam wal Muslimeen (JNIM)	77	279
5	Balochistan Liberation Army (BLA)	30	233
6	Islamic State West Africa (ISWA)	65	219
7	Boko Haram	64	204
8	Tehrik-e-Taliban Pakistan (TTP)	90	137
9	Islamic State – Sinai Province	27	71
10	Indigenous People of Biafra (IPOB)	40	57

Causes of conflict

Conflicts are the result of incompatibilities of ideas, goals, thoughts and interests. In trying to understand a conflict, we have to understand the reasons and causes behind it. The deeper we manage to go into the causes, the better the resolution process will be. Conflicts have many layers. At first glance we only see the outside, which is the position of the parties in the conflict. We see what the actors say the conflict is about, or what the media tells us the conflict is about. If we peel off the different layers, we will find old unaddressed issues that have ended up hidden from general view.

Understanding the causes does not mean immediate success for the conflict's resolution. **Intractable** conflicts (those that persist over time and resist resolution) such as Israel-Palestine, Azerbaijan and Armenia over Nagorno Karabakh, or the dispute over the Western Sahara between Morocco and the Polisario Front, are well understood. Despite numerous efforts, the resolution process has presented numerous failures. It is also important to consider that conflicting parties may have different interpretations or understanding of the causes of the conflict.

Advancements in *Technology* have allowed terrorist and criminal organizations to extend their activities across *Borders* and other spheres such as the Internet. *Technology* has also brought advancements in weapons, military technology and intelligence.

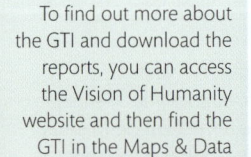

To find out more about the GTI and download the reports, you can access the Vision of Humanity website and then find the GTI in the Maps & Data section:

Thematic studies

One way in which the causes of conflict can be understood is by identifying the positions, interests and needs of the actors involved. *Positions* are what actors say they want. These are often public and explicit and can be expressed in speeches, declarations, official notes, press conferences, etc. The *interests* are what actors really want. Often these are expressed publicly and explicitly, but sometimes these are not immediately clear. For example, two countries may be fighting over the control of territory by claiming historical rights to it; however, control of specific and strategic natural resources in the territory may be what they are actually interested in. Lastly, *needs* represent the most basic necessities of the actors involved. These are often hidden from the general view because they may involve feelings and emotions or intangible things. For example, in a fight over territory, even though the control of natural resources for economic purposes seems to be what is in dispute, it is in fact the need for self-determination, independence, recognition, identity or security that is at stake.

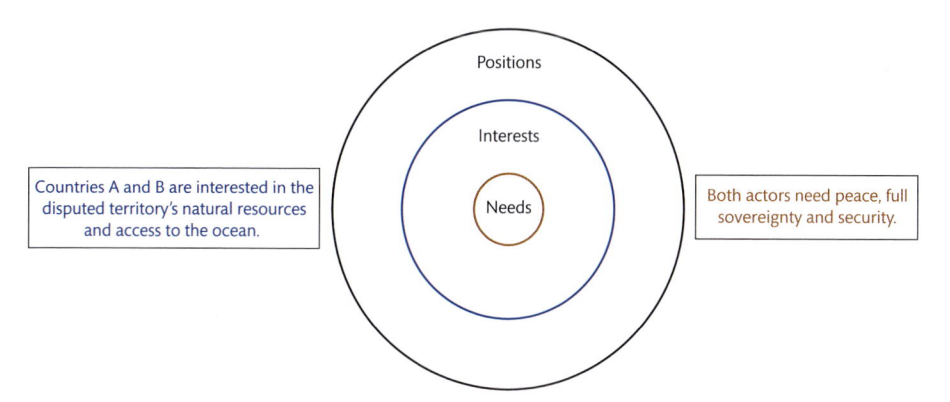

Positions / Interests / Needs

Countries A and B are interested in the disputed territory's natural resources and access to the ocean.

Both actors need peace, full sovereignty and security.

Figure 4.2 Example of Positions, Interests, Needs in a diagram.
Positions = what we say we want
Interests = what we really want
Needs = what we must have

A conflict may have begun years ago as a result of one particular issue (for example, colonization). Over time, other factors build up in relation to that initial issue (such as poverty, inequality, scarce natural resources, oppression by a majority, ethnic divisions, violation of human rights, etc.). This creates an armed conflict that may seem to be about, for example, political discontent. In reality, the conflict is more complex. If policymakers only address the political discontent, the conflict will not only not be resolved, but will escalate over and over again. The outbreak of violence in Sudan that started in 2023 between the Rapid Support Forces (RSF) and the Sudanese Armed Forces (SAF) seemed to be the result of a political dispute and a disagreement over the integration of the RSF into the military as part of a transition toward civilian rule. However, the conflict in Sudan is much older. For decades, the country has suffered from foreign interventions (and colonization), ethnic and religious tensions, and disputes over resources. Since 1956, Sudan has experienced over 15 military coups and two civil wars, demonstrating that internal political, economic and social instability is not the result of the clash between the RSF and the SAF.

Identifying positions, interests and needs can help and, in some cases, solve conflicts, even intractable ones. This can be done by using the Mediator's Iceberg Diagram. This diagram helps identify the three variables for different actors, while also visualizing those interests and, ideally, the needs that are shared by conflicting parties. Finding this overlap can help alleviate animosity and work towards a resolution based on common/shared points.

It is almost impossible to pinpoint the root cause of a conflict (different sides to a conflict will rarely agree upon the cause), but it is possible to highlight the most prominent causes that led to the conflict. In almost every case, despite there being a core issue, several causes are involved in the creation of a conflict.

You can see the Mediator's Iceberg Diagram here, or do a general search online:

TOK
Conflict is made by humans. Violence is inflicted by humans against other humans. The personal traits (personality, emotions, character, personal history, etc.) of an individual can influence the course of a conflict and its resolution. To what extent do you think personal traits of global leaders can influence other global issues?

199

Peace and conflict

As a result, we can categorize conflicts. One category is based on the *dimensions* of the conflict:

Table 4.5 Possible dimensions for conflict

Dimension	Variables
Conflicts with *cultural* dimensions	Religion, language, identity, ethnicity, etc.
Conflicts with *socio-economic* and *geographical* dimensions	Territory, population, organized crime, human security, informal economy, socio-economic inequality, etc.
Conflicts with *political* dimensions	Type of government, military capabilities, citizenship, national security, etc.
Conflicts with *external* dimensions	International relations, borders, diasporas (people settled far from their homeland), regional factors, migrations, etc.

Another categorization can be based on five different *types* of conflict:

- Conflict of interests: this appears as a belief that, in order to satisfy one's own needs, it must be at the expense of others' needs
- Conflict of relations: this stems from stereotypes, lack of communication, negative emotions and misconceptions
- Structural conflict: this is the result of oppressing structures
- Conflict of information: this results from lack of information or incomplete information, that leads to misinterpretations
- Conflict of values: this stems from different beliefs in a context where one belief imposes itself upon the others.

A final categorization can be made based on the *contradictions* behind the conflict. Here are just a few:

- nationalistic
- ethnic
- religious
- ideological
- territorial or geographical
- environmental
- diplomatic
- racial
- gender-based.

Regardless of the categorization used, conflicts can be symmetric or asymmetric.

Table 4.6 Symmetric and asymmetric conflicts

Symmetric Conflicts	Asymmetric Conflicts
The parties involved have a similar or relatively similar situation at the start of a conflict	There is a clear superiority of one involved party over another (economical, political, military, strategic or structural)
For example, a conflict between two nuclear powers	For example, a conflict between a state's military and a secessionist group

Thematic studies

Conflict dynamics

Some conflict cannot be avoided. This does not mean conflicts should be left unaddressed; that would be a huge mistake. Instead, we must learn how to manage and resolve conflicts. The first step is to understand the stages conflicts can go through. Conflicts rarely move through a linear progression toward winning or losing. All conflicts are dynamic and changing. There are a number of stages in the evolution and transformation of a conflict.

Table 4.7 Stages of a conflict

Stage	Characteristics
Pre-conflict	There is an underlying incompatibility of goals between two or more parties. Localized tension can be found, but the conflict is hidden from general view (latent conflict).
Confrontation	Conflict is more open, with confrontational behavior, occasional fighting and other low levels of violence. Polarization appears as relations become strained. The conflict is open (overt conflict) and confrontation begins.
Crisis	The peak of a conflict, when tension/violence becomes more intense. There is a cessation of normal communication.
Outcome	Several possibilities: victory of one side, ceasefire, surrender of one party, negotiations, imposition of an end to fighting by a third party.
Post-conflict	The conflict is resolved in a way that leads to an ending of violent confrontation, to a decrease in tension and to more normal relations. The process of post-conflict peacebuilding begins.

Table 4.7 shows five different stages a conflict can go through, but this process is rarely linear. Conflicts typically escalate and de-escalate more than once. In some cases, conflicts can remain in the confrontation stage for long periods of time, without ever reaching a crisis. Others can go from a crisis to a confrontation to another crisis, without ever reaching an outcome. In some cases, despite reaching an outcome, a conflict can go back to a confrontation. Moving from one stage to the other has its challenges, particularly from a crisis to an outcome. The most difficult is to move from an outcome to a post-conflict stage. Often conflicts are deemed solved once an outcome has been achieved, but this does not mean the end. Post-conflict peacebuilding is an essential step for a conflict to truly end.

Activity

Work in a small group. Research the conflict between North Korea and South Korea. Trace the stages the conflict has gone through in the past 20 years. Where is the conflict situated now? Has there been one or more crises? If so, how many? What have been the outcomes? Has the conflict reached a post-conflict stage?

Approaches to conflict analysis

Conflict and peace theorists have developed models to understand conflicts better and to design approaches to resolving them. These models help us to visualize ideas

Peace and conflict

and simplify conflicts to better understand them. One example is Galtung's Conflict Triangle (or ABC Triangle)[14], which represents conflict as having three main aspects: (A) the attitudes, (B) the behavior and (C) the contradiction. The triangle provides a tool for understanding what the underlying contradiction (the conflict) is, the attitudes adopted by involved parties, and the behavior and actions taken by the parties, in violent and non-violent conflicts.

Figure 4.3 Galtung's Conflict Triangle shows the relationship between attitudes, contradictions and behavior in conflict situations.

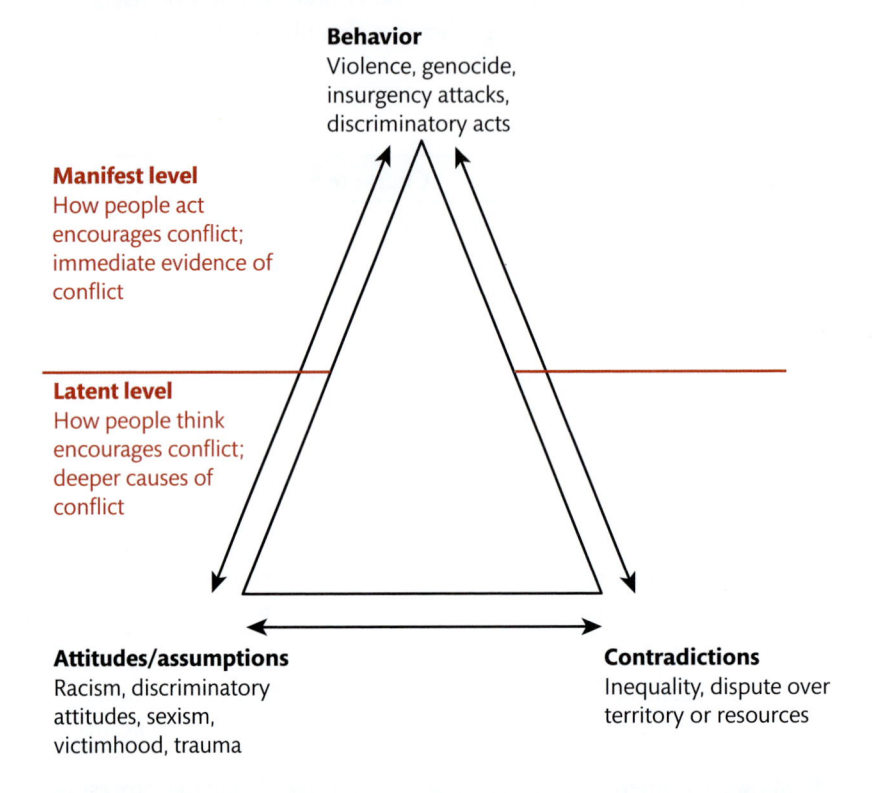

Behavior
Violence, genocide, insurgency attacks, discriminatory acts

Manifest level
How people act encourages conflict; immediate evidence of conflict

Latent level
How people think encourages conflict; deeper causes of conflict

Attitudes/assumptions
Racism, discriminatory attitudes, sexism, victimhood, trauma

Contradictions
Inequality, dispute over territory or resources

Similar to Galtung's triangle of violence (see page 188), the ABC Triangle represents three interrelated factors, any of which has aspects that may be the starting point for a conflict to develop. A violent act can lead to an attitude (such as deepening feelings of grievance or injustice), which creates a contradiction. An attitude can lead to behaviors that transform the contradiction. Or an already existing contradiction can lead to hostile attitudes that result in a specific behavior. According to Galtung, the three factors often reinforce each other. In order to stop a conflict, all three factors must be addressed.

Another model is John Burton's Human Needs Theory[15], an approach to conflict focused on psychological and physiological aspects. According to Burton, human needs are universal and, if these are not met satisfactorily, conflict will occur. It is important to distinguish between:

- needs: basic and universal – non-negotiable
- values: customs and beliefs – non-negotiable
- interests or wants: material goods – negotiable.

This theory states that, in terms of conflict resolution, if a conflict is about needs, it is likely the conflict will be intractable (it will persist over time, resisting resolution) and negotiation will not be possible.

> **TOK**
> Reflect on the merits and limitations of using models in human sciences. To what extent can models simplify reality for us and help us to understand it better, plan policies and make predictions. When it comes to conflict, are the merits and limitations of using models the same?

Thematic studies

There are other models that can help us understand and analyze conflicts. Some of these include: the Onion, the Conflict Tree, the Pyramid and the Force Field Analysis tool. Different models suit different needs, and different models may be needed at different stages of a particular conflict.

Identifying the stages of a conflict allows policymakers to identify the best responses to address the conflict at that particular stage. The hourglass model[16] provides a visual representation of the different possible stages of an ongoing conflict and the different possible conflict resolution approaches for each of them.

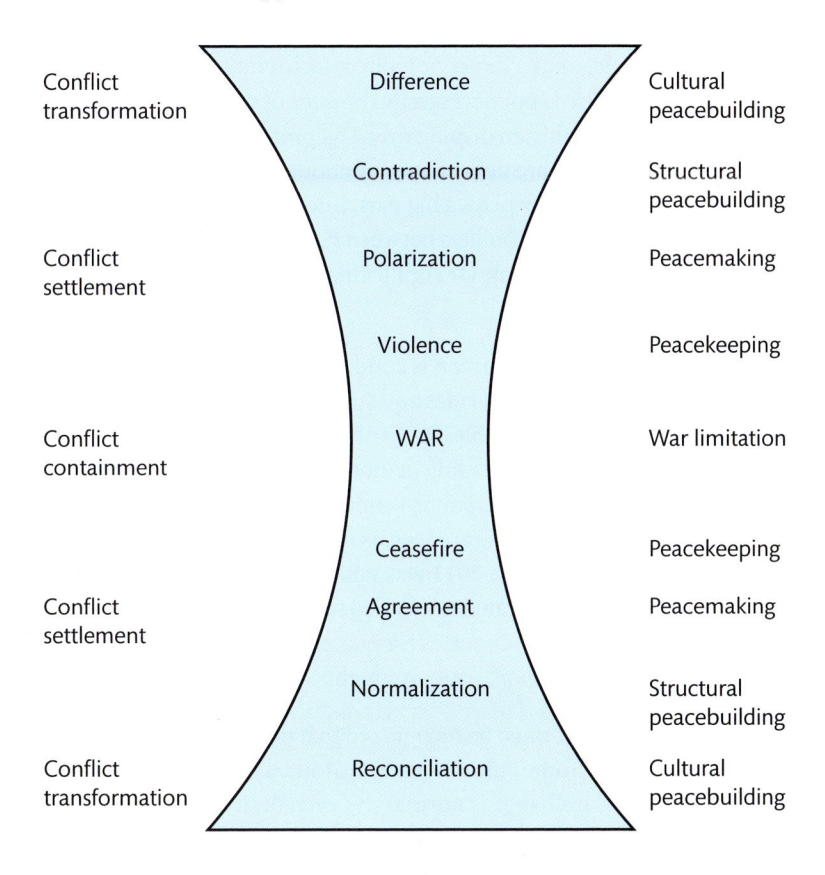

Conflict transformation	Difference	Cultural peacebuilding
	Contradiction	Structural peacebuilding
Conflict settlement	Polarization	Peacemaking
	Violence	Peacekeeping
Conflict containment	WAR	War limitation
	Ceasefire	Peacekeeping
Conflict settlement	Agreement	Peacemaking
	Normalization	Structural peacebuilding
Conflict transformation	Reconciliation	Cultural peacebuilding

Figure 4.4 The hourglass model shows the possible stages of an ongoing conflict and possible approaches to resolution.

Exercises

8. After the Cold War, there was an increase in intrastate conflicts and a decrease in interstate conflicts. Evaluate if this tendency is still happening.

9. In trying to understand armed conflict, identify a level of analysis (political, environmental, economic, ideological, cultural, etc.) that you think is the most helpful in understanding contemporary conflicts. Why?

10. Explain how you think terrorism can be prevented.

11. Analyze the reasons for politicians and global leaders labeling or not labeling a conflict as genocide, and an individual or group as a terrorist organization. Why do you think genocides are sometimes referred to as war crimes, and acts of terrorism as hate crimes?

Peace and conflict

Justifying violence

Pacifism sees war and violence as unjustified under any circumstance or context. For others, violence and war can be morally and legally justified. These justifications can be found in different arenas, such as culture, religion and the law.

Culture and conflict

Culture is embedded in every conflict because culture is part of human life. Culture is our identity. It defines our behaviors, attitudes and perceptions. We see the world and we see conflict from our own cultural perspective. Culture is always present in conflict, whether in the central role, or as a direct or indirect factor influencing how the conflict evolves and is solved (culture is not necessarily the *cause* of conflict though). Intractable conflicts, such as the India-Pakistan dispute over Kashmir, or the dispute between Morocco and Western Sahara, are not exclusively about territory, political control and sovereignty. Cultural identity plays a big part. Interpersonal conflicts are also affected by culture. Think about conflicts between parents and their children, in which generational culture comes into play. Or conflict inside a relationship, influenced by gender culture.

> Culture refers to the social behavior, institutions, norms, knowledge, beliefs, arts, laws and customs found in all human societies.

For most societies, killing another human is condemned, unless it is done during war. Warfare is managed through cultural rules and structures that define which behaviors are allowed and which are unacceptable. States always refer to their own wars as moral, having a higher ethical purpose (spreading democracy, liberating the oppressed, protecting human rights, etc.). Military interventions are sometimes referred to as humanitarian interventions, for these are seen as morally necessary to stop violence. The military intervention in Libya in 2011 was said to be carried out to protect civilians, though actions demonstrated it was also seeking regime change by removing Muammar Gaddafi from power. Advocates for peace and for war have resorted to cultural values and ethics to support their arguments.

From a cultural perspective, it must be recognized that not all cultures agree on what constitutes a conflict. Some cultures are accustomed to calm discussions. For others, a highly emotional exchange is normal and even desirable. So, in some cases, a cultural justification for more physical and emotional reactions to conflict might be used. In other cases, this might be regarded as an overreaction or rude behavior. Some approaches to conflict resolution minimize or ignore cultural factors and their influence. They consider that culture, when belonging to a large majority, makes things seem normal and natural. However, acknowledging culture can often lead to a breakthrough in finding possible solutions to conflicts.

Activity

Discuss with your classmates how disagreements are dealt with amongst your own family and friends. After listening to other experiences, compare how these are similar or different. Can you find cultural traits in how your family deals with confrontation?

Religion and conflict

The decision of any state or armed group over whether to wage war can be influenced or determined by ethical principles and religious beliefs. Judaism, Christianity, Islam,

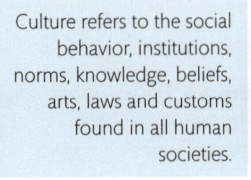

Thematic studies

Hinduism and Buddhism share the idea of aiming to bring peace among people. Yet all of these religions have used their sacred writings and beliefs to legitimize war against what they regard as evil.

Religious scriptures (the documents that the majority of followers recognize as the foundation of their faiths) include stories of fights, swords, soldiers and wars. All major religions acknowledge the legality of war and have been involved in conflicts. The three Abrahamic religions (Judaism, Christianity and Islam) possess aggressive elements and components in their history. The Old Testament refers to the 'commanded' wars urged by God. The Crusades were carried out as 'holy wars' and the concept of 'jihad' can refer to a military struggle.

Throughout history, religion has been used to oppose violence, and also to justify it, by religious and secular actors. Even though the idea of a **just war** appeared in medieval Christianity, justified war theories are not solely Christian, Western or European. They are global.[17] Hinduism has a military tradition, with some texts referring to the duty of devout Hindus to fight for causes they may disagree with. Buddhism, although permeated with the idea of peace, often refers to this as an internal peace. Although it discourages violence for resolving conflicts, there are extremists in Buddhism, for example, the Ma Ba Tha organization that encourages hatred and violence against Muslims in Myanmar. A scripture comparison shows that, while all religions advocate for peace, violence is accepted by all of them under certain circumstances and for certain causes (although these causes are not the same across religions). When religion is important within a state, violence can be morally justified and also legitimate.

As with culture, religion can also facilitate peace. Religion is not in itself a reason for conflict. The historical influence of religion on war does not mean that modern day attitudes toward religion are violent, nor that violence is always supported by religion. Many other factors are involved when deciding to wage war or use violence. However, being aware of the religious influence and implications in a conflict can contribute to the conflict resolution and the peace process by providing a better understanding of personal and communal justifications.

> **TOK**
> Culture and language are inextricably linked. Culture shapes our beliefs and ethics, and these are expressed through language. To what extent can a change in culture change language? Can you think of an example?

Peace and conflict

> Can you think of an example in which war was justified because it led to an improvement in the situation? Can you think of an armed conflict that was necessary? Reflect on the arguments on which the war was justified and the narrative used.

Just war theory

Justifying war and violence is not exclusive to religion and culture. Nowadays, we find legal justifications that allow for armed conflict to take place. The just war theory deals with justifying why and how wars are fought. Presuming that there are legitimate uses of war, the theory sets moral boundaries on how to fight wars to preserve a level of humanity even in our worst moments. It aims at answering the question of when it is morally and legally justified to wage a war. Historically, rules and traditions or mutually agreed rules of combat have applied through the ages across different wars. While war is abhorrent, there are times when it seems to be necessary. The just war theory suggests that it is in the interests of all the actors involved to conduct war because it minimizes the harm done to civilians and non-combatants.

The idea of a just war originated in medieval times, particularly from Christian philosopher Thomas Aquinas, although it was developed further by legal scholars. The just war theory addresses the morality of war in terms of:

- when it is right to resort to violence (*jus ad bellum*)
- what is acceptable when using violence (*jus in bello*).

Jus ad bellum is supported by the UN Charter principle of self-defense (Article 51), while *jus in bello* can be sustained by International Humanitarian Law and the Geneva Conventions.

Jus ad bellum requires that there is the following:

- **Just cause:** For it to be just, the objective of the war should be oriented toward establishing or re-establishing peace. War should not be used as a way of punishing someone.
- **Right authority making the decision:** Those starting the violence should have the legitimate authority to do so. Civilians, a guerrilla group or a criminal organization are not considered competent authorities.
- **Right intention:** Force can be used if the cause is just and solely for that cause. Material gains are not considered acceptable.
- **War as a last resort:** Once other peaceful alternatives have been used and exhausted, then war can be considered an option.
- **Probability of success:** War should not be used where its use is futile.
- **Proportionality:** It should be considered that the overall harm caused by the war does not outweigh the good.

Once the violence has begun, *jus in bello* then provides the guidelines of behavior for combatants:

- **Military necessity:** War should be conducted as a means to help defeat an enemy, once other peaceful options have failed, while limiting unnecessary and excessive damage and death.
- **Distinction:** War should be directed toward armed combatants, never against civilians or non-combatants. Targeting civilian residential areas, infrastructure such as schools and medical facilities, religious places and neutral targets is prohibited. Combatants who have surrendered should not be targeted.
- **Proportionality:** Combatants must take into consideration the level of harm that will be inflicted on civilians and civilian property, ensuring that this is not excessive

> Child soldiers are any child (boy or girl) under age 18, associated with an armed force or armed group, recruited or used in any capacity. It does not refer only to a child who is taking a direct part in hostilities.

Thematic studies

in relation to the advantage that will be obtained from attacking a legitimate objective.
- Treatment of Prisoners of War (POWs): Combatants held captive during or after an armed conflict, or POWs (protected under the 1949 Third Geneva Convention) must at all times be treated humanely, protected from violence and intimidation, receive adequate medical attention and be able to maintain relations with the outside world, especially friends and family.
- *Malum in se* (wrong or evil in itself): Combatants must refrain from actions or methods considered evil such as rape, the use of child soldiers or the use of weapons of mass destruction.

Exercises

12. Explain how you would define a just war. Are some wars more just than others? Why?
13. Describe how culture can facilitate peace when there are so many cultural differences even within countries.
14. Most countries do not treat terrorists as POWs, but refer to them as 'enemy combatants.' Evaluate this term.

To find out more about the use of children as a weapon of war, you can read the International Committee of the Red Cross's report on Child Soldiers. Navigate to the ICRC website or use the QR code below then search for 'Children Associated with Armed Forces or Armed Groups' and download the free PDF.

The path toward resolution

Conflicts stop, but they rarely end. Historically, we have seen armed conflicts coming to an end, with the Second World War being one of the best examples. Violence between European countries ceased and there has been lasting peace among them, although the Cold War and the conflict between Ukraine and Russia may pose exceptions to the success of the Paris Peace Treaties. Yet, there are numerous examples that demonstrate that conflicts rarely end. This is not to say that efforts for conflict resolution are useless, or that we are doomed to live in a world where armed conflicts are the norm. We must always work to reduce armed conflict, because of its political, economic and environmental consequences, and because of its human impact.

As seen with the hourglass model on page 203, different stages of a conflict require different pathways to resolution. Conflicts, regardless of their similarities, are always unique. When it comes to solving conflicts, there is no single solution. However, there are several processes that, together with their own unique features for each conflict, have proven to be useful.

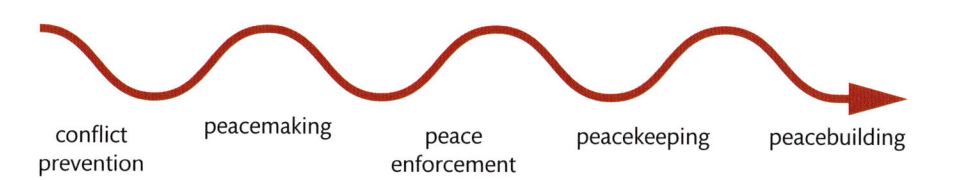

HL Armed conflict and wars are closely related to the *Environment*. Weapons cause environmental harm to land, air and water because of the chemicals they are made of or release when used. War destroys the environment by damaging agriculture, killing animals and polluting water sources, etc. These impacts have significant implications for the affected population's health. Environmental degradation is an indirect cause of conflict, and will increasingly be so as climate changes and environmental impacts increase, leaving places uninhabitable.

conflict prevention — peacemaking — peace enforcement — peacekeeping — peacebuilding

Figure 4.5 The path toward resolution.

According to the UN, these processes should be mutually reinforcing. If they are used individually, it is highly likely that the overall process will fail.

207

Peace and conflict

Conflict prevention

Preventing conflict has become more popular since the end of the Cold War, particularly the decade of the 1990s that saw an increase in the number of intrastate conflicts. Policy and academic debates shifted from a conflict resolution perspective to a more preventive approach, although prevention is still underprioritized and underfunded. **Conflict prevention** addresses the humanitarian implications of armed conflict. It also has close links to economic degradation and the political implications that can be avoided by addressing a conflict before it escalates. Understanding that violent conflicts rarely stay within their own borders, and that the repercussions affect us all, is essential. Although complicated and time-consuming, conflict prevention is extremely important.

Conflict prevention refers to a series of diplomatic measures aimed at keeping tensions and hostilities from escalating into an armed conflict or a full-scale war. These pre-emptive measures can neutralize potential triggers if there is early warning (through information gathering), and a careful analysis of the factors and drivers of the conflict. Conflict prevention is about 'making societies resilient to violent conflict by strengthening the local capacities for peace (systems, resources, structures, attitudes, skills).'[18]

The methods or approaches used in conflict prevention are often divided into direct/operational prevention and structural prevention.

- Direct/operational prevention refers to short-term interventions that take place in a particular moment to reduce escalation of tensions and violence. These are reactive measures (for example, mediation).
- Structural prevention refers to long-term initiatives aimed at institutional and structural changes that seek to create a lasting and sustainable peace. Structural prevention tries to address the sources of the conflict in order to avoid a relapse in the hostilities.

Conflict prevention efforts tend not to be noticed because there is no violence. Also because it is often applied before a conflict intensifies and becomes more visible. Conflict prevention efforts from the UN, the EU and other organizations have proven successful (up to a point) in preventing different disputes from escalating. Tensions in the South China Sea have seen phases of increasing tension but no military action, and the same goes for recurring disputes between the United States and Russia, or the United States and North Korea.

Peacemaking

Chapter VI of the UN Charter describes **peacemaking** as a series of peaceful, diplomatic and judicial efforts through which conflicts can be solved. Peacemaking seeks to bring the opposing parties to the negotiating table and reach an agreement through different methods such as good offices (where a third party serves as intermediary to persuade parties to negotiate), mediation, **conciliation**, arbitration, court settlements and negotiation. These methods of peacemaking can be executed between the conflicting parties, or can involve external actors, such as the UN Secretary General, envoys, other governments, regional organizations, non-governmental groups or another person working independently.

Thematic studies

Signing the UN charter in 1945.

Mediation is a peaceful conflict resolution tool mentioned in Article 33 of the UN Charter, referring to a non-violent process in which the parties to the conflict accept help from a third party (an individual, organization, group or country) in order to change perceptions and/or behaviors. This third party is chosen by the conflicting actors. The UN is the most commonly chosen mediator, though regional organizations such as the European Union (EU) or the African Union (AU) have increasingly been given the task. Some countries have been traditionally chosen as mediators due to their neutrality or their historical role as conflict mediators, such as Switzerland, Norway, Türkiye or Qatar.

In conciliation, the dispute is sent to an existing organ, or an *ad hoc* organ specifically constituted to address that conflict. Its task is to clarify the issues and suggest proposals to find a resolution. It is the conflicting parties who must make the decision to submit their dispute, and it is also the conflicting parties who designate the conciliators. After conducting a thorough investigation of the dispute, the conciliator offers suggestions for the resolution, which the conflicting parties are free to accept or reject.

In 2016, Timor-Leste initiated compulsory conciliation proceedings under the United Nations Convention on the Law of the Sea (UNCLOS) against Australia due to a maritime boundary dispute. By 2018, the conciliation led to the successful settlement of the long-standing deadlock between the parties, which had not been able to be resolved previously by negotiation.

While diplomatic methods such as mediation and conciliation are more flexible and give more room for negotiation, they merely *suggest* ways for the conflicting parties to make peace without any legal obligation. Judicial means have the advantage of proposing binding solutions. These include arbitration, in which the decision is taken by a single arbitrator or court of arbitration, and court settlements, in which an established and permanent or *ad hoc* tribunal makes the decision. Both methods rely on legal decisions that are binding for the parties and must be carried out in good faith.

Peace and conflict

In arbitration, the arbitrator acts in a private manner outside of tribunals. It is chosen by the conflicting parties and often its decision is final. It is considered efficient and equitable, and gives more flexibility than court settlements because conflicting parties can have a voice in the process that will be followed. Court or judicial settlements are achieved by an international tribunal operating under the norms of international law. Some of these are permanent, such as the Inter-American Court of Human Rights, the European Court of Human Rights, the European Court of Justice, and the ICJ. Others are *ad hoc*, such as the Special Tribunal for Lebanon and the Special Court for Sierra Leone.

Activity

Divide your class into two groups. One group identifies the positive and negative aspects of mediation. The other group identifies the positive and negative aspects of arbitration. As a class, discuss which tool may give the best results.

Peace enforcement

Peace enforcement refers to the use of a range of coercive measures, including military assets, to enforce peace. Because of the use of military power, it must be approved by the UN Security Council, and the council needs to unanimously agree that there is a threat to international peace and security. In order to execute peace enforcement, following the UN Charter, the Security Council may use organizations or agencies to enforce the military action. Peace enforcement rarely brings lasting peace because it does not address the underlying conflict. It only enforces peace by compelling combatants to halt the violence, even if one or more parties in the conflict do not wish to stop the fight.

An example of peace enforcement is NATO's intervention in Kosovo, in which NATO used military force (under the name Operation Allied Force) against Serbia between March and June 1999 to halt the violence between the two parties. This military intervention was used until an agreement was reached, and afterward the UN Interim Administration Mission in Kosovo (UNMIK) **peacekeeping** operation was established. It is important to note that this case was rejected by Russia and the PRC in the Security Council. Operation Allied Force actually violated Chapter VII of the UN Charter.

After Iraq invaded and occupied Kuwait in 1990, the UN Security Council did agree unanimously that Iraq had to immediately and unconditionally withdraw their forces from Kuwait. Several resolutions were adopted, which if not met by Iraq would lead to member states using all necessary means to restore peace and security. After the deadline passed without Iraq complying with the resolutions, air attacks against Iraq began on January 16, 1991, under Resolution 687. A ceasefire was implemented, which Iraq eventually agreed upon. There then followed the establishment of the UN Iraq-Kuwait Observation Mission (UNIKOM) in order to monitor the conflict resolution and peace process in the region.

Abandoned Iraqi battle tanks.

Thematic studies

Peacekeeping

Peacekeeping is intended to create and maintain the conditions that favor a long-lasting peace. Within the UN, peacekeeping is an instrument created to help countries affected by conflict to transition to a state adequate for peace. Peacekeepers perform several activities, all of which serve to monitor and observe the peace process, such as providing assistance to electoral processes, strengthening the rule of law, aiding economic and social development, etc. The peacekeepers used to achieve these activities (also known as Blue Helmets or Blue Berets) include a wide range of experts, from soldiers to civilians.

Nepalese peacekeepers in South Sudan.

In contrast to peace enforcement, peacekeeping operations are deployed with the consent of the parties involved and usually as an additional measure to previously agreed ceasefires or peace agreements. This is why peacekeeping forces are lightly armed or unarmed, and mandated to use force minimally and only in exceptional circumstances. UN Peacekeeping operations are guided by the following three principles:

- consent of the parties
- impartiality
- non-use of force except in self-defense and defense of the mandate.

The authorization to conduct a peacekeeping operation must come directly from the UN Security Council under Chapter VII of the UN Charter. These operations are implemented by the UN, with troops that serve under UN control but remain as members of their national armies. This means that there is no UN Army, but an *ad hoc* coalition of willing states. Financing is dependent on the UN Member States. The UN is not the only organization that can conduct a peacekeeping operation. They can also be carried out by organizations or even single states. Two non-UN peacekeeping operations that are still in place are the Kosovo Force (KFOR), which is a NATO-led peacekeeping operation in Kosovo until Kosovo's Security Force becomes self-sufficient, and the Multinational Force and Observers (MFO) tasked with overseeing the terms of the Egypt-Israel peace treaty signed in 1979. The MFO is made up of several countries, including Canada, France, Japan, the USA, New Zealand and Fiji.

Peace and conflict

According to Lisa Hultman, Jacob Kathman and Megan Shannon (2013 and 2014), there is evidence of peacekeeping operations reducing the risk of renewed armed conflict, making peace last longer, reducing the intensity of fighting and saving civilian lives.[19] Yet, criticism of peacekeeping still persists. Critics claim that peacekeepers have been given too many responsibilities outside of their scope that should fall under the peacemaking and peacebuilding processes, such as:

- facilitating electoral processes
- protecting civilians
- aiding in disarmament, demobilization and reintegration (DDR) processes
- conducting social development programs
- promoting human rights
- restoring the rule of law.

Peacekeepers are supposed to be deployed to support and observe the implementation of a previously agreed-upon peace agreement or ceasefire, but often they are deployed without peace being there to keep. This is why there is evidence demonstrating that, while peacekeeping forces have positive effects during times of peace, they also can have negative effects in times of conflict.[20]

> **Activity**
>
> Work in a small group. Research the three principles on which peacekeeping missions must operate. Discuss how there are strengths and weaknesses to the success of peacekeeping operations. As a class, discuss the positive and negative aspects of the peacekeeping process.

It is important to understand that peacekeeping involves numerous cultures intermingling. This can complicate interactions and effectiveness, and can also lead to friction with the populations they are supposed to be working with. As retired Lieutenant-General and humanitarian Roméo Dallaire states in his book, *Shake Hands with the Devil*[21], language barriers, cultural and social differences, and a lack of political and contextual knowledge about a conflict represent insurmountable obstacles to peacekeeping. Even among peacekeepers, cultural differences can be an obstacle, as well as differences in training, equipment, procedures, command and control, and techniques in terms of operations. All these elements can result in divisions within the peacekeeping forces themselves.

It could be said that peacekeeping, although helping in a few cases to bring long-lasting peace (positive peace), often brings negative peace, because it does not address the core issues of the conflict and limits itself to only avoiding direct violence from happening.

It should not be forgotten that peacekeeping forces have been the targets of criticism and have been accused of abuse, sexual assault and human trafficking. Such complaints have been recorded in Cambodia, Mozambique, Kosovo, Bosnia, East Timor, Haiti, the Democratic Republic of Congo and West Africa.

In the case of Haiti, there has been evidence that Nepalese peacekeeping troops triggered a cholera epidemic in 2010.

Thematic studies

Peacebuilding

Peacebuilding, or post-conflict peacebuilding (PCPB), is the process of healing and reconstruction after the damages inflicted by an armed conflict. It entails a broad scope of work that requires well-thought-out solutions for peace to be long-lasting and sustainable. Peacebuilding involves diverse activities, such as:

- the re-establishment of institutions
- the fight against corruption
- implementation of humanitarian programs
- disarmament, demobilization and reintegration processes
- strengthening the rule of law
- reforms (economic, political, judicial, etc.)
- improving and monitoring the respect of human rights
- assisting in democratic processes to reconstruct or strengthen the legitimacy of the government
- providing medical and psychological assistance to the population.

The objective of peacebuilding is to reduce the risk of falling into a conflict, or back into one and to build solid foundations for development and peace to be sustainable. This means that PCPB must include reconciliation strategies. Without them, the conflict will not end because all armed conflict leaves deep emotional scars. However, this process is complex, takes a long time, may not show results for a while and is costly. This is why in many instances this process is addressed superficially or abandoned after a short period of time, leaving space for the conflict to restart or for new conflicts to appear.

Peacebuilding aims to resolve injustices and transform the structural conditions that led to the conflict, by working at all levels of society. If previous structural conditions do not change, it is expected that the conflict will re-emerge. There must be a gradual sharing of power, integration of diverse actors in the decision-making process and repartition of responsibilities. A crucial part of peacebuilding is reconciliation. This is the process by which the conflicting parties build trust, transform their beliefs and attitudes (during war, myths and stereotypes are strengthened to justify the atrocities committed), learn to cooperate, and create a stable and durable peace. The process of reconciliation may involve dialogues, admission of guilt, truth commissions, judicial processes and forgiveness. Reconciliation must go through several psycho-social recovery processes.

Peacebuilding is designed to achieve *positive* peace by addressing the structural, institutional and cultural causes of the conflict.

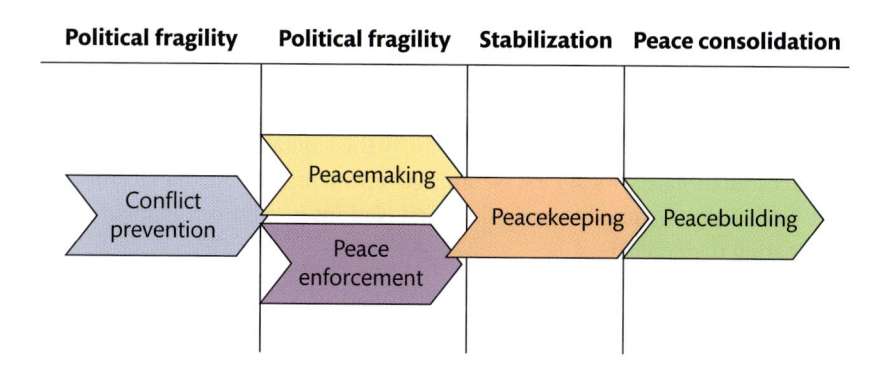

> Legitimacy is the right and acceptance of an authority. It is the belief that a rule, institution or leader has the right to govern, and manifests in the popular acceptance of a government, political regime or system of governance. During peacebuilding operations, it is essential for the stakeholders involved (governments, organizations, companies, tribunals, etc.) to enjoy legitimacy. This means that they need to be considered as trustworthy, capable and transparent. If the general population has no confidence in those in charge of the peacebuilding process, it is highly likely efforts will fail. In order to increase legitimacy, the active participation of citizens is needed.

Figure 4.6 A visual model of the peacekeeping process.

Peace and conflict

> Reconciliation is the process in which conflicting parties reach a truce and agree to make amends, build trust, transform their beliefs and attitudes, learn to cooperate, and create a stable and durable peace.

Truth and Reconciliation Commissions (TRCs) are useful agencies to work on these processes. They are bodies tasked with finding out the truth about what happened during an armed conflict, which often involves investigating human rights abuses. This is because there are often missing people, deaths that are unexplained and truths that are hidden from the public. After a conflict there tends to be *denialism* (during war, antagonistic parties tend to deny what the other side claims to have experienced) and *revisionism* (the whitewashing of the past).

Violence leaves deep trauma in victims and perpetrators, and the emotional toll of war must be acknowledged and confronted. TRCs look to take account of past injustices, violence and abuses of all sorts. They investigate what happened during a specific period of time, and when they have collected this information, they seek to find reconciliation with the past events through memory, reparation or recognition. 'Failure to remember, collectively, injustice and cruelty is an ethical breach. It implies no responsibility and no commitment to prevent inhumanity in the future. Even worse, failures of collective memory stoke fires of resentment and revenge.'[22]

The goal of TRCs is to facilitate national healing. They can be formed by citizens or by governments. This can lead to one of the main criticisms of TRCs. Some people believe that, if it is a government behind a TRC, reconciliation is imposed on the people and is not natural. The process of reconciliation, although providing some emotional closure, also requires an apology to the victims, and this rarely happens, because an apology would imply that the perpetrators acknowledge guilt, thus exposing them to prosecution. Critics claim that TRCs grant clemency to the perpetrators without bringing justice to the victims and their relatives, and that criminal punishments seem to be exchanged for reparations.

In the absence of truth and reconciliation, trauma persists, reminding people of past wrongdoings that have not been addressed. Leaders often manipulate this for their own interests.

Case – Canada's road toward reconciliation

Since the 17th century, when European settlers arrived in Canada, the assumption that European civilization was superior to others (especially over the territory's first inhabitants, who were seen as savage and ignorant) was established within European society. A sense of a responsibility to civilize them was created among the settlers.

In 1867, together with other assimilation policies, the Canadian government set up an educational system for over 150,000 indigenous First Nations, Métis and Inuit children. This was a system of indoctrination into the Euro-Canadian and Christian way of living in mainstream white Canadian society. Residential schools, administered by the Anglican, Presbyterian, United and Roman Catholic churches, forbade children from acknowledging their heritage, culture and language, and kept children far from their families and communities for long periods of time.

By 1920, it was mandatory for indigenous children to attend a residential school under the Indian Act, first introduced in 1876 by the federal government to administer Indian status, local First Nations governments and the management of reserve land. This law aimed to assimilate First Nations into Euro-Canadian society by eliminating their culture.

Education in residential schools was different from that of public schools. Records show that education was very poor in residential schools, with a focus on religion,

Thematic studies

domestic work for girls, and manual labor, agriculture, carpentry and tin smithing for boys. Many children studied part-time while spending the rest of the time working for the school (doing chores that were necessary for the schools to exist) without remuneration. Children were severely punished, physically, emotionally, sexually and psychologically. According to some testimonies, children were 'being beaten and strapped; some students were shackled to their beds; some had needles shoved in their tongues for speaking their native languages.'[23] There was poor sanitation, poor healthcare, inadequate nutrition and overpopulation. These conditions resulted in children dying in the residential schools and at home, after they had been sent back because they were severely ill.

By 1969, the number of residential schools began to decline. In 1996, the last residential school, Gordon Reserve Indian Residential School in Saskatchewan, closed. It was not until the 1990s that the government and the churches involved began to recognize their responsibility for the devastating effects of their educational system on indigenous communities. Today, the Canadian residential school system is considered as a form of genocide because of its attempts to eradicate indigenous cultures.

Former students took legal action against the government's role in this discriminatory and violent system. This led to the creation of the Truth and Reconciliation Commission (TRC) of Canada in 2008, whose aim was to provide all those affected, directly or indirectly, with an opportunity to share their experiences and their stories. The TRC of Canada was born out of the Indian Residential Schools Settlement Agreement in 2006, which was an agreement between survivors, the Assembly of First Nations, Inuit representatives, the governments and the churches, in which:

- the damage inflicted by the residential school system was formally recognized
- an Independent Assessment Process for claims of sexual and serious physical abuse, health and healing measures was established
- commemorative activities were organized
- a $1.9 billion Canadian dollar compensation was promised.

The TRC of Canada worked to document and preserve the experiences of survivors, their families and communities, contributing to truth, healing and reconciliation as established in the Mandate for the Truth and Reconciliation Commission.

The TRC of Canada conducted a six-year research project across Canada, gathered information from over 6500 witnesses (including former staff of the schools), and organized national events to promote awareness and public education about the history and the impacts of residential schools, while also sharing and honoring the experiences of former students and their families. In 2015, the TRC presented its final executive summary, split into six volumes, together with 94 recommendations (Calls to Action) on how to bring about further reconciliation between indigenous peoples and Canadians.

The former Canadian Prime Minister Stephen Harper acknowledged in 2009 in the House of Commons the intergenerational damage caused by the residential school system, apologized and asked for forgiveness from the indigenous peoples. In 2017, Prime Minister Justin Trudeau also apologized, recognizing the responsibility and failure of the Canadian government, and calling on all Canadians to get involved in the healing process. Since 2021, September 30 is recognized as Canada's National Day for Truth and Reconciliation.

Children in a Canadian residential school.

Peace and conflict

> Full reconciliation has not been achieved. For many, the trauma is still fresh, and it is up to individuals to accept or reject the apologies. Critics of the TRC of Canada say the healing process has focused on the residential school system, but has failed to address the fact that the schools were just one of many aspects within a discriminatory colonialist system that lasted for centuries, which has not disappeared entirely. Structural inequalities and discrimination persist, showed by disproportionate poverty rates, unequal access to healthcare, racial bias at work, racial profiling, or violence against women (declared a national emergency by Canadian lawmakers in 2023). As long as indigenous communities in Canada continue being marginalized and vulnerable, there will never be true reconciliation.

Peacebuilding should go beyond just patronage. This is support, such as political or electoral support, economic control over revenues, etc., given by an organization, government and individual, which often demands something in return. Patrons have influence over those who receive the assistance. Peacebuilding should aim toward building local capacity and partnership. Humanitarian aid and donor tools can help the process, but these tend to be short-term solutions that provide immediate assistance. Local priorities must be identified, and there must be local participation in the planning, coordination and execution of the process, involving vulnerable and marginalized groups (people living in poverty or groups that are excluded due to race, gender, identity, sexual orientation, age, physical ability, etc.), in order to end the dependency of people on the aid provided. If the interests of the elites are disconnected from those of the local communities, who actually suffer the most, conflict is likely to recur.

An example of this is the ongoing instability and violence in Sudan and South Sudan after several decades of civil war. Peace agreements have focused on the politico-military elites at the expense of ignoring young people, the psychological and emotional trauma, the destruction of social and communal values, and the needs of the people. In the case of Sudan/South Sudan:

> These deals often focus on elite power and resource-sharing arrangements, while ignoring the communal and societal dynamics that fed the war and leave embers in its wake… In essence, these elite pacts, important as they are in the reduction of violence, lead to a variety of other contests, including competition to seize the renewed flow of money and resources which usually follows peace agreements. As for ordinary citizens, their experience typically is one of disappointment or the status quo. The absence of meaningful change to their lives often becomes a catalyst for a swift return to conflict.[24]

Any road to resolution needs to take a bottom-up approach, taking into consideration what the people involved need, what their concerns are, what difficulties they face and how they see the conflict. For peace to last, local values and culture must be involved.

It is easy to destroy societies, institutions and systems, but it is difficult to build them, or repair them after they have been damaged. Conflict, particularly armed conflict, affects every aspect of a country. War is not only about the human losses, the injured, the maimed or the disappeared. It is more than the economic and commercial toll of disrupted relations and destruction of supply chains. It is not merely about strained political and diplomatic relations. Armed conflicts affect societies to their very core and leave scars that cannot be erased. Peace and conflict studies cannot stop conflicts from happening, but it can work on possible strategies and solutions that reduce their frequency and their humanitarian impact, and strengthen peace as a means to solve conflict.

HL Armed conflict and wars need to be addressed from a *Security* perspective that takes into consideration the fact that peace is not exclusively the absence of physical violence. National and international security are threatened by conflict. However, human security suffers greatly from violence. Human insecurity can also be a cause of violence that can escalate to a war.

Thematic studies

Practice questions

1. Negative peace does not entail cultural and/or structural peace in its entirety. Analyze why international attention and the media often ignore conflicts once direct violence ceases.
2. Some say that legal measures for conflict resolution may be more useful since they entail binding results to which actors must abide. However, diplomatic measures are more commonly used. Evaluate successes and failures in diplomatic measures for conflict resolution.
3. Explain what could motivate people to use violence despite non-violence proving effective in some cases.
4. Justify the claim that in certain cases military intervention is necessary to stop further violence.
5. TRCs have been successful for several intrastate conflicts, although with limitations, particularly when it comes to the population's trust and acceptance of the legitimacy of those in charge of the TRCs. Discuss whether TRCs could apply to interstate conflicts. What could be some of the obstacles?

Summary

In this chapter, you have learned:

- The definition of peace is contested depending on context. It can be seen simply as the absence of direct violence (negative peace), or as the absence of cultural and structural violence (positive peace). Tools like the Global Peace Index attempt to measure peace around the world, but its contested meaning presents an obstacle.

- Peace and conflict are not opposite sides of a line; both exist within wider spectrums. Peace can be seen as a means of making progress, as the end result, or as both. Differing views result in different approaches to peace, like peace movements, pacifism, or the idea of a balance of power.

- There is a direct relation between positive peace and economic growth, as the Positive Peace Index (PPI) shows.

- Conflict is inevitable, but violence can be avoided. This results in violent and non-violent conflicts. Violence can be direct, cultural or structural. Violence can find justifications in cultural norms, religion, and even legal support.

- Armed conflict is not exclusive to states; numerous actors can be directly and indirectly involved in armed conflicts. For the same reason, the causes behind a conflict are often numerous and hard to trace, and therefore address.

- Conflicts are rarely linear, but instead occur with varied dynamics. Different tools to analyze conflicts exist that can help understand and solve the conflicts.

- The path towards conflict resolution has numerous diplomatic, legal and military tools among which are conflict prevention, peacemaking, peace enforcement, peacekeeping and peacebuilding.

- With the use of Truth and Reconciliation Commissions, peacebuilding seeks to bring positive peace to countries, communities and individuals affected by conflict.

Peace and conflict

> **Notes**

1. Hedges, C. (2002). *War is a Force That Gives Us Meaning*. Random House.
2. Hedges, C. (2022). *The Greatest Evil is War*. Seven Stories Press.
3. Barash, D.P. and Webel, C. (2018). *Peace and Conflict Studies*. SAGE, p.9.
4. Barash, D.P. and Webel, C. (2018). *Peace and Conflict Studies*. SAGE, p.9.
5. Institute for Economics & Peace. (2022, January). *Positive Peace Report 2022: Analyzing the factors that build, predict and sustain peace*. Retrieved in March 2023 from: http://visionofhumanity.org/resources
6. Cortright, D. (2008). *Peace: A History of Movements and Ideas*. Cambridge University Press, pp.67–92.
7. Galtung, J. (1969). 'Violence, Peace, and Peace Research'. *Journal of Peace Research*, 6(2), pp.167–91.
8. ilga world database. (2023). 'Criminalisation of consensual same-sex sexual acts'. Retrieved in July 2023 from: https://database.ilga.org/criminalisation-consensual-same-sex-sexual-acts
9. Ackerman, P. and Kruegler, C. (1994). *Strategic Nonviolent Conflict*. Praeger.
10. Kaldor, M. (2012). *New and Old Wars. Organised violence in a Global Era*. Polity Press.
11. Lt. Col. Long, J. (2012, December). 'What is War? A New Point of View'. *Small Wars Journal*. Retrieved in April 2023 from: https://smallwarsjournal.com/jrnl/art/what-is-war-a-new-point-of-view
12. Republika Srpska is a political entity that grew from the violent dissolution of the former Yugoslavia. It is part of Bosnia and Herzegovina (not Serbia), but it is independent in some ways. In 1992, the Bosnian Serb assembly declared Republika Srpska the independent Republic of the Serb people of Bosnia and Herzegovina. The status of the territory was recognized in the Dayton Agreement in 1995, which also ended the war. Most of its population is ethnically Serb.
13. *Global Terrorism Index 2023*. Institute for Economics and Peace, p.12.
14. Galtung, J. (1969). 'Violence, Peace, and Peace Research'. *Journal of Peace Research*, 6(3), SAGE, pp. 167–191.
15. Burton, J.W. (1990). *Conflict: Human Needs Theory*. Palgrave Macmillan.
16. Ramsbotham, O. Woodhouse, T. and Miall, H. (2011). *Contemporary Conflict Resolution*. Polity.
17. Dorn, W.A. (2009, July). *The Justifications for War and Peace in World Religions*. Defense R&D Canada. Retrieved in March 2023 from: https://apps.dtic.mil/sti/pdfs/ADA509464.pdf
18. Swedish International Development Cooperation Agency (SIDA). (2017, December). *Conflict Prevention: Opportunities and challenges in implementing key policy commitments and priorities*. Retrieved in April 2023 from: https://cdn.sida.se/app/uploads/2020/12/01125316/s209461_thematicoverview_conflict_prevention_webb_final.pdf
19. Hultman, L., Kathman, J. and Shannon, M. (2013, October). 'United Nations Peacekeeping and Civilian Protection in Civil War'. *American Journal on Political Science*, 57(4), pp.875–91.
    Hultman, L., Kathman, J. and Shannon, M. (2014). 'Beyond Keeping Peace: United Nations Effectiveness in the Midst of Fighting'. *American Political Science Review*, 108(4), pp.737–53.
20. Blair, R. (2021). 'UN Peacekeeping and the Rule of Law'. *American Political Science Review*, 115(1), pp.51–68.
21. Dallaire, R. (2004). *Shake Hands with the Devil*. Da Capo Press.
22. Barash, D.P. and Webel, C. (2018). *Peace and Conflict Studies*. SAGE, p.604.
23. Hanson, E., et al. (2020). 'The Residential School System'. *Indigenous Foundations*. First Nations and Indigenous Studies, UBC. Retrieved in April 2023 from: https://indigenousfoundations.arts.ubc.ca/the_residential_school_system/
24. Jok, M.J. (2021). 'Lessons in Failure: Peacebuilding in Sudan/South Sudan'. McNamee, T., Muyangwa, M. (eds) *The State of Peacebuilding in Africa*. Palgrave Macmillan. Retrieved in April 2023 from: https://doi.org/10.1007/978-3-030-46636-7_20

Global political challenges

HL EXTENSION

Global political challenges

> **Concepts**
>
> Poverty, Technology, Health, Identity, Borders, Security, Equality, Environment

> **Learning outcomes**
>
> In this chapter, you will learn about:
> - different topic areas (poverty, technology, health, identity, borders, security, equality and environment), emphasizing the interconnection between them
> - the complexities of global challenges and the different ways of addressing them, focusing on possible courses of action
> - how HL topic areas are not disconnected topics, but overlapping areas of study that can contribute to and complement understanding of the core knowledge, thematic studies and other challenges.

Introduction

Students taking the HL course conduct extended inquiries around global political challenges, with an emphasis on:

- the interconnected nature of these challenges
- the complexities and historical tensions involved in addressing these challenges
- a solution-oriented focus that highlights possible courses of action.

While there is no additional content prescribed for the HL extension, the students' explorations of global political challenges should build on the core topics and thematic studies. The concepts, content and contexts explored as part of the common syllabus should serve as a foundation for the HL extension. (Taken from the Global Politics Guide.)

As part of the extended inquiry, students are expected to consider the following guidelines of inquiry related to the analysis of global political challenges and how these can be addressed:

- What connections can be established between the HL topic areas and the core topics?
- What connections can be established between the HL topic areas and the thematic studies?
- To what extent are the HL topic areas interconnected? What are some of the links in how they are studied and/or addressed?
- How are these topic areas perceived and addressed in different contexts?
- Which are some of the frameworks, systems, organizations and mechanisms put in place for addressing global political challenges?
- How can looking at particular cases from different topic areas change the way global political challenges are perceived or addressed?

In a similar way to the thematic studies, these HL topic areas can be seen as areas of study in global politics that provide additional analysis tools, models, frameworks and terminology for analyzing political issues. Additionally, exploring the links between multiple topic areas will most likely provide examples of the complexities of global

HL extension

political challenges, and ways to address them. For example, students might look into the links between poverty and health to research into the impacts in vulnerable populations, while others might explore how technology is used to address security concerns or to reduce environmental risks.

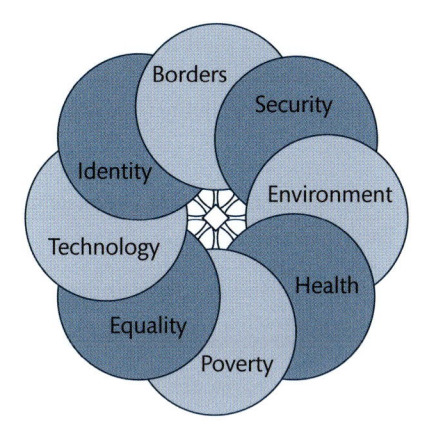

Figure 5.1 Interconnected nature of the global political challenges and HL topic areas (taken from the Global Politics Guide).

Two main approaches to conducting the HL extended inquiries are suggested:

- Using HL topic areas as entry points: If a student is interested in one of the HL topic areas, they may begin an in-depth study of it and then select an appropriate case through which to investigate it further.
- Using cases as entry points: If a particular case or topic is of special interest to the student, they may explore the case and make links to multiple topic areas that they consider relevant. (Taken from the Global Politics Guide.)

Poverty

Learning outcomes

In this section, you will learn about:

- how poverty is not only measured by income, but it is multidimensional and must be addressed by considering different factors
- poverty cannot be solved by raising salaries, but by looking at quality of life and standards of living from a range of perspectives
- education is a crucial factor in addressing poverty worldwide, but education is not useful without social mobility
- poverty is a human security problem, and may be a wider security issue for communities and countries
- poverty is related to inequalities that stop people from achieving access to quality services such as healthcare
- environmental degradation has global implications, though people living in poverty are much more vulnerable to it
- poverty is the main reason for cross-border migration.

Conceptual question

What is poverty and how is it defined?

Global political challenges

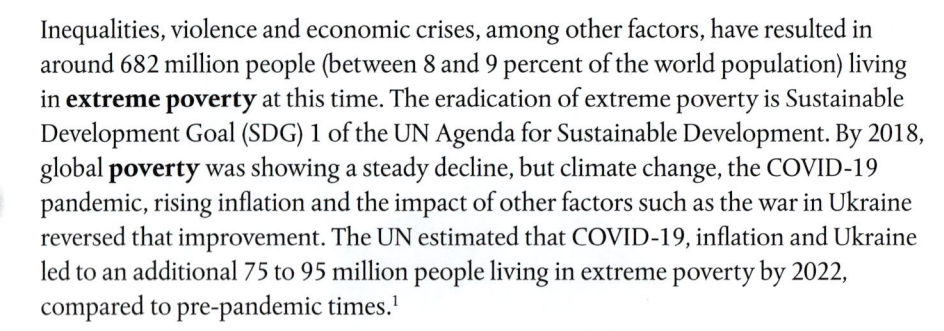

Inequalities, violence and economic crises, among other factors, have resulted in around 682 million people (between 8 and 9 percent of the world population) living in **extreme poverty** at this time. The eradication of extreme poverty is Sustainable Development Goal (SDG) 1 of the UN Agenda for Sustainable Development. By 2018, global **poverty** was showing a steady decline, but climate change, the COVID-19 pandemic, rising inflation and the impact of other factors such as the war in Ukraine reversed that improvement. The UN estimated that COVID-19, inflation and Ukraine led to an additional 75 to 95 million people living in extreme poverty by 2022, compared to pre-pandemic times.[1]

Poverty is not only the lack of financial means to meet basic needs, like clothing, food and shelter. As The World Bank describes it:

> Poverty is hunger. Poverty is lack of shelter. Poverty is being sick and not being able to see a doctor. Poverty is not having access to school and not knowing how to read. Poverty is not having a job, it is fear for the future, and living one day at a time. Poverty has many faces, changing from place to place and across time, and has been described in many ways. Most often, poverty is a situation people want to escape. So poverty is a call to action – for the poor and the wealthy alike – a call to change the world so that many more may have enough to eat, adequate shelter, access to education and health, protection from violence, and a voice in what happens in their communities.[2]

> Poverty is closely linked to development, human rights and conflict, as a cause and a consequence. The number of people living in poverty is higher in less developed and developing countries. Human rights violations and marginalization are more likely to be faced by people living in poverty. Armed conflict can cause an increase in poverty, while poverty can also be a driver for conflict.

Poverty zones in Lima, Peru.

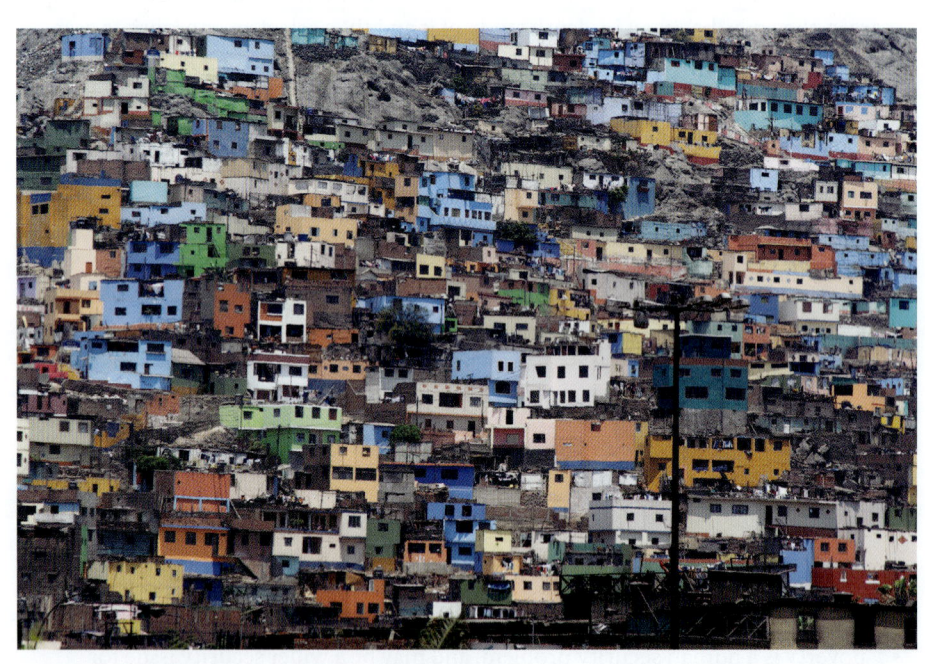

Definitions and measurements of poverty are contested. It is understood that poverty is not only a lack of money, but also an inability to actively participate in society and enjoy its benefits. When people face economic problems, they are unable to consider the expenses around education, healthcare or recreational activities. Global poverty is one of the most pressing challenges in global politics. Globalization, economic integration and international cooperation have resulted in efforts to address poverty, but, in order for progress to happen, we need to understand poverty and all its variables and how it changes.

Defining poverty tends to be influenced by a nation's context. One country may define the **poverty line** at $24.00 (US dollars – USD) a day, while another country

> Poverty is a state or condition in which a person or community lacks the financial resources and essentials for a minimum standard of living. Poverty is a lack of financial means, and also the inability to actively participate in society, enjoy basic human rights and have the possibility of development.

HL extension

may set it at $2.00 a day. Rich and poor countries set different poverty lines to measure poverty, according to the level of income of their citizens. Being poor in Sweden is very different to being poor in Botswana, and being poor in Russia is different to being poor in Ecuador. Regardless of the poverty line set, poverty is a very complex societal issue.

Poverty can be measured in two ways: **absolute poverty** and **relative poverty**.

Table 5.1 Absolute vs relative poverty

Absolute Poverty	Relative Poverty
A person or household lacks the minimum amount of income to meet their basic needs (the poverty line) over an extended period of time, causing their survival to be threatened.	Depends on context, being relative to the economic climate of the particular country in which a person lives.
The United Nations (UN) used to define absolute poverty as living with less than $1.90 USD per day. However, countries set their own poverty lines.	The standard of living a person or household enjoys compared to the standard enjoyed by others within the same society.
A person is considered to be poor if their income, consumption or wealth fall below the poverty line.	In absolute poverty, quality of life is considered low. In relative poverty quality of life is better than in absolute poverty, but lower than for others within the same environment.

Activity

Research the poverty line in the country you live in. How does it compare to other countries in the same region? Every country can set its own poverty line. Analyze and discuss with a partner the implications that this has for measuring poverty. How do these implications influence results and policies?

Measuring and mapping poverty

People living in poverty are the most vulnerable in society. They lack resources to satisfy their basic needs to enjoy a life in dignity (a life in which one has the opportunity to fulfil one's potential, with healthcare, education, income and security). They also tend to experience other vulnerabilities such as:

- higher infant mortality rates
- lower access to education and quality education
- bigger health challenges
- a lack of **social mobility**.

To address poverty and improve the livelihoods of the millions living in poverty, policymakers need access to accurate information regarding who lives in poverty, where they live, and why they live in poverty.

The UN's SDG 1 seeks to 'End poverty in all its forms everywhere.'[3] Although the SDGs are not numbered by priority, this conveys the fact that poverty is directly related to all

Social mobility refers to the change in a person's socio-economic situation, in relation to their parents (*intergenerational mobility*) or throughout their lifetime (*intragenerational mobility*).

Global political challenges

other factors necessary for sustainable development. Understanding economic poverty levels, distributions and trends is central to understanding how people experience poverty and where reduction efforts are most needed.

Measuring poverty is contextual, and there are several indicators that different governments use when measuring it. One of these is **purchasing power parity (PPP)**, which measures the price of specific goods in different countries and compares the absolute purchasing power of other countries' currencies. More simply, a US dollar in New York City will not buy you the same amount of things as a US dollar will in Accra. PPP takes into account different costs of living around the world. It is the reason why different countries set different poverty lines. Gross Domestic Product (GDP), income, inflation and employment rates are often also used to measure poverty within countries. Although there are different approaches to measuring poverty, it is still important to measure it in order to design and implement actions that can address the problem.

The tent city established after the 2010 earthquake that struck Haiti. Living conditions were deplorable.

For more interactive maps on poverty, you can access:

The World Bank has graphs for different indicators for each country available at:

The **extreme poverty line** is the international standard for measuring poverty (absolute poverty) with a threshold equivalent to $2.15 USD per person per day. Two other poverty lines are used internationally: $3.65 USD and $6.85 USD per person per day. The $2.15 USD line is considered by The World Bank as typical for low-income countries. For lower middle-income countries, the line is typically set at $3.65 USD. For upper middle-income countries, the line is typically set at $6.85 USD.[4] The extreme poverty line is standardized using PPP currency conversions, reflecting the real buying power of a currency, instead of the exchange rate of a currency against the US dollar.

Global poverty is measured using data available from national databases. However, some countries do not report their data, or do not have the means to collect the data. For example, national surveys may not consider homeless people, or may consider irregular employment as employment. There may be big delays between data collection, analysis and reporting. Yet, there are global efforts at gathering data from different countries to generate international, regional and national poverty statistics.

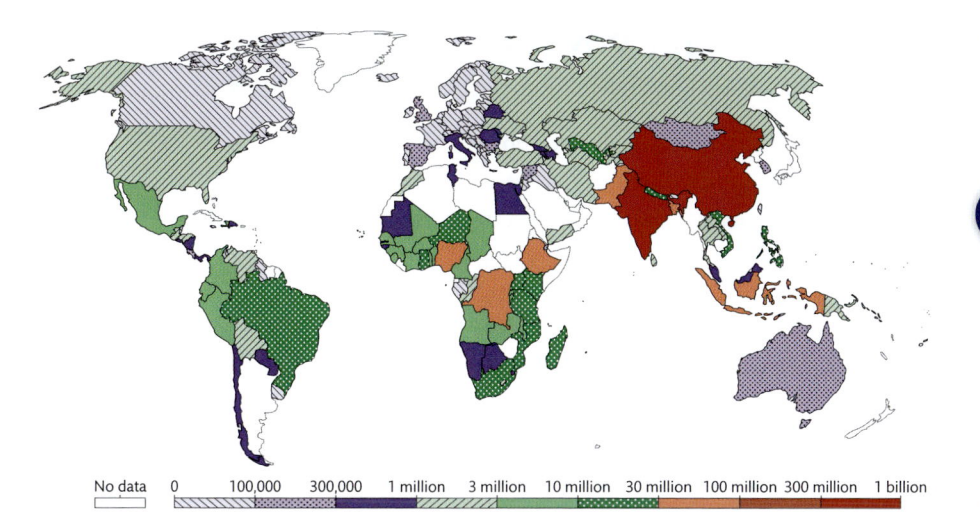

HL extension

Figure 5.2 Number of people living in extreme poverty by 2001.

> Context must be taken into consideration when studying global politics. We tend to rely on data presented by governments. However, we must be critical of the accuracy of the data. Pay close attention to the variables included, and the methodology used to measure the data.

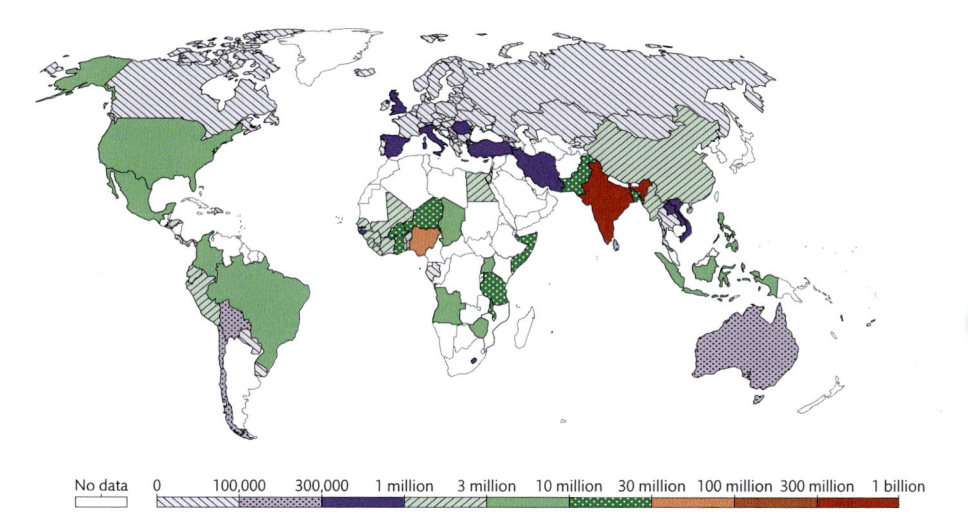

Figure 5.3 Number of people living in extreme poverty by 2021. Data is missing from many countries. This can be the result of a lack of means to measure extreme poverty, an unwillingness to do so, or inconclusive data.

TOK

Extreme poverty in upper middle-income countries is set at $6.85 USD. This means that if you earn $7.00 USD per day you are not absolutely poor, yet you might feel quite poor. How arbitrary are statistics and their thresholds? How much can we rely on them? To what extent do statistics and their thresholds shape our knowledge and our policies to address issues such as poverty?

Since 1990, there has been progress in reducing global economic poverty. However, other quality of life indicators that are considered within the definition of poverty have been an obstacle to reducing poverty. Countries' circumstances, consumption patterns, respect for human rights, armed conflicts and inequalities vary and influence measurements of poverty.

By 2022, global trends indicated that the COVID-19 pandemic, inflation, recession, conflict and climate change affected the number of people in poverty. In 2020, it was estimated that around 26 percent of the world's population lived under the threshold of $3.65 USD a day, and 46 percent under the threshold of $6.85 USD a day. Extreme poverty was concentrated in Sub-Saharan Africa. Thirteen of the 15 countries with the largest increase in population living in extreme poverty were in this region, with the Democratic Republic of Congo (DRC), Madagascar and Nigeria being the poorest. Another two countries were Yemen and Syria. The PRC and India experienced the greatest reductions in extreme poverty. In fact, in 2020, the PRC had a smaller proportion of its population living in extreme poverty than Canada, the UK or the USA.[5]

Global political challenges

Multidimensional poverty

In line with The World Bank's definition, the UN refers to poverty as:

- a state in which a person is denied choices and opportunities
- a violation of human dignity
- the lack of capacity to participate effectively in society.

> It means not having enough to feed and clothe a family, not having a school or clinic to go to, not having the land on which to grow one's food or a job to earn one's living, not having access to credit. It means insecurity, powerlessness and exclusion of individuals, households and communities. It means susceptibility to violence, and it often implies living in marginal or fragile environments, without access to clean water or sanitation.[6]

This means that people living in poverty do not enjoy human security, and cannot be sure they will be able to feed or clothe themselves and their families. They tend to have lower levels of education and health, and poor access to water and sanitation. They often lack a voice in their societies, and have little access to opportunities to improve their lives.

Poverty is multidimensional. But in order to measure global poverty, a consistent line must be drawn across countries. That is why the International Poverty Line, set by The World Bank, has been established at $2.15 USD per day. With this poverty line set, the **Multidimensional Poverty Measure (MPM)**[7] seeks to understand poverty beyond monetary deprivation – it also measures how much people's needs are met with regards to essentials such as education and basic infrastructure services. However, this measure is far from perfect. For instance, the 2022 results showed that around 4 out of 10 people were not classed as living in poverty on a financial basis, but only in regard to the services and infrastructure they were able to access.

The MPM is made up of six indicators:

- monetary consumption or income
- level of educational attainment
- level of educational enrollment
- access to drinking water
- access to sanitation
- access to electricity.

The six indicators are categorized into three *dimensions* of well-being: monetary, education and basic infrastructure services. All dimensions (and all indicators) are weighted equally, as Table 5.2 shows.

Table 5.2 Multidimensional poverty: measure dimension and parameters[8]

Dimension	Parameter	Weight
Monetary	Daily consumption or income is less than $2.15 per person	1/3
Education	At least one school-age child up to the age of grade 8 is not enrolled in school	1/6
	No adult in the household (age of grade 9 or above) has completed primary education	1/6
Access to basic infrastructure	The household lacks access to clean drinking water	1/9
	The household lacks access to adequate sanitation	1/9
	The household has no access to electricity	1/9

▲ Boy collecting rubbish that can be resold or reused.

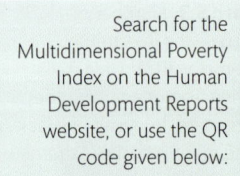

Search for the Multidimensional Poverty Index on the Human Development Reports website, or use the QR code given below:

HL extension

An additional tool to measure poverty is the **Multidimensional Poverty Index (MPI)**[9] developed by the UN Development Program (UNDP). Before the MPI was developed, the Human Poverty Index (HPI) was used. The MPI measures poverty using 10 indicators:

- nutrition
- child mortality
- years in schooling
- school attendance
- cooking fuel
- sanitation
- drinking water
- electricity
- housing
- assets.

These are categorized into three main dimensions: health, education and standard of living (Figure 5.4).

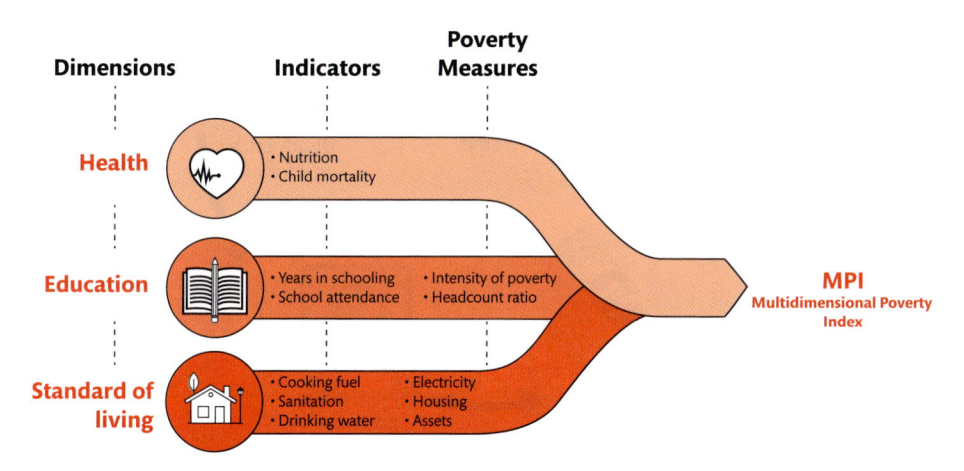

> **TOK**
> The MPM gives the same weight to its three dimensions: monetary, education and access to basic infrastructure. Each dimension has different numbers of parameters. To what extent can these parameters explain to us the gravity and urgency of addressing poverty?

Figure 5.4 MPI dimensions and indicators. In addition to the MPI's 10 indicators, this diagram includes the two poverty measures used for the education dimension.[10]

Deprivation is defined using the indicators as the following:

- Nutrition: any child, or adult under the age of 70, is undernourished
- Child mortality: a child under the age of 18 has died in the family in the five-year period before the survey
- Years of schooling: when no household member above the age of six has completed at least six years of schooling
- School attendance: when any school-aged child is not attending school to the age at which they would complete eighth grade.

With regards to standard of living, deprivation exists when:

- a household cooks with dung, wood, charcoal or coal
- sanitation facilities do not fulfill SDG standards
- access to drinking water does not fulfill SDG standards or there is at least a 30-minute walk to access it (round trip)
- a household has no electricity
- housing materials are inadequate
- a household does not own more than one radio, television, telephone, computer, animal cart, bicycle, motorbike or refrigerator, and does not own a car or truck.

> Undernourishment is the main indicator that the Food and Agriculture Organization (FAO) of the UN uses to measure food supplies and nutrition. It is determined by the calorie (energy) intake, without considering the quality and variety of someone's diet.

227

Global political challenges

Among the key findings of the MPI in 2022, 1.2 billion people were multidimensionally poor, 593 million of those were children under the age of 18 and 579 million lived in Sub-Saharan Africa, followed by 385 million living in South Asia.

The poverty trap

People living in poverty are the most vulnerable in a society. Not only do they lack the economic means for survival and a life of dignity, but they also cannot escape poverty. This is referred to as the **poverty trap**, which is a spiraling cycle that forces people to remain poor. While it generally happens in developing countries, all people living in poverty experience hard times when trying to escape poverty.

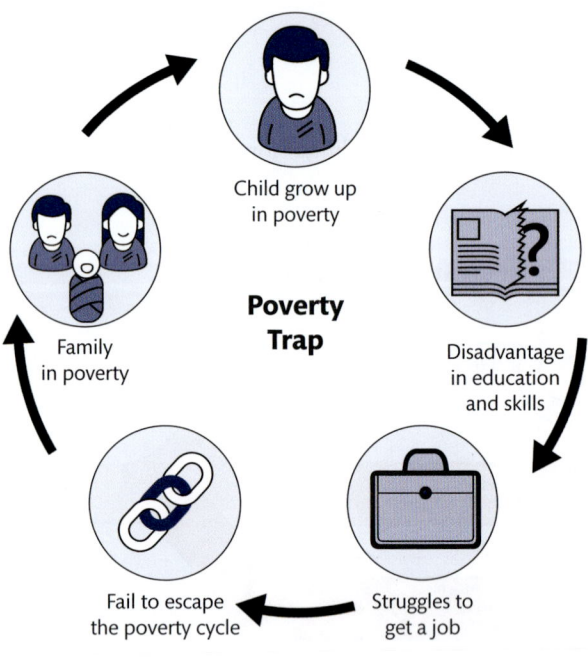

Figure 5.5 Being born into, or growing up in, poverty leads to disadvantages and harsh realities that become obstacles to escaping a lifetime of poverty.

Some of the factors that contribute to people staying in poverty include:

- capital shortage
- inadequate credit facilities
- inadequate infrastructure
- weak education system
- inefficient public healthcare system
- corruption
- weak governance
- armed conflict
- climate change and environmental factors.

The poverty trap is a cycle in which poverty persists for generations. Many governments conduct efforts and programs to decrease the level of poverty in a country, but at times there is not enough capital for subsidizing poverty. Poor people often have limited access to credit because they are seen as unreliable when it comes to repayments. Societies can also face high unemployment, and the few employment opportunities that are available often provide low wages. This results in large percentages of the population being deprived of affordable and quality education, forcing children to work at a young age.

Homeless man begging on a city street in Glasgow, Scotland.

HL extension

Healthcare is also poor in the poverty trap because people struggle to pay medical bills. Communities in poverty often deal with poor sanitation, which results in higher risks of illnesses and epidemics. Climate change and environmental factors can worsen living conditions due to droughts, floods and natural disasters, etc. Armed conflict and war often consume the country's wealth and leave the population vulnerable to worsening living conditions. Governments might fail to manage funds to fight poverty, and so fail to provide adequate access to services and infrastructure for the most vulnerable.

When income is limited, people have to make hard choices, such as:

- Will they use their money to eat, or to send their children to school?
- Will they use their money to buy medicines, or to buy a means of transportation to go to a job in another town?

There is no right answer. It is a matter of immediate survival, where the future cannot be considered. This is why escaping poverty is so hard.

Sometimes, governments are behind the continuous deprivation of people, blocking access to the resources and services people deserve. Inequality causes people to live in poverty, and it can be institutionalized, culturally sustained and entrenched in values and beliefs. Discrimination, segregation and marginalization send people into poverty and contribute to making it difficult (or impossible) for them to improve their conditions.

Poverty leaves people without the possibility of social mobility. Their socio-economic situation cannot change when so many factors and dimensions are involved. A person born in poverty will be unlikely to leave that situation if the social conditions do not provide them with the possibilities to improve their life conditions, especially if their society does not consider them to be worthy of assistance to reach a level of equality with the rest of the population.

The role of governments and other actors in fighting poverty

All governments have the responsibility to address their population's needs and provide them with the tools for an adequate standard of living. They can do this by ensuring that policies do not support the wealthy at the expense of those in poverty. Governments can:

- provide subsidized services for the parts of their population that cannot afford additional expenses
- enforce regulations and standards for companies when it comes to salaries, working conditions or the quality of education
- provide resources and programs to ensure everyone has access to what they need
- eradicate values, institutions or beliefs that discriminate and marginalize those in poverty.

It is essential for governments to listen to and include the voices of those living in poverty, who policies are intended to help, to achieve better and long-lasting results.

In the USA, the cost of healthcare prevents many people from accessing it. This increases the risk of serious illness, death and the spread of diseases. Health insurance is also costly. During the COVID-19 pandemic, there were reports of people who decided not to seek medical assistance out of fear of being unable to pay the bills. Human Rights Watch reported that during this period there were at least 28 million

---

HL Poverty is a state of absence of human *Security*, making people vulnerable to poor health. People in poverty face more inequalities in terms of education, or political participation. Climate change and environmental factors affect those in poverty more. Economic migration is the main cause for people to leave their country and cross *Borders*, seeking better life opportunities.

Not being able to eat, provide a home for your family, have access to clean water or have a decent job (that pays a fair income, guarantees a secure form of employment and safe working conditions), and being forced to drop out of school to work or get married because you live in poverty, are all human rights violations.

Global political challenges

Americans without health insurance. Having lost work (and health insurance) due to the pandemic, many were left with no healthcare. Due to the correlation between race and poverty in the country, communities of color were disproportionately impacted.

> **Case – Poverty and child marriage in Niger**
>
> In spite of being a violation of the UN Convention on the Rights of the Child, child marriage is still practiced in many countries. **Child marriage** refers to any formal marriage or informal union between a child under the age of 18 and an adult or another child.
>
> Child marriage is more prevalent in the poorest regions in the world such as Sub-Saharan Africa and parts of South Asia. Countries with low GDPs tend to have a higher prevalence of child marriage. Niger is one of the poorest countries in the world. According to The World Bank, Niger has a poverty rate of 42.9 percent. In 2021, the UN rated Niger as the least developed country in the world. This situation is made worse by insecurity, hunger, a harsh natural environment and frequent droughts. Poverty in Niger mostly affects women, with girls and women representing around 75 percent of people living below the poverty line.
>
> In Niger, child marriage is driven by factors such as gender inequality and gender violence, displacement, education, customs and religion. Yet, poverty is at the core of this practice. Families marry daughters (or sons) to wealthier older men (or women), in the hope of improving their own economic and social situation. When marrying off a daughter, families receive a payment (bride price). In some cases, families marry children off to settle debts.
>
> In Niger, the minimum legal age for marriage is 15 for girls and 18 for boys. The United Nations Children's Fund (UNICEF) estimates that 76 percent of girls are married in Niger before the age of 18 and 28 percent are married before the age of 15. In the case of boys, 6 percent are married before the age of 18. Girls are likely to be pregnant or to have at least one child by the time they are 17.
>
> Globally, child marriage most often occurs among populations with the lowest educational levels. In Niger, approximately 81 percent of women aged 20–24 with no education, and 63 percent with primary education, are married by the age of 19, compared to 17 percent who have secondary or higher education. When girls are forced to marry, they drop out of school because they become pregnant or because they must focus on their role as wives. Lower levels of education are more commonly found in rural areas, and instances of child marriage are higher in these areas. Around 84.6 percent of women aged 20–24 living in rural areas are married by 18, compared to 43.5 percent in urban areas.[11]
>
> Child marriage causes harm to already vulnerable communities. It leaves many girls vulnerable to violence, and far from schools, jobs and life opportunities. They are also vulnerable to multiple health risks, abuse, exploitation and further poverty.[12]

Governments can contribute to the increasing number of people living in poverty when they prioritize efficiency, by using technology and automation, without considering the impact on people's access to a job. In some cases, they fail to invest in social protection programs that ensure people's economic security when a crisis

HL extension

strikes. In Cambodia, many low-wage workers who lost their jobs due to the COVID-19 pandemic turned to microloans (small amounts of money borrowed that must be paid back with interest in a set period of time) to pay for essential services. Many microloan providers pressured people into selling their land and housing when they could not pay back their loans. The government of Cambodia failed to protect these people.

Microfinance is a tool often used to alleviate poverty. Its intention is to provide credit, through governmental or private agencies, to the marginalized and poor in order to improve their socio-economic well-being and reduce poverty. Microfinance allows people to receive immediate funds to satisfy their basic needs, or even to start a new business that can provide them with a steady income. These loans should come with reasonable terms and conditions regarding interest rates and payback programs, to avoid poor people from acquiring an even bigger debt.

However, several studies have shown that microfinance is not the solution it seems to be. Reasons why it can fail to alleviate poverty include the following:

- Loans are often used to cover short-term needs, eliminating the possibility of that money transforming into long-term economic growth.
- Microfinance can create dependence that results in debt.
- Loans tend to rely on high interest rates in order to meet operating costs. This is because sustaining microcredit can be more expensive than commercial bank loans.
- Microfinance promotes economic inefficiency. New businesses created with the acquired loan exist within limited local markets. This can damage existing businesses and competition, and the business can fail due to low consumer demand.
- Microfinance can exploit those they are supposed to help. Studies have shown that exploitative tactics (including extortion) are frequently used to ensure debts are paid back.[13]

For microfinance and other financial aid to provide solutions to poverty, financial education and awareness need to exist. Education provides knowledge and skills that can be used to improve living conditions. It can empower individuals to change their economic situation, while also improving their communities. When a population is deprived of quality education due to their poverty status, values, structures and institutions need to be changed to ensure no one is left behind.

Microloans, donations and humanitarian assistance are seen as tools to help the poor. However, these are short-term solutions.

Exercises

1. Suggest indicators that could contribute to more accurate measurements of poverty inside a country.
2. Evaluate if it is useful to set a global poverty line. Why yes or why no?
3. Discuss how microfinance can be transformed to become more than a short-term solution, which people can use for long-term sustainable improvements in their quality of life.
4. It is often believed that, if governments provide public assistance to people in poverty, they will become accustomed to governmental support and not have the motivation to work. Discuss if you think this is true, and if so, how can this problem be addressed?

Global political challenges

Summary

In this section, you have learned:

- Poverty not only refers to a lack of material means to meet basic needs. Poverty is living with insecurity about the future, and it is a human security problem.
- Poverty is multidimensional; it affects a person's enjoyment of their human rights and hinders their ability to develop.
- Measuring poverty is widely contested. One option is to consider only economic and financial means and establish a poverty line, which is used to define absolute and relative poverty.
- The extreme poverty line is the international standard for measuring poverty (absolute poverty) with a threshold equivalent to $2.15 USD per person per day. However, poverty is multidimensional and depends on the context of a person (relative poverty).
- Different measurements of poverty include a variety of education, health and infrastructure indicators, such as the Multidimensional Poverty Index.
- Specific circumstances, consumption patterns, the respect for human rights, armed conflict, and inequalities vary among countries. These influence measurements of poverty, as well as the way governments address this issue.
- People living in poverty are the most vulnerable in society. As well as poverty, they also face lower and inadequate access to services like healthcare and education, and face a lack of social mobility.
- The vulnerabilities and inequalities faced by people living in poverty create a poverty trap from which it is almost impossible to escape because cultural, systemic and institutional conditions do not allow it.
- Measures to alleviate poverty, such as microloans, donations and humanitarian assistance must be designed to provide sustainable solutions, and they need to be accompanied by financial education and awareness.

Technology

Learning outcomes

In this section, you will learn about:
- how technology has brought advancements for humans, but has also brought about important legal and security challenges
- communication and information technologies have eliminated traditional borders
- technology has enabled and accelerated globalization, creating wealth and global development, but the benefits are unequally distributed
- development of, access to and use of technologies are not equal across or within countries, and poorer societies do not have equal access to technology and its benefits that the rest of the population enjoys
- technology has contributed to greener environmental solutions, but technological advancement also has environmental impacts

HL extension

- the field of health has experienced some of the greatest technological advancements, but these can come with ethical implications
- self-esteem, self-image, and individual and collective identities have been transformed by the Internet and social media.

Conceptual question

What is technology and what role does it play in global politics?

Technology has brought amazing advancements for humans. Technological advancements in communications, transportation, information dissemination, health, energy and entertainment have improved and brought benefits to our daily lives. Globalization is the result of these technological advancements. Today's global arena would not be what it is without technology, including its positive and negative aspects.

Technology refers to the application of scientific knowledge to the practical aims of human life. It allows us to change and manipulate our environment, often for the common good. Its purpose is to meet a human need or solve a human problem. Today, technology can help us find faster, cheaper and more efficient solutions to problems such as the need for affordable housing, green sources of energy, information, and medicines and vaccines.

Technological innovation has boosted human well-being. In the last 70 years, it has given humans the ability to live relatively comfortably within society. Some of the benefits of technological innovation include:

- quick access to information
- facilitated learning
- simplification of tasks
- breaking of distance barriers
- increased productivity and efficiency
- increased life expectancy
- creation of new jobs
- provision of entertainment
- greener solutions to the need for energy
- ability to explore the unknown (outer space).

Technology offers many advantages, but it also comes with disadvantages. It can:

- create addiction
- come with ethical dilemmas
- dehumanize societies
- damage the environment
- reduce our privacy and, sometimes, our security.

It is essential that we use technology wisely and responsibly, and make sure that its benefits are enjoyed everywhere. However, technological research and development are not equal among countries. This is known as the **technology gap**. Many countries, even industrialized ones, are dependent on technology leaders (such as Japan and the PRC for communication technologies, South Korea for medical technologies, and

> When studying technology in global politics, it is important to consider what all technological advancements mean at the individual, societal and global levels.

> Technology is the application of scientific knowledge to the practical aims of human life.

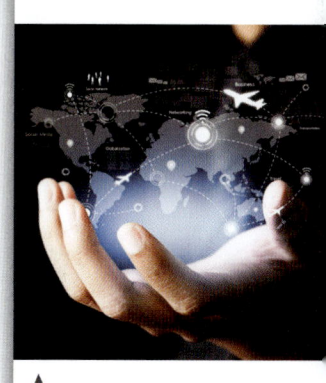

Communication and transportation advances in technology have contributed to globalization, connecting countries, societies and individuals.

Global political challenges

the USA for scientific advances), contributing very little themselves to technological advancement. This is even more true in the case of developing countries, which lack the resources, knowledge and infrastructure to participate in the development of technology. In areas like new energy sources, biotechnology or genetic engineering, the gaps in technological capability are especially large.

> **Activity**
>
> To what extent is it true that the biggest economies are the most competitive when it comes to technological development? To what extent have these economies and their technological advancements contributed to development? Discuss with your classmates.

As a consequence of these gaps, several problems appear. First is the increasing dependency of many countries on a few other countries to access technology that can boost economic growth and bring about development. Second, in order to have access to necessary technology, countries have to spend enormous amounts of money to acquire it, which generates big debts. Alternatively, they may have to settle for older and outdated technology, which is more affordable but means that they continue to lag behind the most technologically advanced countries.

Technologically dependent countries often have to rely on their membership of cooperative regional associations or similar groupings to obtain technological benefits second-hand. While these dependent countries may have access to the technology, many of them lack the knowledge and skills necessary to use it.

> **Activity**
>
> Research the technological innovation and competitiveness of the country you live in. Is your country a leader in technological innovations, or does it depend on other countries? In what areas is it stronger and weaker? In what areas does it depend on others? Write down the impacts this has on your country's power at the regional and global level.

Being behind in technological development can result in:

- lack of research and development funding
- lack of infrastructure
- companies doing the development being too small, or not protected or adequately assisted by their governments
- financial returns on research and development being low, causing a low demand for innovation, which reduces the incentive to innovate
- weak technical infrastructure
- inadequate networks between universities and industries
- regulatory costs for new inventions, which may discourage innovation.

Least economically developed countries (LEDCs) are at the bottom of the scale when it comes to technological innovation and effective usage. These countries tend to be dependent on others, and breaking this dependency is challenging. The UN Conference

HL extension

on Trade and Development's Commodities and Development Report 2021 showed 'over 75% of African LEDCs depend on commodity production for over half of their export earnings.'[14] Producing and exporting high-value sophisticated technologies generates much more income than primary or semi-processed goods, but most LEDCs can only produce and export primary goods.

Infrastructure such as electricity, reliable and high-speed Internet connectivity, and digital skills are necessary to be able to use technology efficiently. But, only 52.8 percent of LEDCs' populations had access to electricity by 2019, compared to a 90.1 percent global average (although contexts within LEDCs vary greatly).

Gross expenditure on research and development as a percentage of GDP is a good indicator of the commitment of governments to devoting resources to technological innovation. Inequalities are huge. The World Bank data from 2020 showed that Israel spent almost 5 percent of its GDP on research and development, with no LEDC country reaching even 1 percent. Cambodia spent 0.1 percent and Uganda spent 0.2 percent. The LEDCs that spent the most were Burkina Faso and Rwanda with 0.7 percent.[15] Even some industrialized countries demonstrated little investment in technological innovation, such as Chile (0.4 percent), Lithuania (0.9 percent) and Canada (1.5 percent). Instead, these countries choose to depend on other countries' efforts.

Information and communication technology (ICT)

One of the most evident changes that technology has brought revolves around communication and the dissemination of information. The fact that you are reading this book (especially if you are reading the electronic version) is the result of faster and more efficient communication methods that allowed for the information and data to be gathered and presented to you. As IB students, you are expected to become communicators, by listening carefully to each other and engaging in respectful dialogue, discussion and debate, for which technology is essential. Advancements in communication allows societies to exchange information, ideas and knowledge, and to share experiences, values and ideologies.

Technology includes any digital tool we can use for practical purposes, such as sending and receiving information, moving around, producing something, etc. This can include computer programs, software, technological devices and messaging systems. The Internet and social media have revolutionized the way people connect and communicate. We can exchange messages with someone on the other side of the world, learn about their culture, share ideas, get to know each other, and organize and mobilize across national borders in seconds. To think about a world without the Internet or cell phones is very hard (although, this is still a reality for many people around the world).

There is a global consensus that information and communication technologies, particularly the Internet, have reshaped our lives and the ways we interact with other individuals, societies and states. They have provided huge opportunities for economic, political and social development. In 1995, during the World Summit for Social Development, it was recognized that global access to 'education, information, technology and know-how is an essential means for enhancing communication and participation in civil, political, economic, social and cultural life, and for ensuring respect for civil, political, economic, social and cultural rights.'[16]

In rural Africa, electricity is generated using the sun's energy and solar panels to reduce greenhouse gas emissions.

Gross national expenditure refers to the sum of household final consumption expenditure, general government final consumption expenditure and gross capital formation (also called gross domestic investment).

HL Technology has been at the core of globalization and the disappearance of *Borders*. While political and natural borders still exist, technology has overcome those obstacles to create an interconnected world without boundaries.

Global political challenges

Figure 5.6 Between 1960 and 2020, the adoption of communication technologies has increased worldwide. The largest increase has been in cell phone subscriptions, followed by Internet users. Landline phone subscriptions have decreased.

- Mobile phone subscriptions
- Internet users
- Landline internet subscriptions
- Landline phone subscriptions

Technologies have contributed to human rights in contested ways. Technology has brought advancements and benefits that have contributed to millions of people being able to access basic services faster and at a cheaper cost (for example, healthcare and education). This has helped many societies to enjoy the tools of technology for development. However, certain technologies have hindered human liberties and civil rights, especially concerning privacy. Everything we do online leaves a trace, reducing our privacy. Governments can use technology to conduct surveillance on us, people and information may be censored, or activists can suffer from online harassment.

Indian rural farmer using a laptop.

The digital divide refers to the gap between demographics and regions in terms of access to modern information and ICT.

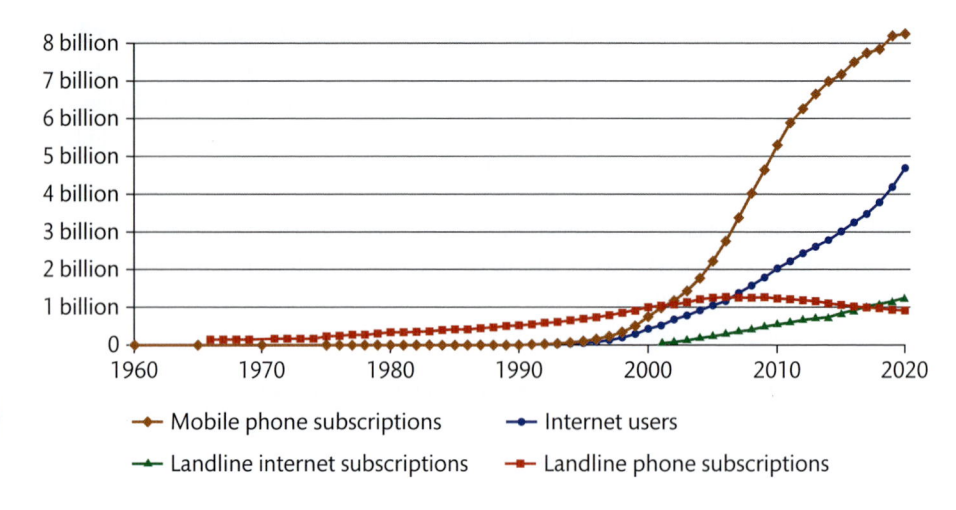

The idea of having global access to technology as a means for enhancing development and the enjoyment of human rights has received wider global acceptance. ICT is seen as a key to eradicating poverty, and building people-centered, inclusive and development-oriented societies. The goal is to live in a world where everyone can create, access, use and share information and knowledge. This would enable individuals and societies to achieve their full potential, improve their quality of life and promote sustainable development.

Governments now rely heavily on ICT to share information with their citizens. Improved access to these technologies bridges the **digital divide** (the technology gap concerning digital technologies), and also improves communication between governmental authorities and citizens, and promotes more informed and organized societies. Figures from 2022 showed that 5.3 billion people (out of a total of 8 billion) used the Internet, while three quarters of people aged 10 and over owned a cell phone. Younger people also represented the most connected, with 75 percent of 15–24-year-olds online, compared to 65 percent of the rest of the population.[17] These numbers show, first, that the number of people having access to the Internet and using cell phones is increasing. Second, that younger generations are the most connected, so it makes sense for governments to use ICT to appeal to their public and to reach their audience. However, relying on modern ICT to establish communication between authorities and citizens leaves out an important portion of the population (older generations and communities living in poverty.) that still relies on more traditional means of communication.

Unfortunately, access to this technology is still unequally distributed within and between countries. The digital divide refers to the gap between demographics and regions that have access to modern ICT, and those that do not have access, or have restricted access.

This technology gap typically exists between urban and rural areas, the educated and less well educated, between socio-economic groups, and between more and less industrialized countries. It does not only refer to the total absence of ICT. It can also be demonstrated by factors such as the use of lower-performance computers, lower-speed Internet connections and higher-priced Internet services.

A 2019 report showed that one million rural American households did not have access to broadband Internet. That same year, Venezuela, Paraguay, Egypt, Yemen and

HL extension

Gabon had some of the lowest digital access speeds.[18] The Organization for Economic Cooperation and Development's (OECD) data from 2022 showed that in South Korea, 100 percent of households had Internet access, followed by Norway with 99 percent and the Netherlands with 98.3 percent. In Colombia, only 60 percent had access by 2021.[19] That same year, the whole African continent had an Internet penetration rate of 43.1 percent compared to a global 66.2 percent.[20]

The digital divide can be caused by the following:

- Usage gap: This is the lack of digital skills to use ICT on a personal and professional level.
- Access gap: Certain groups are unable to access ICT due to socio-economic inequalities, lack of funding to implement the necessary infrastructure to use them or lack of economic means to afford the technologies (devices and services).
- Generation gap: Data suggest that people aged 65 and over have fewer digital skills. This gap widens among people with lower purchasing power and those living in rural areas.
- Digital gender gap: Women still face reduced access to ICT (one of the reasons why fewer girls choose Science, Technology, Engineering and Mathematics (STEM) careers). Worldwide, 62 percent of men use the Internet compared to 57 percent of women, with some countries where gender inequality persists facing bigger divides.

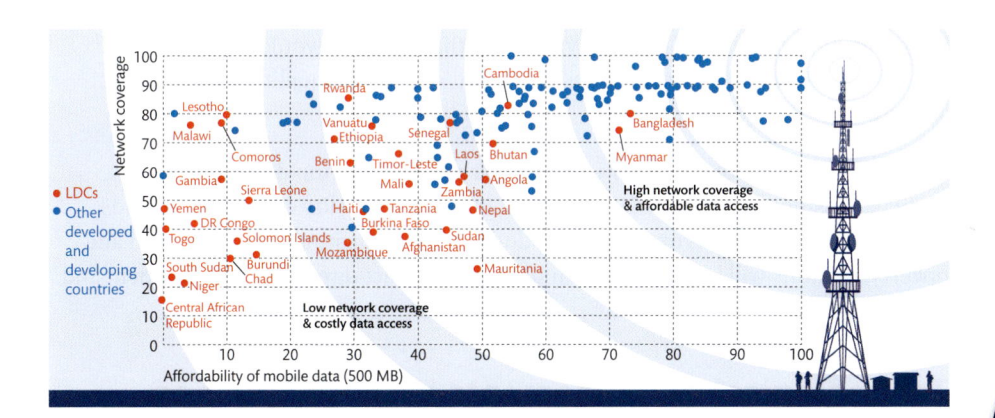

To find more figures and data on Internet access and ICT usage among OECD countries, you can visit:

Figure 5.7 LEDCs suffer a digital divide in mobile connectivity. According to the UN Conference on Trade and Development, network coverage is much lower in LEDCs than in the rest of the world, and their mobile data usage is also significantly more expensive.

HL Access to ICT and other types of technology is still not equal as a result of *Poverty* and inequalities.

The lack of equal access to ICT increases other inequalities because different population groups are excluded from the benefits of technology. During the lockdowns resulting from the COVID-19 pandemic, children were forced to continue their education online, but millions of children did not have an Internet connection or the appropriate devices to work online. This same problem was faced by adults who were forced to work from home. People who live in rural communities lack easy access to medical technologies that can help cure, or even prevent, diseases, which raises death rates for treatable and preventable diseases or conditions (measles, malaria, pre-eclampsia in pregnant women, etc.) in those areas.

Activity

Research how many children dropped out of school in your local area during the COVID-19 lockdown period. What were the main reasons behind this? Compare your results with a classmate and discuss the differences or similarities found.

Global political challenges

Some consequences of the digital divide are included in Table 5.3.

Table 5.3 Consequences of the digital divide[21]

Consequences of the digital divide	
Isolation	People living in rural areas or in poverty are virtually cut off from communication services and experience social isolation.
Difficulty in accessing education	Children and adults may face difficulties when accessing or continuing their education without access to ICT.
Difficulty in accessing work	People face greater challenges in finding a job because digital knowledge is necessary and because many job opportunities are only offered online.
Social differences	Unequal access to the digital world increases other types of differences between groups.
Geographical differences	Differences are intensified between regions and countries and directly affect possibilities for growth.
Dependence and vulnerability	Some people remain dependent on older, costly and slower processes to fulfill certain tasks. The lack of access and knowledge of ICT makes them more vulnerable to digital crimes.

Supporters of bridging the digital divide argue that doing so would improve digital literacy, digital skills democracy, social mobility, economic equality and economic growth.

Consider the contribution of ICT to education and information dissemination, particularly since the COVID-19 pandemic. If access to quality education depends on access to ICT then it is expected that, due to marginalization, discrimination and poverty, millions will be left behind, and this will impact directly on development and economic growth.

Technological advancements in global politics

Technology has transformed the way individuals interact, and it has also transformed the way political actors interact. Technological advances have given rise to new forms of power and influence. In today's technological world, a new geopolitical panorama is taking shape. Digital technologies, AI, 5G and blockchain are becoming important for global cooperation and rivalry.

Why are countries such as the USA and the PRC so invested in the development of technologies? Perhaps the most important reason is the value of these technologies. The World Economic Forum has projected that 5G will generate $13 trillion USD in global economic value and 22 million jobs by 2035. AI is projected to add over $15 trillion USD to the global economy by 2030. This does not necessarily mean that technology is a source of rivalry between countries. Technology partnerships are growing across the globe with countries bringing together knowledge, research, workforces, finance and other factors in cross-border coordination. An example of this is the deal between Gulf-Israel Green Ventures (GIGV) and the United Arab Emirates' (UAE) United Stars Group that allows the exchange of Israeli green technologies in the Gulf region, while introducing Emirate technologies in Israel.

TOK
How might technology exacerbate or mitigate divides in our access, to knowledge?

HL
Health is one of the fields in which advances in technology have had the greatest effect. For example, technological advances in the pharmaceutical industry, the development of medical devices, IT systems, algorithms, artificial intelligence (AI), cloud and blockchain (a record that facilitates the process of recording transactions and tracking assets in a business network), the development of surgical and medical robots, brain computer interfaces, genetic testing and modification, and the use of 3D printing.

HL
Technology has become a source of *Power* in modern times. Strong and influential states in the global arena are no longer those that rely on economic and military power exclusively, but also those who develop and have access to data, information, knowledge and advanced technologies. Those technologies strengthen economic and military power (hard power).

HL extension

There are five Big Tech companies (also known as the 'Big 5') that lead the information technology industry globally: Google, Amazon, Apple, Meta and Microsoft.

Many technologies are increasingly being nationalized and weaponized, to be used as tools of power and influence. Power now depends on access to and control of data and knowledge, and access to the most advanced technologies. Such control and access strengthens economies, military capabilities, education, production, infrastructures, etc. The control of data and information in such a digitalized world is now an important geopolitical tool. The PRC's Digital Silk Road (DSR), part of its Belt and Road Initiative (BRI), allows the PRC to provide aid, political support and other assistance to other states. The DSR also provides support to Chinese exporters.

Many technologies are still in need of global norms and protocols for their development, usage, access, etc. Countries can still exploit many of these gaps for their own interests (which can be detrimental to global security). Communication technologies are mostly provided by Big Tech companies. These companies are barely accountable to the states they work in (for example, Facebook and the US Congress have clashed over social media privacy, and the use and abuse of data).

Activity

Discuss with your classmates to what extent you believe governments use Big Tech companies for their own interests. Research an example of a Big Tech company and its relations with a specific government.

The problem is not technology itself, but who controls it and how it is used. This will define how technology is shared and under what conditions, and what the interests behind the decision of sharing this technology are. As more advanced technologies appear, suspicion among governments might increase, the sense of vulnerability might increase and interstate tensions may heighten. The balance of global economic and political power is shifting and will continue to do so as more technological advances appear, especially with emerging technologies like AI and robotics.

States with advanced scientific medical capabilities were seen as the heroes of the COVID-19 pandemic. However, they also used their power to shape diplomatic relations, and to acquire multimillion dollar contracts and political concessions.

Global political challenges

Cyber capabilities have been and will be used to engage in espionage, challenge national sovereignty, disrupt critical infrastructure and conduct propaganda campaigns.

Case – The 2016 US election

Evidence was found that during the US Presidential campaigns of 2016, Russia conducted a series of operations in favour of candidate Donald Trump and in order to harm Hillary Clinton's campaign. According to the US intelligence community (IC), these activities were ordered directly by Russian president Vladimir Putin. Numerous contacts between Russian officials and Trump's campaign were found, as well as the use of fake accounts on social media that spread fabricated articles and disinformation in support of Trump and against Clinton. According to the IC, Russian military intelligence also infiltrated information systems of the Democratic National Committee, the Democratic Congressional Campaign Committee and Clinton's campaign officials, stealing files and emails.[22]

As Samir Saran, President of the Observer Research Foundation, mentions, an almost impossible dilemma will emerge, presenting national and global concerns.[23]

Governments are not the only powerful actors in the technological arena anymore. Many powerful actors are big multinational corporations (MNCs) and individuals (such as Elon Musk). This will continue to have profound effects on geopolitical trends. The impact of technologies at the individual level, in areas such as human rights and equality, will become an increasing dilemma.

Figure 5.8 According to Saran, a growing dilemma with technology will be how to find sustained economic growth with its usage, while respecting and fostering individual rights, without increasing insecurity.

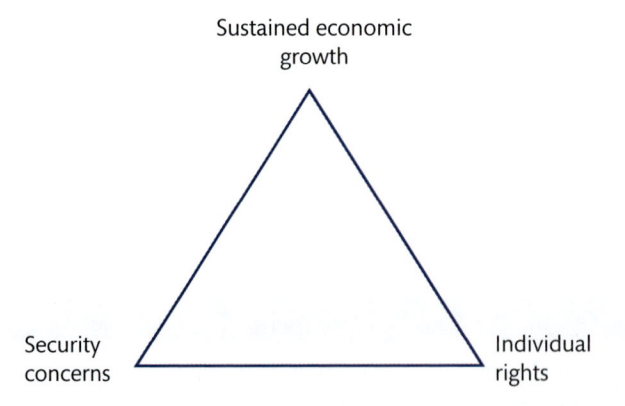

(Triangle diagram: Sustained economic growth — Security concerns — Individual rights)

Data is one of the most valuable assets today. Whoever owns data has influence on public and private entities, human rights, group action and even social cohesion. Yet, technologies put at risk data and information from governments, companies and individuals.

> Data is not just an issue of individual vs big business vs country sovereignty. It is an issue of community and the common good. Many types of valuable data are easily obtained, transported and used to influence large groups of the population. As a result, only global and regional institutions and agreements can ensure equity for all.[24]

Global technological competition is very likely to continue increasing, and it will extend to different fields, such as space exploration, education, infrastructure, green energies and health. This does not need to be a matter of conflict. However, it may be. Technologies are advancing at a very fast pace, but global efforts to agree upon the necessary regulations, norms and legislations that technologies need regarding their creation, use, management and spread require long and strenuous debates and discussions. Technology moves faster than us, leaving important legal vacuums.

Technological advancements, privacy and security

Technological innovations were thought to bring about progress in democratic politics. But the opposite is also happening. Democracies struggle with finding the right balance between economic innovation, financial benefits, protecting user privacy, guarding against surveillance misuse and counter disinformation. Many of these advancements are also enabling authoritarian governments to manipulate information, monitor dissent, track political opponents and censor communications.

During the COVID-19 crisis, several governments used the opportunity to introduce or strengthen restrictive measures that prohibited public gatherings, censored online speech and reduced user privacy. In Singapore (among other countries) people had to scan QR codes that logged their entry into restaurants, malls, shops and even office buildings. There were also Bluetooth apps that traced close contact with any other person. While for many citizens, this was relatively normal, the government of Singapore used the opportunity to propose and introduce other restrictive measures.

By March 2021, the Singapore government had installed 90,000 police cameras across the country as tools to investigate and solve crimes. The use of facial scanners and biometric identifiers is the main tool for immigration clearance. However, facial recognition and verification is being used more and more by the government for things like paying taxes. In 2020, a parliamentarian called for the use of technology to monitor and enforce bans on smoking even out of the windows and on the balconies of people's homes. The argument was that this would help deal with the harm of second-hand smoke.[25]

Some technologies legitimately attempt to solve a security problem, fight crime or control a pandemic. The problem is that many lack the basic regulations to protect citizens' privacy. It is always uncertain when governments will retract those extreme measures (if ever), what is done with the data obtained, who gets access to it and for what purposes.

Western influence on technology is slowly decreasing compared to that of emerging competitors. We are now seeing several different Internets[26], governed by different norms and rules, that answer to different political interests. As long as norms and standards on technology continue to differ across political systems, the potential for conflict will be present.

Technological competition is very likely to increase, which might increase competition in many other areas. The security dilemma posed by technological advances (on people, companies or whole countries) and whether it should be solved at a national and contextual level or globally will continue to be debated. However it is solved, who will set the rules?

It is also important to keep in mind that Big Tech has its own interests (mainly economic), and in some cases these also serve someone else's bigger interests (such as governmental interests). The problem is not only how governments will compete and use these technologies and our data, but also what corporations will do with our data, and how far they are willing to go to increase their own monetary value.

Facial recognition on CCTV camera surveillance.

In May 2021, the government of India attacked Twitter after the social network put a 'manipulated media' tag on a tweet by an official of Prime Minister Narendra Modi's party. After this, a special unit of the Delhi police raided Twitter's offices. The Nigerian government suspended Twitter altogether after the platform removed a tweet by Nigerian President Muhammady Buhari because the message was considered by Twitter to violate their community guidelines.

As anti-government protests swept Iran in late 2022 and early 2023, the government retaliated with violence and also with digital repression. Cell phone and Internet users across the country reported network blackouts and app restrictions, among other disruptions.

Global political challenges

The impact of technologies on societies

For individuals and communities, ICT has brought about important changes in how they connect and organize themselves. Human interaction has suffered from dehumanization, fostering social isolation. It is common to see groups of people, families or friends staring down at their screens instead of interacting face-to-face. Whether this happens at school, during dinner time or parties with friends, the dependency on and addiction we have to technology has transformed our social interactions.

Many students use the Internet or social media to find information to work on assignments instead of asking a teacher or using the school's library. Many people inform themselves about events around the world (sports, weather, politics, the economy) from social media instead of accessing a trustworthy newspaper. Millions of people now trust social media more than their own governments.

Studies have shown that excessive use of cell phones and social media:

- increases social isolation and psychological maladaptation
- decreases self-esteem
- distorts self-image
- contributes to poor academic performance
- causes poor sleep
- exacerbates social conflict.

Checking and scrolling through social media has become an addiction for many people. Psychologists in the USA consider that around 10 percent of Americans suffer from social media addiction[27], which is a behavioral addiction characterized by being overly concerned about social media, having an uncontrollable urge to use it and devoting so much time to it that it impairs other aspects of life.

This is explained by the dopamine-inducing features of social media. These features are associated with positive affirmations that contribute to addiction, such as likes, followers, shares and retweets, and train us to repeat the behavior. Children and adolescents are more susceptible to developing this addiction because their brains are still developing.

TOK
How does technology extend or transform different modes of human cognition and communication?

Dr Anna Lembke, an addiction expert, wrote *Dopamine Nation*[28], in which she explains how social media has generated a behavioral addiction caused by dopamine, a chemical hormone (also known as the feel-good hormone) that translates into pleasure. Dopamine makes us seek more and more for that thing that makes us feel good, but as Dr Lembke warns, with every high comes a low.

HL extension

Such addiction is a problem that must be addressed. But, individuals and communities also have access to new tools for power. Social media and the Internet have led to new forms of political and social activism. Politicians, civil organizations and individuals have benefited from tools that allow them to spread their message, faster, to a wider audience, and often with the advantage of anonymity, to influence masses of people for different purposes. Movements like #MeToo, #BlackLivesMatter, #FridaysForFuture or #OccupyWallStreet would not have had the impact they did without technology.

Online platforms provide global access to organizations and movements that have managed to increase their visibility and impact through digital sharing and networking. Technology has given voice to many that otherwise would not have been heard.

> As a non-state actor (NSA), the role of the media in this globalized world is increasingly important. The use of modern ICT, social media and the Internet have evolved from sources of information to sources of knowledge, movement, engagement, inspiration and political influence at the local, regional and global levels.

Case – The Arab Spring

In the early 2010s, a series of anti-government movements, protests and uprisings spread across North Africa and the Middle East. What could have been seen as a random act by a young Tunisian caused massive social changes, removed decades-long dictatorships from power, and globally demonstrated the power of social action with the help of the Internet.

Mohamed Bouazizi, a young man who sold vegetables from a barrow to support his widowed mother, died after setting himself on fire outside a government building in protest of police harassment, corruption and economic stagnation. His gesture went viral, causing widespread protests across Tunisia that eventually spread through an entire region. The impact of the Arab Spring cannot be attributed exclusively to social media, but social media played a crucial role.

Bouazizi's action and the subsequent social protests cost Tunisia's authoritarian President Zine El Abidine Ben Ali's his legitimacy and, in the end, his power. Ben Ali had ruled the country for 23 years until he was forced to flee to Saudi Arabia, becoming the first leader of an Arab country to be pushed out by popular protests. Tunisia's example, widely documented and shared by mobile devices, inspired a wave of revolts against authoritarianism, corruption and poverty from Morocco to Syria.

Crowds at Freedom Square in the Yemeni city of Taiz in the Arab spring.

By January 2011, millions of Egyptians took to the streets in several cities demanding President Hosni Mubarak, who had ruled Egypt for 30 years, to step down. Mubarak had no choice but to resign and hand control to the military. The country elected Mohammed Morsi from the Muslim Brotherhood to rule Egypt, although he was later overthrown by now President Abdel Fattah el-Sisi.

Global political challenges

On February 15, 2012, Bahrain saw protesters take over Pearl Square in the capital city, demanding a constitutional monarchy among other reforms, and the release of political prisoners. That same day, the Libyan police were dealing with similar issues. Governmental force was used against protesters, turning Libya's case into a civil war in which French, British and American forces intervened until the former leader, Muammar Gaddafi, was captured and killed by rebels. A year later, Ali Abdullah Saleh, who had ruled Yemen for 22 years, also handed power to his deputy, Abdrabuh Mansur Hadi, after a year of protests. In Kuwait, the parliament was dissolved in response to public pressure.

In some cases, these revolutions worked against authoritarian regimes. However, government repression and foreign interference pushed several countries further into civil war, from which some have not recovered, for example, Syria.

The Arab Spring has often been referred to as the Facebook revolutions or Twitter revolutions. One thing was clear: nowadays, revolutions will be posted, tweeted, blogged, texted and organized online. One of the characteristics of the Arab Spring was the number of young protesters using social media to organize, raise awareness and document their experiences.

An analysis of more than three million tweets, gigabytes of YouTube content and thousands of blog posts found that social media played a major role in the Arab Spring and the political debates it triggered. The results of the project, led by associate professor in communication at the University of Washington, Philip Howard, stated:

> Our evidence suggests that social media carried a cascade of messages about freedom and democracy… and helped raise expectations for the success of political uprising… People who shared interest in democracy built extensive social networks and organized political action. Social media became a critical part of the toolkit for greater freedom.[29]

The week before Mubarak resigned in Egypt, tweets from Egypt and across the world about political change in the country went from 2300 to 230,000 per day. Videos featuring protests, political commentary and online content from opposition groups also increased. In the case of Tunisia, the day before Ben Ali's resignation, 20 percent of blogs were focused on debating his leadership, compared to just 5 percent the previous month. The primary topic in Tunisian blogs was revolution.

Anti-government protesters with banners and flags during protests in Tahrir Square, Cairo, Egypt (2011).

HL extension

Online discussions and content crossed borders. Two weeks before Mubarak's resignation, there were on average 2400 tweets a day about the political situation in Egypt from people in neighboring countries. In Tunisia, there were about 2200 tweets every day after Ben Ali left the country. This shows how social media drew people throughout the region into a wider conversation on social uprisings.

Neither the successes nor the failures of the Arab Spring can be attributed to social media, but social media had an important impact on the capacity of citizens to affect domestic and international politics. Even when governments tried to crack down on social media, this only incited more protests. Societies that were fragmented used the Internet to find shared points of interests and shared goals and to build solidarity.

Internationally, social media helped spread the ideals of the Arab Spring to the outside world, showing that millions of people in the Muslim world believe in and desire democratic governance and free expression. As journalist Jamal Khashoggi expressed, 'The debate about the relationship between Islam and democracy conclusively ended with the coming of the Arab Spring.'[30]

> Jamal Khashoggi was a Saudi journalist and dissident who fled his country because of political persecution. While living in Türkiye, he was murdered inside the Saudi consulate in Istanbul in 2018.

The use of social media in political movements can document violence, help exercise freedom of speech, create spaces for civic engagement and reinforce the relevance of citizen journalism.

The ethical dilemma

Technology has brought incredible advantages for societies. As well as communication and transportation advancements, humans have developed technologies that allow doctors to conduct surgeries with full precision with the use of robots, data has become so digitalized that it can be accessed by different people at different places at the same time, education has been revolutionized using virtual reality, and development has been brought much closer to many people who may otherwise not have access to it.

Technology has also brought legal and ethical dilemmas. Only a few years ago, it seemed like something out of a science-fiction movie to see robots and AI playing major roles in our everyday lives. Yet, this reality is fast approaching. This may not be a problem in itself, but it does pose some ethical questions.

For instance, how far will these new technologies go? Robots and AI are, according to some, advancing too fast. Tech leaders had agreed by the beginning of 2023 that AI development should be slowed down until we learn how to use it properly and understand its dangers. For example, the development of ChatGPT introduced new tools for students, teachers, engineers, lawyers, diplomats and doctors. The software can write entire essays, poems, song lyrics and instructions to perform any task or explain any topic. Educational institutions have begun to wonder whether students are learning and are capable of critical thinking when their papers are made entirely by AI and so are not the students' own work.

This question moved to other fields. The law bar exam in the USA was passed by AI, and so were some other prestigious graduate-level exams (with some errors, but still passed). The Sony World Photography Award was given to (though later turned down by)

> **TOK**
> Is it ethical to use AI to write a school essay, the lyrics of a song or answer a test? What happens with intellectual property? Can we demonstrate individual knowledge and critical thinking when using AI? If so, how? How do the tools that we use shape the knowledge that we produce?

Global political challenges

an artist who admitted to not having taken the winning photograph, but creating it with AI.[31] How can we be sure AI is not creating artificial intelligence that will later be used by doctors, lawyers or civil engineers? How are we going to define art or music? Based on what criteria will a book receive a Nobel Prize in Literature? How will global challenges be addressed without the human touch?

Another question that may arise, particularly regarding robots, is whether these technologies will eventually be able to think for themselves or even have feelings. Nowadays, robots are being used for different purposes, one of these being in hospitals. Their roles range from filtering incoming patients to carrying out some routine tasks done by doctors or nurses, such as measuring and recording vital signs. Another use is to keep patients company, particularly elderly or incapacitated patients. Many argue that the use of robots for these purposes promotes dehumanization by removing all human contact, feelings, connection and touch, and replacing it with algorithms. Robots can help us perform complicated tasks with more precision, and reduce the time it takes us. They can also perform almost any task. Does this mean they will replace humans?

Another area in which there have been great technological advances is genetic testing and modification. We will be able to prevent children from being born with certain diseases. Will we also be able to choose physical traits and characteristics for our children? And, if so, is this ethical? If we can modify our bodies to prevent and cure diseases, will the average life span increase? What will be the social and economic implications of having larger, older populations?

Our whole lives can now be found online. The same way that social media allows people to organize themselves is already used to trace, profile, arrest, imprison and sometimes kill. Companies, individuals and whole states are vulnerable to the dangers lurking on the Internet. And consequences can be fatal.

Several actors have been working on the way technology can be regulated. The United Nations founded the International Telecommunication Union (ITU) with the aim of facilitating international connectivity networks, by allocating global radio spectrum and satellite orbits, as well as by developing technical standards to ensure networks and technologies are available to all communities around the world.[32] Although its work began with the standardization of the use of Morse code and the world's first radiocommunication and fixed telecommunication networks, the ITU continues working via conferences and meetings to ensure technology services are available to everyone, to put in place standards for the operations of ICTs, and to bridge the digital divide.

At a regional level, efforts have been made by the European Union. In 2022, European policymakers approved the Digital Services Act (DSA) along with the Digital Markets Act.[33] The goal of the DSA was to update the EU's legal framework concerning illegal content on intermediaries, transparent advertising and disinformation, by aligning national laws within the EU. The EU aims to create a safer digital space that protects the rights of users, and fosters safe growth, innovation and competitiveness for businesses.

Technology has benefits and drawbacks, and it is up to us to use it for global benefit. If we focus exclusively on economic gains and on our own interests, technology may end up turning against us. Global cooperation is necessary to make its benefits reach everyone equally, but we also need to find global ways of regulating its use.

TOK

How may the relationship between Big Tech companies and governments impact our knowledge in global politics?

HL extension

Exercises

5. Suggest what states and the international community could do to bridge the technology gap and secure more global access to technology.

6. Discuss how we could fight disinformation and fake news on social media.

7. Evaluate whether it is possible to find a balance between security and privacy.

8. To what extent do you think technology will alter the future of work and social relations?

Summary

In this section, you have learned:

- Technology plays a crucial role in globalization and our current global political context.

- Technology has improved the well-being of humans around the world, although its benefits are not enjoyed by everyone equally. There are still big technological gaps across countries and within societies, and this can hinder the development of entire countries, communities and individuals.

- In spite of the great advancements technology has brought, there are negative aspects, such as ethical dilemmas, lack of regulation and legislation on the use of technologies, as well as social and health problems like addiction.

- Access to technology and the capacity to develop it have positioned countries and big multinational corporations as leading competitors, while many other actors still depend on the technologies of others. This hierarchy influences politics and transforms the way power is understood in Global Politics. Least developed countries (LDCs) are at the bottom of the ladder when it comes to technological innovation and effective usage.

- Information and communication technologies (ICTs) have brought societies closer, diluting the traditional concept of borders. However, with this growing interconnectedness, global issues easily become international issues.

- Technology contributes to development and the enjoyment of human rights. However, the access and enjoyment of technologies is still unequal, particularly for those living in poverty and in rural areas. This inequality also persists across genders and ages.

- A major problem with technology is who has control over it, and how. Different actors can develop, share and/or use specific technologies for specific purposes, which may not contribute to a society's well-being but instead can threaten human rights and liberties.

- An increasing dilemma with technologies is, and will continue to be, how to promote sustained economic growth, while protecting human rights and avoiding security concerns.

Global political challenges

- Technology has given a voice to those who previously had no platform to express themselves. It can help organize transnational movements, exert pressure over governments, denounce human rights violations and strengthen entire revolutions (like the Arab Spring). But technology also contributes to the mass spread of misinformation, hate speech and fake news that can destabilize entire societies.

Health

Learning outcomes

In this section, you will learn about:
- how access to healthcare (physical and mental) is essential for development
- destigmatizing mental health has a long way to go, and invisible illnesses are still greatly ignored across the globe
- infectious diseases can cross borders and transform into global pandemics, and securitizing the problem can leave many affected populations at a disadvantage
- medical advances can improve global health, such as maternity healthcare and child life expectancy, but benefits have not reached populations equally
- poverty leaves individuals more vulnerable to health issues, due to lack of adequate nutrition, lack of access to water and sanitation, and issues with access to and affordability of medical services
- identity is a factor for unequal health services around the world and across communities
- environmental degradation, climate change and environmental disasters contribute to the creation and spread of diseases and viruses.

Conceptual question

How do we define 'health' in such a complex and diverse world?

Even though global health has improved in recent decades, this benefit has not reached everyone, everywhere. This is especially true in rural communities and among the most vulnerable and impoverished. Our health and that of those we care about is our greatest concern. Regardless of age, gender, socio-economic background, ethnicity or religion, health is essential. Without good health, we cannot fulfill our duties as parents, students or active members of society.

Health is a fundamental part of our human rights and our capacity to live a life with dignity. Article 25 of the 1948 Universal Declaration of Human Rights (UDHR) refers to health as an essential factor in the right all humans have to an adequate standard of living. The right to health was also recognized as a basic human right in the 1966 International Covenant on Economic, Social and Cultural Rights (Article 12), which recognizes the right to health as essential for:

- gender equality
- health-related education
- healthy working and environmental conditions
- adequate housing.

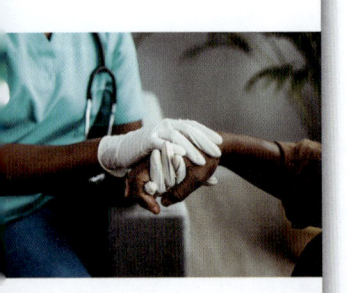

Physical and mental health are recognized as human rights.

HL extension

In 1946, the World Health Organization (WHO) articulated in its Constitution the right to enjoy the highest standard of physical and **mental health** as innate to every human. Health is defined as 'a state of complete physical, mental and social well-being and not merely the absence of disease or infirmity'[34] and extended to mean that this right must be enjoyed without discrimination on the basis of race, religion, political beliefs, economic or social conditions. This means that, even though we tend to think about health in only physical terms, health is a physical, emotional and psychological state of well-being that every person around the world should enjoy. Health services must also be culturally appropriate.

As with any other human right, the right to health depends on and contributes to the realization of other human rights. Think about the right to water (safe access to clean, drinkable water and adequate sanitation). Without this, a person cannot fully enjoy their right to health since clean water is necessary for hygiene. Ingestion of or contact with unsafe water causes water-borne diseases, such as cholera. Or we can think about a child who has no access to basic healthcare services to treat their diabetes, which leaves them vulnerable to other health issues. Health issues do not allow them to enjoy their right to education because they are frequently ill.

Mental health is just as important as our physical health if we wish to live a fulfilling life. Consider the anxiety and psychological stress experiences when the principal earner in a household cannot access a job due to structural discrimination. This can result in anxiety and depression, but also in other physical conditions that can further affect other spheres of their life.

All states are concerned about health, and there have been several international efforts, as well as domestic legislation, oriented toward addressing it. Today, public health is of concern to global politics. The disappearance of borders has led to diseases and epidemics spreading around the globe faster than any country is prepared to deal with. The COVID-19 pandemic showed that even the most technologically advanced, or strongest, healthcare systems did not have enough resources to deal with a pandemic of such scale. We have come to understand that health is closely related to other socio-economic factors, as well as to security, economic growth and development.

SDG 3 addresses the topic of ensuring healthy lives and promoting well-being for all at all ages. According to this SDG, there are 13 targets to cover, including the following:

- Reduce global maternal mortality to less than 70 per 100,000 births.
- End preventable deaths of newborns and children under the age of 5. All countries must aim at reducing neonatal mortality.
- End the epidemics of AIDS, tuberculosis, malaria and neglected tropical diseases, while also combating hepatitis, water-borne and other communicable diseases.
- Reduce premature mortality from non-communicable diseases through prevention and treatment. Mental health and well-being must also be promoted.
- Strengthen campaigns to prevent and treat substance abuse.
- Ensure universal access to sexual and reproductive healthcare services.
- Achieve universal health coverage that includes financial risk protection, the access to quality essential healthcare services, medicines and vaccines (in a safe, effective, qualitative and affordable manner).
- Reduce the number of deaths and illnesses from hazardous chemicals, as well as air, water and soil pollution and contamination.

Health is a state of complete physical, mental and social well-being and not merely the absence of disease or infirmity.

Technology has greatly advanced in the sphere of health, although its benefits are still not enjoyed by everyone. *Poverty* often leaves people marginalized from adequate healthcare services. Inequality can make people more vulnerable to diseases that could be cured or treated if they had access to healthcare. Health can also become a *Security* issue, especially when facing epidemics and pandemics. Climate change and environmental factors can also negatively affect the health of millions of people around the world, contributing to the appearance and spread of diseases.

Global political challenges

Considering the interconnected world in which we live, and the increasing interdependence between countries and societies, strengthening the capacities of all countries is crucial for an improvement in global health.

Such targets must be supported by research and development into the creation of vaccines and medicines, an increase in financial investment into health, and the strengthening of capacities in all countries toward early warning, risk reduction and management of health policies.

Mapping global health

By 2022, the SDG agenda reported several advances, but also several setbacks. COVID-19 was one of the most significant obstacles in attaining the targets. It was estimated that over 6.9 million people died because of the virus as of June 28, 2023, although the real number has been estimated to be three times higher. The pandemic also disrupted health services, shortened life expectancy and worsened inequalities in access to basic health services.

Globally, the under-5 mortality rate fell from 43 to 37 deaths per 1000 live births between 2015 and 2020. Neonatal mortality rates fell from 19 to 17 deaths per 1000 live births in the same period. However, in 2020, five million children died before reaching their fifth birthday.

In terms of reproductive health, Sub-Saharan Africa saw the biggest improvements. In Central and Southern Asia, there was a large reduction in the number of adolescents giving birth. However, in the field of infectious diseases, 2020 saw an increase, with 680,000 deaths occurred due to AIDS-related causes and around 1.5 million new HIV infections. This increase has been explained by the fact that healthcare services focused on battling COVID-19. Around 10 million people contracted tuberculosis the same year, with deaths increasing. Something similar happened with regard to malaria, with cases and deaths also increasing. Africa remained the region most affected by malaria.

The probabilities of dying from any of the main four non-communicable diseases (cardiovascular disease, cancer, chronic respiratory disease or diabetes) between the ages of 30 and 70 declined 2.1 percent from 2010 to 2020. Suicide rates also declined by 29 percent from 2019 to 2020, although the mental health impact of the COVID-19 pandemic is not yet measured in these results. Only anxiety and depression were measured, seeing an increase of 25 percent.

Figure 5.9 shows how low-income and lower middle-income countries suffer more from communicable diseases than upper middle-income and high-income countries. These diseases could be prevented and cured with adequate healthcare. Upper middle-income and high-income countries show increases in non-communicable diseases that can be attributed to specific lifestyles and diets, such as hypertensive heart disease, some types of cancer and diabetes. Wealth can be said to cause harm as well as improve health.

In spite of the improvements in different fields, these improvements will not be enough to achieve the goals set to be achieved by 2030. Unequal access to healthcare is one of the biggest problems in achieving this. The benefits of medical technology and advancements, and access to vaccines and medicines, have not reached everyone equally. Health as a basic right is far from being achieved when considering its close relation to other human rights.

HL extension

Leading causes of death in low-income countries
○ 2000   ● 2019

1. Neonatal conditions
2. Lower respiratory infections
3. Ischaemic heart disease
4. Stroke
5. Diarrhoeal diseases
6. Malaria
7. Road injury
8. Tuberculosis
9. HIV/AIDS
10. Cirrhosis of the liver

Number of deaths (in millions)

Leading causes of death in lower middle-income countries
○ 2000   ● 2019

1. Ischaemic heart disease
2. Stroke
3. Neonatal conditions
4. Chronic obstructive pulmonary disease
5. Lower respiratory infections
6. Diarrhoeal diseases
7. Tuberculosis
8. Cirrhosis of the liver
9. Diabetes mellitus
10. Road injury

Number of deaths (in millions)

● Non-communicable
● Communicable
● Injuries

Leading causes of death in upper middle-income countries
○ 2000   ● 2019

1. Ischaemic heart disease
2. Stroke
3. Chronic obstructive pulmonary disease
4. Trachea, bronchus, lung cancers
5. Lower respiratory infections
6. Diabetes mellitus
7. Hypertensive heart disease
8. Alzheimer's disease and other dementias
9. Stomach cancer
10. Road injury

Number of deaths (in millions)

Leading causes of death in high-income countries
○ 2000   ● 2019

1. Ischaemic heart disease
2. Alzheimer's disease and other dementias
3. Stroke
4. Trachea, bronchus, lung cancers
5. Chronic obstructive pulmonary disease
6. Lower respiratory infections
7. Colon and rectum cancers
8. Kidney diseases
9. Hypertensive heart disease
10. Diabetes mellitus

Number of deaths (in millions)

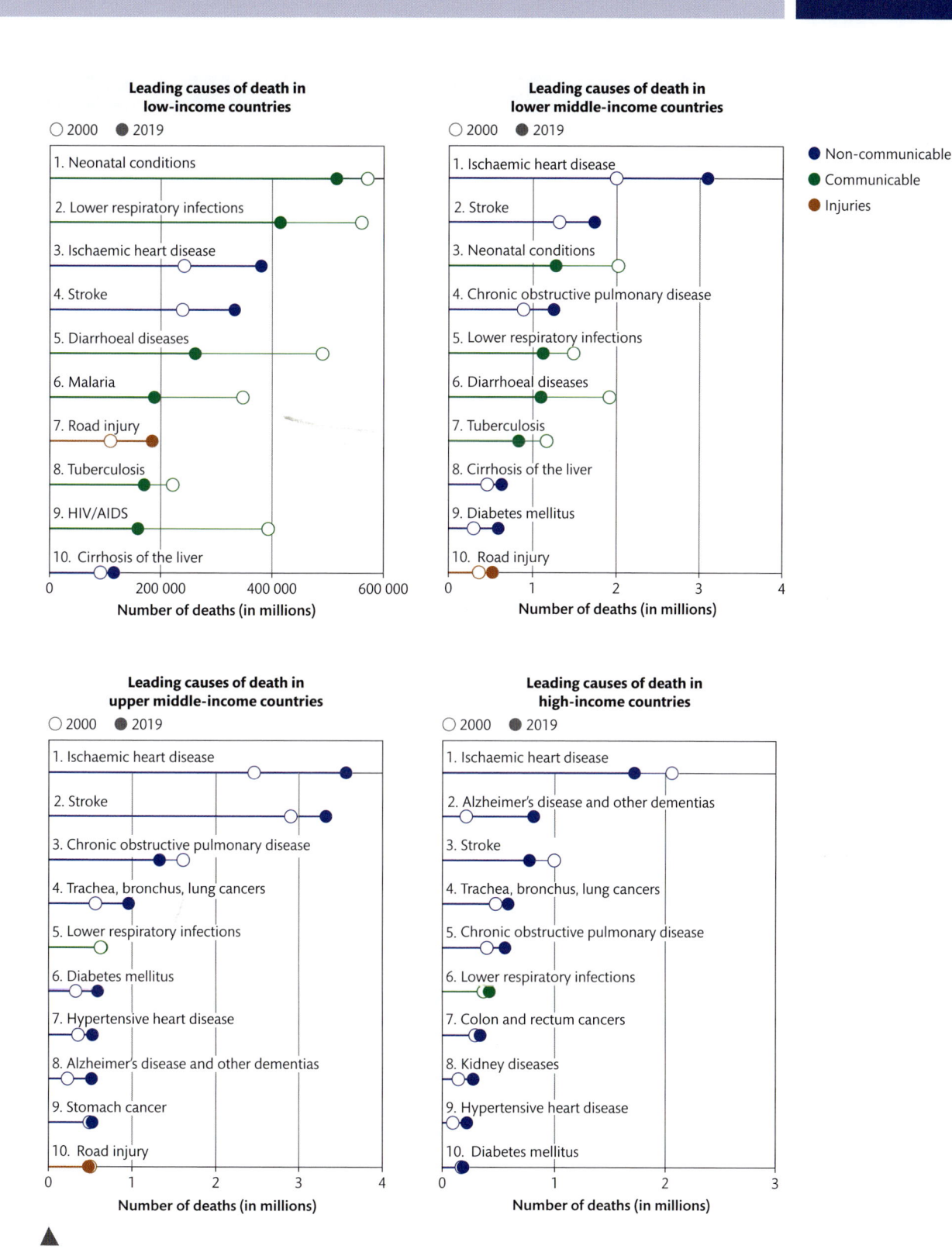

▲
Figure 5.9 The graphs from WHO highlight the top 10 causes of death in four income groups based on gross national income (low, lower middle, upper middle and high). The white circles show the number of deaths in the year 2000, while the other circles (green for communicable diseases, blue for non-communicable diseases, black for injuries) show the number of deaths in 2019.[35]

Global political challenges

> **Activity**
>
> Research the main cause of death in the country you live in. What relationships can you find between the incidence of health issues and other socio-economic challenges (like poverty and inequality)?

The role of global actors

Healthcare services are seen as the responsibility of individual states. However, the UN has a specialized agency responsible for international public health in WHO. With headquarters located in Geneva, Switzerland, WHO has six regional offices and 150 field offices around the world. Established in 1948, WHO is not only a forum for discussion on health issues, but it also works worldwide to promote health and well-being, by monitoring public health risks, advocating that every person around the world should have access to universal healthcare coverage, and coordinating responses to health emergencies. Among its tasks is the provision of technical assistance to countries to achieve international health standards. As with any other UN agency, it relies on the contributions of member states and private donors.

WHO's principles established in its Constitution[36] include the following:

- Health is a state of complete physical, mental and social well-being and not merely the absence of disease or infirmity.
- The enjoyment of the highest attainable standard of health is one of the fundamental rights of every human being without distinction of race, religion, political belief, economic or social condition.
- The health of all peoples is fundamental to the attainment of peace and security and is dependent on the fullest cooperation of individuals and states.
- The achievement of any state in the promotion and protection of health is of value to all.
- Unequal development in different countries in the promotion of health and control of diseases, especially communicable diseases, is a common danger.
- Healthy development of the child is of basic importance; the ability to live harmoniously in a changing total environment is essential to such development.
- The extension to all peoples of the benefits of medical, psychological and related knowledge is essential to the fullest attainment of health.
- Informed opinion and active cooperation on the part of the public are of the utmost importance in the improvement of the health of the people.
- Governments have a responsibility for the health of their peoples that can be fulfilled only by the provision of adequate health and social measures.

WHO measures health using a wide range of indicators, including some of those that are part of SDG 3. It also considers several other indicators, such as:

- nutrition
- healthy workforce
- violence against women
- sexually transmitted infections
- priority health technologies
- assistive technology.

▲ Director-General of WHO, Tedros Adhanom Ghebreyesus. He was appointed on July 1, 2017, and re-appointed on May 24, 2022.

HL extension

WHO recognizes health not only as a human right, but one closely linked to the enjoyment of other human rights such as access to safe drinking water and sanitation, adequate housing, nutritious foods, education and safe working conditions. WHO promotes a people-centered approach to healthcare, believing that outcomes are better and health systems much more efficient when people are active participants in their own care. This means that the individual should have control of their own health and body, and the right to privacy.

An analysis of the role of global treaties, conventions, institutions and other international agreements[37] found that there were 71 identified agreements with a global role in health. Within these, a wide range of diseases were addressed, as well as vulnerable populations and the environment. However, only 34 of these agreements are binding under international law. Less than one-third of them included pandemic preparedness and response (PPR).

The role of governments

States are responsible for providing and satisfying the basic needs of all citizens. They must ensure that the population has access to basic services. These services must be of high enough quality to ensure that humans thrive in dignity and also contribute to the country's development. States must ensure access to health without discrimination, and develop specific legislation and plans of action to ensure the realization of this goal.

In practice, this is not always possible. It is often argued that states do not have the means to afford what is necessary to ensure the right to health or may even delay their obligations as a result of a difficult financial situation. The availability of resources and the development context of a country are important factors. Other issues such as poverty, war, climate change or political instability can constrain the state's capacity to ensure quality health for everyone.

To ensure that the state is fulfilling its obligations, mechanisms of accountability are crucial, whether at national, regional or international level. These mechanisms can be set up by the state, international bodies, non-governmental organizations (NGOs) and human rights organizations. International human rights law cannot prescribe the exact mechanism by which a state must ensure the fulfillment of the right to health (or any other right), making a government entirely responsible. The way the right to health is realized and monitored should be accessible, transparent and effective. If these mechanisms (administrative, political and judicial) exist and function adequately, the population is more likely to enjoy the fulfillment of their rights.

National health policies and strategies, together with participatory budgets and right-based indicators, can help. Some national health services have internal or independent services that offer policymakers assistance in the implementation and monitoring of healthcare. The incorporation of international instruments into domestic laws can strengthen effectiveness.

In 2017, India introduced a new National Health Policy. The previous policies from 1983 and 2002 had served well for several years, but the government recognized a changing context within the country. Its health priorities changed. Previously, they had focused on maternal and child mortality, but, by 2017, battling non-communicable

TOK
Do political leaders and officials have different ethical obligations and responsibilities compared to members of the general public?

!
When writing about national, regional and global policies and strategies regarding health, we need to consider the context. Children need different medical attention than adults, and the same goes for men and women. We also need to demonstrate awareness of any cultural and religious aspects to healthcare. Certain diseases may be eradicated from certain countries, but not from all of them. Diseases can also reappear, and it is important to change strategies to tackle them.

Global political challenges

diseases and other infectious diseases became the priority. A growing healthcare industry and a changing economic environment motivated the government to adopt a new health policy that could respond to contextual changes.

Governments can also rely on the assistance of other actors. The private health sector consists of individuals and profit or non-profit organizations that are neither owned nor controlled directly by governments which can have a domestic or international scope. These include health insurance providers, global health donors, pharmaceutical companies, manufacturers of health products and equipment and private hospitals. Their efforts are crucial to the production of healthcare services as well as producing materials and equipment for all healthcare. However, some are unsure about the relationship between the need to provide care and the need to make a profit which are the two aims of many private companies in the health sector.

Case – Purdue Pharma

In the 1990s, the pharmaceutical company Purdue Pharma introduced the opioid painkiller OxyContin, marketing it as a non-addictive medicine. A wave of deaths linked to the use of legally prescribed opioids swept the USA and an epidemic of addiction began. OxyContin, promoted as a revolutionary pill that would release the patient from pain for 12 hours, became the most prescribed narcotic drug by 2001. Although successful, Purdue Pharma's marketing campaign was unethical. The company was aware of the addictiveness of its narcotic, and the fact that it was widely abused, and it gave fraudulent information about its drug. Reports have shown how the opioid manufacturers bribed politicians and doctors in their favour, medical articles with false and misleading information were often published, and the company created fake pain awareness societies.[38]

After years and thousands of lawsuits that blamed the pharmaceutical company for fuelling the opioid crisis, Purdue Pharma filed for bankruptcy in 2019 and opted for a settlement for $6 billion USD. However, by July 2023, the case was still ongoing, and the USA still faces a serious public health issue with addiction.[39]

There are numerous NGOs whose activities focus on or support the health sector. These can operate at the national, regional or international level. They can cover particular groups (for example, Save the Children, which operates globally), or particular aspects of health (such as National Alliance on Mental Illness (NAMI), operating in the USA). These can be of special assistance to governments by providing medical, social and psychological services. They can also contribute to health advocacy, educational and information training. Other NGOs that promote health are:

- International Crisis Group
- Médecins Sans Frontières (Doctors without Borders)
- Oxfam
- Norwegian Refugee Council
- World Vision USA
- Alertnet
- Humanitarian Practice Network
- Health Link.

HL extension

Health and development

When defining development as a qualitative improvement in the lives of people, health is a crucial factor. Development comes with an improvement in health. Education and health are two of the most important aspects for development, allowing for the realization of other developmental objectives, contributing to economic growth and more prosperous communities. Investing in healthcare is an investment in human capital, creating an increase in individual and national productivity.

An ongoing debate exists, with some believing that development leads to progress in health, while others believe the opposite. In the Millennium Development Goals (which existed between 2000 and 2015 and preceded the SDGs), three out of the eight goals were directly related to health:

- Goal 4: reduce child mortality
- Goal 5: improve maternal health
- Goal 6: combat HIV/AIDS, malaria and other diseases.

Healthier populations contribute to development, and development improves the health of a population.

Throughout history, health has passed from being seen as a consumption to an investment. Robert Fogel, Nobel Prize laureate in economics in 1993, pointed out the connection between improvements in a population's health and economic development, by relating historical declines in mortality rates with economic growth. It seems obvious that a healthier labor force works more efficiently and effectively, resulting in increased productivity. Health is not the only factor in a country's productivity. A correlation between economic development and health can be seen in developing countries that have poor healthcare systems. Lack of funds and access to adequate healthcare can result in needless deaths from curable diseases among a working population. Healthy children are more able to learn and to become productive members of their communities. Healthy parents are better suited to care for their children.

Health is an important tool for improving the economic and social future of populations, but also of individuals. A state of health improves an individual's capacities. Improved health can be the result of specific health program interventions, but it can also result from improved economic and social conditions. Historical records show that interventions and improved conditions are important, although their importance differs from country to country and from era to era.

Health and security

Health is an important asset for national, regional and global security. Pandemics transcend borders and have important social and economic impacts, affecting individuals, families, communities and entire economies. Sometimes, such as with the COVID-19 pandemic, health issues get politicized, making them matters of national security. Historically, illness and diseases have weakened entire armies, and that remains a reality today.

Some argue that the health of the population is fundamental to a state's security. 'If people are unhealthy, they can't work. If they can't work, they can't contribute to the economy. If they can't contribute to the economy, the government can't

> When defining development as a qualitative improvement in the lives of people, health is a crucial factor. Development comes with an improvement in health.

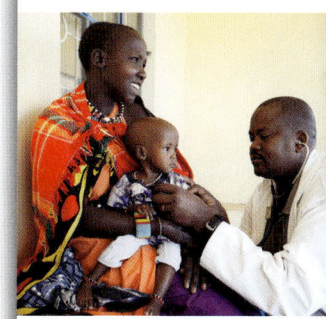

Pediatrician uses a stethoscope while examining a baby held by a carer at a clinic in Kenya.

provide services and infrastructure. If the government can't provide services and infrastructure, then they are persistently vulnerable to security threats from state and non-state actors or from natural threats like climate change and diseases.'[40]

National security cannot exist without human security. The threat to health security is not limited to infectious diseases, but the proliferation of biological weapons and the threat of bioterrorism bring health and national security closer together.

Health as a security issue is not new, although efforts to strengthen this connection have grown since the beginning of the 21st century, even before the September 11, 2001 attacks on the Twin Towers, in New York, USA, and the following attacks with anthrax.[41] Journalists, academics, think tanks and NGOs started referring to public global health as a security issue. The Center for Strategic and International Studies did so in 2000, as did the International Crisis Group, the Council on Foreign Relations and the Milbank Memorial Fund in 2001. In 2003, the RAND Corporation published an article titled 'The Global Threat of New and Reemerging Infectious Diseases: Reconciling US National Security and Public Health Policy.' David P. Fidler, in his 2003 article 'Public Health and National Security in the Global Age: Infectious Diseases, Bioterrorism, and Realpolitik', argues that infectious disease affects a state's capacity, contributes to poverty, state failure, and national and regional destabilization.[42]

In 1994, the UNDP's annual report, *New Dimensions of Human Security*, included health security among its seven fields of human security. In the report, health security encompassed infectious diseases in the developing world as well as the diseases of lifestyle (cancer, diabetes and heart disease) in the developed world. It also suggested that both worlds shared a common vulnerability, which was the unequal distribution of resources to combat diseases and unequal access to health services.

Health security as a dimension of human security entails good health as essential for human survival and a life of dignity. There are other threats to health closely related to other dimensions of human security, such as food and environmental security (for example, the effect of contaminated water, soil or food due to pesticides and toxic chemicals, or the effects of genetically modified food on human health).

Poverty is also closely related to the incidence of infectious diseases. Lack of access to basic sanitation, inadequate access to water, and hunger exacerbate a person's vulnerability to health problems. Disease and infections also exacerbate poverty. Armed conflicts cause substantial human casualties and also the destruction of healthcare systems. This results in a deterioration of basic living conditions and healthcare, contributing to the mass spread of diseases. During armed conflict, biological agents may be used as weapons. Weapons, in general, pollute the air, water and soil.

Climate change and natural disasters are also threats to health and human security. These can directly impact human life and destroy physical, biological and social environments, and have long-term effects on human health. In 2011, Japan was struck by a magnitude 9 earthquake that caused a tsunami in which over 15,000 people died. The two disasters led to the release of radioactive material from the Fukushima nuclear power plant. Estimates are that the release of radioactive material has increased, and will continue to increase, cancer rates, thyroid diseases, circulatory diseases and reproductive dysfunctions, among other health problems.[43]

HL extension

Health challenges can represent a national security threat. Health issues can have important impacts on a country's stability, for example, the epidemic of Ebola in Sierra Leone in 2014, and the H5N1 outbreak in Vietnam in 2008. In Sierra Leone, the government's poor management of the Ebola crisis caused frustration and exposed the citizens' lack of trust in their authorities. Economically, there was a loss in the gross domestic output, an increase in unemployment, a decline in foreign investment and an increase to food insecurity. The crisis also had an impact on education (around two million children stopped attending school), and general standards of living were affected, impacting mainly the elderly, the poor and those with a chronic illness or disability. Social cohesion was weakened by the 'do not touch' policies adopted to reduce the spread of the virus.[44] The erosion of state borders increases the risk of transnational health challenges.

Addressing mental health

Health and national security are not just related to diseases, pandemics and the use of biological weapons. Mental health is still widely ignored, and in some places is an issue of shame and taboo, and mental illness is punished. In recent years, acknowledgment of mental health and its importance has increased. Mental health conditions and their diagnoses are increasing worldwide. However, people with mental health conditions keep facing human rights violations, discrimination and stigma.

The gap between people in need of mental care and those with access to it remains significant, while effective treatment coverage remains low. According to data from WHO, 'Depression is one of the leading causes of disability. Suicide is the fourth leading cause of death among 15–29-year olds, and people with severe mental health conditions die prematurely – as much as two decades early – due to preventable physical conditions.'[45] Mental health conditions have effects on all areas of life, including work and school, relationships with family and friends, and participation in society.

Mental health is not merely the absence of mental disorders. It is a state of mental well-being that allows people to cope with the daily stresses of life, while also realizing their potential, learning and working, and contributing to their communities. Although often seen as affecting only the individual, mental health is integral to collective health and well-being, affecting our ability to make individual and collective decisions, build relations, and contribute to personal and community development.

Mental health problems can worsen due to exposure to unfavorable social, economic, geopolitical and environmental circumstances, such as poverty, violence, inequality and environmental deprivation.

In order to address this, mental health awareness needs to increase, together with access to quality care and treatments. According to Human Rights Watch, in approximately 60 countries around the world, men, women and children are still chained or locked in confined spaces because they have a mental health condition. These countries include Afghanistan, Burkina Faso, Cambodia, Liberia, Mexico, Nigeria, Russia and South Sudan.[46] This inhumane practice results from stigmatization, but in many cases also from the inadequate existence and support of mental health services.

Global political challenges

While mental health is not dealt with through inhumane practices everywhere (such as chains), it is still not addressed adequately around the world. Human Rights Watch has estimated that one in ten people across the world has a mental health condition. Countries tend to spend less than 2 percent of their healthcare budgets on addressing mental health.[47] Even in some developed countries, national health insurance schemes do not cover mental health services. The disregard toward mental health services has psychological and physical consequences, such as malnutrition, infections and cardiovascular problems. However, when provided with adequate mental health services, people with mental conditions can thrive in their communities and be productive members of society, contributing to its development.

Health and technology

Public health has received growing scientific attention in the last few decades, but public health has also been politicized. Technological advancements in the field of medicine are growing the fastest. This is important, considering the demand for healthcare is expected to rise with increasing populations, particularly, an aging population, and increasing life expectancies.

Varying levels of access to medical technological advancements have worsened the global North-South divide. Wealthy countries are constantly developing and having access to medicines, vaccines and advancements in medical treatments, while the majority of countries in Asia, Africa and Latin America increasingly depend on wealthy countries sharing these advancements with them.

The development of coronavirus vaccines is an example of this. Only a small number of countries have developed vaccines against COVID-19, while the rest of the world depends on these countries to receive vaccine supplies. 'This raises the spectre of a new geopolitical arrangement – one in which patron-client relationships are determined by the asymmetry in vaccine supply versus demand.'[48] This new geopolitical arrangement leaves countries that do not have their own vaccine production vulnerable to diplomatic coercion. Countries like Russia, for example, supplied vaccines in exchange for favorable foreign policy concessions. In February 2021, Russia successfully obtained the release of an Israeli citizen held in Syria in exchange for Israel funding Sputnik V vaccines for Syria.[49]

Intellectual property laws and infrastructure constraints have resulted in a **monopolization** of vaccine and medicine production. This has created a trade hierarchy from which only a few obtain advantages and preferences, leaving the majority at their mercy. COVAX is an initiative to coordinate Covid vaccines research and production in order to guarantee a fair and equitable distribution. This program has not been entirely successful. Leading countries have imposed even greater restrictions, with some exploiting their advantage as a diplomatic instrument.

Within the global pharmaceutical market, the USA is the main actor, though it is increasingly facing competition from countries like the UK, Germany, Russia, the PRC, Israel and India, some of whom have become leading suppliers of generics (generic medicines). Israel's Teva Pharmaceuticals has become an essential source of affordable medicines for a large part of the Global South. These technological and scientific advancements can be beneficial for all humans (if distributed adequately), but the global power distribution may change from what we know today. So far, inequalities in access to medical technological advancements are worsening.

> Monopolization refers to the act or process of taking full control or control of the largest part of something. This prevents other people or companies from having any share or influence.

HL extension

Case – The development of generic medicines in Africa

Over the past few years, it has become noticeable that, when global medical needs exceed supply, wealthier countries use their power to get priority over poorer ones. This is one of the reasons why there is a growing interest in Africa, as well as outside the region, to expand the continent's capacity to manufacture medical products, pharmaceuticals and medical equipment. One of the main reasons is that the continent bears the burden of 75 percent of the world's HIV cases, 90 percent of deaths from malaria and a rapid increase in non-communicable diseases.

Africa's generics production, as with vaccines, is still at early-stage development. However, this production offers great opportunities for the private sector to focus investments and build capacity for production. African producers could become competitive at a global scale with tablet formulations and injectable generics. Injectables are pharmaceuticals that can be injected by healthcare workers or by patients. These are being increasingly used for trauma, cancer and surgery. Even though the generics market is still dominated by drugs taken in pill form, injectable generics are gaining in popularity because they act faster.

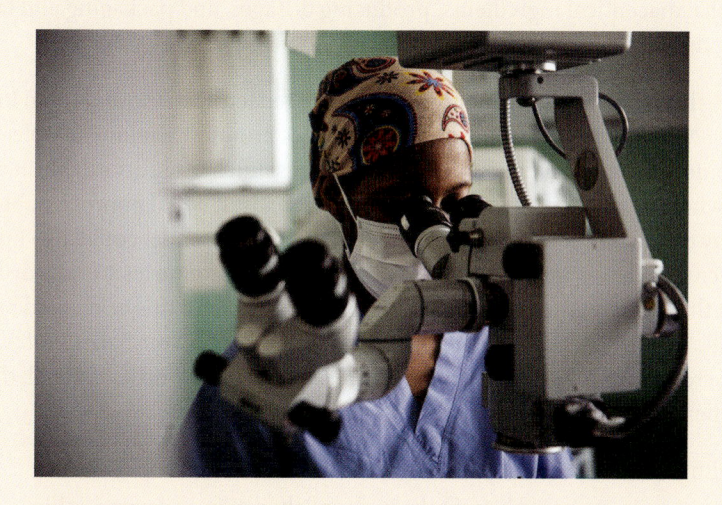

Doctor looking through operating microscope equipment in Cape Town, South Africa.

In 2007, the African Union (AU) endorsed the Pharmaceutical Manufacturing Plan for Africa (PMPA). This is a non-binding framework that was set up with the aim of local production of generics in the continent with the support of different partners. The idea behind the PMPA included benefits such as:

- saving on foreign exchange
- creating jobs and alleviating poverty
- promoting Intra-African trade
- fostering new skills and technologies
- stimulating exports
- enhancing self-sufficiency in drug supply
- responding to emergencies and urgent demands.

By 2030, WHO is expecting deaths in Africa to result not only from communicable and nutritional diseases, but to be exceeded by deaths from lifestyle diseases

Global political challenges

(cancer, heart disease and diabetes). Currently, between 70 and 90 percent of the medicines needed in the continent are still imported from other regions. Other existing obstacles to Africa's success include:

- access to finance
- size of local markets and few economies of scale
- pharmaceutical ingredients still coming mostly from India and the PRC
- cost of production development
- underdeveloped supporting industries
- unreliable infrastructure
- underdeveloped talent base.

The capacities of African countries vary greatly. Nigeria has hundreds of registered manufacturing companies, but other countries do not have any. In some countries, a manufacturing hub is unlikely to be economically viable. In others, it could be viable if several obstacles were overcome. The level of production is also not the same everywhere, resulting in comparatively different results (the costs and benefits of manufacturing raw materials, synthesizing the active pharmaceutical ingredients, producing dosages, and packaging and labeling are very different).

By 2023, the continent had roughly 375 drug manufacturers, most of them located in North Africa, expected to serve a population of around 1.3 billion people. The development of a local industry could make drugs much more affordable in a region where costs are often an impediment for many. It could improve public health by enhancing access and availability of medicines, and it could also impact the system regulating quality and safety (many African countries still use drugs that are past their expiry date). Additionally, the development of this field could bring economic diversification, GDP growth, a positive impact on the balance of trade and the creation of jobs. Even if in the overall economy the impact is small, the total sum of benefits would be remarkable:

- Health would improve in particular countries.
- The entire region could benefit through collaboration and partnership.
- In the long term, it could contribute to alleviating the global challenges faced regarding health.

African countries will find their comparative advantage in the field of generics to be able to serve the continent's population better, by improving public health while reducing dependency on other countries.

Exercises

9. To what extent are mandatory vaccinations a moral duty of all, going alongside public safety and security?

10. Analyze possible reasons why mental health is not a priority in many public health policies and often not included in basic medical coverage.

11. Discuss whether governments should guarantee and provide conditions for equal access to good quality health services or if that should be primarily a job for private institutions.

Summary

In this section, you have learned:

- Health is a fundamental part of our human rights and our capacity to live a life with dignity. The right to the enjoyment of the highest standard of physical and mental health belongs to every human, and it goes beyond the absence of disease or infirmity, being a state of complete physical, mental and social well-being.

- The field of health has experienced some of the greatest advancements in the last years, but these benefits are not enjoyed by everyone, everywhere. Poverty and inequality prevent millions of people from receiving adequate healthcare services. Varying levels of access to medical technological advancements exacerbate the global North-South divide.

- Although healthcare services are the responsibility of individual states, international efforts and cooperation is essential. WHO provides an international forum for discussion, monitors public health risks, and coordinates responses to health emergencies.

- Health is closely linked to the enjoyment of other human rights such as the access to safe drinking water and sanitation, adequate housing, nutritious foods, education, and safe working conditions.

- Governments can rely on the private health sector to provide healthcare services. Among these are health insurance providers, global health donors, pharmaceutical companies, manufacturers of health products and equipment, private hospitals, and others. There are also numerous NGOs whose activities focus on assisting the health sector.

- Health promotes development, and with greater development comes an improvement in health. Although health is not the only factor in a country's productivity, there is a connection between improvements in a population's health and economic development.

- National security requires human security, and this depends on health. Health security is a dimension of human security that considers good health as essential for human survival and a life with dignity.

- Issues like infectious diseases, pandemics, the proliferation of biological weapons, and the threat of bioterrorism bring health and national security closer together.

- The gap between people in need of mental healthcare and those with access to it remains significant, while effective treatment coverage remains extremely low.

Global political challenges

Identity

Learning outcomes

In this section, you will learn about:
- how humans have a biological need to belong, and a sense of belonging can be found in families, friends, communities, sports teams or nations
- we identify ourselves by recognizing what and who we are not, which does not mean conflict is inevitable but identity labels can create tension and conflicts
- having an identity is not enough in itself; it is necessary for that identity to be recognized by others to ensure equal access to basic human rights
- identity is shaped by culture, family, religion, gender and socio-economic background
- social media has transformed our individual identities, and many people embrace a global identity in which physical borders are no longer relevant
- identity is still a factor for unequal health services around the world and across communities
- global crises, such as climate change, indicate that identity must evolve and adapt to a global world.

Conceptual question

What is identity and why does it matter?

In an increasingly interconnected world, we are becoming more aware of our own identity, the identities of others and the political implications. Conventional boundaries are fading, and local identities have more and more transnational and global effects. Global crises, such as climate change, appear to indicate that **identity** must evolve and adapt to a global world.

Answering the question 'Who are we?' is complex because the answer is not self-evident. In many cases, the answer is not as as simple as: 'I am *this* because I am not *that*.' Instead, it is an answer involving interactive processes (social interactions, personal experiences, family environments or maturity) and multidimensional contexts, allowing actors to acquire multiple identities.

Since the attacks in the USA on September 11, 2001, global attention on cultural and religious identity has increased. Ethnic identity and nationalism have been ever-present, and gender identity has greatly transformed and its political effects have strengthened. The concept of identity has evolved from being based on national loyalty (nationality) to a much more complex issue.

Identity often refers to the traits, characteristics or beliefs a person or a community uses to define themselves. Every human has a personal identity and a **collective identity**, which is basic to the nature of the self. Personal identity is associated with the distinctive qualities or traits that make a person individual and unique. Collective identity is associated with the membership and role-behavior a person fulfills in a community or group. Both of these make up who we are and the role we play within our societies. All humans need an identity to develop their self-image, self-concept,

HL extension

individuality and their self-esteem. Humans also need a collective identity that provides them with belonging. 'Identity is an inescapable dimension of being. Nobody could be without it.'[50]

A collective identity serves to create a feeling of belonging, while also strengthening cooperation and a sense of community. It gives every human a role, rights and responsibilities, and a purpose. For example, a person may identify as a woman because they are biologically not a man. At the same time, they identify as mixed race, a mother, a Muslim, a scientist, a volleyball player and a **leftist**. Within these labels, some refer to them as an individual, such as being a woman and a mother. Some refer to them as a member of a community, such as being Muslim and a scientist.

> Identity refers to the traits, characteristics and beliefs that define a person or community. It is the result of a long process of self-definition and social constructs.

Table 5.4 Types of identity

Type of Identity	Description
Political identity	Political inclinations, the lean toward certain policies, specific governmental candidates.
National identity	Results from the international architecture of nation-states. People may lack a national identity as a result of statelessness, or may seek a new national identity due to a desire for independence. Some people may have a national identity based on their belonging to a nation, without the existence of a state (such as the Kurds). Some people have more than one national identity.
Cultural identity	Ideas, values and traditions that result from the culture we belong to. It is possible to choose traits that are more appealing to the individual within a culture, and reject others.
Ethnic identity	Identification with an ethnicity. Ethnicity is often created and imposed by external actors. For example, are Mexicans ethnically Latinos, Hispanic or something else?
Gender identity	The gender to which a person identifies, being within the traditional binary division of men and women, or something outside of this.
Religious identity	The religious beliefs and practices to which we do or do not adhere.
Professional identity	The identification with a profession, its roles and responsibilities.

Individual identity and collective identity are not fixed. A person's identity is the result of a life-long process of self-definition, often influenced by character and personality, as well as through **social constructs** that result from socialization. Identity defines who we are, and this is usually the answer to who are we not. An individual can have cultural, ethnic, political, national, gender, religious and professional identities, etc. All of them can change throughout a person's life. Identity is constructed and performed. Each individual has a wide array of identities that constantly shift according to specific circumstances. Identities appear at some point in a person's life and can gradually develop and transform over time.

Global political challenges

> **Activity**
>
> Write down some aspects of your individual and collective identity. Compare it to that of other classmates.

Think about the woman who identifies, at the moment, as mixed race, a mother, a scientist and a leftist. She will not always have been a mother, and before she became a scientist, she would have been student. She might have one nationality, or have dual-nationality, but never lived in any country other than the one she was born in. She may identify as leftist because of liking a particular political candidate rather than it being her whole political identity.

Identity is not only of concern to individuals. It has for many years played an important role in politics. Identities provide a starting point and frame of reference for states from which political leaders conduct, maintain and shape relations with other states and actors. All states need a sense of self. Identity shapes relations, and relations also shape identity. Identity generates and shapes interests, and vice versa.

Understanding an actor's identity helps us to understand why they act in a certain way and their motives. Identifying a state's identity is also crucial for understanding how and why it behaves the way it does, and can help us to predict, up to a certain point, its reactions. Critical theories in international relations place identity at their core. They consider that an actor's identity is integral to understanding global politics. A state's identity not only structures how it behaves, but also how other states and actors respond to it.

North Korea is a country whose identity shapes its actions while defining how other countries behave toward it (a militarily powerful state to which countries militarily react, or perhaps it is a state that strengthens militarily because other countries behave that way toward it). European Union (EU) members claim to share a common identity of being European (a cultural identity of shared values and a political identity based on democratic practices). Historically, the importance of identity was huge during the Cold War years (and still is today). In the 2003 military intervention in Iraq, the USA wanted to preserve its identity as a champion of political freedom and liberal democracy, against undemocratic authoritarian regimes.

Identity matters at the individual, community, national, regional and international levels.

Othering

Every regional, national and global conflict has some form of group-based difference as a cause behind it. Although identity is essential for every human and for the existence of communities, there is a risk to identity. Identities function as labels, creating a difference between *me* and *you*, and *us* and *them*.

The phenomenon that defines individuals or groups as not fitting with certain norms is called **othering**. This influences how people perceive and behave toward those that are seen as outsiders. The problem with othering is that it involves a negative categorization of the outsiders, transforming identity into a *me* vs *you* and an *us* vs *them*

▲ Flags of the USA and former Soviet Union. During the Cold War era, identity was strongly shaped by the belonging to or alliance with either of the competing powers, or to neither.

Constructivism explains global politics by focusing on norms and identities. This theory recognizes that actors shape their identities and behavior through interactions.

Identity is not exclusive to individuals and communities. All actors in the international system (states, intergovernmental organizations (IGOs), MNCs and terrorist groups) have an identity. Understanding that identity can help us to understand their actions and motivations, as well as predict their future actions. However, identity is not fixed.

Identity is related to *Equality*. Respect for one's identity is not enjoyed by everyone, everywhere, leaving many people suffering from marginalization.

HL extension

dynamic. Othering is 'a set of dynamics, processes, and structures that prompt marginality and persistent inequality across any of the full range of human differences based on group identities.'[51]

Othering ignores other people's or communities' humanity, potentially seeing them as less worthy of dignity, respect and the enjoyment of basic rights and liberties. This means othering can play a role in the weakening of tolerance, the formation of prejudices and the dehumanization of entire groups. Results can be catastrophic when authorities or governments use this to persecute marginalized groups, to deny communities their basic rights and even to inflict violence on others. Using narratives or speech, and with support of the media, the 'other' becomes a threat, is dangerous, goes against our values or lifestyle, does not fit with 'us' and therefore it is acceptable to treat them differently and even suppress them.

Othering can be very subtle and often occur subconsciously. How often do we adhere to gender stereotypes despite disagreeing with them? How often do we give a recommendation from our own perspective without considering the identity of others? Without intending to harm anyone, we resort to *othering* when those who are similar to us are attributed with positive qualities, are not considered a threat to us or our way of living, and seem trustworthy and easy to relate to, compared to the *others*.

Whether othering is the result of social cohesion, protection, lack of knowledge, out-group bias (the idea of the other not belonging to one's own group), the role of the media or any other reason, the effects can be terrible. Consider, for example:

- the exclusion and discrimination of certain minority groups when accessing housing, education or healthcare, such as Roma communities in many European countries
- the effects of homophobia, such as Uganda's anti-homosexuality law that bans and criminalizes identifying oneself as LGBTQI+
- sexism in Saudi Arabia with an entrenched system of gender-based discrimination in terms of marriage, divorce or child custody.

If this dehumanization becomes internalized as part of a people's identity, it becomes even harder to eradicate the division between us and them. Around the world, there are countless cases in which inequality exists and human rights are constantly being violated due to othering. This occurs at the individual, local, state and global level. The way the European Union welcomed refugees from Ukraine, as opposed to refugees from Syria, is an example of othering.

Activity

Define your identity. Evaluate how many of the traits were chosen by you instead of being given to you by your family, school and society.

Manipulating identity

The appearance of multiple and more complex actors in global politics, together with the blurring of the traditional structure of the international system, has raised questions about the volatility of borders, nationalism, loyalties and how these can be manipulated.

Every conflict, armed or unarmed, involves identity. Achieving peace is often supported by a global identity of humanity.

In-group bias exists when individuals gives preferential treatment to people within their social or identity group. Out-group bias exists when dislike, distrust, negative stereotypes and/or discrimination are expressed towards other people or groups.

Global political challenges

National identity, seen as the identification of the national public with the state, allows political leaders to speak and represent the people with one voice. This is particularly true when a government or authority enjoys legitimacy.

When national identities become politicized, this can have serious implications both internally and externally. 'Identities provide a frame of reference from which political leaders can initiate, maintain, and structure their relationships with other states.'[52] This can also happen within states.

In some cases, governments transform identities (the *we* related to allegiance to a nation) as a political tool of control and manipulation. During the disintegration of the former Yugoslavia, a national identity of Yugoslav disappeared to give birth to identities based on nationalism (Serbs, Croats, Bosniaks and Kosovars). These were controlled by their own leaderships, and in turn adopted ethnic and religious characteristics. The result was a decade of brutal wars that devastated the whole region. In cases like this, the political identity and national identity become entrenched and determine a state's interests and priorities.

Sometimes, identity does not serve any bigger purpose than to create a collective identity. For example, there is the ethnic division of the Rwandan people between Hutus and Tutsis. This identity existed long before the ethnic conflict began. Belgium, as the former colonial power, recognized how to exploit this identity for their own political purposes. The Tutsis were, according to the Belgians, less African than the Hutus in their physical traits (noses and foreheads were measured to classify Hutus and Tutsis) and were seen as more capable of holding public posts. The Hutus were discriminated against by the Belgians and relegated to more menial jobs. This division helped the economic and political purposes of the colonizers to exploit the country's natural resources, until they left the country. When they did, the Tutsis (the minority in Rwanda) were left in charge of the country, and the majority (the Hutus) harbored deep grievances. The same was seen in the USA under the presidency of Donald Trump, who managed to manipulate nationalism to create internal divisions, but also to define the country's domestic and foreign policies.

Identity can be found at the core of every conflict. It is not just religion, nationalism and ethnicity that can define conflicts. They are often the result of multiple identities. In the same way that identity is formed and malleable, so is conflict between identities. Our narratives shape identity, and also manipulate identities for different purposes. The violence that the Rohingya have been subjected to in the last few years has been mainly the result of shaping identities through discourse and hate speech spread throughout the media, including social media networks (particularly Facebook).

In general, identity is made up of labels. Without these, we cannot express ourselves and exist freely. However, labels also exacerbate the differences that exist between all peoples.

Identity as a human right

Every human has a name, a date of birth and an identity. Or, this should be the case. According to Article 8 of the UN Convention on the Rights of the Child (UNCRC), every child has the right to an identity and for this to be protected from any interference. This identity includes a name, a nationality and family relations, and must be recorded by the government. A confirmed identity, or legal identity, grants the individual access to resources, basic rights and liberties, economic and social

---

Government legitimacy is the result of a belief in the rightfulness of a hierarchy between a rule or ruler and its subjects, and the subordinate's obligations toward the rule or ruler.

Nationalism refers to the exaltation of one's own nationality, seeing it as superior to others.

TOK
To what extent is our perspective determined by our membership of a particular culture?

HL extension

structures, and services like education and healthcare. It allows them to have a job, open a bank account, rent a car or buy a plane ticket. Having a registered identity guarantees the individual their existence and recognizes it.

A legal identity is a human right established by international law, included in the UDHR as well as in a range of declarations and conventions. Without a legal identity, individuals cannot fully exercise their rights. However, around 1 billion people around the world do not have access to one.[53]

According to 2023 data from The World Bank, 81 percent of people without a legal identity live in Sub-Saharan Africa and South Asia, and 85 percent are from low-income or low to middle-income economies, with women being particularly affected. UNICEF states that one in four children under the age of five do not legally exist because they lack a birth registration.[54]

The exclusion of people from an identity can have severely negative consequences. It increases the vulnerability of everyone and affects those already vulnerable the most. Many people across the world are unable to or cannot afford to obtain government-issued identity documents for several reasons, including costs, difficulties in accessing and bureaucracy.

In Mexico, more than a million people were not registered as citizens by the government in 2023, although the right to an identity is stipulated in Article 4 of the Mexican Constitution. Among them, six out of every 10 were children. The Constitution establishes that identity is a universal right, and the process to register a child and obtain a government-issued identity document must be free and accessible to everyone. However, there are many challenges faced, particularly by vulnerable groups (irregular migrants, households where there is domestic violence, addiction or poverty, and rural and indigenous communities) to obtain a legal identity.

The three poorest regions of Mexico are the ones where a lack of legal identity mostly persists. Some of the most common obstacles are the absence of trained personnel working in governmental offices, the lack of information and knowledge about legal identity (especially within indigenous communities, due to language barriers), few available services and difficulties in accessing governmental offices.

In order to register a child, the government of Mexico requires a birth certificate from a certified medical institution or midwife, or a DNA test. People living in poverty in rural communities or indigenous communities often give birth outside medical facilities. Therefore, they lack the necessary documents to acquire a legal identity that can provide them with the rights, benefits and services that all Mexican citizens are entitled to receive. According to UNICEF data, eight out of 10 children between the ages of 3 and 11 who lack an identity do not go to school, while around 1500 indigenous children have no governmental identity document.[55]

Similar problems to those in Mexico are faced across the world. Internal issues and contexts are not the only causes. Migration poses an identity challenge, especially if it is done irregularly. Often, migrant parents refuse to seek a legal identity that could provide them with benefits in their host country, out of fear of being detained or deported. This frequently happens with irregular migrants who have given birth to children in a foreign country. However, doing so leaves both parents and children excluded from basic rights and services.

▲ All humans are entitled to a nationality and the legal documentation that comes with it, such as a passport, identity card or birth certificate.

Although it is claimed to be a free and universal right to obtain a government-issued identity document, in 2023, passports in Mexico were not free, and acquiring them entailed a very long process. A three-year passport had a cost of $88 USD, a six-year passport $120 USD and a 10-year passport $210 USD. Even printing your own birth certificate at home through the government website had a cost of $4.75 USD.

Global political challenges

We must also consider people fleeing war, persecution or conflict. These people, most of the time, have no way to prove their identity. This is because their documents get destroyed, lost or stolen, or because there was no time to gather them before fleeing. During armed conflict, governmental institutions in charge of issuing identity documents are rarely in operation. These are some of the main reasons why so many people around the world turn to smugglers to migrate. There are also millions of people who find themselves **stateless**.

The 1954 UN Convention relating to the Status of Stateless Persons defines stateless people as individuals who are not considered citizens or nationals under the operation of the laws of any country. A lack of birth registration is a common cause of statelessness.

Case – The world's largest stateless population

For decades, the Rohingya population, a Muslim ethnic minority living in Rakhine State inside Myanmar (formerly Burma), have faced persecution and abuse, have been forced to live in camps, marginalized and violently expelled from their homes. They also lack a nationality and are denied citizenship by their home country, Myanmar.

The UN has referred to the Rohingya as one of the most persecuted minorities in the world. Neglected and unrecognized, they lack access to basic rights and services, including education, healthcare, job opportunities and even freedom of movement. In 2017, after successive violent campaigns from the Myanmar military against the Rohingya, over one million have sought refuge abroad, including in Cox's Bazar, Bangladesh (the world's largest and most densely populated refugee camp). In Cox's Bazar, the people (the majority of whom are women and children) live under inhumane conditions where disease outbreaks are common. The camp is overcrowded, with limited interaction with the outside world, and it lacks access to basic needs such as food and water. These mass migrations have placed significant pressure on Bangladesh's security concerns.

In 1982, Myanmar introduced the Citizenship Law, under which the Rohingya were left without citizenship. Citizenship was now to be based on membership of what were considered national races. The Rohingya, being one of the many minorities in the country, were left unrecognized. Instead, they were to be regarded as foreigners. Although living in Myanmar, this country considers the Rohingya the responsibility of Bangladesh. But Bangladesh denies all connection to them and even refuses to recognize as refugees those who have entered their territory seeking refuge from the violence of Myanmar's military. The Rohingya face persecution in Myanmar, discrimination in their home country and others, and a serious violation of their human rights.

Denied nationality and citizenship, the Rohingya are today the largest stateless population in the world. As such, their identity is unclear and often unrecognized. This puts them in a dire situation, with the escalation of violence between the Arakan Rohingya Salvation Army (ARSA) and the military in Myanmar affecting civilians the most. The government of Myanmar has declared the ARSA a terrorist organization and has conducted what are seen as legitimate arbitrary arrests, gang rapes, extrajudicial killings, infanticides, arson, looting and all kinds of brutalities against the population. Over 100,000 Rohingya are still living in Myanmar in camps for internally displaced people, vulnerable to marginalization and violence.

The countries in which the majority of Rohingya have chosen to take refuge (Bangladesh, India, Malaysia and Thailand) are not signatories to the 1952 Refugee Convention. This leaves those Rohingya without the opportunity to claim their rights as refugees. Migration to other countries is complicated because they lack an official identity.

Unrecognized, the Rohingya have been left out of their communities. Their unequal treatment compared to other members of society means they cannot access basic services such as education and health. They cannot enjoy their basic human rights. They are more vulnerable to environmental disasters and environmental factors. Their human security and their physical safety are in permanent danger. They are more vulnerable to crime and violence, and they will continue living in extreme poverty without any possibility of living in dignity.

The statelessness of the Rohingya has serious consequences for every aspect of their everyday lives, but has also spread over borders. The problem must be addressed at the core, where identity is denied as a result of structural violence, and a long-term solution found for this forgotten and ignored population.

The Rohingya crisis is related to the core topics of the Global Politics course, including human rights, development, and peace and conflict. It also exemplifies the HL topic areas of *Borders, Security, Poverty, Equality, Identity* and *Health*.

To learn more about statelessness, you can visit:

Toward a global identity

More than ever, a **global identity** seems to be shaping the individual identity of many. Increased globalization, the forces of modern information, communications and transportation technologies are creating a stronger idea of a global community to which millions of people feel attached to, aware of their individual and collective actions contributing to global politics. This global identity is not a rejection or abandonment of one's own identity built on nation, religion, culture, etc. Instead, it is an additional identity layer with responsibilities associated with being part of a globalized world.

A global identity recognizes that we all share a common humanity and are equally worthy. It is open to engaging positively with other identities, understanding that differences exist and are to be celebrated. Without a global identity, we cannot be **global citizens**.

Diversity.

Global political challenges

A global identity can be developed and strengthened through education. The idea is for young people to see themselves as citizens of a culturally diverse and interdependent world. To recognize that globalization has profoundly influenced the notion of citizenship helps to instill a global perspective in which students challenge the core principles of citizenship as a concept related to the traditional view of a nation-state.

Identity is an exclusionary concept frequently used (and often exploited by leaders) to separate individuals from others. But, a global identity is inclusive. In it, there is a universality that encourages people to exist with this identity without compromising other multiple collective identities. Because it promotes the idea that we are all members of a community, it recognizes that, in spite of borders and distance, humans share norms and ideals, and social relations are no longer tied to territories and locations.

> **TOK**
> Does a neutral position exist from which judgements about competing claims from different groups with different traditions can be made?

Identity is slowly passing from being prescribed by social roles to being more dependent on individual choices. Today's identities are much more complex and include a sense of belonging to the whole world. The existence of a global identity opens up the possibility of the creation of global citizens. Global citizens share an awareness that global politics is not just about states or big and powerful actors, but it is also about the fact that borders are not fixed and interconnectedness is also social and cultural. Global citizens also share an interest in participating in global issues with a sense of responsibility for bettering the world.

The UN recognizes global citizenship as an umbrella term for social, political, environmental and economic actions of individuals and communities who are globally minded. Global citizens do not identify as single actors affecting isolated societies, but instead embrace their social responsibility to act for the benefit of all humans. SDG 4 (relating to inclusive and quality education) refers to global citizenship as a target. The international community has recognized the need to ensure an education that includes the promotion of global citizenship. This means that all individuals can contribute to the world community.

Global citizens, living in a constantly changing world community, have the following responsibilities:

- To understand one's own perspective and that of others regarding global issues: Only through the understanding of different perspectives can we search for long-lasting and integrative solutions.
- To respect cultural diversity: Understanding that the existence of varied cultural beliefs is not an obstacle but instead brings added value to the search for solutions to the global challenges we face.
- To make connections and build relations with people from other backgrounds: Living in isolated communities limits our understanding on global issues.
- To understand the multiple ways in which societies and countries are interconnected and interdependent.
- To understand global issues.
- To advocate for greater international cooperation.
- To advocate for a stronger implementation of international treaties, conventions and agreements on global issues.
- To advocate for global equity, justice and respect for human rights.

Identities are labels that we all need to exist and be recognized. While they strengthen differences, these differences are not a cause of conflict. Instead, they enrich the global community.

HL extension

Exercises

12. Discuss if it is naturally and biologically easier to establish good relations with those who look like us, or if we learn to do that.

13. Explain why and how ethnicity can become a dangerous label.

14. Evaluate whether nationalism can serve as a positive force for internal cohesion and peaceful foreign relations.

Summary

In this section, you have learned:

- Identity refers to the traits, characteristics or beliefs a person or a community use to define themselves.

- Every person has a personal and a collective identity. Personal identity refers to the distinctive qualities or traits that make every person unique. Collective identity is associated with the membership and role-behavior a person fulfils in a community or group.

- Individual and collective identities are not fixed. Everyone performs a wide array of identities that constantly shift according to specific circumstances.

- Identities provide a starting point and frame of reference for states from which political leaders conduct, maintain and shape the relations with other states and actors. All states need a sense of 'self'.

- Critical theories in international relations place identity at the very core. These believe an actor's identity is integral to understanding global politics. A state's identity defines how it behaves and how other actors respond to this behavior.

- Identity also creates distinction. The process of 'othering' defines who does not fit within a group and therefore is seen as an outsider. Othering comes with negative effects: it neglects other people's or communities' humanity, seeing them as less worthy of dignity, respect and the enjoyment of basic rights and liberties.

- National identity, seen as the identification of the mass national public with the state, allows political leaders to speak and represent the people with one voice. When national identities become politicized, this can have serious implications internally and externally. Governments can use identities as a political tool of control and manipulation.

- Identity is a human right. A confirmed identity, or legal identity, guarantees a person's 'existence' and recognizes this. It grants the individual access to resources, basic rights and liberties, economic and social structures, and to services like education and healthcare. However, around 1 billion people around the world do not have access to a confirmed identity.

- Increased globalization, information, communications and transportation technologies are creating a stronger idea of a global community. The awareness of individual and collective actions contributing to global politics, and understanding the responsibility everyone has, has also transformed the traditional view of state-related identity towards a global citizenship.

Global political challenges

Borders

Learning outcomes

In this section, you will learn about:
- how borders are at the core of national sovereignty, but technology and globalization have blurred the traditional concept of borders
- borders are an important tool to preserve national security
- global challenges affect how we perceive borders, and our own identity as global citizens
- the importance of territory relies not only on its natural resources, but also on its location, size, governance and cultural meaning
- new global challenges, such as those related to global health issues, need us to rethink the way we see borders
- issues such as poverty are of global concern, yet borders allow us to map them more clearly and provide a starting point for solving national problems.

Conceptual question

Are borders real and still relevant?

Borders are at the heart of the modern international system, defining what sovereignty is and looks like. A state's sovereignty is defined by its territorial borders. The current international system agrees that borders are to be respected at all times. These can be defined as real or artificial lines that separate geographical areas, countries, states, cities, provinces, etc. This means that borders are political boundaries that outline an area controlled by a particular governing body.

Sometimes, borders can be defined by natural boundaries such as rivers, deserts or mountain ranges. The Rio Grande separates Mexico and the USA, while the Pyrenees lie between Spain and France. However, most borders are a political construct, which defines power (such as the Schengen area in the EU), affects international relations (such as the conflict between Pakistan and India over Kashmir) and plays a role in global challenges (such as global migration problems).

Borders define the structure of the international system of nation-states, but borders are not static and can be redefined over time. Changes to borders can be the result of diplomatic agreements (when territory is traded or sold peacefully), war or decolonization. This means that, in today's world, we can find nations without a state, such as the Kurds, and states with multiple nations, such as Belgium. While some enjoy stability, harmony and peace, many others do not. That is particularly true of borders that have been defined by violent means or occupation (for example, the Korean Demilitarized Zone, which is the border between North and South Korea, is the most heavily militarized border in the world).

The importance of geographical borders has been strongly contested in the past decade. It seems we would like to relax our borders, yet we are hesitant to do it. The global challenges faced today are no longer exclusive to one actor, but have become multinational and international challenges in which everyone, in spite of distance,

Borders are at the core of sovereignty and closely related to power. Borders determine how far a government's power reaches within a geographical area, from which foreign powers are excluded. The importance of borders is becoming contested by the increasing interdependence of a globalized world.

HL extension

is affected. Terrorism, criminal organizations, poverty, pandemics, financial crises, migration and climate change affect us all. If these challenges know no boundaries, we might wonder then what the point is of having borders.

When states recognize that, in order to address these challenges, the solution is cooperation and collaboration, softening borders seems beneficial. However, these issues remind us that borders are a way of protecting our own territories, people and national interests. For example, the COVID-19 pandemic was a period in which many countries chose to close borders to protect themselves from a global threat. Although, in the end, certain factors affected everyone, such as the economic impacts of the lockdown.

The need for borders

Certain issues have driven some countries to tighten or close their borders and focus on themselves. Other countries keep looking for ways to relax their borders and expand cooperation in different areas with other countries. Yet, borders are still at the core of every state's sovereignty and are far from disappearing. This is because territory is more than just a piece of land, but it is part of a country's identity, its external image, and its power and capabilities.

Territory has significant importance for every country and for their populations, making it a recurrent factor behind interstate and intrastate conflicts. This importance can be classified into three categories:

- Economic value: Territory means natural resources. From water to oil, gas, minerals, cereals or fauna, territory plays an important part in a country's economy and its population's income and means of survival. Neither the type of resources nor their amount define a country's economic success, as the resource curse (or *paradox of plenty*) shows. This occurs when resource-rich countries fail to benefit from their natural resource wealth and are unable to exploit it for their own advantage. This can be the result of their particular allocation of capital and labor, a lack of technology, corruption, weak institutions, etc. For example, the DRC produces around 70 percent of the world's cobalt, yet its benefits do not contribute to the country's development, being one of the countries most impacted by armed conflict and instability.
- Strategic value: The geographical location and position of a country can signify important geopolitical and strategic power. An example is Russia, which is the largest country in the world, bordering 14 different countries. Or Türkiye's position as the bridge between Europe and Asia. This can also bring disadvantages, as bordering 14 countries requires good diplomatic relations or coercive measures to maintain your security, and connecting East and West can represent a challenge to national security when you become a passage for migrants.
- Symbolic value: Territory is closely linked to a country's and its people's identity, due to its cultural, historical and/or religious meaning. Many societies have a deep identity connection to their land due to its historical meaning, such as indigenous communities in Peru. For others, territory is strongly linked to religion. For example, the Serbian Orthodox Church sees Kosovo as the cradle of its faith, and Jerusalem holds religious meaning for the three Abrahamic religions. Borders are a tool to control these territories and preserve the symbolic value they represent to the nation's identity.

Some examples of natural borders are:
- Mount Roraima between Venezuela, Guyana and Brazil
- Rio Grande between Mexico and the USA
- Detian Falls between the PRC and Vietnam
- Iguazu Falls between Argentina and Brazil
- Mount Everest between the PRC and Nepal
- Rhine River between France and Germany
- Panj River between Afghanistan and Tajikistan
- Epupa Falls between Angola and Namibia.

Borders are natural or human-made territorial divisions central to a state's sovereignty. They are often the result of diplomacy, conflict or decolonization. They are essential in the protection of national interests, yet they can be used to control and oppress.

Global political challenges

> Territorial disputes are common. From independence or separatist movements to control over natural resources, borders are an important factor within many conflicts.

Borders and conflict

Delimiting and protecting territory is of vital importance to a state's sovereignty, power and security, making borders still necessary around the world. But borders are also a frequent source of conflict.

The partition of the African territory agreed upon at the Berlin Conference 1884 and subsequent decolonization processes left a continent characterized by conflict. Nowadays, Africa is made up of 54 countries, with two disputed areas: Western Sahara and Somaliland. These two disputed areas are not the only ones facing constant violence.

Table 5.5 Colonial rule in Africa, 1939

Colonial Ruler	Occupied Area (Current Country Name)
Spain	Part of Morocco, Western Sahara
Italy	Angola, Eritrea, Mozambique
France	Algeria, Benin, Burkina, Cameroon, Chad, Congo, Cote, d'Ivoire, Gabon, Gambia, Ghana, Guinea, Guinea Bissau, Mali, Mauritania, Niger, Senegal, Togo
Britain	Botswana, Gold Coast, Kenya, Lesotho, Nigeria, Sierra Leone, Somalia, Swaziland, Tanzania, Uganda, Zimbabwe
Portugal	Angola, Mozambique
Belgium	Burundi, Democratic Republic of Congo, Rwanda
South Africa	Namibia
Egypt	Sudan, South Sudan

> When studying borders, two concepts are relevant. A nation is defined as a large group of people united by common traits, whether language, history, culture, traditions, religion and/or identity. A nation-state is made up of a nation, living within a defined territory, under the control of a government, enjoying international recognition.

Considering that African countries enjoyed a pre-colonial political organization and afterwards were forced to live together or separated from those of their same groups, it is not surprising that tension, hostility, differences and conflict exist. The challenges faced by many African countries are not only the result of colonialism, but the creation of political borders according to European interests is an important factor. This also applies to former colonies in Asia, Latin America and the Middle East. This is because a delimited territory is essential for nations as part of their identity.

> Borders are related to *Identity* in several ways. A territory can have important cultural, historical or religious significance to a community. A defined territory is essential to identity. The effective control over this territory is also crucial. A government unable to protect its territory is seen as weak, unstable or even failed.

States with multiple nations (multinational states) can live in peace, such as Switzerland, Belgium or Canada. Others find borders at the heart of their current or protracted conflicts, such as Spain, Great Britain or Armenia. Some nation-states have managed to cooperate in different areas because of what unites them, in spite of their differences, changing the traditional concept of borders. The best example is perhaps the EU. This supranational political and economic organization is made up of 27 states, and it is one of the most significant standards of peace, democracy and cooperation, in which borders are (up to a certain point) open.

HL extension

The Kurdish people in Türkiye, Iran, Iraq and Syria, have been a cause, target and factor in several of the conflicts present in these countries. One of the desires of the Kurds is to stop being a nation living in a foreign territory and to establish their own nation-state (Kurdistan). The desire to transform from a nation to a nation-state has been a reason for conflict around the world for many years (for example, in Catalonia, Scotland, Republika Srpska, Quebec and South Ossetia). This is not only the result of an interest in controlling resources, but also because international recognition provides the nation with identity and the legitimacy to play a role in international relations, forums and organizations. Sometimes, this desire to become a recognized nation-state is looked for diplomatically, but in other cases, violence is used.

Borders are not in themselves a problem, except when they are used as a tool for control, power or oppression. Control over natural resources or disputes over internationally agreed borders are also common causes of conflict (including territorial waters). A recent example of a conflict over territory is the dispute between Russia and Ukraine over Crimea and the Donbass region inside Ukraine. Other conflicts have been going on for a long time, such as the disputed territory of Nagorno Karabakh between Armenia and Azerbaijan. The International Court of Justice (ICJ), one of the UN's principal organs, plays an important role in solving disputes between countries, including territorial disputes. Some of the cases that have been brought to the ICJ are the sovereignty over the Sapodilla Cayes (Belize vs Honduras), the dispute over the status and use of the waters of the Silala (Chile vs Bolivia), and the land and maritime delimitation and sovereignty over islands (Gabon/Equatorial Guinea).

To learn more about the ICJ and its role in solving territorial disputes, you can visit:

Borders and migration

Borders are closely related to travel and migration. For the purposes of national interest, borders are used to control the movement of people, goods and services, by establishing rules and conditions for entry. While some countries have flexible and porous borders, others apply extremely hard migratory and travel rules, as well as strict measures for trade. Borders can have negative impacts on the human rights of many, particularly migrants and refugees. This is especially true when border control is left in the hands of corrupt and abusive authorities.

A **migrant** is a person who leaves their place of residence as a result of diverse reasons, ranging from economic to professional or personal, or even external. You might change cities because of work opportunities, or move to another country because your partner is there, or move to another continent as a result of personal life-long interests. Migration is often voluntary.

We are all entitled to the right to migrate, but sovereignty, security reasons and national interests give states the full right to accept, deny or make conditions of entry to foreigners. The UDHR asserts in Article 13 that 'everyone has the right to freedom of movement and residence within the borders of each state' and 'everyone has the right to leave any country, including his own, and to return to his country.'[57] But, for different reasons, some countries require visas for certain travelers from specific countries, and different types of visas and permits exist. In the end, it is up to a state to decide whether a foreigner can enter their territory or not.

Global political challenges

In order to provide a global framework for the control of migration, in 1951, the International Organization for Migration (IOM) was established. With 175 member states, the IOM works for several purposes:

- to promote humane and orderly migration
- to promote cooperation on migration
- to provide services and advice to governments and migrants
- to assist in the search for solutions to migration
- to provide humanitarian assistance to migrants in need.

The IOM, as per other international organizations, has no supranational powers, its recommendations are non-binding and it has no obligation or responsibility over migrants. This means that, if you wanted to move to another country because of a job opportunity, or personal interest, and you were rejected, the IOM could not intervene on your behalf.

Activity

Look at the picture on page 275 depicting toy figures of the US border patrol and a group of people trying to cross the border. We are asuming the people are migrants, but they may be refugees. Discuss with your classmates the push factors that lead people to migrate. Which of these are similar among migrants? Which of these differ between migrants and refugees?

Refugees migrate because they are forced to. The 1951 Convention Relating to the Status of Refugees defined a refugee as 'someone who is unable or unwilling to return to their country of origin owing to a well-founded fear of being persecuted for reasons of race, religion, nationality, membership of a particular social group, or political opinion.'[58] In order to qualify as a refugee, a person must cross borders to a different country. Migrants can move because of economic purposes, but refugees do not migrate voluntarily, but because their life is in danger back home.

The term refugee applies to people escaping (leaving their country) from an armed conflict, a war, persecution (including political persecution), or because staying at home means arrest, unjustified detention, torture, execution or even death.

People migrating carrying nothing but what fits inside a backpack.

HL extension

Because of this, the 1951 Convention Relating to the Status of Refugees also establishes the rights that individuals given asylum are entitled to, as well as the responsibilities and obligations governments have toward these people. Among others, the rights refugees have are:

- the right to return to their home countries
- the right to non-refoulement (not to be forcibly returned to the place they are escaping from)
- family reunification
- the right to travel
- the right to have dignified work
- the right to education
- the right to naturalization and assimilation.

As with any other convention treaty or agreement, there is no body or mechanism to enforce compliance, which leaves many asylum seekers and refugees without the legal protection they are entitled to.

During the Syrian refugee crisis between 2013 and 2017, around five million Syrians (as well as Iraqis and Afghans) migrated to Europe in search of asylum. Most of them tried to reach safety by crossing the Mediterranean or by traveling through south-eastern European countries. Several states within the EU welcomed refugees, such as Germany, Sweden, France and the UK.

Other governments adopted tighter migratory measures, leaving hundreds of thousands of refugees without access to safety. One example was the Hungarian government, which adopted strongly restrictive measures against migrants and refugees entering the country. Among these were the closure of crossing points at its borders, declaring a state of emergency and giving special powers to police (including the use of force against migrants). The Hungarian government also made it a criminal offense, punishable by deportation or prison, to damage any erected border defenses (such as barbed-wire fences) and effectively barred future asylum applications. While these border measures violated the human rights of many, it served the country's security interests.

Where migration becomes a social, political and security problem, countries tend to apply stronger measures to protect their borders. This can be done by securing the political borders, and also by erecting additional barriers to deter foreigners from entering. During the Trump administration, several contested efforts were made to deter migration. One of them was Executive Order 13769, Protecting the Nation from Foreign Terrorist Entry into the USA, which banned people entering the USA from seven majority-Muslim countries for 90 days without exception (Iran, Iraq, Libya, Somalia, Sudan, Syria and Yemen). This measure also suspended refugee resettlement for 120 days and banned Syrian refugees indefinitely.

This order was blocked by the Supreme Court, but three months later, a revised travel ban was proposed, removing Iraq from the list and exempting people who had visas and green cards. Several executive orders came after that, with modifications to the list of banned countries and other small details. The Trump administration was characterized by an attempt to close borders. Even during Trump's presidential campaign, a critical point of his proposed policies was the promised expansion of the wall on the border with Mexico.

To learn more about refugees, you can visit the UN High Commissioner for Refugees official website:

In 2018, the UN General Assembly adopted the Global Compact on Refugees, providing a framework to improve global responses to the needs of refugees. One hundred and eighty-one countries voted in favor, with Hungary and the USA voting against.

Global political challenges

Irregular migration from Mexico to the USA. Migrants climb the fence in an attempt to cross or at least wave to their friends and family across the border.

Borders can be a useful tool for deterring terrorism, crime and other challenges. However, borders can be a dangerous place for people who want to migrate or seek asylum. Traffickers and smugglers operate at borders, and people can also experience violence and inhumane conditions in which their human rights are at risk and often violated.

Borders for national and global security

Historically, rulers have always regarded the control of territory as essential to their sovereignty. Many borders were natural borders. Occasionally human-made borders were erected to deter enemies or foreigners from invading. During the Han dynasty in China (202 BCE–9 CE, 25–220 CE), the use of passports (*zhuan*) was in place, with passes that allowed the movement of people within the country. These passes detailed the physical characteristics of the person possessing it. The Ottoman Empire used quarantine stations within its borders to control the spread of infectious diseases.

Border control as a means to security is not new, but it has increased with mass migrations and globalization. The permeability of borders has allowed a freer movement of people, cultures and ideologies, but also of extremist ideas, weapons and drugs. Depending on their needs and priorities, different countries apply different border control measures. India enjoys open borders with Bhutan and Nepal. Although boundaries are defined between the three, there is free movement of people for which passports and visas are not necessary. The EU enjoys safe free movement of people among the Schengen area countries, but this is not a privilege enjoyed around the world.

Underfunded border control, hard to defend borders and corruption allow for the continuous irregular movement of people, illegal movement of goods and services, and trafficking and smuggling, all of which pose a security threat to countries. Examples include drug trafficking between the Philippines and Mexico, human

HL extension

trafficking from Thailand to South Korea, or Islamic State of Iraq and Syria (ISIS) members coming into Europe posing as migrants. Intangible issues, like diseases, can also pose a threat to countries, and strengthening borders can help to manage or keep these threats away. For example, during the COVID-19 pandemic, New Zealand had an absolute closed borders policy.

In order to address these security challenges, many countries make efforts to protect their territories, often strengthened by the use of technology. Since the September 11, 2001 attacks against the USA, border security has taken a different approach to that during the 20th century. Airport security used to be much less intrusive. Metal detectors existed, but passengers were allowed to keep their coats and shoes on. Liquids over 100 ml, lighters and other items were allowed onboard. Airport security could be almost invisible. Today, there are full body scanners, 3D imaging X-ray machines, bomb sniffer dogs, long processes checking the contents of bags, and possibly even verbal harassment and long interrogations.

Many believe these measures are too much, and perhaps violate our privacy, but others believe they are necessary. Studies on the effectiveness of these measures often show contradictory results. A 2022 poll by YouGov America showed that 79 percent of Americans believe airports should prioritize security[59], but since the formation of the Transportation Security Administration (TSA), the US governmental agency in charge of security at airports, not one terrorist has been detained trying to board an aircraft. However, security measures certainly act as deterrents.

▲ Airport security checking passengers' luggage with X-rays.

HL *Technology* plays a crucial role in securing borders nowadays. Digital technologies, AI and other technologies have become important assets for preserving the *Security* of countries.

Activity

Discuss how the technology used in airports has changed since the year 2000. Do you think the changes in security measures answer to a specific national and/or global context? If so, discuss which one(s).

Additional security measures include border walls/fences and checkpoints. Border checkpoints are places where people or goods are inspected before crossing a national or international border. Walls and fences usually fulfill a desire to limit unwanted migration and travel. Examples include the wall Iran built on its border with Pakistan, the walls at Melilla and Ceuta (Spain) at their border with Morocco, the barbed-wire fence between Hungary and Serbia, and the 300-mile electrified fence built in 2003 by Botswana on the border with Zimbabwe. This fence is allegedly intended to keep cattle out (and their diseases). Other walls like the Berm (a sand wall) in the Western Sahara territory delimit contested land.

The reasons behind these measures include the control of irregular migration and the movement of illegal products (weapons, animal and plant species, or drugs), and to act as a deterrent to terrorism and organized crime. They all have the purpose of preserving national security. Evidence shows that border enforcement can but may not always work, leading to a growing debate around expenditure on border control.

Global political challenges

Case study – Human trafficking in Nepal

It is estimated that 27.6 million people (although real numbers are unknown) are victims of human trafficking around the world. Trafficking is an international crime that does not discriminate in terms of backgrounds, nationalities or ages, and men, women and children are prey to human traffickers. Estimates show that around 71 percent of trafficked people are women and girls, and around 29 percent are boys and men.

The UN Office on Drugs and Crimes defines human trafficking as the recruitment, transportation, transfer, harboring or receipt of people through force, fraud or deception, with the aim of exploiting them for profit.[60] Given the scale of the issue, and its hidden nature, it is almost impossible to fully grasp the scope of this crime. Human trafficking consists of three core elements: the act, the means and the purpose.

The crime of human trafficking consists of three core elements: the act, the means and the purpose. The purpose is always the same: exploitation.

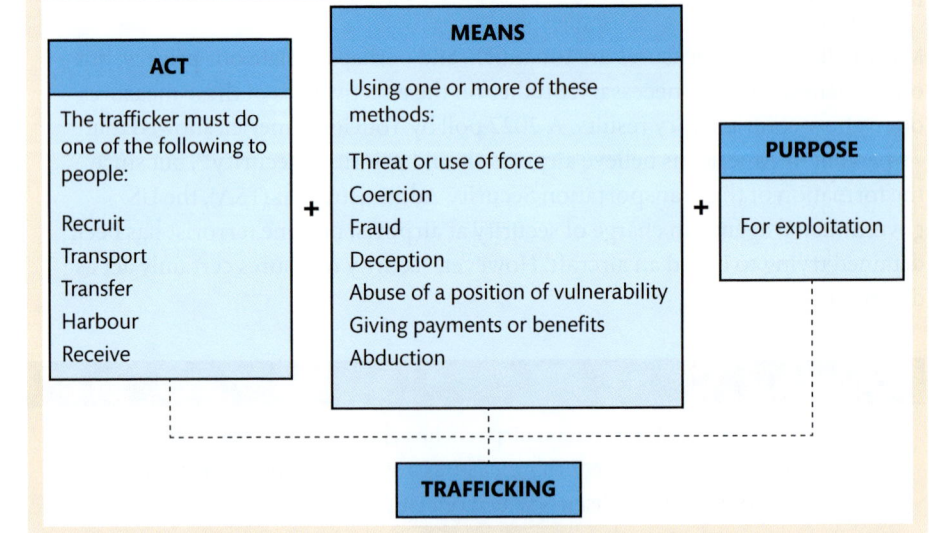

ACT
The trafficker must do one of the following to people:
- Recruit
- Transport
- Transfer
- Harbour
- Receive

+

MEANS
Using one or more of these methods:
- Threat or use of force
- Coercion
- Fraud
- Deception
- Abuse of a position of vulnerability
- Giving payments or benefits
- Abduction

+

PURPOSE
For exploitation

→ **TRAFFICKING**

Human traffickers prey on people in every region of the world, often using violence, manipulation, blackmail, fraud and fake promises to trick and coerce their victims. People can become victims of human trafficking within their home country, during migration or in a foreign country. It always has the same purpose: exploitation. This can include exploitation in the sex, entertainment and hospitality industries, in forced marriages or for labor purposes. Some victims can be coerced or tricked into having their organs removed, while some, mainly children, can be forced to serve as soldiers or commit crimes for the benefit of criminal organizations. Some victims, particularly women, can be forced into domestic servitude.

It is estimated that, on a daily basis, 50 women are trafficked from Nepal to India. The National Human Rights Commission of Nepal found 35,000 Nepali victims between 2018 and 2019, with more than a million currently at risk of becoming victims. According to an article by Rohit Sharma, the scale and persistence of this crime is partly the result of weak border controls at the Indian-Nepalese border[61], although socio-economic and human rights issues are also to blame.

The border between these two countries is 1751 km of open and porous passage, where no immigration control exists (under the 1950 Peace and Friendship Treaty

HL extension

between India and Nepal). This treaty was established to ensure a close strategic relationship between the two countries, allowing free movement of people and goods, as well as a close relationship and collaboration on matters of defense and foreign policy. This has strengthened social, economic and cultural ties. Citizens of both countries may freely move across, reside or work in either country. But these benefits have come at a human cost.

People cross between India and Nepal without any border control.

Nationals do not require a passport or visa to cross over into each other's territory. Every day, thousands of people move across borders using the official trade and transit routes, but there are also informal routes. To distinguish between migrants and victims of trafficking is extremely difficult.

The government of India guards the border through the Sashastra Seema Bal, while Nepal uses the Armed Police Force. Procedures to intercept victims or traffickers are not yet institutionalized. This is exploited by traffickers to make themselves and their victims go unidentified.

In 2015, the Indian and Bangladeshi governments passed a memorandum of understanding concerning human trafficking, in which both parties agreed to take steps relating to illicit cross-border activities. The plan included provisions for the rescue, recovery, repatriation and reintegration of victims. Although there have been efforts to reach a similar agreement with Nepal, this has not yet happened. So far, the only legal measure in place is a no objection letter issued to Nepalese citizens who travel to third countries via India, verifying the reasons for their journey, with diplomatic approval. However, nothing has limited the production of fake letters, and the openness of the border persists. In November 2020, the UN adopted the Protocol to Prevent, Suppress and Punish Trafficking in Persons. As of 2023, there were 181 countries party to the Protocol, including Nepal and India.

Poverty, lack of education and awareness are important factors behind human trafficking in Nepal. However, a different approach to border control is essential to deter criminal organizations from operating.

Global political challenges

Flexible borders can be beneficial for trade and for economic growth. Iceland, Liechtenstein, Norway and Switzerland created the European Free Trade Association (EFTA) to promote free trade and economic integration for the benefit of the member countries, as well as their trading partners around the globe. 'EFTA is the ninth largest trader in the world in merchandise trade and the fifth largest in trade in services. EFTA is the third most important trading partner in goods for the EU and the second most important when it comes to services.'[62]

Borders have a significant role in global politics. They can function as important tools for security, peaceful relations among states, international order, identity and power. They can also be controversial for their role in armed conflicts and international security. Most borders have been agreed upon, but some borders have not yet been agreed, and borders are not fixed. New states continue to be created, while others are still pending recognition. Borders give shape to the actors in the global arena. A change in borders has political, geographical, economic, diplomatic and social effects. When borders change, so does the structure of the international system.

Exercises

15. Explain what makes territorial conflicts so complicated to manage and solve. Is it because of the economic, strategic or symbolic meaning of territory?

16. Discuss whether borders should be open to welcome environmentally induced migrants.

17. Identify what the implications are of closing borders to refugees seeking asylum.

Summary

In this section, you have learned:

- Borders are at the heart of the modern architecture of the international system, defining what sovereignty is and looks like. Borders can be defined by natural boundaries (like the Rio Grande separating Mexico and the United States), although most borders are a political construct (such as the Schengen area in the European Union) that defines power, affects international relations, and plays a role within global challenges.

- The importance of borders is strongly contested. Many countries would like to relax their borders considering that international challenges need cooperation and collaboration, yet some are hesitant to do so because borders are a way of protecting territories, people and national interests. This dilemma was seen during the COVID-19 pandemic.

- Territory has economic, strategic and symbolic value, making it a recurrent factor in interstate and intrastate conflicts. This also makes territory an often non-negotiable issue.

- The desire to transform from a nation to a nation-state has been a reason for conflict around the world for many years, for example, in Catalonia, Spain. This results from an interest in controlling resources, and a desire for international recognition that provides the nation with identity and the legitimacy to play a role in international relations, forums and organizations.

HL extension

- Borders are used to control the movement of people, goods and services, by establishing rules and conditions for entry. Some countries have flexible and porous borders (such as the one between Nepal and India), while others apply extremely hard migratory and travel rules, as well as strict measures for trade.
- Although we are all entitled to the right to migrate, sovereignty, security reasons and national interests give states the full right to accept, deny or make conditions to entry to foreigners.
- The International Organization for Migration (IOM) promotes humane and orderly migration, assists governments in the search for solutions to migration, and helps migrants in need.
- Border control as a means to security has increased as mass migrations and globalization have. To address these security challenges, technology is a useful tool.

Security

Learning outcomes

In this section, you will learn about:
- how security is essential for states, global stability and human development
- borders help states in achieving security for their territories and people
- people living in poverty and those facing inequalities face greater threats to their human security
- technology serves security purposes at the individual, state and international levels, but technology poses security risks
- human security entails equal access to basic human needs like shelter, food, education and health
- threats are defined by authorities according to their specific contexts, but the process of securitization can be controversial
- environmental protection and degradation are a global security problem
- security measures often discriminate based on identity factors.

Conceptual question

What is security and who needs to be secure?

Security is at the core of human life. Whether as individuals, families, communities or societies, we need and wish to live in the absence of danger or fear. Security is associated with peace and stability, while insecurity is often associated with war and violence or the threat of them. Security is the foundation upon which we build our individual and collective lives, and is perhaps the most basic of all human needs.

Security studies have often focused on states and the international arena. This narrow understanding of security emphasizes the use and control of military power against internal and external threats. Humans also need to be secure. Many people around the

Global political challenges

world do not live in peaceful and prosperous circumstances. In some places, the security of communities and whole countries is taken for granted. In other places, everyday life involves insecurity, making safety and survival common preoccupations.

To desire security is a self-protecting response to the fact that harm or the threat of harm exists. This can come from other humans, other countries, the environment or the international system. This is especially true in an interconnected world, where national and global threats are also threats to the security of people.

> The concept of power is at the core of security studies. When we refer to national and international security, power is often demonstrated in military, political and economic strength that helps deter or destroy enemies.

Activity

Think of a moment when you felt threatened or insecure? What were you afraid of? What were the circumstances?

Security is often defined as the absence of danger, threat and harm. This definition is very broad, and the word security is used for many different contexts in many different ways. For example, threats are not the same for everyone everywhere. A person living in New York City may consider it dangerous to walk alone in the streets at night, even the streets close to home, while for someone living in Tokyo, walking the streets alone at night may not be a matter for fear. For a girl in Liberia, it might be a threat to go to school, but for a girl in Stockholm, attending school is not only normal but safe.

The biggest obstacle to defining security is reaching an agreement on what are considered dangers, threats and harms. These include the physical (such as war, disease, accidents, kidnappings or street crime), the emotional (such as harassment, discrimination or marginalization), and the environmental (such as vulnerability to natural disasters). There is a difference between *security from* (which refers to being safe

HL extension

from a specific harm) and *security to* (which refers to having the conditions to pursue a goal). In the name of security, people, governments and organizations have adopted a wide range of courses of action that have resulted in intended and unintended outcomes. Some of these are positive, but some are not.

As a fundamental component of all global issues faced around the world, security is a central theme of global politics. Different debates around security revolve around:

- Who is its target (is security about the protection of individuals, the states or both)?
- Who or what should provide this security (the state, international organizations or private organizations)?
- Through what means should security be provided?
- What is a threat?

Jennifer Jackson-Preece considers four key assumptions underlying the idea of security[63]:

- Security in (or of) what? The assumption recognizes that humans who live in social circumstances always face vulnerabilities.
- Security from what? According to Thomas Hobbes, the 'state of nature'[64] of humans entails a constant potential threat because we all struggle for survival, in a war of all against all. Regardless of our capabilities, we can all inflict harm upon others. So, there is always a large or small possibility of insecurity.
- Security by means of what? Different measures and approaches can be taken to live securely. These range from the use of police forces and armed forces, to walls, locks, barriers, alarms, etc. Security exists when no one threatens to harm someone else.
- Security for what? The goal of security is to provide a state of enjoyment of social life while limiting risks and harm.

Such assumptions see insecurity as always present whenever humans live in societies, because other humans can always pose a threat, one way or another. Individuals live in societies, so there is always a risk of another society causing harm. The same applies to nations and states. In today's world we are all connected. Hence, we are always, at any level, at risk of insecurity from direct threats or from the spillover effects of threats faced somewhere else.

Approaches to security

Within the study of international relations, there are two approaches to address security: normative and instrumental.

The normative approach is based upon values, identities and ideas. It sees security as normative, because without it human life is reduced to a basic struggle for survival. This approach to security often finds itself choosing between competing values. For example, should human security come before national security? To what extent can privacy be diminished at the expense of increasing security? Can individual liberties be hindered to increase national security? These questions are a series of moral dilemmas, with questions about the ends and goals of security, as well as the means to pursue them.

The instrumental approach focuses on outcomes. It believes security policies should be judged by their results, without considering any moral implications. The moral

---

Security is closely related to human rights, especially when talking about human security. However, even in the pursuit of national and international security, measures adopted can hinder the human rights of many around the world at the expense of providing a real, or perceived, security.

Security refers to a state of absence of threats and harm against one's physical integrity, interests or values.

Radioactive waste barrels. If this waste is not managed adequately, it can pollute the environment or produce life-threatening accidents.

dilemmas from the normative approach are not only ignored, but are often seen as a distraction from the rational pursuit of security interests.

Table 5.6 Approaches to security

Normative Approach	Instrumental Approach
Security is a frequent struggle of competing values, between the ends and the means to pursue it.	Security is judged only by its results. Moral implications are an obstacle to security policies and measures.
For example, in the war against terror, can the use of enhanced techniques of interrogation be justified to acquire intelligence? Is the acquisition of intelligence superior to the respect of human rights and liberties of many innocent people?	For example, in the war against terror, were enhanced interrogation techniques appropriate because they provided useful intelligence, leading to the capture of Osama bin Laden?

> Security depends on specific situations and contexts. Threats are not the same for everyone, nor for every state. Dangers do not pose the same level of threat to all countries and societies around the world. As a result, the way we react to solve a security threat or to prevent it from becoming a threat varies from one place to another and throughout time.

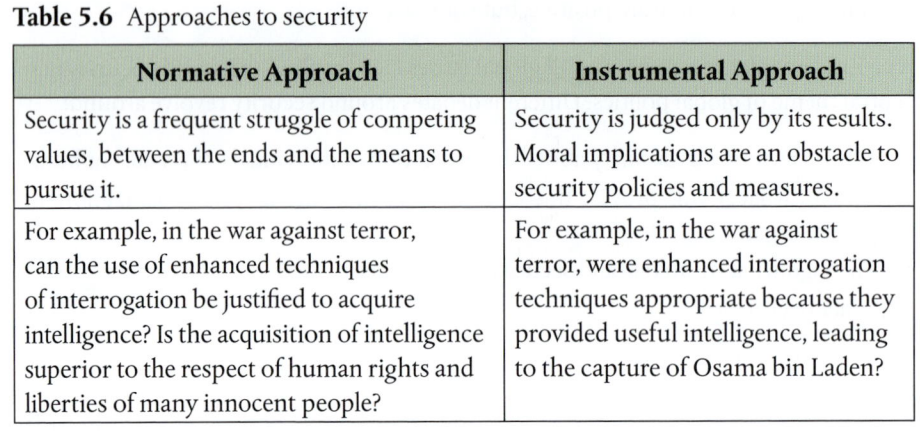

The debate between normative and instrumental views of security is not only present in the ways security is sought. It is also present when defining a threat, choosing the means to act or react to threats, or choosing preventive or pre-emptive measures, and when evaluating the results.

This makes evaluating national security measures a difficult task. There are several methods of measuring cybersecurity, human security, food security or health security (meaning that we *can* measure the global scale of such issues). However, measuring national (and international) security is not possible if there is no agreement on what constitutes a threat, nor is it possible when national security encompasses so many other aspects.

The focus on national security has not diminished, despite growing globalization and interconnectedness. However, challenges such as poverty, hunger, violations of human rights, armed conflict and diseases are responsible for human suffering, and have drawn increasing attention to the importance of global security and human security. This means that all the topics covered in this book are closely linked to security, due to its political, cultural, social, human, technological and economic dimensions.

National security

Historically the idea of international relations revolving around states as the most important actors emphasized the security of states, focusing on their territorial integrity, political stability, military power and economic capabilities. Traditional realist conceptions of security focus on military power and survival (Morgenthau[65] and Mearsheimer[66]) where the state has the monopoly over the means to protect itself. But how can we be safe in a global system by protecting national interests (what is commonly referred to as national security), when this cannot be separated from global security?

National security is the ability of a state to ensure the protection and defense of its territory, population and sovereignty. Several writers, academics and scholars have provided definitions of national security including the 'freedom from foreign dictation'[67] and the 'capacity to control… domestic and foreign conditions that the public opinion of a given community believes necessary to enjoy its own self-determination or autonomy, prosperity, and wellbeing.'[68]

For most of the 20th century, national security depended on military power and strength, but with the 21st century came a new set of threats that required a redefinition of national security. This new definition of national security does not consider military prowess as sufficient to address all the demands of national security: economic, political, homeland, human, environmental, energy and cyber/technological. Some countries have continued to focus on military capabilities (hard power) as a means to protect their national interests (for example, North Korea). Others (for example, Germany) have reshaped their domestic policies to shift funds and resources away from the military and into other spheres by adopting a range of military measures, and also political, economic and diplomatic (soft power) measures to safeguard their security.

Today, a huge amount of state resources is directed toward maintaining and developing armed and security forces, using intelligence to detect and counter external attacks as well as internal subversion, and using diplomacy and cooperation to strengthen alliances. Many governments equate strength with security, so they use military force as a way to coerce opponents or deter potential enemies. Some national security policies do consider international threats, but others do not. While some policies successfully deter international threats, others fail to do so. Conventional national security measures are not entirely adapted to the current and constantly changing security reality. There are security measures that protect national interests but at the same time endanger human security.

The unpredictable characteristics of the international arena, the growth and influence of NSAs and threats, the increase of non-conventional warfare mechanisms (such as domestic political extremism, international terrorism, climate change, the use of child soldiers, drug cartels and digital threats), among other factors, have made national security policies and priorities much more complicated.

Traditional views on national security assume that we live in a world where states are sources of security *and* security threats. It is this view of our existence in an anarchical world that strengthened the idea of an arena in which every state is capable of harming another. This view increasingly includes other actors, even NSAs, where these are viewed as having the capacity, potential and, at times, desire to harm other actors.

National security policies also involve measures designed to deal with internal threats. Such threats include crime, terrorism, insurgency, diseases, natural disasters, etc. Regardless of their impact at the human level, these do pose a threat to the state. They can have harmful economic consequences, damage diplomatic relations, destabilize entire countries, or threaten governments and those in power.

National security has different dimensions based on the potential causes of insecurity. All of these are related to the concepts of power and sovereignty, and are also related to one another.

> Sovereignty exists at the core of national security. National security, in all its forms, aims at protecting the interests and sovereignty of a country.

Global political challenges

Table 5.7 Types of security and their definitions

Type of Security	Definition
Military security	The management of physical threats to a state requires the capacity to mobilize military forces.
Political security	Refers to the organizational stability of states, their legitimacy and the effectiveness of political institutions.
Economic security	The ability of a state to develop and strengthen its economy, access resources and markets, provide employment and economic growth.
Cybersecurity	The technological and digital capacities of the state to develop, protect and manage the use of hardware, software and data belonging to the state and its people.
Environmental security	Encompasses the integrity and protection of ecosystems and their capacity to sustain life, addressing the degradation of these due to human-made and natural processes (natural disasters, soil erosion, deforestation, etc.). Environmental security is related to migration issues, economic impact and development.
Energy security	The availability of natural resources (such as water, minerals, land and other sources of energy) for energy consumption. Energy security is linked to environmental factors and the economic security of a state.

Thomas Hobbes' book *Leviathan or The Matter, Form, and Power of a Commonwealth, Ecclesiastical and Civil*[69], published in 1651, stated that the natural basic state of humankind is one of anarchy, with the strong dominating the weak. Therefore, we live in a constant and permanent competition for survival. The leviathan is a mythical creature referenced in several books of the Hebrew Bible. It is usually represented in the form of a sea serpent.

The goal of national security is to deter, prevent or defeat existing and potential threats to the state and its population. National security in conventional terms derives from military strength, and results in a zero-sum game, where the more one side obtains, the less there is for the other side. Resolving internal security issues often creates a new problem of insecurity between states. This view creates enemies for the state that otherwise would not exist. With the end of the Cold War, national security has come to mean different things to different countries and is not seen exclusively as a military issue.

Local Italian police officer observing people in a square.

Within national security, we can find non-military definitions, some of which are shown in Table 5.7. For example, political security relies on law enforcement. Economic security focuses on the degree to which a government and its people can control their economic and financial decisions, and the country's wealth. Energy security often refers to the degree to which a nation has access to energy resources. Cybersecurity seeks to protect the government's and the people's data, systems and infrastructure from interference. Environmental security focuses on environmental problems, the protection of climate and the threat of its degradation.

To gain complete national security would involve addressing every single dimension – an extremely complicated task for any government. Many governments do not have the means, the infrastructure or the capacity to deal with all these threats. Some

HL extension

countries prefer to focus on a few of them, and address them properly, but ignore others. Some countries put great efforts into trying to solve everything, just to dramatically (and expectedly) fail. Others are much better prepared to address national threats. First, the state must:

- define what or who is a threat to its security
- ask itself whether this threat can be tolerated, or if it should be eliminated
- ask itself whether the threat can be dealt with using the resources at hand, and what the cost will be of doing so.

National security does not always translate into security for the people. Liberal political theory sees the state as belonging to the people because it is created by the people, and the people's security is core to the state's security. In theory, the state cannot and would not pose a threat to its citizens. In practice, this is not always the case. Many states are unable to provide security for their citizens (these are often referred to as weak or failed states), while others intentionally threaten their own population (such as totalitarian regimes).

Global security

The line between national and global security has become increasingly blurred due to growing interconnectedness between countries and societies, and the international role of global actors and threats. Globalization has made it necessary for states to reformulate security measures that national security is not capable of handling on its own, thus drawing states into increasing their cooperation in different arenas.

Since the end of the Cold War, international security has changed. While conflict between states has diminished, regional instabilities, intrastate conflicts and non-traditional threats have increased. Nowadays, a state's security cannot be fully achieved without considering the security needs of other states.

Some of the major global security threats faced today around the world include the following:

- Terrorism: National and international extremist groups have been on the rise, aided by the use of communication technologies and a global trend of growing nationalism and xenophobia.
- Weapons of mass destruction: Disarmament has been a slow process and military technology keeps advancing.
- Cybersecurity: Digital technologies, and advances in technology, in general, have evolved faster than societies have been able to adapt to and regulate. The existing legal vacuums also pose a growing global threat.
- Space security: Although planned to be used for the benefit of humans, the use of space has become a new arena for conflict and competition, raising concerns of its use and potential misuse.
- Criminal organizations: Access to illegal markets, the increasing demand for cheap goods and services, and the porosity of borders allow for drug trafficking, arms trafficking, people smuggling and trafficking, organ trafficking and animal trafficking, etc.

HL One of the main purposes of *Borders* is to provide security for a territory and its people. Climate change and the *Environment* are now considered important to human, national and global security. Global public *Health*, especially in the form of diseases and pandemics, have increasingly been considered a security problem. *Technology*, while playing a crucial role in providing new and more advanced tools for security, has become a cause of insecurity.

Global political challenges

- Climate change: The effects of global warming, extreme weather events and rising sea levels affect a country's economy, infrastructure and population.
- Diseases and pandemics: Despite the eradication of several deadly and widespread diseases, health services in many countries lack funding, while in others they have been devastated by armed conflict. The spread of new diseases and infections is still a global threat, exacerbated by climate change.

A globalized world is a mixture of cooperation and competition. States are not the only responsible actors in this world, nor are they the only ones capable of providing international security. In the international system (compared to national and human security), there are no external threats (so far, our planet is not threatened by an external factor, such as another life form, for example), but only internal threats. This is because global threats are the consequences of actions of other members *within* the international arena. Any action by any state that violates international law is a disruption to the general condition of peace and order.

UN Security Council meeting at the UN Headquarters in New York, USA.

International efforts to address global security threats have resulted in the creation of global and regional organizations. One of the most important is the UN, whose principal goal is to ensure global peace and security, assigning most of this responsibility to the UN Security Council. Other organizations have come into existence to address global threats. In the military field, the North Atlantic Treaty Organization (NATO) was created in 1949 and currently has the involvement of 31 states in its collective security system. NATO has been involved in military operations around the world and is one of the most important actors in the international security field.

Another organization is the Organization for Security and Co-operation in Europe (OSCE), whose area of work includes arms control, conflict prevention and resolution, border management, policing, economic activities, elections, human rights and protection of freedoms. Created during the Cold War as a forum for communication and conflict resolution between the Western and Eastern blocs, the OSCE works with the political commitment of 57 governments, signatories of the Helsinki Final Act.

HL extension

The Shanghai Cooperation Organization (SCO), founded in 2001, focuses on regional security issues, the fight against regional terrorism, ethnic separatism and religious extremism, but its priorities also include regional development,

In the field of worldwide police cooperation and criminal control, Interpol, created in 1923, is one of the leading international organizations, with 195 member states. Despite not being a law enforcement agency (it does not conduct military operations or have the capacity to conduct detentions or arrests), Interpol provides expertise and training to law enforcement and investigative support for every kind of crime through the use of criminal databases and communication networks where national law enforcement institutions collaborate with each other. Some of the security threats addressed by Interpol include cybersecurity, organized crime, terrorism, child pornography, drug trafficking, drug production, intellectual property and political corruption.

These organizations are just a few examples of global efforts in the search for security. Within these global efforts, the following principles are considered paramount:

- Collective defense: This is an official arrangement among states to offer defense support to others in case of attack. It is the basis on which NATO was created and still exists.
- Collective security: This is mutual security commitments and various types of arrangements, often delimited to a regional area (although they can be global), within which international law, international aid and governance are found. It tends to have a hybrid character because collective security recognizes the importance of collective action, but also respects individual sovereignty.

Global security rests on the premise that no single country can be safe unless everyone is safe, and that global security can only exist from collective efforts. Thus it highlights the importance of international law, aid and global governance. Global security sees force as a last resort, and preferably limited to specific situations and contexts.

Human security

Different global challenges around the world have led to human suffering. Poverty, inequality, violation of human rights and liberties, discrimination, violence, diseases and natural disasters have all affected the people's sense of security in terms of the absence of threats and harm. In *Leviathan*, Thomas Hobbes declared that the solution to the problem of personal security is the creation of a political order or a sovereign to protect the people. This can only exist if the population agrees to give up some of their personal freedom in exchange. It is a collective security agreement in which people receive security from their sovereign, and the sovereign obtains power from the people.

Without human security, humans cannot flourish. Security allows people to pursue their own goals and interests without the fear of harm by others. It is a state of peace of mind. However, it is not exclusively related to physical security. The UDHR makes equality and dignity the right of every human. The UDHR also mentions the idea of a 'freedom from fear and want.'[70] This idea helps us to understand human security not only in terms of physical security and integrity, but also in terms of human rights as a means to satisfy basic human needs, with quality and welfare that allow for sustainable human growth and development.

> Human security is an essential aspect of human rights. Every person should live in a state of freedom from fear and want. At the same time, if human security exists, the conditions for development are also present.

Global political challenges

The UN Trust Fund for Human Security published in 2016 a Human Security Handbook for practitioners and policymakers. This diagram shows the connection between freedom from fear, freedom from want and the freedom to live in dignity as interdependent on each other, an essential for the realization of the SDGs.

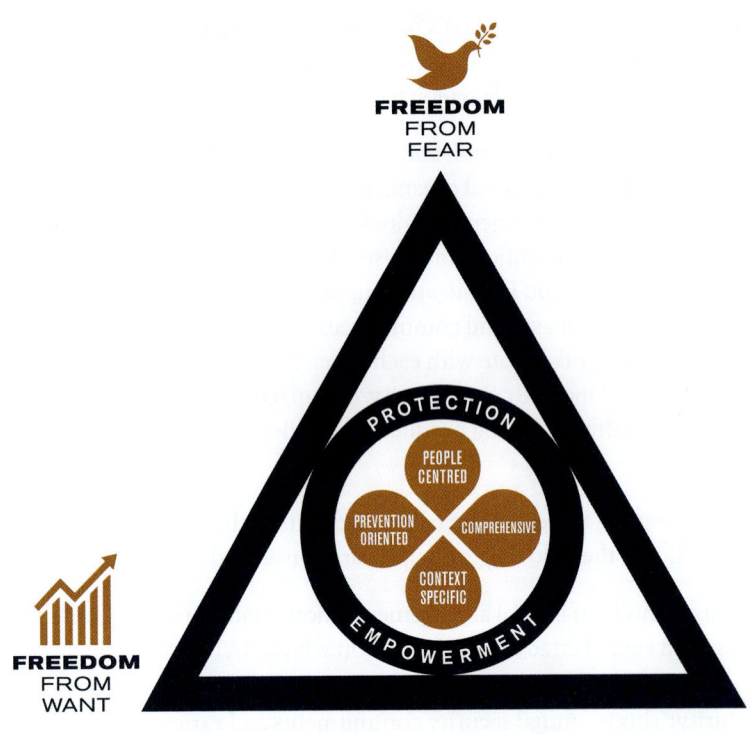

FREEDOM FROM FEAR

FREEDOM FROM WANT

FREEDOM TO LIVE IN DIGNITY

PROTECTION — EMPOWERMENT
- PEOPLE CENTRED
- PREVENTION ORIENTED
- COMPREHENSIVE
- CONTEXT SPECIFIC

HL *Human security is much more than the absence of physical threats and harms. It is also the absence of threats and harm from everyday aspects such as education and Health, which should be enjoyed by everyone equally.*

The UDHR, together with other human rights instruments, has laid the foundations for defining human security. The UNDP in its 1994 *Report on Human Development*[71] introduced the concept of human security in which it became as important as the territorial security of states, but focused on development rather than military capacity. According to the report, human security entails:

- investment in human development
- the engagement of policymakers
- defining a clear mandate within the UN
- enlarging the concept of development cooperation
- the use of national budgets and foreign aid for human development
- the establishment of an Economic Security Council.

This concept aimed at relieving people from threats (such as hunger, disease and repression), while also providing protection from disruptions to everyday life (job opportunities, and access to education and healthcare).

In January 2001, in response to the UN Secretary-General's request at the 2000 Millennium Summit, a Commission on Human Security was created. The Commission's 2003 report *Human security now: protecting and empowering people* defines human security as:

> protect(ing) the vital core of all human lives in ways that enhance human freedoms and human fulfilment… It means protecting people from critical (severe) and pervasive (widespread) threats and situations. It means using processes that build on people's strengths and aspirations. It means creating political, social, environmental, economic, military and cultural systems that together give people the building blocks of survival, livelihood and dignity.[72]

The 1999 UNDP report classifies human security into seven categories (Table 5.8).

HL extension

Table 5.8 Types of security and some main threats

Type of Security	Examples of Main Threats
Economic security	Persistent poverty, unemployment
Food security	Hunger, famine
Health security	Deadly infectious diseases, unsafe food, malnutrition, lack of access to basic healthcare
Environmental security	Environmental degradation, resources depletion, natural disasters, pollution
Personal security	Physical violence, crime, terrorism, domestic violence, child labor
Community security	Inter-ethnic, religious and other identity-based tensions
Political security	Political repression, human rights abuses

Among these types of human security, there are several links and overlaps. Consider, for example, poverty and its link to child labor, hunger and environmental degradation. Or think about political repression, and its overlap with religious conflict, physical violence and the lack of access to basic healthcare. We can also find connections between maternal health during pregnancy, gender rights and equality, access to a social safety net and the protection of indigenous peoples.

It is important to note that, as with national and global security, states have different capacities to address these threats. Some countries are more prone to natural disasters (for example, Kiribati), while others have the technology to be more resilient to environmental changes (for example, the Netherlands). Some countries may have strong economic security yet face big challenges when addressing health insecurity (for example, the USA).

Table 5.9 Types of human security and their indicators[73] (continued on the next page)

Type of Human Security	Indicators
Economic security	Income, access to social safety nets, reliability of incomes, standard of living, employment, risk of joblessness, protection against unemployment
Food security	Availability and supply of food, quality of nutrition, share of household budget for food, access to food during natural or human-made disasters
Environmental security	Assessment on pollution of water and air, prevention of deforestation, land conservation and desertification, concern over environmental problems, ability to solve environmental problems, protection from toxic and hazardous wastes, natural hazard mitigation
Health security	Assessment of the status of health, access to safe water, exposure to illegal drugs, accessibility to healthcare systems (physical and economic), accessibility to safe and affordable family planning, quality of medical care, prevention of HIV/AIDS and other diseases, health trends
Personal security	Fear of violence (physical torture, war, ethnic tension, suicide, etc.), level of crime, efficiency of institutions, prevention of harassment and gender violence

Global political challenges

Type of Human Security	Indicators
Community security	Fear of multinational/multiregional conflicts, fear of internal conflicts, conservation of traditional/ethnic cultures, languages and values, abolishment of ethnic discrimination, protection of indigenous people
Political security	Level of democratization, protection against state repression (freedom of press, speech, voting, etc.), respect of basic human rights and freedom, democratic expectations, abolishment of political detention, imprisonment, systematic torture, ill treatment, disappearance, etc.

The problem with addressing human insecurities is that, in contrast to global threats where international cooperation is necessary, human security is the responsibility of governments and their institutions. Cooperation through foreign aid, foreign investment, IGOs, NGOs, the private sector or humanitarian assistance is possible, but the main responsibility remains that of the state. Human security requires more than just protecting people from harm, but also providing the tools and capacity for individuals and communities to fully develop and to make this development sustainable.

As with many other global challenges and issues, measuring human security is complex. Depending on the context and the place, different priorities exist and different values are assigned to different aspects of human security. There have been several attempts at measuring human security to provide a starting point for policy making. For example, the Global Development Research Center highlights several indicators in the measurement of human security.

> **TOK**
> To what extent is it feasible to precisely measure qualitative aspects of human life, such as human security?

> The Anthropocene is our current geological epoch. It is viewed as the period during which human activity has been the dominant influence on climate and the environment.

> To read the UNDP's report *New threats to human security in the Anthropocene*, you can visit:

Activity

What aspects do you think should be included in the measurement of human security? Do you think a global human security index can exist? Work in a group. Choose one type of insecurity and make a list of the indicators you would include to measure human security. Present these to your classmates and discuss whether anyone would add, change or remove any indicator, and explain why.

In 2022, the UNDP published a report titled *New threats to human security in the Anthropocene*.[74] In it, the UNDP points to digital technology, violent conflict, inequalities and assault on human dignity, and healthcare as the current main challenges for human security. It is important to note that, as with national and global security, human security depends on someone, usually an authority, to determine what is considered a threat. Once a threat has been determined, it is often that same authority that decides upon the measures to be taken to address the threat.

Securitization

One of the principal questions in the field of security studies is who and what defines a threat to security. According to securitization theory, threats are designated by governments and/or authorities in a process of politicization of an issue by labeling it as dangerous, harmful and threatening. This means that security issues are defined as such by specific actors who have the power to transform social, economical or even cultural issues into political concerns that require security measures. The threat can be an actor, an idea, an object or an entire population. As Clara Eroukhmanoff points out, 'it is by referring to them as "security" issues that they become security problems.'[75] This results in different actors identifying different threats, and designing different measures and policies to address them. What are defined as security measures depend on the context and the subject, and they have both positive and negative effects.

Consider, for example, the securitization of Maras (or gangs) in El Salvador under President Nayib Bukele's administration. This process has transformed the Maras into what the government labels as terrorists, and the government has adopted a complex police and military operation that has put into question the excessive force used and the violation of human rights of those detained under this securitzation. The exceptional measures adopted by the government have weakened the gangs. However, this has been at the expense of hindering the liberties of the general population through the use of excessive force and arbitrary detentions.

An important part of the securitization process is the use of rhetoric and discourses (speeches that use language designed to have a persuasive or impressive effect on the audience) to convince the audience about the threat posed by the selected object, and to justify the measures (often excessive) used against it. The authority then draws attention to the threat and exaggerates the urgency with which it must be addressed (by using words such as 'terrorism' or 'existential threat'), spreading fear and panic among the population. This sees excessive measures as acceptable regardless of their negative effects even on the general population: measures that would seem undemocratic under normal circumstances. In the case of El Salvador, it all adds up to the **populist** authoritarian approach Bukele has adopted since reaching power. A populist approach tries to appeal to ordinary people who feel their concerns are disregarded by established elite groups. In extreme circumstances, even liberal democracies restrict civil liberties in the name of security.

Without the support of the population, the securitization process fails. This is because of two reasons. The first is that the authority needs public support to carry on with the repressive measures. The second is that, by having public support, some responsibility falls into the hands of the public and not the government: you, the people, wanted us, the government, to act in this way to protect you. Therefore, a de-securitization process will not begin until the securitization target no longer serves a political or personal interest, and when the public no longer supports the security measures adopted. Examples of this include the Guantanamo Bay Detention Camp, the use of torture as a means of interrogation, and the use of mass surveillance technology during the COVID-19 pandemic.

Security comes at a price, and this is paid by citizens. They pay through their taxes, obligation to obey the law, performance of military duty in times of war and in accepting an authority overstepping their liberties when circumstances seem to require it. Within liberal democracies at least, the freedom to express discontent against the price paid tends to exist. However, in many other places, especially authoritarian or failed states, there is no freedom to do so, or it is limited.

Global political challenges

Case – The securitization of child soldiers

Around the world, thousands of children are recruited and used in armed conflicts despite legal prohibitions. UNICEF reported that between 2005 and 2020 over 93,000 children were recruited and used by different parties in conflicts. These boys and girls, often referred to as child soldiers, suffer from exploitation and horrific abuse. Armed groups, whether state or non-state, use children in any capacity, from cooks, porters, guards and messengers, to human shields or fighters.

Child soldiers are not only children used in the front lines of conflict, but they are also children associated with armed groups performing combat support roles or any other task. These children fall victim to armed groups as a result of abduction, threats, intimidation or manipulation, often driven by poverty, seeking survival or protection for themselves. Despite efforts to stop the recruitment and use of children in armed conflicts, it continues to be a worldwide practice with severe consequences. Their use in armed conflicts is a serious violation of international humanitarian law and the rights of children.

These children are seen as victims of violence, trafficking and exploitation. However, one of the most debatable factors around this issue is the fact that many of them have committed crimes during their association with an armed group. In some cases, children are recruited and used by armed groups that have been labeled as terrorists or have committed acts of terrorism. This complicates the approach taken toward child soldiers.

In 2018, the UN Security Council emphasized in Resolution 2427 a need 'to pay particular attention to the treatment of children associated with all non-State armed groups, including those who commit acts of terrorism.'[76] Increasing awareness of the topic has increased attention on how to reform child protection and juvenile standards in counter-terrorism.

This is of particular importance because counterterrorism laws and policies place children in a complex position. This is due to the existing debate on what constitutes a terrorist, and also because the children used by these groups are often labeled terrorists, as well. As such, their detention and treatment within the criminal justice system leaves children at risk of capital punishment, perpetuates their separation from their family and communities, and exposes them to further violence. In some cases, child soldiers themselves become a security problem.

The UN estimated that in 2016 alone, more than 2000 children were recruited by Boko Haram in Nigeria and were increasingly being used as human bombs. That same year, another estimation considered around 1100 children between the ages of 8 and 15 indoctrinated by ISIS.[77] These children were named the Cubs of the Caliphate. They were mostly Syrian and Iraqi, but many foreign children also filled these ranks, receiving not only constant indoctrination, but also training in basic weapons and soldiering.

The Paris Principles (principles and guidelines on children associated with armed forces or armed groups from 2007) recognizes that children associated with armed groups should be considered victims and not perpetrators. The Rome Statute of the International Criminal Court (ICC) and the Optional Protocol to the Convention on the Rights of the Child add a special protection to be given to children in this context because of their innocence and vulnerability.

HL extension

There is growing debate on the fact that these views neglect children's agency and their own perception of their role within an armed group. This debate occurs frequently, especially under counterterrorism frameworks that see children as threats and address them from a security perspective that highlights their role as perpetrators, forgetting their role as victims.

Resolution 2396 of the UN Security Council states that all countries are obliged to bring anyone participating in terrorist acts to justice, including foreign terrorist fighters, their spouses and children. In many countries, children are detained on suspicion of being associated with designated terrorist groups. Some countries refuse to **repatriate** foreign fighters and their children because they are deemed a security threat.

In 2019, a court in The Hague demanded that the Dutch government repatriate (send back to their own country, in this case, the Netherlands) 56 children born to mothers who joined ISIS in the war in Syria, stating that the children were not to be blamed for the actions of their parents. That same year, a court ordered Germany to repatriate the German wife and three children of an ISIS fighter. One of the most well-known cases was that of Shamima Begum, a British woman who traveled to Syria to marry an ISIS member, who was stripped of her citizenship and banned from traveling back to the UK. The debatable issue in her case is that she traveled to Syria when she was only 15 years old. Opinions on her case are strongly divided, with some declaring that at the time she was already conscious of her actions, with others stating that she was still a child, making her vulnerable to manipulation and grooming, as per any other child associated with armed forces.

Numerous efforts have focused on trying to mitigate and prevent the future use of child soldiers. However, efforts have been hampered for several reasons. One is that the recruitment and use of child soldiers continues to be viewed as a human rights problem, rather than a human and national security issue (regarding it as a security issue does not mean it stops being a human rights concern). It must be understood that the use of children in war is a deliberate and strategic way for armed groups, of any kind, to sustain conflict. Children are used as a weapon of war.

The issue of child soldiers is a moral and ethical dilemma, and it is a security concern. But in trying to address the problem from this perspective, child soldiers have been revictimized, falling prey to a securitization process. This is particularly true when children are recruited and used by so-called terrorist organizations. Are these children a security threat, or victims?

Security is a state we all desire. We cannot eliminate all threats around us, but we can improve security once we understand that human security is essential to national security, which in turn strengthens global security. Tolerating personal insecurity risks the spread of insecurity to other countries and to the international arena. Today, the world is so interconnected that a minority rights violation in one state can spark mass migration across borders, which creates a problem of refugees for other countries, eventually becoming a problem of global concern. Terrorism, civil war, natural hazards or poverty can produce a similar insecurity chain effect.

Global political challenges

Exercises

18. To what extent do you agree with the statement that it is impossible to distinguish between national security and the security interests of political leaders?

19. Compare whether the same answer holds true for developed states and developing states. Why or why not?

20. Discuss whether organized crime should be securitized. Why or why not?

Summary

In this section, you have learned:

- Security is at the core of human life; we all need and wish to live in the absence of danger or fear. Security is a self-protecting response to the fact that harm or the threat of harm exists, whether from other human beings, other countries, the environment, or the international system. This is especially true in such an interconnected world, where national and global threats are also threats to the security of the people.

- Threats are not the same for everyone everywhere, so the biggest obstacle in defining security is reaching an agreement on what are considered dangers, threats and harms.

- A normative approach to security sees it as a frequent struggle of competing values, between the ends and the means to pursue it. An instrumental approach sees security as judged by its results.

- Traditional realist conceptions of security focus exclusively on military power and survival where the state has the monopoly over the means to protect itself. The new set of threats require a redefinition of national security. Some countries have continued focusing on military capabilities as a means to protect their national interests (for example, North Korea), while others have reshaped their domestic policies to shift funds and resources away from the military and into other spheres (for example, Germany).

- The line between national and global security has become increasingly blurred due to growing interconnectedness between countries and societies, and the international role of global actors and threats. Globally speaking, some major security threats come from terrorism, weapons of mass destruction, cybersecurity, climate change, among others.

- Poverty, inequality, violation of human rights and liberties, discrimination, violence, diseases and natural disasters have all hindered people's sense of security. Human security encompasses economic, food, health, environmental, personal, community and political security.

- As with national and global security, human security depends on someone, usually an authority, to determine what is considered a threat. It is that same authority that decides upon the measures to be taken to address the threat. This process of securitization often involves the application of 'exceptional measures' that can restrict human rights and liberties in the name of security. An example of this are the measures adopted by the government of El Salvador to eliminate gang violence in the country.

HL extension

Equality

Learning outcomes

In this section, you will learn about:
- how we live in an increasingly unequal world despite globalization and its benefits, rising global wealth, lower poverty rates, technological, medical and scientific advances
- the advantages we enjoy depend on where we were born
- inequality of opportunities persist based on nationality, ethnic identity, skin color and social class
- equity (recognizing that people do not all start from the same place and we must make adjustments to existing imbalances) may be necessary to achieve development
- inequalities exist between and within countries
- inequalities can create conflict and generate security threats, even for democratic countries
- environmental degradation and climate change exacerbate economic and social inequalities.

Conceptual question

What is inequality and why is the world still so unequal?

Every human is born equal in dignity and rights. The rights and freedoms stipulated in the UDHR are to be enjoyed by every single person, equally. This means being able to live without any discrimination of any kind whatsoever. However, living in such a state is almost impossible. We do not have to look far to find inequalities. 'Leave no one behind' is at the heart of the 2030 Agenda for Sustainable Development, but millions of people are still discriminated against in one way or another. They are seen as less, treated as less and enjoy less.

Inequality is a worldwide problem. This phenomenon, in which people are not seen as equal, where opportunities and resources are unequally, and unjustly, distributed, and where human rights, liberties and services are not enjoyed by everyone, persists across countries. The state of *not* being equal, especially in status, rights and opportunities, is a core concept of social justice theories. However, inequality means different things to different people, and it is faced differently by different people in different contexts. Inequality also encompasses overlapping economic, social and political dimensions.

Some focus on inequality as a monetary issue, as in economic inequality or income inequality. Some focus on the legal approach, as in inequality of rights, unequal political power, and inequality before the law. Others focus on social issues, as in social inequality, gender inequality and racial inequality. Regardless of the approach, inequality is concerned with the unequal opportunities that affect one's potential outcomes and the unequal outcomes that may result from circumstances beyond our control.

Equality of opportunities exists when differences in life outcomes are not determined by personal and social circumstances (age, gender, disability, education level, customs,

> Equality means no discrimination of any kind in access to the opportunities and the tools necessary to achieve the same outcomes.

Global political challenges

and culture, etc), but opportunities are equally available to everyone in order for people to have the freedom to pursue a life of their own choosing.

Equality of opportunities means that, regardless of who we are, or where we come from, we all have access to the same tools to thrive. However, results will vary because we have the freedom to choose what to do with those tools. In principle, it means that we all have the same opportunities, that there is a fair starting point for everyone and outcomes depend on decisions for which we are responsible. In practice, equality of opportunity only exists if there are policies that compensate individuals facing disadvantageous circumstances. This is where the equality, equity and social justice debate arises.

Equality means that every individual or group receives the same resources or opportunities. In reality, not every person or group lives through the same circumstances. Think about the right to access free and quality education. In a country where education is provided by both public and private institutions, one may be free while the other is not. In some countries, cost is not the only difference, but the quality of education may be different (in some cases, public education is better, while in others, private education is better). When quality education is only provided by private institutions, which are costly, then there is inequality because not everyone has the economic wealth to access that quality education.

Equity recognizes that each person experiences different circumstances, and there should be some additional support for those who are disadvantaged. In the case of only private education being quality education, it means that if we expect people to reach equal outcomes, then there should be support (such as grants or scholarships) that allows people without the economic means to access that quality education. Social justice means long-term equity. It is the creation and maintenance of equity in systems as well as in individuals.

Equality, equity and social justice. Equality provides the same tools to everyone. Equity provides custom tools that consider disadvantageous positions. Whilst social justice fixes the system itself, to offer equal access to tools and opportunities.

EQUALITY EQUITY

Income inequality

In spite of global and national efforts to reduce poverty and increase economic growth, economic inequality continues to be a problem. The UN has declared that **income inequality** between countries has seen a decline since the 1990s to today. This means that average incomes in developing countries are increasing at a faster rate than ever before. Different countries across the world have managed to grow

HL extension

economically. There are emerging economies in Asia (such as Singapore, South Korea, Indonesia), Africa (South Africa, Nigeria, Egypt), Latin America (Mexico, Colombia, Chile) and the Middle East (Saudi Arabia, the UAE). However, this does not mean the gap between countries has disappeared. The average income of people who live in North America was, by 2020, 16 times higher than that of people living in Sub-Saharan Africa.[78]

At the same time, income inequality within countries has increased. By 2020, it was estimated that 71 percent of the world population lived in countries within which inequality had increased. This is of particular importance, because inequalities within countries affect people on a daily basis in every aspect of their lives. For example, in some middle-income countries, like India, income inequality has increased, and in Latin America and the Caribbean, levels of income inequality remain high.

Despite improvements in some regions and countries, income and wealth are still concentrated at the top. An Oxfam report from 2019 showed that the number of billionaires had almost doubled in just 10 years, with their fortunes reaching record levels. In 2018, the 26 richest people in the world had as much wealth as half of the global population.[79] This rapid rise in incomes at the top exacerbates income inequality for the rest. Even within social groups (including families), income inequality persists, determined by factors such as sex, age and sexual orientation.

▲ Income inequality and economic inequality persist due to social class, gender, age and other personal characteristics.

To measure income inequality, countries and economists use different indexes and variables that suit particular contexts, but also have limitations. Among these are the Lorenz curve, decile ratios, the Palma ratio and the Theil index. Choosing the best tool to measure economic inequality depends on the choice of what to measure (such as consumption, wages, taxes or employment, etc.), and where inequality is measured.

The Gini coefficient, or Gini index, is used to measure and represent income inequality, wealth inequality and consumption inequality within a nation or a social group. Its coefficient ranges between 0 and 1, with 0 representing perfect equality and 1 perfect inequality. This measurement for the distribution of income across a population shows that the higher the Gini coefficient, the greater the inequality, resulting in high-income individuals receiving much larger percentages of the population's total income.

The data used by the Gini coefficient is obtained primarily from household survey data obtained from government statistics and The World Bank. However, this measurement has several limitations. Among these are the possibility of information about income distribution not being covered thoroughly by its source countries, plus demographic information not being taken into account (for example, age, birth rates, taxes).

To further explore the Gini coefficient, you can access the World Bank Open Data website:

The Gini coefficient supports its source countries' data by using The World Bank's Poverty and Inequality Platform (PIP). The PIP is an interactive computational tool that offers graphic information on The World Bank's estimates of poverty and inequality, including global, regional and country-specific trends for over 160 countries around the world. The PIP allows users to look at specific country profiles, or create estimates and graphs based on their own selection of data.

HL Measuring income inequality goes hand in hand with *Poverty*. Poverty depends on income, so it is included when measuring economic inequalities.

Global political challenges

Figure 5.10 A Gini coefficient map for wealth inequality within countries for 2021. Income distribution is expressed as a number between 0 (perfect equality) and 1 (perfect inequality).

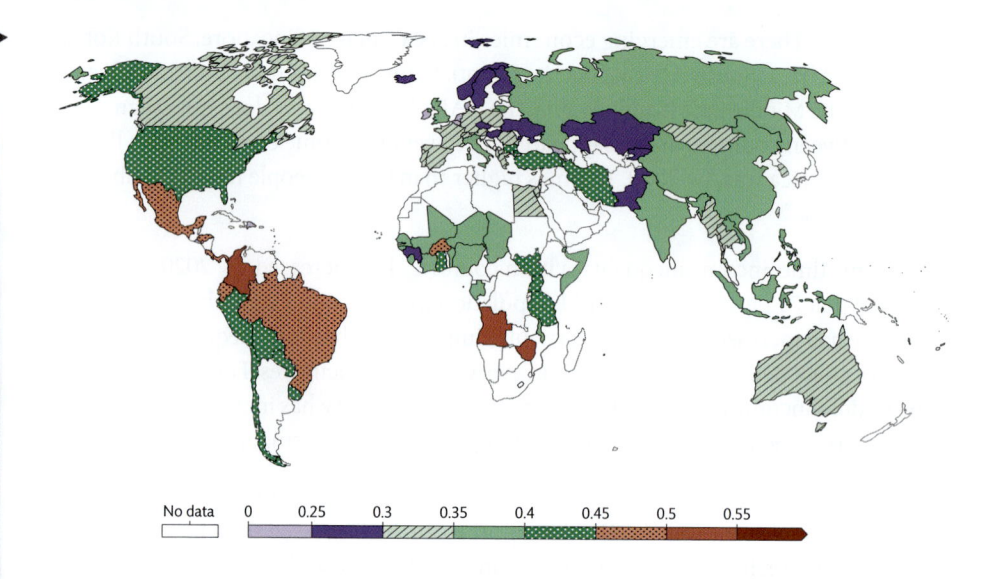

The poverty and inequality estimates within the PIP come from the poverty and inequality indicators used in the World Development Indicators database, as well as several of the indicators of SDG 1 ('No poverty') and SDG 10 ('Reduced inequalities'), particularly the following:

- 1.1.1: share of population below the international poverty line
- 1.2.1: share of population below the national poverty line
- 1.2.2: share of population in multidimensional poverty according to national definitions
- 10.1.1: growth of the poorest 40 percent
- 10.2.1: share of population below 50 percent of median income.[80]

To learn more about the PIP, you can visit:

Activity

Research the results and trends presented by the Gini coefficient and the PIP. Discuss with your classmates the strengths and limitations of these measurements.

What causes inequality? To answer this, we have to look at a wide range of global and domestic (country-specific) factors that affect income inequality trends.

Table 5.10 Factors that contribute to income inequality

Global Factors	Domestic Factors
Technological progress, globalization, commodity price cycles	Financial integration, redistributive fiscal policies, liberalization and deregulation of labor and product markets

Despite the difficulties in measuring income inequality, it is still essential to direct greater efforts to this. Significant inequalities can lead to political polarization, erode social cohesion, lead to grievances among the people, and affect individuals beyond the economic arena.

HL extension

Social inequality

Inequality goes far beyond income and purchasing powers. Inequalities affect people's everyday lives in many different ways, including access to basic services, political and social participation, and respect of their basic rights and liberties. **Social inequality** refers to a condition of unequal access to the conditions every human should enjoy. In equal societies, all citizens are equally able to contribute to their society's well-being, and they are equally able to enjoy the benefits that come with their membership within a society.

Social inequality is related to income and wealth, but social inequalities can also be derived from:

- socio-economic origin and position
- gender
- ethnicity
- disabilities or health issues
- age
- religious beliefs
- class.

These factors, among others, continue to affect inequalities of opportunities around the world. In some countries, this is more pronounced than in others, but social inequalities are a global phenomenon and issue.

Social inequality usually results from biases and prejudices, often strengthened by, or affecting, governmental decisions. This can be seen in two ways: **direct social inequality** and **indirect social inequality**. Direct social inequality is the result of deliberate unfair treatment of a group or individual. It intentionally removes opportunities from some and not from others, for example, legislation that segregates people along racial lines, or businesses that refuse to serve clients due to their socio-economic class. Indirect social inequality results from policies or actions that unintentionally remove opportunities from some people, for example, legislation that prohibits mail-in voting as a way to mitigate voter fraud, but which leaves many people without the ability to vote, or prohibits buying food that contains palm oil extracted in a non-responsible manner, resulting indirectly in the overexploitation of people and ecosystems.

The UN Agenda on Sustainable Development highlights the importance of addressing social inequality, beyond considering only economic factors. SDG 3 ('Good health and well-being'), SDG 4 ('Quality education') and SDG 5 ('Gender equality') consider the importance of eradicating social inequalities around the world. Other goals, while not

> When referring to reports and statistics on inequality (social or economic), it is important to recognize that each source or measuring mechanism sees and expresses inequality in a different way.

> **HL** Social inequality involves unequal opportunities to access and enjoy basic services such as education, and *Health*. Additionally, *Identity* plays an important role, as it is often because of someone's identity (born with or created) that people face inequalities around the world.

> Inequalities are often found to be causes for *conflict*. A grievance resulting from discrimination, regardless of its form, can push societies or groups to demand, either peacefully or through violent means, a change. In order to achieve positive peace, inequalities must always be addressed.

Global political challenges

> **HL** When inequalities exist, people often feel insecure. This insecurity can stem from economic and income inequalities that keep people in an economic state of uncertainty, as well as social inequalities that hinder people or groups from enjoying a state of human *Security*.

directly referencing social inequality, finish with the statement 'for all', meaning that the benefits of sustainable development and its factors must be enjoyed by everyone without discrimination.

In many ways, inequalities have been diminishing, but we are far from achieving equality. Social inequalities 'curtail a person's human rights, through discrimination, abuse and lack of access to justice.'[81] They cause uncertainty, vulnerability and insecurity to persist, increase social discord, undermine trust in institutions and governments, and can trigger violence and conflict.

Gender inequality

> **HL** We are increasingly facing inequalities in areas related to the *Environment* and *Technology*. Environmental degradation and climate change do not impact all societies equally. In addition, the consequences of this increases inequality within and between countries. In terms of technology, it is imperative to consider that access to it is not equal for everyone around the world, not even within societies.

Gender inequality refers to discrimination on the basis of sex or gender. This problem is mainly demonstrated between males and females, where one sex is routinely privileged and prioritized over the other. This discrimination can occur everywhere and at every stage of life. Some people are discriminated against based on sex from childhood, others when they reach adulthood, and others before birth. Millions of people are also discriminated against based on the gender they identify with.

Gender discrimination can be present in families, communities and entire societies. It is partly the result of culture and religion, as well as gender norms. **Gender** refers to a system of roles, expressions, identities, performances and qualities that are attributed as a social construct associated with masculinity and femininity. Although assigned based on sex, these vary with time and across cultures and contexts.

> Sex and gender are not the same thing. Sex refers to the biological characteristics a person is born with – female or male. Gender refers to a personal identity, often as a man or a woman. However, an increasing number of people feel that neither of these genders fully reflects their identity.

Gender norms are the social principles that dictate the behaviors expected from girls and boys, women and men in a society. They include expected gender roles. These are the behaviors, attitudes and actions that are expected of people based on traditions and cultural norms. For example, if men are seen as brave and aggressive, they are expected to engage in armed combat to protect their countries or communities, but women are not expected to do this. These expectations discriminate within the binary view of gender, and also do not consider other gender identities.

> **TOK** We often believe that we no longer live according to strict and traditional gender norms. To what extent does society's unconscious adherence to traditional gender norms influence individuals' behavior?

Activity

Gender roles have changed over time. List some gender roles that have changed in your society over the past 20 years. Which gender roles are still applicable and lead to inequality and/or human rights violations?

> Gender roles and gender norms are also discussed in the Core chapter under feminism as a theoretical perspective in Global Politics, as well as the concept of intersectionality from bell hooks.

The problem with gender norms and roles is that the discrimination they carry has negative impacts on *everyone*, although they still affect women and girls disproportionately. One example of these is the gender pay gap, which is the difference between the earnings of men and women in the workforce. According to *Harvard Business Review*, in 2022, women in the USA earned 77 cents USD for every dollar a man made. This disparity is often exacerbated by other factors such as race, ethnicity, origin and age. That same year, the same report estimated that rural Black and Hispanic women earned just 56 cents USD for every dollar a rural white, non-Hispanic man made, and that Native American women earned only 60 cents in the same comparison.

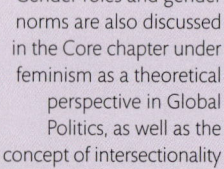

HL extension

The gender pay gap is also affected by parenthood, where norms and roles also come into play. Parenthood and domestic work are still expected to be mostly the responsibility of women (a woman is supposed to leave work during her childbearing years).

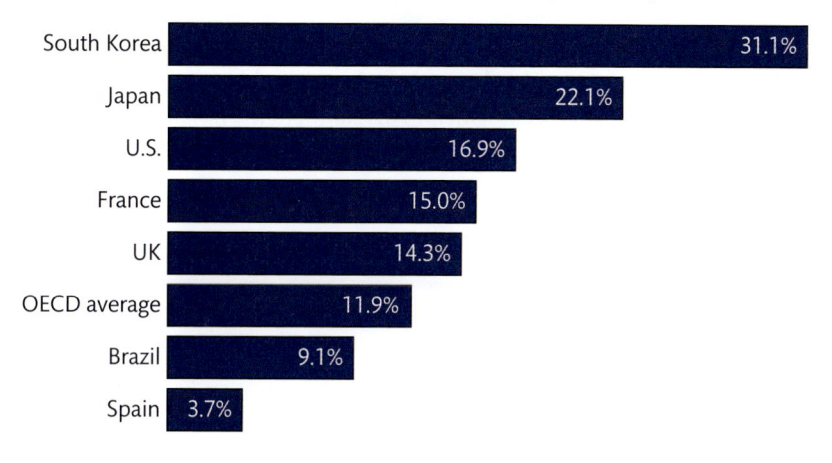

OECD gender pay gap still wide open at 12 percent

Country	%
South Korea	31.1%
Japan	22.1%
U.S.	16.9%
France	15.0%
UK	14.3%
OECD average	11.9%
Brazil	9.1%
Spain	3.7%

Figure 5.11 2021 results show a difference in the median full-time earnings of men and women in selected OECD countries. In countries like South Korea, the difference is over 30 percent.

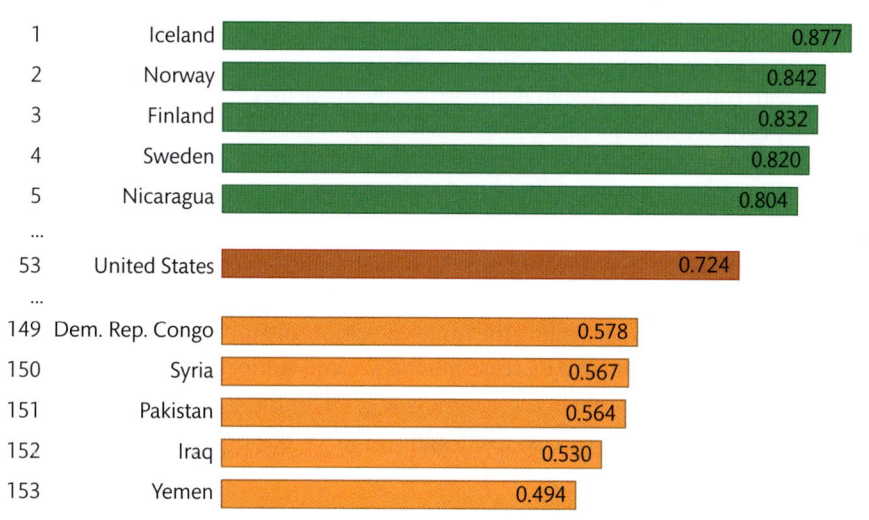

Where the gender gap is most and least pronounced

Rank	Country	Score
1	Iceland	0.877
2	Norway	0.842
3	Finland	0.832
4	Sweden	0.820
5	Nicaragua	0.804
...		
53	United States	0.724
...		
149	Dem. Rep. Congo	0.578
150	Syria	0.567
151	Pakistan	0.564
152	Iraq	0.530
153	Yemen	0.494

Figure 5.12 Global Gender Gap Index shows full gender parity with a rank of 1. This graph shows where the gender gap was most and least pronounced by 2020.

Another example of gender inequality is found in education. According to Save the Children, girls are more likely than boys to miss out on their education. In countries affected by armed conflict, girls are 2.5 times more likely than boys to be out of school. Several gender norms and roles encourage boys to get an education in order to find a job to provide for their future families. It is believed that girls, in charge of household responsibilities, do not need to study. Even if girls do attend school, household chores take away from the time that could be used for their education. Even with equal access to education, the outcome will not be equal.

Gender-based violence (GBV) refers to all harm inflicted on or suffered by humans on the basis of gender differences, influenced by gender norms. This type of violence seeks to establish or reinforce power imbalances between genders and perpetuate

The #MeToo movement is an awareness movement around the issue of sexual harassment and abuse of women in the workplace that grew to prominence in 2017. The movement has helped to raise awareness, give voice to survivors, and bring in important cultural and workplace changes.

305

Global political challenges

inequalities. GBV impacts all genders, though women are particularly at risk. It is estimated that one in three women globally experience physical and/or sexual violence in their life. Data from 2017 showed that around 15 million girls between the ages of 15 and 19 have experienced forced sex[82], while UNICEF data from 2023 showed that 200 million girls and women may have experienced female genital mutilation (FGM) around the world.[83]

However, GBV against boys and men also occurs. There is a stigma surrounding the topic of violence against men that keeps them from speaking up against their abusers, or reporting their cases and seeking help. This same stigma has not allowed equal services and attention to exist for male survivors.

GBV includes:

- pre-natal sex selection
- female infanticide
- neglect
- female genital mutilation
- rape
- child marriage
- forced prostitution
- honor killing.

To address gender inequality, we have to understand the enormous benefits that can come with equality, and design policies that involve actors at different levels. Gender equality can do the following:

- Save lives: by removing risks, harms and violence
- Improve health: by giving women and men the same medical attention, and conducting medical research without sexism. Children will be healthier and become more productive assets for their communities and societies
- Help the economy: providing the same education and job opportunities while considering diversity can increase innovation and competitiveness. An increased participation of women in the economy is good for the country's economy
- Reduce poverty: equal access to education and job opportunities can help individuals to escape the poverty cycle and thrive
- Reduce racial inequality: by addressing gender inequality, inequality due to race can be reduced, for example, reducing the gender pay gap will reduce racial differences in salaries
- Promote peace: by recognizing the equal worth of every single individual and promoting equal opportunities and rights that can foster development and reduce conflict.

Racial and ethnic inequality

Discrimination based on race and ethnicity is widespread in developed and developing countries. This political, social and economic inequality disadvantages certain groups, being unfair, and also detrimental to economic growth and development. It affects two main groups: long-term settled communities that have often lived within the boundaries of modern states, as well as more recent minority groups that have arrived through migration in the past centuries. Racial inequality targets specific groups based

---

GBV is used to strengthen and perpetuate power imbalances across societies. It is the result of gender norms, but also of unequal power hierarchies.

Race and ethnicity are two different concepts, although both relate to human ancestry. Race refers to a category where people share specific physical characteristics or traits, such as skin color. Ethnicity refers to the state of belonging to a shared social or cultural group – it depends on one's own identity.

HL extension

on race, while ethnic inequality does it based on ethnicity. These two are often found to be correlated.

Although recent evidence suggests that inequality is rising, research is still lagging behind in looking at its relation to income inequality, development and conflict. Wealth and income continue to be unevenly distributed across ethnic and racial lines. This affects minorities in terms of economic wealth, and it can also exacerbate differences and tensions related to group identity, limit social cohesion, hinder institutional development and lead to conflict. Racial and ethnic inequalities are often the cause and consequence of discriminatory policies that leave certain individuals with unequal access to public goods and services.

Women supporting an anti-racist movement with a group of people on city streets.

Racial and ethnic inequalities can be seen in how certain societies marginalize indigenous communities (such as indigenous communities in Brazil), immigrants (such as Syrian refugees in Poland), Roma populations (such as Roma people in Italy), people with darker skin colors (such as African Americans in the USA) or minorities in general (such as Rohingya in Myanmar). The caste system in India determines access to education, income and health. By 2019, India's upper caste households earned 47 percent more than the national average annual household income.

Even in developed countries like Germany, inequalities persist between German-born and immigrants. The children of immigrants lag behind in educational attainment from that of the native population. Immigrants of all backgrounds have reported experiencing discrimination in access to jobs and housing, as well as in daily life interactions. In spite of big governmental efforts, unemployment among foreign-born is still higher than that of native workers, with immigrant entrepreneurs also seen in smaller numbers.

Deutsche Welle (DW), a German public, state-owned international broadcaster, reported that of a total of 5617 cases of discrimination reported in 2021 to the Federal Anti-Discrimination agency, 37 percent were related to race (the rest of the cases were related to disability, gender, age, religion and sexual orientation).[84]

Global political challenges

In 2023, Oxfam declared that inequality contributed to the death of approximately 21,300 people every day.[85] These figures are shocking. However, it is a conservative estimate of deaths that result from hunger, lack of access to healthcare, climate change in poor countries, as well as GBV.

In 2022, the UK's unemployment rates were higher for ethnic minorities (12.9 percent) than for the rest of the population (6.3 percent). There was also a smaller percentage of ethnic minorities working in senior positions within companies.[86] Ethnic minorities, earn less than the majority. This exacerbates income inequalities and widens the gap between rich and poor. Income inequality leads to many other social problems.

Activity

Discuss with a partner how you would feel if you earned less and lived a less comfortable life, in spite of working just as hard as they did. To what extent do you think addressing this inequality would help reduce conflicts and promote human rights and development?

Health inequalities also exist within the UK as a result of race. In 2021, the BBC reported that black women were four times more likely to die during childbirth as a result of a lack of acknowledgment of cultural differences as well as bias. 'Often, the concerns of minority patients are dismissed due to racial stereotypes and microaggressions.'[87]

A 2021 survey from Pew Research Center showed concerns about racial and ethnic discrimination in most of the 17 advanced economies studied.[88] According to the majority of adults, especially younger adults, this discrimination is a somewhat or very serious problem in their own societies, including Italy, France, Sweden, Germany, the USA, Japan and Singapore.

To achieve racial and ethnic equality, it is essential to acknowledge that such discrimination is institutional and that education is key to break biases and eradicate negative stereotypes. It is also important to understand the relation between different types of inequality. Inequalities based on race or ethnicity are linked to gender inequality, age inequality and religious inequality. For development to exist, they must all be addressed.

Case – Roma people in Europe

The Romani, known as the Roma, are an Indo-Aryan ethnic group present predominantly in Europe, although they are located around the world. The word 'Roma' means 'man' and refers to a range of sub-groups that include the Kalderash, Romanichals Sinti, Kalé and Gitano. The term 'gypsy' is considered offensive and is rejected by the Roma. The term 'Roma' was globally accepted in 1971, when Roma communities also adopted a flag, an anthem and an international day (April 8). Roma people identify themselves according to their sub-group's history, variants in language, and profession, although many characteristics are also shared, such as the language Rromanës, which includes many dialects.

Young Roma girl in India.

HL extension

Historians believe the Roma first arrived in Europe from northern India, crossing through what is now Iran, Armenia and Türkiye. Over the centuries, they have spread across Europe and the rest of the world. Although traditionally a nomadic group, the majority of them are now settled. They usually work as artisans, farmers, blacksmiths, musicians, fortune-tellers and entertainers. In the beginning, the Roma were welcomed for their skills, until governments and churches began to consider them to be suspicious outsiders.

Throughout history, they have suffered from discrimination, marginalization and inequality. In some regions, they were forced into slavery, a practice that continued during the 19th century. In medieval England, Switzerland and Denmark, thousands of them were sentenced to death. Germany, Poland and Italy ordered their expulsion from their territories. Between 1970 and 1990, the Czech Republic and Slovakia forcibly sterilized 90,000 Romani women. Today, many of them continue to face persecution and are discriminated against, suffering from the fear of forced evictions, police harassment and violence.

> In the 1930s, Nazi Germany considered Roma as racially inferior, causing hundreds of thousands of them to be victims in concentration camps.

Numbers of worldwide Romani populations are unknown and unofficial. It is estimated that between 10 and 12 million Roma live in Europe, most of them in central and eastern European countries. WHO believed Roma constituted the biggest ethnic minority in Europe in 2017.[89] Yet, this ethnic minority faces economic and social inequalities, often living in isolated slums without electricity, running water or waste-removal systems, and struggling to obtain adequate healthcare and education. There is a big pay gap between Roma and non-Roma people, and Roma are more likely to be unemployed.

Roma people face more health problems than other populations. Their life expectancy is 15 years less than that of others. They suffer from higher rates of communicable and non-communicable diseases, and poorer child and maternal health.[90] One in three children faces malnutrition and lives in households where someone goes to bed hungry. In particular, Roma women face unequal treatment, showing an overlap between gender-based and ethnic-based discrimination.

A 2020 study conducted by the European Public Health Alliance[91] showed that inequalities persisted in member countries of the EU, regardless of their social and economic contexts. These inequalities included employment, housing, education and healthcare, and also involved systemic discrimination and lower human rights protection. During the COVID-19 pandemic, human rights organizations made an urgent call to European countries to address health inequalities for the Roma.[92] The risk of spreading and contracting the virus was much higher than for non-Roma, since more than 30 percent of Roma lived in households with no running water, while around 80 percent lived in overpopulated neighborhoods. With most Roma people living in poverty, and 80 percent at risk of poverty (compared to 17 percent of EU population in poverty), buying medication and even basic protective equipment was a major challenge. At the same time, access to doctors and pharmacies are scarce in Roma neighborhoods.

Roma children are often limited to basic and poor-quality education, or face discrimination inside schools where they are the minority (evidence has shown they are often sent to separate classes or are kept separate from other children within classrooms[93]). Some children are sent to special education centers, which are schools for children with learning difficulties. In some countries, Roma children are denied access to education because of a lack of documentation. By 2017, throughout Europe, they had lower school registration and attendance rates, and a higher dropout rate than the general population. In central and south-eastern Europe, only about 20 percent of Roma children had completed primary school (compared to 90 percent of non-Roma).

Despite efforts by the EU, the lack of legally binding mechanisms has been a significant obstacle to eradicating the gap between Roma and non-Roma. Their situation is not the result of poverty, but of centuries of inequalities that have left them in a dire situation. Governments, institutions and individuals have perpetuated negative stereotypes. Roma are usually associated with poverty, high crime rates, and are accused of preferring to beg or steal than work.[94] A 2019 Pew Research poll found that 83 percent of Italians saw the Roma negatively, followed by 76 percent of Slovaks and 68 percent of Greeks.[95]

By the same year, reports of anti-Roma incidents were increasing in Europe. In 2008, following the rape and murder of an Italian woman at the hands of a Romani man, the Italian government declared the Romani population a national security risk. Although the majority of Roma living in the EU are EU citizens, many people in Western Europe see them as foreigners and outsiders. Ukrainian refugees were welcomed when fleeing from war, but Roma women, men and children did not experience the same warm welcome. They struggled to find housing because people did not want to rent to them. Settling in Poland was almost impossible, forcing many to move to hostels or other countries. Institutional assistance was not provided to them, leaving them at the mercy of private donors and humanitarians.[96]

The inequalities faced by Roma are the result of social stigma, and also governmental and systemic discrimination. With equal treatment and access to the same opportunities, the Romani could greatly contribute to the economic growth and development of European countries. Institutional measures need to address the poverty in which the majority of them live, and also the discrimination they face on a daily basis. However, efforts must come not only from the top, but also from within society itself.

The extreme concentration of money, power and influence with the few has negative effects on the rest of us. Poverty, hunger, crime or violence cannot be eradicated as long as such inequalities persist. Consider global warming – the consequences of this are suffered globally, while it is the world's healthiest 1 percent that produces twice the carbon emissions of the bottom 50 percent.

HL extension

Exercises

21. Compare and discuss the possible impacts and limitations of equality and equity in terms of gender over a country's economy.

22. To what extent should equality be related to justice: everyone gets what they deserve?

23. Evaluate how equal access to a good quality education can help to achieve other types of equality.

Summary

In this section, you have learned:

- Inequality is a prevailing problem around the world. Discrimination persists in the access to opportunities and necessary tools (inequality of opportunities) to thrive.

- Inequality is not merely a monetary issue, but is also seen in inequality of rights, unequal political power, inequality before the law, social inequality, gender inequality, racial inequality, among others.

- Equality and equity are often debatable concepts. Equity recognizes the different circumstances of individuals, and the need for additional support to those who are disadvantaged.

- Poverty has reduced, and average incomes have increased, but income inequality between and within countries continues being a problem.

- Income inequality is determined by factors such as sex, age, sexual orientation, among others.

- The Gini coefficient, or Gini index, measures and represents income inequality, wealth inequality and consumption inequality within a nation or a social group. However, this measurement has many limitations, for example, the lack of accurate data.

- Social inequality keeps people from access to basic services, political and social participation, and violates their basic rights and liberties.

- Gender discrimination exists around the world and can be found in gender norms, gender roles, gender-based violence, and the gender pay gap.

- Discrimination based on race and ethnicity is widespread, found in developed and developing countries.

- Political, social and economic inequality leads to grave disadvantages for certain groups, being not only unfair, but also detrimental to economic growth and to development.

- Social inequality creates and strengthens other problems such as poverty, hunger, crime or violence.

Global political challenges

Environment

Learning outcomes

In this section, you will learn about:

- how the environment refers to our natural surroundings, and also to the human-made changes to those surroundings
- environmental effects and climate change are two of the most pressing global problems – causes and consequences affect everyone, everywhere, although not equally
- technology can help us in the fight against climate change, providing us with greener options and more environmentally friendly ways of life, but technology has also contributed to environmental degradation
- not every country and individual contributes to global warming to the same extent, and those who damage the environment the least tend to be affected the most
- environmental degradation increases health problems
- green technologies are a way of reducing carbon footprints, but they are not accessible to everyone, especially poor and marginalized communities
- global environmental policies can address the problem as a security issue
- addressing environmental problems strengthens the idea of a global community and global citizenship.

Conceptual question

Why has the environment become such an important issue for global politics?

In the last decade or so, environmental protection and awareness has become a top priority in the global agenda. Individuals, communities and entire societies have agreed upon the fact that if we do not care about our environment, we might experience human extinction. Some say that this is not going to happen any time soon, because, historically, we have faced massive environmental changes and the planet and humans have learned to adapt to these. Others believe this is our last chance to save our environment.

The environment refers to our immediate surroundings: social, natural or built. It is where all living and non-living elements coexist, and where humans, animals, plants, ecosystems and our human-made reality takes place.

The environment serves several purposes:

- It sustains life.
- It provides us with a supply of resources, without which no living creature could exist.
- If used adequately, it can enhance our quality of life.

We can define the environment in two ways:

- Geographical environment: This is made up of all the elements provided by nature, so it is called the natural environment. It is the physical environment that allows

---

Environment refers to our immediate surroundings in which all living and non-living elements coexist.

Planet Earth seen from space.

HL extension

life to exist, and it is made up of conditions that are not dependent on the existence of humans. Often we have no control over these conditions. The geographical environment includes natural resources, mountains, water, deserts, the weather, etc.

- Human-made environment: This refers to the environment created by humans in order to regulate, monitor and control our geographical environment. This can be divided into the inner environment (traditions, institutions, culture, customs, etc.) that is essential for human life to flourish and the outer environment (technology, infrastructure, commodities, etc.) that we have created to improve our quality of life in our geographical environment.

Environmental changes are not only the result of human activities (although they are an important part of environmental changes). The natural environment has its own natural cycles. These are changes that occur to the planet without human influence. The axial tilt (Earth's orbit around the sun) is not dependent on us, yet it contributes to the planet's natural climate change. Other factors include:

- the output of energy from the sun
- the ocean's natural cooling and warming cycles
- volcanic activities
- glacial advances and retreats.

Have you experienced colder winters, warmer summers, changes in seasonal weather patterns, more frequent natural disasters or even suffered from stronger allergies? Earth's natural cycles have contributed to a **natural climate change** that we must adapt to, even though we are not entirely responsible for it. However, humans have contributed greatly to climate change. This human-induced climate change, also known as **anthropogenic climate change**, results from burning fossil fuels, **aerosol** releases and land alterations due to, for example, agriculture and deforestation.

In 2009, a group of scientists proposed that the functioning of our planet can be understood through nine elements:

- climate change
- new things that humans have incorporated into the ecosystems (such as plastics)
- the ozone layer
- the amount of aerosols (a suspension of fine solid or liquid particles in gas) in the atmosphere
- ocean acidification
- **biogeochemical flows** (the ways by which elements like carbon, phosphorus, nitrogen and sulfur flow between living organisms and the environment)
- freshwater use
- the degree of transformation of natural ecosystems
- loss of biodiversity.

This framework, also known as **Planetary Boundaries**, helps us understand global sustainability by providing a scale and framework with which we can evaluate how much pressure our activities are exerting on the environment. It describes the impacts our human activities have on the Earth according to the nine categories, or boundaries, and shows us the limits the planet has. The idea behind this framework is to show how the planet is capable of resilience and continuing to provide for our long-term social and economic development.

In the last 650,000 years, the Earth has experienced seven ice ages. The most recent one ended 12,000 years ago.

The Earth has its own natural cycles and the capability to adapt to environmental changes. Even though we may be concerned about the environment (and with good reason), we must keep in mind that some processes are natural and the planet can adapt to these. However, it is up to us to avoid pushing the planet to its limits.

To learn more about the Planetary Boundaries framework and where we are right now, you can visit:

Anthropogenic climate change is defined by the human impact on the Earth's climate. It is human-induced climate change. It refers to the amount of fossil fuels burned, aerosols released and land alterations from agriculture and deforestation.

Global political challenges

> The environment is one of the best examples of the increasing interdependence we are experiencing. *Globalization* has connected the whole world in one way or another, but the environment has no geographical, political or social boundary. Any environmental effect, regardless of where it happens, has direct consequences everywhere and for everyone.

It is important to note that, if we push the planet beyond its limits, the environment will not be able to self-regulate. This means that the Earth will stop being capable of sustaining life as we know it. Any crossing of a Planetary Boundary will cause high risks of abrupt and irreversible global environmental change.

Since the beginning of the Industrial Revolution, the world has experienced a significant increase in its temperature. Burning fossil fuels emits enormous amounts of greenhouse gases, particularly carbon dioxide, which traps heat in the atmosphere. This has contributed to the effects of global warming. Evidence of anthropogenic climate change is seen in the overall rise in sea level, temperature rises, melting ice sheets and glaciers, as well as the increase in the frequency and intensity of events such as hurricanes, cyclones, extreme weather, precipitation, floods, droughts, etc.

Such phenomena put enormous amounts of pressure on entire ecosystems, causing irreversible damage to the ecosystems, human-made environments and humans.

Two of the most concerning topics in today's global agenda are environmental problems and climate change. We have come to understand that the activities of one actor directly impacts everyone else. Environmental problems know no boundaries, and affect everyone without discrimination. Global environmental challenges require international political cooperation and action.

Figure 5.13 The Doughnut model of social and planetary boundaries. This model can help us visualise the connections between many of the HL topic areas.

> The Doughnut model[97] can help us understand what is needed for humans to thrive in the 21st century. Formed by two concentric rings (a social foundation that includes life's essentials, and an ecological ceiling that shows the planetary boundaries that protect our planet's supporting systems), we can find in between a doughnut-shaped space in which humans can thrive because it is socially just and ecologically safe.

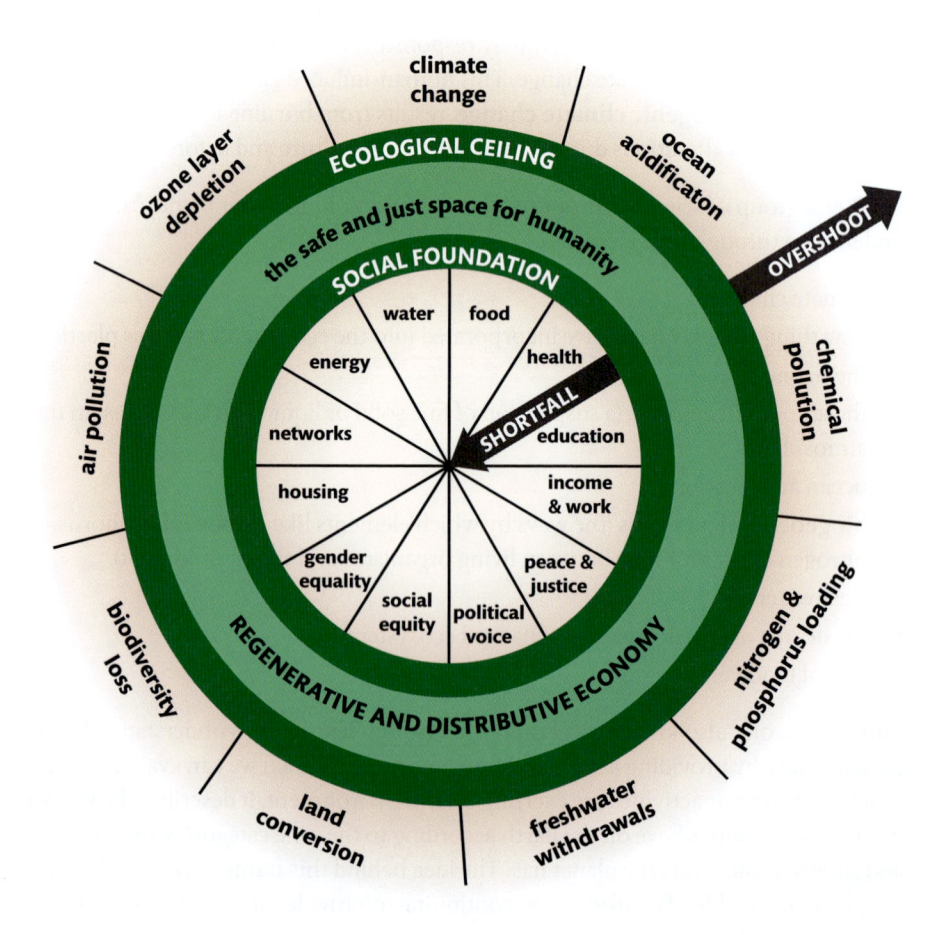

HL extension

Global environmental politics

Global environmental politics is a relatively new field of study within global politics. It focuses on issues related to the interaction between the natural world and humans. For several decades, thinkers have looked at the importance of natural resources to global security and political economy, but this has mainly focused on resource extraction and development issues. Little was done, until recently, to connect resource extraction with other environmental problems. We are now recognizing that the environment concerns geography, economics, politics, law, sociology, biology and other fields of study.

Environmental problems do not respect borders, but they pose a challenge to international politics and international cooperation. Economic, political and ecological problems, though different across countries and places, require some sort of collective governance. We know that the greenhouse gas emissions of one country impact communities across the world, and that the pollution of beaches in one country impacts entire oceans.

Not every country (or individual, or company) contributes to environmental degradation to the same extent. Usually, it is those who damage the environment the least who suffer the most. The same happens within countries. We can measure this through the calculation of **carbon footprints**. A carbon footprint is the measure of the total greenhouse gas emissions (particularly carbon dioxide and methane) produced by an individual, community, organization, company or state. These gases absorb and emit thermal radiation, creating a greenhouse effect that traps heat near the Earth's surface and results in global warming.

These gases help maintain the Earth's temperature at a habitable level. However, in excess, these gases are dangerous. Generally, developed nations have higher carbon footprints. This is due to their energy industries, which burn large amounts of fossil fuels to produce electricity, together with the use of automobiles, airplanes and high individual consumption of energy.

HL Environmental changes may not affect everyone equally, but they do affect everyone. Regardless of the efforts we put into our *Borders*, the environment does not respect them.

Activity

How environmentally aware are you? Discuss with a couple of classmates what actions you perform at home that are environmentally friendly. Are there any actions taken by your peers that you do not do? If so, what do you think are the reasons for that?

Identify the various cognitive biases that can prevent us from understanding how serious of a the threat climate change is.

Global political challenges

Carbon footprint is typically expressed in units of carbon dioxide, CO_2: metric tons (1000 kg [2205 lb] = 1 t), million tons (1,000,000 t = 1 Mt) or gigatons (1 billion metric tons [1000 Mt] = 1 Gt). According to the EU's Joint Research Centre, total CO_2 emissions around the world increased from 34.1 Gt in 2010 to 37.9 Gt by 2019.[98] The COVID-19 pandemic reduced this to 35.96 Gt in 2020 (because of restrictions on travel and transportation). However, emissions have again increased. To avoid a 2 °C rise in global temperatures (which presents a catastrophic scenario), the average global carbon footprint per year must drop to under 2 tons by 2050.

In 2020, the USA emitted 12.6 percent of the total gas emissions. The UN Conference on Trade and Development declared that in 2022 the world's 46 LEDCs, although home to about 1.1 billion people, contributed minimally (less than 4 percent) to global CO_2 emissions. It should not be assumed that countries with higher carbon footprints do not care about the environment, nor that their citizens are big polluters. It is important to note that the top three emitters in the world are also the most populous countries. That is why carbon footprint is also measured per capita (per person).

In 2020, the top five countries with the highest CO_2 emissions per capita were[99]:

- Palau: 55.29 t
- Qatar: 35.64 t
- Trinidad and Tobago: 21.97 t
- Bahrain: 21.60 t
- Kuwait: 20.91 t

Per capita, the USA only totaled 13.68 tons, Russia was in 28th place with 8.20 tons and India in 110th place with 1.74 tons per capita. In fact, a number of developing countries occupy the top places. This is largely the result of less regulated energy, industry and transportation industries. Although, in general, developed countries have higher CO_2 emissions due to more developed infrastructures and higher standards of living, developing countries and emerging economies are seeing a rise in their gas emissions as their infrastructure catches up to their growing populations.

For more interactive maps and figures on national and per capita carbon footprints, you can visit:

Inequalities in carbon footprint are partly the result of *Poverty*, access to technologies and development. Not every individual pollutes to the same extent because not everyone enjoys the same quality of life. Not everyone can afford a car (let alone a hybrid or electric car), can travel by plane or has access to electricity in their homes.

Activity

Calculate your individual or household carbon footprint using the following tool by searching for 'Wren systemic change' in a search engine or using the QR code below:

List 10 changes you or your household could make to reduce this footprint.

Highly developed countries are the best-positioned when it comes to the development and use of more efficient environmentally friendly technologies (such as solar and wind power, or renewable energy systems). Denmark, Luxembourg and Switzerland are some of the most environmentally friendly countries, leading the development and implementation of green initiatives to reduce their carbon footprint and CO_2 emissions.

HL extension

> **Activity**
>
> Work in a small group. Research the top 10 countries in CO_2 emissions in 2023. These can be found at:
>
> [QR code]
>
> Discuss some of the main reasons why these countries may be greater or lesser polluters.

Earth Overshoot Day (EOD) was developed by Andrew Simms of the New Economics Foundation (a UK think tank) to raise awareness about Earth's limited resources. It shows dates on which humanity's resource consumption for a year exceeds the Earth's capacity to regenerate those resources that year. It represents the level by which human demand overshoots the sustainable amount of biological resources regenerated on the planet. The EOD shows the day by which humans enter environmental deficit spending, by calculating the world's biocapacity (the amount of natural resources generated naturally by the Earth), by our ecological footprint (our consumption of resources), multiplied by 365 days in a year.

Figure 5.14 shows how every year our human activities have moved the EOD earlier and earlier into the year. It is up to global efforts to move future EODs to later dates.

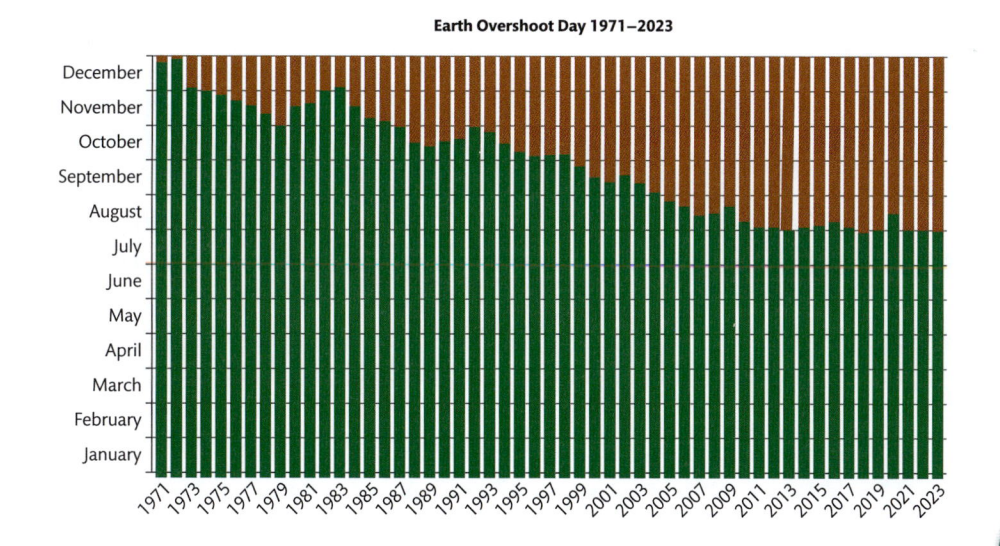

Earth Overshoot Day 1971–2023

Figure 5.14 How the EOD has varied from 1971 to 2023. It is possible to see how, with the passing of years, the overshoot day has moved closer to the beginning of the year.

This measurement is also applicable to individual countries, also known as a Country Overshoot Day.[100] This is the date on which EOD would fall if all humans consumed like the people in that country. It reflects the ecological footprint of a country by comparing the population's demand and the nation's biocapacity. Country overshoot days are published every year on January 1. The dates are calculated the previous December by using that year's National Footprint and Biocapacity Accounts.

Learn more about EOD at the Earth Overshoot website:

[QR code]

Global political challenges

> ### Activity
> What is the overshoot day for the country you live in? How does the country you live in rank when it comes to its ecological footprint? How can you relate the two?

Even this measurement recognizes the unequal participation and contribution to environmental degradation. Not all countries have an overshoot day. This is because, in order to have one, the ecological footprint per person must be greater than the global biocapacity per person. But, not every person enjoys the same standard of living, hence, not everyone has the same carbon footprint.

Environment, human rights and development

All humans depend on the Earth's environment. It is the only place we can live (so far), it provides us with the necessary resources to survive and, with human-made contributions, can improve our lives. A safe, clean, healthy and sustainable environment is essential to the full enjoyment of our human rights. In an environment without these characteristics, we cannot enjoy our right to life, health, food, water or sanitation. Without a safe, clean, healthy and sustainable environment we cannot fulfill our aspirations. We would not even have access to the minimum standards of human dignity.

The realization of human rights and the promotion of development require a safe, clean, healthy and sustainable environment.

Thousands of protesters took part in the Walk for Your Future climate march ahead of COP 27 in Brussels, Belgium on October 23, 2022.

Protecting the environment protects human rights. Protecting human rights protects the environment. The recognition of this link has greatly increased, and international and domestic laws, environmental policies and academic studies are increasingly focusing on the environment.

The Special Rapporteur on human rights and the environment, first created in 2012 and later extended in 2018, has several mandates, among which is 'Promote and report on the realization of human rights obligations relating to the enjoyment of a safe, clean, healthy

HL extension

and sustainable environment.'[101] This mandate promotes best practices related to human rights in environmental policy making. This means that even though the environment is not directly mentioned in the UDHR, a safe, clean, healthy and sustainable environment is recognized as essential to the fulfillment of all individuals' lives.

As the world continues with urbanization and industrialization, environmental crises increasingly affect the lives, health and livelihoods of millions of people around the world. People living in poverty lack access to clean water and sanitation, which in turn affects their health. Deforestation and heavy-polluting industries destroy access to natural resources that are vital for populations to survive (in terms of food and shelter, for example), and they also reduce the amount of these resources. This pushes people toward hunger, homelessness and even starvation. The same occurs when natural disasters or environmental degradation occur.

As in many other cases, the most affected are impoverished and marginalized communities, which have limited opportunities to participate in decision-making and policies on environmental issues. In many countries, activists and citizens who try to defend their rights to land and a safe environment face intimidation, harassment and violence.

A report by the NGO Global Witness records around 200 environmental and land-defense activists killed around the world annually. In 2021, 54 of these cases occurred in Mexico alone, considered the deadliest country for environmentalists.[102] Over 40 percent of the murders are committed against indigenous people. It has been found that activists also experience a wide range of tactics to silence them, such as death threats, surveillance, sexual violence or criminalization. This violence can come from big corporations or governments, whose economic interests require the destruction of the environment at the expense of violating the human rights of many.

People whose human rights are violated and who live in poverty, and without education, are prone to activities that harm the environment without the intention of doing so. Environmental awareness requires people to be educated about what they are doing. The importance of reusing and recycling is partly known to us because of environmental education.

It is not only wealthy people that have disproportionately large carbon footprints. Those on lower income levels do too. Development, in terms of quality of life and access to technologies that contribute to it, is still a far-off reality for many.

A more environmentally friendly lifestyle often requires economic means. For example, vegan alternatives of food and organic products are more expensive. Installing solar panels in our homes is a very good investment. However, the initial cost of installing them is too high for most people, who instead continue to rely on fossil fuels on a daily basis. Without adequate sanitation systems, human waste continues to pollute the air, land and water, causing further damage to the environment. Water treatment plants, energy saving light bulbs or electric cars are not accessible to everyone.

Global environmental efforts

In addition to national and individual initiatives, global efforts have taken place to try to reduce our impact on the environment, mitigate climate change, reduce **vulnerability** to environmental impacts and increase **resilience** (the capacity

---

HL An unsafe, unhealthy and unclean environment has direct implications on *Health*, *Poverty*, and economic and social inequalities.

Disposed garbage polluting the environment.

HL Environmentally friendly lifestyles are often costly, depend on access to *Technology*, education and other characteristics that people living in *Poverty* or marginalized, together with social and economic inequalities, find very hard to attain.

Global political challenges

to withstand or recover), especially of those most affected. As early as the 1990s, countries have debated how to combat climate change, and global efforts have included numerous climate negotiations, forums, bilateral and multilateral agreements.

The UN Framework Convention on Climate Change (UNFCCC) established an international environmental treaty in 1992. It is still the main international treaty on fighting climate change considering the human impact on the climate system. It was originally signed by 154 states at the UN Conference on Environment and Development (informally known as the Earth Summit). Today, there are 197 parties to the Convention. The treaty calls for ongoing scientific research, and for negotiations and future agreements that can contribute to ecosystems naturally adapting to climate change, ensure food production is secure and promote economic development in a sustainable manner.

Signed in 1997, and in place between 2005 and 2020, the Kyoto Protocol was the first implementation of UNFCCC measures. It was, before 2020, the world's only legally binding instrument regarding cutting greenhouse gas emissions. The Kyoto Protocol was ratified by 192 of the UNFCCC parties – the USA was not one of these. In addition, Canada withdrew in 2012. The Protocol has two agreed periods for the reduction of emissions. The first one, between 2008 and 2012, sought for industrialized countries to reduce emissions to 5 percent below 1990 levels. The second period, between 2013 and 2020, committed parties to a reduction of least 18 percent below 1990 levels. Aside from the lack of participation of highly relevant countries like Canada and the USA, it also had the weakness of not compelling developing countries to reduce their emissions.

▲ UN climate change conference COP 28 taking place in Dubai, UAE.

The UNFCCC's supreme decision-making body, the Conference of the Parties (COP), meets every year to assess progress in dealing with climate change. All parties to the convention can take part in these annual meetings, with international organizations, representatives of business, interest groups and associations being able to attend as observers.

You can find an interactive video on how global temperatures have changed in the last century at:

In 2016, the Kyoto Protocol was replaced when the Paris Agreement came into force. This agreement was signed by all UNFCCC parties in 2015 (in 2020, the USA withdrew, although it rejoined in 2021) and is the first universal, legally binding global climate agreement. The **Paris Agreement** covers climate change mitigation, adaptation and finance. One of its main goals is to keep the world temperature below 2 °C above pre-industrial levels, preferably limiting it to 1.5 °C, considering this could reduce effects on climate change. It also hopes to reach greenhouse gas emissions of net-zero by 2050, also known as being climate neutral or **carbon neutral**.

To learn more about the Paris Agreement, visit:

The Paris Agreement aims for global cooperation through financing to help countries to adapt to climate change effects. Under this agreement, each country, developed or developing, must determine its own national plan (known as nationally determined contributions) and regularly report on its advances. The problem is that there are no enforcement mechanisms, and some countries have not and may not continue to adhere to their individual commitments.

Other examples of international forums in which several countries participate to strengthen environmental efforts are:

- Intergovernmental Panel on Climate Change (IPCC)
- G7
- G8 and G20

HL extension

- Major Economies Forum on Energy and Climate (MEF)
- OECD
- International Energy Agency (IEA).

The UN Agenda for sustainable development has given high priority to the environment, too. Some of its goals recognize the importance of global access to a safe and clean environment that allows all individuals to enjoy a quality of life that is sustainable. The following SDG goals focus directly on the topic:

- SDG 6: Clean water and sanitation
- SDG 7: Affordable and clean energy
- SDG 9: Industry, innovation and infrastructure (human-made environment)
- SDG 11: Sustainable cities and communities
- SDG 12: Responsible consumption and production
- SDG 13: Climate action
- SDG 14: Life below water
- SDG 15: Life on land

Eight out of 17 goals address the environment as essential to sustainable development. Governments have collectively pledged to slow global warming. In general, they agree on the science behind climate change. It is globally understood that:

- without a safe and clean environment, other aspects of development are not possible
- resilience must be strengthened
- global cooperation is needed.

However, governments still disagree on who is most responsible for environmental damages, how we should act or react toward these countries, and where the sovereignty line should be drawn upon in an issue that affects every single individual. The world is already facing the consequences of climate change and we can only expect them to become worse.

If we do not manage to keep the Earth's temperature below an increase of 1.5 °C, the IPCC[103] forecasts the following:

- Heat waves: About 14 percent of the people in the world will be exposed to periods of severe heat at least once every five years.
- Droughts and floods: Farming will become much more difficult, lowering crop yields and causing global food shortages.
- Rising sea levels: Tens of millions of people who live in coastal regions will be submerged in the coming decades. Small island nations are particularly vulnerable.
- Ocean changes: Up to 90 percent of coral reefs will be wiped out as oceans become more acidic. World fisheries will become less productive.
- Arctic ice thaws: The Arctic will experience a summer with no sea ice at least once every 100 years (something that has not happened in the last 2000 years). 40 percent of the Arctic's permafrost will thaw by the end of the current century.
- Species loss: More insects, plants and animals will be at risk of extinction.

Most experts believe the Paris Agreement's efforts are not enough, and still expect the global temperature to rise above 2 °C by the end of the present century. As individuals, we have a critical role to play in combating climate change and huge responsibilities toward the environment.

Manage forests, combat desertification, halt and reverse land degradation and halt biodiversity loss are the targets of SDG 15: Life on Land.

TOK

There is abundant scientific evidence to demonstrate that we are exerting too much pressure on our environment. However, we do not all seem to be considering the topic as urgent. Reflect on how people decide to trust or not to trust experts on the issue of climate change.

Global political challenges

> **Activity**
>
> Research how the country you live in is performing on SDG 13. Suggest ways in which these efforts could be improved.

Environment, peace and conflict

With global temperatures expected to continue increasing, industries such as fashion and meat production not seeing any decline in their carbon footprint in the short-run, and technologies quickly advancing for the sake of development, our future scenario seems somewhat hopeless.

The UN Environment Programme works on understanding how environmental degradation and climate change can have an impact on peace and security dynamics. Based on their understanding, effective measures are necessary to protect the environment, ensure resilience and promote peace in politically complex and fragile contexts. The unprecedented pace and scale of population growth, resource depletion and global environmental change require a global redefinition of security. We need to define what exactly is being secured, what it is being secured against, who is to provide security and through what methods.

Some environmental security efforts are focused toward the root causes of environmental problems and the enhancement of human, economic and international security. Other efforts focus on preventing or containing specific threats or effects of environmental problems (for example, floods or air pollution in cities). As well as these differing approaches, disagreement also extends to the institutions, tools and means that actors should use to apply solutions to these problems. This is because environmental security measures can often have detrimental effects on other aspects of life.

Consider the ban on single-use plastics and plastic bags in different countries. While this contributes to the reduction of pollution and waste, it affects economically those who produce, distribute and sell these products. In addition, it can contribute to pushes for an increased production and consumption of products made of Styrofoam or paper, which also damages the environment.

Viewing the environment as a security concern does not necessarily mean approaching it through a traditional view of security associated with military strength. It is instead seen from the view that global, regional and local environmental problems seriously threaten human life, health, well-being and economic factors. If a country does not manage its forests sustainably, it could lose an important part of its export base. Such deforestation can also lead to changes in climate, increase flooding, degradation of arable land and decimation of fisheries. The costs of rebuilding or repairing an environment, if even possible, would be huge.

Regarding the environment, a traditional view of security is not entirely out of the question. The environment is connected to regional tensions and conflict. Causes of conflict can range from control over vital environmental resources to contestations over natural resources. Results can range from disagreements at the local level to outright wars. In fact, environmental factors have played and do play a part in historic, contemporary and current conflicts, in which actors fight for control over resources (water, land, oil, gold, diamonds, gas, coltan, etc).

HL

Environmental change can be seen from a human, national and global *Security* perspective. However, there is still debate on defining what is being secured, what it is secured against, who provides security and what means are acceptable.

Columbite-tantalite, or coltan for short, is a metallic ore found in large quantities in the eastern Congo. When refined, it becomes a heat-resistant powder that can hold a high electrical charge. These properties make it vital in the creation of electronic elements. In spite of little knowledge about it, it is an essential component of your cell phone and laptop. However, numerous reports have referred to exploitation of coltan from Congo by foreign countries involved in the current war. Neighboring countries like Rwanda, Uganda and Burundi are also involved in smuggling coltan, using the revenues generated from the high price of this mineral to sustain their war efforts.

Conflict minerals are raw materials that come from a particular part of the world where conflict is occurring and which are commonly extracted through forced labour, including the use of children. Among these materials are gold, tin, tantalum, tungsten, coltan, cobalt and diamonds.

HL extension

With the degradation of the environment and climate change, environmental tensions will only increase. If there is an environmental pressure (for example, droughts) in a specific region within a country, then people will increasingly struggle to find water. Water is vital for themselves, their animals and agriculture, so the reduced amounts of water resources can lead to a conflict that can escalate to the use of violence.

◀ Dead cattle on dry Masai land in Kenya.

This is not a hypothetical case. Such conflicts are seen more and more often across the world. Diminishing water resources in Lake Chad has created conflicts and undermined livelihood-sustaining activities in Cameroon, Chad, Niger and Nigeria. In the Rwandan genocide, land was not the primary cause, but it was an important one. Ordinary citizens, whose livelihoods were increasingly vulnerable because of shrinking sizes of land and increasing demographics, were incited to kill and take their neighbor's land and belongings. Experts point to Sudan's civil war as an example of a climate change-induced conflict. The UN found connections between desertification, diminished rainfall, rising temperatures and water insecurity, and the resulting popular rebellion, that led to violence.

A growing body of evidence suggests there are strong links between climate and conflict in developed and developing countries. It is still not globally accepted that climate change directly causes conflict. According to the International Committee of the Red Cross, of the 25 countries deemed most vulnerable to climate change, 14 are going through armed conflict.[104] Armed conflict, in turn, makes societies more vulnerable and less capable to adapt to environmental factors.

Another security issue is that related to human displacement. Around the world, people are increasingly being forced to leave their homes because of the effects of climate change, natural disasters and other environmental factors that are leaving their homes completely uninhabitable. The United Nations High Commissioner for Refugees (UNHCR) and the Institute for Economics and Peace estimate that by 2050 there will be 1.2 billion environmentally induced migrants.[105] This is an enormous amount of people who will be leaving their place of origin, not just in search of better life opportunities, but for survival, because the environment back home is not safe to sustain their quality of life, their lifestyles or their actual lives.

Such migration can generate two problems. First, groups of people will be forced to seek a new home. In their new home, they will exert demographic pressure that will come at the cost of consuming resources. These resources may be already in use by the local population, who will not be happy having to share them with more people, thus creating tension over the sharing of resources. Migrants might encounter other types of tension with the local population due to ethnic differences, religious beliefs, political ideas, or gender, etc.

Second, countries will face the issue of how to cope with an increasing influx of migrants. It is important to note that, by 2023, people migrating to other countries because of climate change or environmental disasters were still considered economic

> Environmental degradation and climate change have been found to be important factors behind violent and non-violent conflicts. These factors currently contribute to push factors for migration (and will increasingly do so). However, the environment can also be a factor for peace. Environmental peacebuilding advocates for environmental protection and cooperation as a factor for the creation and strengthening of peaceful relations.

migrants. As such, they have no international protection and states are not obliged to welcome these migrants. This topic has sparked increasing debate concerning environmentally induced migration, with some believing these migrants should be included in the 1951 definition of refugees, receiving the international protection other refugees have. However, others believe climate change and environmental disasters are not valid reasons to ask for asylum.

Case – Pacific island nations

Rising sea level is a global danger, particularly in coastal areas. Entire cities around the world are slowly losing land to the rising sea. It affects developed and developing countries. Some have the technology, financial means and infrastructure to delay the loss of land. The Netherlands has shown an incredible capacity to adapt with the use of dams. Japan has built underground tunnels so the water caused by floods can go underneath cities without affecting their infrastructure and population. In other parts of the world, artificial islands are being built to gain territory. There are also engineering projects as well as nature-based flood defenses (mangrove forests and saltmarshes) that can be adopted.

Scientists have found that the global mean sea level has risen 10.1 cm since 1992. The increase by the early 1990s was 2.5 mm per year. However, over the past decade, the rate of sea-level rise has been 3.9 mm per year.[106]

In spite of several efforts, sea levels on US coastlines are expected to rise 30 cm by 2050. By 2100, they are likely to have risen 60 cm. Coastal flooding will become much more frequent in the next 30 years. Moderate floods will occur 10 times more often than they do today (almost 40 percent of the US population lives on the coastline).[107]

Sea-level rise will not be the same everywhere. Around the world, 1.47 billion people are at risk of intense flooding, out of whom 600 million live in poverty.[108] Regardless of our efforts, sea-level rise can be slowed down, but not stopped.

Photographer walking on the streets during a flood (*acqua alta* or high water) in Venice, Italy, 2019.

Countries like Bangladesh, India, Egypt, the Netherlands, the USA, Australia and New Zealand are some of the countries most at risk. But smaller islands are much more vulnerable. Their territories are smaller, which means there is not much land available to relocate people affected by floods and rising sea levels. Many of them are also developing countries that lack the financial means, technological knowledge and capabilities, as well as the infrastructure to deal with a problem that will affect their entire populations.

Pacific island nations are home to a relatively small population, with just over 2.3 million people. The region is one of the most affected by the impacts of climate change. Many of the islands are low-lying, and some rise only a few feet above sea level.

HL extension

The current pace of sea-level rise in the region has not been seen for 5000 years. It is predicted that, by 2050, on average the sea level will rise between 25 and 58 cm. This rise will be devastating. Ninety percent of the coral reefs in the region will suffer severe degradation, and marine species and entire ecosystems may disappear. Scientists estimate that:

▶ Village on South Tarawa atoll, Kiribati. Communities use natural barriers like mangroves to deter floods.

> In the most likely climate change scenario, the rate of sea level rise would triple, groundwater sources will be permanently lost in the next few decades, with islands becoming unstable in the second half of this century. Under a more negative climate change scenario, the sea level would rise by a meter, rendering the islands unstable in the next 20 to 40 years and exposing many human communities to intolerable levels of risk by the year 2060.[109]

The Pacific island nations rely on the oceans and their coasts for natural resources, food, clothing and many other essential materials. They are responsible for only 0.03 percent of global greenhouse gas emissions.

Pacific islands such as Tonga, Fiji, Tuvalu, Kiribati and the Solomon Islands are facing disappearance. It is no longer a matter of *if* but *when*. In the case of Tonga, sea levels are rising at almost twice the global average rate. Being a country with active volcanic activity, this intensifies the threats of tsunamis. In turn, tsunamis will:

- damage agricultural soil (from the sea water that washes ashore), leaving it useless for years
- exacerbate coastal erosion and destroy natural buffers such as coral reefs and mangroves
- affect individuals, households and the country's economy.

Tuvalu is also struggling. Every year between January and March, the country faces its seasonal king tides, and these are causing severe flooding and destroying everything in their way. Since 2014, Prime Minister Enele Sopoaga has urged industrialized countries to reduce their greenhouse gas emissions. By 2018, the government had in place official programs with countries like Fiji, Australia and New Zealand to help relocate Tuvaluans, but many people do not want to move as their roots and identity are in those places. In addition, Australia has not always been the best neighbor. In 2014, the government launched its No Way campaign to deter asylum seekers from going to Australia, while the country also used offshore detention centers for these migrants. New Zealand and Fiji are also threatened by climate change.

Environmental changes, combined with other factors like poverty and health, can exacerbate inequalities, affect livelihoods and be a driver for displacement and migration. In the Solomon Islands, cyclones, flash floods and other weather-related events forced more than 26,000 people to relocate between 2008 and 2023. The country's Ministry of Environment, Climate Change, Disaster Management and Meteorology believes sea levels will rise 1 meter by the year 2100. This will cause

Global political challenges

coastal erosion, coastal saltwater intrusion and will decrease levels of fresh water supplies, affecting food security. By 2016, the country had seen five of its islands completely lost to sea-level rise, with six others severely affected by erosion. These, and other countries like Vanuatu and Fiji, are facing category five (severe tropical) cyclones every two or three years, instead of one every 10 years.

When we look at the Pacific island nations, we now see a likely future of total disappearance due to climate change. Pacific islanders are expected to be among the first groups of climate refugees, because the effects of climate change are forcing them to leave their homes. Even if they do not want to leave, they will reach a point where no other option is available. The political, social, cultural, economic and human implications go beyond what we can currently grasp. As a global community, we must act to slow down this process as much as possible, but we also need to consider a future scenario where there are no Pacific island nations anymore.

The protection and conservation of *our* environment (because we all share the same planet) is of global importance, and as such requires global cooperation and efforts. No single organization or country, or group of countries, has the capacity to solve this challenge on its own. If we continue relying on governments and corporations to find a solution to environmental degradation, global warming and climate change, little will be done. It is up to the international community, including us as individuals, to find a solution that respects the human rights and dignity of the millions of people who are already suffering and will continue to do so as a result of environmental changes. Every living creature and human deserves a safe environment in which to live. We not only deserve it, but we NEED it.

Exercises

24. Evaluate whether environmental issues should be securitized. If so, what is the threat, who should be protected, who should provide the security and through what means?
25. Identify the environmental problems with electric cars.
26. Discuss how environmental education can, at an individual and community level, help countries achieve the national goals presented in the Paris Agreement.

Summary

In this section, you have learned:

- Environmental protection and awareness require urgent attention and action. Even if climate change is the result of natural processes (natural climate change), human activities (anthropogenic climate change) are driving the planet closer to its limits, as seen with the planetary boundaries.
- Environmental problems do not respect borders. They pose a challenge to international politics and international cooperation. Economic, political and ecological problems, though different across countries and places, require some sort of collective governance.

- The countries with bigger carbon footprints are not always the ones with bigger carbon footprints per capita. Least developed countries can have big carbon footprints because of less regulated energy, industry, transportation industries, lack of access to environmentally friendly technologies, lower levels of education and higher levels of poverty, among other reasons.

- A safe, clean, healthy and sustainable environment is essential to the full enjoyment of our human rights. In an environment without these characteristics, we cannot enjoy our right to life, health, food, water or sanitation.

- The Paris Agreement signed by all UNFCCC parties in 2015, is the first-ever universal, legally binding global climate agreement. It aims to hold the increase in the global average temperature to well below 2°C above pre-industrial levels, reach greenhouse gas emissions of net-zero by 2050, and global cooperation through financing and helping countries to adapt to climate change effects.

- Governments strongly disagree on who is most responsible for environmental damages, how should we act or react towards these countries, and where the sovereignty line should be drawn upon in an issue that affects every single individual.

- Environmental change can be seen from a human, national and global security perspective, although there is still debate on defining what is being secured, what it is secured against, who provides security, and what means are acceptable.

- Climate change is creating and accelerating the conditions necessary for armed conflict to occur as well as mass migrations, by increasing the frequency and intensity of natural disasters and leaving entire places uninhabitable.

Practice questions

1. Compare and contrast the strengths and weaknesses of measuring poverty in absolute terms and in relative terms, and consider the implications these can have when developing national policies to address poverty.
2. Discuss how education and social mobility could help break the poverty trap in which millions of people find themselves.
3. Suggest what indicators could be added to the Multidimensional Poverty Index in order to measure poverty in a more holistic way.
4. Discuss ways in which the use of AI in the academic field could be regulated.
5. Evaluate positive and negative aspects of the use of technologies used by social and political movements.
6. Explain health in terms of national security. Use a contemporary real-life example to justify your response.
7. Discuss the feasibility of medicines and vaccines being developed in LEDCs and what the political, social and economic impacts could be.
8. To what extent should governments rely on private stakeholders to address public healthcare? Suggest regulations that should be in place to ensure healthcare is accessible to everyone.
9. Explain what is needed to achieve a global identity that can help to address global challenges.

Global political challenges

10. National identities have changed since the COVID-19 pandemic. To what extent do you agree? Justify your answer.
11. Recommend ways in which identity can be used by governments to bring social cohesion and peace instead of enhancing differences and promoting conflict.
12. Examine the political and geographical implications of Scotland becoming independent from the United Kingdom. How would this affect identity, political relations and social relations?
13. Discuss the claim that historical territorial divisions are the cause of recurrent or enduring conflicts of secession. Use a current real-life example to justify your answer.
14. To what extent are we moving closer to a global nation as borders are becoming more fluid, or are globalization fallouts making governments rethink and strengthen their borders?
15. Climate change is the greatest threat to countries' national security nowadays. To what extent do you agree?
16. Suggest how the international community can work together to address global security threats without compromising sovereignty.
17. Discuss to what extent anti-terrorist measures that disproportionately affect particular groups in a society are justifiable.
18. Discuss social inequality in terms of social mobility and its relation with human rights.
19. Explain the main reasons behind the unequal access to technological and scientific advances on a global level.
20. Discuss poverty and inequality from ethical and economic perspectives.
21. Evaluate the most significant obstacles that are hindering more effective global climate cooperation and governance.
22. Suggest how governments can exert more pressure on corporations to reduce their carbon footprint, and discuss the implications this governmental pressure could have on corporations.
23. To what extent is nuclear energy a viable option for fighting climate change and global warming?

Notes

1. United Nations. Statistics Division. 'End Poverty in All Its Forms Everywhere'. Retrieved in May 2023 from: https://unstats.un.org/sdgs/report/2022/goal-01/
2. New Brunswick, Canada. Economic and Social Inclusion Corporation. 'What is Poverty?' Retrieved in May 2023 from: www2.gnb.ca/content/gnb/en/departments/esic/overview/content/what_is_poverty.html
3. United Nations. Department of Economic and Social Affairs. Sustainable Development Goal 1. 'End poverty in all its forms everywhere'. Retrieved in July 2023 from: https://sdgs.un.org/goals/goal1
4. The World Bank. (2022). 'Fact Sheet: An Adjustment to Global Poverty Lines'. Retrieved in April 2023 from: www.worldbank.org/en/news/factsheet/2022/05/02/fact-sheet-an-adjustment-to-global-poverty-lines
5. Development Initiatives. (2023). *Economic poverty trends: Global, regional and national factsheet*. Retrieved in April 2023 from: https://devinit.org/documents/1285/Economic_poverty_factsheet_February_2023_JRJ2Y4f.pdf
6. Gordon, D. (2005). *Indicators of Poverty & Hunger*. Retrieved in April 2023 from: www.un.org/esa/socdev/unyin/documents/ydiDavidGordon_poverty.pdf

7. The World Bank. 'Multidimensional Poverty Measure'. Retrieved in May 2023 from: www.worldbank.org/en/topic/poverty/brief/multidimensional-poverty-measure#:~:text=What%20is%20the%20Multidimensional%20Poverty,more%20complete%20picture%20of%20poverty
8. The World Bank. 'Multidimensional Poverty Measure'. Retrieved in July 2023 from: https://www.worldbank.org/en/topic/poverty/brief/multidimensional-poverty-measure
9. UNDP. Human Development Reports. *2022 Global Multidimensional Poverty Index (MPI)*. Retrieved in April 2023 from: https://hdr.undp.org/content/2022-global-multidimensional-poverty-index-mpi#/indicies/MPI
10. UNDP. Human Development Reports. *2022 Global Multidimensional Poverty Index (MPI)*. Retrieved in April 2023 from: https://hdr.undp.org/content/2022-global-multidimensional-poverty-index-mpi#/indicies/MPI
11. 'Girls Not Brides'. Retrieved in May 2023 from: https://www.girlsnotbrides.org/learning-resources/child-marriage-atlas/regions-and-countries/niger/
12. Fatratra Andriamasinoro, L. and Abdou Soumaila, I. 'Ending child marriage in Niger'. UNICEF. Retrieved in May 2023 from: www.unicef.org/niger/stories/ending-child-marriage-niger
13. fivetalents. (2016). 'Five Reasons Microcredit Fails in the Fight Against Poverty'. Retrieved in June 2023 from: https://fivetalents.org/blog/2017/8/15/five-reasons-microcredit-fails-in-the-fight-against-poverty
14. UN Conference on Trade and Development. (2021). *Escaping from the Commodity Dependence Trap through Technology and Innovation*. Retrieved in May 2023 from: https://unctad.org/system/files/official-document/ditccom2021d1_en.pdf
15. The World Bank. (2020). TC Data 360. 'Gross Expenditure on R&D (GERD)'. Retrieved in May 2023 from: https://tcdata360.worldbank.org/indicators/5b985527?country=AGO&indicator=40353&countries=BDI,BEN,BFA,BGD,BTN,CAF,CHE,COM,KIR,VNM&viz=line_chart&years=2013,2020
16. United Nations. Department of Economic and Social Affairs. 'Information and communication technologies (ICTs)'. Retrieved in April 2023 from: www.un.org/development/desa/socialperspectiveondevelopment/issues/information-and-communication-technologies-icts.html
17. GSMA. *The Mobile Economy 2022*. Retrieved in June 2023 from: www.gsma.com/mobileeconomy/wp-content/uploads/2022/02/280222-The-Mobile-Economy-2022.pdf
18. Horrigan, J.B. (2019). 'Analysis: Digital Divide Isn't Just a Rural Problem'. The Daily Yonde. Retrieved in May 2023 from: https://dailyyonder.com/analysis-digital-divide-isnt-just-a-rural-problem/2019/08/14/
19. OECD Data. 'Internet Access'. Retrieved from: https://data.oecd.org/ict/internet-access.htm
20. Statista. 'Internet penetration rate in Africa as of December 2021, compared to the global average'. Retrieved in June 2023 from: www.statista.com/statistics/1176654/internet-penetration-rate-africa-compared-to-global-average/
21. Repsol Global. (2023). 'What is the digital divide?'. Retrieved in June 2023 from: https://www.repsol.com/en/energy-and-the-future/people/digital-divide/index.cshtml
22. Nakashima, E. and Harris, S. (2018). 'How the Russians hacked the DNC and passed its emails to Wikileaks'. *The Washington Post*. Retrieved in July 2023 from: https://www.washingtonpost.com/world/national-security/how-the-russians-hacked-the-dnc-and-passed-its-emails-to-wikileaks/2018/07/13/af19a828-86c3-11e8-8553-a3ce89036c78_story.html

    Geller, E. (2016). 'Russian hackers infiltrated podesta's email, security firm says'. Politico. Retrieved in July 2023 from: https://www.politico.com/story/2016/10/russia-responsible-podesta-wikileaks-hack-230095
23. Saran, S. (2021). '7 views on how technology will shape geopolitics'. World Economic Forum. Retrieved in June 2023 from: www.weforum.org/agenda/2021/04/seven-business-leaders-on-how-technology-will-shape-geopolitics/
24. Songwe, V. (2021). '7 views on how technology will shape geopolitics'. World Economic Forum. Retrieved in June 2023 from: www.weforum.org/agenda/2021/04/seven-business-leaders-on-how-technology-will-shape-geopolitics/
25. Han, K. (2021). 'In Singapore, Covid vs privacy is no contest'. Lowy Institute. Retrieved in May 2023 from: www.lowyinstitute.org/the-interpreter/singapore-covid-vs-privacy-no-contest

26. Council on Foreign Relations. (2022). 'The Three Internets'. Retrieved in June 2023 from: www.cfr.org/podcasts/three-internets
27. Addiction Center. 'Social Media Addiction'. Retrieved in June 2023 from: www.addictioncenter.com/drugs/social-media-addiction/
28. Water, J. (2021). 'Constant craving: how digital media turned us all into dopamine addicts'. *The Guardian*. Retrieved in June 2023 from: www.theguardian.com/global/2021/aug/22/how-digital-media-turned-us-all-into-dopamine-addicts-and-what-we-can-do-to-break-the-cycle Lembke, A. (2021). *Dopamine Nation: Finding Balance in the Age of Indulgence*. Hachette.
29. Howard, P. in O'Donnell, C. (2011). 'New study quantifies use of social media in Arab Spring'. University of Washington News. Retrieved in May 2023 from: www.washington.edu/news/2011/09/12/new-study-quantifies-use-of-social-media-in-arab-spring/
30. Khashoggi, J. (2018). 'Why the Arab World Needs Democracy Now'. *The New York Times*. Retrieved in May 2023 from: www.nytimes.com/2018/10/22/opinion/khashoggi-mbs-arab-democracy.html
31. Parshall, A. (2023). 'How This AI Image Won a Major Photography Competition'. *Scientific American*. Retrieved in June 2023 from: www.scientificamerican.com/article/how-my-ai-image-won-a-major-photography-competition/
32. ITU. (2023). 'About International Communication Union'. Retrieved in July 2023 from: https://www.itu.int/en/about/Pages/default.aspx
33. European Commission. (2023). 'The Digital Services Act package'. Retrieved in July 2023 from: https://digital-strategy.ec.europa.eu/en/policies/digital-services-act-package
34. WHO. (2023). 'Constitution'. Retrieved in July 2023 from: https://www.who.int/about/governance/constitution
35. WHO. (2020). 'The top 10 causes of death'. Retrieved in May 2023 from: www.who.int/news-room/fact-sheets/detail/the-top-10-causes-of-death
36. WHO. 'Constitution'. Retrieved in May 2023 from: www.who.int/about/governance/constitution
37. Rouw, A., Wexler, A., Kates, J., et. al. (2023). 'Assessing the Role of Treaties, Conventions, Institutions, and Other International Agreements in the Global COVID-19 Response: Implications for the Future'. Retrieved in June 2023 from: www.kff.org/global-health-policy/issue-brief/assessing-the-role-of-treaties-conventions-institutions-and-other-international-agreements-in-the-global-covid-19-response-implications-for-the-future/
38. White, C. (2022). *The Rise of OxyContin: How Purdue Pharma and the Sackler Family is Responsible For the Epidemic Behind the Pandemic Family is Responsible For the Epidemic Behind the Pandemic*. Dominican University of California. Retrieved in July 2023 from: https://scholar.dominican.edu/cgi/viewcontent.cgi?article=1011&context=history-senior-theses
39. Gale, A. (2022). 'Sacklers Sacked But Purdue Still Caused Opioid Epidemic'. *The Journal of the Missouri State Medical Association*, 119(2): 109. Retrieved in July 2023 from: https://www.ncbi.nlm.nih.gov/pmc/articles/PMC9339402/
40. Beauregard, J. and Kazemi, R. (2020). 'Health Security is National Security'. Retrieved in May 2023 from: www.newsecuritybeat.org/2020/04/health-security-national-security/
41. Soon after the terrorist attacks of September 11, 2001, letters laced with anthrax began appearing in the US mail.
42. Fiddler, D.P. (2023). 'Public Health and National Security in the Global Age: Infectious Diseases, Bioterrorism, and Realpolitik Diseases, Bioterrorism, and Realpolitik'. ResearchGate.
43. World Nuclear Association. (2023). 'Fukushima Daiichi Accident'. Retrieved in June 2023 from: https://world-nuclear.org/information-library/safety-and-security/safety-of-plants/fukushima-daiichi-accident.aspx
44. Rohwerder, B. (2014). *Impact and Implications of the Ebola Crisis*. GSDRC, University of Birmingham. Retrieved in June 2023 from: www.gsdrc.org/docs/open/hdq1177.pdf
45. WHO. (2023). 'Mental Health'. Retrieved in May 2023 from: www.who.int/health-topics/mental-health#tab=tab_1
46. Human Rights Watch. (2020). 'Living in Chains'. Retrieved in June 2023 from: www.hrw.org/report/2020/10/06/living-chains/shackling-people-psychosocial-disabilities-worldwide
47. Human Rights Watch. (2021). 'With Pandemic, Mental Health Services Even More Critical'. Retrieved in May 2023 from: www.hrw.org/news/2021/09/29/pandemic-mental-health-services-even-more-critical

HL extension

48. Frankel Pratt, S. and Levin, J. (2021). 'Vaccines Will Shape the New Geopolitical Order'. Retrieved in May 2023 from: https://foreignpolicy.com/2021/04/29/vaccine-geopolitics-diplomacy-israel-russia-china/

49. Kingsley, P., Bergman, R. and Kramer, A.E. (2021, February 24). 'Israel Secretly Agrees to Fund Vaccines for Syria as Part of Prisoner Swap'. *The New York Times*. Retrieved in June 2023 from: www.nytimes.com/2021/02/20/world/middleeast/israel-syria-prisoner-swap-vaccines.html

50. Campbell, D. (1992). *Writing Security: United States Foreign Policy and the Politics of Identity*. Manchester University Press.

51. Powell, J.A. (2017). 'Us vs them: the sinister techniques of "Othering" – and how to avoid them'. *The Guardian*. Retrieved in April 2023 from: www.theguardian.com/inequality/2017/nov/08/us-vs-them-the-sinister-techniques-of-othering-and-how-to-avoid-them

52. Cronin, B. (1999). *Community under Anarchy: Transnational Identity and the Evolution of Cooperation*. Columbia University Press.

53. Desai, V.T., Diofasi, A. and Lu, J. (2018). 'The global identification challenge: Who are the 1 billion people without proof of identity?' Retrieved in May 2023 from: https://blogs.worldbank.org/voices/global-identification-challenge-who-are-1-billion-people-without-proof-identity

54. UNICEF. (2019). 'Birth Registration for Every Child by 2030: Are we on track?' Retrieved in May 2023 from: https://data.unicef.org/resources/birth-registration-for-every-child-by-2030/

55. García, A.K. (2023). 'Niñas y niños sin identidad: entre la marginación, las fronteras y la pobreza'. *El Economista*. Retrieved in June 2023 from: www.eleconomista.com.mx/arteseideas/Ninas-y-ninos-sin-identidad-entre-la-marginacion-las-fronteras-y-la-pobreza-20230414-0032.html

56. Overy, R. (2004). *The Times Complete History of the World*, Times Books, pp.284-85.

57. United Nations. 'Universal Declaration of Human Rights'. Retrieved in July 2023 from: https://www.un.org/en/about-us/universal-declaration-of-human-rights

58. USA for UNHCR. (2023). 'What is a Refugee?' Retrieved in July 2023 from: https://www.unrefugees.org/refugee-facts/what-is-a-refugee/#:~:text=A%20refugee%20is%20someone%20who,in%20a%20particular%20social%20group

59. YouGovAmerica. (2001). 'Airport Security Despite Inconvenience'. Retrieved in May 2023 from: https://today.yougov.com/topics/travel/articles-reports/2021/12/23/airport-security-despite-inconvenience-most-americ

60. UN Office on Drugs and Crime. 'Human Trafficking'. Retrieved in June 2023 from: https://www.unodc.org/unodc/en/human-Trafficking/Human-Trafficking.html

61. Sharma, R. (2020). 'India and Nepal Must Develop a Formal Agreement to Prevent Human Trafficking'. Retrieved in May 2023 from: https://blogs.lse.ac.uk/socialpolicy/2020/10/20/india-and-nepal-must-develop-a-formal-agreement-to-prevent-human-trafficking/

62. The European Free Trade Association. Retrieved in June 2023 from: www.efta.int

63. Jackson-Preece, J. (2011). *Security in international relations*. University of London. Retrieved in May 2023 from: www.london.ac.uk/sites/default/files/uploads/ir3140-security-international-relations-study-guide.pdf

64. Stanford Encyclopedia of Philosophy. (2022). 'Hobbes's Moral and Political Philosophy'. Retrieved in June 2023 from: https://plato.stanford.edu/entries/hobbes-moral/#StaNat

65. Morgenthau, H.J. (1978). *Politics Among Nations: The Struggle for Power and Peace*. Alfred A. Knopf.

66. Mearsheimer, J.J. (1983). *Conventional Deterrence*. Cornell University Press.

67. Lasswell, H. (1950). *National Security and Individual Freedom*. Da Capo Press.

68. Maier, C.S. (1990, 12 June). *Peace and security for the 1990s*. Unpublished paper for the MacArthur Fellowship Program, Social Science Research Council.

69. Hobbes, T. (1651). *Leviathan; or, The Matter, Form, and Power of a Commonwealth, Ecclesiastical and Civil*. Retrieved in June 2023 from: https://www.google.com.mx/books/edition/Leviathan_Or_The_Matter_Form_and_Power_o/L3FgBpvIWRkC?hl=en&gbpv=0

70. United Nations. 'Universal Declaration of Human Rights'. Retrieved in July 2023 from: https://www.un.org/en/about-us/universal-declaration-of-human-rights

71. UNDP. (1994). *Human Development Report*. Retrieved in June 2023 from: https://hdr.undp.org/content/human-development-report-1994

72. United Nations Digital Library. (2003). *Human security now: protecting and empowering people/ Commission on Human Security,* Retrieved in May 2023 from: https://digitallibrary.un.org/record/503749?ln=en
73. Global Development Research Center. 'Human Security: Indicators for Measurement'. Retrieved in May 2023 from: www.gdrc.org/sustdev/husec/z-indicators.html
74. UNDP. (2022). *New threats to human security in the Anthropocene.* 2022 Special Report. Retrieved in June 2023 from: https://hs.hdr.undp.org/pdf/srhs2022.pdf
75. Eroukhmanoff, C. (2018). 'Securitisation Theory: An Introduction'. Retrieved in May 2023 from: www.e-ir.info/2018/01/14/securitisation-theory-an-introduction/
76. United Nations. (2018). 'Security Council Seeks to Strengthen Protections for Children in Armed Conflict, Unanimously Adopting Resolution 2427 (2018)'. Retrieved in June 2023 from: https://press.un.org/en/2018/sc13412.doc.htm
77. Mahmood, S. (2016). 'Cubs of the Caliphate: The Islamic State's Focus on Children'. *Counter Terrorist Trends and Analyses,* 8(10), pp.9–12. Retrieved in April 2023 from: www.jstor.org/stable/26351458
78. United Nations. (2020). *World Social Report 2020. Inequality in a Rapidly Changing World.* Retrieved in April 2023 from: www.un.org/development/desa/dspd/wp-content/uploads/sites/22/2020/01/World-Social-Report-2020-FullReport.pdf
79. Oxfam International. (2023, January). 'Richest 1% bag nearly twice as much wealth as the rest of the world put together over the past two years'. Retrieved in June 2023 from: https://www.oxfam.org/en/press-releases/richest-1-bag-nearly-twice-much-wealth-rest-world-put-together-over-past-two-years
80. UN Department of Economic and Social Affairs. (2023). 'Sustainable Development'. Retrieved in May 2023 from: https://sdgs.un.org/goals/goal1 and https://sdgs.un.org/goals/goal10
81. United Nations. 'Inequality – Bridging the Divide'. Retrieved in May 2023 from: www.un.org/en/un75/inequality-bridging-divide
82. SEMA International. (2023). 'Effects of Child Abuse'. Retrieved in June 2023 from: https://sema-sy.org/effects-of-child-abuse/
83. Unicef. (2023), 'Female genital mutilation'. Retrieved in June 2023 from: https://www.unicef.org/protection/female-genital-mutilation#:~:text=Despite%20being%20internationally%20recognized%20as,in%20Egypt%2C%20Ethiopia%20and%20Indonesia
84. Strack, C. (2022). 'Racial discrimination still prevalent in Germany'. Retrieved in June 2023 from: https://www.dw.com/en/discrimination-remains-a-major-problem-in-germany/a-62819504
85. Oxfam International. (2023). 'A Deadly Virus: 5 shocking facts about global extreme inequality'. Retrieved in June 2023 from: https://www.oxfam.org/en/5-shocking-facts-about-extreme-global-inequality-and-how-even-it
86. Waugh, C. (2022). 'Race and Inequality – Do We Really Understand It?' Retrieved in May 2023 from: https://sites.manchester.ac.uk/global-social-challenges/2022/07/06/race-and-inequality-do-we-really-understand-it/
87. Mundasad, S. (2021, 11 November). 'Black women four times more likely to die in childbirth'. Retrieved in May 2023 from: www.bbc.com/news/health-59248345
88. Silver, L., Fetterolf, J. and Connaughton, A. (2021). 'Diversity and Division in Advanced Economies'. Retrieved in May 2023 from: www.pewresearch.org/global/2021/10/13/diversity-and-division-in-advanced-economies/
89. WHO – Europe. 'Roma Health'. Retrieved in June 2023 from: www.euro.who.int/en/health-topics/health-determinants/roma-health
90. Cook, B., Wayne, G.F., Valentine, A., Lessios, A. and Yeh, E. (2013). 'Revisiting the evidence on health and health care disparities among the Roma: a systematic review 2003–2012'. *International Journal of Public Health,* 58(6), pp.885–911.
91. European Public Health Alliance. (2020). 'Health inequalities: a persistent obstacle for Roma equality and inclusion'. Retrieved in June 2023 from: https://epha.org/health-inequalities-a-persistent-obstacle-for-roma-equality-and-inclusion/
92. European Union Agency for Fundamental Rights. (2020). 'Persistent Roma inequality increases COVID-19 risk, human rights heads say'. Retrieved in June 2023 from: http://fra.europa.eu/en/news/2020/persistent-roma-inequality-increases-covid-19-risk-human-rights-heads-say

HL extension

93. Bryant, A. (2017). 'Europe's Roma Do Not Have Equal Education'. Retrieved in June 2023 from: https://learningenglish.voanews.com/a/europes-roma-still-struggle-to-get-good-education/4108678.html
94. Carlo, A. (2019). 'We need to talk about the rising wave of anti-Roma attacks in Europe.' *Independent*. Retrieved in June 2023 from: www.independent.co.uk/voices/roma-antiziganist-romani-discrimination-italy-matteo-salvini-ukraine-a9024196.html
95. Pew Research Center. (2019, October). *European Public Opinion Three Decades After the Fall of Communism*, p.86. Retrieved in June 2023 from: www.pewresearch.org/global/wp-content/uploads/sites/2/2019/10/Pew-Research-Center-Value-of-Europe-report-FINAL-UPDATED.pdf
96. Strzyżyńska, W. (2022). '"Meet us before you reject us": Ukraine's Roma refugees face closed doors in Poland'. *The Guardian*. Retrieved in March 2023 from: www.theguardian.com/global-development/2022/may/10/ukraine-roma-refugees-poland
97. Doughnut Economics Action Lab. (2023). 'About Doughnut Economics'. Retrieved in July 2023 from: https://doughnuteconomics.org/about-doughnut-economics
98. European Commission. (2023). Retrieved in April 2023 from: https://data.jrc.ec.europa.eu/
99. *Ibid.*
100. Earth Overshoot Day. (2023). 'Country Overshoot Days'. Retrieved in April 2023 from: www.overshootday.org/newsroom/country-overshoot-days/
101. United Nations Human Rights Office of the High Commissioner. (2023). 'About the mandate'. Retrieved in May 2023 from: https://www.ohchr.org/en/special-procedures/sr-environment/about-mandate
102. Hines, A. (2023). 'Decade of defiance'. Retrieved in June 2023 from: www.globalwitness.org/en/campaigns/environmental-activists/decade-defiance/#decade-killings-globally
103. IPCC. 'Global Warming of 1.5°C'. Retrieved in June 2023 from: www.ipcc.ch/sr15/
104. ICRC. (2020, 9 July). 'ICRC report: Climate change and conflict are a cruel combo that stalk the world's most vulnerable'. Retrieved in June 2023 from: www.icrc.org/en/document/icrc-report-climate-change-and-conflict-are-cruel-combo-stalk-worlds-most-vulnerable
105. Institute for Economics and Peace. (2020). *Over one billion people at threat of being displaced by 2050 due to environmental change, conflict and civil unrest*. Retrieved in May 2023 from: www.economicsandpeace.org/wp-content/uploads/2020/09/Ecological-Threat-Register-Press-Release-27.08-FINAL.pdf
106. NASA earth observatory. (2022). 'Tracking 30 Years of Sea Level Rise'. Retrieved in May 2023 from: https://earthobservatory.nasa.gov/images/150192/tracking-30-years-of-sea-level-rise#:~:text=By%20the%20early%201990s%2C%20it,(0.15%20inches)%20per%20year
107. US Department of Commerce. National Oceanic and Atmospheric Administration. (2022). 'US coastline to see up to a foot of sea level rise by 2050'. Retrieved in May 2023 from: www.noaa.gov/news-release/us-coastline-to-see-up-to-foot-of-sea-level-rise-by-2050
108. Rentschler, J. and Salhab, M. (2020). '1.47 billion people face flood risk worldwide: for over a third, it could be devastating'. Retrieved in June 2023 from: https://blogs.worldbank.org/climatechange/147-billion-people-face-flood-risk-worldwide-over-third-it-could-be-devastating#:~:text=Using%20the%20latest%20high%2Dresolution,third%20of%20them%2C%20almost%20600
109. Parsons, C. (2022). 'The Pacific Islands: The front line in the battle against climate change'. Retrieved in May 2023 from: https://new.nsf.gov/science-matters/pacific-islands-front-line-battle-against-climate

Assessment support

An overview of Paper 1

Paper 1 is a four-document source paper with four questions that assess knowledge of the core topics of Global Politics and your source analysis skills. Through Paper 1, you are expected to demonstrate knowledge and understanding of:

- power relationships in Global Politics between state and non-state stakeholders
- political key concepts and related concepts from your core topics and thematic studies
- relevant source material from your core topics and thematic studies
- political issues and challenges from your core topics and thematic studies.

Paper 1 gives you the chance to demonstrate the skills, knowledge and abilities that you have been developing since the Global Politics course began, including:

- application of relevant concepts and tools to analyze contemporary political issues and challenges in a variety of contexts
- identification and analysis of information, claims and perspectives in source material
- synthesis and evaluation of source material evidence and own knowledge about Global Politics
- synthesis and evaluation of different perspectives and approaches to Global Politics
- examination and synthesis of different perspectives on political beliefs, positions and biases.

Table 6.1 Paper 1 question structure for SL and HL (continues on following page)

Question	Assessment Objective (AO)	Description
Question 1 (3 marks)	AO1	Question 1 tests understanding of a source. This can be demonstrated, for example, by identifying specific elements present in a source or by describing or summarizing information included in a diagram or table.
Question 2 (4 marks)	AO2	Question 2 tests the application of knowledge for the analysis of a source. This can be demonstrated, for example, by explaining a term used in a source or by explaining a claim expressed by the source.
Question 3 (6 marks)	AO3	Question 3 tests the comparison and/or contrast of the views, ideas, claims and information presented in two of the sources.
		Candidates should focus on comparing and/or contrasting specific points in the sources but may make use of their wider understanding of global politics to provide context, if relevant.
		Candidates should organize the material into a clear, logical and coherent response. For the highest marks, a detailed running comparison and/or contrast is expected.

Paper 1 is a 25-mark, 75-minute (1 hour 15 minutes) paper that draws from the common SL and HL core topics. You will answer four structured questions using the sources provided. Paper 1 is the same for SL and HL and is worth 30% of the overall mark for SL and 20% of the overall mark for HL.

Paper 1 will be based on one of the thematic studies: Rights and justice, Development and sustainability, Peace and conflict. You will not know the focus in advance, so be prepared for all three. The concepts that make up the core topics (power, sovereignty, legitimacy and interdependence) will likely appear explicitly or implicitly in each of the Paper 1 questions.

You need to manage your time effectively. You have 75 minutes to interpret four sources and answer four questions. You can boost your success by planning to spend a certain amount of time on each question.

You will have 5 minutes reading time at the start of Paper 1. You are not allowed to write anything during this time. Use it to read through the four questions and make mental notes about the expectations of each question. Then read through the document sources with the expectations of the questions in mind. Consider the origin of each source. What kind of stakeholder is the source coming from? When was is created? Make mental notes on each of the questions and the sources they are connected to. Begin to formulate your response to Question 1 during your reading time.

Exam papers

Question	Assessment Objective (AO)	Description
Question 4 (12 marks)	AO3	Question 4 tests the evaluation of sources and synthesis of source material and previous knowledge. Candidates should evaluate the sources and synthesize relevant evidence from them with their own knowledge about the prescribed content of the course. Candidates should organize the material into a clear, logical and coherent response.

(Taken from the Global Politics Guide)

Approaching Question 1: knowledge and understanding (3 marks)

'Syrian Refugees' by Paresh Nath from 8 February 2013.

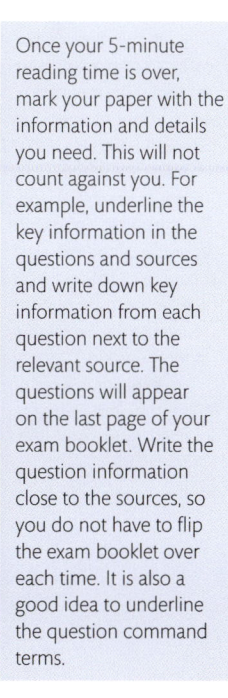

Question 1 is usually an interpretation of a political cartoon, data table, diagram, image or images, infographic or some other visual representation of political issues in global politics. It is worth 3 marks, so you need to identify three specific ideas from the source based on the question.

You should expect to spend about 5 minutes responding to this question.

Reference the source directly in your response. Make sure you are answering the question being asked.

Command terms used in Question 1
You will generally find the following command terms in Question 1:

- Describe: Give a detailed account.
- Define: Give the precise meaning of a word, phrase, concept or physical quantity.

Once your 5-minute reading time is over, mark your paper with the information and details you need. This will not count against you. For example, underline the key information in the questions and sources and write down key information from each question next to the relevant source. The questions will appear on the last page of your exam booklet. Write the question information close to the sources, so you do not have to flip the exam booklet over each time. It is also a good idea to underline the question command terms.

335

Assessment support

- Identify: Provide an answer from a number of possibilities.
- Outline: Give a brief account or summary.

Follow the expectations of the command term as this will be key to meeting the expectations of the question.

Your Question 1 response

Your answer needs to be focused and to the point. There is no need for long paragraphs. Interpret Source A, provide the required three points and move on.

You could begin your response with 'According to Source A…' and include the type of source and its origin (author, where it was published and date if available).

You can respond in full sentences or use bullet points. Each point should have details that link it to the source and the question. One complete and detailed sentence per point should be enough.

> As you read Question 1 and analyze Source A, consider the ways in which the source relates to the key concepts of the relevant thematic study. For example, for Development and sustainability, see where these concepts as well as the themes of poverty and inequality are found.

Activity

Consider the political cartoon 'Syrian Refugees' by Paresh Nath. Use the strategies above to answer this question: 'Identify three things this political cartoon says about the nature of human rights.' Note that this means the prompt is from the thematic study Rights and justice, so you will need to show how the cartoon relates to the concepts of rights, justice, liberty and equality.

Approaching Question 2: application of knowledge (4 marks)

Question 2 tests your application of knowledge in the analysis of a specific source. As a 4-mark question, you are expected to identify, include and develop two ideas related to the question. Give each idea its own paragraph so each idea is clear. You will earn 1 mark for identifying an idea and 1 mark for developing support for that idea.

You should expect to spend about 10–15 minutes responding to this question. Each paragraph should be about 100–125 words (200–250 words in total).

Underline important information in the question and source that will help you in your response. Keep in mind that Question 2, as with all the questions in Paper 1, will be connected to a specific thematic study.

> Some questions in Paper 1 may ask you to include 'your own knowledge' or 'an example you have studied'. This means you need to consider what you have learned in Global Politics about the focus and include this in your response, along with your use of the required source or sources. You can demonstrate this, for example, by explaining a term used in a source or explaining a claim expressed by the source as it relates to the question.

Command terms in Question 2

You can expect to find the following command terms in Question 2:

- Analyze: Break down, in order to bring out the essential elements or structure.
- Distinguish: Make clear the differences between two or more concepts or items.
- Explain: Give a detailed account, including reasons or causes.
- Suggest: Propose a solution, hypothesis or other possible answer.

Follow the expectations of the command term as this will be key to meeting the expectations of the question.

Your Question 2 response

Your answer should be in paragraph form, with two well-structured paragraphs of 3–4 sentences each. Restate the question at the start of each paragraph. Consider using the following paragraph structure:

- Restate the question and include source details to clarify your main point: Make this the main statement of the paragraph and be sure to use the language and origin of the source.
- Evidence or example: The longest part of your paragraph should include specific quotes and/or paraphrasing from the source.
- Analyze: Make it clear how the evidence you presented in the previous sentence(s) supports the point you made in your first sentence. This should back up your point.
- Link and reconnect to the main point: A summary sentence that relates what you wrote in the previous sentence back to the question.

You are expected to provide your own knowledge of global politics *as well as* using the source to respond to Question 2 if the question asks for this. Be sure to include the specific information required. You can modify your approach to your second paragraph in this way:

- Use the specific language of the case study or example you are bringing in from your own knowledge.
- Include evidence from your example or case study so that it is clear it is relevant to the source.

> Think about Question 2 when you read a relevant article or report. As you read, ask yourself: 'How is this relevant to what I am learning in Global Politics right now?'

> Question 2 will likely ask you to identify and explain, examine or suggest recommendations based on a specific Global Politics key concept or related concept. Keep in mind that such concepts can be interpreted from different perspectives and are generally multifaceted and contested depending on the perspective you are coming from.

Approaching Question 3: compare and/or contrast (6 marks)

Question 3 is worth 6 marks and is based on one of the most important analytical skills used by political scientists and other professionals in global politics: the ability to compare and/or contrast the views, ideas, claims and information presented in two different sources.

You should expect to spend about 20 minutes responding to this question. Each of your three paragraphs should be roughly 75–100 words (225–300 words in total).

You should focus on comparing and/or contrasting specific points in the sources, but you can make use of the wider context of global politics to provide relevant background information. For the highest marks, you are expected to provide a detailed compare and/or contrast of the sources.

> Use a T-Chart to draft a brief outline of the main compare and/or contrast points you find in the sources. You can boost your success by drawing a T-Chart in your exam booklet. Keep this in front of you as you write your response.

Command terms in Question 3

You can expect to find the following command terms in Question 3:

- Compare and contrast: Give an account of similarities and differences between two (or more) items or situations, referring to both (all) of them throughout.
- Contrast: Give an account of the differences between two (or more) items or situations, referring to both (all) of them throughout.
- Compare: Give an account of the similarities between two (or more) items or situations, referring to both (all) of them throughout.

Assessment support

Follow the expectations of the command term as this will be key to meeting the expectations of the question.

Your Question 3 response

Be sure to read the sources carefully and underline the key ideas in each source as they relate to Question 3. Double-check that you have identified and are using the correct command terms.

You need to be clear in terms of what you will be comparing and/or contrasting. Look for ways in which the sources connect to each other. You can do this by identifying and using **comparison benchmarks** for each source. Your use of these benchmarks will be important in how your response is structured as you have to find ideas in each source that connect in some way.

The two sources in Question 3 will likely contain some of these benchmarks. You need to be able to identify them and use them. Below is a non-exhaustive list of possible benchmarks you can use to compare and/or contrast the two sources in Question 3.

> Comparison benchmarks are used to address compare, contrast and compare and contrast analytical activities. A benchmark is something that you look for in each source that you will compare or contrast. Global Politics is full of possible benchmarks. These are the analytical tools you have been using during the course, the scope or levels from which you create your analyses as well as the perspectives that you have studied.

Table 6.2 Sample table with select comparison benchmarks (non-exhaustive)

Benchmarks	Source C	Source D
Treatment of key concepts and related concepts from the *thematic study of focus*		
Treatment of key concepts and related concepts from the *core topics*		
Power relationships in global politics between state and non-state stakeholders		
Role of *state and non-state stakeholders* in the sources, including countries and marginalized groups		
Scope of the sources (local, national, regional, international, global)		
Political issues, challenges and *events* in each of the sources		
Themes or topics addressed in the source (political, economic, social, cultural)		
Perspective of each source (neorealist, neoliberal, postcolonial, sustainable development, human rights, gender, etc.)		
Tone of each source (positive, optimistic about what is at stake, solution oriented, or negative and more pessimistic, more critical)		
Purpose of each of source (the perspective of the source and what the source wants you to think)		
Origin of the sources (where does each source come from and why might this be relevant)		

Your response should be in the form of three short and focused paragraphs (2–3 lines for each is enough). Each paragraph should contain the following:

- specific comparison/contrast pairs from the sources
- clear benchmarks for each pairing
- reference to and quotes/paraphrasing from each source
- evidence from both sources to support the comparison/contrast being made
- a brief summary of the comparison/contrast made, referring back to the benchmark explicitly.

A sample answer might be:

> Both Source C and D refer to *the role and effectiveness of international organizations with regards to the protection of migrants and asylum seekers* in need of international protection. Source C states that 'significant efforts have been made by UNHCR to convince EU member states to relax their restrictions on migrants and asylum seekers coming to Europe through the Mediterranean' whereas Source D makes clear that the UNHCR is limited in its ability to influence EU policy due to 'the close relationship that the UNHCR has with each EU member state as well as the EU itself for purposes of funding.' Source C is expectedly more complimentary of the role of international organizations like UNHCR as it is their own report, whereas Source D, from an NGO, is critical of this role, mentioning a specific limitation of UNHCR in this context.

The mention of *the role and effectiveness of international organizations* in the response is your benchmark of comparison in each source for this pairing. The origin of each source is clearly identified with some analysis of the source itself, evidence is provided in the form of quotes from the sources and the comparison/contrast is summarized in one clear sentence that uses the original benchmark of comparison.

You should have three of these pairings with the required details in each.

Activity

Think about Question 3 throughout your study of Global Politics. Find two short sources that are related in some way to some aspect of a thematic study. Use a T-Chart and list 3–5 benchmarks of comparison. See which benchmarks can be found in both sources, in one of the sources or in neither of them. Try again until you find two sources where at least three of your benchmarks can be found in both sources. Then create compare or contrast pairings for each benchmark using each source.

Approaching Question 4: mini-essay (12 marks)

Question 4 is worth 12 marks and tests your ability to evaluate *all* of the sources *and* synthesize the source material with your own relevant knowledge. You should organize your response like you would a standard 5-paragraph essay so that it is clear, logical and coherent (see the hints for success for Paper 2 for more details).

You should expect to spend about 30 minutes responding to this question. Each of your main paragraphs should be 100–125 words, with an introduction paragraph of around 75–100 words and a conclusion paragraph of around 75–100 words (a total word count of 550–700 words).

Assessment support

Question 4 demands a longer, well-structured response based on the issues raised by the sources. Think of this question as a Paper 2-style question, but one where you use some sources to help you.

Command terms in Question 4

You can expect to find the following command terms in Question 4:

- Discuss: Offer a considered and balanced review that includes a range of arguments, factors or hypotheses. Opinions or conclusions should be presented clearly and supported by appropriate evidence.
- Evaluate: Make an appraisal by weighing up the strengths and limitations.
- Examine: Consider an argument or concept in a way that uncovers the assumptions and interrelationships of the issue.

Follow the expectations of each command term as this will be key to meeting the expectations of the question.

Your Question 4 response

Be sure to read Question 4 carefully so you are aware of the expectations of the question. You are expected to use all four sources *and* your own knowledge. Some sources will be more valuable than others, but you *must* use all four. Make sure that you are complementing each source with your own knowledge.

Your own knowledge comes in the form of a deep and thorough understanding of the key concepts and related concepts of the focus. Relate and connect your response to these concepts.

Your own knowledge also comes in the form of detailed and relevant examples and case studies.

The structure of your Question 4 response should include the following:

- Introduction: This is where you restate the question, provide your initial and informed argument or thesis in response to the question, a possible justification of the argument and views from different perspectives (counterclaims). Address any important views and related concepts that will be important in your exploration of the question. Make clear how you intend to explore these important issues raised by the question.
- Body paragraphs: Each of your four body paragraphs could be organized as follows. Try not to focus each paragraph on a separate source, but compare and contrast ideas and sources within each paragraph.
  - Restate the question and include source details to make clear your main point: Make this the main statement of the paragraph and be sure to use the language and origin of the source and the specific language of the case study or example you are bringing in from your own knowledge.
  - Evidence or example: This should be the longest part of your paragraph and include evidence from your relevant and detailed example or case study *as well as* specific quotes from the sources and/or paraphrasing so that it is clear that it is relevant.

> ⚠ Underline each source when you use it in your Question 4 response. For example, when you reference Source A, make sure that you include the key details of the source and underline it. This will help you when you review your essay before time is up. You should see all four sources underlined throughout your writing. If you do not, it means that you missed a source and you will lose marks.

> ⚠ Review the key concepts and related concepts from the thematic studies and the core topics as part of your revision for Paper 1. Make sure that you have recent and relevant examples of these concepts in practice through case studies. You can boost your success by including specific and relevant details from your case studies. Case studies that can be explored and discussed from multiple perspectives are more effective and useful.

340

- ○ Analyze: Make it clear how the evidence you presented in the previous sentence supports the point you made in your first sentence. This should back up your point.
- ○ Balance: Include other perspectives and other approaches to the points you are making. See this from the perspective of other state and non-state stakeholders. High marks are available if you use effective claims and counterclaims in your responses. Put forward one side of the argument and then contrast it with other views and state which, on the balance of the evidence, is more powerful *and* why this might be.
- ○ Link and reconnect to main point: A summary sentence that relates the paragraph you just wrote back to the question you raised in the first sentence.
- Conclusion: Summarize the points you have made. Explain, for example, what the balance of evidence leads you to conclude, and which side is most persuasive and why. Be sure to provide an explicit answer to the question and include the text of the question in your conclusion.

Question 4 markbands

In addition to the analytical mark scheme for each question, the marks for Question 4 are also allocated using the markbands in Table 6.3, applied holistically using a best fit approach. The stronger and more informed your writing is, the higher the markband.

Table 6.3 Markbands for Question 4

Marks	Level Descriptor
0	The work does not reach a standard described by the descriptors below.
1–3	The response shows a limited understanding of the demands of the question. • Little relevant knowledge is demonstrated. • References to the sources are made, but they are mostly descriptive or no clear evidence is integrated in the response. • Different perspectives are not identified.
4–6	The response shows some understanding of the demands of the question. • Some knowledge is demonstrated, but this is not always relevant or accurate. • Evidence from the sources is partially integrated into the response. • Different perspectives are identified, but not explored.
7–9	The response shows adequate understanding of the demands of the question. • Relevant and accurate knowledge is demonstrated. • There is synthesis of own knowledge and source material. • Different perspectives are explored.
10–12	The response shows an in-depth understanding of the demands of the question. • Relevant and accurate knowledge is demonstrated throughout. • There is effective synthesis of own knowledge and source material, with appropriate examples integrated in the response. • Different perspectives are explored and evaluated.

(Taken from the Global Politics Guide)

Draft or sketch a short outline as soon as you begin to respond to Question 4. Highlight key information in the question as well as key information in the sources that can help you. Taking a couple of minutes to do this will help you organize your response. After reading the question and understanding its demands, come up with 3–5 perspectives, arguments, claims and counterclaims that could be used to help address the question. Take note of your own knowledge that might be useful to answer the question from the different perspectives you have identified. This will help to bring balance to your response.

Keep in mind that the sources provided are not facts to be accepted at face value, but a collection of perspectives that you can and should analyze based on the skills you have developed. You can boost your success, especially in Question 4, by being explicit about the perspectives found in the sources and critically evaluating these perspectives. This counts as your own knowledge.

Assessment support

Final thoughts on Paper 1

Paper 1 is designed to develop your skills, not to trick you.

Spend time practicing Paper 1 questions with your classmates as well as on your own. Practice creating T-Charts for Question 3 and draft outlines for Question 4. This will help you develop an understanding of how you can best meet the demands of the question and utilize the sources. When you practice, set a timer and allow yourself plenty of time for Question 4. You could distribute the 75 minutes of Paper 1 as follows:

- Question 1 (3 marks): 5 minutes
- Question 2 (4 marks): 10 minutes
- Question 3 (6 marks) 20 minutes
- Question 4 (12 marks): 35 minutes
- Reviewing work after completing questions: 5 minutes

Be concise in your responses. Keep them focused on the demands of the question, the sources and your own knowledge. Remember the following:

- Rewording and paraphrasing the question will help you to answer it, as well as signalling to the examiner that you have understood the demands of the question.
- Use the origin of the source in your response.

This should ensure you are answering the question being asked.

Read different documents related to relevant and recent case studies and real-world examples. Each case study you explore should include newspaper articles as well as reports from state and non-state stakeholders, including think tanks and testimonies from populations and marginalized groups impacted by the events or policies you are researching. As you use these sources, practice each of the Paper 1 skill sets.

An overview of Paper 2

Paper 2 is the same for SL and HL and is an essay paper in response to open-ended prompts or questions. Paper 2 has two sections, each with three questions. You will be required to answer one question from each section, with each question being worth 15 marks.

- Section A includes questions from each of the thematic studies: Rights and justice, Development and sustainability, and Peace and conflict.
- Section B includes integrating questions, and requires you to make connections across two of the three thematic studies as well as the core topics.

You will have 105 minutes (1 hour 45 minutes) to complete Paper 2 and it is worth 40% of the total IB mark for SL students and 30% of the total IB mark for HL students.

Exam papers

Paper 2 is designed to assess your ability to *synthesize* elements from the prescribed content (see the Global Politics Guide), key concepts and diverse real-world contexts. Given the number of times that you will be required to show your ability to synthesize, it is important that you have a clear understanding of what this requires of you. In an academic context, synthesis refers to the process of combining information from multiple perspectives to create a new understanding or perspective on a particular topic. It involves analyzing, evaluating and integrating different ideas, theories or arguments to generate new insights, draw conclusions, or develop a comprehensive and balanced understanding of a topic or issue. The process of synthesis involves organizing and structuring information in a logical and coherent way, highlighting key points or arguments, and presenting a balanced view of the topic. It goes beyond summarizing individual perspectives or real-world examples by identifying the connections, intersections, overlaps or divergences between them. Through synthesis, you should develop a nuanced understanding of an issue and identify broader trends or patterns.

It is also important that you demonstrate a conceptual understanding of global politics by making use of key concepts in your responses. This is true even when key concepts are not explicitly included as part of the question/prompt. If you make a reference to a political key concept, you need to make sure that you develop it in the context of the question/prompt and demonstrate its relevance to the argument or points being made.

The Paper 2 markbands are shown in Table 6.4. You will be awarded marks for demonstrating relevant knowledge and understanding of political concepts and prescribed content. Marks will also be given for the extent to which your arguments are coherent and justified with reference to relevant and contemporary real-world examples and cases. If you do not include references to diverse perspectives, it is unlikely that your response will score more than 6 marks out of a possible 15 marks, and so it is critically important that you identify different perspectives that are relevant in the context of the prompt or question you are answering. The more you explore diverse perspectives by considering different views on the question/prompt and claims and counterclaims, the more likely your response will score highly. If you do this and evaluate any arguments you have proposed and any examples you have used to support these arguments, then this will increase the likelihood of your response scoring in the top markband (13–15 marks).

> It is very important that you have a good understanding of all the prescribed content for each topic as this is where the language of a Paper 2 question/prompt will be taken from.

> A *balanced understanding* does not mean that you cannot argue in favor of one particular perspective, but rather, that you must consider more than one point of view.

> A *contemporary* real-world example is interpreted as one that comes from your lifetime. The IB can be flexible here and sometimes it may be appropriate to refer to an historical event that occurred before you were born, but in such cases it is your responsibility to connect it to more contemporary phenomena or issues. For example, the 1994 Rwandan genocide is not a contemporary example but it could be referenced in order to help explain and understand a more contemporary real-world example such as the genocide of the Rohingya in Myanmar.

Table 6.4 Markbands for Paper 2 (continues on following page)

Marks	Level Descriptor
0	The work does not reach a standard described by the descriptors below.
1–3	The response shows limited understanding of the demands of the question. • The arguments are poorly structured and unclear. • There is little relevant knowledge present. • The response is descriptive or is based in unsupported generalizations.

Assessment support

> It is perfectly acceptable to take a black and white approach to including different perspectives in your Paper 2 responses to meet this requirement. However, a more compelling approach involves exploring the different shades of gray that exist in global politics. Engaging with the *it depends* question is often a good way to ensure that 'diverse perspectives are explored *and* evaluated', which is a key feature of the highest markband in the Paper 2.

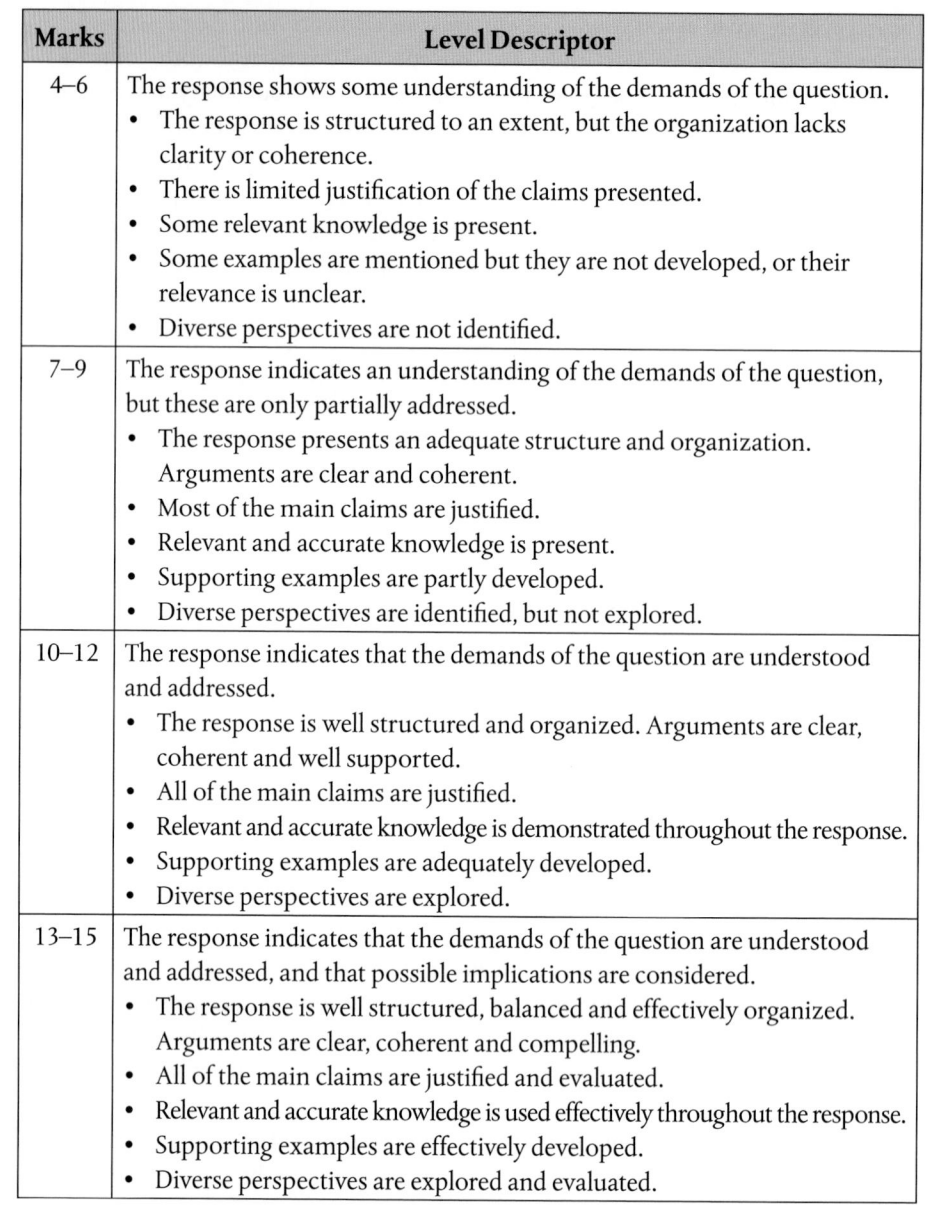

Marks	Level Descriptor
4–6	The response shows some understanding of the demands of the question. • The response is structured to an extent, but the organization lacks clarity or coherence. • There is limited justification of the claims presented. • Some relevant knowledge is present. • Some examples are mentioned but they are not developed, or their relevance is unclear. • Diverse perspectives are not identified.
7–9	The response indicates an understanding of the demands of the question, but these are only partially addressed. • The response presents an adequate structure and organization. Arguments are clear and coherent. • Most of the main claims are justified. • Relevant and accurate knowledge is present. • Supporting examples are partly developed. • Diverse perspectives are identified, but not explored.
10–12	The response indicates that the demands of the question are understood and addressed. • The response is well structured and organized. Arguments are clear, coherent and well supported. • All of the main claims are justified. • Relevant and accurate knowledge is demonstrated throughout the response. • Supporting examples are adequately developed. • Diverse perspectives are explored.
13–15	The response indicates that the demands of the question are understood and addressed, and that possible implications are considered. • The response is well structured, balanced and effectively organized. Arguments are clear, coherent and compelling. • All of the main claims are justified and evaluated. • Relevant and accurate knowledge is used effectively throughout the response. • Supporting examples are effectively developed. • Diverse perspectives are explored and evaluated.

(Taken from the Global Politics Guide)

> You can use old Paper 2 questions (2017–25) as practice questions. If you look at Paper 2, you will see that, in each pair of questions, there is one that is grounded in one topic while the other links different topics. This mirrors the Section A and Section B structure of Paper 2. The 2017–25 markbands are not the same as the markbands in Table 6.4, although many of the requirements remain roughly the same.

General advice

The open-ended nature of a Paper 2 prompt/question may seem daunting at first, and so it is important that you practice similar types of question and old IB exam questions. You should practice thinking about and reflecting on different types of questions to make sure that you correctly identify the key demands of each question and you understand any terms that have been used. It is important that you answer the prompt you were given and not the prompt that you wish you had been given. It is very difficult for an examiner to award a high mark if you have not answered the question, no matter how familiar you may be with the course content in general.

There may be the temptation to reproduce a response, especially if a question is similar to one that you have practiced in class or as part of your own review process.

It may also be tempting to include real-world examples or cases studied in class when they relate well to the question you are attempting to answer. Both temptations should be avoided – the process must always proceed from the question to the example(s) rather than the other way around. It is painfully apparent to examiners when a candidate has reused a real-world example, case or conceptual approach without determining its relevance in the context of the question. Such approaches generally do not score well.

Some specific guidance

- Plan out your response before you begin: There may be the temptation to start writing immediately once your 5-minute reading time is up, but it is worth taking 5–10 minutes more to plan your responses before you start writing. This ensures that you have a better chance of accurately identifying the key demands of the question/prompt you are answering.
- You must have an introduction: This should not be too long. You could begin by defining any key terms you think need to be defined. You should clearly show early in the response that you understand any key terms/concepts that are part of the prompt/question.
- Your introduction should have an overall thesis around which a response can be structured: Ideally, your thesis should include some sense of how it will be justified in the paragraphs that follow.
- Use paragraphs: Each paragraph should be focused on a single point or argument. Each paragraph should have a topic sentence that clearly states this point or argument.
- Each paragraph should include a clear reference to at least one relevant, contemporary real-world example or case: You must clearly connect any real-world example or case you include to the point or argument you are making.
- Do not conclude a paragraph by simply asserting that a point or argument has been proved: The point or argument needs to be clearly established and demonstrated in the preceding discussion. Whatever you say at the end of your paragraph should be the logical conclusion of everything you have said in that paragraph. You should also end each body paragraph by making a clear link between what you have said in that paragraph and the key demands of the question/prompt.
- There should be a logical structure to your overall response: One possible approach, bifurcation, is shown below.
- You must have a conclusion: You should not include any new arguments or information in your conclusion. This is often an ideal place to inject some nuance into your response if you have not already done so. Nuance often takes the form of acknowledging the complex, contingent and uncertain nature of much of global politics.

One possible approach: bifurcation

Bifurcation (a dichotomy) is one possible approach that you might take in answering a Paper 2 question. There is no IB-prescribed format that a Paper 2 response must take and there are many possible options depending on what you may have been taught. As long as your response fulfills the criteria given in the Paper 2 markbands, it will score highly.

Assessment support

Bifurcation works well if the open-ended nature of a Paper 2 prompt/question is challenging because you are struggling to decide which of your thoughts or ideas are most relevant to the question – you have so many ideas that you do not know where to start. This approach gives your response a straightforward and relatively simple base upon which you can then add greater complexity and sophistication.

Look at this previous Paper 2 question (2017–25): *Justify the claim that the debate between universal rights and cultural relativism is useful for codifying and protecting human rights.*

Bifurcating the response give us:

- Yes, the debate is useful.
- No, the debate is not useful.

You now have the basis for your first two body paragraphs. Each paragraph needs to give some reasons and examples to support each side of this bifurcated argument. For example:

> The debate is useful because it highlights real differences in position, and if what we truly care about is that people's human rights are promoted and protected then we need to have a better idea of any points of difference that exist across different cultures. However, the debate may not be useful because it is often used as window dressing for other, more instrumental or strategic concerns. That is, states and other political actors often dress up strategic considerations in the language of human rights rather than being genuinely concerned about them, per se.

This shows that you understand the demands of the question, and you will have demonstrated an understanding of the prescribed content and a familiarity with global politics.

To push your response into the higher markbands, you need to consider how real-world global politics is more complex than a simple and crude bifurcation would suggest. This is where you would introduce the *it depends* angle of your response. That is, what might the answer to the question depend upon? By asking this question you are more likely to demonstrate your critical thinking and synthesis skills. There are a number of *it depends* dimensions in Global Politics, including:

- It depends on the level of analysis: local, national, regional, international, global.
- It depends on the political actor or stakeholder under consideration: state, IGO, NGO, informal forum, social movement, individual, etc. It further depends on variation within single categories. That is, not all states, IGOs, NGOs, etc. are the same.
- It depends on the timeframe: short term, medium term, long term.
- It depends on the conceptual lens through which we or political actors/stakeholders view the world.
- It depends on where we are in the world: the Global North or the Global South.
- It depends on how we define a key concept: most concepts in Global Politics are multidimensional and contested.

With respect to the question/prompt above, the answer might depend on the degree to which universal human rights are better articulated and protected if they are first filtered through a national or even local cultural lens. Doing so allows those affected and/or responsible for fulfilling these rights to see them as something that has come from below rather than having been imposed from above.

However, the way in which you bifurcate a question may not be as clear as this. Here is another Paper 2 question that may seem more challenging: *Discuss reasons why the legitimacy of a state may need to be questioned.*

Bifurcating this question requires a little more thinking, but it is still possible:

- The legitimacy of a state may need to be *internally* questioned when the state/government threatens or does not meet the needs of its domestic constituency of legitimation, that is, domestic society.
- The legitimacy of a state/government may need to be *externally* questioned when the state/government acts in ways that the international community believes to be illegitimate or unacceptable.

This gives us the first two body paragraphs. The following body paragraphs could then engage with the complexity of real-world global politics by arguing that the increasingly globalized and interdependent nature of the world means that this ideal separation of the internal and external is not as clear cut as the first two paragraphs suggest. For example:

> The boundaries between the inside and the outside of a state have become increasingly porous with respect to legitimacy and the legitimate basis of statehood. Whereas, in the past, Westphalian sovereignty (non-interference in domestic affairs) may have reigned supreme, it is now the case that what states do inside their own borders matters to the international community or society of states. External legitimacy can be seen to rest on internal legitimacy. And, so, domestic crises of legitimacy may have international repercussions, and vice versa. This is, essentially, the basis of Responsibility to Protect (R2P) and humanitarian intervention.

Some final advice

Students often ask what the tone of their Paper 2 response should be. You should imagine that you are writing for an audience of students who have just started the Global Politics course, which means that you need to provide enough explanation of content and concepts so that someone with a limited knowledge of global politics can understand what you are discussing. This means that you need to clearly justify any assertions or claims you make. It also means that it is up to you to connect any point you make to the real-world examples or cases you include in your response.

Global Politics is contextual and contingent. Figuring out how context matters and how a situation is (historically, culturally, politically, etc.) contingent is a good way of acknowledging and assessing the complexity of a specific event, phenomenon or process, etc.

Assessment support

You should practice, practice, practice. The more you practice Paper 2 questions throughout the duration of your course (and do so in exam-like situations, assessed according to IB standards) the more likely it will be that you will do well in your IB exams.

HL

An overview of HL Paper 3

The Global Politics Paper 3 is HL only. Paper 3 is a stimulus-based paper and is focused on the HL extension global political challenges. Your knowledge of concepts, content and contexts from the core topics and thematic studies with regards to policy, policy-making, policy implementation and the impacts of policies on different stakeholders and actors at different scopes or levels of analysis in Global Politics will be extremely useful in preparing for Paper 3.

Paper 3 also tests your ability to apply these concepts to the HL global political challenges case studies you have independently researched.

The main difference between Paper 1 and Paper 3 is that Paper 3 draws on your independent research from your chosen HL global political challenge topic areas, and you will be expected to develop policy recommendations based on the stimulus provided in the paper. While the stimulus will be important, the relevant evidence for the responses will mostly draw from the case studies you have researched.

Paper 3 has three questions that address your understanding of the core topics as they relate to your chosen HL topic areas. Through Paper 3, you are expected to demonstrate knowledge and understanding of:

- power relationships in global politics between state and non-state stakeholders
- political key concepts and related concepts from the core topics and thematic studies
- relevant source material from the core topics and thematic studies
- political issues and challenges from the core topics and thematic studies.

Paper 3 is an opportunity for you to demonstrate your ability to make connections across the entirety of your work in Global Politics.

Paper 3 is worth 28 marks, and makes up 30% of your overall mark in Global Politics HL.

You will have 1 hour and 30 minutes (90 minutes) to answer all three questions. You will have 5 minutes reading time before your 90 minutes begins.

> A stimulus-based paper introduces materials like text, images or data with the aim of getting you to think about the implications or impacts of what is contained in the stimulus. Responses to stimulus-based papers are usually in the form of informed policy recommendations or suggestions based on the stimulus as well as your own knowledge and research.

> In Paper 3, you need to show your understanding of the policy-making challenges and policy implementation challenges for various stakeholders and actors at different levels of analysis in the various HL topic areas.

Table 6.5 Paper 3 question structure (continues on following page)

Question	Assessment Objective (AO)	Description
Question 1 (3 marks)	AO2	Question 1 requires understanding and analysis of the presented stimulus, as well as knowledge on global political challenges.

Exam papers

Question	Assessment Objective (AO)	Description
Question 2a (4 marks)	AO2	Question 2a requires demonstration of knowledge, understanding and analysis of an identified political issue.
Question 2b (6 marks)	AO3	Question 2b requires a recommendation of a possible course of action or solution to the identified political issue.
Question 3 (15 marks)	AO3	Question 3 requires synthesis and evaluation of researched case studies and global political challenges. The question will be based on the guiding lines of inquiry for the HL extension.

(Taken from the Global Politics Guide)

Paper 3 gives you the chance to demonstrate the skills, knowledge and abilities that you have been developing since the course began regarding your chosen HL global political challenges, including:

- application of relevant concepts and tools to analyze contemporary political issues and challenges in a variety of contexts
- identification and analysis of information, claims and perspectives in the stimulus
- synthesis and evaluation of stimulus evidence as well as your own knowledge about Global Politics
- synthesis and evaluation of different perspectives and approaches to Global Politics
- examination and synthesis of different perspectives on political beliefs, positions and biases.

You *must* answer all three questions in Paper 3.

Question 1 (3 marks)

Question 1 is worth 3 marks and tests your understanding of the stimulus along with your knowledge of the HL topic areas you have independently researched. You can demonstrate this, for example, by identifying specific elements present in the stimulus as they relate to your political challenges. There is no generic Question 1 mark scheme, but a question-specific mark scheme is developed for each paper.

You should expect to spend 8 minutes responding to this question.

Question 2a (4 marks)

Question 2a is worth 4 marks and tests your demonstration of knowledge, understanding and analysis of an identified political issue referred to in the stimulus. You can demonstrate this, for example, by using your researched case studies to explain a political issue that evidences the tensions or gaps between national decision-making and global solutions. This might also come through explaining a term used in a stimulus or by explaining a claim expressed by the stimulus. You might also be asked to consider the role of stakeholders or actors relevant to the political issue identified in the stimulus.

You should expect to spend 12 minutes responding to this question.

You will have 5 minutes reading time at the start of Paper 3. You are not allowed to write anything during this time. Read through the three questions and make mental notes about the expectations of each of question. Then read through the stimulus document with the expectations of the questions in mind. Consider the following:

- the origin of the stimulus
- what policy implications the stimulus is referring to
- what kind of stakeholder the stimulus is coming from
- when it was created.

Make mental notes on the questions and the stimulus they are connected to. Begin to formulate your response to Question 1 during your reading time.

Once your 5-minute reading time is over, mark the paper with the information and details you need. This will not count against you. Underline key information in the questions and the stimulus and write down key information from each question next to the relevant stimulus. The stimulus and questions appear on the same page of your exam booklet.

Assessment support

Table 6.6 Markbands for Question 2a

Marks	Level Descriptor
0	The work does not reach a standard described by the descriptors below.
1–2	The demands of the question are partially addressed. • The response is mostly descriptive. • Some knowledge of the political issue is demonstrated, but it is not all relevant or accurate.
3–4	The demands of the question are addressed. • The response provides a clear analysis of a political issue. • Relevant and accurate knowledge of the context is demonstrated.

(Taken from the Global Politics Guide)

Question 2b (6 marks)

Question 2b is worth 6 marks and tests your ability to develop a coherent and relevant policy, course of action, or solution to the identified political issue. You can do this by recommending how a government could work with other stakeholders to address the global political challenge identified. Or, you could recommend a course of action that would increase the influence of a specific state or non-state actor. Alternatively, you could make a recommendation for how global governance could be improved to address global political challenges more effectively.

Your policy recommendation will be considered well-supported if you provide specific evidence of similar policies from your case studies.

You should expect to spend 20 minutes responding to this question.

Table 6.7 Markbands for Question 2b

Marks	Level Descriptor
0	The work does not reach a standard described by the descriptors below.
1–2	A recommendation is presented, but it is vague or unclear. • The recommendation does not clearly address the identified political issue.
3–4	An adequate recommendation is presented. • The recommendation addresses the identified political issue. • Possible challenges or implications are not considered.
5–6	A clear and well-supported recommendation is presented. • The recommendation addresses the identified political issue effectively. • Possible challenges, implications or unintended consequences are considered.

(Taken from the Global Politics Guide)

Question 3 (15 marks)

Question 3 is worth 15 marks and tests your ability to put the political issue raised by the stimulus document into the larger context of the case studies from your chosen HL topic areas. It is your opportunity to demonstrate your ability to synthesize your work to produce an effective evaluation of the identified global political challenge.

You can do this by connecting your case studies to your global political challenge topic areas by emphasizing the interconnected nature of the factors involved. This might include examining the links between the two global political challenges you have researched. You might consider the ability of state and non-state stakeholders to address the identified challenges through policies at the international, regional, national or local scopes or levels.

You should respond to Question 3 in an essay format, so you can draw on your Paper 1 Question 4 skills as well as your Paper 2 skills. In addition, since you will be comparing and contrasting policies from different case studies and perhaps different political challenge topic areas, you can draw on Paper 1 Question 3 compare and/or contrast.

You should expect to spend 45 minutes responding to this question.

Command terms in Question 3

You can expect to find the following command terms in Question 3:

- Discuss: Offer a considered and balanced review that includes a range of arguments, factors, or hypotheses. Opinions or conclusions should be presented clearly and supported by appropriate evidence.
- Evaluate: Make an appraisal by weighing up the strengths and limitations.
- Examine: Consider an argument or concept in a way that uncovers the assumptions and interrelationships of the issue.

Follow the expectations of the command term as this will be key to meeting the expectations of the question.

Question 3 may ask you to discuss, evaluate or examine a particular global political challenge topic area using the political issue from the stimulus and two or more case studies you have researched in that political topic area category. Or Question 3 may ask you to discuss, evaluate or examine one of the case studies you have researched using two of the global political challenge topic areas you have studied.

Your Question 3 response

The structure of your Question 3 response could include the following:

- Introduction: This is where you restate the question, provide your initial and informed reaction to the question, and give a possible position on the question with some explicit mention of the perspectives and the positions that might be taken on the political issue raised. When you restate the question, you should make clear the global political challenge topic areas you will be using to discuss, evaluate or examine the question. You might consider including other positions from different perspectives as counterclaims. Include any key concepts and related concepts that will be important in your exploration of the question. Make clear how you intend to explore the issues raised by the question and include some introductory information about your case studies so it is clear how they are relevant to the political issue.
- Body paragraphs: Each of your body paragraphs could be organized as follows:
  - Restate the question and political issue and include relevant details to make clear your main point: Make this the main statement of the paragraph and be sure to use the language of the global political challenge topic areas you are using and the specific language of the case studies or examples you are bringing in from your own knowledge.

Assessment support

- Evidence or example: This should be the longest part of your paragraph and include evidence from your relevant, accurate and detailed case studies. Make it clear how these link to the global political challenge topic areas you are using.
- Analyze: Make it clear how the evidence you presented in the previous sentence supports the point you made in your first sentence. This should back up your point.
- Balance: High marks are available if you use effective claims and counterclaims in your responses. Put forward one side of the argument and then contrast it with other views and state which, on the balance of the evidence, is more powerful *and* why this might be.
- Link and reconnect to main point: A summary sentence that relates the paragraph back to the question you raised in the first sentence, which should be connected to the political issue.

- Conclusion: Summarize the points you have made. Explain, for example, which points might lead you to support one side or the other, or both equally, and why. Be sure to provide an explicit answer to the question and include the actual text of the question in your conclusion.

Make sure that you are using the language of Question 3 as well as the language of the stimulus throughout your response.

Table 6.8 Markbands Question 3 (continues on following page)

Marks	Level Descriptor
0	The work does not reach a standard described by the descriptors below.
1–3	The response shows limited understanding of the demands of the question. • The arguments are poorly structured and unclear. • There is little relevant knowledge present. • The response is descriptive or is based in unsupported generalizations.
4–6	The response shows some understanding of the demands of the question. • The response is structured to an extent, but the organization lacks clarity or coherence. • There is limited justification of the claims presented. • Some relevant knowledge is present. • Some examples are mentioned, but they are not developed, or their relevance is unclear. • Diverse perspectives are not identified.
7–9	The response indicates an understanding of the demands of the question, but these demands are only partially addressed. • The response presents an adequate structure and organization. Arguments are clear and coherent. • Most of the main claims are justified. • Relevant and accurate knowledge is present. • Supporting examples are partly developed. • Diverse perspectives are identified, but not explored.

> The stimulus provided in Paper 3 is not a fact to be accepted at face value, but a perspective that you should analyze based on the skills you have developed. You can boost your success, especially in Question 3, by being explicit about the perspective found in the stimulus and critically evaluating this perspective.

Marks	Level Descriptor
10–12	The response indicates that the demands of the question are understood and addressed. • The response is well structured and organized. Arguments are clear, coherent and well supported. • All of the main claims are justified. • Relevant and accurate knowledge is demonstrated throughout the response. • Supporting examples are adequately developed. • Diverse perspectives are explored.
13–15	The response indicates that demands of the question are understood and addressed, and that possible implications are considered. • The response is well structured, balanced and effectively organized. Arguments are clear, coherent and compelling. • All of the main claims are justified and evaluated. • Relevant and accurate knowledge is used effectively throughout the response. • Supporting examples are effectively developed. • Diverse perspectives are explored and evaluated.

(Taken from the Global Politics Guide)

Activity

Look at an example Question 3 and start a timer. In 5 minutes, come up with 3–5 perspectives, arguments, claims and counterclaims that could be used to help address the question. Take note of any of your own knowledge that might be useful to answer the question from the different perspectives you have identified. Working with a classmate, compare your perspectives and knowledge. Use this opportunity to expand your knowledge and add details to your case studies and examples. Consider the perspectives that you found and those that you did not. Make sure that you keep a record of your responses so you can come back to these during your revision.

Final thoughts on Paper 3

You could distribute the 90 minutes of Paper 3 as follows:

- Question 1 (3 marks): 8 minutes
- Question 2a (4 marks): 12 minutes
- Question 2b (6 marks) 20 minutes
- Question 3 (12 marks): 45 minutes
- Reviewing work after completing questions: 5 minutes

Be concise in your responses. Keep them focused on the demands of the question, the stimulus and your own research.

HL end

Assessment support

The Engagement Project

An overview of the Engagement Project

A key component of the IB Global Politics course is the Engagement Project, where you have the opportunity to explore power and agency in practice by investigating a political issue of your choice and then writing an analytical report exploring the issue. You do this by organizing a project that allows you to research and experience a political issue first-hand.

The Engagement Project provides the opportunity for you to involve yourself in a community issue of which you have first-hand experience or which is particularly relevant to your own experiences in some way. This allows you to engage with the opinions of stakeholders on all sides.

The Engagement Project report is 2000 words for SL and 2400 words for HL. The report combines research, engagement activities and an analysis of the chosen political issue.

The engagement activities are intended to allow you to explore and to reflect on the ways in which politics has an influence on, and is influenced by, people at local, regional or global levels. This section describes the requirements for the Engagement Project and offers some practical advice toward completing it.

HL

HL students are expected to conduct further research in order to formulate a policy recommendation for addressing the challenges raised by their identified political issue. This gives HL students the opportunity to design their recommendation for a specific stakeholder or policymaker. The evidence provided to support the recommendation will be very important.

HL end

The Engagement Project connects to the wider context of Global Politics

The Engagement Project offers you the opportunity to:

- learn more about issues and manifestations of power in practice
- develop in-depth knowledge about a particular topic or subject, which might include further, in-depth research in secondary or specialist areas
- apply knowledge and theory gained during the course by talking to other students and professionals
- receive positive social support from other students, professionals and the teacher throughout the process
- connect your learning to the world beyond the classroom
- at HL level, formulate a recommendation for addressing a challenge created by the political issue.

You need to write a report that shows:

- analysis of a political issue and the political challenges resulting from that issue
- exploration, and active and direct investigation of the chosen issue through the project organized, which may also require secondary research to develop further understanding

---

In the Global Politics course, a political issue is any situation or matter that deals with how power is distributed and how it operates within a social organization.

Power is about being able to determine outcomes and not having outcomes determined for you. Your Engagement Project should involve partners, stakeholders and policymakers who are trying to determine outcomes, as well as those who are impacted by those outcomes.

An analysis of power relationships and power dynamics between the different stakeholders and policymakers you engage with through your Engagement Project should be explicit in your Engagement Project.

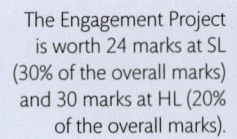

The Engagement Project is worth 24 marks at SL (30% of the overall marks) and 30 marks at HL (20% of the overall marks).

The Engagement Project recommendation component gives HL students the opportunity to include a well-supported policy recommendation that effectively addresses the political issue engaged with throughout the project. This component is worth 6 marks out of a total of 30 marks.

- at the HL level, a recommendation for addressing a challenge created by the political issue.

The Engagement Project tests and develops a number of key real-world skills. Each of these can be thought of as separate stages or tasks to complete:

- identifying a political issue of interest and planning an effective and suitable project that will allow the political issue to be properly analyzed
- researching a political issue through active engagement: organizing, making sense of, and *synthesizing* evidence gained through the engagement activities, Global Politics coursework and secondary research
- writing a report that investigates the political issue and synthesizes information gained through the engagement activities with secondary research
- at the HL level, including a well-evidenced recommendation for addressing a challenge created by the political issue.

A good Engagement Project keeps the focus on the challenges created by the political issue and how the different stakeholders and policymakers who are involved with the issue work with and through these challenges.

Organizing your Engagement Project

As the Engagement Project is intended to be a longer-term project with a number of possible ways for you to engage with the political issue you have chosen, it is important to plan and organize your Engagement Project step by step.

You should think about an Engagement Project that helps you to gain an experiential perspective on a political issue, so the project should:

- be linked to a political issue that you have an interest in
- allow you to experience the power dynamics of real-world politics
- include opportunities for you to observe and analyze these dynamics in a community or society that you have some stake in and experience of
- provide some meaningful and appropriate participation in these dynamics
- bring you into contact with others who are interested in, or have a stake in, the political issue.

Your Engagement Project could be organized like this workflow taken from the Global Politics Guide.

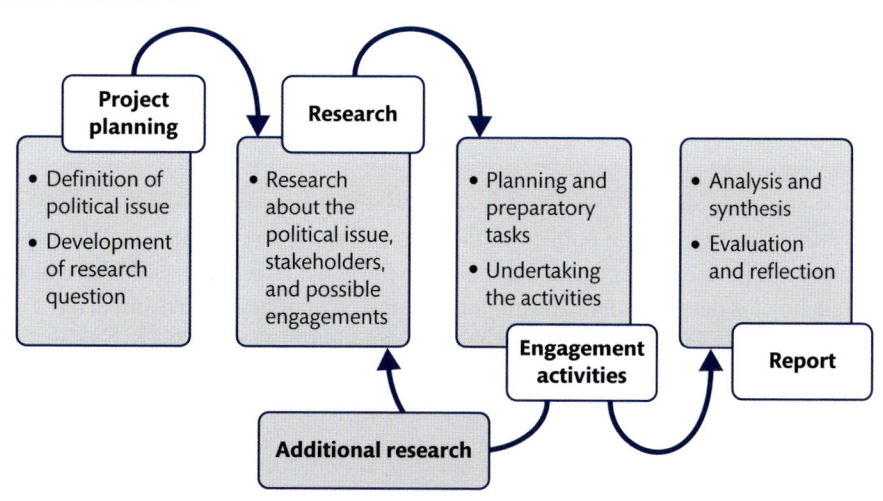

> Your Engagement Project needs early planning and organization. You can increase your Engagement Project mark by planning a schedule that includes specific deadlines and expectations for each of these deadlines.

> The recommendation should be an advisable course of action to be taken by stakeholders or policymakers to address the political challenge created by the explored political issue.

> The HL policy recommendation needs to be supported by appropriate evidence. Evidence could be in the form of:
> - analyzed statistical data
> - a comparison of your recommendation to the impacts of a similar policy
> - explorations of similar recommendations found through different political theories
> - models that have been used to test and evaluate similar recommendations.

Project planning
- Definition of political issue
- Development of research question

Research
- Research about the political issue, stakeholders, and possible engagements

Engagement activities
- Planning and preparatory tasks
- Undertaking the activities

Additional research

Report
- Analysis and synthesis
- Evaluation and reflection

Assessment support

Because power is at the core of your Engagement Project, consider partners, stakeholders and policymakers who are trying to determine outcomes, as well as those who are impacted by those outcomes.	

Step 1: Identifying a political issue that relates to power and agency

First, choose your political issue, consider the political challenges created by that issue, confirm that these political challenges involve power dynamics in some meaningful way, then see if you have access to different stakeholders and policymakers who engage with or are impacted by these challenges.

In other words, make sure that your Engagement Project:

- has a valid political issue
- is something you are genuinely interested in and passionate about
- is both manageable and achievable.

This is a crucial part of the process and sufficient time should be devoted to choosing the political issue and the different engagement activities that will make up the Engagement Project. It is recommended that you first choose a political issue that is of genuine interest or concern to you. Having a connection to or interest in the issue will help you develop meaningful activities.

> Synthesizing, here, is making connections between the activities and the full breadth of the course.

Activity

Make a list of the political issues you have come across in Global Politics as well as in your Creativity, Activity and Service (CAS) activities and your conversations with others. Discuss your ideas in a group. Ask each other about the different stakeholders and policymakers that might be impacted by your political issue. Do you have any access to or contact with these stakeholders and policymakers? Can someone you know help make this contact? Your school might have an Advancement Office or an Alumni Office. Reach out to them and see if they can help you make meaningful contacts.

> Be prepared: a great deal of the time invested in the Engagement Project happens outside of class when you are meeting with stakeholders and policymakers and engaging in meaningful activities related to exploring your political issue in practice.

Political challenges can come from different interpretations of concepts within Global Politics and they often appear as an issue, policy, problem or controversy created by or linked to a political issue.

Political issues that impact multiple stakeholders and policymakers will likely have several different power interactions to consider. For example, you might look at:

- the specific role played by legislators in drafting certain laws or regulations
- the role of the government agency that has to implement these laws or regulations
- the different populations or groups that are impacted by the implementation of these laws or regulations.

> Start thinking about your Engagement Project as early in the Global Politics course as possible. You will likely need exposure to many of the concepts in Global Politics such as Rights and justice and Development and sustainability, before you can identify the political issue that is of interest to you. This means that engaging with stakeholders will probably come later in the Global Politics course, once you have covered the concepts and political issues raised in the thematic studies. Finding the right time to start depends on how you have organized your Global Politics course.

Once you have a suitable political issue, look for activities that will allow for a proper exploration of the issue.

Example

A student is interested in public health issues and wants to consider possible power relationships and power dynamics related to the issue. They might consider which stakeholders develop public health policy, implement policy and are impacted by the policy being implemented. There may be additional questions of power related to funding certain public health initiatives, especially those involving more expensive medicines in middle-income and low-income countries where bilateral and multilateral official development assistance is more common.

356

Engagement Project

Step 2: Identifying how you might engage with the political issue

Once you have identified a suitable political issue and its links to power, power relationships and power dynamics are clear, you can now consider whether it is possible to engage with this issue through the Engagement Project.

During this step, it is important to do stakeholder audit and find out which stakeholders involved with the chosen political issue you might need to have contact with. It is important to analyze the political issue from a number of different stakeholder perspectives.

It might be that you have a connection to and are passionate about your political issue and it does raise a number of relevant and significant political challenges. Keep in mind that you need willing and accessible stakeholders to effectively engage with your chosen political issue. If your chosen stakeholders are inaccessible, your engagement will be limited. It is best you find a political issue where stakeholders can be found.

Activity

Ask your teacher to invite your CAS coordinator, school external relations officer, alumni officer or advancement officer to your class so that they can share the different stakeholders that make up your school community. Share your political issues with them. You might be surprised by how many parents are working at different levels or scopes that might be useful to your Engagement Project.

Example

A student wanted to develop an Engagement Project around a political issue linked to public health issues. The stakeholders they found included government health officials, local health clinics and hospitals, NGOs working with public health issues in marginalized and vulnerable communities (such as WHO or Doctors without Borders), as well as bilateral and multilateral organizations that provided technical expertise and funding for such issues.

Step 3: Connecting with resources (Global Politics coursework and stakeholders)

In most cases, coursework in Global Politics will form a rich basis from which you can identify relevant resources to develop your understanding of political issues.

You may begin your Engagement Project after the core concepts of the course have been introduced, but before the thematic studies (and HL extension topic areas) have been explored in more detail. This creates a challenge as you might not be aware of a political issue that you could be interested in related to sustainable development, for example, because this has not yet been covered in class.

It is important to engage early on with a range of possible political issues touching on the thematic studies (and HL extension topic areas), with suitable resources available in case you feel a particular interest in one of these topics.

As important as the Global Politics coursework, key concepts and related concepts are to the Engagement Project, it is also important to make sure that you have significant knowledge of the stakeholders and policymakers you will be in contact with through your Engagement Project.

! Discuss the ideas you have about different political issues you are interested in with your classmates, parents or guardians, and your teacher. If you can explain your political issue to someone who is not in your Global Politics class and they understand what you are doing, this means you are on the right track. It will help make identifying a suitable political issue that can be effectively explored easier.

! Choose a political issue first. Some students have been driven toward their issue because they have an activity ready and waiting. They then attempt to create a political issue out of an activity that is not very political.

! Having different stakeholder perspectives in your Engagement Project is a good way to better understand the political challenges created by the identified political issue. If you only have non-governmental stakeholder perspectives, you miss the opportunity to have meaningful discussions with state policymakers or citizens impacted by the intended policies, as well as missing the opportunity to gain the perspective of an IGO like the UN.

! One way to find political issues that might be explored through the Engagement Project is to review local news sources for stories that you might find interesting.

! The Engagement Project asks you to describe the different levels of analysis in Global Politics (local, national, regional and international). .

Assessment support

The stakeholder audit undertaken in Step 2 should form the basis of deeper research into the various duties and expectations of the identified stakeholders and policymakers. You should access the websites of the different stakeholders and research the specific activities of the stakeholders that match the political issue.

This way, you will have a general (or even deeper) understanding of the work of each stakeholder before reaching out. This will likely lead to better informed questions and a stakeholder that is excited to provide more details and access.

Step 4: Developing the initial research question

Once the political issue is clear and it looks like it can be addressed given the available stakeholders, it is important to design an initial research question that can help guide the Engagement Project.

The design of the initial research question should consider and may include the following:

- a political challenge created by the political issue
- a reference to a thematic study (or an HL extension topic area)
- a key concept or related concept
- details about the policy or decision that is the focus of the political issue
- some concrete details like geographic location, timeframe/timespan and stakeholders.

> Reaching out to your stakeholders early in your Engagement Project is important. Remember that stakeholders are generally busy working on the political issue that you have identified. They might need time to arrange an interview or a visit to their project site.

> It is not mandatory for your Engagement Project to focus solely on the key concepts and related concepts from the core of Global Politics or just one thematic study. However, it is a good idea to make sure that your political issue is linked to at least one of the four key concepts of Global Politics.

> If your Engagement Project focuses on an issue such as the challenges facing refugee resettlement and you are looking at relevant government policies, the position of the UN High Commissioner for Refugees and the work of a local NGO supporting this resettlement, it is a good idea to research the *specific* work of these different stakeholders before you correspond with them or meet them. Informed questions generally receive better answers than those where the answers can be found on a website.

Example

A student, whose chosen political issue was 'the role of funding (government, bilateral and multilateral) for public health programs (HIV/AIDS treatment) in middle-income country X', developed this issue into a research question: 'What impact does the reliance on official development assistance to fund domestic HIV/AIDS health programs have on developing country X's ability to fund such public health initiatives for itself?' This initial question was asked of a range of appropriate stakeholders, including government health officials, bilateral or multilateral donors, local and international public health NGOs and recipients of the health programs.

As per any good research in the human and social sciences, as evidence presents itself, the initial research question will likely change and develop. What makes the Engagement Project so valuable is that contact with experts in the political issues being investigated often leads to the development of better research questions.

Activity

Ask your teacher to organize a shark tank activity where students have 90 seconds to pitch their initial research question to a panel of Global Politics students and teachers. The panel can evaluate the research question, and provide some helpful guidance on how the research question might be improved as well as suggestions for how to engage with the research question through the Engagement Project.

Organizing your Engagement Project: a summary

You will be on track in the early stages of the Engagement Project if the following have been considered:

- You have selected a political issue that is of interest to you.
- The political issue relates to power.
- The political issue is linked to the key concepts and learning outcomes of Global Politics.
- The political issue can be explored given the available stakeholder base.
- There are sufficient resources available to support any practical engagement.
- The initial guiding research question is answerable.

If these six planning expectations are met, you can then select and design appropriate engagement activities.

Step 5: Selecting and designing appropriate and meaningful engagement activities

Finding appropriate and relevant engagement activities can be a challenge. There are a number of factors and conditions, including the following:

- accessibility to stakeholders relevant to the political issue
- physical distance between stakeholders and your school, including traffic issues
- political climate
- health, safety and security
- the willingness of stakeholders to meet.

However, an appropriate and meaningful engagement activity can take place anywhere as long as the following expectations are met:

- It is linked to a political issue that you have an interest in.
- It allows you to experience the power dynamics of real-world politics.
- It includes opportunities for you to observe and analyze these dynamics in a community or society that you have some stake in and experience of.
- It provides some meaningful and appropriate participation for you within these dynamics.
- It puts you in contact with others who are interested in, or have a stake in, the political issue.

Step 6: Determining the local, national, regional or global scope and nature of the engagement activity

As long as stakeholders are available and the health, security, safety and ethical conditions for the engagement activity are in place, effective and meaningful activities can happen anywhere.

It is important to consider the value of engaging in political issues that are more local in scope and nature. Consider choosing a political issue and stakeholders working on this political issue that are in the country you are living in or are easily accessible from where your school is located. This is not mandatory, but it might help you have a more meaningful and less stressful experience. It also puts your teacher in a good position to be able to help you out.

> **!** Bring balance to your Engagement Project in the early stages by thoroughly researching your stakeholders. If you only use the website or reports coming from your stakeholder, you will likely get a good understanding of your stakeholder's perspective on the political issue, but little else. Try to find reports from other organizations, agencies or in the media that provide a more critical look at the work of your stakeholder. Once you have met and discussed your political issue with the stakeholder, review and confirm their responses through additional research. Your research is part of your engagement. One of the resources should provide a critical view of the activities of that stakeholder, where possible.

> **!** Try not to overload a stakeholder with requests for information and support. Make sure you coordinate with other students who are working on similar political issues. Maybe you can reach out to the same stakeholders together?

> **!** Want to improve your research question? Share it with the stakeholders and policymakers you come into contact with and ask them for suggestions.

Assessment support

The experiential expectation of the Engagement Project might make it difficult for you to effectively engage with a political issue if, for example, your stakeholders or your engagement activities are in your home country and you only spend a few weeks visiting your home country when you have a break from school.

For example, engagement activities with stakeholders to view development project sites in a remote village or attend high level meetings of policymakers, especially busy senior ones, are often are canceled at the last minute and, if you are not around to reschedule, this opportunity for engagement is lost.

Effective and meaningful engagement activities can take place outside the community or even the country where your Global Politics class takes place, especially if you are extremely interested in your chosen political issue. It is important to consider health, safety, security and ethical factors, as well as your own motivation, all of which will be beyond the control of your teacher if engagement activities take place far from your school.

> It helps to consider local political issues and engage with local stakeholders. They are usually more accessible, and you can develop working relationships with them, leading to more fulfilling engagement activities.

Example

A student was going to school in a country not their own. The student was interested in exploring the political issue of marriage migration. In the initial discussions with the teacher, the student wanted to focus on the impacts of marriage migration in a low-income country, far from where the student was going to school. After a few discussions with the teacher and further research, the student designed an Engagement Project that focused on marriage between women from the country where the student was going to school (a middle-income country) and men from the student's home country (a high-income G20 member). The student was able to take their genuine interest in the political issue and effectively engage with this issue with stakeholders in both countries, as well as an intergovernmental stakeholder.

Step 7: Finding the balance between meeting stakeholders, research and engaging with the political issue

Meeting stakeholders who are related to the political issue is a crucial part of your Engagement Project. Effective and meaningful Engagement Projects need to include multiple perspectives, and this often comes from meeting with stakeholders, policymakers and other actors. However, these meetings are not the only source of such perspectives. What is learned from those meetings, how that knowledge is used and what happens afterward are all valuable contributions to a fully realized Engagement Project.

Meetings and discussions with stakeholders should be designed to deepen your knowledge of the political issue from the perspective of that stakeholder. A stakeholder may add to what you already know about the political issue, contradict what you know or cause you to see the issue differently. These are all excellent outcomes of stakeholder interactions.

You should compare the information you receive from different stakeholders. Keep in mind that stakeholders represent certain national or organizational perspectives.

This makes it very important to continually compare and contrast the information received from stakeholders. Because multiple and different perspectives are important elements of the Engagement Project, comparing what is being received from stakeholders as the engagement activity progresses might reveal the need to find perspectives not yet represented.

You should follow up with research on the information you receive about the political issue from stakeholders. In many cases, stakeholders introduce something new to the discussion. It is important to remember that stakeholders are often representing their own perspective and understanding of the political issue. Make sure to confirm and verify the information that you receive, especially if it contradicts what you know about the issue.

You should use the opportunities you have with stakeholders to expand your contact base for the exploration of your political issue. This means that you need to practice professionalism in any contact with stakeholders by arriving on time for any scheduled meetings, dressing professionally, being prepared and thanking them. Stakeholders will be more likely to pass on other possible contacts to help with further research if you behave in this way.

Stakeholders who often have the greatest influence on the understanding of the deeper consequences of political issues are those who work closest with those most impacted by the issue.

In meetings, be sure to keep the focus on the political issue and the research question being used to explore the issue.

> After meeting with a stakeholder, you should summarize your meeting and what you took away in terms of a deeper or different understanding of your political issue. Meet with your teacher after each stakeholder meeting whenever possible to share the results of these important interactions. Use these conversations to find additional sources to complement what you have found out.

> When meeting with stakeholders, it is important to be prepared. Be sure you know how the stakeholder is connected to the political issue and what they do with regards to the issue. Your discussion with stakeholders should deepen your knowledge and should also lead to further discussions with stakeholders, and other possible stakeholders or actors recommended to you by the initial contact.

Example

To engage with their chosen political issue of informal workers and trade unions, a student met with a local NGO that provided language classes for migrant workers. The student arrived on time and had done a significant amount of preliminary research on the topic from the perspective of informal workers and an understanding of the labor laws of the country. The director of the NGO was so impressed with the professionalism of the student that they were invited to attend some of the language classes, where the student was introduced to several of the workers who spoke to the student about their experiences. The director of the NGO put the student in contact with a member of a trade union who provided them with additional information.

Step 8: Designing out-of-school engagement activities

The Engagement Project allows you to experience the political issue in some practical way. Visiting a school in a developing region of a country, volunteering at a shelter for vulnerable populations, observing a civil or criminal trial, taking part in a meeting of an IGO, watching a panel discussion about human rights or attending a demonstration for action against climate change are all excellent ways to see the political issue in practice and to deepen understanding of the issue.

Assessment support

If these opportunities are available, they need to be well-planned. The purpose of taking part in these engagement activities needs to be clear, and there should be a strong connection to the political issue, research question and chosen concepts that are part of the Engagement Project.

Most importantly, you need to make sure that these engagement activities are a necessary part of your engagement with the political issue. For example, watching a trial is interesting but will count as limited engagement unless you can connect it to your Engagement Project through the concepts you are exploring (rule of law) and your political issue makes the activity meaningful learning.

Similar to working with stakeholders, it is important to complement any out-of-school engagement activities with research, especially if what was observed or witnessed does not match the theoretical or conceptual understanding.

These engagement activities should not be taken as isolated events but integrated and synthesized into the overall understanding of the political issue. They should be critically evaluated, and there might be value in returning to some of your stakeholders to discuss what you experienced given what you previously learned from them.

There is not always time to engage with the political issue for as long or as frequently as you might want. Keep in mind that, in some places, engagement activity opportunities are limited or not available due to reasons beyond your control.

You will often engage with stakeholders or take part in these activities without your teacher present. Your health, safety and security is a priority, so it is a good idea to make sure that a responsible adult is informed as early as possible about the Engagement Project and the various engagement activities that might make up the project. They may wish to accompany you on some visits.

> **!** If legally, ethically and practicably possible, and if your health, safety and security are not at risk, record the interactions you have through your out-of-school engagement activities. Images, video and any materials you collect help to serve as evidence of your engagement with the political issue in practice. Be sure that you have been clear with stakeholders how you will use these recordings and images. You might need written consent.

> **!** After taking part in an engagement activity, you should summarize your experience and what you took away in terms of a deeper or different understanding of your political issue. Meet with your teacher after each activity whenever possible to share the results of these important experiences. Use these conversations to find additional sources to complement what you have found out.

Example

A student was exploring the political issue of state responsibility for vulnerable groups, specifically refugees. The country where the student went to school hosted a refugee camp, initially funded by UNHCR but later transferred to local authority control. The camp was more like a village. The refugees in the camp were from a country going through recent post-conflict reconstruction. The host government was in the process of regulating the legal status of many of the families within the camp, and also looking to repatriate those who wished to return. The student organized a visit to the camp after reaching out to its director. While there, the student met with a number of families who wished to return to their home country rather than apply for citizenship in the host country. The process was completely voluntary. This was a surprise to the student, whose previous research had revealed a certain tension between host countries and refugee populations, and it changed the nature and focus of the student's Engagement Project and research question.

Engagement Project

Step 9: How the school community might be a part of the engagement activity

Well-constructed questions on surveys can help inform you about different perceptions and opinions your own school community has about your political issue. These surveys may also lead to getting contacts for additional stakeholders from the parent/guardian and teacher community.

Meeting with existing community service or service learning clubs or performing CAS activities with themes that link to the political issue may be valuable to an Engagement Project. These existing clubs and activities will have potential stakeholder contacts, and many of them will be active with local social movements, NGOs or grassroots and community organizers, engaged in the political issue in some practical way.

Finding ways for simulation activities, such as a mock trial or a model United Nations to contribute meaningfully to an Engagement Project depends on your motivation and the connection you have to those activities. For example, if you were to invest a great deal of time in researching a political issue and drafted and debated a resolution in a model Human Rights Council on a topic relevant to your political issue, it could be interesting to observe points being made by other delegates. There might be some limited insight into the significance of the political issue through this activity, but it would be unclear what impact this would have on your understanding of the political issue.

Remember that your school faculty, as well as members of the wider community, might have experiences relevant to the exploration of the chosen political issue and their perspective might be valuable to include in the Engagement Project.

Example

A student interested in the perceptions of gender norms and expectations in a certain national community knew that there were members of that community on the faculty at school. The student crafted a three-question survey, where the third question asked: 'Would you be interested in having a further conversation with me about some of the issues raised in this survey?' Three respondents said yes to this question and these later discussions were extremely valuable in deepening the student's understanding of the political issue. One discussion led to contact with an additional stakeholder who proved valuable to the student's overall Engagement Project.

Writing the report

The earlier the Engagement Project begins, the earlier the draft report can begin to take shape.

You are required to write a (maximum) 2000-word report for SL or 2400-word report for HL. This needs to include the following:

- an explanation and analysis of the political issue
- a justification of the selection of sources for research and engagement activities

Assessment support

- an evaluation and synthesis of perspectives presented
- a critical reflection on the project as a learning experience.

HL students need to carry out further research to formulate and present a recommendation to address the political issue.

The Engagement Project report is assessed against five criteria for SL and six criteria for HL. The report is marked out of 24 for SL and out of 30 for HL. The Criteria are shown in Table 6.10.

Table 6.9 shows the two most common mistakes that students make when presenting the first draft of their reports.

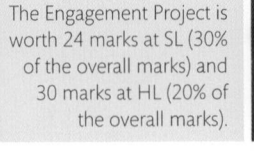

> The Engagement Project is worth 24 marks at SL (30% of the overall marks) and 30 marks at HL (20% of the overall marks).

Table 6.9 Common Engagement Project first draft mistakes

Report is dominated by the activity, with no analysis	Report forgets about the activity, with or without analysis
• The student writes only about the activity and does so as a narrative, rather than an analysis. • The report reads like an account of who they met, what they did, what they saw, what they were told, how they felt about what they saw and heard. • There is little analysis of what their experiences tell us about the political issue or how it links to and helps us understand the key concepts or learning outcomes of the course.	• The student writes only about the political issue, perhaps analyzing it, but in the style of an Extended Essay. • There is no link between the activity and the issue, and it feels as if the student has focused more on secondary research. • There is a sense that the activity was of little importance or relevance to the political issue, which is why the student rarely mentions the activity.

> The Engagement Project word length is 2400 for HL and 2000 words for SL. This means that the Criterion F: Recommendation will be about 400 words.

The report should be a balance between these two extremes, aiming to clearly demonstrate how the engagement activity helped build an analytical understanding of the political issue.

HL students are expected to conduct further research in order to formulate a recommendation for addressing the political issue in practice. The recommendation can be focused on a specific stakeholder or target structural elements that contributed to the challenge created by the political issue.

> If the Criterion F: Recommendation is targeting a specific stakeholder, the stakeholder should be one that was part of your Engagement Project.

The recommendation should present an advisable course of action with appropriate supporting evidence. The evidence could come from statistical information, similar initiatives implemented in other contexts, or political theory and models.

Table 6.10 Assessment criteria for the Engagement Project report (continues on next page)

Criterion	Student Will…	Marks and Level Descriptors
A: Explanation and justification (4 marks)	• clearly identify and explain what the political issue is • clearly explain why the particular engagement activities were chosen and conducted in the way they appear in the Engagement Project report • explain how the issue links to the key concepts and prescribed content of the Global Politics course.	0 The work does not reach a standard described by the descriptors below. 1–2 The report includes a limited explanation and justification of the Engagement Project. A political issue is identified, but not clearly explained. There is a limited explanation of the importance and suitability of the project. The engagement activities are described, but their relevance is not justified. 3–4 The report includes an appropriate explanation and justification of the Engagement Project. A political issue is identified and clearly explained. There is a clear explanation of the importance and suitability of the project. The engagement activities are explained, and their relevance is justified.
B: Process (3 marks)	• plan their engagement process well • integrate research throughout the engagement process.	0 The work does not reach a standard described by the descriptors below. 1 The report evidences a limited research and engagement process. 2 The report evidences an adequate research and engagement process. 3 The report evidences a well-planned and integrated research and engagement process.
C: Analysis and synthesis (8 marks)	• analyze the political issue explored and explained in the specific context of the engagement • demonstrate a good understanding and application of course concepts and content • synthesize diverse perspectives of sources and engaged stakeholders.	0 The work does not reach a standard described by the descriptors below. 1–2 The report is mostly descriptive. There is a vague reference to relevant course concepts and content. The political issue is identified, but not analyzed. There is no synthesis of perspectives. 3–4 The report presents limited analysis and synthesis of the political issue. The analysis demonstrates a limited understanding of relevant course concepts and content. Analysis of the political issue is limited. There is limited synthesis of the perspectives of stakeholders and sources. 5–6 The report presents an adequate analysis and synthesis of the political issue. The analysis demonstrates an adequate understanding of relevant course concepts and content. The political issue is partially analyzed. Perspectives of stakeholders and sources are partially synthesized, but not always clear. 7–8 The report presents an effective analysis and synthesis of the political issue. The analysis demonstrates a good understanding and application of course concepts and content. The political issue is clearly analyzed. There is an effective synthesis of the perspectives of involved stakeholders and sources.

Assessment support

Criterion	Student Will…	Marks and Level Descriptors
D: Evaluation and reflection (6 marks)	• evaluate the selected sources • evaluate the engagement activities • explain personal positions and biases • provide evidence of critical reflection about the project as a learning experience.	0 The work does not reach a standard described by the descriptors below. 1–2 The report demonstrates limited evaluation and reflection. The research and engagement activities are not evaluated. Personal positions and biases related to the political issue are not identified. There is limited reflection on the Engagement Project as a learning experience. 3–4 The report demonstrates an adequate evaluation and reflection. The research and engagement activities are partially evaluated. Some personal positions and biases related to the political issue are identified. There is adequate reflection on the Engagement Project as a learning experience. 5–6 The report evidences a critical evaluation and reflection. The research and engagement activities are critically evaluated. Personal positions and biases related to the political issue are explained. There is an in-depth reflection on the Engagement Project as a learning experience.
E: Communication (3 marks)	• communicate information clearly • communicate points presented clearly • submit a well-organized report.	0 The work does not reach a standard described by the descriptors below. 1 Communication is limited. The organization and clarity of the report are limited and do not support understanding. 2 Communication is adequate. The report is adequately organized and supports understanding. 3 Communication is effective. The report is well organized and coherently supports understanding.
HL HL Only		
F: Recommendation (6 marks)	• present an effective recommendation • support the recommendation with relevant and specific evidence • effectively address the political issue within the particular context studied • explain possible implications or challenges.	0 The work does not reach a standard described by the descriptors below. 1–2 A limited recommendation is presented. The recommendation is partially supported, with limited reference to specific evidence. The recommendation partly addresses the political issue with some considerations of the context studied. Possible implications or challenges are not identified. 3–4 An adequate recommendation is presented. The recommendation is supported by relevant evidence. The recommendation adequately addresses the political issue within the particular context studied. Possible implications or challenges are identified. 5–6 An effective recommendation is presented. The recommendation is well supported by relevant and specific evidence. The recommendation effectively addresses the political issue within the particular context studied. Possible implications or challenges are explained.

(Adapted from the Global Politics Guide)

Engagement Project

Step 10: Organizing and structuring your report (power and other key concepts)

You should start to draft an outline as soon as the Engagement Project begins. However, the report should *not* be structured according to the sections that reflect each of the assessment criteria, nor should it be organized along the lines of 'stakeholder meeting 1', 'activity 1' and 'stakeholder meeting 2', etc. as this demonstrates little understanding of or engagement with the principles of the Engagement Project.

Each section of the report should be authentic to the exploration of the research question through the Engagement Project. In each section, the criteria should be met using the activities of the Engagement Project, and the relevant key concepts and related concepts of Global Politics.

Apart from power, not all the key concepts (sovereignty, legitimacy and interdependence) and thematic concepts (rights, justice, liberty, equality, development, poverty, inequality, sustainability, peace, conflict, violence and non-violence) need to be explicitly represented and analyzed in each Engagement Project. It is crucial to select only the most relevant concepts and their interpretations and apply those throughout the Engagement Project. It will require some interaction with stakeholders, and other engagement activities, to determine the most significant concepts (other than power) at stake.

Make sure that you:

- define and explain the interpretations of the concepts that you use
- connect and demonstrate how these concepts relate to the activities of the Engagement Project
- provide examples of these concepts from Global Politics
- explore those concepts that are relevant to the engagement activities and the political issue in the report.

Step 11: Organizing and structuring your report (creating an outline)

Drafting and maintaining an outline throughout the Engagement Project is important. Your outline should begin with your political issue and the research question you are using to explore the political issue.

Each section of your outline will develop as you engage with stakeholders and activities. It is fine to begin your outline with placeholder sections such as 'introduction', 'overview of political issue', 'definition of key concept 1' and 'stakeholder interview 1'.

As your Engagement Project develops, these sections should grow and synthesize to better reflect how you have engaged with your political issue and what that engagement has revealed about the political issue and the challenges created by the political issue.

The Engagement Project gives a total of 24 marks at SL and 30 marks at HL. In addition, there are five SL criteria and six HL criteria. The difference between them is that HL includes Criterion F: Recommendation.

Power is an important focus of the engagement with the political issue. It would be a mistake to assume that there is only one agreed interpretation of power or that all possible interpretations of power are present in each Engagement Project. The interpretations and types of power present will be specific to the particular Engagement Project and will need to be explicitly identified and analyzed throughout the Engagement Project.

Emphasis is placed on analysis and synthesis at SL and HL. Additional marks can be earned by communicating in a professional way.

Keep track of all your sources using a citation generator such as Noodletools, and make sure that you create and maintain a properly formatted works cited list for all the sources you cite and consult, right from the start of your Engagement Project.

Assessment support

> **Example**
>
> A student developed their Engagement Project with a focus on the political issue of governmental approaches to sustainability in the tourism industry in a middle-income country. The initial outline had not taken into consideration the possibility of the value of weak sustainability, but did have a section defining strong sustainability. As the Engagement Project and more stakeholders kept referring to the importance of weak sustainability, it became clear that this concept needed to be included and discussed in more detail. The student's outline already had some details on sustainability, so it was clear where this concept might fit.

Step 12: Meeting the expectations of the criteria

The Engagement Project and political issue should link to some part of the prescribed content of the Global Politics course. This is best done with a review of the main concepts of the core topics and thematic studies. In addition, it would be useful to review the main elements of the prescribed content for the core topics and thematic studies, including:

- role of stakeholders and actors
- definitions and understandings of the key concepts
- the nature, practice and study of each relevant concept
- important debates and contested issues related to the relevant concepts
- case studies that highlight the relevant concept in practice.

Criterion A: Explanation and justification (4 marks)

Criterion A asks you to clearly identify and explain your political issue. You are also expected to explain how the political issue links to the key concepts and prescribed content of the Global Politics course.

To score full marks, you should explain *why* you participated in this activity in the first place. The key here is to explain why the activity helped you explore the political issue chosen and to provide a clear account of the engagement activity and its connection to your studies in Global Politics. This is probably the most descriptive section in that you are being asked to describe all aspects of your activity as it relates to your studies of the prescribed content of the course.

Criterion B: Process (3 marks)

Criterion B assesses your ability to demonstrate that you carried out well-planned and integrated research for the Engagement Project. Moderators will be looking for evidence of a well-developed process of research and engagement.

This evidence can be in the form of documentation of a well-organized engagement process, evidence of accurate use of the key concepts of Global Politics and effective use of stakeholder engagement and complementary research.

Engagement Project

Criterion C: Analysis and synthesis (8 marks)

Criterion C asks you to analyze the political issue chosen, drawing on everything that you have learned in the Global Politics course.

This criterion assesses your ability to examine political issues from a variety of perspectives. One way to think about this aspect of the Engagement Project is to use the key concepts of the course. Power and the analysis of power relationships and dynamics between stakeholders and within policy development and implementation will be instrumental in meeting the expectations of this criterion.

However, additional relevant key concepts and related concepts need to be included in the analysis.

> **Example**
>
> A student living in a high-income country was interested in exploring the ways in which candidates use both hard power and soft power to exercise influence and convince voters in an election. Discussions with stakeholders led the student to inquire about the role that fundraising and campaign finance laws play in voter choice. The student was given access to polling data that identified voting patterns and trends. The student had access to several candidates running for local office and had the chance to observe each candidate's behavior. The student also looked at similar data and practices in other countries to get some context. This helped the student to make a judgment as to how effective these practices were based on the evidence at hand.

Criterion D: Evaluation and reflection (6 marks)

Criterion D asks you to evaluate your research, including the selected sources and the engagement activities.

There is an expectation that, as part of your critical reflection about the Engagement Project as a learning activity, you explain your personal positions and biases that were developed or challenged through the Engagement Project.

Criterion E: Communication (3 marks)

Criterion E evaluates the extent to which you have submitted a well organized and coherent report.

HL

Criterion F: Recommendation (6 marks)

Criterion F asks HL students to develop and articulate an effective recommendation. It is expected that the recommendation is well-supported by relevant and specific evidence, that the recommendation effectively addresses the political issue within the particular context studied and that possible implications of or challenges for the recommendation are explained.

This additional HL section should be about 400 words.

Global Politics and Theory of Knowledge

Let us begin with two questions:

- How do Global Politics and Theory of Knowledge (TOK) intersect?
- How can Global Politics strengthen your TOK experience, and what TOK methodology might help you in Global Politics?

We will try to answer these questions in this chapter.

TOK provides you with a set of practical tools, some activities and a safe space for critical thinking and discussion to help bring clarity to your understanding of the significance of knowledge.

We will look at the expectations and assessments of the TOK course. Then, we will look into the connections you can make between Global Politics and TOK.

> Your TOK Exhibition is an excellent opportunity for you to apply your knowledge and understanding of global politics by choosing an assessment prompt that you can directly connect to what you are learning in Global Politics, such as prompt 19: 'What counts as a good justification for a claim?' With this prompt, you might make a connection to an object such as a quote that is critical of a country's human rights record or an image showing the negative environmental consequences of development.

What is Theory of Knowledge?

A core component of the IB DP is the TOK course. TOK is taught differently at different schools, but what all TOK courses have in common is a focus on knowledge, how we know what we know, the potential limitations to our knowledge, and the impact that knowledge has on our decision-making. TOK asks you to consider the roles that certainty, evidence and truth play in your decision-making.

There are two assessed components of TOK:

- The TOK Exhibition is an internally assessed component (your teacher will mark it) made up of a maximum 950-word written exploration of a TOK prompt/question using three objects or artifacts that you choose. This means about 300 words for each object or artifact, with 50 words for an introduction to your exhibition. Your objects or artifacts can be physical, or they might be images, or they could be text. How do you know which objects or artifacts to pick? To help you, the IB has made available 35 different assessment prompts (you can find these in the IB's TOK Guide). Each prompt is phrased like a general question about knowledge, such as prompt 25: 'How can we distinguish between knowledge, belief and opinion?' Your goal is to find three significant real-world objects that can each be used to have a 300-word discussion about the prompt. TOK provides you with a framework and series of categories that you can use to help make better sense of the prompts and connect these prompts to objects or artifacts. We have provided a brief overview of the framework and categories to help you. Your TOK Exhibition is usually completed by the end of your first DP year.

> TOK emphasizes analytical balance. If you were to choose prompt 19 and your object was a quote critical of the human rights record of a country, you could boost your success by considering the position of the country that is the target of the criticism and looking at their response or how they have justified what someone considers a human rights violation.

- The TOK Essay is an externally assessed component (an IB examiner will mark it, although your teacher might provide a preliminary mark) where you have a maximum of 1600 words to respond to one of six prompts designed as a knowledge question or claim about knowledge. These six prompts are usually released by the IB early during the first semester of your second DP year. Once you have chosen your prompt, you are expected to explore the *knowledge at stake* in the prompt.

Theory of Knowledge

You can do this by using real-world examples from different TOK categories and applying the TOK framework. The TOK Essay is not a traditional argument essay where you are expected to reach a clear and definitive conclusion based on relevant facts and evidence. Instead, the TOK Essay is designed to get you to think about what might be considered a valid argument and under what conditions might evidence be extremely valid or less valid. It is a challenging and stimulating activity that usually takes about 3–4 months to write.

Both of these assessments provide you with an opportunity to explore issues of importance in global politics while keeping your focus on knowledge.

To help keep you focused on knowledge, TOK has a structure that gives you the chance to explore questions related to knowledge. Below is a short overview of that structure. You should review the IB's TOK Guide for more specific details about TOK.

Activity

Working with a classmate, reflect on and discuss the painting by Francisco Goya, *The Third of May 1808 in Madrid*, also known as *The Executions*. Where might you find power in this painting? Do you see power in the soldiers with their rifles pointed at the man in the white shirt? Is it in the actions of the man in the white shirt? Can you find power elsewhere in the painting? How do you know? Consider how and why you and your classmate define and consider power.

'Knowledge at stake' comes up frequently in TOK. It means you need to think about what is important or significant about the knowledge raised in the TOK Essay prompt or TOK Exhibition prompt.

The TOK Essay is an excellent opportunity for you to apply your knowledge and understanding of global politics by choosing a prompt that enables you to explore more deeply and from different perspectives something you are studying in Global Politics.

Since the TOK Essay challenges you to consider different approaches or perspectives, you can boost your success by using examples that can be explored in many different ways.

How is power defined in Global Politics? How is power discussed in TOK? What connections can you make between these two approaches to the fundamental concept of power? What is the difference between defining something and discussing it?

◀ Goya's *The Executions*.

TOK includes five optional themes relating to knowledge and technology, knowledge and language, knowledge and politics, knowledge and religion, and knowledge and indigenous societies. The optional theme of knowledge and politics is an excellent opportunity to explore core and related concepts in Global Politics through TOK.

371

Knowledge in TOK and in Global Politics

TOK introduces 12 concepts (power, perspective, responsibility, truth, values, culture, evidence, certainty, interpretation, justification, explanation and objectivity) and you can boost your success by considering how knowledge in global politics might be considered using one or more of these concepts.

TOK exhibition prompt 25: How do we distinguish between knowledge, belief and opinion?

Early thinkers and philosophers of knowledge, such as Aristotle, considered knowledge to be justified true belief. Mid-20th century philosopher Edmund Gettier examined and challenged the idea that knowledge is only based on justification, truth and belief through a series of counterexamples in what is called the Gettier Problem. You will probably explore this in more detail in your TOK course.

The core unit of TOK is about you as a knower in our world. This means you will discuss your relationship to knowledge, certainty and truth, and what you know (or think you know).

Knowledge shapes and guides our existence. It would be difficult to function in our world as an individual or with other individuals without some sense of a common understanding about knowledge and the impact that knowledge has on our existence.

Our knowledge, use of that knowledge or lack of application of that knowledge may lead to our extinction, especially when we consider weapons of mass destruction or the impact of climate change.

As a result, knowledge and our study and understanding of knowledge is more than academic. It may also be about our survival.

Your exposure to knowledge in TOK will likely begin with the statement that knowledge is considered by some to be justified true belief.

From that starting point, you will discuss that knowledge is sometimes classified as experiential knowledge (I have experienced it, so I know it), procedural knowledge (this is the process you follow in order to do something), practical knowledge (I have done this so many times, I know it) and theoretical knowledge (I have learned about it, so I know it).

Knowledge in TOK will then likely discuss personal knowledge (what I know and believe to be true) and shared knowledge (what we know and believe to be true).

The impact of the study of knowledge and the application of knowledge is controversial and contested because, as Sir Francis Bacon once wrote, 'knowledge is power'.

With 'knowledge is power' in mind, let us consider what might be considered knowledge in global politics. What can we know in global politics, and how can we be sure we know it? Knowledge in global politics comes in many forms.

Knowledge might be a theoretical understanding of a concept like sovereignty and the different interpretations or understandings of sovereignty, like internal or external sovereignty, Westphalian or Post-Westphalian sovereignty, shared or pooled sovereignty. Sovereignty might also be looked at through the lens of personal or collective sovereignty, self-determination, autonomy, semi-autonomy or independence.

Knowledge in global politics also comes in the application of these concepts through policies, and how political scientists and others analyze the application of these policies. Consider the independence of South Sudan in 2011 from Sudan, following a civil war and public referendum. This is the application of sovereignty in practice.

In the context of the independence of South Sudan, TOK asks us to consider what might have counted as valid evidence for those who supported independence and for those who were against it. How was independence justified? How do we determine whether the justification was valid? Might there have been another option and how do we know what that option might be?

Theory of Knowledge

Knowledge comes from those who have been impacted by policies. Stakeholders are a valuable source of knowledge. Once completed, the Grand Ethiopian Renaissance Dam on the Blue Nile is projected to provide enough electricity to meet Ethiopia's energy needs. The energy generated may also be able to be sold within the region. There were many groups and countries who opposed the building of the dam. The Gumuz people of Ethiopia, for example, will be displaced once the dam is complete. They have complained and petitioned for the dam not to be built, yet construction is underway.

> TOK expects an analysis of the knowledge at stake and the different perspectives regarding any real-world example rather than a definitive conclusion. You can boost your success by paying close attention to the language that you use by including words such as 'may', 'might' and 'could' rather than 'must' or 'should'.

Activity

Consider the case of the Gumuz community and apply this real-world example from global politics to TOK Exhibition prompt 13: 'How can we know if current knowledge is an improvement over past knowledge?'

TOK asks us to consider why the claims of the Gumuz, for example, were not persuasive enough to halt the construction of the dam. Why were their justifications not considered valid evidence for the dam to be built differently, elsewhere or not at all? We have the knowledge about the displacement of the Gumuz, so why has this not pushed us to act on their behalf? How do we know how to value the energy needs of a country when they conflict or endanger the livelihoods of tribal or traditional populations? What do we consider to be a good justification for a policy or action?

By addressing real-world examples in this way, you can see how TOK can support you in Global Politics.

While, at the start, it is a bit challenging to look at global politics through the lens of TOK, it is also very rewarding because it adds an additional analytical dimension to your thinking.

Activity

Consider South Sudan's 2011 independence. How do we know it was successful? Was it because it was respected by Sudan? Was it due to South Sudan's subsequent membership of the African Union and United Nations? Using the same approach, to what extent can we consider Kosovo or Kurdistan independent? How do we know if a people or group should be independent or not? Complete a concept map and share a list of possible circumstances or conditions that might be used to justify or not justify independence. Who might agree with these points and who might disagree? Share your thoughts with your class.

The TOK areas of knowledge and optional themes

TOK uses five areas of knowledge (AOK) and five optional themes to help us explore knowledge using fundamental questions such as: 'How do we know what we know?', 'To what extent can we know?' and 'To what extent can we be certain about what we know?'.

> Areas of knowledge are like different school subjects or professional disciplines.

373

Not everyone sees things in the same way. Do you see this face from the front or the side?

It is common that TOK Essay prompts mention the production of knowledge. You can boost your success in the TOK Essay by being aware of the production of knowledge process in each AOK that you study and using what you know to identify interesting real-world examples to explore through your essay.

Demonstrations like this are one way that people engage in politics.

Optional themes in TOK give you the opportunity to explore how knowledge is produced and how our knowledge impacts and is impacted by each of the themes.

The areas of knowledge

The AOKs are similar to subject areas in high school, university academic departments, fields of study and professions. What happens in an AOK? Knowledge is produced. By produced, we mean that knowers in any given AOK (groups of knowers like physicists, doctors, choreographers, historians, directors, mathematicians, authors, political scientists, engineers or artists) pursue, construct, develop, apply, obstruct, debate, replace and challenge knowledge in the field that they work in.

This is known as the production of knowledge process. This happens within and between different AOKs.

The IB has identified five AOKs (IB TOK Guide page 10):

- History (political, social, economic, diplomatic, cultural schools of historiography, etc.)
- The human sciences (political science, psychology, economics, etc.)
- The natural sciences (physics, biology, chemistry, astronomy, etc.)
- The arts (music, theater, literature, film, dance, visual arts, etc.)
- Mathematics (theoretical, applied, etc.)

Each AOK explores the knowledge at stake and the relevant production of knowledge process.

The idea of separating knowledge into different AOKs is based on the assumption that the production of knowledge process is different in each of these AOKs *and* that this difference has a significant impact on the form, type and relevance of the knowledge being produced and what is at stake.

It raises the question as to the extent to which mathematicians, for example, approach knowledge, what they know and how they know it differently to a film maker or political scientist.

We can locate global politics as part of the human sciences (or social sciences). Global politics uses the analytical framework of political science and political scientists. But, the example of the Gumuz people of Ethiopia shows that knowledge in global politics comes from more than just political scientists.

The optional themes

The IB has identified five optional themes (IB TOK Guide page 10) that operate in a similar way to the AOKs with regards to the production of knowledge.

These optional themes are intended to be more flexible than the AOKs, linked to contemporary themes, and have a significant impact on ourselves and our world (similar to the AOKs).

The TOK optional themes are:

- Knowledge and technology
- Knowledge and language
- Knowledge and politics
- Knowledge and religion
- Knowledge and indigenous societies.

Theory of Knowledge

The expectation within the study of the optional themes is to discuss how and why knowledge might impact politics and how politics might impact knowledge. The IB recommends that at least two optional themes are covered in your TOK course.

Themes or issues in Global Politics can be discussed in (and are relevant to) all five of the optional themes. Knowledge and politics is where you can focus specifically on what influences what we know and how stakeholders make and are impacted by decisions and policies. Knowledge and politics gives you the chance to consider the different perspectives that go into human rights, national security or development policies and strategies. How does a country know when it is right to intervene or to sanction or sign a treaty or agreement?

You might consider, for example, why a country might want to join an IGO like the European Union or not. Norway and Switzerland have continually rejected EU membership. The UK voted to leave the EU in 2016, and Croatia joined in 2013. As of 2023, Montenegro, Ukraine and Moldova all wish to join.

TOK nudges you to consider how we might know if EU membership is the right choice. TOK asks us to consider what different factors, conditions and circumstances might lead someone from the UK to argue for continued membership while someone else might want to leave. Why do some countries decide to have their parliament vote on membership while others choose a public referendum? Regarding the UK's Brexit, TOK asks us to contemplate what were considered valid justifications and evidence that guided some to vote remain, others to vote leave, and others to not vote at all.

In Global Politics, we are not limited only to knowledge and politics. Technology and the influence that technology has on what we know in global politics is extremely important. Consider the most recent election process that you have followed and the extent to which artificial intelligence or the use of algorithms has had an impact on the way in which people vote. How do we know what a political candidate's true opinion or position on an issue is? How do we know when technology influences our political choices?

Knowledge and language is important in global politics as well. Consider how news headlines are crafted and framed to highlight the success of one policy or to criticize another policy. In global politics, we are concerned about the persuasive nature of language and how we react, vote or support something depending on the language being used. How can we distinguish between knowledge, belief and opinion? (TOK exhibition prompt 25)

Knowledge and religion is also relevant to global politics. Consider the communities and countries where the religious belief system is interconnected with the political system. How do we know what the relationship should be between religion and government policy?

As we saw with the example of the Gumuz community in Ethiopia, knowledge and indigenous societies is of interest to global politics as well. Underrepresented, indigenous communities are often marginalized and therefore vulnerable. Why might some societies disregard the knowledge from these communities while others find such knowledge useful?

> Knowledge and politics is an excellent opportunity for you to consider different perspectives in global politics, such as why neorealists and neoliberals have different world views and ways of interpreting and understanding events.

> Global Politics fits naturally into the AOK of the human sciences and the optional theme of Knowledge and politics, although issues relevant to global politics can be found throughout all the AOKs and optional themes.

TOK is less about right or wrong answers and more about how you might look at or analyze something from different perspectives and how these perspectives might influence what we know. You can boost your success by using different perspectives and balanced language in TOK when analyzing a question about knowledge.

All five of the optional themes in TOK offer a unique opportunity for you in Global Politics to explore important questions related to knowledge.

Activity

Consider the following question, create a concept map and discuss three possible explanations with a partner: 'With access to the same information and evidence, why do neorealists and neoliberals have different world views and ways of interpreting and understanding events?'

The AOK and optional themes knowledge frameworks

Each of the AOKs and optional themes are organized into analytical categories that we call a knowledge framework. A knowledge framework should help you break down and evaluate how, why and what knowledge is being produced and the knowledge at stake in a given AOK or optional theme.

The knowledge frameworks should also help you in comparing and contrasting the production of knowledge processes in different AOKs and optional themes.

The IB currently recommends the following four knowledge framework elements (IB TOK Guide pages 12–15):

- the scope, nature and area of application of the knowledge produced and the production of knowledge in an AOK and optional theme
- the perspectives and context of the knowledge produced and the production of knowledge in an AOK and optional theme
- the methods, tools and practices that are used to produce knowledge in an AOK and optional theme
- ethics and ethical considerations raised by the knowledge produced and the production of knowledge in an AOK and optional theme.

In Global Politics, we often rely on the opinions and analysis of experts, usually political scientists or other stakeholders with an interest in a policy. Knowing the perspective of the expert is important in order to understand why they take the positions they take on certain issues. Political scientists and others in global politics use a knowledge framework very similar to the one you will be working with in TOK.

Other knowledge framework elements include:

- the language, terms and definitions used in the production of knowledge process
- the core concepts, ideas, laws, axioms and assumptions that support and drive the production of knowledge
- the historical development of the AOK and optional themes
- the role of experts in the production of knowledge
- the role of self-justification, and how biases impact the production of knowledge
- the limitations of application of knowledge produced
- the links between shared knowledge and personal knowledge.

The TOK knowledge framework is an important tool. You can boost your success by finding different real-world examples and practice applying the knowledge framework. Be sure to consider any ethical questions or considerations that your real-world example might raise.

This knowledge framework should be used when considering knowledge in each of the AOKs and optional themes. The primary knowledge framework in Global Politics is political science. We therefore generally follow the methodology of political scientists.

Theory of Knowledge

> **Activity**
>
> Look at a real-world example in global politics with a classmate where the causes or the impacts of the event have been analyzed by a journalist or political scientist. Using TOK Exhibition prompt 32: 'What makes a good explanation?', identify three pieces of evidence presented that you would consider a good explanation for the event. Compare these pieces of evidence with other pairs of students. Did you come up with the same good explanations? Discuss what makes an explanation good or valid to you.

The 12 TOK concepts

TOK introduces 12 important concepts that are integrated throughout the course. The concepts are evidence, certainty, truth, interpretation, power, justification, explanation, objectivity, perspective, culture, values and responsibility (IB TOK Guide, page 6). They are intended to guide your thinking and analysis of any real-world situations or events that you might consider exploring. In other words, TOK expects you, the knower, to use these concepts as you investigate how you know what you know.

In addition, you are expected to integrate relevant components of these concepts in both your TOK Exhibition and TOK Essay, so you need to use them clearly and explicitly.

Regardless of the AOK or optional themes you are exploring, the production of knowledge process is influenced and impacted by these concepts.

In Global Politics, it is very useful to approach these concepts through the following questions and considerations directly connected to Global Politics. You should use these questions in Global Politics to help you create stronger and more meaningful TOK connections.

- What impacts what is considered evidence of knowledge and knowing in Global Politics?
- What conditions impact what is considered a justification of knowledge and knowing in Global Politics?
- What does pure objectivity look like in Global Politics and how might it be achieved?
- In Global Politics, how do we evaluate what might be considered a good explanation?
- How do we measure the role that perspective plays in the production of knowledge in Global Politics?
- What role does the need for certainty play in the acceptance of knowledge in Global Politics?
- In Global Politics, who determines what is considered the truth?
- Who do we trust most with regards to the interpretation of knowledge in Global Politics and why?

- In Global Politics, in what ways does culture impact knowledge and the production of knowledge?
- In what ways do values impact knowledge and the production of knowledge in Global Politics?
- In Global Politics, what is the responsibility of someone who has knowledge?
- How do we measure the relationship between power and knowledge in Global Politics?

Each of the 12 TOK concepts has relevance to Global Politics. It is useful to have a discussion about these questions together with your classmates early on in your Global Politics course. This will have benefits for you both in TOK and in Global Politics.

> The twelfth question (power) is an excellent opportunity for you to discuss more deeply the understanding of power that we address in Global Politics.

Activity

Consider the third question (objectivity) above. Reflect on your understanding of human rights. Consider the role that objectivity might play in proving or making a claim for a human rights violation. Consider what objectivity looks like in Global Politics.

> If you choose to explore real-world situations and examples from Global Politics in your TOK Exhibition or TOK Essay, be sure that you are considering the significance of one or two of the 12 TOK concepts to boost your success.

Activity

Reflect on Albin Egger-Lienz's painting *The Nameless 1914,* painted in 1916. What interpretation do you have as to what this painting might mean? What message do you think the painter was intending to communicate? Do artists have an ethical responsibility to share knowledge? Do political scientists? How do you know?

Egger-Lienz's *The Nameless 1914.*

Theory of Knowledge

The Global Politics and TOK connection: what is at stake?

Global Politics and TOK helps us to question and consider our understanding of other cultures and our own culture.

If knowledge is power, then there is a great deal at stake. You should take advantage of what TOK can offer you as a student of Global Politics. But is all knowledge equally important? How do we go about figuring this out? Who decides? Remember that knowledge is sometimes interpreted as justified true belief. (If I know it to be so, then it must be so.) If that were true, would that make life much simpler?

In Global Politics, this should raise a number of significant questions for you to address throughout your experience, including:

- Who decides what justifies something as knowledge and what might be considered a true belief?
- How certain can I be, or should I be, about what I know?
- How do I determine the accuracy, value or use-value of this knowledge?
- Who decides if, and when, knowledge changes?
- Can old knowledge still be relevant?
- Is new knowledge always correct (and how do we know, etc.)?

These are just some of the TOK-related questions that you should consider addressing through Global Politics.

More significantly, TOK allows you to have a little fun as you explore the impacts of what we know, how we know it, why we know it and what we do with knowledge once we think we know something in Global Politics.

Enjoy your exploration of knowledge through TOK and let it enhance your understanding of Global Politics.

Activity

Think about what you have learned throughout this chapter and compare it with what you are currently working on or have already covered in TOK. What do you see as the most important take-away from this chapter?

Summary

In this chapter, you have learned:

- The meaningful ways you can include Global Politics in both TOK assessments: TOK Exhibition and TOK Essay. The TOK Exhibition prompts are designed to get you to think about knowledge and, if you choose objects or artifacts relevant to Global Politics, these can be explored through one of the 35 TOK Exhibition prompts.
- How knowledge is defined and used in TOK and how we might use the TOK approach to knowledge to help us better understand knowledge and the production of knowledge process in Global Politics.
- Of the areas of knowledge in TOK, the human sciences is the natural home for Global Politics, but Global Politics has application to and through all the AOKs.
- Knowledge and politics is just one of the five optional themes that can be connected to your work in Global Politics. The strength of this connection will depend on how you identify and select different real-world situations and examples to explore using the optional themes.
- Elements of the TOK knowledge framework resemble the methods used by political scientists to carry out their analyses and evaluations. Global Politics consists of a number of different knowers or stakeholders, all of whom can contribute to the production of knowledge process in Global Politics, not just political scientists.
- The importance of thoroughly investigating and including one or two of the 12 concepts in the work that you submit in TOK. These concepts can be useful in your Global Politics analysis of real-world examples.
- There is a strong connection between Global Politics and TOK. If you take the time to explore this connection, you will deepen your understanding of and appreciation for the world we live in.

The Extended Essay

Students starting in 2025 onwards

The Extended Essay Subject Guide is being updated for 2025. This chapter will be revised in 2025. You will find any updates to this chapter by accessing this page of your eBook.

Introduction

The IB DP programme offers you the opportunity to engage in an in-depth research project known as the Extended Essay (EE). Global Politics provides a rich and relevant subject area for you to delve into, encouraging you to apply your understanding of global political issues to real-world contexts.

The EE provides you with an opportunity to engage in independent research on a topic of your choice. It encourages you to develop your critical thinking, and your analytical, research and writing skills, fostering an appreciation for intellectual inquiry and deepening your understanding of a subject area. The EE also serves as preparation for university-level work, giving you a taste of academic research and the opportunity to explore your own interests within a structured framework. This chapter focuses on understanding the purpose of the EE, highlighting the skills developed through the process and discussing the benefits it provides, with a specific focus on Global Politics as the subject area for the EE.

The EE plays a crucial role in the development of various skills that are valuable for your academic and personal growth. These skills include:

- *Critical thinking and analytical skills:* The EE requires you to critically analyze and evaluate information, theories and arguments. It promotes the development of analytical skills by challenging you to think deeply about your research question, consider different perspectives and draw well-reasoned conclusions.
- *Research and writing skills:* Conducting extensive research, gathering relevant sources and synthesizing information are integral parts of the EE. Through the process, you will learn how to navigate academic sources, evaluate their quality and reliability, and effectively cite and reference your work. The EE also enhances your writing skills, as you learn to structure your arguments coherently, present evidence and articulate your ideas concisely.
- *Preparation for university-level work*: Engaging in the EE provides you with a taste of the academic rigor you can expect at university level. It prepares you for the demands of independent research, critical analysis and academic writing, ensuring a smoother transition into higher education.
- *Independent learning and time management*: The EE is a self-directed project, requiring you to manage your time effectively and take ownership of your learning. It fosters independence, self-motivation and the ability to set and meet deadlines – a skill set that is invaluable in university and beyond.
- *Personal growth and confidence*: Completing an in-depth research project such as the EE allows you to explore your interests, cultivate intellectual curiosity and gain confidence in your ability to tackle complex topics. It empowers you to develop your own voice, take ownership of your learning and contribute to the body of knowledge in Global Politics.

- *Subject mastery*: The EE enables you to deepen your understanding of Global Politics, allowing you to develop expertise and knowledge that goes beyond the syllabus. It encourages a passion for learning and provides an opportunity for you to engage with real-world issues and apply theoretical concepts.
- *Enhanced critical awareness*: By undertaking the EE, you will gain a deeper understanding of the complexity and nuance of Global Politics. You will learn to critically evaluate different sources of information, distinguish between reliable and biased perspectives, and engage in nuanced discussions on global political issues.

Formulating a research question

The first step once you have chosen to write your EE in Global Politics is formulating your research question. It is important to take some time to think about your question as this will form the basis for all the research and writing that you will do for your EE. While the wording of your question may change a little as you do more research, it is recommended that the core of your question is solid from the start.

Formulating a research question for an EE in Global Politics requires careful consideration and planning. Here is some advice to help you in this process:

- *Choose a topic of personal interest*: Select a topic that genuinely interests you. This will make the research process more enjoyable and motivating. Additionally, your passion for the subject will likely reflect in the quality of your work.
- *Review the syllabus and assessment criteria*: Familiarize yourself with the Global Politics syllabus and the assessment criteria for the EE. This will help you understand the expectations and requirements of the assignment, ensuring that your research question aligns with them.
- *Narrow down your focus*: Global Politics is a broad field, so it is important to narrow down your research question to a specific area or issue. Consider focusing on a particular region, conflict, policy, international organization or theoretical framework. You only have 4000 words, so your question must be manageable and allow you to explore your chosen topic in depth within this constraint.
- *Consider real-world relevance*: Global Politics is all about understanding and analyzing real-world events, policies and conflicts. Aim to formulate a research question that addresses a current or historical issue (ideally, within the last ten years) with significant global implications. This will make your research more meaningful and relevant.
- *Formulate a clear and concise question*: Your research question should be focused, specific and open-ended. It should clearly state what you intend to investigate and leave room for analysis and critical evaluation. Avoid vague or overly broad questions that are difficult to address within the scope of the EE. Avoid compound questions – your question should not contain the word *and*.
- *Ensure feasibility and availability of sources*: Before finalizing your research question, conduct a preliminary search to determine whether there is a sufficient amount of credible and accessible sources available. This will help ensure that you can gather the necessary evidence to support your arguments.
- *Seek guidance and feedback*: Consult with your Global Politics teacher or supervisor throughout the process of formulating your research question. They can provide valuable insights, suggestions and guidance based on their expertise and experience.

Your issue cannot have happened more than 20 years ago.

Keep in mind that research questions in the Human/Social Sciences generally, and in Global Politics more specifically, will evolve as you look at new sources and access new material. You should expect your question to develop as you grow your understanding of the political issues at stake in your research.

Your research question will serve as the foundation for your EE. Take your time to refine and develop it, ensuring that it is both manageable and intellectually stimulating.

Conducting background research

Conducting background research is a crucial step in writing an EE in Global Politics. It involves immersing yourself in the existing literature and scholarly work related to your chosen topic. By engaging with academic books, scholarly articles, reports and other relevant sources, you lay the foundation for a well-informed and evidence-based research project. Thorough background research helps you gain a solid understanding of the topic. It allows you to explore different perspectives, theories and arguments that exist within the field of global politics. Imagine that you have arrived late to a party and there is an interesting conversation going on. You sit and listen to what is being said for a while, then you add your contribution to the discussion. You leave the party knowing that the conversation will continue after you have left. In many ways, this is what is involved with your EE. By familiarizing yourself with key debates and concepts, you can situate your research question within the broader academic discourse, ensuring that your essay makes a meaningful, but not final, contribution.

Background research enables you to identify gaps or areas that require further investigation. It helps you identify existing research limitations, unanswered questions or emerging issues within your chosen topic. This identification of gaps can shape the direction and focus of your own research, allowing you to provide a fresh perspective or explore new angles within Global Politics.

Conducting thorough background research equips you with the necessary knowledge and context to develop a well-informed and rigorous EE. By immersing yourself in the existing literature, you can gain insights into key debates, theories and arguments, while identifying opportunities for your own research to contribute to the field of global politics.

Developing a research plan

After choosing a research question and conducting background research, the next step in the EE process is to develop a research plan. It is important to create a comprehensive plan, breaking down the research process into manageable steps and applying appropriate research tools and techniques to the context of Global Politics.

- *Creating a timeline and setting deadlines:* Developing a research plan begins with creating a timeline and setting realistic deadlines. Time management is crucial to ensuring that all aspects of the EE are completed within the given timeframe. By setting specific milestones and deadlines, you can effectively manage your time and avoid unnecessary stress.
- *Breaking down the research process into manageable steps:* The EE requires a significant amount of time and effort. Start early to allow yourself ample time for research, planning and writing. Break down the tasks into smaller, manageable parts and stay organized and meet deadlines. This approach allows you to tackle each aspect of the EE systematically by getting a little bit done on a regular basis. Some key steps to consider include:

- *Formulating research objectives:* Clearly define the specific objectives that will guide the research process. These objectives should align with the research question and provide a framework for conducting the research.
- *Gathering and evaluating sources:* Identify and gather credible sources, including academic articles, books, reports and other relevant materials. Evaluate the quality and reliability of each source to ensure the inclusion of accurate and authoritative information.
- *Outlining the structure of the essay:* Create a preliminary outline that organizes the structure of the EE. This outline should include sections such as an introduction, literature review, methodology, analysis and findings, and discussion and conclusion. Even if you do not eventually use these headings, this step provides a clear roadmap for the research and writing processes.
- *Use questions to guide your outline:* By creating questions for each section of your outline, it will be easier to fill in what you need in that section of your outline. For example, if you have a section titled 'Methodology', you might want to try to answer the questions: 'What sources did I use to get a better understanding of the important concepts in my EE?' and 'What additional research did I need to carry out outside of my Global Politics course work to address my research question?' and 'What primary research did I undertake and how has that impacted my EE?'. These questions will help guide your writing in each section of your outline.
- *Analyzing data and interpreting findings:* Plan how the collected data will be analyzed and interpreted. Identify appropriate frameworks, models or theories that can support the analysis and allow for a comprehensive interpretation of the findings.

- *Planning primary research methods:* If primary research methods are used, such as interviews or surveys, it is essential to plan and design these methods effectively. Consider the target population, sample size, question design and any ethical considerations. Develop a clear plan for data collection, storage and analysis to ensure the reliability and validity of the research.
- *Utilizing research tools and techniques:* Select tools and techniques that are appropriate for the research question and objectives, and ensure that you have a thorough understanding of how to use them effectively.

Developing a research plan is a critical step in the EE process. A well-thought-out research plan is the foundation for a successful and structured approach to the EE, ensuring the attainment of research objectives and timely completion of the project.

Writing the Extended Essay

Once you have conducted thorough research and developed an outline for your EE in Global Politics, it is time to start writing. The essay should be structured and organized, presenting your arguments and analysis in a clear and concise manner.

Begin with an engaging but brief introduction that sets the stage for your essay. The introduction should capture the reader's attention and create interest in your topic. By the end of your first paragraph, you should have introduced your research question and provided the relevant context. You should state your thesis statement, which outlines the main argument or position you will be defending in the essay in the second paragraph, while also signposting how you will answer your question and justify your thesis statement in the rest of the essay. The reader should not have to wait until the end of your essay to know what it is all about.

In the body paragraphs, develop your arguments and support them with evidence and analysis. Each paragraph should focus on a specific aspect of your research question, and present coherent and well-supported points. Use relevant examples, case studies, data and scholarly sources to strengthen your arguments. When analyzing data, apply appropriate frameworks, models or theories relevant to Global Politics. Use qualitative or quantitative methods, depending on the nature of your research question, and present your findings in a clear and organized manner. Ensure that there is a logical flow between paragraphs, allowing the reader to follow your thought process and understand the connections between different ideas.

Global Politics involves complex and multifaceted issues. Acknowledge and consider multiple perspectives and viewpoints when analyzing and discussing your research findings. This demonstrates critical thinking and a nuanced understanding of the subject. In the discussion and conclusion, reflect on the implications and significance of your research findings. Consider the broader context of your research question and discuss how your findings contribute to existing knowledge or have practical implications in Global Politics.

Pay attention to the clarity, conciseness and coherence of your writing. Use clear and concise academic language to convey your ideas effectively. Make sure your sentences and paragraphs are well-structured, and consider using headings and subheadings to organize the content and enhance readability. Use appropriate academic writing conventions, such as proper citations and referencing systems (such as MLA, APA or Chicago) to avoid plagiarism and demonstrate academic integrity. By following these guidelines, you can write a compelling and well-structured EE in Global Politics.

Revising your Extended Essay draft

Once you have a complete first draft of your EE, the next stage is to revise and edit your work before finalizing your essay. The revision and editing stage is crucial in the process of writing an EE and involves refining your first draft to ensure clarity, coherence and effectiveness in conveying your arguments and addressing the research question. Here are the key steps to follow during this stage:

- *Check for clarity and coherence:* Review your essay to ensure that your arguments are presented in a clear and logical manner. Check for any ambiguous or confusing statements and revise them for clarity. Ensure that your ideas flow smoothly from one paragraph to another, maintaining coherence throughout the essay.
- *Grammar, spelling and punctuation:* Proofread your essay for grammar, spelling and punctuation errors. Pay attention to sentence structure, verb tenses, subject-verb agreement and the proper use of punctuation. Correct any mistakes to enhance the overall quality and readability of your essay. There are online tools that will help you with this.
- *Evaluate arguments and evidence:* Assess the strength of your arguments and the evidence used to support them. Ensure that your arguments are supported by credible sources, examples and analysis. Check if there are any gaps or weaknesses in your reasoning and address them by providing additional evidence or refining your arguments.

- *Address the research question:* Check that your essay effectively addresses the research question. Revisit your thesis statement and ensure that each section of your essay contributes to the overall goal of answering the question. Make necessary adjustments to the content if certain sections are not directly relevant to, or align with, the research question.
- *Seek feedback:* Share your essay with your supervisor or teacher and request their feedback. They can provide valuable insights and suggestions for improvement. According to IB rules, your EE supervisor can provide formal written feedback only once on your draft, so make sure that it is as complete as possible before you ask them do this. Consider their feedback carefully and make revisions accordingly. Their perspective can help identify areas where your essay can be strengthened or clarified. You can, of course, have other people read your work.
- *Finalize formatting and citations:* Review the formatting guidelines provided by the IB and ensure that your essay adheres to them. Double-check the accuracy of your in-text citations and ensure that your bibliography or references page is complete and follows the prescribed format.
- *Check that your essay meets the required word count limitations:* Make sure that your EE is at or under the 4000 word limit.

Once you have incorporated the feedback and made necessary revisions, polish your essay by proofreading it once again. Pay attention to the details to ensure that your final version is error-free and meets the highest standards of academic writing. By revising, editing and finalizing your essay, you can enhance its quality, coherence and adherence to the research question and IB guidelines. This stage is essential for producing a well-crafted and polished EE in Global Politics.

The EE is an opportunity for you to engage deeply with a topic in Global Politics and showcase your academic and research skills. Stay organized, manage your time effectively and approach the process with curiosity and enthusiasm. Good luck with your EE!

GLOSSARY

absolute poverty lacking the minimum amount of income to meet basic needs over an extended period of time. When the income received falls below the poverty line.

actors entities with three key features: (a) autonomous determination of their purposes and interests, (b) the ability to mobilize resources for their goals, and (c) the capacity to significantly impact the behavior of other actors in global politics.

adaptive development an approach to development that emphasizes the importance of a wide range of data and stakeholder inclusion through a 'partnership' that changes the nature of the relationship between official development assistance donors and recipients.

aerosol a suspension of fine solid or liquid particles in a gas.

alliances formal or informal agreements between two or more states to cooperate for mutual benefit, often involving security, economic or diplomatic cooperation.

anarchy a condition of the international system where there is no central authority or world government, leading to the absence of a higher power regulating states' interactions.

anthropogenic climate change alteration in climate change resulting from the human burning of fossil fuels, release of aerosols and land alterations.

authoritarian a system of governance where power is concentrated in a central authority, often with limited political freedoms, and without the same degree of checks and balances found in democratic systems.

autocratic or authoritarian states describes a country with a government characterized by centralized power and limited political freedoms, often led by a single leader or a small ruling elite with minimal checks on their authority.

balance of power a concept where states or alliances seek to maintain equilibrium by countering or aligning with one another to prevent the dominance of any single actor, promoting stability in international relations.

Beijing Consensus a proposed development model emphasizing state-led economic growth and authoritarian governance, often associated with the PRC's influence in international politics.

biogeochemical flows the ways by which elements like carbon, phosphorus, nitrogen and sulfur flow between living organisms and the environment

bipolarity a situation where two major superpowers or blocs hold significant influence and act as the primary poles in the international system.

borders boundaries that outline an area. These can be natural (real) or human-made (artificial).

boycotts deliberate and organized efforts to abstain from economic, political or social interactions with a specific entity, often a country or organization, as a form of protest or to achieve a political goal.

capitalist an economic and political system in which private individuals or corporations own and control the means of production, and market forces play a central role in resource allocation.

carbon footprints the measure of the total greenhouse gas emissions (particularly carbon dioxide and methane) produced by an individual, community, organization, company or state.

carbon neutral the existence of a balance between emitting carbon and absorbing carbon from the atmosphere in carbon sinks, such as soil, oceans and forests.

ceasefire temporary stop in direct fighting between the parties involved in a conflict. It is a temporary period of truce.

child marriage any formal marriage or informal union between a child under the age of 18 and an adult or another child.

civil disobedience the refusal to obey the demands or commands of a government or authority, without resorting to violence or active measures of opposition.

civil society the realm of organized, non-governmental groups, institutions and individuals that operate independently from the government and play a role in shaping public policies, advocating for various causes, and promoting civic engagement.

classical realism a theoretical perspective that emphasizes the importance of human nature, power and state interests as key drivers of international relations, often viewing the international system as inherently competitive and conflict-prone.

coalition an alliance or partnership formed by multiple states or actors to achieve a common goal or address a specific issue, often involving cooperation on political, military or economic matters.

codification the process of systematically organizing and standardizing rules, norms or laws, often in international agreements or treaties, to regulate various aspects of international behavior and relations.

colonialism the practice of one nation or state establishing and maintaining control over other territories, often exploiting their resources and imposing its governance, typically during the period of European expansion in the 15th to 20th centuries.

coloniality the enduring legacy and influence of colonialism, including its social, economic and cultural structures, which continue to shape global power dynamics and inequalities.

communist/socialist political ideologies or systems that advocate for collective ownership of resources and the means of production, with the aim of reducing class disparities and promoting social equality.

collective bargaining the negotiation process between organized groups of workers and employers to reach agreements on labor conditions, wages and other employment-related matters.

collective identity the shared sense of belonging, values and interests among a group of people, often with a common cultural, political or social background, which can influence their political actions and interactions with others.

collective rights the rights and privileges granted to a group, often based on shared characteristics like ethnicity or culture, and are distinct from individual rights, aiming to protect and promote the group's interests and identity.

collective security an international system in which multiple states commit to mutual defense and cooperation to deter or respond to aggression, aiming to maintain peace and stability.

communitarian a political and social philosophy that emphasizes the importance of community, shared values and the common good, often advocating for collective responsibility and social cohesion alongside individual rights.

comparison benchmarks what specifically you are comparing and/or contrasting in a response, usually a specific list of ideas that the writer will be looking at in both sources.

complex interdependence a concept that acknowledges multiple channels of interaction, beyond just military force, between states, including economic, social and political ties.

conciliation a conflict resolution instrument in which parties voluntarily seek for a third party's intervention (conciliator) who provides a non-binding settlement proposal.

conflict disputes or disagreements between states, non-state actors or individuals, which may involve political, military, economic or ideological tensions and can vary in intensity from minor disagreements to full-scale wars.

conflict prevention a diplomatic approach that refers to a variety of activities and strategies deployed to pre-empt and subsequently neutralize potential triggers to widespread violent conflict.

constitutive theory an approach that focuses on how international actors, norms and structures shape the identity and behavior of states and other global entities, emphasizing the mutual constitution of international relations.

constructivism a theoretical perspective that emphasizes the role of ideas, norms, and identities in shaping international relations and believes that actors' perceptions and beliefs influence their behavior in the global arena.

context the broader circumstances, conditions and factors that surround and influence international events, decisions and interactions, providing the background and environment in which they occur.

contingency the idea that events and outcomes are subject to unforeseen and unpredictable factors or events, emphasizing the role of chance and uncertainty in global politics.

country a geographic or territorial entity, typically with defined borders and its own system of laws and institutions.

critical theory encompasses a range of perspectives that question and analyze the underlying power dynamics, inequalities and ideological constructs that shape international relations, aiming to challenge and transform existing systems and structures.

cultural power the influence and impact that a nation's cultural products, such as art, music, literature and media, can have on shaping the perceptions, values and behavior of people around the world, contributing to a country's soft power.

cultural relativism the perspective that cultural practices, beliefs and norms should be understood and judged within the context of their own culture, rather than using one's own cultural values as a standard for evaluation.

cultural violence the subtle forms of harm and discrimination that are perpetuated through cultural norms, practices and symbols, which may reinforce inequalities and social divisions.

culture the shared values, beliefs, traditions, customs and ways of life of a particular group or society, which can influence international relations and the behavior of states and non-state actors.

customary international law a body of legal principles and rules that have evolved over time through consistent state practice and are considered legally binding on states, even in the absence of formal written agreements.

decoloniality a movement and perspective that seeks to challenge and dismantle the enduring legacies of colonialism, aiming to promote postcolonial societies and systems that address historical injustices and inequalities.

Glossary

decolonization the process by which formerly colonized nations gain independence, sovereignty and self-governance, often marking the end of colonial rule and the restoration of autonomy.

defensive realism a theoretical perspective that focuses on states' efforts to maintain their security and survival by seeking defensive capabilities and forming alliances, emphasizing caution and balance of power.

democracy a system of government in which political power is vested in the people, typically through free and fair elections, allowing citizens to participate in decision-making and holding leaders accountable.

democratic systems, practices or institutions that uphold the principles of democracy, including free and fair elections, individual rights and rule by the people.

development the process of improving living standards, economic growth and social well-being in a country or region, often involving factors such as infrastructure, education and healthcare.

digital divide the gap between demographics and regions that have access to modern information and communications technology, and those that do not, or have restricted access.

direct social inequality the result of deliberate unfair treatment of a group or individual that intentionally removes opportunities from some and not from others.

direct violence the immediate action of hurting someone physically, emotionally or psychologically.

disciplinary power the use of institutions, norms and practices to control and regulate the behavior of individuals or groups, often promoting compliance with established rules and social order.

dominant narratives the prevailing, widely accepted stories or interpretations that shape how events, issues and cultures are understood and can influence public opinion and policymaking.

duplication in the context of official development assistance: investments, actions or supports that are done by multiple state and/or non-state actors often leading to waste, insufficient funding or support for other projects as well as corruption.

economic neoliberal in the context of development, economic liberalism refers to a relationship between countries and within countries that promotes free trade, access to markets and limited government intervention or interference in trade relations between states, as well as investments within states.

economic partnerships agreements or collaborations between countries or entities to facilitate trade, investment and economic cooperation, often aimed at mutual economic benefits and development.

economic power a nation's ability to influence international affairs through its economic resources, including GDP, trade, investment, and control over key industries and resources.

embargo an official ban (typically imposed by a country, group of countries or organization) on trade or other commercial activity with a country or countries.

emerging powers a group of countries that are increasing in economic strength, political influence and international prominence, often challenging the traditional power dynamics within the international system.

environment the physical and ecological conditions of the planet, including natural resources, ecosystems, and the impact of human activity on the Earth's sustainability.

equality the principle of fairness and uniform treatment, where individuals, groups and nations have similar rights, opportunities and access to resources, to promote social justice and reduce disparities.

equity the promotion of fairness and justice by addressing systemic inequalities and ensuring that resources and opportunities are distributed to achieve more balanced outcomes, particularly in policies and international relations.

explanatory theory a theoretical approach that seeks to understand and describe international phenomena by providing explanations and insights into the causes and consequences of various events and behaviors in the global arena.

external sovereignty the principle that a state has full control over its external affairs, including its relations with other states, without external interference or domination.

extreme poverty a condition of severe deprivation of basic human needs, including food, safe drinking water, sanitation facilities, health, shelter, education and information.

extreme poverty line defined by the international community as living on less than USD $1.90 per person per day.

feminism a multifaceted ideology and movement that advocates for gender equality, challenging the historical and contemporary structures of power and oppression that disproportionately affect women.

First World a term that historically referred to the capitalist, industrialized and economically developed countries, often aligned with the Western bloc during the Cold War, although this term is now less commonly used due to changes in global politics.

Food and Agriculture Organization (FAO) a United Nations agency dedicated to addressing food security, agriculture and nutrition issues worldwide.

fragile or failed states states that lack effective governance, experience political instability, and struggle to provide basic public services, often resulting in significant social and economic challenges.

gender the social and cultural roles, expectations, and identities associated with being male, female or other gender categories, and how these roles influence power dynamics, discrimination, and opportunities in society and international relations.

Gender Development Index (GDI) introduced in 1995 through UNDP's Human Development Report with the aim of adding a specific gender-sensitive measurement to development that focuses on gaps between economic access, income, education and life expectancy.

gender inequality discrimination on the basis of sex or gender.

genocide any of the following acts committed with intent to destroy in whole or in part a national, ethnical, racial or religious group, as such: (a) killing members of the group; (b) causing serious bodily or mental harm to members of the group; (c) deliberately inflicting on the group conditions of life calculated to bring about its physical destruction in whole or in part; (d) imposing measures intended to prevent births within the group; (e) forcibly transferring children of the group to another group.

Gini coefficient in the context of development, a useful tool to measure income inequality between countries as well as within countries. Often used together with the Lorenz curve to visually illustrate income inequality.

global citizens individuals and communities whose social, political, environmental and economic actions are globally minded.

global civil society a network of non-governmental organizations, activists and individuals from around the world who engage in transnational advocacy, humanitarian efforts and social change, often addressing issues that transcend national boundaries.

global governance the collective efforts and mechanisms, often involving international organizations and treaties, that aim to address and manage transnational issues, such as climate change, trade and human rights, to achieve global stability and cooperation.

global identity being part of a culturally diverse and interdependent world, with an awareness that global politics is not exclusively about states or big and powerful actors and an interest in participating in global issues with a sense of responsibility for bettering the world.

globalization the process of increased interconnectedness and interdependence among countries and societies, driven by the flow of information, goods, services and ideas across borders, often resulting in economic, cultural, environmental and political changes.

Global North typically, the economically developed, industrialized former colonial countries, which often wield significant economic and political influence on the global stage.

Global Reporting Initiative (GRI) a set of standards that help state and non-state stakeholders measure the impacts of their practices on issues such as climate change, human rights and corruption.

Global South generally, the less economically developed often postcolonial countries, often facing social and economic challenges and seeking to address historical inequalities in the international system.

Great Green Wall an initiative from the African Union and other stakeholders rooted in the United Nation's 1994 Convention to Combat Desertification in order to restore degraded land in the Sahel Region.

great powers states that hold significant economic, military and political influence and are often central actors in shaping the international system and global affairs.

green theory an environmentalist perspective that emphasizes the importance of sustainability, ecological responsibility, and addressing environmental challenges in shaping international relations and policies.

greenwashing the making of false or misleading statements about the environmental or sustainability benefits of actions, measures or initiatives by state and non-state stakeholders, especially for-profit corporations.

gross expenditure the sum of household final consumption expenditure, general government final consumption expenditure, and gross capital formation.

Group of Twenty (G20) an international informal forum or informal intergovernmental organization comprising 19 major economies, the European Union and the African Union, aimed at addressing global economic challenges and fostering international economic cooperation.

hard power a state's ability to influence and shape international affairs through military force, economic coercion or other forms of tangible coercive means.

health a state of complete physical, mental and social well-being.

healthcare the system of institutions, policies and practices that provide medical services and access to health-related resources to a country's or region's population.

Glossary

heavily indebted poor countries (HIPCs) countries with significant debt burdens.

hegemon a dominant and powerful state or entity that exercises significant influence over the international system, often setting the rules and norms of the global order.

hegemony a situation in which one state or country controls others.

horizontal enforcement mechanisms or processes by which states or actors hold one another accountable for compliance with international agreements or norms through peer pressure and diplomacy, rather than through external authorities or enforcement.

human capital knowledge, skills and health that people invest in and accumulate throughout their lives, enabling them to realize their potential as productive members of society.

Human Development Index (HDI) a measure of average achievement in key dimensions of human development including life expectancy, education and gross national income per capita.

humanitarian intervention the use of military force or diplomatic means by one or more states or international organizations to protect populations in another state from grave human rights abuses or humanitarian crises, often without the consent of the affected state's government.

human rights the fundamental, inalienable rights and freedoms to which all individuals are entitled, including the right to life, liberty and equality, which are protected by international agreements and laws.

human security an approach that prioritizes the protection of individuals and communities from a wide range of threats, including armed conflict, disease, poverty and environmental disasters, recognizing that security extends beyond traditional military concerns.

income inequality disparity in the distribution of income between individuals, groups, populations, social classes or countries.

ideational the realm of ideas, beliefs and norms that influence and shape international relations, often encompassing ideologies, cultural values and shared identities.

identity how individuals, groups, nations or states perceive themselves and are perceived by others, often based on shared characteristics, values or affiliations, which can influence their political behavior and interactions.

indirect social inequality results from policies or actions that unintentionally remove opportunities from some people.

individual rights the inherent, inviolable entitlements and freedoms that individuals possess, which are often protected by legal and ethical principles and are crucial for safeguarding personal autonomy and dignity.

indivisible rights the principle that human rights are interconnected and interdependent, such that the violation of one right can often lead to the violation of others, highlighting the need for comprehensive protection and promotion of all rights.

inequality the disparities in wealth, opportunities, power and access to resources among individuals, groups or nations, often leading to social, economic and political imbalances and challenges.

informal forum/informal intergovernmental organisation (IIGO) an unofficial setting where states or other global actors engage in discussions, negotiations or cooperation on specific issues or agendas, often without the constraints and formality of official diplomatic channels.

institutional violence indirect form of violence inflicted by governments or any other authority through institutions, systems or established structures.

interdependence the condition in which states and actors are mutually reliant on one another for various aspects, such as trade, security and economic stability, creating shared interests and vulnerabilities in the international system.

interest group an organized association or entity that represents the common interests or concerns of a specific sector, industry or issue, and seeks to influence policies or decisions, often through advocacy and lobbying.

intergovernmental organisation (IGO) a formal institution comprised of member states that collaborate on various international issues, often with the goal of addressing common challenges, establishing norms or promoting cooperation.

internally displaced people (IDPs) persons or groups who have been forced or obliged to flee or to leave their homes or places of habitual residence, as a result of, or in order to avoid, the effects of armed conflict, situations of generalized violence, violations of human rights or natural or human-made disasters, and who have not crossed an internationally recognized border.

internal sovereignty a state's exclusive authority to govern within its own borders, make and enforce laws, and maintain order without interference from external actors or authorities.

International Bill of Rights encompasses a set of international agreements, including the Universal Declaration of Human Rights and related covenants, that outline fundamental human rights and freedoms to be protected and upheld worldwide.

International Criminal Court (ICC) a permanent tribunal established to prosecute individuals for the most serious international crimes, such as genocide, war crimes and crimes against humanity, when national jurisdictions are unwilling or unable to do so.

International Fund for Agricultural Development (IFAD) a specialized agency of the United Nations that works to address poverty and hunger in rural areas of developing countries.

international institution formal or informal organizations or structures that facilitate cooperation, provide governance, and address common issues at the international level.

international level pertains to activities, interactions and issues that transcend national borders, and are addressed through international agreements, institutions and cooperation.

International Monetary Fund (IMF) an international organization that provides financial assistance, policy advice and economic stability support to member countries facing balance of payments problems and economic challenges.

intersectional the approach that recognizes how various forms of identity, such as race, gender and socioeconomic status, intersect and interact, shaping individuals' experiences and positions in society and international relations.

intersectionality the analytical framework that acknowledges how various social identities and power structures intersect, interact and influence an individual's experiences, often used to understand and address discrimination and inequalities.

intersubjective the shared understanding and meaning-making among individuals, states or actors in the international system, shaping perceptions and behavior based on common norms and ideas.

intractable hard to control or deal with. Intractable conflicts are those that persist over time and resist resolution.

justice the principle of fairness and equity in the treatment of individuals, groups and states, often associated with international legal standards and ethical considerations.

just war the just war theory deals with justifying why and how wars are fought, based on when it is right to resort to violence (*jus ad bellum*) and what is acceptable when using violence (*jus in bello*).

labor unions organized associations of workers formed to advocate for better working conditions, fair wages and workers' rights through collective bargaining and activism.

latent conflict the situation where there are differences of viewpoint and things that bother individuals or parts of a group, but these are not great enough to modify the status quo.

leftist having left-wing political views.

legitimacy the acceptance and recognition of a government's authority and actions as valid, often based on consent from the governed, adherence to rules, and the moral or legal justifiability of its decisions and policies.

liberal democracy a political system that combines the principles of liberal values, individual rights and democratic governance, typically characterized by competitive elections, political pluralism and the rule of law.

liberal institutionalists theorists who emphasize the role of international institutions and cooperation in promoting stability and cooperation among states, often arguing that these institutions facilitate peaceful interactions and mitigate conflict.

liberalism a political ideology that advocates for individual rights, democratic governance, the rule of law and free-market capitalism, emphasizing the importance of cooperation, diplomacy and international institutions in achieving peace and prosperity.

liberty the fundamental principle of individual freedom and autonomy, often protected by laws and norms, which allows people to make choices, express themselves, and pursue their own goals without undue interference or coercion.

Lorenz curve a graphical representation of income inequality used in cooperation with the Gini Coefficient.

mandate typically, the official authorization or instruction granted to a government or political leader, often through an electoral victory, to govern and make decisions on behalf of a specific constituency or population.

Marxism a social and economic theory that emphasizes class struggle and the eventual transition to a classless, communist society, often critiquing capitalism and inequality in the international system.

media various communication channels and platforms, including television, radio, newspapers and the internet, used to disseminate news, information and perspectives to a wide audience, influencing public opinion and political discourse.

mediation a diplomatic process in which a neutral third party facilitates negotiations and dialogue between conflicting parties to help them resolve disputes and reach a mutually acceptable agreement.

mental health emotional, psychological and social well-being.

microcredit small, short-term loans generally targeting minority, marginalized and/or vulnerable populations, and usually with very low to no interest rates.

Glossary

microfinance financial services provided to low-income individuals or groups who are typically excluded from traditional banking.

migrant an individual who relocates from one place to another, often across international borders, for various reasons, such as seeking employment, refuge or improved living conditions.

modernization theory in the context of development, the impact that increased investment and increased exposure to more economically developed countries will lead to better economic benefits for lower economically developed countries.

monopolization the act or process of taking full control or control of the largest part of something.

Multidimensional Poverty Measure (MPM) a means to capture the complexity of poverty that considers dimensions of well-being beyond just monetary poverty, including monetary poverty, education and basic infrastructure services.

Multidimensional Poverty Index (MPI) international measure of acute multidimensional poverty covering over 100 developing countries. Complements traditional monetary poverty measures by capturing the acute deprivations in health, education and living standards that a person faces simultaneously.

multilateral actions, agreements or interactions involving multiple states or international actors working together to address common issues or challenges, often within a framework of shared rules and institutions.

multinational corporations (MNCs) a large business entity that operates in more than one country, conducting business activities and trade on a global scale, often with subsidiaries and operations worldwide.

multiplexity the complex, multifaceted relationships and interactions between states and non-state actors, involving various dimensions such as diplomacy, trade, the environment, security and culture, often contributing to the interwoven nature of international relations.

multipolar a world order characterized by the presence of multiple major powers or centers of influence, each capable of shaping international affairs, often resulting in a more balanced distribution of power and competing interests.

multipolarity a system where several major powers or centers of influence exist, each with the ability to shape international relations, leading to a complex and often competitive global landscape.

nation a group of people who share a common identity, often based on factors such as culture, language, history and geography, and may seek self-determination and statehood.

national development agencies the government offices or agencies that manage bilateral and multilateral official development assistance programmes and investments for a country.

national identity the sense of belonging, shared culture and common values that individuals in a particular nation associate with, often influencing their political loyalties and affiliations.

national security the protection of a nation's sovereignty, territorial integrity and the well-being of its citizens from external and internal threats, encompassing various aspects, including military defense, intelligence and economic stability.

nation-state a sovereign political entity characterized by defined borders, a permanent population, a government, and the capacity to conduct foreign relations, often based on a shared national identity.

natural climate change Earth's natural cycles and changes.

natural law the idea that there are inherent moral principles and ethical standards that transcend human-made laws and serve as a basis for evaluating the legitimacy of government actions and international relations.

negative liberty the absence of external constraints, coercion or interference in an individual's actions and choices, often seen as a fundamental aspect of individual freedom and rights.

negative peace the absence of direct, physical or immediate violence.

neoliberalism a theoretical approach that emphasizes the interconnected, interdependent and cooperative nature of stakeholders within global politics towards the promotion of peace, justice and security.

neoliberal institutionalism a theoretical perspective that emphasizes the role of international institutions and regimes in promoting cooperation among states, often focusing on the benefits of formal agreements, rules and regimes for addressing various global issues.

neorealism a theoretical approach that emphasizes the role of power and the anarchic structure of the international system in shaping the behavior of states, often focusing on security concerns and the distribution of power among states.

non-aligned countries or states that adopt a policy of not aligning with any major power bloc, aiming to maintain their sovereignty and independence in international relations.

non-governmental organisations (NGOs) private, nonprofit entities that operate independently from governments, often engaged in various humanitarian, social and advocacy activities on the international stage.

non-state actor (NSA) entities or actors that are not states but still play significant roles in international affairs, such as multinational corporations, non-governmental organizations and insurgent groups.

non-violence the use of peaceful means to bring about political or social change.

normative theory a theoretical framework that focuses on evaluating and establishing principles of ethics, morality and justice to guide international relations, often aiming to inform and improve global behavior and decision-making.

norms shared expectations, standards and rules of behavior that guide and shape the interactions and conduct of states and non-state actors.

offensive realism a theoretical perspective that emphasizes the competitive and expansionist nature of states in their pursuit of power, often focusing on the importance of military capabilities and dominance in shaping international relations.

official development assistance (ODA) a country's contributions to other countries through bilateral and/or multilateral channels.

othering set of processes, structures and dynamics that promote marginality and inequality based on group identities, defining individuals or communities as outsiders.

overt conflict when people openly disagree and choose to confront.

pacifism the belief that violence (and war) is unjustifiable under any circumstances, promoting peaceful means, exclusively, for conflict resolution.

Paris Agreement an international treaty within the United Nations Framework Convention on Climate Change, aimed at addressing climate change by limiting global warming to well below 2 degrees Celsius above pre-industrial levels and fostering climate resilience.

peace a state of non-violence, stability and the absence of armed conflict, often accompanied by the presence of diplomacy, cooperation and security.

peacebuilding the comprehensive efforts and strategies aimed at establishing and maintaining peace in conflict-affected regions, often addressing the root causes of conflict, promoting reconciliation, and supporting the recovery and transformation of societies.

peace enforcement the use of a range of coercive measures (force or threats), including military assets, to enforce peace.

peacekeeping an instrument of active involvement that seeks to maintain the conditions needed to transition from conflict to peace.

peacemaking a series of peaceful, diplomatic and judicial means through which conflicts can be solved.

peace movements a type of social movement in which people organize and sustain a campaign in support of a social goal, looking for the implementation or the prevention of a change in the society's structure or values.

people-centred development (PCD) an approach to international development that focuses on improving a local communities' self-reliance, social justice and participatory decision-making.

Planetary Boundaries the environmental limits within which humanity can safely operate.

polarity the distribution of power and influence among states in the international system, often categorized as unipolar (dominated by one major power), bipolar (split between two major powers), or multipolar (with multiple significant powers).

political power the ability to influence or control decisions, policies and events, often exercised by governments, leaders and institutions to shape the direction and behavior of a nation or the international system.

pooled sovereignty the practice of multiple states voluntarily ceding certain powers and responsibilities to international organizations or supranational entities while retaining their overall sovereignty, often to achieve common goals or address shared challenges.

populist a political style or movement that seeks to appeal to the concerns and sentiments of the general population, often by presenting itself as the voice of the people against established elites or institutions.

positive liberty the capacity and opportunity for individuals to actively pursue their goals and fulfil their potential, often with the assistance of government or societal resources, emphasizing self-realization and empowerment.

positive peace the absence of direct, cultural and structural violence.

postcolonial the period and discourse that emerges after the end of formal colonial rule, often focused on the examination of the lasting legacies, power dynamics, and cultural impacts of colonialism in former colonies.

postcolonialism a theoretical framework and perspective that critically analyzes the historical, cultural and political effects of colonialism, often addressing issues of identity, power and decolonization.

poverty a state of economic deprivation and lack of basic necessities that significantly hinders individuals' or communities' quality of life, often linked to social, political and economic factors.

poverty line the minimum amount of money a person needs to fulfil the basic necessities of life.

Glossary

poverty trap a situation or cycle that keeps people in poverty unable to escape poverty.

power the capacity of states, actors or institutions to influence and shape international affairs.

power-over the ability of one entity or state to exert control, dominance or coercion over others, often through force, coercion or manipulation.

power-to the capacity of individuals, groups or states to act in ways that promote their own interests, often emphasizing agency, autonomy, and the ability to achieve goals through cooperation and self-determination.

power-with collaborative efforts and the ability of multiple actors to work together and influence outcomes through shared decision-making and cooperation.

pressure group a type of interest group that actively seeks to influence government policies and decisions by advocating for specific issues, often through lobbying, public campaigns and other forms of advocacy.

public health the science of protecting and improving the health of people and their communities.

purchasing power parity (PPP) the rate of currency conversion that tries to equalize the purchasing power of different currencies by eliminating the differences in price levels between countries.

ratification the formal process through which a state's government or legislative body approves and adopts an international agreement or treaty, thereby binding the state to its terms and obligations.

realism a theoretical perspective that emphasizes the role of power, self-interest and state-centric behavior in shaping international relations, often viewing the international system as driven by competition and the pursuit of national security and survival.

realists theorists who adhere to the realist perspective, emphasizing the importance of power, state-centric behavior and the pursuit of self-interest as primary drivers of international relations.

realpolitik a pragmatic approach that prioritizes practical, often power-based considerations and national interests in foreign policy and international relations, sometimes overlooking moral or ideological concerns.

reconciliation the process of mending and restoring relationships between individuals, groups or states that have been in conflict or divided, often through efforts to address grievances, promote forgiveness and build trust for a more peaceful coexistence.

refugees individuals who have been forced to leave their home countries due to well-founded fears of persecution, conflict or violence, seeking safety and protection in other nations.

regime the system of government and the set of rules, institutions and practices that guide political authority and decision-making in a country, often encompassing formal structures and informal norms.

relational power the ability of actors to influence and shape the behavior and actions of others through interpersonal dynamics, networks and interactions, often based on trust, persuasion and cooperation.

relative poverty the standard of living a person or household enjoys compared to the standard enjoyed by others within the same society.

repatriate to send someone back to their own country.

representation the act of advocating for the interests, views and concerns of a specific group, constituency or entity within international or national decision-making processes, often through elected officials or diplomatic representatives.

resilience the capacity to withstand or recover from difficulties.

resistance movements organized groups or individuals who oppose and challenge oppressive governments, occupations or authorities, often using a variety of strategies, including protests, armed struggle and civil disobedience.

responsibility to protect (R2P) a principle that holds states responsible for protecting their populations from mass atrocities, and, when states fail to do so, the international community may intervene to prevent genocide, war crimes, ethnic cleansing and crimes against humanity.

rhetoric the art and use of persuasive language and communication strategies, often employed by leaders, states and organizations to influence public opinion, shape perceptions, and achieve political or diplomatic goals.

rights legally recognized entitlements and freedoms, often protected by international agreements, laws and norms, that individuals and groups possess and are entitled to enjoy.

Rome Statute the treaty that established the International Criminal Court (ICC), outlining its jurisdiction, functions and legal framework for prosecuting individuals for genocide, war crimes, crimes against humanity, and the crime of aggression.

sanctions punitive measures imposed by one or more states or international organizations to pressure another state or entity into changing its behavior, often involving trade restrictions, asset freezes or diplomatic penalties.

Second World a term used during the Cold War to describe countries aligned with the socialist or communist bloc, often led by the Soviet Union.

security a term used to describe the protection of a state or entity from various threats and risks, such as military aggression, terrorism, economic instability and environmental hazards, often achieved through measures like defense, diplomacy and law enforcement.

Security Council a principal organ of the United Nations responsible for maintaining international peace and security, consisting of five permanent members with veto power and ten non-permanent members.

security dilemma a situation in which the actions taken by one state to enhance its security, such as military build-ups, can inadvertently lead to increased insecurity and tensions with other states, often resulting in an arms race or conflict.

self-determination the principle that allows nations or peoples to freely choose their political status, establish their own government, and pursue their economic, social and cultural development without external interference.

sharp power the use of non-military, often covert or deceptive means, such as disinformation, propaganda and economic leverage, by states or actors to influence and shape the policies, opinions and actions of other countries.

smart power a strategy that combines both hard power (military force and coercion) and soft power (persuasion and attraction) to achieve foreign policy objectives, emphasizing a balanced and effective approach to international relations.

social constructs a concept that exists as a result of human interaction or socialization.

social development an emphasis placed on initiatives that focus on enhancing individual and group well-being, health, and quality of life outcomes.

social inequality disparities in wealth, access to resources, opportunities, and social privileges among individuals and groups, often influenced by factors such as class, race and gender.

social media digital platforms and technologies that enable individuals and organizations to create, share and exchange information, opinions and content, often with significant implications for public discourse, activism and diplomacy.

social mobility the change in a person's socio-economic situation, either in relation to their parents or throughout their lifetime.

social movements organized groups of individuals who mobilize to advocate for social or political change, often addressing issues such as human rights, environmental protection or civil liberties through collective action and activism.

social power the influence, control or authority that individuals, groups or societies hold within a given social context, often affecting norms, values and decision-making processes.

soft power the ability of states or actors to shape and influence the behavior of others through attraction, persuasion, and the appeal of their culture, values and policies, as opposed to coercion or force.

sovereign states political entities with recognized borders, a permanent population, a government, and the exclusive authority to make and enforce laws within its territory, often considered the highest authority in the international system.

sovereignty the supreme and independent authority of a state to govern itself and make decisions within its own territory without external interference, often a foundational organizing principle of international relations.

stakeholders individuals, groups or entities with a vested interest or concern in a particular issue, policy or international affairs, often including governments/states, non-governmental organizations, businesses and civil society.

state a sovereign and independent political entity with defined borders, a permanent population, a government, and the capacity to engage in international relations.

stateless not recognized by any country. Often used to refer to people – a stateless person.

strategic alliances formal or informal partnerships between states or entities based on shared interests and goals, often aimed at enhancing security, economic cooperation or diplomatic influence.

strikes organized work stoppages or labor actions carried out by employees or labor unions to demand better working conditions, higher wages or other labor-related concessions from employers or the government.

strong sustainability within development, an approach within the for-profit sector that recognizes the finite nature of natural resources and the need for these resources to be preserved, protected and replenished in all business practices. Often contrasted with weak sustainability.

structural inequalities disparities in access to resources, opportunities and social advantages that result from systemic and long-standing factors, often rooted in economic, social and political structures.

structural power the influence and control that states, institutions or entities hold over international systems, norms and rules, often shaping the behavior and outcomes of actors within that structure.

structural realism a theoretical framework that emphasizes the systemic structure of the international system, where states' behavior is primarily shaped by the distribution of power and their pursuit of security in a self-help environment.

structural realists theorists who adhere to the structural realist perspective, emphasizing the significance of the international system's structure, distribution of power and state behavior in shaping global politics.

Glossary

structural violence the harm and suffering experienced by individuals or groups due to systemic social, economic or political inequalities and injustices, rather than direct physical violence, often linked to poverty, discrimination or oppressive systems.

subaltern marginalized or oppressed groups and individuals who lack political and social power, often associated with postcolonial and critical theory perspectives.

substate political entities or regions within a sovereign state that have a degree of autonomy and governance distinct from the central government, often related to federal or decentralized systems.

supranational entities or organizations that exist above and beyond the authority of individual states, often involving the delegation of certain powers or decision-making to a collective body, as seen in the European Union.

sustainability the goal of meeting the needs of the present without compromising the ability of future generations to meet their own needs, often involving environmental, economic and social considerations.

Sustainability Accounting Standards Board (SASB) within development, an element of Corporate Social Responsibility that seeks to set standards and guidelines for sustainable business practices in manufacturing and other sectors.

sustainable development a comprehensive approach to economic and social progress that seeks to balance present needs and growth with the preservation of natural resources and the well-being of future generations.

Sustainable Development Goals (SDGs) a set of 17 global objectives established by the United Nations to address various social, economic and environmental challenges, and promote sustainable development by 2030.

systemic inequalities pervasive and deeply ingrained disparities in power, resources and opportunities that affect individuals and groups on a large scale, often connected to the structural characteristics of society and the international system.

technology the application of scientific knowledge and tools to address international challenges, improve communication, influence warfare, enhance economic productivity, and shape global interactions.

technology gap the unequal development and access to technological production, innovation and usage, including digital technologies.

terrorism the use of violence, often targeting civilians or non-combatants, by non-state actors to create fear, coerce governments, or advance political, ideological or religious objectives.

theory as a lens the use of theoretical frameworks and concepts to analyze and interpret international events, offering insights and perspectives on complex political phenomena.

Third World historically referred to countries that were not aligned with either the Western capitalist bloc (First World) or the Eastern socialist bloc (Second World) during the Cold War, often associated with postcolonial developing nations facing economic and social challenges.

three faces of political power as described by Steven Lukes, representing the different dimensions of power: the first face involves direct, observable influence; the second face involves shaping perceptions and agendas to control issues; and the third face involves influencing the beliefs and desires of individuals to prevent conflicts or challenges from arising.

Three Pillars of Sustainability as described by John Elkington, representing the need to consider the economic, environmental and social impact of stakeholder practices.

totalitarian states states that are characterized by an all-encompassing government that exercises control over every aspect of public and private life, often suppressing opposition, limiting individual freedoms, and tightly regulating the economy and society.

trade unions an organized association of workers formed to protect and advocate for their collective rights, interests and working conditions through negotiations and collective bargaining with employers or government entities.

transnational advocacy networks coalitions of non-governmental organizations, activists and individuals that operate across national borders to advocate for specific causes, policies or social issues, often leveraging the power of global connectivity to influence international decision-making.

Truth and Reconciliation Commissions (TRCs) official bodies established in post-conflict or transitional societies to investigate and address past human rights abuses, often aiming to uncover the truth, promote healing, and facilitate national reconciliation.

unipolarity a system in which one state or actor holds dominant power and influence, often characterized by a single superpower or hegemon shaping international affairs and maintaining unchallenged authority.

Universal Declaration of Human Rights (UDHR) a foundational document adopted by the United Nations in 1948, outlining fundamental human rights and freedoms to be protected and upheld worldwide.

universalism the idea and concern over every human being, regardless of origin, nationality, race, gender or any other affiliation, being as important as any other.

universal jurisdiction a legal principle allowing a state to prosecute individuals for certain serious crimes, such as war crimes or crimes against humanity, regardless of where the crimes occurred or the nationality of the perpetrators.

vertical enforcement the exercise of power and authority from higher levels of government or authority, often influencing and regulating the actions of lower-level entities or institutions within a hierarchical system.

violence the use of physical force or coercion, whether by states or non-state actors, to achieve political, social or ideological objectives, often resulting in harm, conflict or suffering.

vulnerability the quality or state of being easily exposed to harm or potential harm.

Washington Consensus an economic policy framework, often associated with the recommendations of international financial institutions, emphasizing free-market policies, liberalization and privatization as a means of promoting economic growth and stability.

weak sustainability within development, an approach within the for-profit sector that sees the possibility of replacing natural resources with manufactured resources. Often contrasted with strong sustainability.

Western imperialism historically, the expansion and domination of Western powers, particularly European colonial powers, over other regions and peoples through military, economic and political means, often driven by the pursuit of resources, territory and influence.

Westphalian sovereignty the principle of state sovereignty established by the Peace of Westphalia in 1648, emphasizing the idea that each state has exclusive control over its own territory and affairs, and other states should not interfere in its internal matters.

Westphalian states system a framework that emerged from the Peace of Westphalia in 1648, emphasizing the notion of sovereign states coexisting within a system based on non-interference in each other's internal affairs and territorial integrity.

World Bank, The an international financial institution that provides financial and technical assistance to developing countries for development projects and poverty reduction efforts.

World Food Programme (WFP) a United Nations organization that provides food assistance worldwide.

World Health Organization (WHO) a specialized agency of the United Nations responsible for international public health, including monitoring, coordinating and providing assistance for global health issues and emergencies.

World Trade Organization (WTO) an international organization that deals with the global rules of trade between nations, promoting and regulating international trade and resolving trade disputes.

Index

A

activism 61, 112, 244
activists 15–16, 315–16
actors and stakeholders 10–19
   and equality 87
   identity 263
   and legitimacy 16, 46, 50–2
   and liberty 85–6
   and power 28–9, 30–1
   role in conflict 193–4
   role in development 147–61
   role in fighting poverty 230–2
   role in global governance 55–62
   role in health 252–4
   role in multiplex systems 25–6
   role in rights and justice 80, 81, 83, 85, 91–5, 102–16
   role in sustainable development 168–9
   structural effects on 19–20, 24–5
Africa 259–60, 272–3
African Commission 107–8
African Union (AU) 97, 107–8, 135, 259–60
Al Shabaab 50–1, 158, 198
Albania 165
Amnesty International (AI) 111
anarchy 23, 28–9, 67
Arab Quartet, Qatar crisis 191–3
Arab Spring 37, 84, 191, 244–6
artificial intelligence (AI) 15, 121, 246–7
Asian values debate 118
Australia 167
authoritarian states 11, 33, 104, 244–6
authority 46–7, 49
autocratic states 11, 15, 104

B

Bahrain 33, 191–3, 245
Bangladesh 147, 267–8, 280
Banjul Charter 97, 107–8
bifurcation 343–5
biological weapons 256
Bolivia 157
borders 249, 270–2, 281
   border control 276–8
   and conflict 272–4
   and migration 274–7
   and security 276, 277–81
Brazil 17, 44, 88, 140
BRICS group 13
Brundtland Commission 143

C

Canada 121, 213–15, 316
carbon footprints 312, 315, 316
carbon neutral 165, 317
cartels 158–9
ceasefire 180, 210
child marriage 230–1
child soldiers 294–5, 296–7
China, People's Republic of (PRC) 32, 56, 60–1, 144, 145, 225, 240, 312
citizenship 266–8, 269–70, 295
civil disobedience 184–5
civil society actors 11, 15–16, 36, 51, 62
   and development 158, 169
   and human rights 80, 92, 112–13
   and multiplexity 26
Civil Society Organizations (CSOs) 36, 51, 62, 92
climate change 44, 61, 309, 310
   climate justice 85, 120
   and conflict 319–20
   and development 147, 165
   global warming 310, 312, 325, 327
   and health 256
   and inequality 307, 322
   sea level rise 320–2
   and security 288, 318–22
   treaties and agreements 316–18
colonialism 22, 40, 94–5, 140, 272–3
   colonial matrix of power 35–6
   and postcolonialism 69
communitarian values 118, 119
Community Climate Change Project (CCCP) 147
community groups 159–60
Conference of the Parties (COP) 317
conflict 50, 77, 179, 180, 186–7
   armed 187, 193–8, 212, 215–16, 294–5
   and borders 272–4
   categorization 199–200
   causes of 198–200, 201–2, 264, 272–4, 319
   child soldiers 296–7
   and climate change 319–20
   conflict analysis 201–2
   and culture 203–4
   and identity 203, 263, 264, 265–6
   justifying violence 203–6
   media narratives 15
   non-violent 187, 190–3
   prevention 207–8
   reconciliation 84, 212–15
   and religion 204–5
   resolution 198, 201, 202, 204, 205
   resolution pathways 206–16
   stages of 200–1, 202
   stakeholders and actors 193–4
constructivism 66–7, 120
Costa Rica 165
countries 10, 11, 149–51, 168
   carbon and ecological footprints 311–14
   Global North vs Global South 173–4
   peace indexes 181–3
   technology gaps 233–5
   vulnerable to climate change 318, 319–22
COVID-19 pandemic 117–18, 230, 231, 238, 255, 258–9, 306
criminal organizations 280, 288
critical theories 63, 68–70, 263
Critical Theory 68
critical thinking 10, 246, 379
cultural relativism 83, 98, 118–19
cultural violence 180, 188–9, 190
culture, and conflict 203–4
cybersecurity 286, 288

D

decoloniality 35–6
decolonization 272–3
deep ecology 174

development 76–7, 128–30, 162
   adaptive 146–7
   contested concepts 129
   and environment 147, 148, 154–5, 165, 314–16, 317
   and health 249–50, 255
   international development goals 135, 143–7, 163, 223–4, 249–50, 255, 300–1, 317
   international level 148–54, 158–9
   local level 147, 157, 158, 159–60
   measuring 130–2, 133, 134, 136–7, 155
   national level 155–7, 159, 165
   official development assistance (ODA) 143, 149–51, 155, 156, 172–3
   policies 148, 155, 157, 158
   political and institutional 132–4, 148, 154–5
   regional level 154–5
   social 134–7, 148, 154–5, 255
   stakeholders 147–61
   sustainable 138, 145–6, 168–74, 249–50, 317
   see also economic development
digital divide 236–9
direct violence 180, 188, 189, 190, 211
discrimination 88, 264, 300, 301, 303–4, 305, 306–7
doughnut model 314

E

Earth Overshoot Day (EOD) 317
ecological footprints 313–14
economic development 130–2, 139–47, 148, 154–5, 158
   Beijing Consensus 60–1
   and health 255
   modernization theory 139–41
   neoliberal economic policies 141–3
economic partnerships 58–60
Egypt 191–3, 244, 245–6
elections 48–9, 106, 240, 373
embargoes 190, 192
Engagement Project 354
   assessment criteria 365–69
   engagement activities 359–63
   political issue and research question 353–7
   report writing 354–5, 361–2, 365–6
environment 70, 84, 308–22, 325
   carbon footprints 311–13
   definitions 308–9
   and development 147, 148, 154–5, 158, 314–16, 317
   ecological footprints 313–14
   environmental justice 84
   global environmental efforts 316–18, 322
   global environmental politics 311–14
   global warming 310, 311–12, 317–18
   and human rights 120, 314–16
   impact of armed conflict and war 207
   Planetary Boundaries 313–14
   and security 318–22
   and sustainability 164–7, 169, 317
   and technology 169, 313
   see also climate change

393

Index

equality 87–9, 92, 296–307
  definitions 87, 297
  othering and identity 264
  racial and ethnic 305
  and social development 135
  see also inequality
equity 135, 297
Ethiopia, Gumuz people 372
European Union (EU) 24, 45, 54, 102, 154–5, 263, 305–7, 373
Eurovision Song Contest 30
exam assessment support 334
  Paper 1 334–42
  Paper 2 342–8
  Paper 3 (HL) 348–53
Extended Essay 381–85

F

failed states 11, 287
feminism 36, 69–70
foreign aid 102–3, 172–3
foreign direct investment (FDI) 141, 173
fossil fuels 61, 309, 310, 312, 316
fragile states 11, 158
France 24, 56

G

G20 (Group of Twenty) 61
Gambia 108
gender inequality 69–70, 237, 301–3
genocide 195–6, 214, 319
Germany 84, 304, 306
Gini coefficient 132, 298–9
global challenges 44–5, 61, 85, 220–1, 310, 323–5
global citizenship 269–70
global civil society 15–16
global environmental politics 311–14
Global Freedom Index 133
global governance 53, 55–62
global identity 268–70
Global North 14, 85, 102, 115, 173–4
Global Peace Index (GPI) 181–2, 183
global politics 1–2, 9–10, 71–2
  actors and stakeholders 10–19
  before and after Peace of Westphalia 20–3
  interdependence 52–62
  legitimacy 46–52
  non-Western influences 22–3, 25
  polarity and multiplexity 25–6
  power 27–38
  sovereignty 38–46
  structures 19–20, 23–5
  as a system 19–20, 22, 23
  theoretical perspectives 62–70
Global South 13, 14, 22, 85, 115, 119, 173–4
globalization 11, 13–14, 23, 44
  and conflict 194–5
  of human rights 119
  and identity 268–70
  and legitimacy 50, 51
  and security 287–9
  and sustainability 169–71, 172, 173–4
  and technology 236
governance 53, 55–62, 166

governments 12, 156, 172, 253–4
  anti-government protests 184–5
  legitimacy 46–50
  and national security 285–7
  and poverty 229, 230–1
  and security 292–3
  and technology 236, 239–40, 241–2
  and violence 189, 190
Greece 142, 156
green theory 70
greenwashing 158
gross domestic product (GDP) 130–1, 132, 183
gross national income (GNI) 130–1, 132
gross national product (GNP) 130–1, 132, 143
gun laws 38

H

health 135, 152, 248–61
  and development 249–50, 255
  inequality 305, 306
  mapping global health 250–1
  mental health 249, 257–8
  and poverty 227–8, 229, 256
  public health 249, 258
  role of governments 253–4
  role of WHO 252–3
  and security 255–7, 288
  and technology 239, 247, 249, 258–60
  vaccines and medicines 258–60
hegemony 34
Human Development Index (HDI) 136
human needs 133–4, 202
human rights 42, 79, 83, 119–22
  abuse of *see* human rights violations
  courts and legal protections 99–100, 105–10, 113
  definition 91
  economic incentives 102–3
  and environment 120–1
  generations of 82–3, 94
  health as 248–9, 253
  human security 289–90
  identity as 266–8
  laws and treaties 94–8, 105, 107
  national level 96–7, 113
  origins and evolution 81–2, 89–94, 120–1
  perspectives on 90–1
  politicization 99–101, 109–10
  promotion and protection 102–16
  regional level 97–8, 107–8, 113
  responsibility to protect (R2P) 100–1
  role of actors and stakeholders 102–16
  role of UN 91–6, 105–7, 108, 113
  and technology 236
  UDHR 83, 92–4, 98, 266, 275, 289–90
  universal jurisdiction 99–100
human rights violations 91–3, 95, 99, 197, 258
  accountability for 84, 99–101
  child soldiers 294–5
  and environment 315–16
  highlighting 16, 111–12, 115
  humanitarian intervention 100–1, 103
  and legitimacy 50
  reporting and assessment 105–6, 107, 108–10
  responding to with force 110

  role of the state 104–5
  sanctions for 103, 106–7
  securitization 292–3
human trafficking 278, 279–80
humanitarian intervention 14–15, 100–1, 103

I

ideational structures 23–4
identity 48, 203–4, 261–70, 272
income 132, 149, 298–9, 301–2
India 144, 170, 253–4, 279–80, 304
Indigenous peoples 16–17, 371, 373
  Canadian residential schools 214–16
  citizenship and legal identity 266–7
  rights 97, 120–1
  sustainable development 159–60
Indigenous sovereignty 44
individuals 14, 17–18, 49, 159, 241
  identity 262–3, 266, 269
  and power 34–5, 36, 37, 240–1
  rights 81–2, 89–91, 116–19, 120
inequality 87, 88, 138, 139, 229, 296–7
  and climate change 307, 322
  critical theories 68–70
  gender 69–70, 237, 301–3
  income 298–9, 301–2, 304
  racial and ethnic 303–7
  social 139, 300–1
  see also equality
informal forums 13, 14, 18, 61, 317
informal intergovernmental organization (IIGO) 13, 14, 18
information and communication technology (ICT) 235–9, 240
institutional violence 189–90
interdependence 9, 30, 52–62, 88–9
  complex interdependence 29, 66
  global governance 53, 58–62
  international law 53–5
  and legitimacy 50
  role of the UN 55–8
  and sovereignty 41, 43, 44–5
interest groups 17, 18
intergovernmental organizations (IGOs) 12–13, 14, 18, 20
  and development 151–2, 153–4
  and human rights 105–11, 115–16
  and justice 85
  role in global governance 55–61
internally displaced people (IDPs) 181, 182, 267–8
International Court of Justice (ICJ) 14, 55, 56, 57, 108, 274
International Criminal Court (ICC) 108–10, 196
international financial institutions (IFIs) 60, 141, 152–3
international institutions 24, 29, 31, 54–5, 66
international law 40, 42, 53–5, 289
  genocide 195–6
  human rights 94–8, 105, 108
  international criminal tribunals 99–100, 108–10, 196
  peacemaking 209
  universal jurisdiction 99–100
International Monetary Fund (IMF) 60, 141, 153

Index

international multilateral stakeholders 151
Interpol 289
intersectionality 36, 70, 87
intersubjectivity 67
interventions 40–1, 43–4, 85
   conflict prevention 207
   humanitarian intervention 100–1, 103, 203
   military intervention 100–1, 110, 203, 209–10
   peace enforcement 209–10
Iran 184, 190, 191
Iraq 15, 210
Israel 33, 180, 235, 239

J

Japan 10, 150, 156, 256
just war theory 205–6
justice 76, 79–80, 83–5, 88–9
   application in global contexts 84–5
   climate justice 85, 120
   courts 55, 99–100, 107–10
   responsibility to protect (R2P) 100–1
   social justice 36, 112–13, 114, 296–7
   universal jurisdiction 55, 99–100

K

Kazakhstan 157
Kosovo 101, 210
Kyoto Protocol 316–17

L

labor unions 113–14
law enforcement 157, 289
legitimacy 9, 46–52, 57
   challenges to 16, 50, 51
   humanitarian intervention 100–1
   international law 55
   and non-state actors (NSA) 50–1
   peacebuilding 212
   and power 37, 46–7, 48
   sources of 48–9, 50–1
less economically developed countries (LEDCs) 173–4, 234–5, 312
liberalism 29–31, 65–6, 70, 105
liberty 80, 85–7, 88–9
Libya 100, 110, 203, 245
Lorenz curve 132

M

Malaysia 157
malnutrition 152
Marxism 68–9, 70, 81
material structures 23–4
media 14–15, 18, 157, 159, 190, 191
Mexico 158–9, 266–7
microcredit 147
microfinance 231–2
Middle East 33, 191–3, 244–6
migration 267–8, 274–7, 278, 320, 322
Millennium Development Goals (MDGs) 144–5, 146, 255
modernization theory 139–41
monopolization 258, 259
more economically developed countries (MEDCs) 173–4

multilateral agreements 12–13, 316–17
multinational corporations (MNCs) 11, 14, 18, 160–1
   and development 158
   and global governance 61–2
   and human rights 113
   and sustainability 168, 170
   technology and data 240–1
multinational states 10, 273–4
multiplexity 25–6
Myanmar 108, 267–8

N

national development agencies (NDAs) 150
national human rights institutions (NHRIs) 113
national identity 48, 265, 272
national security 104, 284, 285–7, 295
nationalism 81, 273–4
nations 10, 11, 273–4
nation-states 10–12, 14, 18, 20
   borders 271, 272–3
   and development 148–51, 154–7
   legitimacy 46–50
NATO (North Atlantic Treaty Organization) 58, 59, 288, 289
   military interventions 110, 210
   and Russia's war on Ukraine 29
natural law 81
negative peace 179–80, 211
neoliberalism 66, 141–3
neorealism (structural realism) 28–9, 65, 185
Nepal 279–80
Niger 230–1
Nigeria 156, 169, 260, 294
non-governmental organizations (NGOs) 14, 15–16, 18, 61
   and development 158
   and health 254
   and sustainability 168
non-state actors (NSAs) 11, 14–18, 20, 26, 86
   armed 50–1
   and development 158–9
   and human rights 111–16
   and legitimacy 50–1
   role in conflict 193–4
   role in global governance 61–2
   soft power 30–1
norms 24, 48, 50, 67, 301
North Korea 55, 107, 263
nuclear weapons 24, 55, 69, 184

O

official development assistance (ODA) 143, 149–51, 155, 156, 172–3
Organization of Islamic Cooperation (OIC) 97–8
Organization for Security and Co-operation in Europe (OSCE) 107, 290
organized crime organizations 50, 158–9
Orientalism 69
othering 264

P

Pacific island nations 14, 320–2
pacifism 185, 190
Paris Agreement 84, 320, 321
peace 77, 178–86, 205, 211
   contested meanings 178–83
   measuring 181–3
   road to 183–6, 190, 206–7
peace enforcement 209–10
peace movements 183–4
peacebuilding 212–16
peacekeeping 210–11
peacemaking 208–9
people-centered development (PCD) 136
Planetary Boundaries 309–11
polarity 25
political authority 20
political issues 10, 19, 220–1, 332, 333, 347–50, 352–67
political movements 244–6
political parties 157, 159
pollution 144, 160, 163, 168, 169, 319
pooled sovereignty 44–5
populist authoritarian approach 293
positive peace 179, 180–1
Positive Peace Index (PPI) 182–3
postcolonial states 94–5, 100, 101, 119
postcolonialism 22, 69, 70
poverty 138–9, 221–32, 324
   absolute 223, 224
   defining poverty lines 222–3, 224
   extreme 222, 224, 225
   and health 227–8, 229, 256
   indicators 226–8
   measuring and mapping 223–5, 226–8, 298–9
   microfinance 231–2
   multidimensional 226–8
   poverty trap 228–9
   reduction 143–4, 152
   relative 223
   role of governments 229, 230–1
power 27–38
   balance of 185
   coloniality/decoloniality 35–6
   hard power 28–9, 31, 32, 103
   and individuals 14, 17–18, 34–5, 36, 37, 240–1
   and influence 33
   and legitimacy 37, 46–7, 48
   liberalism 29–31, 66
   military power 28, 64, 209–10, 285
   negative and coercive 28–36
   political power 10, 25, 29, 34, 48, 60–1, 69
   positive and cooperative 37–8
   realism 28–9, 64, 65
   and security 28–9, 285
   smart power 32
   in societies 34–5, 36, 37–8
   soft power 29–32, 33
   of states 28–33, 64–6, 103, 285
   and sustainability 162
   and technology 239–41
   three faces 34, 111
power-over 27–36
power-to 27–8

Index

power-with 28, 36, 37–8
pressure groups 17, 18
private sector companies 156–7, 158, 166–7, 169, 170, 171, 172
   see also multinational corporations
public services 50, 141
public-private partnerships 61
purchasing power parity (PPP) 224

Q
Qatar crisis 191–3

R
racial discrimination 112, 114, 303–5
realism 28–9, 41, 64–5, 105, 185
reconciliation 84, 212–15
refugees 15, 181, 182, 267–8, 275–6, 320
regimes 47, 48–9, 104
religion 90, 204–5
resistance movements 16–17, 18
responsibility to protect (R2P) 100–1
revolutions 46, 49, 191, 244–6
rights 76, 79–80
   civil-political rights 82, 83, 105, 112
   collective rights 82, 116–19
   concept and contested meanings 80–3, 88–9
   cultural rights 82
   culturally relative 118–19
   disability rights 88
   and economic conditions 105
   economic rights 82, 83
   general/special 81, 90
   of Indigenous peoples 97, 120–1
   individual rights 81–2, 89–91, 116–19, 120
   indivisible 83
   LGBTQI+ rights 83, 189, 264
   and liberty 86–7
   migrants and refugees 275–6
   natural rights 81–2
   politicization and weaponization 100–1, 109–10
   prioritizing 83, 116–17
   privacy rights 86–7
   and social development 134–5
   social rights 82, 83
   solidarity rights 82
   universal 83, 118–19
   of women 112, 134–5
   of workers 113–15
   see also human rights
Rohingya population 108, 265–6, 267–8
Roma ethnic group 305–7
Rome Statute 104–5, 109–10
Russia 24, 56, 103, 109–10
   war on Ukraine 29, 109, 184, 185
Rwanda 266, 323

S
sanctions 103, 106–7, 192, 193
Saudi Arabia 33, 103, 191–3
sea level rise 318, 320–2
security 281–4
   and borders 276, 277–81
   collective 58, 59, 288–9
   and environment 318–22
   global 287–9, 295
   and health 255–7, 288
   human 70, 226, 256, 289–92, 295
   and liberty 86–7
   national 104, 284, 285–7, 295
   and power 28–9, 285
   role of IGOs 13, 58, 59, 288–9
   securitization 292–5
   and technology 241–2, 286, 287
   threats to and human rights 104–5
   types/categorization 286, 291–2
security dilemma 29
self-determination 44, 95, 100, 119
separatist movements 40, 44
slavery 89–90, 114–15
social constructs 263
social inequality 139, 300–1
social justice 112–13, 114, 297
social media 15, 17, 112, 243–6
   ethics and regulation 247
   manipulating identity 266
   and security 242
social mobility 223–5, 229
social movements 16–17, 18, 112–13, 157, 159–60, 244
social services 50, 169
Somalia 50, 51, 110, 158
South Africa 156–7, 189
South Korea 140
South Sudan 215, 370
sovereign states 10, 11, 20–2, 38–40, 54–5, 90, 104
sovereignty 9, 10, 11, 38–46, 56, 119, 185
   and borders 271, 272
   challenges to 43–5
   contingent sovereignty 42, 45
   internal/external 42–3
   and international law 54–5, 99–100
   not an absolute principle 99–101
   and Peace of Westphalia 20–2
   pooled sovereignty 44–5
   sources of 39–42
stakeholders *see* actors and stakeholders
stateless nations 158
stateless populations 267–8
states 10–13, 18
   and conflict 194
   defining terms 10, 11, 12
   and human rights 90, 91–2, 102–5
   interdependence 41
   international law 53–5
   and justice 85
   legitimacy 46–9
   and liberty 85, 86
   multinational 10, 273–4
   postcolonial states 94–5, 100, 101, 119
   and power 28–33, 64–6, 103, 285
   and security 104, 285–9
   strategic alliances 58–60
   strategic non-violence 190–3
   see also borders; nation-states; sovereignty
strategic alliances 58–60
strategic non-violence 190–3
Structural Adjustment Loans (SALs) 141, 142
Structural Adjustment Programmes (SAPs) 141, 142
structural realism *see* neorealism
structural violence 180, 189–90
substate groups 13, 30
Sudan 199, 216
sustainability 76–7, 161–75
   actors and stakeholders 168–9
   contemporary debates 172–4
   contested understandings 163
   economic 164–7, 169
   environmental 164–7, 169, 317
   globalization impacts 169–71, 172, 173–4
   measuring 165–7
   Planetary Boundaries 309–11
   social 164–7, 169
   strong/weak 163
   three pillars 164–5, 166
sustainable development 138, 145–6, 168–74, 249–50, 317
Sustainable Development Goals (SDGs) 145–6, 163, 223–4, 249–50, 269, 300–1, 317
Syria 276, 295

T
technology 232–48, 324–5, 373
   advancement and security 241–2
   advantages/disadvantages 233, 246
   border control 278
   climate change adaptation 320
   competition 241, 242
   cybersecurity 286, 288
   environmentally friendly 169, 313
   ethics and regulation 246–7
   and health 239, 247, 249, 258–60
   impact on societies 243–6
   information and communication technology (ICT) 235–9, 240
   source of power/influence 239–41
   technology gaps 233–5, 236–9
territorial integrity 40
terrorism 196–8
terrorist groups 15
terrorist organizations 17, 50–1, 191, 196–8, 268, 293, 294–5
theoretical perspectives 62–70
   critical theories 63, 68–70
   middle ground theories 66–7
   traditional theories 64–6
   types of theory 62–3
Theory of Knowledge 370–80
   TOK and themes 373–5
   assessments 370–77
   concepts 377–8
think tanks 144–5, 159, 256, 313
torture 95, 96, 104
totalitarian states 11, 49
trade 172–3, 281
trade agreements 60, 281
trade unions 113–14, 156–7, 159, 170
trafficking/smuggling 278–80, 288
transnational advocacy networks 11, 30–1, 61, 112
treaties 12–13, 54, 55, 58–60, 148
   climate change 316–18

Index

free movement 279–80
global security 288–9
human rights 94–8, 105, 107
refugees 275–6
Truth and Reconciliation Commissions (TRCs) 84, 213–15
Tunisia 244, 245–6

U

Uganda 189, 264
Ukraine, Russia's war on 29, 109, 184, 185
UN (United Nations) 17, 55–8
  adoption of UDHR 92–4
  and climate change 316–17, 318
  courts and tribunals 14, 55, 56, 57, 108–9, 196, 274
  creation 91–2
  and development 136, 143–6, 151–2
  and human rights 91–6, 105–7, 113
  and human security 290–1, 292
  peacekeeping 210
  peacemaking 208–9
  and sustainability 162–3, 168
UN Charter 89, 91, 92, 110
UN Convention on the Law of the Sea (UNCLOS) 24–5, 43, 209
UN Development Programme (UNDP) 136, 151, 290–1, 292
UN General Assembly 56, 57, 93, 109
UN Security Council 56–7, 58, 100, 101, 106–7, 110, 209, 210, 288, 294, 295
United Arab Emirates (UAE) 33, 239
  Qatar crisis 191–3
United Kingdom (UK) 10, 15, 24, 56, 91, 169, 305, 373
United States of America (USA) 15, 17, 56, 110, 114, 263, 320
  2016 election 240
  borders and migration 276–7
  carbon footprint 313
  foreign aid 103
  government structure 12
  healthcare 230
  and human rights 91, 104–5
  investment policies 141–3
  and UNCLOS 43
Universal Declaration of Human Rights (UDHR) 83, 92–4, 98, 266, 275, 289–90
universal jurisdiction 99–100
universalism 184

V

violence 180, 187–90, 315–16
  gender based (GBV) 305–6
  justifying 203–6
  non-violent conflict 187, 190–3
  persecuted minorities 267, 268
  social/resistance movements 16, 17
  terrorism 196–8
  violent conflict 187, 194–8
voting 30, 48–9, 57, 153, 300

W

war 179, 188, 203–6
  'new wars' 194, 195
  opposition to 183–5
Washington Consensus 60, 141–3
water 16–17, 148, 157, 161, 249, 319
wealth 169, 298–9, 304
well-being 134, 136, 137, 143–4
Western bias 118
Westphalian states system 14, 20–2, 39–40, 56, 119
women 146, 147, 237, 301–3
  feminism 36, 69–70
  rights 112, 134–5
World Bank 60, 141, 149, 152–3
  poverty data 224, 226, 298–9
World Health Organization (WHO) 152, 249, 252–3
World Trade Organization (WTO) 60, 153–4

Acknowledgments are continued from Copyright page (ii)

Non-Prominent Text Credit(s):

38 North: Ramon Pacheco Pardo "Pressure and Principles: The EU's Human Rights Sanctions on North Korea," 38 North (26 March 2021). Retrieved from https://www.38north.org/2021/03/pressure-and-principles-the-eus-human-rights-sanctions-on-north-korea/. 107, **African Union:** African Charter on Human and Peoples' Rights, Article 24. African Union (27 June 1981). Retrieved from https://achpr.au.int/en/charter/african-charter-human-and-peoples-rights. 97, African Charter on Human and Peoples' Rights, Article 29. African Union (27 June 1981). Retrieved from https://achpr.au.int/en/charter/african-charter-human-and-peoples-rights. 97, **Association of Southeast Asian Nations:** ASEAN Human Rights Declaration, Article 28. ASEAN (2013). Retrieved from https://www.asean.org/wp-content/uploads/images/resources/ASEAN%20Publication/2013%20(7.%20Jul)%20-%20ASEAN%20Human%20Rights%20Declaration%20(AHRD)%20and%20Its%20Translation.pdf. 98, ASEAN Human Rights Declaration, Article 29. ASEAN (2013). Retrieved from https://www.asean.org/wp-content/uploads/images/resources/ASEAN%20Publication/2013%20(7.%20Jul)%20-%20ASEAN%20Human%20Rights%20Declaration%20(AHRD)%20and%20Its%20Translation.pdf. 98, ASEAN Human Rights Declaration, Article 35 and 36. ASEAN (2013). Retrieved from https://www.asean.org/wp-content/uploads/images/resources/ASEAN%20Publication/2013%20(7.%20Jul)%20-%20ASEAN%20Human%20Rights%20Declaration%20(AHRD)%20and%20Its%20Translation.pdf. 98, ASEAN Human Rights Declaration, Article 7. ASEAN (2013). Retrieved from https://www.asean.org/wp-content/uploads/images/resources/ASEAN%20Publication/2013%20(7.%20Jul)%20-%20ASEAN%20Human%20Rights%20Declaration%20(AHRD)%20and%20Its%20Translation.pdf. 98, ASEAN Human Rights Declaration, Article 8. ASEAN (2013). Retrieved from https://www.asean.org/wp-content/uploads/images/resources/ASEAN%20Publication/2013%20(7.%20Jul)%20-%20ASEAN%20Human%20Rights%20Declaration%20(AHRD)%20and%20Its%20Translation.pdf. 98, **BBC World Service:** Repression in the name of rights is unacceptable. (n.d.). BBC World Service. Retrieved April 30, 2023, from www.bbc.co.uk/worldservice/people/features/ihavearightto/four_b/casestudy_art30.shtml 118, **Bloomsbury:** Mathur, S. and Acharya, A. 'Towards Global International Relations' in, McGlinchey, S. (ed.) (2022). Foundations of International Relations. Bloomsbury Academic, p.49. 25, Mathur, S. and Acharya, A. 'Towards Global International Relations' in, McGlinchey, S. (ed.) (2022). Foundations of International Relations. Bloomsbury Academic, p.50. 26, **Bulletin of the Atomic Scientists:** English, E. (2023, May 22). High camp and soft power: How Eurovision explains modern Europe-and more. Bulletin of the Atomic Scientists. Retrieved from: https://thebulletin.org/2023/05/high-camp-and-soft-power-eurovision-explains-europe/ 30, **Business & Human Rights Resource Centre:** Statement on behalf of a Group of Countries at the 24rd [sic] Session of the Human Rights Council. (2013, September). Retrieved April 29, 2023, from https://media.business-humanrights.org/media/documents/files/media/documents/statement-unhrc-legally-binding.pdf 113, **Cambridge University Press:** Reus-Smit, C. (2013). Individual Rights and the Making of the International System. Cambridge University Press, p.170. 90, Reus-Smit, C. (2013). Individual Rights and the Making of the International System. Cambridge University Press, p.211. 90, Vincent, J. (1986). Human Rights and International Relations. Cambridge University Press, p.13. 91, Reus-Smit, C. (2001). 'Human rights and the social construction of sovereignty'. Review of International Studies, 27(4), p.521. 91, Reus-Smit, C. (2001). 'Human rights and the social construction of sovereignty'. Review of International Studies, 27(4), p.182. 93, Reus-Smit, C. (2001). 'Human rights and the social construction of sovereignty'. Review of International Studies, 27(4), p.188. 94, Reus-Smit, C. (2001). 'Human rights and the social construction of sovereignty'. Review of International Studies, 27(4), p.186. 94, Reus-Smit, C. (2001). 'Human rights and the social construction of sovereignty'. Review of International Studies, 27(4), p.535. 95, Reus-Smit, C. (2001). 'Human rights and the social construction of sovereignty'. Review of International Studies, 27(4), p.537. 95, Jo, H. and Simmons, B. A. (2016)., 'Can the International Criminal Court Deter Atrocity?' International Organization 70(3), pp. 443–75. 110, Vincent, J. (1986). Human Rights and International Relations. Cambridge University Press, p.3. 116, Cortright, David. (2008)."Peace: A History of Movements and Ideas." Cambridge University Press, pp.67-92 185, **CBC/Radio-Canada:** CBC/Radio Canada. (2017, October 10). The gun lobby doesn't always win: The Democratic Workaround that best the NRA. CBC Radio. CBCnews. Retrieved on May 6, 2023, from www.cbc.ca/radio/day6/episode-358-outsmarting-the-nra-canada-s-magnitsky-act-ham-radios-for-puerto-rico-music-in-dna-and-more-1.4329733/the-gun-lobby-doesn-t-always-win-the-democratic-workaround-that-beat-the-nra-1.4329884 38, **Central Intelligence Agency:** Adapted from CIA World Factbook (https://www.cia.gov/the-world-factbook/). 41, **Columbia University Press:** Cronin, Bruce. (1999). "Community under Anarchy: Transnational Identity and the Evolution of Cooperation." Columbia University Press. 266, **Economics Help:** Quoted in "Do You Know When Sustainability First Appeared?," Acciona. https://www.activesustainability.com/sustainable-development/do-you-know-when-sustainability-first-appeared/?_adin=01874690616 162, **E-International Relations:** Eroukhmanoff, Clara. (2018). "Securitization Theory. An introduction." E-International Relations. Available at: www.e-ir.info/2018/01/14/securitisation-theory-an-introduction/ (accessed May 2023). 295, **Encyloepaedia Britannica:** Wivel, A. (n.d.). Security dilemma. Encyloepaedia Britannica. Retrieved on May 3, 2023, from www.britannica.com/topic/security-dilemma. 29, **European Environment Agency:** "GDP Map (the territory size shows the proportion of worldwide wealth measured as GDP, based on exchange rates with the USD, that is found there)," European Environment Agency. https://www.eea.europa.eu/data-and-maps/figures/top-gdp-map-the-territory-size-shows-the-proportion-of-worldwide-wealth-measured-as-gdp-based-on-exchange-rates-with-the-usd-that-is-found-there-bottom-total-gdp-in-the-pan-european-region-and-the-rest-of-the-world-in-2005-based-on-constant-2000-usd 130, **European Free Trade Association:** The European Free Trade Association. Available at: www.efta.int/about-efta/european-free-trade-association#:~:text=The%20European%20Free%20Trade%20Association%20(EFTA)%20is%20an%20intergovernmental%20organisation, trading%20partners%20around%20the%20globe (accessed June 2023). 282, **First Nations and Indigenous Studies:** Hanson, Eric, et al. (2020). "The Residential School System." Indigenous Foundations. First Nations and Indigenous Studies UBC. https://indigenousfoundations.arts.ubc.ca/the_residential_school_system/ (accessed April 2023) 215, **Forbes:** "7 Views on How Technology Will Shape Geopolitics." Forbes (7 Apr. 2021). Available at: https://www.forbes.com/sites/worldeconomicforum/2021/04/07/7-views-on-how-technology-will-shape-geopolitics/?sh=564968cb31e7. 240, **Foreign Affairs:** Keohane, R. O., & Nye Jr, J. S. (1998). Power and interdependence in the information age. Foreign Aff., 77, 81, p.83. 29, Ignatieff, M. (2001, November 1). The Attack on Human Rights. Foreign Affairs. Retrieved April 29, 2023, from www.foreignaffairs.com/articles/2001-11-01/attack-human-rights 118,"The Attack on Human Rights," Foreign Affairs (1 Nov 2001). Retrieved from https://www.foreignaffairs.com/articles/2001-11-01/attack-human-rights. 118, **Foreign Policy:** Nye, J. (1990). Soft Power. Foreign Policy, p.167. 30, Nye, J. (1990). Soft Power. Foreign Policy, p.166. 31, Frankel Pratt, Simon and Levin, Jamie, (2021). "Vaccines Will Shape the New Geopolitical Order." Foreign Policy. Available at: https://foreignpolicy.com/2021/04/29/vaccine-geopolitics-diplomacy-israel-russia-china/ (accessed May 2023). 258, **George Allen & Unwin:** Russell, B. (1938). Power: A New Social Analysis. George Allen & Unwin, p.35. 27, **Global Development Research Center:** Global Development Research Center, Human Security: Indicators for Measurement. Available at: www.gdrc.org/sustdev/husec/z-indicators.html (accessed May 2023). 293, **HarperCollins:** Arendt, H. (1972). Crises of the Republic. Harcourt, pp.140. 37, **Global Footprint Network:** National Footprint and biocapacity Accounts 2023 Edition. data.footprintnetwork.org 317, **HBS Working Knowledge:** Nye, J. (2004, February 8). The benefits of soft power. HBS Working Knowledge. Retrieved on May 5, 2023, from https://hbswk.hbs.edu/archive/the-benefits-of-soft-power 31, **Helgi Library:** Helgi Library. https://www.helgilibrary.com/ 131, **Houghton Mifflin Harcourt:** Arendt, H. (1979). The Origins of Totalitarianism. Harcourt, Brace and Co., p. 291. 119, **Institute for Economics & Peace:** Institute for Economics & Peace. (2022, January). Positive Peace Report 2022: Analyzing the factors that build, predict and sustain peace. Available from: http://visionofhumanity.org/resources (accessed March 2023). 183, Global Terrorism Index 2023, Institute for Economics and Peace, p.12. 198, **International Baccalaureate Organization:** IB Learner Profile. International Baccalaureate Organization. Retrieved from https://www.ibo.org/contentassets/fd82f70643ef4086b7d3f292cc214962/learner-profile-en.pdf 22, **International Monetary Fund:** "IMF Members' Quotas and Voting Power, and IMF Board of Governors," IMF (14 Mar 2024). https://www.imf.org/en/About/executive-board/members-quotas 153, **International Organization for Migration:** "Environmental Migration". International Organization for Migration. Retrieved from https://environmentalmigration.iom.int/environmental-migration#:~:text=%E2%80%9CEnvironmental%20migrants%20are%20persons%20or, and%20who%20move%20either%20within. 182, **International Publishers:** Du Bois, W.E.B. (1996, 1946). The World and Africa: An Inquiry into the Part Which Africa has Played in World History. International Publishers, p. 80 22, **Landgeist:** "Global Freedom Index 2021." https://landgeist.com/2021/03/08/global-freedom-index-2021/ 133, **Lawfare:** Wuerth, I. (2019, March 22). A Post-Human Rights Era? A Reappraisal and Response to Critics. Lawfare. Retrieved April 27, 2023, from https://www.lawfareblog.com/post-human-rights-era-appraisal-and-response-critics. 97, **Manchester University Press:** Campbell, David. (1992). "Writing Security: United States Foreign Policy and the Politics of Identity." Manchester University Press. 263, **McGraw Hill Education:** Laswell, Harold. (1950). "National Security and Individual Freedom". Fb&c Limited. 287, **National Endowment for Democracy:** Walker, C. and Ludwig, J. (2017). From 'Soft Power' to 'Sharp Power': Rising Authoritarian Influence in the Democratic World. Sharp Power: Rising Authoritarian Influence. National Endowment for Democracy, p.6. 33, Walker, C. and Ludwig, J. (2017). From 'Soft Power' to 'Sharp Power': Rising Authoritarian Influence in the Democratic World. Sharp Power: Rising Authoritarian Influence. National Endowment for Democracy, p.13. 33, **National Science Foundation:** Parsons, Chris. (2022). "The Pacific Islands: the Front Line in the Battle Against Climate Change." National Science Foundation. Available at: https://new.nsf.gov/science-matters/pacific-islands-front-line-battle-against-climate (accessed May 2023). 325, **Net0:** Fominova, Sofia. (2022). "Top 5 Carbon Emitters by Country," Net0. Available at: https://net0.com/blog/top-five-carbon-emitters-by-country (accessed April 2023). 316, **New Security Beat:** Beauregard, Jordan. and Kazemi, Roxana. (2020). "Health Security is National Security." 2020. Available at: www.newsecuritybeat.org/2020/04/health-security-national-security/ (accessed May 2023). 255, **New York University Press:** In, Held, D. (ed.) (1983). States and Societies. New York University Press, p.111. 12, **Nordic Statistics Database:** "The extreme poverty rate has dropped significantly in most developing regions," in The Millennium Development Goals Report 2015. United Nations. https://www.un.org/millenniumgoals/2015_MDG_Report/pdf/MDG%202015%20rev%20(July%201).pdf 145, **Office of the High Commissioner for Human Rights:** United Nations Human Rights, Office of the High Commissioner (2023), About the Mandate. Available at: https://www.ohchr.org/en/special-procedures/sr-environment/about-mandate (accessed May 2023) 318, **Organisation for Economic Co-operation and Development:** "Covid 19 related ODA expenditures for top donors," OECD. 149, **Our World in Data:** "Number of people living in extreme poverty, 2001," Our World in Data. https://ourworldindata.org/grapher/total-population-in-extreme-poverty?time=2001 225,"Number of people living in extreme poverty, 2021," Our World in Data. https://ourworldindata.org/grapher/total-population-in-extreme-poverty?time=latest&country=IND~CHN~MDG~NGA~BGD 225, "Adoption of communication technologies, World," Our World in Data. https://ourworldindata.org/grapher/ict-adoption 236, "Income inequality: Gini coefficient, 2021," Our World in Data. https://ourworldindata.org/grapher/economic-inequality-gini-index?time=latest 302, **Oxford University Press:** Lake, D.A. (2008). The State and International Relations. In The Oxford Handbook of International Relations (Ser. The Oxford Handbook of Political Science). Oxford University Press, p.43. 11, Qin, Y. (2016). A Relational Theory of World Politics. International Studies Review, 18(1), p.36. 33, Qin, Y. (2016). A Relational Theory of World Politics. International Studies Review, 18(1), p.42 33, Barker, R. (1990). Political Legitimacy and the State. Oxford, p.11. 46, Clapham, A. (2015). Human Rights: A Very Short Introduction. Oxford University Press, p.42. 93, Clapham, A. (2015). Human Rights: A Very Short Introduction. Oxford University Press, p.48. 94, Clapham, A. (2015).

Human Rights: A Very Short Introduction. Oxford University Press, pp. 49–51. 96, **Palgrave MacMillan:** Lukes, S. (2005). Power: A Radical View (2nd ed.). Palgrave MacMillan, p.27. 34, Jok, Madut Jok. (2021). Lessons in Failure: Peacebuilding in Sudan/South Sudan. In: McNamee, T., Muyangwa, M. (eds) The State of Peacebuilding in Africa. Palgrave Macmillan. https://doi.org/10.1007/978-3-030-46636-7_20 (accessed April 2023). 217, **Penguin Books:** Hobbes, T. (1985 [1641]). Leviathan. Penguin Books, p. 150. 27, Foucault, M. (1998). The History of Sexuality: The Will to Knowledge. Penguin, p.63. 34, **Pinter Publishers:** Strange, S. (1988). States and Markets. Pinter Publishers, p.24. 32, **Polity Press:** Ramsbotham, Oliver, Woodhouse, Tom, and Miall, Hugh. "Contemporary Conflict Resolution" (3rd ed.). Cambridge, UK: Polity, 2011 203, **Progress Publishers:** Marx/Engels Selected Works, Volume One, p. 13 - 15 (1969). Progress Publishers. 68, **Public Affairs:** Nye, J. (2004). Soft Power: The Means to Success in World Politics. Public Affairs, p.8. 31, **Random House:** Hedges, Chris. (2002). "War is a Force That Gives Us Meaning". Random House. 179, **Repsol:** Repsol Global. (2023). A Gap That Must Be Bridged. Available at: https://www.repsol.com/en/energy-and-the-future/people/digital-divide/index.cshtml (accessed June 2023) 238, **SAGE Publications, Inc:** Barash, David P. and Webel, Charles. (2018). Peace and Conflict Studies. SAGE. 180, 185, Galtung, Johan. (1969). "Violence, Peace, and Peace Research." Journal of Peace Research, 6(2), pp. 167–191. 188, Barash, David P. and Webel, Charles. (2018). "Peace and Conflict Studies". SAGE, p.604. 214, **SpringerNature:** Bull, H. (1995). The Anarchical Society: A Study of Order in World Politics. London, p.8. 42 **Stanford University Press:** Alagappa, M. (1995). Introduction, in Alagappa, M. (ed.). Political Legitimacy in Southeast Asia: The Quest for Moral Authority. Stanford, p.15. 46, Alagappa, M. (1995). The Anatomy of Legitimacy, in Alagappa, M. (ed.). Political Legitimacy in Southeast Asia: The Quest for Moral Authority. Stanford, p.15. 48, Alagappa, M. (1995). The Anatomy of Legitimacy, in Alagappa, M. (ed.). Political Legitimacy in Southeast Asia: The Quest for Moral Authority. Stanford, p.24. 49, **Swedish International Development Cooperation Agency:** Swedish International Development Cooperation Agency (SIDA). (2017, December). "Conflict Prevention: Opportunities and challenges in implementing key policy commitments and priorities". Available at: https://cdn.sida.se/app/uploads/2020/12/01125316/s209461_thematicoverview_conflict_prevention_webb_final.pdf (accessed April 2023) 208, **Taylor & Fancis:** Hooks, b. (2015 [1984]). Feminist Theory: From Margin to Center. Routledge, pp.90–91. 37, Belloni, R. (2006). 'The Tragedy of Darfur and the Limits of the "'Responsibility to Protect"'. Ethnopolitics, 5(4), p.331. 100, **The Guardian:** Guterres, A. (2019, March 15). The climate strikers should inspire us all to act at the next UN summit. The Guardian. Retrieved on 18 June, 2023 from https://www.theguardian.com/commentisfree/2019/mar/15/climate-strikers-urgency-un-summit-world-leaders 18, Kaminski, I. (2019, December 20). Dutch Supreme Court upholds landmark ruling demanding climate action. The Guardian. Retrieved April 30, 2023, from www.theguardian.com/world/2019/dec/20/dutch-supreme-court-upholds-landmark-ruling-demanding-climate-action. 120, Quoted from John McArthur & Krista Rasmussen "How successful were the millennium development goals?," The Guardian (30 Mar 2017). https://www.theguardian.com/global-development-professionals-network/2017/mar/30/how-successful-were-the-millennium-development-goals 145, **The Irish Times:** O'Toole, F. (2022). Would Ukrainians still feel welcome if they were not white and Christian? The Irish Times, 18 June. Retrieved on June 15, 2023 from: www.irishtimes.com/opinion/2022/06/18/fintan-otoole-would-ukrainians-still-feel-welcome-if-they-were-not-white-and-christian/ 15, **The New York Times:** Khashoggi, Jamal. (2018). "Why the Arab World Needs Democracy Now." The New York Times. Available at: www.nytimes.com/2018/10/22/opinion/khashoggi-mbs-arab-democracy.html (accessed May 2023). 245, **The Stanford Encyclopedia of Philosophy:** d'Entreves, M.P. and Tömmel, T. "Hannah Arendt" in Zalta, E.N and Nodelman, U. (eds) (Fall 2022 Edition). The Stanford Encyclopedia of Philosophy. Retrieved on May 3, 2023, from https://plato.standford.edu/archives/fall2022/entries/arendt/ 37, **The University of Chicago Press:** Cohn, C. (1987). 'Sex and Death in the Rational World of Defense Intellectuals'. Signs 12(4), p.715. 70, **The World Bank:** "Poverty and Shared Prosperity 2020: Reversals of Fortune," The World Bank (2020). https://openknowledge.worldbank.org/server/api/core/bitstreams/611fc6f2-140b-551e-9371-468eec64c552/content 226, **U.S. Government Publishing Office:** U.S. GOVERNMENT PUBLISHING OFFICE 12, **United Nations:** United Nations Office of Legal Affairs. (1999, December 31). No. 3802. convention on rights and duties of states adopted by the Seventh International Conference of American States. signed at Montevideo, December 26th, 1933. UN iLibrary, https://doi.org/10.18356/57z42223-en-fr 12, United Nations Charter, Chapter I: Purposes and Principles. United Nations. Retrieved from https://www.un.org/en/about-us/un-charter/chapter-1. 40, 56, United Nations. (n.d.). Growth in United Nations membership. UN. www.un.org/en/about-us/growth-in-un-membership. 41, General Assembly resolution 1514 (XV) (14 December 1960) Declaration on the Granting of Independence to Colonial Countries and Peoples. United Nations. Retrieved from https://www.ohchr.org/en/instruments-mechanisms/instruments/declaration-granting-independence-colonial-countries-and-peoples. 42, United Nations Charter: Preamble. Retrieved from https://www.un.org/en/about-us/un-charter/preamble. 89, United Nations. (1945). United Nations charter, art. 55 and art. 56. United Nations. Retrieved April 25, 2023, from www.un.org/en/about-us/un-charter/full-text 92, Universal Declaration of Human Rights: Article 1 from https://www.un.org/en/about-us/universal-declaration-of-human-rights#:~:text=Article%201,in%20a%20spirit%20of%20brotherhood. 94, United Nations, Yearbook of the United Nations: 1953. United Nations Department of Information, p.386. 94, "Declaration on the Granting of Independence to Colonial Countries and Peoples', General Assembly Resolution 1514 (XV), December 14, 1960. 95, United Nations, Yearbook of the United Nations: 1951. (United Nations Department of Information), p.485. 95, United Nations Charter. 99, General Assembly resolution 2200A (XXI) (16 December 1966) "International Covenant on Civil and Political Rights," United Nations. Retrieved from https://www.ohchr.org/en/instruments-mechanisms/instruments/international-covenant-civil-and-political-rights. 104, Universal Declaration of Human Rights, Article 21(3). United Nations. Retrieved from https://www.un.org/en/about-us/universal-declaration-of-human-rights. 106, Concerned by Unintended Negative Impact of Sanctions, Speakers in Security Council Urge Action to Better Protect Civilians, Ensure Humanitarian Needs Are Met. (2022, February).

United Nations. Retrieved April 28, 2023, from https://press.un.org/en/2022/sc14788.doc.htm 106, "The Convention on the Prevention and Punishment of the Crime of Genocide," (1948) United Nations. Retrieved from https://www.un.org/en/genocideprevention/documents/Genocide%20Convention-FactSheet-ENG.pdf. 195, Eight Millennium Development Goals. United Nations. 144, United Nations, Department of Economic and Social Affairs. Sustainable Development. Goal 1: End poverty in all its forms everywhere. Available at: https://sdgs.un.org/goals/goal1 (accessed July 2023) 223, "Statement of Commitment for Action to Eradicate Poverty Adopted by Administrative Committee on Coordination," United Nations (20 May 1998). https://press.un.org/en/1998/19980520.eco5759.html 226, UN, Department of Economic and Social Affairs "Information and Communication Technologies (ICTs)." Available at: www.un.org/development/desa/socialperspectiveondevelopment/issues/information-and-communication-technologies-icts.html (accessed April 2023). 235, "UN Millennium Development Goals," United Nations. https://www.un.org/millenniumgoals/ 255, United Nations. "Universal Declaration of Human Rights". Available at: https://www.un.org/en/about-us/universal-declaration-of-human-rights (accessed July 2023) 275, "The Crime," United Nations. https://www.unodc.org/unodc/en/human-trafficking/crime.html 280, United Nations, "Universal Declaration of Human Rights". Available at: https://www.un.org/en/about-us/universal-declaration-of-human-rights (accessed July 2023) 291, United Nations Digital Library. (2003). Human security now: protecting and empowering people / Commission on Human Security, p4. Available at: https://digitallibrary.un.org/record/503749?ln=en (accessed May 2023) 292, United Nations (2018), "Security Council Seeks to Strengthen Protections for Children in Armed Conflict, Unanimously Adopting Resolution 2427 (2018)". Available at: https://press.un.org/en/2018/sc13412.doc.htm (accessed June 2023) 296, United Nations. Inequality – Bridging the Divide. Available at: www.un.org/en/un75/inequality-bridging-divide (accessed May 2023). 304,"UN 17 Sustainable Development Goals," United Nations. https://sdgs.un.org/goals 321, **United Nations Conference on Trade and Development:** UN Conference on Trade and Development. (2021). "Escaping from the Commodity Dependence Trap through Technology and Innovation." Available at: https://unctad.org/system/files/official-document/ditccom2021d1_en.pdf (accessed May 2023). 235, "Least developed countries suffer digital divide in mobile connectivity," United Nations Conference on Trade and Development. https://unctad.org/topic/least-developed-countries/chart-april-2021 237, **United Nations Development Programme:** UNDP DGI: www.undp.org/sites/g/files/zskgke326/files/migration/tr/UNDP-TR-EN-HDR-2019-FAQS-GDI.pdf 137, "MPI Dimensions and Indicators," in 2022 Global Multidimensional Poverty Index (MPI). United Nations Development Programme (17 Oct 2022). https://hdr.undp.org/content/2022-global-multidimensional-poverty-index-mpi#/indicies/MPI 227, **United Nations High Commissioner for Refugees:** USA for UNHCR. (2023) "What is a Refugee?" Refugee Facts. Available at: https://www.unrefugees.org/refugee-facts/what-is-a-refugee/#:~:text=A%20refugee%20is%20someone%20who,in%20a%20particular%20social%20group. (accessed July 2023) 276, **United Nations Trust Fund for Human Security:** From "Human Security Handbook," United Nations Trust Fund for Human Security (2016). https://www.un.org/humansecurity/wp-content/uploads/2017/10/h2.pdf 292, **University of California Press:** Geddes, B. (1994). Politician's Dilemma: Building State Capacity in Latin America. University of California Press, p.7. 12, **University of Washington:** Howard, Philip in O'Donnell, Catherine. (2011). "New Study Quantifies Use of Social Media in Arab Spring." University of Washington News. Available at: www.washington.edu/news/2011/09/12/new-study-quantifies-use-of-social-media-in-arab-spring/ (accessed May 2023). 244, **W.W. Norton & Co.:** Mearsheimer, J.J. (2014, 1001). The Tragedy of Great Power Politics. W.W. Norton & Co., p.19. 28, Mearsheimer, J.J. (2014, 1001). The Tragedy of Great Power Politics. W.W. Norton & Co., p.21. 65, **Wall Street Mojo:** "Poverty Trap," Wall Street Mojo. https://www.wallstreetmojo.com/poverty-trap/ 228, **WomenStat:** "Women's Mobility Scaled: Scaled 2022," WomenStats. https://www.womanstats.org/maps.html 135, **World Health Organization:** WHO, Constitution (2023). Available at: https://www.who.int/about/governance/constitution (accessed July 2023) 249,"Leading causes of death in low-income countries," in The top 10 causes of death (9 Dec 2020) WHO. https://www.who.int/news-room/fact-sheets/detail/the-top-10-causes-of-death 251, "Leading causes of death in lower-middle-income countries," in The top 10 causes of death (9 Dec 2020) WHO. https://www.who.int/news-room/fact-sheets/detail/the-top-10-causes-of-death 251, "Leading causes of death in upper-middle-income countries," in The top 10 causes of death (9 Dec 2020) WHO. https://www.who.int/news-room/fact-sheets/detail/the-top-10-causes-of-death 251, "Leading causes of death in high-income countries" in The top 10 causes of death (9 Dec 2020) WHO. https://www.who.int/news-room/fact-sheets/detail/the-top-10-causes-of-death 251, World Health Organization. Constitution. Available at: www.who.int/about/governance/constitution (accessed May 2023). 252, World Health Organization. (2023) "Mental Health". Available at: www.who.int/health-topics/mental-health#tab=tab_1 (accessed May 2023). 257